Fodor's 04

WALT DISNEY WORLD,®
UNIVERSAL ORLANDO®
& CENTRAL FLORIDA

Where to Stay and Eat
for All Budgets

Ratings You Can Trust

Fodor's Travel Publications   New York, Toronto, London, Sydney, Auckland
www.fodors.com

FODOR'S WALT DISNEY WORLD®, UNIVERSAL ORLANDO® & CENTRAL FLORIDA 2004

Editors: Mary Beth Bohman and Emmanuelle Morgen

Editorial Production: Tom Holton
Editorial Contributors: Jennie Hess, Gary McKechnie, Alicia Rivas, Rowland Stiteler
Maps: David Lindroth *cartographer;* Bob Blake and Rebecca Baer, *map editors*
Design: Fabrizio La Rocca, *creative director;* Guido Caroti, *art director;* Melanie Marin, *photo editor*
Production/Manufacturing: Robert B. Shields
Cover Photo (Dueling Dragons at Universal Orlando's Islands of Adventure): © Universal Orlando

SPECIAL SALES

Fodor's Travel Publications are available at special discounts for bulk purchases for sales promotions or premiums. Special editions, including personalized covers, excerpts of existing guides, and corporate imprints, can be created in large quantities for special needs. For more information, contact your local bookseller or write to Special Markets, Fodor's Travel Publications, 1745 Broadway, New York, NY 10019. Inquiries from Canada should be directed to your local Canadian bookseller or sent to Random House of Canada, Ltd., Marketing Department, 2775 Matheson Boulevard East, Mississauga, Ontario L4W 4P7. Inquiries from the United Kingdom should be sent to Fodor's Travel Publications, 20 Vauxhall Bridge Road, London SW1V 2SA, England.

IMPORTANT TIP & AN INVITATION

Although all prices, opening times, and other details in this book are based on information supplied to us at press time, changes occur all the time in the travel world, and Fodor's cannot accept responsibility for facts that become outdated or for inadvertent errors or omissions. So **always confirm information when it matters,** especially if you're making a detour to visit a specific place. Your experiences—positive and negative—matter to us. If we have missed or misstated something, **please write to us.** We follow up on all suggestions. Contact the Walt Disney World, Universal Orlando and Central Florida editor at editors@fodors.com or c/o Fodor's at 1745 Broadway, New York, New York 10019.

PRINTED IN THE UNITED STATES OF AMERICA

10 9 8 7 6 5 4 3 2 1

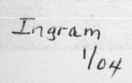

Ingram
1/04

DESTINATION: MAGIC

Sneakers? Check. Sunscreen? Check. Hat, backpack, admission ticket and passes? Check. Once you choose to vacation in Neverland, it's never too soon to begin strategizing. Because no one truly "escapes" to central Florida without fine-tuning a game plan. Will you ride the fantasy conjured up by the golden-spired Cinderella Castle in the Magic Kingdom? Forward-march to the jungles and savanna of Disney's Animal Kingdom? Discover Epcot, half culture, half technology? Rewind to a Hollywood heyday that never was—the star-studded Disney–MGM Studios? Or will you soar beyond Disney's worlds to the thrills and themes of Universal Studios and—extra special—Islands of Adventure? Do you have time for SeaWorld and, due west on Florida's Gulf Coast at Tampa, Busch Gardens? With the rides as joyful diversions among displays of animals as fine as in any aquarium or zoo, they may well be a priority if yours is a family of animal lovers. Take your pick and don't worry if you can't fit everything into the time you have—you can't go far wrong with any choice. Then, provisioned with snacks and water bottles and armed with park maps and this guide, you'll be ready to outmaneuver all the other pixie-dusted travelers who share your mission. Have fun—and hang on to your hat!

Karen Cure, Editorial Director

CONTENTS

ABOUT THIS BOOK

There's no doubt that the best source for travel advice is a like-minded friend who's just been where you're headed. But with or without that friend, you'll have a better trip with a Fodor's guide in hand. Once you've learned to find your way around its pages, you'll be in great shape to find your way around your destination.

SELECTION

Our goal is to cover the best properties, sights, and activities in their category, as well as the most interesting communities to visit. We make a point of including local food-lovers' hot spots as well as neighborhood options, and we avoid all that's touristy unless it's really worth your time. You can go on the assumption that everything you read about in this book is recommended wholeheartedly by our writers and editors. Flip to On the Road with Fodor's to learn more about who they are. It goes without saying that no property mentioned in the book has paid to be included.

RATING THE RIDES

Every visitor leaves the theme parks with a different opinion about what was "the best." To take this into account, our descriptions include Ratings. ★, ★★, or ★★★ rates the appeal of the attraction to the audience noted. In Audience designations, "young children" refers to kids ages 5–7; "very young children" are those (ages 4 and under) who probably won't meet the height requirements of most thrill rides anyway. Since youngsters come with different confidence levels, exercise your own judgment when it comes to the scarier rides.

FODOR'S CHOICE

Fodor's Choice in the margin denotes sights and properties that our editors and writers consider the very best in the area covered by the entire book. These, the best of the best, are listed in the Fodor's Choice section in the front of the book. Fodor's Choice options are also listed on the title page of their respective chapters. Use the index to find complete descriptions.

TIME IT RIGHT

Wondering when to go? Check On the Calendar up front and the individual theme parks' Timing Tips for weather and crowd overviews and best days and times to visit. Then, while you're at the park, use the Strategy notes for each attraction to time your visits so as to waste as little time waiting in line as possible.

SEE IT ALL

Every theme park includes a Blitz Tour that shows you how to squeeze all of the highlights into a single day.

SPECIAL SPOTS

Pleasures & Pastimes focuses on types of experiences that reveal the spirit of central Florida. Watch for Off the Beaten Path sights. Some are out of the way, some are quirky, and all are worth your while. If the munchies hit all of a sudden, look for Need a Break? suggestions.

BUDGET WELL

Hotel and restaurant price categories from ¢ to $$$$ are defined in the opening pages of each chapter-expect to find a balanced selection for every budget. For attractions, we always give standard admission fees for children and adults; reductions are usually available for students and senior citizens. Look in Discounts & Deals in Smart Travel Tips for information on destination-wide ticket schemes.

BASIC INFO

Smart Travel Tips lists travel essentials for the entire area covered by the book. To find the best way to get around, see the transportation section; see individual modes of travel ("By Car," "By Train") for details. We assume you'll check Web sites or call for particulars.

ON THE MAPS	**Maps** throughout the book show you what's where and help you find your way around. Black and orange numbered bullets in the text correlate to bullets on maps.
DON'T FORGET	**Restaurants** are open for lunch and dinner daily unless we state otherwise; we mention dress only when there's a specific requirement and reservations only when they're essential or not accepted—it's always best to book ahead. **Hotels** have private baths, phone, TVs, and air-conditioning and operate on the European Plan (a.k.a. EP, meaning without meals). We always list facilities but not whether you'll be charged extra to use them, so when pricing accommodations, find out what's included.
SYMBOLS	

Many Listings

⊠ Physical address
⟺ Directions
🗐 Mailing address
☏ Telephone
🖷 Fax
⊕ On the Web
✍ E-mail
☉ Open/closed times
▭ Credit cards

Outdoors

🏌 Golf
⚑ Camping

Hotels & Restaurants

🏨 Hotel
⟿ Number of rooms
♨ Facilities
🍴 Meal plans
✕ Restaurant
🏊 Reservations
🏛 Dress code
🚭 Smoking
🍷 BYOB
✕🏨 Hotel with restaurant that warrants a visit

Other

♘ Family-friendly
🎗 Contact information
⇨ See also
⊠ Branch address
☞ Take note

ON THE ROAD WITH FODOR'S

By definition, trips are a break from your everyday reality. But that's especially so when you travel to Central Florida. Alone, the palmy Florida weather is mesmerizing; the roller coasters and simulator rides, not to mention the all-consuming quest for the perfect vantage point on a park's daily parade, complete your transformation from workaday stiff. Concerns of life at home completely disappear, driven away by the far more immediate thoughts involved in getting yourself to the right place at the right time and having a ball doing it. Where does Fodor's come in? We go to extraordinary lengths to make sure that you know all your options, so that you don't miss something that's on the next corner just because you didn't know it was there. And because the best memories of your trip might well have nothing to do with what you came to Central Florida to see, we guide you to a bunch of sights large and small beyond, way beyond, the theme parks. Although you may have left home completely focused on riding in the first car of Island of Adventure's stomach-churning Hulk Coaster, you may find yourself back at home unable to forget the splendid comics in the funky Pleasure Island nightspot known as the Adventurers' Club. With Fodor's at your side, such serendipitous discoveries are never far away.

Our success in showing you every corner of the Central Florida and its theme parks is a credit to our extraordinary writers. Although there's no substitute for travel advice from a good friend who knows your style, our contributors are the next best thing—the kind of people you would poll for travel advice if you knew them.

Jennie Hess is a travel and feature writer based in Orlando. A former newspaper journalist, Hess was a publicist for Walt Disney World Resort from 1988 through 1999, exploring every corner of the evolving kingdom and gathering theme-park details faster than Pooh could sniff out honey. Today, she enjoys sharing the "inside scoop" on Disney with visitors—including insights gleaned from her husband and two sons.

Florida native Gary McKechnie has encyclopedic knowledge of what he thinks is the greatest state in the Union. During his student days, he worked as a Walt Disney World ferryboat pilot, Jungle Cruise skipper, steam-train conductor, double-decker bus driver, and improv comedian at Epcot. His book *Great American Motorcycle Tours* won a silver medal in the 2001 Lowell Thomas Travel Journalism Competition.

Alicia Rivas, our Smart Travel Tips updater, is a freelance broadcast journalist and writer. Though technically a transplant, she considers herself a Central Florida native. Rivas worked at Epcot while she was in college, and she still considers it the best job she's ever had.

Good meals stick to your ribs; great meals stick in your mind. That's the belief of Rowland Stiteler, who has served as editor and dining critic of *Orlando* and *Central Florida* magazines. During the past seven years, he's researched over 300 Florida hotels and restaurants for travel publications and the convention and resort industry.

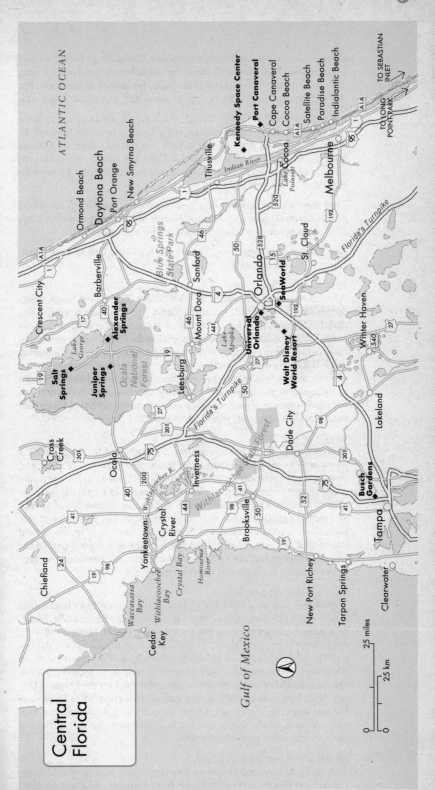

Central Florida

ATLANTIC OCEAN

Gulf of Mexico

Kennedy Space Center
Port Canaveral
Cape Canaveral
Cocoa Beach
Satellite Beach
Paradise Beach
Indialantic Beach

TO SEBASTIAN INLET

TO LONG POINT PARK

Titusville
Cocoa
Lake Cocoa
Poinsett
Indian River
Melbourne

Ormond Beach
Daytona Beach
Port Orange
New Smyrna Beach

Crescent City
Barberville
Blue Springs State Park
Sanford
Mount Dora
Lake Apopka
Leesburg
Lake George
Alexander Springs
Salt Springs
Juniper Springs
Ocala National Forest

Orlando
SeaWorld
Universal Orlando
Walt Disney World Resort
St. Cloud

Winter Haven

Cross Creek
Ocala
Inverness
Withlacoochee R.
Withlacoochee State Forest
Dade City
Lakeland

Florida's Turnpike

Busch Gardens
Tampa

Chiefland
Cedar Key
Waccasassa Bay
Withlacoochee Bay
Crystal Bay
Crystal River
Yankeetown
Homosassa River
Brooksville
New Port Richey
Tarpon Springs
Clearwater

25 miles

25 km

Orlando can be a pretty bewildering place, filled with an endless stream of attractions. Walt Disney World alone can flummox the planner in you, with its 47 square miles (that's about twice the area of Manhattan). But don't let the selection and the enormousness of it all stop you in your tracks.

Let's start with Walt Disney World. Many people are surprised to learn that it isn't a theme park. Instead, it's a huge complex of assorted diversions, including not one theme park but several, along with resort hotels, golf courses, and water parks. There are two shopping and entertainment complexes, Downtown Disney (which includes Pleasure Island) and Disney's Boardwalk.

Then there's Universal Orlando Resort, which is made up of the theme parks Universal Studios Florida and Islands of Adventure as well as CityWalk, a complex of restaurants, nightclubs, and stores.

And that's just the beginning. There's still SeaWorld Orlando and Busch Gardens Tampa to explore.

The Magic Kingdom

What most people imagine to be Walt Disney World—the Magic Kingdom—actually is a small, but emblematic, part of it. Similar to California's Disneyland, the Magic Kingdom is the wellspring of Mickeymania and the most popular individual theme park in the United States, welcoming millions every year. For many of those who have grown up with Cinderella, Snow White, Peter Pan, Dumbo, Davy Crockett, and Pinocchio, it's one of those magical places, "so full of echoes, allusions, and half-memories as to be almost metaphysical," according to renowned travel writer Jan Morris. It's the site of such world-famous attractions as Space Mountain, Pirates of the Caribbean, Splash Mountain, and "it's a small world."

Epcot

Designed to promote enthusiasm for discovery and learning, WDW's Epcot is a sweeping combination of amusement park, world's fair, and class-act entertainment venue. In Future World, anchored by the trademark 17-story silver geosphere known as Spaceship Earth, the focus inside 10 landmark pavilions is on the fascinating discoveries of science and technology. Don't miss the funny, often startling, 3-D film and special-effects attraction *Honey, I Shrunk the Audience*. In the second major area of Epcot, World Showcase, you can tour a good part of the world, minus jet lag, via 11 architecturally realistic pavilions that represent cultures and tastes of nations around the world.

Disney–MGM Studios

With a cast that reads like the credits of the biggest blockbuster ever made—to Walt's name add George Lucas, Jim Henson, the Duke, Bogie, and Julie Andrews—this is Disney's re-creation of Hollywood as it might have been in the good old days. Amazing attractions are the key to "The Studios' " success: there's the Rock 'n' Roller Coaster Starring Aerosmith, and the stunt artist's showcase, the Indiana Jones Epic Stunt Spectacular! Other not-to-be-missed attractions include the Magic of Disney Animation, a behind-the-scenes look at those remarkable Disney animators working at their art. Extras include the fully operational film and television production center and back-lot tours that reveal tricks of the film and video production trade.

Disney's Animal Kingdom

This lushly landscaped theme park is the largest in area of all Disney parks, five times the size of the Magic Kingdom, with rides and up-close safari encounters with exotic animals on a 100-acre savanna. Its centerpiece is the wonderfully detailed 145-ft Tree of Life, which houses a very funny 3-D film and special-effects show, *It's Tough to Be a Bug!* The park has seven major lands, including Africa, where elephants, zebras, lions, and other animals roam freely beyond imperceptible natural barriers. Experience Bengal tigers and a high-speed white-water raft ride in Asia; in other lands you can meet lifelike dinosaurs and enjoy some of the best Disney shows on the property.

Universal Studios

The competition with Disney means that Universal gives plenty of hip originality and a saucy, sassy personality to its rides, as in *Back to the Future,* the simulator ride to end all simulator rides, and the longtime special-effects star among theme-park rides—*Terminator 2* 3-D, which combines a spectacular 3-D film, live Arnold look-alikes whizzing around on bruiser Harley-Davidsons, bone-chilling fog, and more. At the opposite end of the thrill spectrum, A Day in the Park with Barney is a boppin' musical revue and a hands-on educational playground.

Islands of Adventure

It's hard to describe Islands of Adventure as a theme park, since there are so many themes running around. Regardless, the screamfest begins at the Incredible Hulk Coaster and continues at the double coaster known as Dueling Dragons, and people are still shrieking like babies at the Amazing Adventures of Spider-Man. There are plenty of ways to get wet, too: Dudley Do-Right's Ripsaw Falls was the first flume ride with an underwater portion. Little ones have a land all to themselves: Seuss Landing, where they can enter the world of *One Fish, Two Fish, Red Fish, Blue Fish* and *The Cat in the Hat.* All in all, they've done it all—and they've done it all right.

SeaWorld Orlando

It's the animals who are the stars here. Sleek dolphins perform like gymnastic champions, and orca whales sail through the air like featherweight Nijinskys. The world's largest zoological park, SeaWorld is devoted to mammals, birds, fish, and reptiles that live in the oceans and their tributaries. Every attraction is designed to explain the marine world and its vulnerability to human use. Yet the presentations are always enjoyable, and almost always memorable. The highlight is Shamu Stadium, where you can see Shamu and his sidekicks propel their trainers high up into the air. Discovery Cove, a separate attraction, allows you to interact with a dolphin, splash around an artificial reef, snorkel along an artificial river, and wade among real stingrays. It's calming, quiet, and rather expensive.

Busch Gardens

Wildlife at its chest-thumping best is the specialty here: Busch Gardens Tampa is one of America's leading legitimate zoos as well as a great theme park. Going eyeball-to-eyeball with a Western Lowland gorilla will please any budding biologist. Plus, there are spectacular roller coasters and other thrill rides: the twisting Kumba; the inverted Montu, whose cars are suspended from the track rather than placed on top of it; the Tanganyika Tidal Wave, whose 55-ft drop is an outrageous way to test zero gravity; and Gwazi, twin racing wooden coasters.

WHEN TO GO

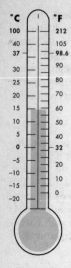

Timing can spell the difference between a good vacation in the theme parks and a great one. Since the Orlando area is an obvious destination for families, the area is at its most crowded during school vacation periods.

If you're traveling without youngsters or with just preschoolers, avoid school holidays. Attendance is light (the parks are busy but not packed) from early September until just before Thanksgiving. Another excellent time is January. The least crowded period of all is from just after the Thanksgiving weekend until the beginning of the Christmas holidays. If you have school-age children, however, the question of when to go is more complicated.

With schoolchildren, it's nice to avoid prime break times, but it's not always possible—or necessary. During certain periods, especially Christmas to New Year's Day, the parks are oppressively crowded, with discouraging lines. However, bigger crowds do not *always* mean longer lines, as the parks staff up and run rides at full capacity to accommodate the larger number of visitors. In addition, busy periods bring longer hours and added entertainment and parades, such as the evening Parade in Disney's Magic Kingdom, that you can't see in quiet seasons. For many children, it's more fun to be in a park with plenty of other kids around.

So if possible, avoid Christmas, March (when most colleges have spring break), the Easter weeks, and mid-June to mid-August, especially around July 4 (it's not fun waiting in lines in the hot sun, anyway). Try to vacation in late May or early June (excluding Memorial Day weekend), as soon as the school year ends; in late August, if you must go in summer; or at Thanksgiving, which is not as busy as other holidays.

Finally, before you finalize your travel schedule, call the theme parks you plan to visit in order to find out about any planned maintenance that will close major attractions you want to see.

Climate

Below are average daily maximum and minimum temperatures for Orlando.

🅵 **Forecasts Weather Channel Connection** ☎ 900/932-8437, 95¢ per minute from a Touch-Tone phone.

ORLANDO

Jan.	70F	21C	May	88F	31C	Sept.	88F	31C
	49	9		67	19		74	23
Feb.	72F	22C	June	90F	32C	Oct.	83F	28C
	54	12		74	23		67	19
Mar.	76F	24C	July	90F	32C	Nov.	76F	24C
	56	13		74	23		58	14
Apr.	81F	27C	Aug.	90F	32C	Dec.	70F	21C
	63	17		74	23		52	11

ON THE CALENDAR

December

Early in the month, Orlando's Loch Haven Park stages a Pet Fair & Winterfest (☎ 407/644–2739). Christmas in the Park (☎ 407/644–8281) in downtown Winter Park is the first weekend in December. Central Park becomes a brilliant place with the Lighting of the Tiffany, when a collection of Tiffany windows is rolled into the park for viewing. The Bach Festival adult and children's choirs provide holiday music. December 8–14, Disney's Wide World of Sports hosts the Pop Warner Little Scholars Super Bowl and the Pop Warner National Cheer & Dance Championships (☎ 407/828–3267). These events bring hundreds of aspiring young football players and cheerleaders to Orlando from across the nation. For a Disney Christmas, Walt Disney World gears up by decorating Main Street in perfect Victorian style, complete with a magnificent Christmas tree in Town Square, special afternoon parades, and holiday entertainment. On select December evenings before Christmas, Mickey's Very Merry Christmas Party (☎ 407/824–4321) special-ticket event in the Magic Kingdom can really get you into the holiday spirit. At Epcot the Candlelight Processional and Holidays Around the World (☎ 407/824–4321) keep things festive. Downtown Disney (☎ 407/824–4321) has some terrific holiday shopping, especially at Disney's Days of Christmas shop; nightly tree-lighting festivities; and appearances by the North Pole's most important citizen. Universal's Grinchmas (☎ 407/363–8000) takes place from mid-November until December 31 with real snow and Whos aplenty. A Norman Rockwell Holiday Showcase at SeaWorld runs from mid-November to after New Year's. The old-time Christmas comes complete with strolling musicians as well as visits from Santa and the Budweiser Clydesdales decked out in their full regalia.

January

The The Capitol One Bowl (☎ 407/423–2476) takes place at the Orlando Citrus Bowl on January 1. In early January, the Walt Disney World Marathon and Half Marathon (☎ 407/939–7810 ⊕ www. disneyworldsports.com) send runners on a 26.25-mi odyssey (or half an odyssey for those with less stamina) around the World. The City of Eatonville, the country's oldest incorporated black community, hosts the annual Zora Neale Hurston Festival of the Arts (☎ 800/972-3310 ⊕ www.zoranealehurston.cc). At the end of January, Scottish Highland Games (⊕ www.flascot.com) are played at Central Winds Park in Winter Springs. The Rolex 24 (☎ 386-253-7223 ⊕ www.daytonaintlspeedway.com) at Daytona International Speedway usually lands on the last weekend of January or first weekend in February.

February

Kicking off a busy February, the Mount Dora Art Festival (☎ 352/383–2165 ⊕ www.renningersflorida.com) opens Central Florida's spring art-fair season. The Orlando Museum of Art's annual Antiques Show and Sale (☎ 407/672–3838) is a significant show with more 30 national dealers. A tradition since 1935, the Bach Music Festival (☎ 407/646-2182 ⊕ www.bachfestivalflorida.org) usually spans late February to early March. February also brings the granddaddy of Nascar races, the Daytona 500 (☎ 386-253-7223 ⊕ www.daytonaintlspeedway.com). Kissimmee's Silver Spurs Rodeo (☎ 407/847–5000) is one of the oldest and largest rodeos in the South, drawing cowboys from all over North America. Bike Week (⊕ www.daytonachamber.com) in Daytona Beach may be the single biggest annual event in Central Florida. Held from the end of February to early March, the 10-day festival attracts hundreds of thousands motorcycle enthusiasts from all over the world.

SPRING

March

March means Universal Studios' Mardi Gras (☎ 407/363–8000), one of the events that has given Universal the reputation for hosting the best parties. The actual Mardi Gras floats from New Orleans are shipped to Universal for huge post-Fat Tuesday celebration. Pleasure Island Mardi Gras (☎ 407/939–2648) at Downtown Disney is another area alternative to the Big Easy itself. The Florida Film Festival (☎ 407-629-1088 ⊕ www.floridafilmfestival.com) is now in early March. The ten day festival was recently voted one of the ten best in the world and is a qualifying festival for the Oscars in the category of live action short films. One weekend in early March, the Kissimmee Bluegrass Festival (☎ 813-783-7205) showcases bluegrass bands and gospel music at the Silver Spurs Rodeo Arena. SeaWorld's All American Barbecue Festival (☎ 407-351-3600) is a four-day, old-fashioned family barbecue celebration, complete with entertainment from top country artists. Midmonth, the Bay Hill Invitational (☎ 407/876–2888 ⊕ www.bayhillinvitational.bizland.com), a regular PGA Tour stop, is held at Orlando's Bay Hill Club. The Winter Park Sidewalk Art Festival (☎ 407/644–8281 ⊕ www.wpsaf.org) takes over Winter Park in mid-March. One of the most prestigious juried shows in the country, the three-day festival attracts close to a half-million visitors. March is also the season for baseball spring training all over Florida. Disney's Wide World of Sports (☎ 407-939-7810 ⊕ dwws.disney.go.com/wideworldofsports) hosts the Atlanta Braves.

April

From early April through early May, the Orlando-UCF Shakespeare Festival (☎ 407/423–6905 ⊕ www.shakespearefest.org) pays tribute to the Bard at Orlando's Lake Eola Amphitheater. From the end of April until early May, the Orlando International Fringe Festival (☎ 407/648-0077 ⊕ www.orlandofringe.com) brings 200 artists and theater troupes to perform in downtown Orlando.

May

Topiaries of Disney characters and beautiful floral designs grace Epcot during its International Flower and Garden Festival (☎ 407/824–4321), which runs from late April through May. There are also howto seminars and nightly entertainment. Sea World's Viva La Musica (☎ 407/351-3600) is a celebration of Hispanic music, food and culture; the festival is held in May and again in September.

SUMMER

June

The city of Orlando hosts the Cultural Heritage Festival (☎ 407/423–6905) during the first weekend in June. The first week of June, Gay Day (⊕ www.gayday.com) activities take place at several major Central Florida attractions, including the Magic Kingdom, SeaWorld Orlando, and Universal Studios Florida. Although they aren't sanctioned as official park events, attendance has grown each year, and they now attract more than 100,000 gay and lesbian visitors to the area. Summer Nights (☎ 407/351–9453) kick off at Wet 'n Wild with late park hours and entertainment by live bands, contests, and hundreds

	of prizes. Late in June and early in July is the Silver Spurs Rodeo (☎ 407/847–5000); there's another in early February.
July	The Fourth of July is a big day in and around Orlando, with fireworks (☎ 407/939–7814 for WDW, 407/363–5871 for Lake Eola, 407/932–7223 for Lakefront Park) everywhere. WDW's Independence Day pyrotechnic displays are legendary; theme-park crowds reach their peak for this holiday. In downtown Orlando, the masses gather around Lake Eola for the city's fireworks. Lakefront Park in Kissimmee has fireworks as part of an old-fashioned celebration that also includes games, rides, entertainment, and food. Three days of racing surround Fourth of July celebrations in Daytona, culminating with the Pepsi 400 (☎ 386-253-7223), which usually lands on July 5th.
August	The 10th annual Christmas in August Craft Fair (☎ 407/860–0092) is held at the Central Florida Fairgrounds.

FALL

October	Legendary bull riders and cowboys compete at the Silver Spurs Rodeo and RibFest (☎ 407/847–4052 or 407/847–3174) held the first weekend in October in Kissimmee. Early in October, the Universal Art Show (☎ 407/295–3247) is held on Orlando's Central Florida Fairgrounds. Mid-October is the time for the Walt Disney World Golf Classic (☎ 407/824–2250), played on two of Walt Disney World's 18-hole golf courses. At the Epcot International Food & Wine Festival (☎ 407/824–4321), mid-October through mid-November, you'll find delicacies, fine wines, and special entertainment from around the world, with wine-tasting seminars and culinary demonstrations daily. The Winter Park Autumn Art Festival (☎ 407/644–8281) takes place at Lake Island Park. For Halloween there are several October weekends of Halloween Horror Nights at Universal Studios, one of the top events of the year in Orlando. Universal creative talents exercise the dark side of their imagination, and there are truly frightening haunted houses here and there on the park grounds, open during the special ticketed events. Shamu's Halloween Spooktacular promises ghoulishly fun shows, trick or treat stations, costume parades and street performers.
November	The American Indian Powwow (☎ 407/295–3247) kicks off the month at the Central Florida Fairgrounds. Early in the month, there's Festival in the Park, an arts-and-crafts show around the shores of downtown Orlando's Lake Eola. The Space Coast Birding & Wildlife Festival (☎ 321/268–5000) in Titusville occurs November 9–12. Field trips, seminars, and art exhibits are all organized. November 8–10 is the Festival of the Masters (☎ 407/934–6743) with 150 top artists exhibiting their creations at Downtown Disney. Daytime drama fans love Super Soap Weekend (☎ 407/824–4321) at Disney–MGM Studios, where they can schmooze for two days with their fave soap stars and participate in soap-related festivities. Beginning around Thanksgiving, the Osborne Family Spectacle of Lights (☎ 407/824–4321), an amazing neighborhood light display that started out in Little Rock, Arkansas, comes to the Residential Street back lot of Disney–MGM Studios—all 4 million lights of it. Universal's CityWalk hosts its annual BeerFest (☎ 407/363–8000), complete with lager tastings from throughout the world.

PLEASURES & PASTIMES

Water Play

Once visitors are land-locked in Central Florida and at least an hour's drive from the nearest ocean, they often are overcome with the instinct to seek an alternative body of water and jump in. No problem. Wet options abound in this land of lakes, water parks, natural springs, fountains, elaborate resort swimming pools, and theme-park attractions designed to spray, splash, and soak all who dare enter. Disney's Typhoon Lagoon can convince you that you're stranded on a tropical island, and Blizzard Beach is awash with whimsical water fun. Beyond Disney, Wet 'n' Wild and Water Mania are fresh-water attractions with plenty of slides and rafting experiences. Natural cool springs refresh at Wekiwa Springs and DeLeon Springs state parks. You can go airboating on Lake Toho in Kissimmee and waterskiing on any number of Orlando-area lakes. If you have only enough time for a theme-park blitz, hit the parks' flume rides for a refreshing dunk, or look for some spray from the nearest dancing fountain.

Roller Coasting

You don't have to be an astronaut or leave the atmosphere to experience G-forces during a visit to Florida. Defying gravity is a thrilling way to pass the time on the many roller-coaster slopes and multiple inversions that dot the parks from Universal to SeaWorld to Disney. Islands of Adventure is packed with the highest-tech rides, exposing you to near-collisions on dueling coasters and stomach-churning action on the high-speed Incredible Hulk Coaster. All 53-inch-tall coaster enthusiasts are dreaming of the extra inch that's their ticket onto SeaWorld's Kraken, the area's highest coaster at 15 stories. Until that anticipated growth spurt, they can test their mettle on the Magic Kingdom's legendary indoor Space Mountain for twists, turns and drops in the dark. The most elaborately-themed ride is Disney–MGM's Rock 'n' Roller Coaster starring Aerosmith, another indoor coaster with limo-like ride vehicles that hug the curves and blast tunes on a speaker system worth screaming about.

Dining Around the World

The world is your oyster, your spring roll, or even your seared maize cake in the wonderful world of Orlando-area dining. Years before Wolfgang Puck came to town with one of his famous cafés and Emeril Lagasse opened his thriving Emeril's Orlando with a bam!, dining options were diverse throughout the metropolitan area. Even the theme parks offer a degree of culinary savvy, whipping up counter-service fare beyond the expected burgers, dogs, and fries and often including vegetarian options. Throughout Orlando, Winter Park and the Disney and Kissimmee area, food lovers have their pick of African, Thai, Cuban, French, Indian and other ethnic cuisines. Many local eateries boast impressive wine cellars. Whether your stomach aches for comfort food or your taste buds beg for the freshest ingredients combined with flair, there's a buffet in town to die for or a restaurant serving a little slice of heaven.

Golf for Everyone

Whether you're a serious golfer or just one who likes to putt around, you have options: indulge on a championship course, take in a scenic nine holes, or aim for par at one of many themed mini-golf attractions. In the city that Tiger Woods, Arnold Palmer, and many famous PGA pros call home, you must have a member's invitation to play at Arnold Palmer's

Bay Hill Golf Resort. But you won't have to pull strings to play on one of Disney's five 18-hole courses or its nine-hole walking course. The picturesque Winter Park Municipal Golf Club is on the National Register of Historic Places and has some of the lowest greens fees in town. Countless resort courses and clubs offer excellent year-round challenges. Colorful mini-golf courses with pirate, jungle and other themes dot the area from International Drive to Lake Buena Vista and Kissimmee. At Disney, you can golf with the hippos from "Fantasia" at Disney's Fantasia Gardens mini-golf course or even with a "snowman" at the chill-inspiring Winter Summerland course next to, you guessed it, Blizzard Beach.

Bird Watching

It's a strange and fascinating sight to see an anhinga, also known as a snakebird, dive for its dinner in one of Central Florida's many lakes. The large water bird, which has no oil glands to waterproof its feathers, plunges underwater, its long, snake-like neck breaking the surface here and there until fishing is done. Back on shore, it spreads its wings to dry in the sun. Orlando's abundant wildlife also includes other birds, from the great blue heron and white ibis to hawks and American bald eagles. At the Audubon Center for Birds of Prey in Maitland, you can see injured or orphaned birds such as owls, falcons, eagles, and kites being cared for and rehabilitated. Many are released back into the wild after recuperating. And two terrific aviaries at Disney's Animal Kingdom show off a variety of bird species native to Africa and Asia, including the carmine bee-eater, hottentot teal, hammerkop, the yellow-throated laughing thrush and timor sparrow finch.

FODOR'S CHOICE

The sights, restaurants, hotels, and other travel experiences on these pages are our editors' top picks—our Fodor's Choices. They're the best of their type in the area covered by the book—not to be missed and always worth your time. In the destination chapters that follow, you will find all the details.

LODGING

$$$$ **Animal Kingdom Lodge,** in Walt Disney World. Live giraffes and zebras browse outside your window at this African-theme hotel.

$$$$ **BoardWalk Inn and Villas,** in Walt Disney World. This elegant re-creation of a beach resort of the early 1900s even extends its homage to the swimming pool, where the 200-ft water slide resembles an old wooden roller coaster.

$$$$ **Hyatt Regency Grand Cypress Resort,** near Lake Buena Vista. The word "grand" in the hotel's name is no misrepresentation—within its 2-⅓ square mi are a nature preserve, an enormous pool, and a bird-filled, 18-story atrium.

$$$$ **Ritz-Carlton Orlando Grande Lakes,** in Southwestern Orlando. With an elaborate pool area that rivals Orlando's best water parks, a huge European-style spa, and what seems like miles of marble floors, this opulent resort has something for everyone and then some.

$$$–$$$$ **Wilderness Lodge,** in Walt Disney World. This majestic hotel, incongruous in Central Florida with its surrounding fuzz of towering pines, is patterned after the Rocky Mountain lodges of the Teddy Roosevelt era.

$$$ **Gaylord Palms Resort,** in Kissimmee. The 4-acre, glass-enclosed atrium contains environments recalling old St. Augustine, Key West, and the Everglades, all exceptionally detailed.

$$$ **Grand Floridian Resort & Spa,** in Walt Disney World. If it weren't for its modern amenities, you might think you were in one of the great hotels of the 19th century when you visit this Victorian-style charmer, Disney's flagship resort.

$$$ **Royal Pacific Resort,** in Universal Studios. The South Pacific theme extends to the beautiful, lagoon-style pool and grounds filled with tropical flora.

BUDGET LODGING

¢   **Studio Plus Orlando,** near Universal Studios. For less than half of what you'd spend on theme-park property, you can get a spacious suite with a full kitchen and extras like a fold-out couch.

RESTAURANTS

$$$$ **Victoria and Albert's,** in Walt Disney World. It's expensive, but menu offerings like grilled prime filet over onion risotto and cabernet jus are well worth the price.

| $$-$$$$ | **Le Coq au Vin,** in Central Orlando. New York critics periodically pay homage to this fine little eatery's French country cooking, especially preparations such as the house namesake dish. |

| $$-$$$$ | **Les Chefs de France,** in Walt Disney World. Very good French food is served daily at this Epcot charmer, which many call Disney's best. |

| $$-$$$ | **Spoodles,** in Walt Disney World. At this stylish spot on Disney's Boardwalk, you can sample wonderful Mediterranean tapas, from Italian to Greek. |

| $-$$ | **La Fontanella Da Nino,** in Thornton Park. The quiet fountain for which this place is named is as special as the fine Italian cooking. |

| $-$$ | **"Once Upon a Time" Character Breakfast at Cinderella's Royal Table,** in Walt Disney World. Getting the reservation requires more strategy than traversing the theme parks, but it's an exceptional photo opportunity for children infatuated with the Disney princesses. |

BUDGET RESTAURANTS

| ¢-$ | **Anthony's Pizzeria,** in Thornton Park. This is the place for great pizza and pasta at great prices. |

| ¢ | **Little Saigon,** in Central Orlando. Both the price and the solid Vietnamese cooking keep locals coming back for more. |

AFTER HOURS

Comedy Warehouse, in Walt Disney World. Talented improv performers deliver quick one-liners and longer sketches—and there's not an off-color joke in the bunch.

House of Blues, in Walt Disney World. In this antidote to Orlando's bubblegum pop slop, real musicians play real music, accompanying real food made by real Southerners.

La Nouba at Cirque du Soleil. Probably the best thing you can do at WDW as a couple or as a family with children over eight. You are likely to alternately hold your breath and exclaim in wonder.

ANIMAL ENCOUNTERS

Green Meadows Farm, in Kissimmee. The pigs will nibble on your shoelaces and you'll get to cuddle a baby chick and milk a cow on this 40-acre family-friendly farm.

Kilimanjaro Safaris, Disney's Animal Kingdom. You might see more wild animals in authentic-looking habitats on this themed 20-minute bus ride than you might if you went all the way to Africa.

Myombe Reserve, at Busch Gardens. While you're enchanted by the lonesome and loving eyes of the gorillas and chimps, they'll be enchanted to have you as their guest. The windows inside the quiet caves bring you a little closer to their world.

Rhino Rally, at Busch Gardens. Mixing the kind of rapid fire jokes you hear on Disney's Jungle Cruise with whitewater rapids and an ersatz safari experience makes this attraction a thrill a second.

FIREWORKS & PARADES

Fantasmic!, Disney–MGM Studios. Lasers, fireworks, music, drama. and more Disney heroes, heroines, and villains than anywhere else on the property.

IllumiNations, Epcot. An amazing fireworks show accompanied by lasers, fountains, and original music.

SpectroMagic Parade, Magic Kingdom. This extravaganza makes for a true "When You Wish upon a Star" finale to any day.

RIDES

The Amazing Adventures of Spider-Man, Islands of Adventure. Easily the best ride in town. The huge leaps in technology and the sensory tricks make this worth the wait—and you will, unless you get up bright and early and head straight over.

Buzz Lightyear's Space Ranger Spin, Magic Kingdom. Even if you don't know Buzz or Woody of *Toy Story* fame, you'll have a blast spinning out in your two-passenger star cruiser and shooting your laser at colorful targets as you try to defeat the evil Emperor Zurg.

Haunted Mansion, Magic Kingdom. Ghoulish wit and cobweb-laced Victorian trappings add up to a delightful scarefest.

Summit Plummet, Blizzard Beach. Dangle your legs on Florida's only "ski lift" as you ride to the top of Mt. Gushmore, a 350-ft-long water slide.

Test Track, Epcot. A wild ride on a General Motors proving ground as your car revs up to 60 mph on a hairpin curve.

Twilight Zone Tower of Terror, Disney–MGM Studios. Scare up some nerve and defy gravity inside this deserted hotel. You'd be better off taking the stairs—if there were any to take. As they say, the 13th story is a killer.

ROLLER COASTERS

Dueling Dragons, Islands of Adventure. With multiple inversions and relative fly-by speeds of up to 120 mph, these coasters can really churn up your stomach.

Rock 'n' Roller Coaster Starring Aerosmith, Disney–MGM Studios. WDW's high-speed, multiple-inversion roller coaster, with the pumped-up volume of Aerosmith, is a hit.

Splash Mountain, Magic Kingdom. Heading over the final 52½-ft drop here, one of the steepest of any flume ride in existence, makes you feel like Wile E. Coyote.

SHOWS, FILMS & TOURS

Animal Planet Live!, Universal Studios. A perfect family show starring a menagerie of animals whose unusually high IQs are surpassed only by their cuteness and cuddle-ability.

Eighth Voyage of Sindbad, Islands of Adventure. Running, jumping, diving, punching. is it another Schwarzenegger action film? No, it's a live and thoroughly pleasing stunt show with a love story thrown in.

Honey, I Shrunk the Audience, Epcot. This side-splitting, chill-inducing 3-D and special-effects show is a wild sensation that ranks among the best in the World.

The Magic of Disney Animation, Disney–MGM Studios. This self-guided tour takes a behind-the-scenes look at the making of Disney's great animated films.

Pets Ahoy, SeaWorld. Starring pets rescued from local animal shelters, this is a show that's fun for everyone.

Sea Lion & Otter Stadium, SeaWorld. The show changes, but the seals, sea lions, otters, and preshow mime are always fantastically funny.

Shamu Rocks America, SeaWorld. How in the world can an Arctic whale make you proud to be an American? Who knows? At this spectacular, Shamu does his bit for the USA.

Tree of Life—It's Tough to Be a Bug!, Disney's Animal Kingdom. Adults and children who don't mind surprises in a dark theater shouldn't miss the music, special effects, and puns found here.

Universal Horror Make-Up Show, Universal Studios. This sometimes gross, often raunchy, but always entertaining demonstration merges the best of stand-up comedy with creepy effects.

GOLF

Osprey Ridge, in Walt Disney World. With its pristine pine groves, this Tom Fazio-designed course is among the most pleasant in WDW, but it's also one of the most challenging, as its tees and greens are as much as 20 ft above the fairways.

Winter Summerland Miniature Golf Course, in Walt Disney World. At this fantasy-driven mini-golf course for all levels, you putt through sand castles and snow that never melts.

MUSEUMS

Charles Hosmer Morse Museum, in Winter Park. Stunning stained-glass windows, lamps, and watercolors designed by Louis Comfort Tiffany are the draw.

Orlando Science Center, in Downtown Orlando. Science meets entertainment in 12 themed display halls with interactive exhibits that cover health, energy, nature, and the solar system, among others.

SPORTS & THE OUTDOORS

Disney's Wide World of Sports Complex, in Walt Disney World. You can watch or sign up to play almost any game at this comprehensive sports center, and you may even walk away with a Mickey-shape medal.

Grand Cypress Equestrian Center, near Lake Buena Vista. You can take a Western trail ride through the Florida scrub or attend a dressage show at this center at the Hyatt Grand Cypress Resort.

Sky Venture, in the I-Drive Area. Here, to get the thrill of sky diving, you don't have to jump out of an airplane or even get very far off the ground.

PARKS & GARDENS

Bok Tower Gardens, in Lake Wales. When you're ready for a peaceful retreat from the parks, take a walk along the quiet path through these colorful gardens, shaded by the arching boughs of ancient trees.

Wekiwa Springs State Park, in Apopka. Bring a picnic and spend the day canoeing, swimming, and looking for water turtles at this 6,400-acre state park.

SHOPPING

Belz Factory Outlet World, in the I-Drive Area. New stores and regular expansions keep the grandfather of all outlet malls on top.

Downtown Disney, in Walt Disney World. After a day of beating your feet around a theme park, reserve an evening for some quiet lakeside shopping and strolling.

Outdoor World, in the I-Drive Area. Sporting goods for every sport in existence, all presented in outdoors-y style inside a massive faux Pacific Northwest lodge. It's all here. *Everything.*

THE SPACE COAST

Kennedy Space Center Visitor Complex, in Titusville. Don't miss the bus tours here—a must if you want a close-up view of the enormous space shuttle.

Merritt Island National Wildlife Refuge, in Titusville. This preserve owes its existence to Kennedy Space Center—it's a buffer zone between civilization and space central. The wildlife and the endless Florida plains make for complete tranquility.

Ron Jon Surf Shop, in Cocoa Beach. Self-promotion turned this 24-hour surf store into an East Coast icon.

Surfing off Cocoa Beach. The "Small Wave Capital of the World" is a great place to laze on the beach or buy a board and learn how to kick a tube.

SMART TRAVEL TIPS

Finding out about your destination before you leave home means you won't squander time organizing everyday minutiae once you've arrived. You'll be more streetwise when you hit the ground as well, better prepared to explore the aspects of the Orlando area that drew you here in the first place. The organizations in this section can provide information to supplement this guide; contact them for up-to-the-minute details. Happy landings!

AIR TRAVEL TO & FROM ORLANDO

BOOKING

When you book, **look for nonstop flights and remember that "direct" flights stop at least once.** Try to avoid connecting flights, which require a change of plane. Two airlines may operate a connecting flight jointly, so ask whether your airline operates every segment of the trip; you may find that the carrier you prefer flies only part of the way. Those traveling from the United Kingdom and Canada can fly directly to Orlando. Air Canada offers 26 flights a week, but smaller planes mean fewer seats. Virgin Atlantic offers 14–20 flights a week, depending on what time of year it is, but has more seats available. Qantas and Air New Zealand do not fly into Orlando, so travelers would have to fly into Los Angeles and grab a domestic flight to Orlando. To find more booking tips and to check prices and make on-line flight reservations, log on to www.fodors.com.

CARRIERS

More than 20 scheduled airlines and more than 30 charter firms operate in and out of Orlando International Airport, providing direct service to more than 100 cities in the United States and overseas.

🔢 Major Airlines **Air Tran** ☎ 800/247-8726. **America West** ☎ 800/235-9292. **American** ☎ 800/433-7300. **Continental** ☎ 800/523-3273. **Delta** ☎ 800/221-1212. **Northwest/KLM** ☎ 800/225-2525. **United Airlines** ☎ 800/241-6522. **US Airways** ☎ 800/428-4322.

🔢 Smaller Airlines **Frontier** ☎ 800/432-1359. **Midwest Express** ☎ 800/452-2022. **Southwest** ☎ 800/435-9792. **GM Spirit** ☎ 800/772-7117.

🔢 From the U.K. **American** ☎ 0208/572-5555 in London; 845/7789-789 via Miami or Chicago. **British Airways** ☎ 0845/773-3377. **Continental** ☎ 0800/

776-464. Delta ☎ 0800/414-767. United ☎ 0845/844-4777. Virgin Atlantic ☎ 01293/747-747.

CHECK-IN & BOARDING

Always **ask your carrier about its check-in policy.** Plan to arrive at the airport about two hours before your scheduled departure time for domestic flights and 2½ to 3 hours before international flights. You may need to arrive earlier if you're flying from one of the busier airports or during peak air-traffic times. At Orlando International Airport (OIA), all baggage and vehicles are subject to search while on airport property, so be prepared to cooperate if authorities ask to search your belongings. OIA has been ranked number one in the nation repeatedly by J.D. Powers and Associates for customer satisfaction in terms of security and service. The Orlando–New York route is the busiest for OIA. To avoid delays at airport-security checkpoints, try not to wear any metal. Jewelry, belt and other buckles, steel-toe shoes, barrettes, and underwire bras are among the items that can set off detectors.

Assuming that not everyone with a ticket will show up, airlines routinely overbook planes. When everyone does, airlines ask for volunteers to give up their seats. In return, these volunteers usually get a several-hundred-dollar flight voucher, which can be used toward the purchase of another ticket, and are rebooked on the next flight out. If there are not enough volunteers, the airline must choose who will be denied boarding. The first to get bumped are passengers who checked in late and those flying on discounted tickets, so **get to the gate and check in as early as possible,** especially during peak periods.

Always **bring a government-issued photo I.D. to the airport;** even when it's not required, a passport is best.

CUTTING COSTS

Since Orlando receives a high volume of visitors, a lot of deals are offered via the Internet and airlines. Last-minute flights purchased over the Internet can be very cheap, but generally the least expensive airfares to Orlando must be purchased in advance and are nonrefundable. The cheapest tickets are also for round-trip travel, though airlines generally allow you to change your return date for a fee. It's smart to **call a number of airlines and**

check the Internet; when you are quoted a good price, **book it on the spot**—the same fare may not be available the next day, or even the next hour. Always **check different routings** and look into using alternate airports. Also, price off-peak flights, which may be significantly less expensive than others. Travel agents, especially low-fare specialists (⇨ Discounts & Deals), are helpful.

Consolidators are another good source. They buy tickets for scheduled flights at reduced rates from the airlines, then sell them at prices that beat the best fare available directly from the airlines. Sometimes you can even get your money back if you need to return the ticket. Carefully read the fine print detailing penalties for changes and cancellations, purchase the ticket with a credit card, and **confirm your consolidator reservation with the airline.**

🎫 **Consolidators** AirlineConsolidator.com ☎ 888/468-5385 ⊕ www.airlineconsolidator.com; for international tickets. **Best Fares** ☎ 800/576-8255 or 800/576-1600 ⊕ www.bestfares.com; $59.90 annual membership. **Cheap Tickets** ☎ 800/377-1000 or 888/922-8849 ⊕ www.cheaptickets.com. **Expedia** ☎ 800/397-3342 or 404/728-8787 ⊕ www.expedia.com. **Hotwire** ☎ 866/468-9473 or 920/330-9418 ⊕ www.hotwire.com. **Now Voyager Travel** ✉ 45 W. 21st St., 5th fl., New York, NY 10010 ☎ 212/459-1616 🖷 212/243-2711 ⊕ www.nowvoyagertravel.com. **Onetravel.com** ⊕ www.onetravel.com. **Orbitz** ☎ 888/656-4546 ⊕ www.orbitz.com. **Priceline.com** ⊕ www.priceline.com. **Travelocity** ☎ 888/709-5983, 877/282-2925 in Canada, 0870/876-3876 in the U.K. ⊕ www.travelocity.com.

ENJOYING THE FLIGHT

En route to Orlando, wear lighter clothing and carry a midweight jacket if you're coming from a colder climate. If you're traveling with children, be sure to bring snacks, games, toys, and books to keep them entertained during the flight.

State your seat preference when purchasing your ticket, and then repeat it when you confirm and when you check in. For more legroom, you can request one of the few emergency-aisle seats at check-in, if you are capable of lifting at least 50 pounds—a Federal Aviation Administration requirement of passengers in these seats. Seats behind a bulkhead also offer more legroom, but they don't have underseat storage. Don't sit in the row in front of the emergency aisle or in front of a bulkhead, where seats may not recline.

Ask the airline whether a snack or meal is served on the flight. If you have dietary concerns, **request special meals when booking.** These can be vegetarian, low-cholesterol, or kosher, for example. It's a good idea to pack some healthful snacks and a small (plastic) bottle of water in your carry-on bag. On long flights, try to maintain a normal routine, to help fight jet lag. At night, **get some sleep.** By day, **eat light meals, drink water** (not alcohol), and **move around the cabin** to stretch your legs. For additional jet-lag tips consult *Fodor's FYI: Travel Fit & Healthy* (available at bookstores everywhere).

Smoking policies vary from carrier to carrier. Many airlines prohibit smoking on all of their flights; others allow smoking only on certain routes or certain departures. Ask your carrier about its policy.

FLYING TIMES

Flying time is 2½ hours from New York, 3½ hours from Chicago, and 5 hours from Los Angeles.

HOW TO COMPLAIN

If your baggage goes astray or your flight goes awry, complain right away. Most carriers require that you **file a claim immediately.** The Aviation Consumer Protection Division of the Department of Transportation publishes *Fly-Rights,* which discusses airlines and consumer issues and is available on-line.

🛈 Airline Complaints **Aviation Consumer Protection Division** ✉ U.S. Department of Transportation, C-75, Room 4107, 400 7th St. NW, Washington, DC 20590 ☎ 202/366-2220 ⊕ www.dot.gov/airconsumer. **Federal Aviation Administration Consumer Hotline** ✉ for inquiries: FAA, 800 Independence Ave. SW, Room 810, Washington, DC 20591 ☎ 800/322-7873 ⊕ www.faa.gov.

RECONFIRMING

Check the status of your flight before you leave for the airport. You can do this on your carrier's Web site, by linking to a flight-status checker (many Web booking services offer these), or by calling your carrier or travel agent. Always confirm international flights at least 72 hours ahead of the scheduled departure time.

AIRPORTS & TRANSFERS

The Orlando airport is ultramodern, huge, and growing all the time. It is also relatively easy to navigate thanks to excellent signs. The airport is divided into terminals A and B. Terminal C is under construction. Monorails shuttle you from gate areas to the core area, where you'll find baggage claim. If you land in the A section, go to the A baggage claim area, if you land in the B section, go to the B baggage claim area, and so forth. The complex is southeast of Orlando and northeast of Walt Disney World.

🛈 **Orlando International Airport (MCO)** ☎ 407/825-2001.

AIRPORT TRANSFERS

Taxis take only a half hour to get from the airport to most hotels used by WDW visitors; they charge about $25 plus tip to the International Drive area, about $10 more to the U.S. 192 area. Depending on the number of people in your party, this may cost less than paying by the head for an airport shuttle. Mears Transportation Group meets you at the gate, helps with the luggage, and whisks you away in either an 11-passenger van, a town car, or a limo. Vans run to Walt Disney World and along U.S. 192 every 30 minutes; prices range from $16 one way for adults ($12 for children 4–11) to $28 round-trip for adults ($20 children 4–11). Limo rates run $44–$60 for a town car that accommodates three or four to $125 for a stretch limo that seats six. Town & Country Transportation charges $35–$55 one way for up to seven people. Public buses, operated by Lynx transportation authority, operate between the airport and the main bus terminal in downtown Orlando. The cost is $1.25.

🛈 Taxis & Limos **Ace Metro Cab** ☎ 407/855-1111. **Town & Country Transportation** ☎ 407/828-3035. **Yellow Cab Co.** ☎ 407/699-9999. 🛈 Buses & Shuttles **Lynx** ✉ 1200 W. South St., Orlando ☎ 407/841-8240 or 800/344-5969 ⊕ www.golynx.com. **Mears Transportation Group** ☎ 407/423-5566 ⊕ www.mearstransportation.com.

BUS TRAVEL TO & FROM ORLANDO

Greyhound is the only major bus line providing service to the Orlando area. Round-trip tickets from other Florida cities, such as Jacksonville, cost $25–$30 and traveling time is 2½ hours, longer than the same trip by car. The Greyhound terminal is in an industrial area of Orlando, outside of downtown proper. There is no shuttle service available from the terminal to area attractions, but you can call for a taxi or wait at the taxi stand outside the terminal.

🚌 **Greyhound Bus Lines of Orlando** ⊠ 555 N. John Young Pkwy. ☎ 800/231-2222.

BUS TRAVEL AROUND ORLANDO

Public buses run by Lynx transportation authority can get you around the International Drive area, Kissimmee, and Orlando proper. To find out which bus to take, ask the information desk at your hotel or contact Lynx Customer Service. Lymmo, operated by Lynx, is a free bus service that circulates downtown Orlando daily until 10 PM (until midnight on Friday and Saturday).

Many hotels run shuttles for guests, although these buses may not run to the places you want to see on the days or at the times you prefer, whether that's back to your hotel at midday or out to the theme parks in late afternoon. Some buses also pick up or drop off guests at several hotels, adding to your ride time and delaying your arrival.

Your hotel may have contracted service with Mears Transportation, or the concierge may be able to call a Mears shuttle for you. During certain times of the year, you can get a good deal on special excursion fares that include both transportation and admission to Busch Gardens, which is more than a half hour's drive away. Sometimes you can negotiate a room rate that includes free transportation, even when it's not routinely available.

If you're staying on International Drive or Universal Boulevard between Vineland Avenue and the Florida Turnpike, and you plan to spend a day visiting just I-Drive attractions, then consider using the I-Ride Trolley to get around. For 75¢ the trolley takes you to Sea World, Wet 'n Wild, the Mercado, the Orange County Convention Center, Orlando Premium Outlets, and Belz Factory Outlet stores, and it'll put you within walking distance of dozens of other attractions, shops, and restaurants.

FARES & SCHEDULES

One-way public bus fare is $1.25, and exact change in coins or a dollar bill is required. Transfers and bus travel in downtown Orlando are free. Daily ($3) and weekly ($10) bus passes let you ride as many times as you want while the pass is valid. A one-way fare on a Mears bus between major hotel areas and the Disney parks usually costs $8–$10 per adult, and a couple of dollars less for children ages 4–11. I-Ride trolleys run daily 8 AM–10:30 PM. Exact change is necessary for the adult fare (75¢); children under 12 ride free. Passes let you ride as many times as you want for a set price: $2 for one day, $3 for three days, $5 for five days, and $7 for one week.

🚌 **Between Hotels & Attractions Lynx Information Office** ⊠ 1200 W. South St., Orlando ☎ 407/841-8240 or 800/344-5969 (LYNX) ⊕ www.golynx.com. **Mears Transportation Group** ☎ 407/423-5566 ⊕ www.mearstransportation.com. **I-Ride Trolley** ☎ 407/248-9590 or 866/243-7483 ⊕ www.iridetrolley.com.

CAMERAS & PHOTOGRAPHY

Central Florida presents lots of opportunities for a great photo, from shots of the family hugging Disney characters to panoramas of beautifully manicured lakeside parks to up-close snaps of gators and crocs. Combat the bright sun with ASA 200 film and keep the sun behind you when you compose a photo.

The *Kodak Guide to Shooting Great Travel Pictures* (available at bookstores everywhere) is loaded with tips.

🚌 **Photo Help Kodak Information Center** ☎ 800/242-2424 ⊕ www.kodak.com.

EQUIPMENT PRECAUTIONS

Don't pack film and equipment in checked luggage, where it is much more susceptible to damage. X-ray machines used to view checked luggage are extremely powerful and therefore are likely to ruin your film. Try to **ask for hand inspection of film,** which becomes clouded after repeated exposure to airport X-ray machines, and **keep videotapes and computer disks away from metal detectors.** Always **keep film, tape, and computer disks out of the sun.** Carry an extra supply of batteries, and **be prepared to turn on your camera,**

camcorder, or laptop to prove to airport security personnel that the device is real.

CAR RENTAL

If you want to visit major theme parks outside Walt Disney World, or move from park to resort to park on Disney property in a single day, or stay in a Disney resort that's served only by buses, or venture off the beaten track, or eat where most tourists don't, **rent a car.** Rates here are among the lowest in the United States but vary seasonally. They can begin as low as $30 a day and $149 a week for an economy car with air-conditioning, automatic transmission, and unlimited mileage. This does not include tax on car rentals, which is 6%. Avis and Budget have car lots on airport property, a short walk from baggage claim. Bus transportation to other car rentals is usually fast and efficient.

🚗 Major Agencies **Alamo** ☎ 800/327-9633 ⊕ www.alamo.com. **Avis** ☎ 800/331-1212, 800/879-2847 or 800/272-5871 in Canada, 0870/606-0100 in the U.K., 02/9353-9000 in Australia, 09/526-2847 in New Zealand ⊕ www.avis.com. **Budget** ☎ 800/527-0700, 0870/156-5656 in the U.K. ⊕ www.budget.com. **Dollar** ☎ 800/800-4000, 0124/622-0111 in the U.K., where it's affiliated with Sixt, 02/9223-1444 in Australia ⊕ www.dollar.com. **Hertz** ☎ 800/654-3131, 800/263-0600 in Canada, 0870/844-8844 in the U.K., 02/9669-2444 in Australia, 09/256-8690 in New Zealand ⊕ www.hertz. com. **National Car Rental** ☎ 800/227-7368, 0870/600-6666 in the U.K. ⊕ www.nationalcar.com.

CUTTING COSTS

For a good deal, **book through a travel agent who will shop around.** Also, **price local car-rental companies**—whose prices may be lower still, although their service and maintenance may not be as good as those of major rental agencies—and **research rates on the Internet.** Remember to ask about required deposits, cancellation penalties, and drop-off charges if you're planning to pick up the car in one city and leave it in another. If you're traveling during a holiday period, make sure that a confirmed reservation guarantees you a car.

INSURANCE

When driving a rented car you are generally responsible for any damage to or loss of the vehicle. You also may be liable for any property damage or personal injury that you may cause while driving. Before you rent, see what coverage you already have under the terms of your personal auto-insurance policy and credit cards.

For about $10 to $25 a day, rental companies sell protection, known as a collision- or loss-damage waiver (CDW or LDW), that eliminates your liability for damage to the car; it's always optional and should never be automatically added to your bill. In most states you don't need a CDW if you have personal auto insurance or other liability insurance. However, **make sure you have enough coverage to pay for the car.** If you do not have auto insurance or an umbrella policy that covers damage to third parties, purchasing liability insurance and a CDW or LDW is highly recommended.

REQUIREMENTS & RESTRICTIONS

In Florida, some agencies require that you be at least 21 to rent a car. Others require that you be 25.

SURCHARGES

Before you pick up a car in one city and leave it in another, **ask about drop-off charges or one-way service fees,** which can be substantial. Note, too, that some rental agencies charge extra if you return the car before the time specified in your contract. To avoid a hefty refueling fee, **fill the tank just before you turn in the car,** but be aware that gas stations near the rental outlet may overcharge. It's almost never a deal to buy the tank of gas that's in the car when you rent it; the understanding is that you'll return it empty, but some fuel usually remains. Surcharges may apply if you're under 25 or if you take the car outside the area approved by the rental agency. You'll pay extra for child seats (about $6 a day), which are compulsory for children under five, and usually for additional drivers (about $10 per day).

CAR TRAVEL

The Beeline Expressway (Route 528) is the best way to get to the International Drive area and Walt Disney World from the Orlando International Airport, though you should expect to pay about $1.25 in tolls. Depending on the location of your hotel, follow the expressway west to International Drive, and either exit at SeaWorld for the International Drive area, or stay on the Beeline to I–4, and head west for Walt Disney World and U.S. 192/Kissimmee or east for Universal Studios and downtown Orlando. Call your hotel for the best route.

I–4 is the main artery in Central Florida, linking the Gulf coast in Tampa to the Atlantic coast in Daytona Beach. Although I–4 is an east–west highway, it actually follows a north–south track through the Orlando area. So **think north when I–4 signs say east and think south when the signs say west.**

In 2002, the Florida Department of Transportation changed the exit numbers of several major interstates, including I–4, which intersects Orlando and Walt Disney World. The WDW exits are 64B, 65, 67, and 68, but locals and older maps may still cite the old exits, 25, 24D, 26D, and 27, respectively. The new highway signs display both the old and new exit numbers.

Two other main roads you're likely to use are International Drive, also known as I-Drive, and U.S. 192, sometimes called the Spacecoast Parkway or Irlo Bronson Memorial Highway. You can get onto International Drive from I–4 Exits 72 (formerly 28), 74A (formerly 29), and 75B (formerly 30B). U.S. 192 cuts across I–4 at Exits 64A (formerly 25A) and 64B (formerly 25B).

EMERGENCY SERVICES

If you have a cell phone, dialing *347 (*FHP) will get you the Florida Highway Patrol. Most Florida highways are also patrolled by Road Rangers, a free roadside service that helps stranded motorists with minor problems and can call for a tow-truck when there are bigger problems. Disney's Car Care Center near the Magic Kingdom is a full service operation that will provide most emergency services, except towing, while it is open (weekdays 7 AM–6 PM, Saturday 7:30 AM–4 PM). On Disney property, you can flag a security guard any day until 10 PM for help with minor emergencies, such as a flat tire, dead battery, empty gas tank, or towing.
🏛 **Florida Highway Patrol** ☎ *347. **Walt Disney World Car Care Center** ☎ 407/824-0976.

PARKING

For information on parking at the theme parks, *see* Parking *in* the A to Z sections of the individual parks *in* chapters 1, 2, and 3.

Parking in downtown Orlando is available both on the street and in garages. Meters on the street take nickels, dimes, and quarters, and parking rules are strictly enforced. Fines start at $15 and can go as high as $35. Meter debit cards are available for purchase at city hall. There are several large parking garages downtown. Most charge 50¢ for the first half hour and $1 for each additional hour. Overnight parking is available only at the Central Boulevard garage and the Market Street and Library garage, both of which offer a flat rate of $4 to park 5 PM–5:30 AM. Private parking is widely available at properties on I-Drive and in Kissimmee and outlying towns.

RULES OF THE ROAD

All front-seat passengers are required to wear seat belts. All children under 4 years old must be in approved child-safety seats. Children older than 4 must wear a seat belt. Florida's Alcohol/Controlled Substance DUI Law is one of the toughest in the U.S. A blood alcohol level of .08 or higher can have serious repercussions even for the first-time offender.

In Florida, you may turn right at a red light after stopping, unless otherwise posted. When in doubt, wait for the green. Be alert for one-way streets, "no left turn" intersections, and blocks closed to car traffic. Watch for middle lanes with painted arrows that point left. These are turn lanes. They are to help you make a left turn without disrupting the flow of traffic behind you. Turn your blinker on, pull into this lane, and come to a stop, if necessary, before making a left turn. Never use this lane as a passing lane.

Expect heavy traffic during rush hours, which are on weekdays 6–10 AM and 4–7 PM. To encourage carpooling, some freeways have special lanes for so-called high-occupancy vehicles (HOV)—cars carrying more than one passenger. The use of radar detectors is legal in Florida and its neighboring states, Alabama and Georgia. Although it is legal to talk on your cell phone while driving in Florida, it is not recommended. Dial *511 on a cell phone to hear I–4 traffic advisory.

CHILDREN IN ORLANDO

Are your children old enough for a Central Florida vacation? There's no question that at 10, or even 8 or 9, many children have the maturity to understand and enjoy the information and entertainment at the theme parks.

Younger children are another matter. It's not that they won't enjoy it, because all the theme parks get high marks from young travelers. But you'll be spending a lot of money and probably battling huge crowds to see the place yourself, and you and your children may have totally different ideas about what's fun. While you're envisioning the Twilight Zone Tower of Terror, ExtraTERRORestrial Alien Encounter, Space Mountain, *Earthquake, Jaws,* and *Back to the Future* . . . The Ride, your youngsters may want to ride Dumbo 100 times, splash in the fountains outside Ariel's Grotto, and collect signatures from people dressed up in funny outfits. And they may well be terrified by the very attractions that adults typically travel to the Orlando area to experience. Although the Baby Swap can be helpful, allowing you and your partner to take turns experiencing an attraction, it's not a perfect solution.

Consider how you feel about forcing your kids to wait repeatedly in the hot Florida sun while you ride, or making them go on rides that are scary for them. Don't forget cost: do you really want to spend $45 a day for your child to do this? And then there's the issue of who you ride with: when you use Baby Swap, you end up experiencing the attractions with total strangers, while your significant other baby-sits back in the queue area. Think about how having young children along slows you down and effectively increases the time you spend in line, and you may decide to hold off until your kids are older.

The alternative, of course, is to bite the bullet and go anyway. But **create an itinerary that builds in your children's interests as well as your own,** understanding that they will delight in details that you might overlook. Allow yourself to appreciate the park from their point of view. And **plan for plenty of family time away from the theme parks.** For a night or two, step out for the fireworks or some other after-dark thrills in or away from the theme parks. Give yourself more time than you think you need, and buy passes rather than tickets so that you can always go back and

see what you've missed another day. (Passes, in theme-park lingo, allow you to visit a number of theme parks on any given day as long as the pass is valid.)

Crowds are often a problem and can overwhelm preschoolers. Do what you can to avoid the times of the year that are likely to be the most crowded (during school holidays, for example) and then plan your itinerary around the days of the week and times of day when the parks and attractions are the least busy. For more information on the busiest and least-crowded times to visit the theme parks, *see* When to Go *in* the Destination chapter, and Timing Tips in the theme park sections of chapters 1, 2, and 3.

So that you won't have to concern yourself with lugging items such as strollers, cribs, high chairs, and backpack carriers, be sure to ask your hotel whether what you need can be provided. If it can't, consider calling A Baby's Best Friend before you leave. The company's employees will deliver high-quality equipment to your accommodations prior to your arrival and pick them up after your departure. If you are renting a car, don't forget to **arrange for a car seat** when you reserve.

Fodor's Around Orlando with Kids can help you plan your days together. For general advice about traveling with children, consult *Fodor's FYI: Travel with Your Baby.* Both guidebooks are available in bookstores everywhere.

🔁 Rental Baby Equipment **A Baby's Best Friend** ☎ 407/891-2241 or 888/461-2229 ⊕ www.abbf.com.

BABY-SITTING

Walt Disney World has strong children's facilities and programs at the BoardWalk, Contemporary, Dolphin, Grand Floridian, Polynesian, Swan, Wilderness Lodge, and Yacht and Beach Club resorts. The Polynesian Resort's Never Land Club has an enchanting Peter Pan–theme clubhouse and youngsters-only dinner show. Parents also rave about the Sand Castle Club at the Yacht and Beach Club resorts. The BoardWalk's child-care facility, Harbor Club, provides late-afternoon and evening baby-sitting.

Many hotels have supervised children's programs with trained counselors and planned activities as well as attractive facilities; some even have mascots. Standouts are the Hyatt Regency Grand Cypress, near Downtown Disney, and the Camp Holiday programs at the Holiday Inn SunSpree Resort Lake Buena Vista and Holiday Inn Hotel & Suites Main Gate East. The Hilton, near Downtown Disney's Marketplace, has the Vacation Station, a hotel within a hotel for the little ones.

Walt Disney World has KinderCare preschool and drop-off day-care facilities in the Lake Buena Vista area. The KinderCare center accepts children who are potty trained and walking and is open weekdays 6 AM–9 PM, weekends 6 AM–6 PM. KinderCare cost $10.00 an hour or $45.00 for a 10-hour day. You don't have to be a Disney hotel guest to use the program. Disney's Kid's Night Out program provides infant care and in-room baby-sitting. Fees start at $13.50 an hour for one child, and increase with the number of children you have. There is a four-hour minimum, plus a transportation fee for the sitter to travel to your hotel room.

KinderCare ☎ 407/827-5437. Kid's Night Out ☎ 407/827-5444.

BABY SWAP

Parents with small children under the height limit for major attractions have to take turns waiting in the long lines, right? Wrong. In what's unofficially known as the Baby Swap, both of you queue up, and when it's your turn to board, one stays with the youngsters until the other returns; the waiting partner then rides without waiting again. Universal Studios calls it a Baby Exchange and has areas set aside for it at most rides.

CHARACTER MEALS

At special breakfasts, brunches, lunches, and dinners in many Walt Disney World restaurants, Mickey, Donald, Goofy, Chip 'n' Dale, Cinderella, and other favorite characters sign autographs and pose for snapshots. Universal's Islands of Adventure has a character luncheon, so your children can enjoy pizza or chicken fingers with their favorite Seuss characters. Talk with your children to find out which characters they most want to see; then call the Disney dining reservations line and speak with the representative about what's available.

Reservations are not always necessary, but these hugging-and-feeding frenzies are wildly popular, so **show up early.** It's a good idea to have your character meal near the end of your visit, when your little ones will be used to seeing these large and sometimes frightening figures; they're also a good way to spend the morning on the day you check out.

WHERE TO EAT

Many Central Florida restaurants have children's menus. And franchised fast-food eateries abound, providing that reassuring taste of home. The McDonald's on International Drive has an elaborate multilevel playground that seems almost bigger than the restaurant. The Rainforest Café chain, with its rainstorms and jungle details, is another child-pleaser. Stagestruck children like the belly dancer in the Marrakesh Restaurant, in Morocco in Epcot's World Showcase. Whispering Canyon Café in Disney's Wilderness Lodge and 'Ohana in the Polynesian have what it takes to please both parents and their offspring.

EDUCATIONAL PROGRAMS

For any behind-the-scenes tours and programs, be sure to **reserve ahead.**

Many of Walt Disney World's backstage tours are good for children. For full descriptions of each, see Guided Tours in the A to Z sections of the individual theme parks in Chapter 1. Two favorites are "Dolphins In Depth" at Epcot, costing $150 for three-and-a-half hours, and Disney's "Family Magic Tour" at the Magic Kingdom, costing $25 for two hours.

SeaWorld's Behind the Scenes Tours offer an up-close look at rescue procedures and caring for killer whales. One-hour tours are $8.95 for adults, $7.95 for children ages 3–9, in addition to park admission price. The seven-hour "Trainer For A Day" program costs $389. There are also more than 16 year-round adventure camps, from half-day to week-long sessions (prices start at $50). The bring-your-own-sleeping-bag "Education Sleepovers" provide kids with the chance to sleep near the sharks or penguins.

Busch Gardens' Multiday Zoo Camps keep children learning here from June through October. There's a different program for each age group, from 3rd grade through 12th, and each program lasts a week ($130–$230 per session). Youngsters can also sign up for classes that last just a few hours ($8–$10 plus general admission), from a hands-on introduction to wildlife for toddlers to a night hike for preteens.

Walt Disney World Resort ☎ 407/824-4321 ⊕ www.disney.com. **SeaWorld** ☎ 407/363-2380 or 800/406-2244 ⊕ www.seaworld.org. **Busch Gardens** ☎ 813/987-5555 ⊕ www.buschgardens.com.

FLYING

Experts agree that it's a good idea to use safety seats aloft for children weighing less than 40 pounds. Airlines set their own policies: If you use a safety seat, U.S. carriers usually require that the child be ticketed, even if he or she is young enough to ride free, because the seats must be strapped into regular seats. And even if you pay the full adult fare for the seat, it may be worth it, especially on longer trips. Do **check your airline's policy about using safety seats during takeoff and landing.** Safety seats are not allowed everywhere in the plane, so get your seat assignments as early as possible.

When reserving, **request children's meals or a freestanding bassinet** (not available at all airlines) if you need them. But note that bulkhead seats, where you must sit to use the bassinet, may lack an overhead bin or storage space on the floor.

SIGHTS & ATTRACTIONS

Places that are especially appealing to children are indicated by a rubber-duckie icon (🦆) in the margin.

STROLLER RENTALS

Stroller rentals are available in theme parks, but you may want to bring your own, since fees run $5–$7 per day (plus a deposit). Also, you will probably need a stroller in places where you can't rent one—to tour Orlando off the beaten track, to explore Orlando's malls, even just to get around an especially large hotel. Theme parks' strollers are sturdy but unyielding, and not optimal for infants.

If you do rent a stroller, there is always the possibility that it will be taken. Although it is tempting, **don't leave packages in your stroller.** Experienced park-goers tape a large card with their name to the stroller; now many of the parks provide the tags.

In addition, you might want to attach some small personal item to mark yours, such as a bandanna, a T-shirt, or even a clear plastic bag with diapers inside; the theory is that people who wouldn't think twice about taking theme-park property that they will subsequently return hesitate to make off with something that belongs to a fellow parent. If your stroller does disappear, you can easily pick up a replacement; ask any park staffer for the nearest location. If you wish to park-hop on the same day there's no need to rent another stroller. Simply turn the old one in when leaving the first park and get a new one upon entrance to the next park. Your deposit receipt is good all day at all Disney theme parks.

WHAT TO BRING

A backpack is a good idea. Sunscreen is recommended year-round, as well as a water bottle that you can refill at drinking fountains, and an assortment of small, uncrushable snacks to tide you over between meals (or even as meals themselves). Some parents bring frozen juice boxes—they'll thaw out by the time your children are ready for them and keep your back cool in the meantime. A bathing suit or a change of clothes can also be helpful, since youngsters like to splash around in theme-park fountains. Clean, dry socks are incredibly soothing to sore feet in the middle of the day. A pen or Sharpie marker is essential for gathering those precious character autographs.

CONCIERGES

Concierges, found in many hotels, can help you with theater tickets and dinner reservations: a good one with connections may be able to get you seats for a hot show or prime-time dinner reservations at the restaurant of the moment. You can also turn to your hotel's concierge for help with travel arrangements, sightseeing plans, services ranging from aromatherapy to zipper repair, and emergencies. Always, **always tip** a concierge who has been of assistance (⇨ Tipping).

CONSUMER PROTECTION

Whether you're shopping for gifts or purchasing travel services, **pay with a major credit card** whenever possible, so you can cancel payment or get reimbursed if there's a problem (and you can provide documentation). If you're doing business with a particular company for the first time, **contact your local Better Business Bureau and the attorney general's offices** in your state and (for U.S. businesses) the company's home state as well. Have any complaints been filed? Finally, if you're buying a package or tour, always **consider travel insurance** that includes default coverage (⇨ Insurance).

🛈 **Council of Better Business Bureaus** ⊠ 4200 Wilson Blvd., Suite 800, Arlington, VA 22203 ☎ 703/276-0100 📠 703/525-8277 ⊕ www.bbb.org. **BBB of Central Florida, Inc.** ⊠ 151 Wymore Rd., Suite 100, Altamonte Springs, 32714 ☎ 407/621-3300 📠 407/786-2625 ⊕ www.orlando.bbb.org.

CUSTOMS & DUTIES

IN AUSTRALIA

Australian residents who are 18 or older may bring home A$400 worth of souvenirs and gifts (including jewelry), 250 cigarettes or 250 grams of cigars or other tobacco products, and 1,125 ml of alcohol (including wine, beer, and spirits). Residents under 18 may bring back A$200 worth of goods. Members of the same family traveling together may pool their allowances. Prohibited items include meat products. Seeds, plants, and fruits need to be declared upon arrival.

🛈 **Australian Customs Service** ✍ Regional Director, Box 8, Sydney, NSW 2001 ☎ 02/9213-2000 or 1300/363-263, 02/9364-7222 or 1800/803-006 quarantine-inquiry line 📠 02/9213-4043 ⊕ www.customs.gov.au.

IN CANADA

Canadian residents who have been out of Canada for at least seven days may bring in C$750 worth of goods duty-free. If you've been away fewer than seven days but more than 48 hours, the duty-free allowance drops to C$200. If your trip lasts 24 to 48 hours, the allowance is C$50. You may not pool allowances with family members. Goods claimed under the C$750 exemption may follow you by mail; those claimed under the lesser exemptions must accompany you. Alcohol and tobacco products may be included in the seven-day and 48-hour exemptions but not in the 24-hour exemption. If you meet the age requirements of the province or territory through which you reenter Canada, you may bring in, duty-free, 1.5 liters of wine *or* 1.14 liters (40 imperial ounces) of liquor *or* 24 12-ounce cans or bottles of beer or ale. Also, if you meet the local age requirement for tobacco products, you may bring in, duty-free, 200 cigarettes and 50 cigars. Check ahead of time with the Canada Customs and Revenue Agency or the Department of Agriculture for policies regarding meat products, seeds, plants, and fruits.

You may send an unlimited number of gifts (only one gift per recipient, however) worth up to C$60 each duty-free to Canada. Label the package UNSOLICITED GIFT—VALUE UNDER $60. Alcohol and tobacco are excluded.

🛈 **Canada Customs and Revenue Agency** ⊠ 2265 St. Laurent Blvd., Ottawa, Ontario K1G 4K3 ☎ 800/461-9999, 204/983-3500, 506/636-5064 ⊕ www.ccra.gc.ca.

IN NEW ZEALAND

All homeward-bound residents may bring back NZ$700 worth of souvenirs and gifts; passengers may not pool their allowances, and children can claim only the concession on goods intended for their own use. For those 17 or older, the duty-free allowance also includes 4.5 liters of wine or beer; one 1,125-ml bottle of spirits; and either 200 cigarettes, 250 grams of tobacco, 50 cigars, *or* a combination of the three up to 250 grams. Meat products, seeds, plants, and fruits must be declared upon arrival to the Agricultural Services Department.

🛈 **New Zealand Customs** ⊠ Head office: The Customhouse, 17–21 Whitmore St., Box 2218, Wellington ☎ 09/300-5399 or 0800/428-786 ⊕ www.customs.govt.nz.

IN THE U.K.

If you plan to bring back large quantities of alcohol or tobacco, check EU limits beforehand. In most cases, if you bring back more than 200 cigars, 800 cigarettes, 10 liters of spirits, 110 liters of beer, and/or 90 liters of wine, you have to declare the goods upon return.

🛈 **HM Customs and Excise** ⊠ Portcullis House, 21 Cowbridge Rd. E, Cardiff CF11 9SS ☎ 0845/010-9000 or 0208/929-0152, 0208/929-6731 or 0208/910-3602 complaints ⊕ www.hmce.gov.uk.

DISABILITIES & ACCESSIBILITY

Central Florida attractions are among the most accessible destinations in the world for people who have disabilities. The hospitality industry continues to spend millions on barrier-removing renovations. Though some challenges remain, most can be overcome with planning.

The main park-information centers can answer specific questions and dispense general information for guests with disabilities. Both Walt Disney World and Universal Studios publish guidebooks for guests with disabilities; allow six weeks for delivery.

WHERE TO STAY

Despite the Americans with Disabilities Act, the definition of accessibility seems to differ from hotel to hotel. Some properties may be accessible by ADA standards for people with mobility problems but not for people with hearing or vision impairments, for example.

If you have mobility problems, ask for the lowest floor on which accessible services are offered. If you have a hearing impairment, check whether the hotel has devices to alert you visually to the ring of the telephone, a knock at the door, and a fire/emergency alarm. Some hotels provide these devices without charge. Discuss your needs with hotel personnel if this equipment isn't available, so that a staff member can personally alert you in the event of an emergency.

If you're bringing a guide dog, get authorization ahead of time and write down the name of the person with whom you spoke. Hotels and motels at Walt Disney World are continually being renovated to comply with the Americans with Disabilities Act. Call the WDW Special Request Reservations line for up-to-the-minute information.

For guests using wheelchairs, staying at Disney-owned resort hotels is particularly convenient, since the Disney transportation system has dozens of lift-equipped vehicles. Most resorts here in every price range have rooms with roll-in showers or transfer benches in the bathrooms. Especially worthwhile and convenient are the luxurious Grand Floridian and the Port Orleans–French Quarter.

One of the most accommodating off-Disney resorts is the Marriott Orlando World Center; its level of commitment is especially apparent on Sunday morning, when the Solaris Restaurant hosts one of the most delicious, hospitable, and wheelchair-accessible Sunday brunches in Central Florida.

In most properties, only elevators are braille-equipped, but some have programs to help employees understand how best to assist guests with visual impairments. Particularly outstanding is the Wyndham Palace Resort & Spa. The Embassy Suites hotels offer services such as talking alarm clocks and braille or recorded menus.

Most area properties have purchased the equipment necessary to accommodate guests with hearing impairments. Telecommunications devices for the deaf, flashing or vibrating phones and alarms, and closed captioning are common; an industry-wide effort to teach some employees sign language is under way. The Grosvenor Resort, on Hotel Plaza Boulevard, has excellent facilities but no Teletype reservations line.

WDW Wheelchair-Accessible Lodgings All-Star Music Resort ☎ 407/939-6000. **All-Star Movies Resort** ☎ 407/939-7000. **All-Star Sports Resort** ☎ 407/939-5000. **Beach Club Resort and Villas** ☎ 407/934-8000. **BoardWalk Inn and Villas** ☎ 407/939-5100. **Grand Floridian Resort & Spa** ☎ 407/824-3000; 407/934-7639 Walt Disney World Central Reservations; 407/828-6799 TTY. **Port Orleans Resort–French Quarter** ☎ 407/934-5000. **Wilderness Lodge** ☎ 407/824-3200. **Yacht Club Resort** ☎ 407/934-7000.

Wheelchair-Accessible Lodgings Elsewhere Embassy Suites Hotel International Drive South ☎ 800/433-7275; 407/352-1400 front desk, which can help callers with hearing problems ⊕ www.embassysuitesorlando.com. **Embassy Suites Hotel Lake Buena Vista Resort** ☎ 407/239-1144 or 800/362-2779; 800/451-4833 TTY ⊕ www.embassysuitesorlando.com.

Good Hotels for Vision-Impaired Guests Embassy Suites Hotel International Drive South ☎ 800/433-7275; 407/352-1400 TTY ⊕ www.embassysuitesorlando.com. **Embassy Suites Hotel Lake Buena Vista Resort** ☎ 407/239-1144 or 800/362-2779; 800/451-4833 TTY ⊕ www.embassysuitesorlando.com. **Wyndham Palace Re-**

sort & Spa in the WDW Resort ☎ 407/827–2727 or 800/327–2990 ⊕ www.wyndham.com.

RESERVATIONS

When discussing accessibility with an operator or reservations agent, **ask hard questions.** Are there any stairs, inside *or* out? Are there grab bars next to the toilet *and* in the shower/tub? How wide is the doorway to the room? To the bathroom? For the most extensive facilities meeting the latest legal specifications, **opt for newer accommodations.** If you reserve through a toll-free number, consider also calling the hotel's local number to confirm the information from the central reservations office. Get confirmation in writing when you can.

🚹 **WDW Special Request Reservations** ☎ 407/ 354–1853.

SIGHTS & ATTRACTIONS

Guests with disabilities can **take advantage of many discounts:** 50% at Busch Gardens for wheelchair users and the visually or hearing impaired; at least 50% at Sea-World for guests with visual or hearing impairments; and 20% at Universal Studios for those with a disability that limits enjoyment of the park.

At Walt Disney World, a new standard of access was set with the opening of Disney's Animal Kingdom; all attractions, restaurants, and shops are wheelchair accessible. Disney–MGM Studios comes in a close second, followed by Epcot, some of whose rides have a tailgate that drops down to provide a level entrance to the ride vehicle. Though the Magic Kingdom, now in its third decade, was designed before architects gave consideration to access issues, renovation plans are under way. Even so, the 20 or so accessible attractions combine with the live entertainment around the park to provide a memorable experience. Universal Studios and Sea-World are both substantially barrier-free.

In some attractions, you may be required to transfer to a wheelchair if you use a scooter. In others, you must be able to leave your own wheelchair to board the ride vehicle and must have a traveling companion assist, as park staff cannot do so. Attractions with emergency evacuation routes that have narrow walkways or steps require additional mobility. Turbulence on other attractions poses a problem for some guests.

Rest rooms at all of these parks have standard accessible stalls. More spacious facilities are available in first-aid stations.

Walt Disney World's *Guidebook for Guests with Disabilities* describes the theme and story of various attractions in its three parks. The guidebook is available in the park at Guest Relations, ticket booths, or the wheelchair rental location; you can also call ahead and request one by mail.

WDW and Universal have produced descriptive cassette tapes that can be borrowed, along with portable tape recorders (deposit required); SeaWorld, with a week's notice, provides an escort or interpreter to take people with visual or hearing impairments through the park. Service animals, although welcome, must be leashed or in a harness; they may board many rides, but not all—usually not those with loud noises, pyrotechnics, and other intense effects that may startle the animals.

WDW has several free devices available for the hearing impaired. The Handheld Captioning Device is available at the attractions themselves. Assistive Listening Devices (deposit, $25) are available at the Guest Relations window of all theme parks. Stage shows with sign language interpreters are listed in the calendar of events. At Epcot, you can rent personal translator units that amplify the sound tracks of seven shows ($4; $40 deposit). At Epcot and in the Magic Kingdom (and in Disney–MGM Studios by special arrangement), four-hour guided tours in sign language are available. Advance reservations are a must; provide two weeks' notice if possible ($5 adults, $3.50 children 3–9).

Both Universal Studios and SeaWorld can also provide guides fluent in sign language with advance notice; Universal has scripts available for all its shows. Busch Gardens does not offer assistance in sign.

🚹 Theme-Park Information for Guests with Disabilities **Walt Disney World** ☎ 407/560–6233; 407/ 827–5141 TTY. **Universal Studios** ☎ 407/224–4414; 407/363–8265 TTY. The TDD (Telecommunications Device for the Deaf) number is 407/363–8000. **Sea-World** ☎ 407/363– 2414 or 407/351–3600; 407/363–2617 TTY; TDD 800/837–4268.

TRANSPORTATION

Outside Disney property there are some lift-equipped vans for rent and some shuttle services available, but you'll need to plan your itinerary beforehand. Inside Disney, every other bus on each route is lift-equipped and there's never more than a 30-minute wait for hotel–to–theme park trips. Consult transportation companies for more information.

Designated parking is available for guests with disabilities. At most parks it's near the turnstile area. The Magic Kingdom's special lot is near the Transportation and Ticket Center, where ferries depart for the Magic Kingdom. From there the monorails depart for Epcot. Monorail entrances are level, but the ramp is quite steep.

◪ Transportation for Travelers with Disabilities **Dor Sar Transport Services** ✉ 1005 S. Lake Formosa Dr., Orlando 32819 ☎ 407/897-6839.

◪ Complaints **Aviation Consumer Protection Division** (⇨ Air Travel) for airline-related problems. **Departmental Office of Civil Rights** ✉ for general inquiries, U.S. Department of Transportation, S-30, 400 7th St. SW, Room 10215, Washington, DC 20590 ☎ 202/366-4648 ♻ 202/366-9371 ⊕ www.dot. gov/ost/docr/index.htm. **Disability Rights Section** ✉ NYAV, U.S. Department of Justice, Civil Rights Division, 950 Pennsylvania Ave. NW, Washington, DC 20530 ☎ ADA information line 202/514-0301, 800/514-0301, 202/514-0383 TTY, 800/514-0383 TTY ⊕ www.ada.gov. **U.S. Department of Transportation Hotline** ☎ for disability-related air-travel problems, 800/778-4838 or 800/455-9880 TTY.

TRAVEL AGENCIES

In the United States, the Americans with Disabilities Act requires that travel firms serve the needs of all travelers. Some agencies specialize in working with people with disabilities.

◪ Agencies for Travelers with Mobility Problems **Access Adventures** ✉ 206 Chestnut Ridge Rd., Scottsville, NY 14624 ☎ 585/889-9096 ✎ dltravel@prodigy.net, run by a former physical-rehabilitation counselor. **Accessible Vans of America** ✉ 9 Spielman Rd., Fairfield, NJ 07004 ☎ 877/282-8267, 973/808-9709 reservations ♻ 973/808-9713 ⊕ www.accessiblevans.com. **CareVacations** ✉ No. 5, 5110-50 Ave., Leduc, Alberta, Canada T9E 6V4 ☎ 780/986-6404 or 877/478-7827 ♻ 780/986-8332 ⊕ www.carevacations.com, for group tours and cruise vacations. **Flying Wheels Travel** ✉ 143 W. Bridge St., Box 382, Owatonna, MN 55060 ☎ 507/451-5005 ♻ 507/451-1685 ⊕ www. flyingwheelstravel.com.

◪ Agencies for Travelers with Developmental Disabilities **New Directions** ✉ 5276 Hollister Ave., Suite 207, Santa Barbara, CA 93111 ☎ 805/967-2841 or 888/967-2841 ♻ 805/964-7344 ⊕ www. newdirectionstravel.com. **Sprout** ✉ 893 Amsterdam Ave., New York, NY 10025 ☎ 212/222-9575 or 888/222-9575 ♻ 212/222-9768 ⊕ www.gosprout.org.

WHEELCHAIRS

Probably the most comfortable course is to bring your wheelchair from home. Access may be difficult, except in theater-style shows, however, if your chair is wider than 24½ inches and longer than 32 inches (44 inches for scooters); consult attraction hosts and hostesses. Thefts of personal wheelchairs while their owners are inside attractions are rare but have been known to occur. Take the precautions you would in any public place.

Wheelchair rentals are available from area medical-supply companies that will deliver to your hotel and let you keep the chair for the duration of your vacation. You can also rent by the day in major theme parks ($7 a day for wheelchairs, plus a $1 refundable deposit); $30 daily for the limited number of scooters, plus a $10 refundable deposit).

In Disney parks, since rental locations are relatively close to parking, it may be a good idea to send someone ahead to get the wheelchair and bring it back to the car; at day's end, a Disney host or hostess may escort you to your car and then return the wheelchair for you. Rented wheelchairs that disappear while you're on a ride can be replaced throughout the parks—ask any staffer for the nearest location. Attaching a small personal item to the wheelchair may prevent other guests from taking yours by mistake.

DISCOUNTS & DEALS

There are plenty of ways to save money while you're in the Orlando area. Coupon books, such as those available from Entertainment Travel Editions for around $30, can be good sources for discounts on rental cars, admission to attractions, meals, and other typical purchases.

Be a smart shopper and **compare all your options** before making decisions. A plane ticket bought with a promotional coupon from travel clubs, coupon books, and direct-mail offers or on the Internet may not be cheaper than the least expensive fare from a discount ticket agency. And always keep in mind that what you get is just as important as what you save.

BEST WAYS TO SAVE

1. Shop around for discounted theme-park tickets, which are widely available. Be sure to **look into combination tickets** and second-day free tickets that get you admission to multiple theme parks or two days' admission for the price of one to a single park. The Orlando FlexTicket is just one example of the various combination tickets available. You can also visit the Orlando/Orange County Convention and Visitors Bureau on International Drive or stop in one of the many ticket booths around town, including the Tourism Bureau of Orlando, Know Before You Go, and the Tourist Information Center of Orlando. Be wary of extra-cheap tickets (they may be expired) and discounts that require you to take time-share tours—unless you're interested in a time-share, that is.

If you're a member of the American Automobile Association, be sure to ask at your local club about getting discounted tickets. Find out if your company belongs to the Universal Fan Club or the Magic Kingdom Club, which offer discount schemes to members' employees. At Busch Gardens, go for the Twilight Tickets, available after 3 PM.

2. Buy your tickets as soon as you know you're going. Prices typically go up two or three times a year, so you might beat a price hike—and save a little money.

3. Stay at hotels on U.S. 192 around Kissimmee and on International Drive that offer free transportation to and from the park. Getting to and from the parks may take a little extra time, but you won't have to pay to rent a car—or to park it.

4. In deciding whether or not to rent a car, do the math. Weigh the cost of renting against what it will cost to get your entire party to and from the airport and the theme parks and any other places you want to go. If you are traveling with a group of more than four, renting a car may be cheaper than other options.

5. Choose accommodations with a kitchen. You can stock up on breakfast items in a nearby supermarket, and save time—and money—by eating your morning meal in your hotel room.

6. Watch your shopping carefully. Theme-park merchandisers are excellent at displaying the goods so that you (or your children) can't resist them. You may find that some of the items for sale are also available at home—for quite a bit less. One way to cope is to give every member of your family a souvenir budget—adults and children alike.

7. Avoid holidays and school vacation times or go off-season. You can see more in less time and lodging rates are lower.

8. If you plan to eat in a full-service restaurant, have a large, late breakfast, and then eat lunch late in the day in lieu of dinner. Lunchtime prices are almost always lower than dinnertime prices. Also look for "early bird" menus, which offer dinner entrées at reduced prices during late afternoon and early evening hours.

For further discount information, if applicable, *see* Disabilities and Accessibility and Senior-Citizen Travel.

🄵 **Central Florida Tickets and Travel** ✉ 3501 W. Vine St., Suite 319, Kissimmee, 34741. ☎ 407/932-2080 ⊕ www.centralfloridatravel.com. **Entertainment Travel Editions** ☎ 800/445-4137 ⊕ www. entertainment.com. **Orlando/Orange County Convention and Visitors Bureau** ✉ 8723 International Dr., Orlando, FL 32819 ☎ 407/363-5871. **Tourism Bureau of Orlando** ☎ 407/363-5800. **Know Before You Go** ☎ 407/352-9813. **Tourist Information Center of Orlando** ☎ 407/363-5871.

DISCOUNT RESERVATIONS

To save money, **look into discount reservations services** with Web sites and toll-free numbers, which use their buying power to get a better price on hotels, airline tickets (⇨ Air Travel), even car rentals. When booking a room, always **call the hotel's local toll-free number** (if one is available) rather than the central reservations number—you'll often get a better price. Always ask about special packages or corporate rates.

🄵 Airline Tickets **Air 4 Less** ☎ 800/AIR4LESS; low-fare specialist.
🄵 Hotels **Accommodations Express** ☎ 800/444-7666 or 800/277-1064 ⊕ www. accommodationsexpress.com. **Central Reservation Service (CRS)** ☎ 800/555-7555 or 800/548-3311 ⊕ www.roomconnection.net. **Hotels.com** ☎ 800/246-8357 or 214/369-1246 ⊕ www.hotels.com. **Quikbook** ☎ 800/789-9887 ⊕ www.quikbook.com. **RMC Travel** ☎ 800/245-5738 ⊕ www.

rmcwebtravel.com. **Steigenberger Reservation Service** ☎ 800/223-5652 ⊕ www.srs-worldhotels.com. **Turbotrip.com** ☎ 800/473-7829 ⊕ www.turbotrip.com.

PACKAGE DEALS

Don't confuse packages and guided tours. When you buy a package, you travel on your own, just as though you had planned the trip yourself. Fly/drive packages, which combine airfare and car rental, are often a good deal. Look into hotel packages that include theme park tickets.

EMERGENCIES

All the major theme parks have first-aid centers. Hospital emergency rooms are open 24 hours a day. For minor emergencies visit the Main Street Physicians clinic (open weekdays 8 AM–7 PM, weekends 8–4) or its minor-emergency mobile service, which offers hotel-room visits by physicians for minor medical care and dispenses nonnarcotic medication. There are several Centra Care centers. One is closer to Orlando (a block east of Kirkman Road) and is open daily 8 AM–midnight. Another Centra Care center is near Downtown Disney and is open weekdays 8 AM–midnight; and another is in Lake Buena Vista, open weekdays 8 AM–8 PM, weekends 9–9. The latter provides free shuttle service from any of the Disney theme park's first aid stations.

🚩 **Police or ambulance** ☎ 911.

🚩 Doctors & Dentists **Dental Emergency Service** ☎ 407/331-2526.

🚩 Hospitals & Clinics **Orlando Regional Medical Center/Sand Lake Hospital** ✉ 9400 Turkey Lake Rd., I-Drive Area ☎ 407/351-8500. **Florida Hospital Celebration Health** ✉ 400 Celebration Pl., Celebration ☎ 407/764-4000. **Main Street Physicians** ✉ 8324 International Drive ☎ 407/370-4881. **Centra Care** ✉ 4320 W. Vine St., Kissimmee ☎ 407/390-1888. **Centra Care** ✉ 12500 S. Apopka Vineland Rd., Lake Buena Vista ☎ 407/934-2273.

🚩 24-Hour Pharmacies **Walgreens** ✉ 5501 S. Kirkman Rd., Universal Studios Area ☎ 407/248-0315 ✉ 7650 W. Sand Lake Rd., off International Drive, Spring Lake ☎ 407/238-0400.

GAY & LESBIAN TRAVEL

Gay Day Orlando, held the first Saturday in June, includes a week's worth of activities. Contact the Gay, Lesbian & Bisexual Community Center of Central Florida

(GLBCC) or visit Gay Day's official Web site for more information. For details about the gay and lesbian scene, consult *Fodor's Gay Guide to the USA* (available in bookstores everywhere).

🚩 Local Information **Gay and Lesbian Community Services** ✉ 946 N. Mills Ave., Orlando, FL 32803 ☎ 407/228-8272 ⊕ www.glbcc.com. **Gay Day at Walt Disney World** ⊕ www.gayday.com.

🚩 Gay- & Lesbian-Friendly Travel Agencies **Different Roads Travel** ✉ 8383 Wilshire Blvd., Suite 520, Beverly Hills, CA 90211 ☎ 323/651-5557 or 800/429-8747 (Ext. 14 for both) 🖷 323/651-3678 ✉ lgernert@tzell.com. **Kennedy Travel** ✉ 130 W. 42nd St., Suite 401, New York, NY 10036 ☎ 212/840-8659 🖷 212/730-2269 ⊕ www.kennedytravel.com. **Now, Voyager** ✉ 4406 18th St., San Francisco, CA 94114 ☎ 415/626-1169 or 800/255-6951 🖷 415/626-8626 ⊕ www.nowvoyager.com. **Skylink Travel and Tour** ✉ 1455 N. Dutton Ave., Suite A, Santa Rosa, CA 95401 ☎ 707/546-9888 or 800/225-5759 🖷 707/636-0951; serving lesbian travelers.

GUIDEBOOKS

Plan well and you won't be sorry. Guidebooks are excellent tools—and you can take them with you. You may want to check out the color-photo-illustrated *Fodor's Exploring Florida* and *Compass American Guide: Florida,* thorough on culture and history; or *Fodor's Road Guide USA: Florida* for comprehensive restaurant, hotel, and attractions listings. All are available at on-line retailers and bookstores everywhere.

HOLIDAYS

Major national holidays are New Year's Day (Jan. 1); Martin Luther King Day (3rd Mon. in Jan.); Presidents' Day (3rd Mon. in Feb.); Memorial Day (last Mon. in May); Independence Day (July 4); Labor Day (1st Mon. in Sept.); Columbus Day (2nd Mon. in Oct.); Thanksgiving Day (4th Thurs. in Nov.); Christmas Eve and Christmas Day (Dec. 24 and 25); and New Year's Eve (Dec. 31).

INSURANCE

The most useful travel-insurance plan is a comprehensive policy that includes coverage for trip cancellation and interruption, default, trip delay, and medical expenses (with a waiver for preexisting conditions).

Without insurance you'll lose all or most of your money if you cancel your trip, regardless of the reason. Default insurance covers you if your tour operator, airline, or cruise line goes out of business. Trip-delay covers expenses that arise because of bad weather or mechanical delays. Study the fine print when comparing policies.

U.K. residents can buy a travel-insurance policy valid for most vacations taken during the year in which it's purchased (but check preexisting-condition coverage).Always **buy travel policies directly from the insurance company**; if you buy them from a cruise line, airline, or tour operator that goes out of business you probably won't be covered for the agency's or operator's default, a major risk. Before making any purchase, **review your existing health and home-owner's policies** to find what they cover away from home.

🚩 Travel Insurers In the U.S.: **Access America** ✉ 6600 W. Broad St., Richmond, VA 23230 ☎ 800/284-8300 📠 804/673-1491 or 800/346-9265 🌐 www.accessamerica.com. **Travel Guard International** ✉ 1145 Clark St., Stevens Point, WI 54481 ☎ 715/345-0505 or 800/826-1300 📠 800/955-8785 🌐 www.travelguard.com.

FOR INTERNATIONAL TRAVELERS

For information on customs restrictions, *see* Customs and Duties.

CAR RENTAL

When picking up a rental car, non-U.S. residents need a reservation voucher for any prepaid reservations that were made in the traveler's home country, a passport, a driver's license, and a travel policy that covers each driver.

CAR TRAVEL

Your driver's license may not be recognized outside your home country. International driving permits (IDPs) are available from the American and Canadian automobile associations and, in the United Kingdom, from the Automobile Association and Royal Automobile Club. These international permits, valid only in conjunction with your regular driver's license, are universally recognized; having one may save you a problem with local authorities.

In Orlando gasoline costs at this writing ranged from $1.48 to $1.88 a gallon. Gas stations closest to Walt Disney World always charge roughly 20¢ more per gallon than elsewhere. Stations are plentiful. Most stay open late; some are open 24 hrs.

Highways are well paved. Interstate highways—limited-access, multilane highways whose numbers are prefixed by "I–"—are the fastest routes. Interstates with three-digit numbers encircle urban areas, which may have other limited-access expressways, freeways, and parkways as well. Tolls may be levied on limited-access highways. So-called U.S. highways and state highways are not necessarily limited-access but may have several lanes.

Along larger highways, roadside stops with rest rooms, fast-food restaurants, and sundries stores are well spaced. State police and tow trucks patrol major highways and lend assistance. If your car breaks down on an interstate, pull onto the shoulder and wait for help, or have your passengers wait while you walk to an emergency phone. If you carry a cell phone, dial *347 (*FHP) to reach the Florida Highway Patrol, noting your location on the small green roadside mileage markers.

Driving in the United States is on the right. Do **obey speed limits** posted along roads and highways. Watch for lower limits in small towns and on back roads. On weekdays between 6 and 10 AM and again between 4 and 7 PM **expect heavy traffic.** To encourage carpooling, some freeways have special lanes for so-called high-occupancy vehicles (HOV)—cars carrying more than one passenger.

Bookstores, gas stations, convenience stores, and rest stops sell maps (about $3) and multiregion road atlases (about $10).

CURRENCY

The dollar is the basic unit of U.S. currency. It has 100 cents. Coins are the copper penny (1¢); the silvery nickel (5¢), dime (10¢), quarter (25¢), and half-dollar (50¢); and the golden $1 coin, replacing a now-rare silver dollar. Bills are denominated $1, $5, $10, $20, $50, and $100, all green and identical in size; designs vary. In addition, you may come across a $2 bill, but the chances are slim. The exchange rate at press time was U.S. $1.52 per British pound, U.S. $.65 per Canadian dollar, U.S. $.58 per Australian dollar, and U.S. $.52 per New Zealand dollar.

ELECTRICITY

The U.S. standard is AC, 110 volts/60 cycles. Plugs have two flat pins set parallel to each other.

EMERGENCIES

For police, fire, or ambulance, **dial 911** (0 in rural areas).

INSURANCE

Britons and Australians need extra medical coverage when traveling overseas.

 Insurance Information In the U.K.: **Association of British Insurers** ⊠ 51 Gresham St., London EC2V 7HQ ☎ 020/7600-3333 🖷 020/7696-8999 ⊕ www.abi.org.uk. In Australia: **Insurance Council of Australia** ⊠ Insurance Enquiries and Complaints, Level 3, 56 Pitt St., Sydney, NSW 2000 ☎ 1300/363683 or 02/9251-4456 🖷 02/9251-4453 ⊕ www.iecltd.com.au. In Canada: **RBC Insurance** ⊠ 6880 Financial Dr., Mississauga, Ontario L5N 7Y5 ☎ 800/565-3129 🖷 905/813-4704 ⊕ www.rbcinsurance.com. In New Zealand: **Insurance Council of New Zealand** ⊠ Level 7, 111-115 Customhouse Quay, Box 474, Wellington ☎ 04/472-5230 🖷 04/473-3011 ⊕ www.icnz.org.nz.

MAIL & SHIPPING

You can buy stamps and aerograms and send letters and parcels in post offices. Stamp-dispensing machines can occasionally be found in airports, bus and train stations, office buildings, drugstores, and the like. You can also deposit mail in the stout, dark blue, steel bins at strategic locations everywhere and in the mail chutes of large buildings; pickup schedules are posted.

For mail sent within the United States, you need a 37¢ stamp for first-class letters weighing up to 1 ounce (23¢ for each additional ounce) and 23¢ for postcards. You pay 80¢ for 1-ounce airmail letters and 70¢ for airmail postcards to most other countries; to Canada and Mexico, you need a 60¢ stamp for a 1-ounce letter and 50¢ for a postcard. An aerogram—a single sheet of lightweight blue paper that folds into its own envelope, stamped for overseas airmail—costs 70¢.

To receive mail on the road, have it sent c/o General Delivery at your destination's main post office (use the correct five-digit ZIP code). You must pick up mail in person within 30 days and show a driver's license or passport.

PASSPORTS & VISAS

When traveling internationally, **carry your passport** even if you don't need one (it's always the best form of I.D.) and **make two photocopies of the data page** (one for someone at home and another for you, carried separately from your passport). If you lose your passport, promptly call the nearest embassy or consulate and the local police.

Visitor visas aren't necessary for Canadian or European Union citizens, or for citizens of Australia who are staying fewer than 90 days.

 Australian Citizens **Passports Australia** ☎ 131-232 ⊕ www.passports.gov.au. **United States Consulate General** ⊠ MLC Centre, Level 59, 19–29 Martin Pl., Sydney, NSW 2000 ☎ 02/9373-9200, 1902/941-641 fee-based visa-inquiry line ⊕ usembassy-australia.state.gov/sydney.

 Canadian Citizens **Passport Office** ⊠ to mail in applications: 200 Promenade du Portage, Hull, Québec J8X 4B7 ☎ 819/994-3500 or 800/567-6868 ⊕ www.ppt.gc.ca.

 New Zealand Citizens **New Zealand Passports Office** ⊠ for applications and information, Level 3, Boulcott House, 47 Boulcott St., Wellington ☎ 0800/22-5050 or 04/474-8100 ⊕ www.passports.govt.nz. **Embassy of the United States** ⊠ 29 Fitzherbert Terr., Thorndon, Wellington ☎ 04/462-6000 ⊕ usembassy.org.nz. **U.S. Consulate General** ⊠ Citibank Bldg., 3rd floor, 23 Customs St. E, Auckland ☎ 09/303-2724 ⊕ usembassy.org.nz.

 U.K. Citizens **U.K. Passport Service** ☎ 0870/521-0410 ⊕ www.passport.gov.uk. **American Consulate General** ⊠ Queen's House, 14 Queen St., Belfast, Northern Ireland BT1 6EQ ☎ 028/9032-8239 🖷 028/9024-8482 ⊕ www.usembassy.org.uk. **American Embassy** ⊠ for visa and immigration information (enclose an SASE), Consular Information Unit, 24 Grosvenor Sq., London W1 1AE ⊠ to submit an application via mail, Visa Branch, 5 Upper Grosvenor St., London W1A 2JB ☎ 09068/200-290 recorded visa information or 09055/444-546 operator service, both with per-minute charges, 0207/499-9000 main switchboard ⊕ www.usembassy.org.uk.

TELEPHONES

All U.S. telephone numbers consist of a three-digit area code and a seven-digit local number. Within many local calling areas, you dial only the seven-digit number. Within some area codes, you must dial

"1" first for calls outside the local area. To call between area-code regions, dial "1" then all 10 digits; the same goes for calls to numbers prefixed by "800," "866," "888," and "877"—all toll free. For calls to numbers preceded by "900" you must pay—usually dearly.

For international calls, dial "011" followed by the country code and the local number. For help, dial "0" and ask for an overseas operator. The country code is 61 for Australia, 64 for New Zealand, 44 for the United Kingdom. Calling Canada is the same as calling within the United States. Most local phone books list country codes and U.S. area codes. The country code for the United States is 1.

For operator assistance, dial "0." To obtain someone's phone number, call directory assistance at 555–1212 or occasionally 411 (free at public phones). To have the person you're calling foot the bill, phone collect; dial "0" instead of "1" before the 10-digit number.

At pay phones, instructions often are posted. You insert coins in a slot (usually 25¢–50¢ for local calls) and wait for a steady tone before dialing. When you call long-distance, the operator tells you how much to insert; prepaid phone cards, widely available in various denominations, are easier. Call the number on the back, punch in the card's identification number when prompted, then dial your number.

MEDIA

NEWSPAPERS & MAGAZINES

The *Orlando Sentinel* is the area outlet for news; *Orlando Magazine* is a monthly publication. Both are mainstream and mundane. The *Orlando Weekly* is the alternative newspaper for the city, covering and criticizing local politics when it's not recommending bars and clubs. The free weekly is found in distinctive red racks throughout the city.

RADIO

WSHE (100.3 FM) is an oldies station. You'll find country music at **WPCV** (97.5 FM) and **WWKA** (92 FM). **WMFE** (90.7 FM) is the local National Public Radio affiliate. **WDBO** (580 AM) is an excellent source of news and traffic. **WFLA** (540 AM) has weak news but several popular talk shows.

TELEVISION

WFTV (channel 9) is the local ABC affiliate; **WKMG** (channel 6) is the CBS affiliate; **WESH** (channel 2) is the NBC affiliate; and **WOFL** (channel 35) is the Fox affiliate.

MONEY MATTERS

Be prepared to spend and spend—and spend some more. Despite relatively low airfares and car-rental rates, cash seems to evaporate out of wallets, and credit card balances seem to increase on exposure to the hot Orlando sun. Theme-park admission averages around $50 per day per person—not counting all the $2 soft drinks and $10–$20 souvenirs. Hotels range so wildly—from $40 a night to 10 or more times that—that you have to do some hard thinking about just how much you want to spend. Meal prices away from the theme parks are comparable to those in other midsize cities, ranging from $5 per person at a fast-food chain to $40 entrées at a fancy restaurant. Prices throughout this guide are given for adults and children. Reduced fees are almost always available for senior citizens.

ATMS

There are ATMs in the entry areas of all theme parks as well as here and there around town. Often there's a $1.50–$2.50 charge if you're not a customer of the specific bank that maintains the ATM.

CREDIT CARDS

Throughout this guide, the following abbreviations are used: **AE**, American Express; **D**, Discover; **DC**, Diners Club; **MC**, MasterCard; and **V**, Visa.

🄵 Reporting Lost Cards **American Express** ☎ 800/441-0519. **Diners Club** ☎ 800/234-6377. **Discover** ☎ 800/347-2683. **MasterCard** ☎ 800/622-7747. **Visa** ☎ 800/847-2911.

PACKING

Comfortable walking shoes or sneakers are essential. The entire area is extremely casual, day and night, so men need a jacket and tie in only a handful of restaurants. For sightseeing and theme-park visits, pack cool, comfortable clothing. On hot summer days, the perfect theme-park outfit begins with shorts with large pockets made of a breathable, quick-drying material, topped by a T-shirt of similar material. Women may want to consider wearing a bathing-suit top under their T-shirts. Most theme parks either have water rides that leave you drenched or interactive fountains that are so tempting on hot days—that is, most of the time—that you're hard put to pass them by. Experienced theme-park visitors also suggest using a waist pack rather than a tote bag or purse. Sunglasses are a must—as is sunscreen. Don't ruin your trip by getting sunburned on the first day.

In winter, be prepared for a range of temperatures: take clothing that you can layer, including a sweater and warm jacket. It can get quite cool in December and January. For summer, you'll want a sun hat, and a poncho and folding umbrella in case of sudden thunderstorms.

In your carry-on luggage, **pack an extra pair of eyeglasses or contact lenses and enough of any medication** you take to last a few days longer than the entire trip. You may also ask your doctor to write a spare prescription using the drug's generic name, as brand names may vary from country to country. In luggage to be checked, **never pack prescription drugs, valuables, or undeveloped film.** And don't forget to carry with you the addresses of offices that handle refunds of lost traveler's checks. Check *Fodor's How to Pack* (available at on-line retailers and bookstores everywhere) for more tips.

To avoid customs and security delays, carry medications in their original packaging. Don't pack any sharp objects in your carry-on luggage, including knives of any size or material, scissors, and corkscrews, or anything else that might arouse suspicion.

To avoid having your checked luggage chosen for hand inspection, don't cram bags full. The U.S. Transportation Security Administration suggests packing shoes on top and placing personal items you don't want touched in clear plastic bags.

CHECKING LUGGAGE

You're allowed to carry aboard one bag and one personal article, such as a purse or a laptop computer. Make sure what you carry on fits under your seat or in the overhead bin. Get to the gate early, so you can board as soon as possible, before the overhead bins fill up.

Baggage allowances vary by carrier, destination, and ticket class. On domestic flights, the limit may be 50 pounds (23 kilograms) per bag. Most airlines won't accept bags that weigh more than 100 pounds (45 kilograms) on domestic or international flights. Check baggage restrictions with your carrier before you pack.

Airline liability for baggage is limited to $2,500 per person on flights within the United States. On international flights it amounts to $9.07 per pound or $20 per kilogram for checked baggage (roughly $640 per 70-pound bag) and $400 per passenger for unchecked baggage. You can buy additional coverage at check-in for about $10 per $1,000 of coverage, but it often excludes a rather extensive list of items, shown on your airline ticket.

Before departure, **itemize your bags' contents** and their worth, and label the bags with your name, address, and phone number. (If you use your home address, cover it so potential thieves can't see it readily.) Include a label inside each bag and **pack a copy of your itinerary.** At check-in, **make sure each bag is correctly tagged** with the destination airport's three-letter code. Because some checked bags will be opened for hand inspection, the U.S. Transportation Security Administration recommends that you leave luggage unlocked or use the plastic locks offered at check-in. TSA screeners place an inspection notice inside searched bags, which are re-sealed with a special lock.

If your bag has been searched and contents are missing or damaged, file a claim with the TSA Consumer Response Center as soon as possible. If your bags arrive damaged or fail to arrive at all, file a written report with the airline before leaving the airport.

🏷 Complaints **U.S. Transportation Security Administration Consumer Response Center** ☎ 866/289-9673 ⊕ www.tsa.gov.

PETS

It's probably best to leave Rover at home, but if you just can't part with your animal, all the parks have kennel facilities. They provide a cage, water, and sometimes food, but you have to do the walking, which, of course, takes up valuable vacation time. On-site Disney resort guests may board their pets for $9 per night; others pay $11 per night. The day rate is $6. The Holiday Inn Maingate West is one of the few area hotels that allows pets to stay in your room. The fee is $75 per pet, of which $25 is refundable if no damage results to the room. The Portofino Bay Hotel, the Hard Rock Hotel, and the Royal Pacific Resort at Universal allow your pet to stay in your room at no extra cost, and they even offer pet room service. However, you must provide a pet health certificate that is no more than 10 days old.

Hard Rock Hotel ✉ 1000 Universal Studios Plaza, Universal Studios 32819 ☎ 407/503–7625 or 800/232–7827 🖷 407/503–7655 🌐 www. loewshotels.com. **Holiday Inn Maingate West** ✉ 7601 Black Lake Rd., Kissimmee 34747 ☎ 407/ 396–1100 or 800/365–6935 🖷 407/396–0689 🌐 www.sixcontinentshotels.com. **Portofino Bay Hotel** ✉ 5601 Universal Blvd., Universal Studios 32819 ☎ 407/503–1000 or 888/322–5541 🌐 www. loewshotels.com.

PLANNING YOUR TRIP

Careful planning is key to the most hassle-free visit to the Orlando area. The first step is to **figure out everything you want to see and do in the area.** Will you be staying put, or do you want to spend some time at the beach? Once you've settled on your sightseeing priorities, you can figure out how long you want to stay, make reservations, and buy tickets.

HOW LONG TO STAY

There are a couple of ways to approach this question. If your objective is to enjoy the complete Orlando resort experience, seven days is a comfortable period to allow; this gives you time to see all of the parks at Universal and WDW and to take in one water park, to sample the restaurants and entertainment, and to spend a bit of time around the pool. Eight days would be better. Figure on an additional day for every other area theme park you want to visit, and then add your travel time to and from home.

If you're coming to the area mostly to go on the rides and see the theme parks, allow one day per theme park. This supposes that you're willing to start out early every day, move quickly, breeze through shops, and hurry through meals. Then add your travel time to and from home.

In either case, add time for exploring Orlando, and for shopping. Orlando has some great high-end and discount shopping. Tenants at the Mall at Millenia include Bloomingdale's, Macy's, Neiman Marcus, Tiffany & Co., and Chanel. The Florida Mall has just added Nordstrom and Lord & Taylor. **Add an extra day or two if you're traveling with small children,** who may have limited patience for marathon touring, or if you're staying off Disney property. Also add in extra time if you're visiting during a busy period, when long lines will make it nearly impossible to see all the most popular attractions unless you have enormous stamina and are willing to be on the go from early in the morning until park closing. You could easily spend more than two weeks in the area and still not see it all.

CREATING AN ITINERARY

Once you know what you want to see and do, **lay out a day-by-day touring plan,** using the Blitz Tours, Tip Boards, and Strategies for Your Visit sections in chapters 1, 2, and 3. Also look at the italicized Crowds and Strategy information following each review. Don't try to plot your route from hour to hour; instead break the day up into morning, afternoon, and evening sections. Make a note of the busiest days in each park you've planned to visit, and schedule yourself accordingly. Then, beginning with the dates on which you plan to visit, **decide which parks you will see on each day.**

Think creatively. If you're staying on Walt Disney World property in a not-too-busy period and have at least five days, **consider spending afternoons at one of the water parks,** at your hotel swimming pool, or at a spa or sports facility. If you buy a multi-day Park Hopper pass, which is good for unlimited visits to WDW's major parks, you can also **visit two or more theme parks in a day**—say, do the Magic Kingdom in the morning, when the park isn't crowded, and spend an afternoon in Epcot's Future World, that area's least busy time. Put each day's plan on a separate index card, and carry the card with you as you explore Orlando.

Finally, **make a schedule for calling for any reservations** you will need. Make a list of all the things you want to do that require reservations. Note on the list how far in advance you can book for each. Then, based on your travel schedule, designate the date on which you should call for the reservations you want. Some reservations can be made as soon as you book your hotel or before; others will have to wait until you're in the area.

BUYING YOUR TICKETS

If you aren't signing up for an escorted tour or travel package, buy your tickets in advance. This will save you time in Orlando, and you may beat a price hike and save a little money as well.

The Orlando airport has Universal Studios, SeaWorld, and Walt Disney World gift shops, where tickets, maps, and information are available. Buying tickets here while waiting for your bags to be unloaded will save time later. Local Disney Stores also sell certain multiday passes. Plenty of other outlets around Orlando sell theme-park tickets, including stores and, most likely, your hotel.

REST ROOMS

Rest rooms at Walt Disney World, Universal, and Seaworld are widely available, frequently cleaned, and there are usually enough stalls so that you rarely have to wait in line; most, including men's rooms, have baby-changing stations. Plus, rest rooms at the airport and at most attractions use the automatic infrared flush trigger, so you never have to touch the toilet.

SENIOR-CITIZEN TRAVEL

Bear in mind that school vacation times can spell ordeal rather than adventure if you have limited energy or patience. Your endurance will go further if you arrive in the theme parks at opening time or before. Take in first those attractions that you most want to see. This way you can take it easy when the day warms up. Then relax in the shade, have a nice long lunch, see some shows in air-conditioned theaters, and maybe even go back to your hotel to relax around the pool, read, or nap. Refreshed, you can return to one of the theme parks, when they're open late, or explore Pleasure Island, Church Street Station, or Orlando's other after-dark options.

To qualify for age-related discounts, **mention your senior-citizen status up front** when booking hotel reservations (not when checking out) and before you're seated in restaurants (not when paying the bill). Be sure to have identification on hand. When renting a car, ask about promotional car-rental discounts, which can be cheaper than senior-citizen rates.

Educational Programs Elderhostel ✉ 11 Ave. de Lafayette, Boston, MA 02111-1746 ☎ 877/426-8056, 978/323-4141 international callers, 877/426-2167 TTY 📠 877/426-2166 🌐 www.elderhostel.org.

SHOPPING

SMART SOUVENIRS

Although it is easy to burn through wads of cash in the gift stores, some of the most popular and unique items are quite affordable. Disney's trading pins are a big hit with kids and can be bought for $6 in all the theme parks. You'll find the largest assortment of pins at Disney's Pin Traders at the Downtown Disney Marketplace. Probably the single most popular item at Disney is the autograph book, which costs less than $20.

SIGHTSEEING TOURS

IN THE THEME PARKS

Guided tours are available in all the area's major theme parks. *See* theme park A to Z sections for tour descriptions, fees, and additional information.

AROUND ORLANDO

Helicopter rides are a great way to get an overall view of the Orlando area. You'll be surprised at the vast number of lakes and open spaces; costs range from $20 per person to $395.

Helicopter Rides Air Florida ✉ 8990 International Dr., Orlando ☎ 407/354-1400 🌐 www.airfloridahelicopters.com.

STUDENTS AT WALT DISNEY WORLD

Don't expect to find discount prices for students at Walt Disney World.

I.D.s & Services STA Travel ✉ 10 Downing St., New York, NY 10014 ☎ 212/627-3111 or 800/777-0112 📠 212/627-3387 🌐 www.sta.com. **Travel Cuts** ✉ 187 College St., Toronto, Ontario M5T 1P7 Canada ☎ 416/979-2406, 800/592-2887, 866/246-9762 in Canada 📠 416/979-8167 🌐 www.travelcuts.com.

TAXES

Tourists pay a 5% bed tax on top of the sales tax, which means you will pay an extra 11%–12% of the rate for your hotel stay. There are no airport departure taxes.

SALES TAX

Orlando-area sales tax varies from 6% to 7%; it's 6.5% in Orange, 6% in Volusia County, 7% in Osceola and Seminole counties. You will pay different sales tax within Walt Disney World depending on where you are in the complex. At other major area theme parks, which are all in Orange County, you pay 6.5%. Sales taxes are levied on clothing, souvenirs, restaurants meals, and snack items.

TAXIS

Taxi fares start at $2 for the first mile and cost $1.50 for each mile thereafter. Sample fares: to WDW's Magic Kingdom, about $22 from International Drive, $12–$16 from U.S. 192. To Universal Studios, $7–$12 from International Drive, $25–$32 from U.S. 192. To Church Street Station, downtown, $20–$26 from International Drive, $34–$42 from U.S. 192. For information on getting to or from the airport by taxi, *see* Airports and Transfers. ⚽ Taxi Companies **A-1 Taxi** ☎ 407/328-4555. **Checker Cab Company** ☎ 407/699-9999. **Star Taxi** ☎ 407/857-9999.

TIME

Florida is in the Eastern U.S. time zone and adopts Daylight Saving Time between April and October (clocks are set one hour ahead).

TIPPING

Whether they carry bags, open doors, deliver food, or clean rooms, hospitality employees work to receive a portion of your travel budget. In deciding how much to give, **base your tip on what the service is and how well it's performed.**

In transit, tip an airport valet $1–$3 per bag, a taxi driver 15%–20% of the fare.

For hotel staff, recommended amounts are $1–$3 per bag for a bellhop, $2 per night per guest for housekeeping, $5–$10 for special concierge service, $1–$3 for a doorman who hails a cab or parks a car, 15% of the greens fee for a caddy, 15%–20% of the bill for a massage, and 15% of a room service bill, which is often already included, so be sure to check.

In a restaurant, give 15%–20% of your bill before tax to the server, 5%–10% to the maître d', 15% to a bartender, and 15% of the wine bill for a wine steward who makes a special effort in selecting and serving wine.

TOURS & PACKAGES

Because everything is prearranged on a prepackaged tour or independent vacation, you spend less time planning—and often get it all at a good price.

BOOKING WITH AN AGENT

Travel agents are excellent resources. But it's a good idea to collect brochures from several agencies, as some agents' suggestions may be influenced by relationships with tour and package firms that reward them for volume sales. If you have a special interest, **find an agent with expertise in that area**; the American Society of Travel Agents (ASTA; ⇨ Travel Agencies) has a database of specialists worldwide.

Make sure your travel agent knows the accommodations and other services of the place being recommended. Ask about the hotel's location, room size, beds, and whether it has a pool, room service, or programs for children, if you care about these. Has your agent been there in person or sent others whom you can contact?

Do some homework on your own, too: local tourism boards can provide information about lesser-known and small-niche operators, some of which may sell only direct.

BUYER BEWARE

Each year consumers are stranded or lose their money when tour operators—even large ones with excellent reputations—go out of business. So **check out the operator.** Ask several travel agents about its reputation, and try to **book with a company that has a consumer-protection program.** (Look for information in the company's brochure.) In the United States, members of the National Tour Association and the United States Tour Operators Association are required to set aside funds to cover payments and travel arrangements in the event that the company defaults. It's also a good idea to choose a company that participates in the American Society of Travel Agents' Tour Operator Program; ASTA will act as mediator in any disputes between you and your tour operator.

Remember that the more your package or tour includes, the better you can predict the ultimate cost of your vacation. Make sure you know exactly what is covered, and **beware of hidden costs.** Are taxes, tips, and transfers included? Entertainment and excursions? These can add up.

Tour-Operator Recommendations American Society of Travel Agents (⇨ Travel Agencies). **National Tour Association** (NTA) ⊠ 546 E. Main St., Lexington, KY 40508 ☎ 859/226-4444 or 800/682-8886 🖷 859/226-4404 ⊕ www.ntaonline.com. **United States Tour Operators Association** (USTOA) ⊠ 275 Madison Ave., Suite 2014, New York, NY 10016 ☎ 212/599-6599 or 800/468-7862 🖷 212/599-6744 ⊕ www.ustoa.com.

TRAIN TRAVEL

Amtrak stops in downtown Orlando and in picturesque Winter Park, about 15 mi north of Walt Disney World. A taxi ride from the Orlando station to the Disney area costs around $47. Although you won't find car-rental agencies at the stations, some agencies will send a shuttle to pick you up or reimburse your cab fare to their location.

If you want to have your car in Florida without driving it there, consider a 900-mi shortcut with Amtrak's Auto Train, which departs for Florida from Lorton, Virginia, near Washington, D.C. Its southern terminus—Sanford, Florida—is 23 mi north of Orlando.

FARES & SCHEDULES

Second-class round-trip Amtrak fare from New York to Orlando costs $180, round-trip fare from Jacksonville costs $32, and round-trip fare from Houston costs $162.

The Auto Train runs daily with one departure at 4 PM (car boarding ends one hour earlier). You'll arrive in Sanford around 8:30 the next morning. Fares vary depending on class of service and time of year, but expect to pay between $229 and $445 for a basic sleeper seat and car passage each way. For a group of four and one car, the cost is about $520 total. You must be traveling with an automobile to ride on the Auto Train.

Amtrak ☎ 800/872-7245 **Auto Train** ☎ 407/321-3873 or 877/754-7495.

TRANSPORTATION AROUND WALT DISNEY WORLD, UNIVERSAL STUDIOS & ORLANDO

If you're staying on Disney property, plan to use Disney's transportation system, which consists of buses and a monorail—all fast, clean, and comfortable—to travel between the parks and your hotel.

Universal is not as spread out as WDW, so if you stay on property, you can walk to most attractions and restaurants. A pleasant boat ride connects the Portofino Bay Hotel and Citywalk.

If your hotel is on International Drive and you plan to spend a day visiting the area, avoid driving in horrendous traffic by taking the I-Ride Trolley (⇨ Bus Travel Around Orlando) to I-Drive's attractions, shops, and restaurants.

Although public buses (⇨ Bus Travel Around Orlando) are available, a car is the fastest and most convenient way to travel if you plan to visit several theme parks and downtown Orlando. Once you're in downtown Orlando, however, park and ride the free Lymmo bus.

TRAVEL AGENCIES

A good travel agent puts your needs first. Look for an agency that has been in business at least five years, emphasizes customer service, and has someone on staff who specializes in your destination. In addition, **make sure the agency belongs to a professional trade organization.** The American Society of Travel Agents (ASTA)—the largest and most influential in the field with more than 20,000 members in some 140 countries—maintains and enforces a strict code of ethics and will step in to help mediate any agent-client disputes involving ASTA members if necessary. ASTA (whose motto is "Without a travel agent, you're on your own") also maintains a Web site that includes a directory of agents. (If a travel agency is also acting as your tour operator, *see* Buyer Beware *in* Tours and Packages.)

Local Agent Referrals American Society of Travel Agents (ASTA) ⊠ 1101 King St., Suite 200,

Alexandria, VA 22314 ☎ 703/739-2782 or 800/965-2782 24-hr hot line 🖷 703/739-3268 ⊕ www.astanet.com. **Association of British Travel Agents** ✉ 68-71 Newman St., London W1T 3AH ☎ 020/7637-2444 🖷 020/7637-0713 ⊕ www.abtanet.com. **Association of Canadian Travel Agents** ✉ 130 Albert St., Suite 1705, Ottawa, Ontario K1P 5G4 ☎ 613/237-3657 🖷 613/237-7052 ⊕ www.acta.ca. **Australian Federation of Travel Agents** ✉ Level 3, 309 Pitt St., Sydney, NSW 2000 ☎ 02/9264-3299 🖷 02/9264-1085 ⊕ www.afta.com.au. **Travel Agents' Association of New Zealand** ✉ Level 5, Tourism and Travel House, 79 Boulcott St., Box 1888, Wellington 6001 ☎ 04/499-0104 🖷 04/499-0786 ⊕ www.taanz.org.nz.

VISITOR INFORMATION

For Disney parks, hotels, dining, and entertainment reservations, contact Walt Disney World Information and Disney Reservation Center. To sit in the audience at a show being taped at Disney–MGM Studios call Production Information.

To get general information packages on the attractions of the Greater Orlando area, contact the convention and visitors bureaus below. For information on destinations outside the immediate Orlando-Kissimmee area, contact the Florida Tourism Industry Marketing Corporation.

🖪 Disney Information **Walt Disney World Information** ✉ Box 10000, Lake Buena Vista, FL 32830 ☎ 407/824-4321; 407/827-5141 TDD ⊕ www.disney.com. **Disney Reservation Center** ☎ 407/934-7639; 407/939-3463 for dining. **Production Information** ☎ 407/560-4651.

🖪 Details on Other Theme Parks **Universal Studios Escape** ✉ 1000 Universal Studios Plaza, Orlando, FL 32819-8000 ☎ 407/363-8000; 407/363-8265 TDD ⊕ www.uescape.com. **SeaWorld Orlando** ✉ 7007 SeaWorld Dr., Orlando, FL 32821 ☎ 407/351-3600 ⊕ www.seaworld.com. **Busch Gardens** ✉ Box 9158, Tampa, FL 33674 ☎ 813/987-5283 ⊕ www.buschgardens.com.

🖪 About Greater Orlando **Orlando/Orange County Convention & Visitors Bureau** ✉ 8723 International Dr., Orlando, FL 32819 ☎ 407/363-5871. **Kissimmee/St. Cloud Convention and Visitors Bureau** ✉ 1925 Irlo Bronson Hwy., Kissimmee, FL 34744 ☎ 407/847-5000 or 800/327-9159. **Winter Park Chamber of Commerce** ✉ Box 280, Winter Park, FL 32790 ☎ 407/644-8281.

🖪 About the State of Florida **Visit Florida** ✉ Box 1100, 661 E. Jefferson St., Suite 300, Tallahassee, FL 32302 ☎ 850/488-5607 🖷 850/224-9589 ⊕ www.visitflorida.com ⊕ www.myflorida.com. In the U.K.: **ABC Florida** ✉ Box 35, Abingdon, Oxon OX14 4TB

☎ 0891/600-555; enclose £2 for a vacation pack, or call at 50p per minute.

🖪 Government Advisories **Consular Affairs Bureau of Canada** ☎ 800/267-6788 or 613/944-6788 ⊕ www.voyage.gc.ca. **U.K. Foreign and Commonwealth Office** ✉ Travel Advice Unit, Consular Division, Old Admiralty Building, London SW1A 2PA ☎ 020/7008-0232 or 020/7008-0233 ⊕ www.fco.gov.uk/travel. **Australian Department of Foreign Affairs and Trade** ☎ 02/6261-1299 Consular Travel Advice Faxback Service ⊕ www.dfat.gov.au. **New Zealand Ministry of Foreign Affairs and Trade** ☎ 04/439-8000 ⊕ www.mft.govt.nz.

FURTHER READING

The most perceptive book on Walt Disney and his works is *The Disney Version*, by Richard Schickel (Ivan R. Dee, third edition 1997). A comprehensive history of the great Disney animation tradition is provided in *Disney Animation: The Illusion of Life*, by Frank Thomas and Ollie Johnston (Hyperion, revised edition 1995). For a good read about Disney and other animators, look for *Of Mice and Magic* (New American Library, revised edition 1990), by Leonard Maltin. *Walt Disney: An American Original* (Hyperion, reprint edition 1994), by Bob Thomas, is full of anecdotes about the development of WDW. Rollins College professor Richard Fogelsong questions the "economic marriage" between Disney and Orlando in his book *Married to the Mouse* (Yale University Press, reprint edition 2003).

WEB SITES

Do check out the World Wide Web when planning your trip. You'll find everything from weather forecasts to virtual tours of famous cities. Be sure to **visit Fodors.com** (⊕ www.fodors.com), a complete travel-planning site. You can research prices and book plane tickets, hotel rooms, rental cars, vacation packages, and more. In addition, you can post your pressing questions in the Travel Talk section.

Check theme park Web sites to get the latest prices and operating hours. To get feedback from fellow visitors who have been there, done that, check out the lively bulletin boards at www.disneyinfo.com and at www.fodors.com. To tap into the thrill-riding community, check out www.thrillride.com. Orlando is heavily represented, although you can also read about other theme parks nationwide.

CONVERSIONS

DISTANCE

KILOMETERS/MILES

To change kilometers (km) to miles (mi), multiply km by .621. To change mi to km, multiply mi by 1.61.

km to mi	mi to km
1 = .62	1 = 1.6
2 = 1.2	2 = 3.2
3 = 1.9	3 = 4.8
4 = 2.5	4 = 6.4
5 = 3.1	5 = 8.1
6 = 3.7	6 = 9.7
7 = 4.3	7 = 11.3
8 = 5.0	8 = 12.9

METERS/FEET

To change meters (m) to feet (ft), multiply m by 3.28. To change ft to m, multiply ft by .305.

m to ft	ft to m
1 = 3.3	1 = .30
2 = 6.6	2 = .61
3 = 9.8	3 = .92
4 = 13.1	4 = 1.2
5 = 16.4	5 = 1.5
6 = 19.7	6 = 1.8
7 = 23.0	7 = 2.1
8 = 26.2	8 = 2.4

TEMPERATURE

METRIC CONVERSIONS

To change centigrade or Celsius (C) to Fahrenheit (F), multiply C by 1.8 and add 32. To change F to C, subtract 32 from F and multiply by .555.

°F	°C
0	-17.8
10	-12.2
20	-6.7
30	-1.1
32	0
40	+4.4
50	10.0
60	15.5
70	21.1
80	26.6
90	32.2
98.6	37.0
100	37.7

WEIGHT

KILOGRAMS/POUNDS

To change kilograms (kg) to pounds (lb), multiply kg by 2.20. To change lb to kg, multiply lb by .455.

kg to lb	lb to kg
1 = 2.2	1 = .45
2 = 4.4	2 = .91
3 = 6.6	3 = 1.4
4 = 8.8	4 = 1.8
5 = 11.0	5 = 2.3
6 = 13.2	6 = 2.7
7 = 15.4	7 = 3.2
8 = 17.6	8 = 3.6

GRAMS/OUNCES

To change grams (g) to ounces (oz), multiply g by .035. To change oz to g, multiply oz by 28.4.

g to oz	oz to g
1 = .04	1 = 28
2 = .07	2 = 57
3 = .11	3 = 85
4 = .14	4 = 114
5 = .18	5 = 142
6 = .21	6 = 170
7 = .25	7 = 199
8 = .28	8 = 227

LIQUID VOLUME

LITERS/U.S. GALLONS

To change liters (L) to U.S. gallons (gal), multiply L by .264. To change U.S. gal to L, multiply gal by 3.79.

L to gal	gal to L
1 = .26	1 = 3.8
2 = .53	2 = 7.6
3 = .79	3 = 11.4
4 = 1.1	4 = 15.2
5 = 1.3	5 = 19.0
6 = 1.6	6 = 22.7
7 = 1.8	7 = 26.5
8 = 2.1	8 = 30.3

CLOTHING SIZE

WOMEN'S CLOTHING

US	UK	EUR
4	6	34
6	8	36
8	10	38
10	12	40
12	14	42

WOMEN'S SHOES

US	UK	EUR
5	3	36
6	4	37
7	5	38
8	6	39
9	7	40

MEN'S SUITS

US	UK	EUR
34	34	44
36	36	46
38	38	48
40	40	50
42	42	52
44	44	54
46	46	56

MEN'S SHIRTS

US	UK	EUR
14½	14½	37
15	15	38
15½	15½	39
16	16	41
16½	16½	42
17	17	43
17½	17½	44

MEN'S SHOES

US	UK	EUR
7	6	39½
8	7	41
9	8	42
10	9	43
11	10	44½
12	11	46

WEDDINGS

Planning on living happily ever after? Then maybe you should tie the knot at Walt Disney World, as do some 1,000 couples every year. At the Fairy Tale Wedding Pavilion near the Grand Floridian Resort, the bride can ride in a Cinderella coach, have rings borne to the altar in a glass slipper, and invite Mickey and Minnie to attend the reception. Or exchange vows in the presence of sharks and dolphins at SeaWorld's *Ports of Call* events and banquet complex. Although it may prove impossible for Shamu to make a guest appearance, the maritime surroundings do make the pavilion tranquil.

🔲 WDW Wedding Information **Fairy Tale Wedding Pavilion** ☎ 407/828-3400 🖨 407/828-3744. **Ports of Call** ☎ 407/363-2200. **SeaWorld Weddings** ☎ 407/363-2273.

WALT DISNEY WORLD® RESORT

1

FODOR'S CHOICE

Buzz Lightyear's Space Ranger Spin, in the Magic Kingdom

Fantasmic! in Disney–MGM Studios

The Haunted Mansion, in the Magic Kingdom

Honey, I Shrunk the Audience, in Epcot

IllumiNations, in Epcot

Kilimanjaro Safaris, in Disney's Animal Kingdom

The Magic of Disney Animation, in Disney–MGM Studios

Rock 'n' Roller Coaster Starring Aerosmith, in Disney–MGM Studios

Splash Mountain, in the Magic Kingdom

SpectroMagic Parade, in the Magic Kingdom

Summit Plummet, in Blizzard Beach

Test Track, in Epcot

Tree of Life—*It's Tough to Be a Bug!*, in Disney's Animal Kingdom

Twilight Zone Tower of Terror, in Disney–MGM Studios

By Catherine
Fredman
Updated by
Jennie Hess

NO MOSS EVER GROWS under the Mouse's trademark yellow clogs (unless it's artfully re-created moss for some lush forest landscape). Since its opening in 1971, Walt Disney World Resort has made it a point to stay fresh, current, and endlessly amusing. Disney Imagineers and producers constantly choreograph new shows and parades, revamp classic theme rides, and periodically replace an entire attraction. Yet amid all the hoopla, much remains reassuringly the same, rekindling fond memories among the generations who return.

Millions of visitors, even those who place Pirates of the Caribbean and Space Mountain among the wonders of the world, are hard-pressed to define Walt Disney World. When you take a Walt Disney World exit off I–4, you're almost on the grounds, even though there's no Cinderella Castle in sight. It's a very big place, and it's crammed with pleasures: from swooping above the Magic Kingdom's starlit London in Peter Pan's Flight to simply sitting under the shade of a Callary pear tree frosted with blooms in Epcot; from enjoying jazz at Pleasure Island and cheering for your favorite team at the ESPN sports bar at Disney's Board-Walk to whooping and hollering down water slides at the cleverly designed water parks.

The sheer enormity of the property—30,000 acres near Kissimmee, Florida—suggests that WDW is more than a single theme park with a fabulous castle in the center. The property's acreage translates to 47 square mi—twice the size of Manhattan or Bermuda, and about the same size as San Francisco. On a tract that size, 107 acres is a mere speck, yet that's the size of the Magic Kingdom. When most people imagine Walt Disney World, they think only of those 107 acres, but there's much, much more.

More than 2,800 acres of the property are occupied by hotels and villa complexes, each with its own theme and swimming pools and other recreational facilities. Epcot, a little more than twice the size of the Magic Kingdom, is the second major theme park. A combination of a science exploratorium and a world's fair sprinkled with thrills throughout, Epcot looks at the future and celebrates the world's cultural diversity. Disney–MGM Studios, devoted to the film business and also known familiarly as the "Studios," is nearby. The fourth major theme park, Disney's Animal Kingdom, salutes creatures real, imaginary, and extinct. Thousands of acres are still undeveloped—grassy plains and pine forests patrolled by deer and other Florida fauna, and swamps patched by thickets of palmettos and filled with white ibis.

In the past several years, Disney has introduced and expanded a way to experience the most popular attractions with little or no wait. FAST-PASS allows you to schedule appointments and avoid the long lines that are so commonplace. Going by a Disney survey, FASTPASS may save as much as two hours of line-standing time. Just step up to the front of the line and book your reservation time by feeding your theme-park admission ticket into a machine.

Walt Disney's original decree that his parks be ever changing, along with some healthy competition from area attractions, keeps the Disney Imagineers and show producers on their toes as they dream up new entertainment and install higher-tech attractions. To avoid missing anything, do plenty of research before you go, make a plan, then try to relax—and have a wonderful time.

MAGIC KINGDOM

The Magic Kingdom is the heart and soul of the Disney empire. Comparable (in scope) to California's Disneyland, it was the first Disney outpost in Florida when it opened in 1971, and it's the park that launched Disney's presence, with modifications, in France and Japan.

For a landmark that wields such worldwide influence, the Magic Kingdom may seem small: at 107 acres, it's smaller than Disney World's other Big Three parks. But looks can be deceiving: the unofficial theme song—"It's a Small World After All"—doesn't hold true when it comes to the Magic Kingdom's attractions. Packed into seven different "lands" are nearly 50 major crowd pleasers, and that's not counting all the ancillary attractions: shops, eateries, live entertainment, Disney-character meet-and-greet spots (all Disney theme-park maps are marked with a "Mickey glove" symbol wherever characters come out to play), fireworks, parades, and, of course, the sheer pleasure of strolling through the beautifully landscaped and manicured grounds.

Many rides are geared for the young, but the Magic Kingdom is anything but a kiddie park. The degree of detail, the greater vision, the surprisingly witty spiel of the guides, and the tongue-in-cheek signs that crop up in the oddest places—for instance, in Fantasyland, the rest rooms are marked "Prince" and "Princess"—all contribute to a delightful sense of discovery that's far beyond the mere thrill of a ride.

The park is laid out on a north–south axis, with Cinderella Castle at the center and the various lands surrounding it in a broad circle. Upon passing through the entrance gates, you immediately find yourself in Town Square, containing City Hall, the park's main information center. Town Square segues into Main Street, U.S.A., a boulevard filled with Victorian-style stores and snack spots. Main Street runs due north and ends at the Hub, a large tree-lined circle, properly known as Central Plaza, in front of Cinderella Castle. Rope Drop, the ceremonial stampede that kicks off each day, occurs at the various points where the end of Main Street intersects the Hub.

As you move clockwise from the Hub, the Magic Kingdom's seven lands begin with Adventureland—home of Pirates of the Caribbean, the Jungle Cruise, and the Swiss Family Treehouse. Next come Frontierland and Liberty Square, containing Splash Mountain, Big Thunder Mountain Railroad, and the Haunted Mansion. Fantasyland is directly behind Cinderella Castle—the castle's rear courtyard, as it were. Mickey's Toontown Fair is just east of Fantasyland. Tomorrowland, directly to the right of the Hub, rounds out the circle.

Numbers in the margin correspond to points of interest on the Magic Kingdom map.

Main Street, U.S.A.

With its pastel Victorian-style buildings, antique automobiles ahoohga-oohga-ing, sparkling sidewalks, and an atmosphere of what one writer has called "almost hysterical joy," Main Street is more than a mere conduit to the other enchantments of the Magic Kingdom. It's where the spell is first cast.

Like Dorothy waking up in a Technicolor Oz or Mary Poppins jumping through the pavement painting, you emerge from beneath the Walt Disney World Railroad Station into a realization of one of the most tenacious American dreams. The perfect street in the perfect small town in

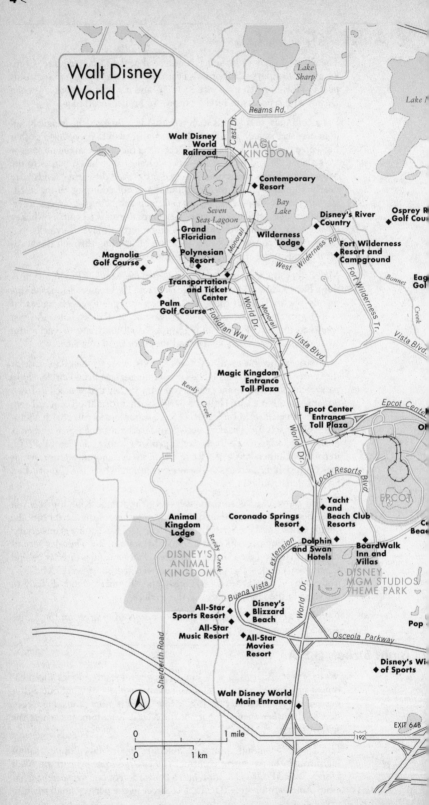

4

Walt Disney World

Walt Disney World Railroad

MAGIC KINGDOM

Cast Dr.

Reams Rd.

Lake Sharp

Lake N

Contemporary Resort

Bay Lake

Seven Seas Lagoon

Disney's River Country

Osprey R Golf Cou

Grand Floridian

Wilderness Lodge

Fort Wilderness Resort and Campground

West Wilderness Rd.

Bonnet

Eagle Gol

Polynesian Resort

Magnolia Golf Course

Monorail

Fort Wilderness Tr.

Vista Blvd

Vista Blvd

Transportation and Ticket Center

Palm Golf Course

Floridian Way

World Dr.

Monorail

Reedy Creek

Creek

Magic Kingdom Entrance Toll Plaza

Epcot Center Entrance Toll Plaza

Epcot Cente

World Dr.

Of

Epcot Resorts Blvd

EPCOT

Yacht and Beach Club Resorts

Animal Kingdom Lodge

Coronado Springs Resort

Reedy Creek

Ce Bea

DISNEY'S ANIMAL KINGDOM

Dolphin and Swan Hotels

BoardWalk Inn and Villas

DISNEY-MGM STUDIOS THEME PARK

Buena Vista Dr. extension

World Dr.

All-Star Sports Resort

Disney's Blizzard Beach

All-Star Music Resort

All-Star Movies Resort

Osceola Parkway

Pop

Disney's Wi of Sports

Shebeth Road

Walt Disney World Main Entrance

EXIT 64B

192

0   1 mile

0   1 km

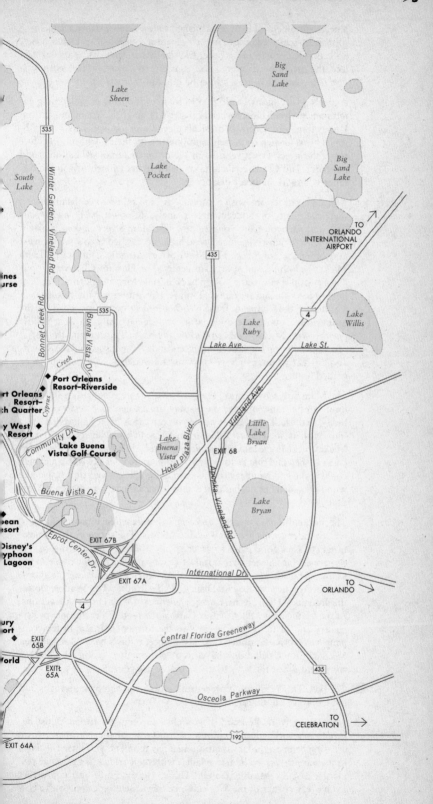

a perfect moment of time is burnished to jewel-like quality, thanks to a four-fifths-scale reduction, nightly cleanings with high-pressure hoses, and constant repainting; neither life-size nor so small as to appear toy-like, the carefully calculated size is meant to make you feel as though you're looking through a telescope into another world.

And it's a very sunny world thanks to an outpouring of welcoming entertainment: live bands, barbershop quartets, and background music from Disney films and American musicals played over loudspeakers. Old-fashioned horse-drawn trams and omnibuses with their horns tooting chug along the street. Street vendors in Victorian costumes sell balloons and popcorn. And Cinderella's famous castle floats whimsically in the distance where Main Street disappears.

Although attractions with a capital "A" are minimal on Main Street, there are plenty of inducements—namely, shops—to while away your time and part you from your money. The Main Street Gallery, a bright yellow, Victorian-style gingerbread building, is filled with animation art and other memorabilia. The Main Street Athletic Club sells "Team Mickey" clothing and sporty souvenirs. The Harmony Barber Shop is a novel stop if you want to step back in time for a quick trim. You can line up for your monogrammed mouse ears and other fun headgear at a millinery, the Chapeau. If the weather looks threatening, head for the Emporium to purchase a signature mouse-ear umbrella or a yellow poncho with Mickey emblazoned on the back. This mammoth shop is often the last stop for souvenir hunters at day's end, so avoid the crowds and buy early. You can have your purchases delivered to your hotel or mailed home.

The Main Street Exposition Hall in Town Square is actually a shop, exhibit, and theater in one; on display are cameras of yesteryear and today. In the hall is a theater where you can catch Disney animated short films such as *Steamboat Willie*, from 1928. In his silver-screen premier, Mickey met Minnie and was inspired to serenade her using a cow's udder. (Walt Disney said that he loved his creation more than any woman, which could make you wonder how his wife, Lillian, felt about this. It was she who persuaded her husband to change the character's name from Mortimer.)

The air-conditioned theater can come in handy when approaching summer thunderstorms give way to downpours. The shops in the Exposition Hall are a good place to stock up on batteries, film, and disposable cameras. Main Street is also full of Disney insider fun for those in the know. For instance, check out the proprietors' names above the shops: Crystal Arts honors Roy O. Disney, Walt's brother. The Shadow Box is the domain of Dick Nunis, former chairman of Walt Disney Attractions. At the Main Street Athletic Club, Card Walker—the "Practitioner of Psychiatry and Justice of the Peace"—is the former chairman of the company's executive committee. At last glance, today's head Mouseketeer, Michael Eisner, still didn't have his own shop; then again, who needs a storefront when the keys to the kingdom are yours?

❶ City Hall. This is information central, where you can pick up maps and guidebooks and inquire about all things Disney.

❷ Walt Disney World Railroad. If you click through the turnstile just before 9 AM with young children in tow, wait at the entrance before crossing beneath the train station. In a few moment, you'll see the day's first steam-driven train arrive laden with the park's most popular residents: Mickey Mouse, Donald Duck, Goofy, Pluto and characters from every corner of the World. Once they disembark and you've col-

Best of the Park

Arrive at the parking lot 45 minutes before scheduled opening, and once in the park, dash left, or hop the **Walt Disney World Railroad,** to Frontierland, where you can claim an early FASTPASS time for **Splash Mountain.** After you've received your ticket, head over for **Big Thunder Mountain Railroad.** Then, catch the next **Country Bear Jamboree** show. By now, if things are going well, your FASTPASS ticket should be valid to ride Splash Mountain. Next head over to Adventureland to the **Jungle Cruise** and pick up another FAST-PASS. After you get your ticket, venture on to **Pirates of the Caribbean,** the **Swiss Family Treehouse,** and **The Magic Carpets of Aladdin.** If the time is still not right to do the Jungle Cruise, grab a bite to eat at **El Pirata y el Perico Restaurante** or the **Sunshine Tree Terrace.** By now, it should be time to take the Jungle Cruise. When you're finished, sprint over to Tomorrowland and pick up your next FASTPASS, this time for **Space Mountain.** Experience the **ExtraTERRORestrial Alien Encounter,** then head to the **Timekeeper** and the **Carousel of Progress** if they're operating. After that, ride the **Tomorrowland Transit Authority.** By now, it'll be time for you to ride Space Mountain. Afterward, pick up your next FASTPASS—this time for **Buzz Lightyear's Space Ranger Spin.** If you haven't done some of the attractions above, now's the time to squeeze them in before returning to help Buzz in his attempt to save the planet.

Around 2:40 find your viewing spot for the 3 PM parade. Once you settle on a curb, send a member of your group to pick up the next set of FAST-PASS tickets for **The Many Adventures of Winnie the Pooh.** If the crowds aren't too thick, the second floor of the train station makes a really nice parade viewing spot. After the parade, hop the train to Mickey's Toontown Fair and pose by the colorful house fronts for some fun photos. From there, stroll right into Fantasyland. By now, your FASTPASS time should be valid for The Many Adventures of Winnie the Pooh. Afterward, get your FASTPASS appointment for **Peter Pan's Flight.** While you wait for your appointment, take a ride on **Snow White's Scary Adventures** and see **Mickey's PhilharMagic.** After a spin on **Cinderella's Golden Carrousel,** head over to **it's a small world.** Then cruise on over for your FASTPASS ride on Peter Pan's Flight.

Meander over to Liberty Square now and scare up some fun at the **Haunted Mansion.** If the line is long, get a FASTPASS appointment and take in the next **Hall of Presidents** show while you wait. Don't miss **SpectroMagic** if you're visiting during peak season. Then return to the Haunted Mansion for your ghostly appointment and depart as **Fantasy in the Sky** fireworks cap the evening; by leaving in the midst of the fireworks display instead of after they finish, you avoid much of the madding crowds rushing to exit.

On Rainy Days

If you visit during a busy time of year, pray for rain. Rainy days dissolve the crowds here. Unlike those at Disney–MGM and Epcot's Future World, however, many of the Magic Kingdom's attractions are outdoors. If you don't mind getting damp, pick up a brightly colored poncho ($6 adults, $5 children) in almost any Disney merchandise shop and soldier on.

With Small Children

At Rope Drop, go directly to Fantasyland and start your day by getting a FASTPASS return-time ticket at **The Many Adventures of Winnie the Pooh.** Then, go on a ride with **Dumbo the Flying Elephant.** Next, check show times for **Mickey's PhilharMagic** 3-D extravaganza and plan to see it before moving on to a new land. While you wait for the show and your appointment with Pooh, take a whirl on **Cinderella's Golden Carrousel** and, moving clockwise, other attractions without prohibitive waits. You can also head for a character greeting (check your guide map for times). By now it should be time to use your FASTPASS ticket at The Many Adventures of Winnie the Pooh. When you've finished, get a FASTPASS for **Peter Pan's Flight.** Next, visit **Ariel's Grotto** to pose for snapshots with the Little Mermaid or go to **Fantasyland Character Festival** to see other Disney "stars." On to **it's a small world,** where lines move quickly; then stroll across the lane for your FASTPASS "night-sky" flight over Peter Pan's domain.

If you want a sit-down lunch, proceed to **Cinderella's Royal Table** at Cinderella Castle or **Liberty Tree Tavern** in Liberty Square (be sure to arrange priority seating in advance). Your best bet for a quick lunch, however, is Disney's ever-improving brand of fast food at **Cosmic Ray's Starlight Cafe** in Tomorrowland, where three counters serve up sandwiches, soups, salads, and rotisserie chicken. Depending on your lunch location, either take the train or walk to Mickey's Toontown Fair. Lunch can digest while the children get their autographs and photos with Mickey Mouse. Then on to **The Barnstormer** to test their coaster mettle. Taking the **Walt Disney World Railroad** is the most relaxing way to return to Frontierland, where you can pick up your FAST-PASS timed ticket for **Splash Mountain.** Then claim a piece of pavement across the street from the Country Bear Jamboree for the 3 PM parade so you can make a quick exit to line up for **Big Thunder Mountain Railroad**—if your kids can handle the thrills and are tall enough. For the shortest lines, go *during* the parade. By now, it should be time for your FASTPASS reservation for Splash Mountain. After the ride, check out either the **Country Bear Jamboree** show or the **Haunted Mansion.**

Late afternoon is a nice time to hitch a raft to **Tom Sawyer Island.** When you return, head straight for Adventureland. Proceed directly across the Adventureland plaza to the **Jungle Cruise.** Pick up another FASTPASS here if the line is long. Then do **Pirates of the Caribbean** and **The Magic Carpets of Aladdin.** If you still have some time and energy left, scramble around the **Swiss Family Treehouse** and then head back for your FASTPASS entry to the Jungle Cruise.

Now stroll across the Main Street hub to Tomorrowland and pick up a FAST-PASS ticket for **Buzz Lightyear's Space Ranger Spin.** While you wait, climb aboard **Tomorrowland Transit Authority** and, if the line's not prohibitive, **Astro-Orbiter.** If you still have time to kill you join Buzz on his intergalactic mission, line up for a spin on the **Mad Tea Party.**

If you're really determined to see it all, have dinner at the **Crystal Palace,** in Main Street, U.S.A. Then hike toward the front of the park to grab a rocker on the porch of **Tony's Town Square Restaurant** or stake out a curb about an hour before the evening **SpectroMagic** parade and **Fantasy in the Sky** fireworks for a spectacular end to your day.

lected the stars' signatures, step right up to the elevated platform above the Magic Kingdom's entrance for a ride into living history. Walt Disney was a railroad buff of the highest order—he constructed a one-eighth-scale train in his backyard and named it *Lilly Belle,* after his wife, Lillian. Another *Lilly Belle* rides the rails here, as do *Walter E. Disney, Roy O. Disney,* and *Roger Broggie* (named for a Disney Imagineer and fellow railroad aficionado). All the locomotives date from 1928, coincidentally the same year Mickey Mouse was created. Disney scouts tracked down these vintage carriers in Mexico, where they were used to haul sugarcane in the Yucatán, brought them back, and completely overhauled them to their present splendor. And splendid they are, with striped awnings, brightly painted benches, authoritative "choo-choo" sounds, and hissing plumes of steam. Their 1½-mi track runs along the perimeter of the Magic Kingdom, with much of the trip through the woods. You'll pass Tom Sawyer Island and other attractions; stops are in Frontierland and Mickey's Toontown Fair. The ride provides a good introduction to the layout of the park and a quick trip with small children to Toontown in the morning; otherwise, it's great as relief for tired feet and dragging legs later in the day. The four trains run at five- to seven-minute intervals. ☞ *Duration: 21 mins. Crowds: Can be substantial beginning in late morning through late afternoon. Strategy: Board with small children for an early start in Toontown, or hop aboard in midafternoon if you don't see a line. Or ride to Frontierland in the early morning to get a jump-start on the Splash Mountain line. Audience: All ages. Rating:* ★★

Fodor's Choice **SpectroMagic.** The magic truly comes out at night when this parade rolls down Main Street, U.S.A., in a splendidly choreographed surge of electroluminescent, fiber-optic, and prismatic lighting effects that bring to life peacocks, sea horses, fountains, fantasy gardens, and floats full of colorful Disney characters. Plenty of old-fashioned twinkle lights are thrown in for good measure, and a powerful musical score produced for the parade is broadcast over 204 speakers with 72,000 watts of power. Mickey, as always, is the star. But Practical Pig, from one of Disney's prewar Silly Symphony cartoons, steals the show. With the flick of a paintbrush, he transforms more than 100 ft of multicolor floats into a gleaming white-light dreamscape. ☞ *Duration: 20 mins. Crowds: Heavy. Strategy: Take your place on the curb 40 mins before it begins. Audience: All ages. Rating:* ★★★

Adventureland

From the scrubbed brick, manicured lawns, and meticulously pruned trees of the Central Plaza, an artfully dilapidated wooden bridge leads to the jungles of Adventureland. The landscape artists went wild here: South African cape honeysuckle droops, Brazilian bougainvillea drapes, Mexican flame vines cling, spider plants clone, and three different varieties of palm trees sway, all creating a seemingly spontaneous mess. The bright, all-American sing-along tunes that fill the air along Main Street and Central Plaza are replaced by the recorded repetitions of trumpeting elephants, pounding drums, and squawking parrots. The architecture is a mishmash of the best of Thailand, the Middle East, the Caribbean, Africa, and Polynesia, arranged in an inspired disorder that recalls comic-book fantasies of far-off places. Even without your Mickey-emblazoned safari hat, you won't want to resist the lure of this adventure.

Adventureland is built around an oblong plaza. To your right as you cross the bridge from the Hub is the Agrabah Bazaar marketplace. Here you can buy Aladdin-wear, including costumes and jewelry, as well as Moroccan-made carpets, carvings, masks, and other goods. In the center of the plaza is the Magic Carpets of Aladdin, where magic-carpet riders are spun around a giant genie's bottle. To your left are the spreading branches of the Swiss Family Robinson's banyan tree. As you continue around the plaza you'll see the entrances to the Jungle Cruise, the Pirates of the Caribbean, and the Polynesian great house containing the Enchanted Tiki Room—Under New Management. Farther along, within the Caribbean Plaza, is another conglomeration of shops. Here the treasures are inspired by the Pirates of the Caribbean, most notably tropical clothing and costume jewelry (how about some pineapple earrings?). Children swoop down on the pirates' swords and hats embroidered with skulls and crossbones.

❸ Swiss Family Treehouse. Inspired by the classic novel by Johann Wyss about the adventures of the Robinson family, who were shipwrecked on the way to America, the tree house shows what you can do with a big tree and a lot of imagination. The rooms are furnished with patchwork quilts and mahogany furniture. Disney detail abounds: the kitchen sink is a giant clamshell; the boys' room, strewn with clothing, has two hammocks instead of beds; and an ingenious system of rain barrels and bamboo pipes provides running water in every room. Small wonder that in the 1960 film, when offered the chance to leave their island, all but one Robinson decided to stay on. As you clamber around the narrow wooden steps and rope bridges that connect the rooms in this split-level dwelling, take a look at the Spanish moss. It's real, but the tree itself— some 90 ft in diameter, with more than 1,000 branches—was constructed by the props department. The 300,000 leaves are vinyl. It all adds up to a species of tree unofficially called *Disneyodendron eximus,* or "out-of-the-ordinary Disney tree." ☞ *Duration: Up to you. Crowds: Artfully camouflaged so you may not see them—and the lines move slowly. Strategy: Visit while waiting for your Jungle Cruise FASTPASS appointment. Audience: All ages; toddlers unsteady on their feet may have trouble with the stairs. Rating:* ★★

❹ Jungle Cruise. On this Disney favorite, you cruise through three continents and along four rivers: the Congo, the Nile, the Mekong, and the Amazon. The canopied launches are loaded, the safari-suited guides make a point of checking their pistols, and the *Irrawady Irma* or *Mongala Millie* is off for another "perilous" journey. The guide's shtick is surprisingly funny, with just the right blend of wry and cornball humor. Along the way, you'll encounter Disney's famed Audio-Animatronics creatures of the African veldt: bathing elephants, slinky pythons, an irritated rhinoceros, a tribe of hungry headhunters, and a bunch of hyperactive hippos (good thing the guide's got a pop pistol). Then there's Old Smiley, the crocodile, who's always waiting for a handout—or, as the guide quips, "a foot out." Be sure to give him your left hand, the guide advises, and you'll be "all right." Kids who might be frightened by the darkness in Pirates of the Caribbean will love this outdoor adventure, and adults love the patter and all the detail—listen for what's playing on the radio of the overturned Jeep. ☞ *Duration: 10 mins. Crowds: Huge, from late morning until dinnertime. Strategy: Use the FASTPASS. Otherwise go first thing in the morning or during the afternoon parade, but not after dark—you miss too much. Audience: All ages. Rating:* ★★★

❺ Shrunken Ned's Junior Jungle Boats. Although cleverly named, these are nothing more than remote-controlled miniatures of the Jungle Cruise boats. Look for them to your immediate right as you exit the Jungle Cruise (they're easy to miss on a crowded day). A change machine spits out to-

When to Go

Most families hit the Magic Kingdom early in their visit, so try to go toward the end of the week instead. Avoid weekends, since that's when local residents tend to visit the park.

Arrive at the turnstiles least 30 minutes before Rope Drop to get your bearings and explore the shops on Main Street.

If you're staying at a Disney resort, arrive at park opening and stay until early afternoon, then head back to the hotel for a nap or swim. You can return to the park in the mid- to late afternoon, when crowds have often thinned out.

Times for after-dark entertainment depend on the day of the week, holidays, and peak times. Check the schedule before entering the park so you can set priorities and plan your day to avoid missing the nighttime festivities.

When You're There

Check Disney's Tip Board at the end of Main Street for good information on wait times—fairly reliable except for those moments when everyone follows the "See It Now!" advice and the line immediately triples.

Staying hydrated is critical in the steamy Central Florida afternoons. Take your own water bottles and refill them at park fountains throughout the day. A 20–24 ounce bottle of water sells for $2–$2.50 in the parks.

Do your shopping in midafternoon, when attraction lines resemble a napping anaconda. During the afternoon parade, store clerks have been spotted twiddling their thumbs, so this is the time to seek sales assistance. If you go at the end of the day, you'll be engulfed by rush-hour crowds.

See or ride one of the star attractions while the parade is going on, if you're willing to miss it, since lines ease considerably. But be careful not to get stuck on the wrong side of the parade route when the hoopla starts, or you may never get across.

Designate a very specific meeting place—such as a particular bench—after rest room stops, when it's easy to miss someone.

At the start of the day, set up a rendezvous point and time, just in case you and your companions get separated. Good places are by the Cinderella Fountain in Fantasyland, the bottom of the staircase at the Main Street railroad station, the benches of City Hall, and the archway entrance to Adventureland.

---

kens ($1 for one, $5 for six), one of which purchases a few minutes' worth of play with the boats. ☞ *Duration: As long as you like and your money holds out. Crowds: Can get thick during midafternoon. Strategy: If you can talk the kids out of it, skip this attraction. Audience: Mostly children, some adults. Rating:* ★

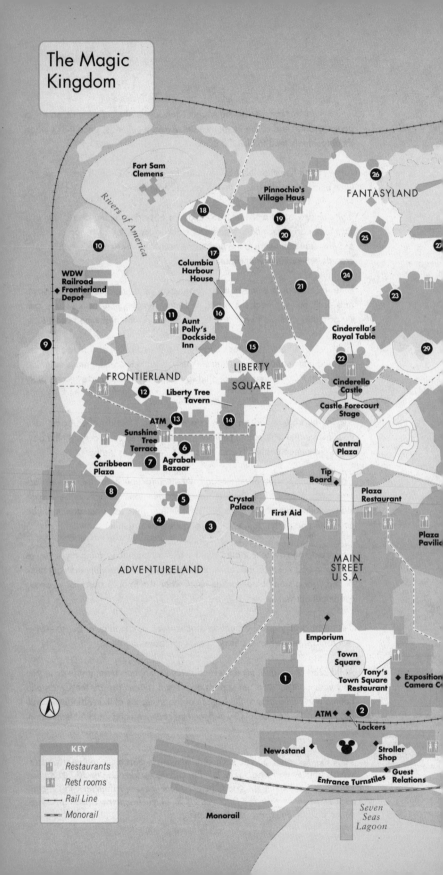

The Magic Kingdom

Fort Sam Clemens

Rivers of America

FANTASYLAND

Pinnochio's Village Haus

WDW Railroad Frontierland Depot

Columbia Harbour House

Aunt Polly's Dockside Inn

FRONTIERLAND

LIBERTY SQUARE

Cinderella's Royal Table

Liberty Tree Tavern

Cinderella Castle

ATM

Sunshine Tree Terrace

Castle Forecourt Stage

Caribbean Plaza

Agrabah Bazaar

Central Plaza

Tip Board

Plaza Restaurant

Crystal Palace

First Aid

ADVENTURELAND

Plaza Pavilion

MAIN STREET U.S.A.

Emporium

Town Square

Tony's Town Square Restaurant

Exposition Camera Ce

ATM

Lockers

Newsstand

Stroller Shop

Guest Relations

Entrance Turnstiles

Monorail

Seven Seas Lagoon

KEY

🖼	Restaurants
🖼	Rest rooms
—+—	Rail Line
====	Monorail

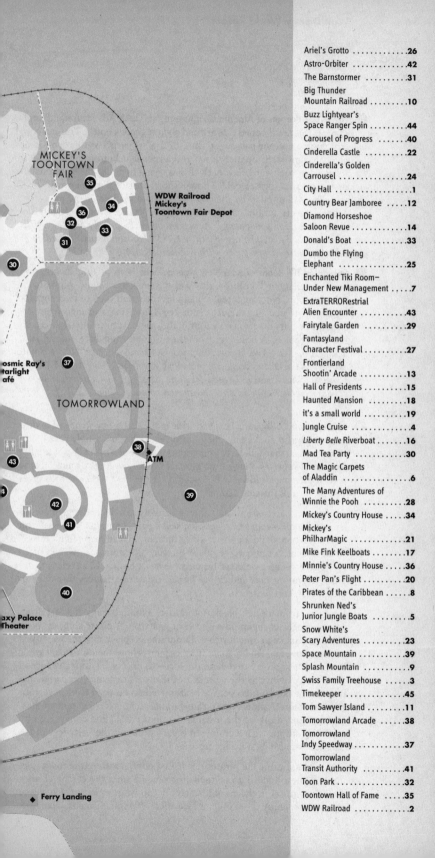

MICKEY'S
TOONTOWN
FAIR

WDW Railroad
Mickey's
Toontown Fair Depot

osmic Ray's
tarlight
afé

TOMORROWLAND

ATM

axy Palace
Theater

Ferry Landing

> ### need a break?
>
> Among the fast munchies here, some of the tastiest and most healthful are the fresh pineapple spears at **Aloha Isle.** You can take your spear to one of the benches scattered throughout Adventureland.

❻ The Magic Carpets of Aladdin. Brightening the lush Adventureland landscape is this jewel-toned ride around a giant genie's bottle. You can control your own four-passenger, state-of-the-art carpet with a front-seat lever that moves it up and down and a rear-seat button that pitches it forward or backward. Part of the fun is trying to dodge the right-on aim of a water-spewing "camel." Though short, the ride is a big hit with kids, who are also dazzled by the colorful gems implanted in the pavement around the attraction. ☞ *Duration: about 3 mins. Crowds: Heavy due to the attraction's newness, but lines move fairly quickly. Strategy: Visit while waiting for your Jungle Cruise FASTPASS appointment. Audience: All ages; parents must ride with toddlers. Rating:* ★★★

❼ Enchanted Tiki Room—Under New Management. In its original incarnation as the Enchanted Tiki Birds, this was Disney's first Audio-Animatronics attraction. Now updated, it includes the avian stars of two popular Disney animated films: Zazu from *The Lion King* and Iago from *Aladdin.* The boys take you on a tour of the original attraction while cracking lots of jokes. A holdover from the original is the ditty "In the Tiki, Tiki, Tiki, Tiki, Tiki Room," which is second only to "It's a Small World" as the Disney song you most love to hate. ☞ *Duration: 12 mins. Crowds: Waits seldom exceed 30 mins. Strategy: Go when you need a sit-down refresher in an air-conditioned room. Audience: All ages. Rating:* ★

❽ Pirates of the Caribbean. This boat ride is classic Disney wrapped in dramatic, colorful packaging: memorable vignettes, incredible detail, and catchy music that will have you chiming "Yo-ho! Yo-ho! A pirate's life for me!" for hours. One of the pirate's "Avast, ye scurvy scum!" is the sort of greeting children will proclaim for the next week—which gives you an idea of the ride's impact.

The gracious arched entrance soon gives way to a dusty dungeon, redolent of dampness and of a spooky, scary past. Lanterns flicker as you board the boats and a ghostly voice intones, "Dead men tell no tales." At this point, a timid voice might quaver, "Mommy, can we get off?" Hugs help. Next, a deserted beach, strewn with shovels, a skeleton, and a disintegrating map indicating buried treasure, prefaces this story of greed, lust, and destruction.

Emerging from a pitch-black tunnel after a mild, tummy-tickling drop, you're caught in the middle of a furious battle. A pirate ship, cannons blazing, attacks a stone fortress. Cannonballs splash into the water just off your bow, and Audio-Animatronics pirates hoist the Jolly Roger while brave soldiers scurry to defend the fort—to no avail. Politically correct nerves may twinge as the women of the town are rounded up and auctioned. "Strike your colors, ye brazen wench, no need to expose your superstructure!" shouts one pirate, but the scene is terrific: pirates chasing chickens, dunking the town mayor in the well, and collapsing into a snoring stupor with a couple of pigs. Check out the hairy legs of the carouser straddling a bridge up ahead.

The wild antics of the pirates result in a conflagration; the town goes up in flames, and all go to their just reward amid the catchy chorus. There's a moral in there somewhere, if you want to look for one—or you can just enjoy the show. ☞ *Duration: 10 mins. Crowds: Waits sel-*

dom exceed 30 mins, despite the ride's popularity. Strategy: A good destination, especially in the heat of the afternoon. Audience: All ages. Rating: ★★★

Frontierland

Frontierland, in the northwest quadrant of the Magic Kingdom, evokes the American frontier. The period seems to be the latter half of the 19th century, and the West is being won by Disney cast members dressed in checked shirts, leather vests, cowboy hats, and brightly colored neckerchiefs. Banjo and fiddle music twangs from tree to tree, and snackers walk around munching turkey drumsticks so large that you could best an outlaw single-handedly with one.

The screams that periodically drown out the string music are not the result of a cowboy surprising an Indian. They come from two of the Magic Kingdom's more thrilling rides: Splash Mountain, an elaborate flume ride; and Big Thunder Mountain Railroad, one of the park's two roller coasters. The rust-red rock spires of Thunder Mountain and Splash Mountain serve as local landmarks. In contrast to lush Adventureland, Frontierland is planted with mesquite, twisted Peruvian pepper trees, slash pines, and many cacti. The unpainted buildings and wooden sidewalks look ramshackle, and even though you know that no dust is allowed to settle unintentionally in Walt Disney World, the scene elicits dusty thoughts.

Shops and eateries are along the avenue bordering the southern curve of a body of water that looks like a lake. However, because it variously represents the Mississippi and Missouri rivers and their tributaries, it is called Rivers of America. Emporia here are generally referred to as "posts," as in the Frontier Trading Post and Prairie Outpost & Supply, which sell sheriff badges, leather work, cowboy hats, and southwestern, Native American, and Mexican crafts as well as sweet treats. Then there's Big Al's, for genuine Davy Crockett coonskin hats. Yee-haw!

The Walt Disney World Railroad makes a stop at Frontierland. It tunnels past a colorful scene in Splash Mountain and drops you off between Splash Mountain and Thunder Mountain.

❾ **Splash Mountain.** At Rope Drop, one of the attractions to which the hordes
Fodor'sChoice are dashing is this incredibly popular log-flume ride, based on the animated sequences in Disney's 1946 film *Song of the South*. Here the Audio-Animatronics creations of Brer Rabbit, Brer Bear, Brer Fox, and a menagerie of other Brer beasts (including Brer Frog and a Heckle-and-Jeckle duo of Brer Crows) frolic in bright, cartoonlike settings. No matter what time you get there, you *will,* repeat *will,* wait in line. So the Disney folks have made the waiting area here as entertaining and comfortable as possible, with trees to shade you and, to entertain you, little critters in tiny houses and toe-tappin' country music wafting from speakers hidden in rocks. When you finally do settle into the eight-person hollowed-out logs, Uncle Remus's voice growls, "Mark mah words, Brer Rabbit gonna put his foot in Brer Fox's mouth one of these days." And this just might be the day.

As the boat carries you through a lily pond—just bopping with Brer Frogs merrily singing the ride's theme song, "Time to Be Moving Along"—past signs for Brer Fox's lair and Brer Bear's den, Brer Rabbit's silhouette hops along in front as the carefree hare seeks out his laughin' place. Every time some critter makes a grab for the bunny, the log boats drop out of reach. But Brer Fox has been studying his book *How to Catch a Rabbit,* and our lop-eared friend looks as if he's destined for the pot.

Things don't look so good for the flumers, either, as the boats creak up and up the mountain, past a pair of pessimistic crows. You get one heart-stopping pause at the top—just long enough to grab the safety bar—and then the boat plummets down a long, sharp flume drop right into a gigantic, very wet briar patch. In case you want to know what you're getting into, the drop is 52½ ft—that's about five stories—at a 45° angle, enough to reach speeds of 40 mph and make you feel weightless. From the boat—especially if you're in the front seat—it looks truly as if you're going to be impaled on those enormous spikes. Try to smile through your clenched teeth: as you begin to drop, a flashbulb pops. You can purchase a photographic memento of the experience before exiting the ride. Brer Rabbit escapes—and so do you, wet and exhilarated—to the tune of "Zip-a-Dee-Doo-Dah," the bouncy, best-known melody from the film. If you want to get really wet—and you will get splashed from almost every seat—ask the ride attendant to seat you in the front row. ☞ *Duration: 11 mins. Crowds: Yes! Strategy: FASTPASS appointment. Otherwise, if you're not in line by 9:45 AM, plan to ride during meal or parade times. Parents who need to Baby Swap can take the young ones to a play area in a cave under the ride. Audience: All except very young children, who may be terrified by the final drop. No pregnant women or guests wearing back, neck, or leg braces. Minimum height: 40". Rating:* ★★★

⑩ **Big Thunder Mountain Railroad.** As any true roller-coaster lover can tell you, this four-minute ride is relatively tame. Despite the posted warnings, you won't stagger off, you won't throw up, and you won't vow never to subject yourself to the experience again. The thrills are there, however, thanks to clever ride engineering, intricate details, and stunning scenery along every inch of the 2,780-ft track.

Set in gold-rush days, the runaway train rushes and rattles past 20 Audio-Animatronics figures—including donkeys, chickens, a goat, and a grizzled old miner surprised in his bathtub—as well as $300,000 worth of genuine antique mining equipment, tumbleweeds, a derelict mining town, hot springs, and a flash flood.

The ride was 15 years in the planning and took two years and close to $17 million to build. This 1979 price tag, give or take a few million, equaled the entire cost of erecting California's Disneyland in 1955. The 197-ft mountain is based on the monoliths of Utah's Monument Valley, and thanks to 650 tons of steel, 4,675 tons of concrete, and 16,000 gallons of paint, it closely resembles the real thing. ☞ *Duration: 4 mins. Crowds: Large. Strategy: Use FASTPASS unless the wait is less than 10 mins. The ride is most exciting at night, when you can't anticipate the curves and the track's rattling sounds as if something's about to give. Audience: All except young children, though it's a good starter coaster for kids who have mastered Toontown's Barnstormer. No pregnant women or guests wearing back, neck, or leg braces. Minimum height: 40". Rating:* ★★★

⑪ **Tom Sawyer Island.** An artfully ungrammatical sign, signed by Tom Sawyer, tells you what to expect: "IF'N YOU LIKE DARK CAVES, MYSTERY MINES, BOTTOMLESS PITS, SHAKY BRIDGES 'N' BIG ROCKS, YOU HAVE CAME TO THE BEST PLACE I KNOW." Aunt Polly would have walloped Tom for his orthography, but she couldn't have argued with the sentiment. Actually two tiny islands connected by an old-fashioned swing bridge, Tom Sawyer Island is a natural playground, all hills and trees and rocks and shrubs. You could always sit this one out on the porch of Aunt Polly's Dockside Inn, sipping lemonade—but why let the kids have all the fun?

The main island, where your raft docks, is where most of the attractions are found. The Mystery Cave is an almost pitch-black labyrinth where the wind wails in a truly spooky fashion. Children love Injun Joe's Cave, all pointy stalactites and stalagmites and endowed with lots of columns and crevices from which to jump out and startle sisters and brothers. Harper's Mill is an old-fashioned gristmill. And, in a clearing at the top of the hill, there's a rustic playground. As you explore the shoreline on the dirt paths, keep an eye out for the barrel bridge—every time someone takes a step, the whole contraption bounces.

On the other island is Fort Sam Clemens, a log fortress from which you can fire air guns with great booms and cracks at the passing *Liberty Belle* Riverboat. It's guarded by a snoring Audio-Animatronics sentry, working off his last bender. Both islands are sprinkled with lookouts for great views to Thunder Mountain and Frontierland, as well as with nice niches—often furnished with benches and water fountains. ☞ *Duration: Up to you. Crowds: Seldom overwhelming, but it wouldn't matter—here, the more the merrier. Strategy: Try it as a refreshing afternoon getaway. Audience: All ages. Rating:* ★★

⑫ Country Bear Jamboree. Wisecracking, cornpone, lovelorn Audio-Animatronics bears joke, sing, and play country music and 1950s rock-and-roll in this stage show. The emcee, the massive but debonair Henry, leads the stellar cast of Grizzly Hall, which includes the robust Trixie, who laments love lost while perching on a swing suspended from the ceiling; Bubbles, Bunny, and Beulah, harmonizing on "All the Guys That Turn Me On Turn Me Down"; and Big Al, the off-key cult figure who has inspired postcards, stuffed animals, and his own shop next door. Don't miss the bears' seasonal show in late November and December, when they deck the halls for a special concert. ☞ *Duration: 17 mins. Crowds: Large, considering the relatively small theater. Strategy: Visit before 11 AM, during the afternoon parade, or after most small children have left for the day. Stand to the far left in the anteroom, where you wait, to end up in the front rows; to the far right if you want to sit in the last row, where small children can perch on top of the seats to see better. Audience: All ages; even timid youngsters love the bears. Rating:* ★★★

⑬ Frontierland Shootin' Arcade. At this classic shooting arcade, laser beams substitute for bullets, as genuine Hawkins 54-caliber buffalo rifles have been refitted to emit electronic beams. When they strike, tombstones spin and epitaphs change, ghost riders gallop out of clouds, and skulls pop out of graves, accompanied by the sounds of howling coyotes, creaking bridges, and the cracks of the rifles blasted over the digital audio system. ☞ *Cost: Roughly 50¢ per 5 shots. Strategy: Bring a pocketful of change. Audience: Older children and adults. Rating:* ★

⑭ Diamond Horseshoe Saloon Revue. "Knock, knock." "Who's there?" "Ya." "Ya who?" "Yaaahooo!" And they're off, with another rip-roaring, raucous, corny, nonstop, high-kicking, elbow-jabbing, song-and-dance-and-fiddling show staged in a re-creation of an Old West saloon—without the booze. Singing cowboys leap from the balconies and swing around columns; Lily's Girls perform an exuberant cancan; and everyone has a hand-clapping good time. Snacks and light refreshments may be purchased. ☞ *Show times: Continuously, starting just after opening. Seating is first-come, first-served. Duration: 30 mins. Crowds: Busy for all shows. Strategy: Go early. You can kill two birds with one stone by eating here—light refreshments such as salads and sandwiches are served. But give it a miss if you're on a tight schedule and have plans to see the Hoop-Dee-Doo Revue at Fort Wilderness Resort. Audience: All ages. Rating:* ★★

Share a Dream Come True Parade. Get ready to feel the magic perpetuated by Walt Disney's legacy during this parade, which proceeds through Frontierland and down Main Street beginning at 3 PM. Bolstered by a powerful orchestral score and beloved songs from Disney films, the six giant themed snow-globe floats reveal Disney characters performing "under glass"—climate-controlled glass, that is. Mickey Mouse leads off in a tribute to his countless film roles through the years, followed by floats celebrating the early film breakthroughs of Pinocchio and Snow White; Disney adventures in flight with Dumbo, Mary Poppins and others; Disney villains from Fantasia's Chernabog to Cruella de Vil; fantasy princesses like Cinderella and Belle who eventually snagged their guy; and a magical finale double snow globe of Cinderella Castle with Tinkerbell and other character favorites. ☞ *Duration: About 15 mins. Crowds: Heavy. Strategy: Arrive 20–30 mins in advance. Audience: All ages. Older kids may want to skip it in favor of rides, which will have shorter lines until the parade ends. Rating:* ★★

Liberty Square

The rough-and-tumble Western frontier gently slides into colonial America as Liberty Square picks up where Frontierland leaves off. The weathered siding gives way to solid brick and neat clapboard. The mesquite and cactus are replaced by stately oaks and masses of azalea. The land of the red, white, and blue continues around the shore of Rivers of America and forms the western boundary of Fantasyland.

The theme is colonial history, which Northerners will be happy to learn is portrayed here as solid Yankee. The small buildings, topped with weather vanes and exuding comfortable prosperity from every rosy brick and spiffy shutter, are pure New England. A replica of the Liberty Bell, crack and all, seems an appropriate prop to separate Liberty Square from Frontierland. There's even a Liberty Tree, a more than 150-year-old live oak found elsewhere on Walt Disney World property and moved to the Magic Kingdom. Just as the Sons of Liberty hung lanterns on trees as a signal of solidarity after the Boston Tea Party, the Liberty Tree's branches are decorated with 13 lanterns representing the 13 original colonies.

As you wander through this area, look into the Yankee Trader for fancy foods—some with a Mickey motif—and cooking items that include Mickey waffle irons. Stop at the Silhouette Cart for profiles, hand-cut and framed while you wait. Ye Old Christmas Shoppe is a favorite among collectors, and Madame Letta's Cart, near the Haunted Mansion, has an ample supply of spooky souvenirs. There are plenty of tree-shaded tables for alfresco meals and plenty of carts and fast-food eateries to supply the goods.

⑮ **Hall of Presidents.** This multimedia tribute to the Constitution caused quite a sensation when it opened decades ago, because it was here that the first refinements of the Audio-Animatronics system of computerized robots could be seen. Now surpassed by Epcot's American Adventure, it's still well worth attending, as much for the spacious, air-conditioned theater as for the two-part show.

It starts with a film, narrated by writer Maya Angelou, that discusses the Constitution as the codification of the spirit that founded America. You learn about threats to the document, ranging from the 18th-century Whiskey Rebellion to the Civil War, and hear such famous speeches as Benjamin Franklin's plea to the Continental Congress delegates for ratification and Abraham Lincoln's warning that "a house divided against itself cannot stand." The shows conveying Disney's brand of patriotism may be a little ponderous, but they're always well researched and lovingly presented; this film, for instance, was revamped to replace a lingering subtext of Cold War fear with the more progressive assertion that democracy is a work in progress, that liberty and justice still do not figure equally in the lives of all Americans.

The second half is a roll call of all 42 U.S. presidents. (Because Grover Cleveland's two terms were nonconsecutive, they are counted separately. This makes George W. Bush's term the 43rd.) Each chief executive responds with a nod—even those who blatantly attempted to subvert the Constitution—and those who are seated rise (except for wheelchair-bound Franklin Delano Roosevelt, of course). The detail is lifelike, right down to the brace on Roosevelt's leg. The robots can't resist nodding, fidgeting, and even whispering to each other while waiting for their names to come up. ☞ *Duration: 30 mins. Crowds: Usually moderate. Strategy: Go in the afternoon, when you'll appreciate the air-conditioning. Audience: Older children and adults. Rating:* ★★

need a break? In season, **Sleepy Hollow** carts sell delicious warm fruit cobblers—a welcome treat not found in many Walt Disney World eateries. The espresso drinks and root beer floats also make great afternoon pick-me-ups.

🔟6️⃣ *Liberty Belle* **Riverboat.** An old-fashioned steamboat, the *Liberty Belle* is authentic, from its calliope whistle and the gingerbread trim on its three decks to the boilers that produce the steam that drives the big rear paddle wheel. In fact, the boat misses authenticity on only one count: there's no mustachioed captain to guide it during the ride around the Rivers of America. That task is performed by an underwater rail. The trip is slow and not exactly thrilling, except, perhaps, to the kids getting "shot at" by their counterparts at Fort Sam Clemens on Tom Sawyer Island. But it's a relaxing break for all concerned, and children like exploring the boat. ☞ *Duration: 15 mins. Crowds: Moderate, but capacity is high, so waits are seldom trying. Strategy: Go when you need a break from the crowds. Audience: All ages. Rating:* ★

🔟7️⃣ **Mike Fink Keelboats.** They're short and dumpy and you have to sit on a bench, wedged tightly between fellow visitors, and listen to a heavy-handed, noisy gag about those roistering, roustabout days along the Missouri. And the Tom Sawyer Island crowd doesn't even bother to shoot you. Just for that we're going to tell you the answer to the guide's extraordinarily lackluster joke: "Firewood." The boats run only when the park is very crowded, such as summer and holidays. ☞ *Duration: 10–15 mins. Crowds: Lines move slowly because of boats' low passenger capacity. Strategy: Skip this on your first visit. Audience: All ages. Rating:* ★

🔟8️⃣ **Haunted Mansion.** The special effects here are a howl. Or perhaps a scream is more like it. You're greeted at the creaking iron gates of this Hudson River valley Gothic mansion by a lugubrious attendant, who has one of the few jobs at Walt Disney World for which smiling is frowned upon, and ushered into a spooky picture gallery. A disembodied voice echoes from the walls: "Welcome, foolish mortals, to the Haunted Mansion. I am your ghost host." A scream shivers down, and you're off into one of the best attractions at Walt Disney World.

Fodor'sChoice

Consisting mainly of a slow-moving ride in a black, cocoonlike "doom buggy," the Haunted Mansion is scary but not terrifying for adults and moderately scary for younger children, mostly because of the darkness throughout. Certainly, the special effects intensify the chill factor. Catch the artfully strung liquid cobwebs; the suit of armor that comes alive; the shifting walls in the portrait gallery that make you wonder if they are moving up or if you are moving down; the strategically placed gusts of damp, cold air; the marble busts of the world's greatest "ghostwriters" in the library; the wacky inscriptions on the tombstones as you wait in line; the spectral xylophone player who enlivens the graveyard shift with bones instead of mallets; the ghostly ballroom dancers; and, of course, the talking disembodied head in the crystal ball. Just when you think the Imagineers have exhausted their bag of ectoplasmic tricks, along comes another one. They've saved the best for last, as you suddenly discover that your doom buggy has gained an extra passenger. As you approach the exit, your ghoulish guide intones, "Now I will raise the safety bar and the ghost will follow you home." Thanks for the souvenir, pal.

An interesting piece of Disney trivia: one of the biggest jobs for the maintenance crew here isn't cleaning up but keeping the 200-odd trunks, chairs, harps, dress forms, statues, rugs, and knickknacks appropriately dusty. Disney buys its dust in 5-pound bags and scatters it throughout the mansion with a special gadget resembling a fertilizer spreader. According to local lore, enough dust has been dumped since the park's 1971 opening to completely bury the mansion. Where does it all go? Perhaps the voice is right in saying that something will follow you home. *Du-ration: 8 mins. Crowds: Substantial, but high capacity and fast loading usually keep lines moving. Strategy: Take advantage of FASTPASS here unless the line is short. Nighttime adds an extra fright factor, and you may be able to queue right up during the evening parade during peak season. Audience: All but very young children who are easily frightened. Rating: ★★★*

Fantasyland

Walt Disney called this "a timeless land of enchantment." Fantasyland does conjure up pixie dust. Perhaps that's because the fanciful gingerbread houses, gleaming gold turrets, and, of course, rides based on Disney-animated movies are what the Magic Kingdom is all about.

With the exception of the slightly spooky Snow White's Scary Adventures, the attractions here are whimsical rather than heart-stopping. Like the animated classics on which they're based, these rides—which could ostensibly be classified as rides for children—are packed with enough delightful detail to engage the adults who accompany them. Although the youngsters are awed by the bigger picture, their parents take a quick trip back to their childhoods via rides that conjure up favorite images of Winnie the Pooh, Peter Pan, and others, and it's hard to remain unmoved by the view of moonlit London in Peter Pan's Flight. If you're traveling without children, stick with Peter Pan, the unforgettable "it's a small world," and the new Mickey's PhilharMagic 3-D extravaganza. Enjoy the rest of the scenery as you pass through. Or save the rides for evening, when a sizable number of the little ones will have departed for their own private dreamland. Unfortunately, Fantasyland is always the most heavily trafficked area in the park, and its rides are almost always crowded.

You can enter Fantasyland on foot from Liberty Square, but the classic introduction is through Cinderella Castle. To get in an appropriately magical mood—and to provide yourself with a cooling break—turn left immediately after you exit the castle's archway. Here you'll find one of the most charming and most overlooked touches in Fantasyland: Cinderella Fountain, a lovely brass casting of the castle's namesake, who's dressed

THE MAGIC BENEATH THE MAGIC

AS YOU STROLL DOWN *Main Street, U.S.A., Disney cast members are dashing through tunnels a floor below you in a bustling underground city that is the nerve center of the Magic Kingdom. The 9-acre corridor system beneath the park leads to top-secret behind-the-scenes areas where employees create their Disney magic. It also ensures that you'll never see a frontiersman ambling through Tomorrowland. There's the Costuming department with miles of racks, and Cosmetology, where Cinderella can touch up her hair and makeup. At the heart of this underground domain is the Digital Animation Control System (DACS), a computer center that directs virtually everything in the Magic Kingdom—from the rides and Audio-Animatronic figures to the parades and fireworks.*

The only way to see what goes on in Disney's underground tunnels is by taking one of two backstage tours: the Keys to the Kingdom lasts four hours and costs $58, including lunch but not mandatory park admission; Backstage Magic lasts seven hours and costs $199, including peeks at attractions in Epcot and Disney–MGM Studios, as well as lunch (park admission not included or required). Tours are restricted to people age 16 and older. The concrete tunnels are lined with cables and pipes, and you never know when you're going to bump into Mickey without his head on. (And don't expect to take photos. Disney guards its underground treasures very carefully!) If you visit in December, you can take a Yuletide Fantasy tour—an insider's look at how Disney's elves transform its parks and resorts for the holidays (more than three hours long; $59). These tours book up quickly, so reserve a spot several months in advance. For details, call ☎ 407/939–8687.

—Ellen Parlapiano

in her peasant togs and surrounded by her beloved mice and bird friends. Water splashing from the fountain provides a cooling sensation on a hot day—as do the very welcome brass drinking fountains at the statue's base. Don't forget to toss in a coin and make a wish; after all, you're in Fantasyland, where dreams do come true.

Photographers will want to take advantage of one of the least-traveled byways in the Magic Kingdom. If you're coming to Fantasyland from the southern end of Liberty Square, turn left at the Sleepy Hollow snack shop. Just past the outdoor tables you'll find a shortcut that provides one of the best unobstructed ground-level views of Cinderella Castle in the park. It's a great spot for a family photo.

⑲ **it's a small world.** Visiting Walt Disney World and not stopping for this tribute to terminal cuteness—why, the idea is practically un-American. Disney raided the remains of the 1964–65 New York World's Fair for this boat ride and then appropriated the theme song of international brotherhood and friendship for its own.

The ride may strain the patience of adults visiting with no children, but it allows parents to soak up the wonder on their little ones' faces. Moving at not quite a snail's pace, your barge meanders through several candy-colored lands, each representing a continent and each crammed with musical moppets, all madly singing. Some claim that it's the revenge of the Audio-Animatrons, as simplistic dolls differentiated mostly by their national dress—Dutch babies in clogs, Spanish flamenco dancers, German oompah bands, Russians playing balalaikas, sari-wrapped Indians waving temple bells, Tower of London guards in scarlet beefeater uniforms, Swiss yodelers and goatherds, Japanese kite fliers, Middle East snake charmers, and young French cancan dancers, to name just a few—parade past, smiling away and wagging their heads in time to the song. But somehow, by the time you reach the end of the ride, you're grinning and wagging, too. You just can't help it—and small children can't wait to ride again. By the way, there's only one verse to the song, and it repeats incessantly, indelibly impressing itself on your brain. Now all together: "It's a world of laughter, a world of tears. It's a world of hope and a world of fears. . . ." ☞ *Duration: 11 mins. Crowds: Steady, but lines move fast. Strategy: Check out all available queues before you line up—one line is sometimes shorter. Go back later if there's a wait, since crowds ebb and flow here. Tots may beg for a repeat ride; it's worth another go-round to see all that you missed on the first trip through. Audience: All ages. Rating:* ★★

㉕ Peter Pan's Flight. This truly fantastic indoor ride was inspired by Sir James M. Barrie's 1904 novel about the boy who wouldn't grow up, which Disney animated in 1953. Aboard two-person magic sailing ships with brightly striped sails, you soar into the skies above London en route to Neverland. Along the way you can see Wendy, Michael, and John get sprinkled with pixie dust while Nana barks below, wave to Princess Tiger Lily, meet the evil Captain Hook, and cheer for the tick-tocking, clock-swallowing crocodile who breakfasted on Hook's hand and is more than ready for lunch. Despite the absence of high-tech special effects, children love this ride. Adults enjoy the dreamy views of London by moonlight, a galaxy of twinkling yellow lights punctuated by Big Ben, London Bridge, and the Thames River. There's so much to see that the ride seems slightly longer than it is. ☞ *Duration: 2½ mins. Crowds: Always heavy, except in the evening and early morning. Strategy: This is in the FAST-PASS lineup, so get an appointment and enjoy other Fantasyland attractions while you wait. Audience: All ages. Rating:* ★★★

㉑ Mickey's PhilharMagic. Join Mickey and Donald on an adventure destined to include many other friends from the silver screen, including Ariel from *The Little Mermaid,* Aladdin and Jasmine from *Aladdin,* and Simba from *The Lion King.* The film is bound to startle with its special-effects technology and its "in-your-face" action on one of the largest screens ever created for a 3-D film: a 150-ft-wide canvas. ☞ *Audience: All ages.*

㉒ Cinderella Castle. This quintessential Disney icon, with its royal blue turrets, gold spires, and glistening white towers, was inspired by the castle built by the mad Bavarian king Ludwig II at Neuschwanstein, as well as by drawings prepared for Disney's animated film of the French fairy tale. Although often confused with Disneyland's Sleeping Beauty Castle, at 180 ft this castle is more than 100 ft taller; and with its elongated towers and lacy fretwork, it is immeasurably more graceful. It's easy to miss the elaborate murals on the walls of the archway as you rush toward Fantasyland from the Hub, but they're worth a stop. The five panels, measuring some 15 ft high and 10 ft wide, were designed by Disney artist Dorothea Redmond and created from a million bits of multicolor Italian glass, silver, and 14-karat gold by mosaicist Hanns-Joachim Scharff. Following the images drawn for the Disney film, the mosaics tell the story of the little cinder girl as she goes from pumpkin to prince to happily ever after.

The fantasy castle has feet, if not of clay, then of solid steel beams, fiberglass, and 500 gallons of paint. Instead of dungeons, there are service tunnels for the Magic Kingdom's less-than-magical quotidian operations, such as Makeup and Costuming. These are the same tunnels that honeycomb the ground under much of the park. And upstairs doesn't hold, as rumor has it, a casket containing the cryogenically preserved body of Walt Disney but instead mundane broadcast facilities, security rooms, and the like (these are off bounds to the public). Upstairs, also, is Cinderella's Royal Table, a full-service dining room popular for character breakfasts.

Within the castle's archway, on the left as you face Fantasyland, is the **King's Gallery,** one of the Magic Kingdom's priciest shops. Here you'll find exquisite hand-painted models of carousel horses, delicate crystal castles, and other symbols of fairy-tale magic, including Cinderella's glass slipper in many colors and sizes.

㉓ Snow White's Scary Adventures. What was previously an unremittingly scary indoor spook-house ride where the dwarves might as well have been named Anxious and Fearful is now a kinder, gentler experience with six-passenger cars and a miniversion of the movie. There's still the evil queen, the wart on her nose, and her cackle, but joining the cast at long last are the prince and Snow White herself. Although the trip is packed with plenty of scary moments, an honest-to-goodness kiss followed by a happily-ever-after ending might even get you heigh-ho-ing on your way out. ☞ *Duration: 3 mins. Crowds: Steady from late morning until evening. Strategy: Go very early, during the afternoon parade, or after dark. Audience: All ages; may be frightening for young children. Rating:* ★

㉔ Cinderella's Golden Carrousel. It's the whirling, musical heart of Fantasyland. This ride encapsulates the Disney experience in 90 prancing horses and then hands it to you on a 60-ft moving platter. Seventy-two of the dashing wooden steeds date from the original carousel built in 1917 by the Philadelphia Toboggan Company; additional mounts were made of fiberglass. All are meticulously painted—it takes about 48 hours per horse—and each one is completely different. One wears a collar of bright yellow roses, another a quiver of Native American arrows, and yet another, for some completely mysterious reason, a portrait of Eric the Red. The horses gallop ceaselessly beneath a wooden canopy, gaily striped on the outside and decorated on the inside with 18 panels depicting scenes from Disney's 1950 film *Cinderella.* As the platter starts to spin, the mirrors sparkle, the fairy lights glitter, and the rich notes of the band organ play favorite tunes from Disney movies. If you wished upon a star, it couldn't get more magical. ☞ *Duration: 2 mins. Crowds: Lines during busy periods but they move fairly quickly. Strategy: Go while waiting for your Peter Pan's Flight FASTPASS reservation, during the afternoon parade, or after dark. Audience: A great ride for families and for romantics, both young and old. Rating:* ★★

㉕ Dumbo the Flying Elephant. Hands down, this is one of Fantasyland's most popular rides. Although the movie has one baby elephant with gigantic ears who accidentally downs a bucket of water spiked with champagne and learns he can fly, the ride has 16 jolly Dumbos flying around a central column, each pachyderm packing a couple of kids and a parent. A joystick controls each of Dumbo's vertical motions, so you can make him ascend or descend at will. Alas, the ears do not flap. Keep an eye out for Timothy Mouse atop the ride's colorful balloon. ☞ *Duration: 2 mins. Crowds: Perpetual, except in very early morning, and there's little shade—in summer, the wait is truly brutal. Strategy: If accompanying small children, make a beeline here at Rope Drop; if you're lucky enough to time your ride during end-of-day fireworks over the castle, you'll be living one of Disney's happy endings. Audience: Toddlers and young children—the modest thrills are just perfect for them. Rating:* ★★

㉖ Ariel's Grotto. This starfish-scattered meet-and-greet locale carries out an "Under the Sea" motif. Ariel the Little Mermaid appears here in person, her carrot-red tresses cascading onto her glittery green tail. Just across the ropes from the queue area are a group of wonderfully interactive fountains that little kids love splashing around in. ☞ *Duration: Up to you. Strategy: Check your map for appearance times, and arrive at least 20 mins ahead. Audience: Young children, especially little girls. Rating:* ★★

㉗ Fantasyland Character Festival. In the former queue-up area of 20,000 Leagues Under the Sea, you can collect autographs from and have your picture taken with Pinocchio, Pluto, Goofy, and other popular characters. ☞ *Duration: Up to you. Strategy: Check your map for appearance times and arrive at least 20 mins ahead. Lines tend to be longer in later morning and early afternoon, when toddlers are at their best. Audience: Young children. Rating:* ★

㉘ The Many Adventures of Winnie the Pooh. The famous honey lover and his exploits in the Hundred Acre Wood are the theme for this ride. You can read passages from A. A. Milne's famous stories as you wait in line. Once you board your honey pot, Pooh and his friends wish you a "happy windsday." Pooh flies through the air, held aloft by his balloon, in his perennial search for "hunny," and you bounce along with Tigger, ride with the Heffalumps and Woozles, and experience a cloudburst. When the rain ends at last, everyone gathers again to say "Hurray!" This ride replaced the late lamented Mr. Toad's Wild Ride; look for the painting of Mr. Toad handing the deed to Owl. ☞ *Duration: About 3 mins. Crowds: Large. Strategy: Use the FASTPASS setup; if the youngsters favor immediate gratification, go early in the day, late in the afternoon, or after dark. Audience: All ages. Rating:* ★★★

㉙ Fairytale Garden. Belle makes an appearance here and brings *Beauty and the Beast* to life, using her audience as members of the cast. Storytelling was never so much fun. *Duration: 25 mins, several times daily (check guide map schedule). Crowds: Heaviest in midday. Strategy: See during the Fantasyland stage show or during the parade. Audience: All ages. Rating:* ★

㉚ Mad Tea Party. This carnival staple is for the vertigo addict looking for a fix. The Disney version is based on its own 1951 film *Alice in Wonderland,* in which the Mad Hatter hosts a tea party for his un-birthday. You hop into oversize, pastel-color teacups and whirl around a giant platter. Add your own spin to the teacup's orbit with the help of the steering wheel in the center. If the centrifugal force hasn't shaken you up too much, check out the soused mouse that pops out of the teapot centerpiece and compare his condition with your own. ☞ *Duration: 2 mins. Crowds: Steady from late morning on, with slow-moving lines. Strategy: Skip this ride if motion sickness is a problem. Rating:* ★

Mickey's Toontown Fair

This concentrated tribute to the big-eared mighty one was built in 1988 to celebrate the Mouse's Big Six-O. Owing to its continual popularity with the small-fry set, it is now an official Magic Kingdom land, a 3-acre niche set off to the side of Fantasyland. As in a scene from a cartoon, everything is child size. The pastel houses are positively Lilliputian, with miniature driveways, toy-size picket fences, and signs scribbled with finger paint. Toontown Fair provides great one-stop shopping (better known as meet-and-greets) for your favorite Disney characters—hug them, get autographs, and take photos. The best way to arrive is on the Walt

MOUSE DETECTIVE

SEARCHING FOR MICKEY? *Character meals and meet-and-greets aren't the only places you can find the "big cheese." If you keep your eyes peeled, you might just spot images of Mickey Mouse cleverly hidden in murals, statues, lighting fixtures, floor tiles, and other decorative elements throughout the resorts' queue areas and rides.*

Hidden Mickeys began as an inside joke among Disney Imagineers, the artists and engineers who design the company's theme parks. When putting the finishing touches on an attraction, they'd subtly slip a Mickey into the motif to see if coworkers and family and friends would notice. Today, hunting for Hidden Mickeys (and Minnies) has become quite popular and can be a great way to pass the time while standing in line. For example, as you wait to board Norway's Maelstrom ride in Epcot's World Showcase, you can scan the big mural for the Viking wearing mouse ears. Playful touches like these abound throughout the resort.

The most common image you'll spy is the outline of Mickey's face. While riding Big Thunder Mountain Railroad in the Magic Kingdom, you'll pass three rusty gears on the ground that actually form his head and ears. (Look to your right toward the end of the ride, just as your train is nearing the station.) But also watch for Mickey in profile. After the final drop in Splash Mountain, he lounges on his back in a cloud to the right of the Steamboat where the characters "zip-a-dee-doo-dah."

You can request a list of Hidden Mickeys at guest services in the theme parks or at Disney hotels, and the non-Disney Web site ⊕ www.hiddenmickeys.org has very full listings. Before you begin your search, keep in mind that some of the images can be quite difficult to discern. (You practically need a magnifying glass to make out the profile of Minnie Mouse in the Hollywood mural at the Great Movie Ride in Disney–MGM Studios; she's above the roof of the gazebo.) If you're traveling with young children, don't count on using Hidden Mickeys as a distraction tactic. *Toddlers and preschoolers might actually become frustrated trying to find him. (And besides, "Let's look for Mickey" means something quite different to a four-year-old.) But school-age kids might welcome the challenge of finding as many Hidden Mickeys as they can and checking them off their list.*

Here are some more clues to help you get started on your mouse hunt:

In the Magic Kingdom
Snow White's Adventures. *In the queue-area mural, look for shorts hanging on the clothesline and at three of the stones in the chimney.*

Haunted Mansion. *There's a Mouse-eared place setting on the table in the ballroom.*

In Epcot
Spaceship Earth. *Mickey smiles down from a constellation just beyond the attraction's loading area.*

The American Adventure. *Check out the lobby's painting of the wagon train heading west, and look above the front leg of the foremost oxen.*

Disney–MGM Studios
Twilight Zone Tower of Terror. *While you wait in line in the boiler room, look for a whimsical water stain on the wall right after the queue splits.*

Rock 'n' Roller Coaster. *A pair of Mickeys hide in the floor tile right before the doors with the marbles.*

Animal Kingdom
Dinosaur. *Stare at the bark of the painted tree in the far left background of the wall mural at the building's entrance.*

Rafiki's Planet Watch. *The main Conservation Station building contains more than 25 Hidden Mickeys. Look in the eyes of animals in the entrance mural, on insects' wings and bodies, and in the tree trunks of the rain forest.*

—Ellen Parlapiano

Disney World Railroad, the old-fashioned choo-choo that also stops at Main Street and Frontierland.

31 **The Barnstormer.** Traditional red barns and farm buildings form the backdrop at Goofy's Wiseacre Farm. But the real attraction is the Barnstormer, a roller coaster whose ride vehicles are 1920s crop-dusting biplanes—designed for children but large enough for adults as well. Hold on to your Mouse ears—this attraction promises tummy-tickling thrills to young first-time coaster riders. If there are any questions in your mind as to whether your offspring are up to Big Thunder Mountain Railroad, this is the test to take. ☞ *Duration: 1 min. Crowds: Heaviest in mid-morning. Strategy: Visit in the evening, when many tykes have gone home. Audience: Younger children. Restrictions: No riders under age 3. Rating:* ★★★

32 **Toon Park.** This spongy green area is filled with foam topiary in the shapes of goats, cows, pigs, and horses. Children can jump and hop on interactive lily pads to hear animal topiaries moo, bleat, and whinny. ☞ *Duration: Up to you. Crowds: Moderate and seldom a problem. Strategy: Go anytime. Audience: Young children mainly, but everyone enjoys watching them. Rating:* ★

33 **Donald's Boat.** A cross between a tugboat and a leaky ocean liner, the *Miss Daisy* is actually a water-play area, with lily pads that spray without warning. Although it's intended for kids, there's no reason for grown-ups not to take the opportunity to cool off on a humid Central Florida afternoon, too. ☞ *Duration: Up to you. Crowds: Can get heavy in late morning and early afternoon. Strategy: Go first thing in the morning or after the toddlers have gone home. Audience: Young children and their families. Rating:* ★★

> **need a break?** The Toontown **Farmer's Market** sells simple, healthy snacks and fruit, plus juices, espresso drinks, and soda. If you're lucky, you can find a place on the park bench next to the cart and give your feet a rest.

34 **Mickey's Country House.** Begin here to find your way to the Big Cheese himself. As you walk through this slightly goofy piece of architecture right in the heart of Toontown Fairgrounds, notice the radio in the living room, "tooned" to scores from Mickey's favorite football team, Duckburg University. Down the hall, Mickey's kitchen shows the ill effects of Donald and Goofy's attempt to win the Toontown Home Remodeling Contest—with buckets of paint spilled and stacked in the sink and paint splattered on the floor and walls. The flowers in the garden, just outside the kitchen, are shaped like Mickey's familiar silhouette, and Mickey's Mousekosh overalls are drying on the clothesline next to oversize tomato plants, cactus plants, and pumpkins (complete with ears, of course). The Judge's Tent just behind Mickey's house is where the mouse king holds court as he doles out hugs and autographs and mugs for photos with adoring fans. ☞ *Duration: Up to you. Crowds: Moderate. Strategy: Go first thing in the morning or during the afternoon parade. Audience: All ages, although teens may be put off by the terminal cuteness of it all. Rating:* ★★

35 **Toontown Hall of Fame.** Stop here to collect an autograph and a hug from Disney characters such as Pluto and Goofy, and check out the blue-ribbon-winning entries from the Toontown Fair. **County Bounty** sells stuffed animals and all kinds of Toontown souvenirs, including autograph books. ☞ *Duration: Up to you. Crowds: Can get heavy in late morning and early afternoon. Strategy: Go first thing in the morn-*

ing or after the toddlers have gone home. Audience: Young children. Rating: ★★

36 Minnie's Country House. Unlike Mickey's house, where ropes keep you from going into the rooms, this baby-blue-and-pink house is a please-touch kind of place. In this scenario, Minnie is editor of *Minnie's Cartoon Country Living* magazine, the Martha Stewart of the mouse set. While touring her office, crafts room, and kitchen, you can check the latest messages on her answering machine, bake a "quick-rising" cake at the touch of a button, and, opening the refrigerator door, get a wonderful blast of arctic air while checking out her favorite ice cream flavor: cheese-chip. ☞ *Duration: Up to you. Crowds: Moderate. Strategy: Go first thing in the morning or during the afternoon parade. Audience: All ages, although teens may find it too much to take. Rating:* ★★

Tomorrowland

The "future that never was" spins boldly into view as you enter Tomorrowland, where Disney Imagineers paint the landscape with whirling spaceships, flashy neon lights, and gleaming robots. This is the future as envisioned by sci-fi writers and moviemakers in the 1920s and '30s, when space flight, laser beams, and home computers belonged in the world of fiction, not fact. Retro Jetsonesque styling lends the area lasting chic.

The ATM near the **Tomorrowland Arcade** is useful when the games begin to deplete your stash of cash.

37 Tomorrowland Indy Speedway. This is one of those rides that incite instant addiction among children and immediate hatred among parents. The reasons for the former are easy to figure out: the brightly colored Mark VII model cars that swerve around the four 2,260-ft tracks with much vroom-vroom-vrooming. Kids will feel like they're Mario Andretti as they race around. Like real sports cars, the gasoline-powered vehicles are equipped with rack-and-pinion steering and disc brakes; unlike the real thing, these run on a track. However, the track is so twisty that it's hard to keep the car on a straight course—something the race car fanatics warming the bleachers love to watch. If you're not a fanatic, the persistent noise and pervasive smell of high-test on a muggy Central Florida afternoon can quickly rasp your nerves into the danger zone. Furthermore, there's a lot of waiting: you can wait up to an hour to get on the track; you wait again for your turn to climb in a car; then you wait one more time to return your vehicle after your lap. All this for a ride in which the main thrill is achieving a top speed of 7 mph. ☞ *Duration: 5 mins. Crowds: Steady and heavy from late morning to evening. Strategy: Go in the evening or during a parade; skip on a first-time visit unless you've been through all the major attractions. Audience: Older children. Minimum height: 52" to drive. Rating:* ★

38 Tomorrowland Arcade. With so much to cover in the Kingdom, it's hard to imagine giving up time and cash to a bank of video games not unlike those lined up in arcades across the country. But this locale inside the Tomorrowland Light and Power Company may be a draw to teens with its emphasis on Formula One racing. Another plus: it never has a line. ☞ *Duration: Up to you. Crowds: Not usually a problem. Strategy: Give it a wide berth unless you love arcade games. Audience: Teens. Rating:* ★

39 Space Mountain. The needlelike spires and gleaming white concrete cone of this attraction are almost as much of a Magic Kingdom landmark as Cinderella Castle. Towering 180 ft high, the structure has been called

"Florida's third-highest mountain." Inside is what is arguably still the world's most imaginative roller coaster. Although there are no loop-the-loops, gravitational whizbangs, or high-speed curves, the thrills are amply provided by Disney's masterful brainwashing as you take a trip into the depths of outer space—in the dark.

The mood for your space shot is set in the waiting area, where a dim blue light reflects off the mirror-and-chrome walls. Above you planets and galaxies and meteors and comets whirl past; strobe lights flash, and the fluorescent panels on the six-passenger rockets streak by, leaving phosphorescent memories. Screams and shrieks echo in the chamber, piercing the darkness and punctuating the rattling of the cars and the various otherworldly beeps and buzzes. Meanwhile, you can't help overhearing rumors about how earrings have been known to be ripped out of earlobes by the centrifugal force, pocketbooks shaken open and upended, and so on.

Finally, you get your chance to wedge yourself into the seat. The blinking sign in front switches from "boarding" to "blast off," and you do. The ride lasts only 2 minutes and 38 seconds and attains a top speed of 28 mph, but the devious twists and invisible drops, not to mention the fact that you can't see where you're going, make it seem twice as long. People of all ages adore this thrilling ride.

For the significant number who dislike it or are afraid they will, there's a bail-out area just before boarding. Keep in mind, though, that although the ride *is* rough, and it's a good idea to stow personal belongings securely, Disney staffers in a control booth constantly monitor the ride on a battery of closed-circuit televisions; at the first sign of any guest having trouble, the ride can be stopped. And that seldom happens. ☞ *Duration: 2½ mins. Crowds: Large and steady, with long lines from morning to night despite high capacity. Strategy: Get a FASTPASS ticket and ride when you have your appointment. Or go either at the end of the day, during a parade, or at Rope Drop (in which case you should wait at the Plaza Restaurant to give yourself a 120-yard head start on the crowd). Audience: All except young children. No pregnant women or guests wearing back, neck, or leg braces. Minimum height: 44". Rating:* ★★★

40 Carousel of Progress. Originally seen at New York's 1964–65 World's Fair, this revolving theater traces the impact of technological progress on the daily lives of Americans from the turn of the 20th century into the near future. Representing each decade, an Audio-Animatronics family sings the praises of modern-day gadgets that technology has wrought. Fans of the holiday film *A Christmas Story* will recognize the voice of its narrator, Jean Shepard, who injects his folksy, all-American humor as father figure through the decades. A preshow, which you see on overhead video monitors while waiting to enter the theater, details the design of the original carousel—Walt himself sings the theme song. Speaking of which, the irritating theme of years past, "The Best Time of Your Life," has been replaced by the ride's original ditty, "There's a Great Big Beautiful Tomorrow"—which fits nicely with the Tomorrowland theme. This attraction is open seasonally, during holidays and summer. ☞ *Duration: 20 mins. Crowds: Moderate. Strategy: Skip on a first-time visit. Audience: All ages. Rating:* ★

41 Tomorrowland Transit Authority. A reincarnation of what Disney old-timers may remember as the WEDway PeopleMover, the TTA takes a nice, leisurely ride around the perimeter of Tomorrowland, circling the Astro-Orbiter and eventually gliding through the middle of Space Mountain. Some fainthearted TTA passengers have no doubt chucked the notion of riding the roller coaster after being exposed firsthand to the screams emanating from within the mountain—although these make the ride sound worse than it really is. Disney's version of future mass transit is smooth and noiseless, thanks to an electromagnetic linear induction motor that has no moving parts, uses little power, and emits no pollutants. ☞ *Duration: 10 mins. Crowds: Not one of the park's most popular attractions, so lines are seldom long and they move quickly. Strategy: Go if you want to preview Space Mountain, if you have very young children, or if you simply want a nice, relaxing ride that provides a great bird's-eye tour of Tomorrowland. Audience: All ages. Rating:* ★

㊷ Astro-Orbiter. This gleaming superstructure of revolving planets has come to symbolize Tomorrowland as much as Dumbo represents Fantasyland. Passenger vehicles, on arms projecting from a central column, sail past whirling planets; you control your car's altitude but not the velocity. The queue is directly across from the entrance to the TTA. ☞ *Duration: 2 mins. Crowds: Often large, and the line moves slowly. Strategy: Visit while waiting out your Space Mountain FASTPASS appointment or skip on your first visit if time is limited, unless there's a short line. Audience: All ages. Rating:* ★★

㊸ ExtraTERRORestrial Alien Encounter. This ride is probably the single scariest attraction in all of Walt Disney World and is not recommended for children under 12. Even older children who frighten easily should skip it. But if you love a good "bump-in-the-night" thrill and can handle some sensory surprises, go for it. Playing on Tomorrowland's Future City theme, the story line is that you're entering the city's convention center to watch a test of a new teleportation system. Representatives from the device's manufacturer, an alien corporation called XS-Tech (pronounced "excess")—whose motto is "If something can't be done with XS, it can't be done at all"—try to transport the company's CEO from their planet to Earth. The attempt fails, however, and the resulting catastrophe consists of a very close encounter with a horrifying "extraTERRORestrial" creature, complete with realistic sound effects, smoke, tactile surprises, and several seconds of complete, seriously inky darkness. *Duration: 20 minutes, including preshow. Crowds: Expect lines. Strategy: Go first thing in the morning or during a parade or the fireworks. Audience: Adults not prone to heart attacks and teens or older children who aren't afraid of the dark and can handle sudden special-effects surprises. Heed warning signs. Rating:* ★★

㊹ Buzz Lightyear's Space Ranger Spin. Based on the wildly popular *Toy Story,* FodorsChoice this ride gives you a toy's perspective as it pits you and Buzz against the world. You're seated in a fast-moving two-passenger Star Cruiser vehicle with a laser gun in front of each rider and a centrally located lever for spinning your ship to get a good vantage point. You shoot at targets throughout the ride to help Disney's macho space toy, Buzz, defeat Emperor Zurg and save the universe—you have to hit the targets marked with a "Z" to score, and the rider with the most points wins. As Buzz likes to say, "To infinity and beyond!" The larger-than-life-size toys in the waiting area are great distractions while you queue. ☞ *Duration: 5 mins. Crowds: Substantial, but lines move fast. Go first thing in the morning, get your FASTPASS appointment time, then return when scheduled. If you're with children, time the wait and ride twice if it's only 15 minutes. Youngsters like a practice run to learn how to hit the targets. Audience: Kids 3 to 100. Rating:* ★★★

㊺ Timekeeper. Walt Disney World buffs may remember this attraction as the former "America the Beautiful," a CircleVision 360° tribute to the natural wonders of the United States. It's now a time-traveling adventure hosted by TimeKeeper, a C-3PO clone whose frenetic personality is given voice by the great Robin Williams, and Nine-Eye, a slightly frazzled droid, who's a graduate of MITT (the Metropolis Institute of Time Travel). Along the way, you meet famous inventors and visionaries of the machine age, such as Jules Verne and H. G. Wells. Don't plan on a relaxing voyage, however; there are no seats in the theater—only lean rails. This attraction is open seasonally, including holidays and summer. ☞ *Duration: 11 mins. Crowds: Moderate, but lines move steadily, since theater capacity is nearly 900. Strategy: Go when the lines at ExtraTERRORestrial Alien Encounter are long. Audience: All ages, although you'll have to hold youngsters or piggyback them so they can see. Rating:* ★★

Magic Kingdom A to Z

To research prices, get advice from other travelers, and book travel arrangements, visit www.fodors.com.

BABY CARE

The Magic Kingdom's soothing, quiet **Baby Care Center** is next to the Crystal Palace, which lies between Main Street and Adventureland. Furnished with rocking chairs, it has a low lighting level that makes it comfortable for nursing, though it can get crowded in midafternoon in peak season. There are adorable toddler-size toilets (these may be a high point for your just-potty-trained offspring) as well as supplies such as formula, baby food, pacifiers, and disposable diapers. Changing tables are here, as well as in all women's rooms and men's rooms. You can also buy disposable diapers in the Emporium on Main Street. The **Stroller Shop** near the entrance to the Magic Kingdom, on the east side of Main Street, is the place for stroller rentals ($7 single, $14 double; plus $1 refundable deposit).

BARBERSHOP

Tucked in a corner on the left side of Town Square, the **Harmony Barber Shop** isn't just for show—it's a for-real place to get a haircut from Disney cast members dressed in 19th-century costumes. Kids get complimentary Mickey Ears and a certificate if it's their first haircut ever. Dads can even get a mustache trim. Open 9–5:30 daily.

CAMERAS & FILM

Disposable cameras are widely available in shops throughout the theme parks and hotels. The **Camera Center,** at Town Square, is staffed by cast members who'll position you and your group for a photo in front of Cinderella Castle. A 5″×7″ photo costs $12.95 for the first print and $9.95 for each additional copy. An 8″×10″ costs $16.95 and $13 for each additional copy. This is also the place for minor camera repairs.

For two-hour film developing, look for the **Photo Express** signs throughout the park; drop your film in the container, and you can pick up your pictures at the Camera Center as you leave the park—virtually instant gratification.

DINING

Dining options are mainly counter-service—and every land has its share of fast-food restaurants serving burgers, hot dogs, grilled-chicken sandwiches, and salads. The walkways are peppered with carts dispensing popcorn, ice cream bars, lemonade, bottled water, and soda.

FULL-SERVICE RESTAURANTS

Priority seating reservations are essential for the three full-service restaurants in the Magic Kingdom. You can make them at all restaurants on the day you want to eat or through the Disney Reservations Line.

The fare at **Cinderella's Royal Table** includes Caesar salads, coconut shrimp, prime rib, and salmon. But the real attraction is that you get to eat inside Cinderella Castle in an old mead hall, where Cinderella herself is sometimes on hand in her shiny blue gown—often escorted by her kindly fairy godmother. An early character breakfast here is a mighty special treat for the entire family—and a good way to get a jump on the Rope Drop stampede. *In Fantasyland.*

Decorated in lovely Williamsburg colors, with Early American–style antiques and lots of brightly polished brass, **Liberty Tree Tavern** is a pleasant place even when jammed. The menu is all-American, with soups, stews, and sandwiches—a good bet at lunch. Dinnertime, hosted by a patriotic crew of Disney characters, is a "revolutionary" feast of ham, turkey, flank steak, and all the trimmings. *In Liberty Square.*

Tony's Town Square Restaurant is named after the Italian restaurant in *Lady and the Tramp,* where Disney's most famous canine couple share their first kiss over a plate of spaghetti. In fact, the video plays on a TV in the restaurant's waiting area. Lunch and "Da Dinner" menus offer pasta, of course, along with Italian twists on seafood and chicken. You also can have breakfast here beginning at 8:30. *Main Street.*

🚹 **Disney Reservation Center** ☎ 407/939-3463.

SELF-SERVICE RESTAURANT

In the **Crystal Palace**, the "buffets with character" are pleasant. Winnie the Pooh and his pals from the Hundred Acre Wood visit tables in this glass-roof conservatory, and the offerings at breakfast, lunch, and dinner are varied, generous, and surprisingly good. Healthy doses of American regional cuisine include offerings inspired by the season, and there's a sizable choice of pastas, soups, freshly baked breads, and salads that varies from day to day. The place is huge but charming with its numerous nooks and crannies, comfortable banquettes, cozy cast-iron tables, and abundant sunlight. It's also one of the few places in the Magic Kingdom that serves breakfast. *At the Hub end of Main Street facing Cinderella Castle.*

DISABILITIES & ACCESSIBILITY

ATTRACTIONS

Overall, the Magic Kingdom gets decent marks from visitors with disabilities. Before your trip, call and request a copy of the *Guidebook for Guests with Disabilities* to help with planning your visit. The guidebook, assisted-listening receivers, captioning systems, Braille and audio guides, and sign-language interpretation schedules are available in the park at Guest Relations.

To board the **Walt Disney World Railroad** at the Main Street Station, you must transfer from your wheelchair, which can be folded to ride with you or left in the station. Alternatively, board at Frontierland or Mickey's Toontown Fair. The **Main Street Vehicles** can be boarded by those with limited mobility as long as they can fold their wheelchair and climb into a car. There are curb cuts or ramps on each corner.

In Adventureland, **The Magic Carpets of Aladdin** has ramped access for guests in wheelchairs and a customized control pendant for manipulating the "carpet's" height and pitch movement. The **Swiss Family Treehouse,** with its 100 steps and lack of narration, gets low ratings among those with mobility and visual impairments. At the **Jungle Cruise,** several boats have lifts that allow access to visitors in wheelchairs; people with hearing impairments who lip-read will find the skippers' punny narration, delivered with a handheld mike, difficult to follow, although sitting up front may make it easier to see. Boarding **Pirates of the Caribbean** requires transferring from a nonfolding to a folding wheelchair, available at the entrance; the very small flume drop may make the attraction inappropriate for those with limited upper-body strength or who wear neck or back braces. Because of gunshot and fire effects, service animals should stay behind.

Frontierland is the only area of the park, aside from Main Street, that has sidewalk curbs; there are ramps by the Mile Long Bar and east of Frontierland Trading Post. To ride **Big Thunder Mountain Railroad** and **Splash Mountain,** you must be able to step into the ride vehicle and walk short distances, in case of an emergency evacuation; those with limited upper-body strength should assess the situation on-site, and those wearing back, neck, or leg braces shouldn't ride. Service animals aren't allowed on these rides. **Tom Sawyer Island,** with its stairs, bridges, inclines, and narrow caves, is not negotiable by those using a wheelchair. The **Diamond Horseshoe Saloon Revue** and the **Country Bear Jamboree** are completely wheelchair accessible; if you lip-read, ask to sit up front, especially at the Diamond Horseshoe (its script is not in the guide for guests with hearing impairments). The **Frontierland Shootin' Arcade** has two guns set at wheelchair level.

The **Hall of Presidents** and *Liberty Belle* Riverboat, in Liberty Square, are completely wheelchair accessible. At the **Haunted Mansion,** those in wheelchairs must transfer to the "doom buggies" and take one step; however, if you can walk as much as 200 ft, you'll enjoy the great preshow as well as the sensations and eerie sounds of the rest of the ride.

Mickey's PhilharMagic has special viewing areas for guests in wheelchairs. **it's a small world** can be boarded without leaving your wheelchair, but only if it's of standard size; if you use a scooter or an oversize chair, you must transfer to one of the attraction's standard chairs, available at the ride entrance. To board **Peter Pan's Flight, Dumbo the Flying Elephant, Cinderella's Golden Carrousel,** the **Mad Tea Party,** and **Snow White's Scary Adventures,** guests using wheelchairs must transfer to the ride vehicles. The Dumbo and Peter Pan rides are not suitable for service animals. For **The Many Adventures of Winnie the Pooh,** people who use wheelchairs wait in the main queue and then are able to roll right onto an individual honey pot to ride, with one member of their party accompanying them. There are amplifiers for guests with hearing impairments.

Mickey's Toontown Fair is completely accessible.

Of the Tomorrowland attractions, **ExtraTERRORestrial Alien Encounter, Timekeeper,** and the **Carousel of Progress** are barrier-free for those using wheelchairs. To board **Buzz Lightyear's Space Ranger Spin, Astro-Orbiter,** and the **Tomorrowland Transit Authority,** you must be able to walk several steps and transfer to the ride vehicle. The TTA has more appeal to guests with visual impairments. To drive **Tomorrowland Indy Speedway** cars, you must have adequate vision and be able to steer, press the gas pedal, and transfer into the low car seat. The cautions for **Big Thunder Mountain Railroad** and **Splash Mountain** also apply to **Space Mountain.** In the **Tomorrowland Arcade,** the machines may be too high for guests using wheelchairs.

🎵 **WDW Guest Information** ☎ 407/824-4321.

RESTAURANTS & SHOPS All restaurants and shops throughout the park have level entrances or are accessible by ramps.

Go to the gift shop to the left of the ticket booths at the **Transportation and Ticket Center** or the **Stroller Shop** inside the main entrance to your right ($7; $1 refundable deposit); the latter also has motor-powered chairs ($30; $10 refundable deposit). If your rental needs replacing, ask any host or hostess.

ENTERTAINMENT

The headliners are, of course, the **Disney characters**, especially if you're traveling with children. In what Disney calls "character greetings," these lovable creatures sign autographs and pose for snapshots throughout the park—line up in Town Square when the gates open or later at City Hall for your turn to pose for a picture, or snag Mickey's autograph in Mickey's Toontown Fair. Ariel's Grotto and the Fantasyland Character Festival in Fantasyland are prime spots for character autographs. Pick up a character-greeting location guide at City Hall or in any shop for times and locations.

The entertainment along Main Street smoothly transports you back in time with lively performances by a barbershop quartet, a ragtime pianist, and a funny, rousing washboard-and-banjo routine by the Rhythm Rascals. Every day just after 5 PM, homing pigeons wing their way to Cinderella Castle from Town Square as part of a **Flag Retreat.** The Cinderella Castle forecourt provides the perfect location for several daily performances of **Cinderella's Surprise Celebration,** a lighthearted gathering of Disney storybook characters who rally to save their kingdom from famous Disney villains. Donald Duck has several comic turns, but when you see the skull and crossbones raised over the castle, you'll be eager for a Disney-style happy ending. Other performances are staged throughout the day in Fantasyland, Adventureland, and Tomorrowland.

For a real nighttime blast, be sure to see **Fantasy in the Sky,** the Magic Kingdom fireworks display, heralded by a dimming of all the lights along Main Street and the wistful strains of "When You Wish upon a Star" playing over camouflaged loudspeakers. A single spotlight illuminates the top turret of the Cinderella Castle and—poof!—Tinkerbell emerges in a shower of pixie dust. Thanks to an almost-invisible guy wire, she appears to fly over the treetops and the crowds, on her way to a Neverland touchdown located, appropriately enough, in Tomorrowland. Her disappearance signals the start of the fireworks, which paint the night sky with colorful abandon for a magical ending to the day.

FIRST AID

The Magic Kingdom's First Aid Center, staffed by registered nurses, is alongside the Crystal Palace.

GETTING AROUND

Once you're in the Magic Kingdom, distances are generally short, and the best way to get around is on foot. The Walt Disney World Railroad, the Main Street vehicles, and the Tomorrowland Transit Authority do help you cover some territory and can give your feet a welcome rest, but they're primarily entertainment, not transportation.

GUIDED TOURS

A number of **guided tours** are available. Arrive 15 minutes ahead of time to check in for all tours. Some companies, such as American Express, offer discounts for some of the tours; make sure to ask ahead about special discounts.

The 4½-hour **Keys to the Kingdom Tour** is a good way to get a feel for the layout of the Magic Kingdom and what goes on behind the scenes.

The walking tour, which costs $58, includes lunch but not admission to the park itself. No one younger than 16 is allowed. Tours leave from City Hall daily at 8:30, 9, and 9:30 AM. Included are visits to some of the "backstage" zones: the parade staging area and the wardrobe area and other parts of the tunnels that web the ground underneath the Magic Kingdom.

The **Family Magic Tour** is a two-hour scavenger hunt in which your tour guide encourages you to find things that have disappeared. Disney officials don't want to reveal the tour's components—after all, it's the Family "Magic" Tour—but they can say that a special character greeting session awaits you at the end of the adventure. Tours leave City Hall at 10 AM daily ($25 for adults and children 3 and up).

Railroad enthusiasts will love the **Magic Behind Our Steam Trains**, which gives you an inside look at the daily operation of the WDW railroad. The two-hour tour begins at 7:30 AM on Monday, Thursday, and Saturday. Those over 10 years old may participate. Cost is $30 per person, plus park admission. No discounts are offered.

Backstage Magic takes you on a tour of the Magic Kingdom, Epcot, Disney–MGM Studios, and the resort's behind-the-scenes Central Shop area, where repair work is done. The cost for the seven-hour tour, which is for those 16 and older, is $199 per person. Tours depart at 9 AM on weekdays. The fee does not include park admission, which is not required for the tour itself.

🚹 **Guided Tours** ☎ 407/939-8687.

LOCKERS

Lockers are available in an arcade underneath the Main Street Railroad Station ($5; plus $2 deposit). If you're park-hopping, you can use your locker receipt to acquire a locker at the next park you visit for no extra charge.

LOST THINGS & PEOPLE

Name tags are available at City Hall or at the Baby Care Center next to the Crystal Palace, if you're worried about your children getting lost. Instruct them to talk to anyone with a Disney name tag if they lose you. If that does happen, immediately ask any cast member and try not to panic; children who are obviously lost are usually taken to City Hall or the Baby Care Center, where lost-children logbooks are kept, and everyone is well trained to effect speedy reunions. City Hall also has a Lost & Found and a computerized Message Center, where you can leave notes for your traveling companions, both those in the Magic Kingdom and those visiting other parks. After a day, found items are taken to the Transportation and Ticket Center.

🚹 **Magic Kingdom Lost & Found** ✉ City Hall ☎ 407/824-4521. **Main Lost & Found** ✉ Magic Kingdom, Transportation and Ticket Center ☎ 407/824-4245.

MONEY MATTERS

ATMs are by the lockers underneath the Main Street railroad station, inside the Tomorrowland Arcade, and in the breezeway between Adventureland and Frontierland. For currency exchange, go to the Guest Relations window in the turnstile area or to City Hall.

PACKAGE PICKUP

Ask the shop clerk to send any large purchase you make to Guest Relations, so you won't have to carry it around all day. Allow three hours. The package pickup area is in Town Square near the firehouse next to the Emporium.

SHOPPING

Everywhere you turn in the Magic Kingdom there are shops and stalls urging you to take home a little piece of the magic. Many of the stores carry items themed to the area where they're found.

The big daddy of all Magic Kingdom shops is the enormous **Emporium.** This 17,000-square-ft store stocks thousands of Disney character products, from key chains to T-shirts to sunglasses and stuffed animals. Although perpetually crowded and absolutely mobbed at closing time, the Emporium is, hands down, one of the best sources for souvenirs. Hang on to your kids in here; they're likely to wander away as they spot yet another trinket they have to have—and near park closing, the crowds are so thick that you'll be hard-pressed to find them before you panic.

The **Harmony Barber Shop,** on the west side of Main Street, is a nifty nook where such old-time shaving items as mustache cups are sold. At **Heritage House,** in Liberty Square, history buffs can find presidential and Civil War memorabilia. Inside Cinderella Castle is the **King's Gallery,** where you can browse imported European clocks, chess sets, and tapestries while artisans perform intricate metalwork that will look just right in your house if you're going for that Olde Europe look.

The **Main Street Athletic Shop** is a source for Disney-themed sports items of all sorts, including golf attire, balls, and other items with Disney logos. Serious collectors of Disney memorabilia stop at **Main Street Gallery,** next to City Hall. Limited-edition sculptures, dolls, posters, and sometimes even park signs are available, and you can have your portrait sketched by Disney-character artists. The **Main Street Market House** sells cooking accessories, Mickey-shaped pasta and candies, and other food items. Freshly baked cookies and pastries are tantalizing at the **Main Street Bakery,** and **Uptown Jewelers** has a dazzling display of Mickey Mouse jewelry and collectibles. **Ye Olde Christmas Shoppe** has a wonderful collection of holiday items.

For Davy Crockett coonskin hats, personalized sheriff badges, and Big Al memorabilia, check out **Big Al's,** across from the Country Bear Jamboree in Frontierland. Among the all-time best Magic Kingdom souvenirs are the pirate hats, swords, and plastic hooks-for-hands at the **Pirate's Bazaar** at the Pirates of the Caribbean exit in Adventureland.

The **Briar Patch,** next door to Splash Mountain, handles all things Winnie the Pooh, and it's one of the places where you can buy those signature yellow ponchos with Mickey smiling on the back—$6 for adults and $5 for kids. To get monogrammed Mouse ears, stop at the **Chapeau,** on the east side of Main Street. Disney character pins are a very popular collectible, and the best selection can be found at the **pushcart** across from the Chapeau. The Fantasyland source for the famous black Mouseketeer hats is **Sir Mickey's.** For children's clothing with Disney characters, go to **Tinkerbell's Treasures,** in Fantasyland, or Toontown's **County Bounty.**

VISITOR INFORMATION

City Hall is the Magic Kingdom's principal information center. Here you can search for misplaced belongings or companions, ask questions of the omniscient staffers, and pick up the *Magic Kingdom Guide Map,* with its schedule of daily event and character greeting and attraction information (if you haven't requested one by mail in advance).

At the end of Main Street, on the left as you face Cinderella Castle, just before the Hub, is the **Tip Board,** a large board with constantly updated information about attractions' wait times—fairly reliable except for those moments when everyone follows the "See It Now!" advice and the line immediately triples.

Signs at the centrally located WDW Ticket and Transportation Center, where you board the monorail or ferry to the park, keep you posted about park hours and activities such as parades and fireworks. And cast members are available at almost every turn to help you. In fact, providing information to visitors is part of the job description of the young men and women who sweep the pavement and faithfully keep litter in its place. ▣ City Hall ☏ 407/824-4521.

EPCOT

Walt Disney World was created because of Walt Disney's dream of EPCOT, an "Experimental Prototype Community of Tomorrow." Disney envisioned a future in which nations coexisted in peace and harmony, reaping the miraculous harvest of technological achievement. He suggested the idea as early as October 1966, saying that EPCOT would "take its cue from the new ideas and new technologies that are now emerging from the creative centers of American industry." He wrote that EPCOT, never completed, always improving, "will never cease to be a living blueprint of the future . . . a showcase to the world for the ingenuity and imagination of American free enterprise."

But with Disneyland in California hemmed in by development, Disney had to search for another location to build this community. He found it in Central Florida. Many of the technologies incorporated into the Walt Disney World infrastructure were cutting-edge at the time. But the permanent settlement that he envisioned wasn't to be and is only now taking shape in Disney's Celebration, an urban planner's dream of a town near fast-growing Kissimmee. Epcot, which opened in 1982, 16 years after Disney's death, is a showcase, ostensibly, for the concepts that would be incorporated into the real-life Epcots of the future. It's composed of two parts: Future World, where most pavilions are colorful collaborations of Walt Disney Imagineering and major U.S. corporations designed to demonstrate technological advances; and World Showcase, where exhibition areas are microcosms of 11 countries from four continents.

Epcot today is both more and less than Walt Disney's original dream. Less because a few of the Future World pavilions remain stuck in a 1964 World's Fair mentality. Less because World Showcase presents views of its countries that are, as an Epcot guide once put it, "as Americans perceive them"—highly idealized.

But these are minor quibbles in the face of the major achievement: Epcot is that rare paradox—an educational theme park—and a very successful one, too. Every year, Epcot experiences change and inspires greater interest among the younger set, and the amount of imagination concentrated in its 230 acres is astounding. Through ingenious architecture, intriguing exhibits, amusing and awe-inspiring movies, some lively rides, and first-rate entertainment, Epcot inspires curiosity, rewards discovery, and encourages the creative spark in each of us.

Although several of the newer attractions, such as Mission: SPACE and Test Track, provide high-octane kicks, the thrills are mostly for the mind. Epcot is best for older children and adults. But that doesn't mean the little ones can't have a great time here. Much of the park's entertainment, and at least half of its attractions, provides a fun diversion for younger children overstimulated by the Magic Kingdom's pixie dust. If you do bring young ones, don't miss the Kid Zones sprinkled

20 ROMANTIC THINGS TO DO AT WALT DISNEY WORLD

NOT EVERYTHING AT DISNEY WORLD *involves children. Get a baby-sitter (available for a fee through WDWR) and enjoy some private time, just the two of you.*

1. Have dinner at the very grand Victoria and Albert's restaurant in the Grand Floridian.

2. Have dinner at the California Grill and watch the Magic Kingdom fireworks.

3. Rent a boat to take a cruise on the Seven Seas Lagoon or the waterways leading to it. Bring champagne and glasses.

4. Take a nighttime whirl on Cinderella's Golden Carrousel in Fantasyland. Sparkling lights make it magical.

5. Have your picture taken and grab a kiss in the heart-shape gazebo in the back of Minnie's Country House.

6. Sit on the beach at the Grand Floridian at sunrise or at dusk—a special time.

7. Have a massage day at the Grand Floridian Spa.

8. Buy a faux diamond ring at the Emporium on Main Street in the Magic Kingdom. Propose to your sweetheart at your favorite spot in the World.

9. Have a caricature drawn of the two of you at the Marketplace.

10. Sit by the fountain in front of Epcot's France pavilion and have some wine or a pastry and coffee.

11. Have a drink at the cozy Yachtsman's Crew bar in the Yacht Club hotel.

12. After dinner at Narcoosee's in the Grand Floridian, watch the Electrical Water Pageant outside.

13. Take a walk on the BoardWalk. Watch IllumiNations from the bridge to the Yacht and Beach Club. Then boogie at Atlantic Dance.

14. Tie the knot all over again at the Wedding Pavilion. Invite Mickey and Minnie to the reception.

15. Rent a hot-air balloon for a magical tour of Walt Disney World.

16. Every night is New Year's Eve at Pleasure Island. Declare your love amid confetti and fireworks.

17. Enjoy a British lager outside at Epcot's Rose & Crown Pub—a perfect IllumiNations viewing spot. Book ahead and ask for a table with a view.

18. Have your picture taken with Mickey at Toontown Fair.

19. Have dinner at Alfredo's in Epcot, right after IllumiNations—request an 8:55 reservation. After dinner, since the park is officially closed, it's incredibly lovely.

20. Have dinner at the Brown Derby in Disney–MGM Studios and book ahead for priority Fantasmic! seating.

throughout World Showcase, where they can make puppets, draw pictures, use chalk on the pavement, and make a Moroccan fez. And bring their swimsuits and a towel so they can play in the interactive fountains by the walkway from Future World to World Showcase.

The northern half of Epcot, Future World, is where the monorail drops you off and where the official entrance is located. The southern half, World Showcase, surrounds the 40-acre World Showcase Lagoon and contains an entrance used by Epcot Resort guests—the International Gateway. You can reach the gateway, between the France and United Kingdom pavilions, via water launches or a walkway from the Dolphin and Swan hotels, Disney's Yacht and Beach Club resorts, and Disney's BoardWalk resort.

Future World

Future World is made up of two concentric circles of pavilions. The inner core is composed of the Spaceship Earth geosphere and, just beyond it, a plaza anchored by the wow-generating computer-animated Fountain of Nations, which is as mesmerizing as many a more elaborate ride or show. Bracketing it are the crescent-shape Innoventions East and West.

Seven pavilions compose the outer ring. On the east side they are, in order, the Universe of Energy, Wonders of Life, Test Track, and Mission: SPACE. With the exception of the Wonders of Life, the east pavilions present a single, self-contained ride and an occasional postride showcase; a visit rarely takes more than 30 minutes, but it depends on how long you spend in the postride area. On the west side there are Living Seas, The Land, and Imagination! Like the Wonders of Life, these blockbuster exhibits contain both rides and interactive displays; you could spend at least 1½ hours at each of these pavilions, but there aren't enough hours in the day, so prioritize.

Spaceship Earth

Balanced like a giant golf ball waiting for some celestial being to tee off, the multifaceted silver geosphere of Spaceship Earth is to Epcot what Cinderella Castle is to the Magic Kingdom. As much a landmark as an icon, it can be seen on a clear day from an airplane flying down either coast of Florida. Spaceship Earth contains the Spaceship Earth Ride.

Everyone likes to gawk at the golf ball, but there are some truly jaw-dropping facts about it: it weighs 1 million pounds and measures 164 ft in diameter and 180 ft in height ("Aha!" you say. "It's not really a sphere!"). Altogether it encompasses more than 2 million cubic ft of space, and it's balanced on six pylons sunk 100 ft into the ground. The anodized aluminum sheath is composed of 954 triangular panels, not all of equal size or shape. And, last, because it is not a geodesic dome, which is only a half sphere, the name "geosphere" was coined; no other like it existed when it was built.

Spaceship Earth Ride. This ride transports you past a series of tableaux that explore human progress and the continuing search for better forms of communication. Scripted by science-fiction writer Ray Bradbury and narrated by Jeremy Irons, the journey begins in the darkest tunnels of time, proceeds through history, and ends poised on the edge of the future.

Audio-Animatronics figures present in astonishing detail Cro-Magnon man daubing mystic paintings on cave walls, Egyptian scribes scratching genuine hieroglyphics on papyrus, Roman centurions building roads, Islamic scholars mapping the heavens, and 11th- and 12th-century Benedictine monks hand-copying ancient manuscripts in order to preserve the wisdom of the past. One monk, not as tireless as history would have us believe, is conked out at his carrel, his candle smoking in the gusts of his snores. As you move into the Renaissance, Michelangelo paints the Sistine Chapel, Gutenberg invents the printing press, and in rapid succession, the telegraph, radio, television, and computer come into being. The pace speeds up, you're bombarded with images from the age of communication, and, just as you begin to think you can't absorb another photon, you're shot through a tunnel of swirling lights into serene space, its velvety darkness sparkling with thousands of stars. In one corner is a photograph of the Earth as taken by an astronaut on one of the *Apollo* moon shots. Toward the conclusion of the ride, you arrive in a "Global Neighborhood" that ties all of the peoples of the

Best of the Park

Plan to arrive in the parking lot 30 minutes before the official park opening. As soon as you're admitted, race over to **Mission: SPACE** and either wait in line to ride it or get a FASTPASS appointment. After you ride Mission: SPACE, be sure to get a FASTPASS ticket for Test Track. Then, ready to have your mind expanded, backtrack to **Spaceship Earth.** Upon leaving Spaceship Earth, people naturally head for the first pavilion they see: either Universe of Energy or the Living Seas. Skip them for now and go directly to the **Wonders of Life** and segue without a pause from Body Wars to *The Making of Me* to Cranium Command. Don't forget to go to your FASTPASS apointment at Mission: SPACE or Test Track, if you haven't already done so.

Then head to **Future World**'s western pavilions. Visit the **Imagination!** pavilion and get another FASTPASS ticket for *Honey, I Shrunk the Audience.* Visit **Journey into Your Imagination with Figment.** Then, if you have a short amount of time left, meander through Image Works before returning to *Honey, I Shrunk the Audience.*

Now enter **The Land**; take the boat ride and see *Circle of Life.* By this time there may be a line at **Living Seas,** but if there isn't, go on in and stay as long as you like. Outside, things should be getting crowded.

Head counterclockwise into World Showcase, toward **Canada,** while everyone else is hoofing it toward Mexico. If it's lunchtime, you may be able to get a table right away at **Le Cellier,** one of Epcot's lesser-known dining gems. Then try to catch a performance of the British Invasion in the United Kingdom before crossing the bridge at International Gateway into **France,** where you can snap up an éclair or napoleon at **Boulangerie Pâtisserie.** Shop in Morocco and Japan; then see the **American Adventure Show,** timing it to a Voices of Liberty or American Vybe performance. If there are lines at **Norway** by the time you get there, grab a FASTPASS for the Maelstrom ride, then head for **Innoventions** or **Ellen's Energy Adventure.**

Now's the time to head back to Norway and Maelstrom, followed by an early dinner at France, Italy, Mexico, or another inviting spot. See any attractions you missed, remembering that parts of Future World sometimes close ahead of the rest of the park. Stick around for **IllumiNations,** and stake out a spot early by the lagoon wall at Italy, on the International Gateway Bridge between France and the United Kingdom, or at an outdoor U.K. table. Make sure the wind is to your back so fireworks and special-effects smoke don't waft your way and obscure the scene. Take your time on the way out—the park seems especially magical after dark.

On Rainy Days

Although attractions at Future World are largely indoors, Epcot's expansiveness and the pleasures of meandering around World Showcase on a sunny day make the park a poor choice in inclement weather. Still, if you can't go another day, bring a poncho and muddle through. You'll feel right at home in the United Kingdom.

Earth together through an interactive global network. Special effects, animated sets, and colorful laser-beam patterns are used to create the experience. If you have time, spend an extra 15 minutes checking out the fun interactive exhibits of the Global Neighborhood. ☞ *Duration: 15 mins. Crowds: Longest during the morning and shortest just before closing. Strategy: Ride first thing in the morning or just before leaving. Audience: All ages. The portion of the ride in total darkness may frighten children or others who are anxious in dark, narrow, or enclosed spaces, but the ride vehicles move slowly and the subject matter is completely educational and nonthreatening, so the scare factor is low. Rating:* ★★

Innoventions

In Innoventions—the two-building, 100,000-square-ft attraction at the center of Future World—new technology that affects daily living is highlighted by constantly changing exhibits, live stage demonstrations, and hands-on displays. Each major exhibition area is presented by a leading technology company or association. Innoventions East focuses heavily on home products for the not-too-distant future. Here, you can explore Whirlpool's House of Innoventions filled with innovative lifestyle conveniences that include a hot tub with a built-in, 43″, high-definition plasma video screen with surround-sound. There's also an oven with built-in refrigerator and warming capabilities that can be programmed to prepare a meal 24 hours ahead. The area's Disney.com Internet Zone is loaded with family-friendly activities, and the Segway Human Transporter offers a cutting-edge alternative to walking. At Innoventions West, IBM's ThinkPlace exhibits a wearable computer and showcases a high-tech playground for children called the "Little Thinkers Playground." Lutron demonstrates an Ultimate Home Theater with fiber-optic lighting and even a romantic "star-field" ceiling. Disney Interactive's Video Games of Tomorrow offers an interactive preview of games to come. You'll be hard-pressed to pull your kids out of here. When you finally do exit, if you're a collector of the myriad Disney pins that sell in nearly all the theme-park shops, you'll want to stop by the Pin Station at Innoventions Plaza—it's headquarters for either purchasing or trading pins with fellow collectors. ☞ *Duration: Up to you. Crowds: Largest around the popular computer displays. Strategy: Go first thing in the morning or after dark during IllumiNations. Audience: All but toddlers. Several games are designed with preschoolers in mind. Rating:* ★★★

need a break? The **Fountain View Espresso and Bakery** sells freshly ground coffees, scrumptious croissants, fruit tarts, and éclairs. You can eat at the circular counter or perch on a chair at one of the high tables. The umbrella-covered tables on the patio have a fine view of the fountain. In the afternoon, this is a great place to sip wine and watch the Fountain of Nations water ballet show without having to crane your neck while standing in the blazing sun.

Ice Station Cool

Stooping low in the ice-tunnel-like entrance to this re-created igloo, you see statues of one Refreshus Maximus, frozen in his hunt for refreshment. Beyond, you come to a room full of soda machines where you can sample Coca-Cola products from around the world, such as Vegitabeta from Japan, Smart Watermelon from China, and Kinley Lemon from Israel. There's no free American Coke here, but there's plenty of Coca-Cola memorabilia to buy. ☞ *Duration: As long as you like. Crowds: Move pretty quickly. Strategy: Visit in midafternoon on a very hot day. Audience: All ages. Rating:* ★

When to Go

Epcot is now so vast and varied that you really need two days to explore it all. The best days to go are early in the week, since most people tend to go to Disney's Animal Kingdom and the Magic Kingdom first.

Don't sleep late, especially if you're attempting to see the park in one day. Count on arriving at the turnstiles 15 minutes before opening. It's the best way to squeeze the most in and to avoid some of the lines. Once you're in, head straight for your first FAST-PASS to either Test Track or *Honey, I Shrunk the Audience*.

When You're There

Plan to have at least one relaxed meal. With children, you may want to make reservations (try to make them 3 to 4 months in advance) for the Princess Storybook Breakfast at Norway's Akershus or for lunch or dinner at The Land's Garden Grill, a revolving restaurant that features character appearances by Mickey and friends. Or opt for an early seafood lunch at the Coral Reef in the Living Seas or a festive meal of Italian fare at L'Originale Alfredo di Roma Ristorante in Italy. A late lunch or an early dinner at one of the World Showcase restaurants is another great option.

Upon entering, check the Tip Board past Spaceship Earth and just outside Innoventions, and modify your strategy if there's a short line at a top attraction.

Walk fast, see the exhibits when the park is at its emptiest, and slow down and enjoy the shops and the live entertainment when the crowds thicken.

Set up a rendezvous point and time at the start of the day, just in case you and your companions get separated. Be specific—deciding on a particular bench or table is a smart idea. Some good places in Future World include in front of Gateway Gifts near Spaceship Earth and in front of the Fountain of Nations; in World Showcase, meet at one of the boat-ramp entrances or in front of your country of choice.

Universe of Energy

The first of the pavilions on the left, or east, side of Future World, the Universe of Energy occupies a large, lopsided pyramid sheathed in thousands of mirrors—solar collectors that power the attraction inside. It's one of the most technologically complex shows at Epcot, combining one ride, a film, the largest Audio-Animatronics animals ever built, 250 prehistoric trees, and enough cold, damp fog to make you think you've been transported to the inside of a defrosting refrigerator. ("We don't want to go through that fog again," one child announced after emerging from a particularly damp vision of the Mesozoic era.)

Ellen's Energy Adventure. In the Universe of Energy show, comedian Ellen DeGeneres portrays a woman who dreams she's a contestant on *Jeopardy!* only to discover that all the categories involve a subject she knows nothing about—energy. Her challengers on the show, hosted by Alex Trebek himself, are Ellen's know-it-all former college roommate (played to the irritating hilt by Jamie Lee Curtis) and Albert Einstein. Enter Bill Nye, the Science Guy, Ellen's nice-guy neighbor and all-around science whiz, who guides Ellen (and you) on a crash course in Energy 101.

First comes the history of the universe—in one minute—on three 70-mm screens, 157 ft wide by 32 ft tall. Next the theater separates into six 96-passenger vehicles that lurch into the forest primeval. Huge trees loom out of the mists of time, ominous blue moonbeams waver in the fog, sulfurous lava burbles up, and the air smells distinctly of Swamp Thing. Through this unfriendly landscape apatosauruses wander trailing mouthfuls of weeds, a tyrannosaurus fights it out with a triceratops, pterodactyls swoop through the air, and a truly nasty sea snake emerges from the swamp to attack the left side of the tram. A terrified Ellen is even cornered by a menacing elasmosaurus.

The ride concludes with another film in which Ellen learns about the world's present-day energy needs, resources, and concerns. It's shown on three screens, each 30 ft tall, 74 ft wide, and curved to create a 200° range of vision. Does Ellen win in her *Jeopardy!* dream? You'll have to travel back in time for the answer. ☞ *Duration: 30 mins. Crowd: Steady but never horrible; 600 people enter every 15 mins. Strategy: To be at the front of the ride and have your experience of the primeval landscape unspoiled by rows of modern heads in front of you, sit in the seats to the far left and front of the theater; to get these seats, be sure to position yourself similarly in the preshow area. Audience: All ages. Rating:* ★★★

Wonders of Life

A towering statue of a DNA double helix outside the gold-crowned dome of the Wonders of Life welcomes you to one of Epcot's most popular attractions. Truly among the wonders of Epcot, it takes an amusing but educational look at health, fitness, and modern lifestyles. The messages come via two terrific films; one of Disney's first flight-simulator rides; a multimedia presentation; and dozens of interactive gadgets that whiz, bleep, and blink.

Body Wars. The flight-simulator technology that's used to train commercial and military pilots adapts perfectly to thrill rides. By synchronizing the action on a movie screen with the movement of a ride vehicle, you're tricked into thinking you're moving in wild and crazy fashion even though you never leave your seat. Probably the mildest flight simulator in Central Florida, Body Wars still offers a nifty experience, thanks to the fascinating film and the ingenious idea. You and your fellow scientists enter a simulator chamber that, like something out of a science-fiction plot, will be miniaturized and injected into the body's bloodstream to remove a splinter, which appears on-screen like a massive rock formation. "How's the weather in there?" calls out one of the specialists on the screen. "Clear and warm, temperature about 98.6," comes the reply from within. And in a couple of seconds, you feel it yourself: shooting through the heart, wheezing through the lungs, and picking up a jolt of energy in the brain. ☞ *Duration: 5 mins. Crowds: Rarely a long line now that Test Track and Mission: SPACE are the biggest draws. Strategy: Go anytime. Audience: All but some young children, who may be frightened by the sensation of movement the film induces and by the lurching and pitching of the simulator chamber. Not recommended for pregnant women or guests with heart, back, or neck problems or motion sickness. Minimum height: 40". Rating:* ★★★

The Making of Me. Show times at Wonders of Life are staggered to pick up as soon as another lets out, so with a little luck you can segue right into this valuable film on human conception and childbearing. Starring

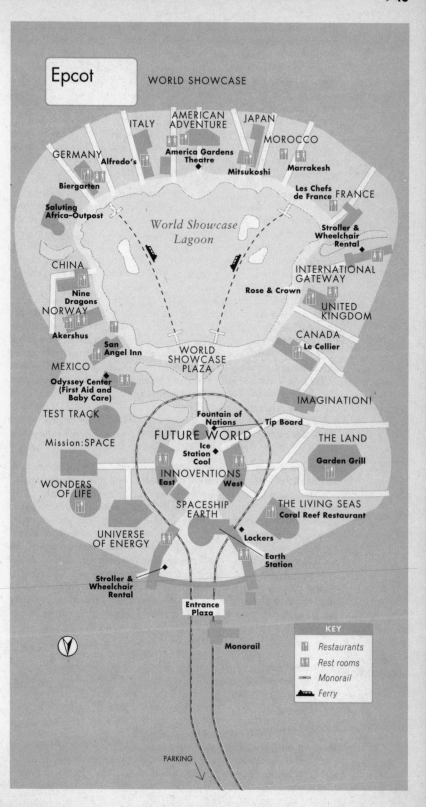

Martin Short as a man who, in search of his origins, journeys back in time to his parents' childhood, youth, marriage, and, eventually, their decision to have him, the film uses both animation and actual footage from a live birth to explain where babies come from. Some scenes are explicit, but all the topics are handled with gentle humor—as when the sperm race for the egg to the tune of "The Ride of the Valkyries"—and with great delicacy. Many adults find the film affecting enough to get out the handkerchiefs for a quick swipe at overflowing eyes, and the film gives children a great opening for talking with their parents about the beginning of life. ☞ *Duration: 14 mins. Crowds: Manageable lines, though the theater is small. Strategy: Line up 5–10 minutes before showtime. Audience: All ages. Rating:* ★★★

Cranium Command. Combining a fast-paced movie with an elaborate set, Disney's Audio-Animatronics, and celebrity cameos, this engaging show takes a clever look at how the cranium manages to make the heart, the uptight left brain, the laid-back right brain, the stomach, and an ever-alert adrenal gland all work together as their host, a 12-year-old boy, dodges the slings and arrows of a typical day. The star is Buzzy, a bumbling Audio-Animatronics Cranium Commando given one last chance to take the helm of an adolescent boy before being consigned to run the brain of a chicken. Buzzy's is not an easy job; as the sign on the way to the theater warns, you are entering THE HOME OF THE FLYING ENDORPHINS. In the flick, Buzzy's 12-year-old wakes up late, dashes off without breakfast, meets the new girl in school, fights for her honor, gets called up before the principal, and, finally, returns home and has a much-needed snack. Buzzy attempts to coordinate a heart, operated by *Saturday Night Live*'s muscle team, Hans and Franz; a stomach, run by George Wendt, formerly of *Cheers,* in a sewer worker's overalls and rubber boots; and all the other body parts. Buzzy succeeds—but just barely. ☞ *Duration: 20 mins. Crowds: Long lines, but they're quickly erased by the big theater, which seats 200 at a shot. Strategy: Go when everyone else is at Body Wars. Audience: All ages. Rating:* ★★★

Fitness Fairground. This educational playground, which teaches both adults and children about good health, takes up much of Wonders of Life. You can pedal around the world on a stationary bicycle while watching an ever-changing view on video, and you can guess your stress level at an interactive computer terminal. "Goofy about Health," an eight-minute multiscreen montage, follows Goofy's conversion from a foul-living "man-dog" to a fun-loving guy. The Sensory Funhouse provides great interactive fun for the little ones and their families. The Frontiers of Medicine, the only completely serious section of the pavilion, demonstrates leading-edge developments in medicine. ☞ *Duration: Up to you. Crowds: Shifting, but they don't affect your visit. Strategy: Hang loose and take turns while you're in the Fitness Fairground. Audience: All ages. Rating:* ★★

need a
break?

Pure & Simple offers healthful snacks and full meals, proving that nutritious can also be delicious. If you take the Wonders of Life message to heart, sample the vegetarian chili spiked with fresh herbs or try the yogurt smoothie. Not even the prices will give you indigestion.

Mission: SPACE

Blast off on a simulated space adventure to Mars as one of four crew members—commander, navigator, pilot, or engineer—in this pavilion, slated for a grand opening in October 2003. The story transports riders to the year 2036 and the International Space Training Center, where you are an astronaut-in-traning preparing for your launch. You'll feel the heart-pounding thrill of lift-off, the rumble of turbulence, and even the sensation of weightlessness in outer space. Mission: SPACE, created with the help of former NASA scientists and astronauts, is the first ride system ever created to take visitors straight up in simulated flight. Each rider encounters simulations of challenges faced by real astronauts and "participates" in carrying out the mission. After landing, you exit your capsule into the Advanced Traning Lab, where you can play Space Race, a dynamic, interactive computer game, and send the little ones to crawl around in the tunnels of the Space Base. The pavilion, looking like its own little galaxy, sits next to Test Track. *Crowds: Since this is Disney's newest and most technologically advanced attraction, everyone will want to go. Fortunately, space travel is fast. Strategy: Race there as soon as the park opens or get a FASTPASS ticket, if available. Audience: Small children should skip this ride. Minimum-height and other restrictions were not available at press time.*

Test Track

Fodor'sChoice This small-scale-with-big-thrills version of a General Motors vehicle proving ground takes you behind the scenes of automobile testing. The queue area showcases many of these tests in informative, action-packed exhibits—and they make the wait fun.

The main draw, however, is the ride itself, billed as "the longest and fastest ride in Walt Disney World's history." Sporty convertible Test Track vehicles take you and five other passengers through seven different performance tests. In the Brake Test your ride vehicle makes two passes through a circular setup of traffic cones, and you learn how antilock brakes can make a wildly out-of-control skid become manageable. In the Environmental Chamber, the ride vehicle is exposed to extreme heat, bone-chilling cold, and a mist that simulates exposure to corrosive substances. After leaving these test chambers, vehicles accelerate quickly up a switchback "mountain road" in the Ride Handling Test. There's also a too-close-for-comfort view of a Barrier Test. The best part, the High-Speed Test, is last: your vehicle goes outside the Test Track building to negotiate a steeply banked loop at a speed of nearly 60 mph. As you leave the pavilion, kids can get a soaking in the Cool Wash, an interactive water area that lets them pretend they are in a car wash. ☞ *Ride duration: 5 mins. Crowds: Expect long lines, as at all popular attractions. Strategy: Go first thing in the morning and get a FASTPASS ticket, or you will wait—a long time. Note that the ride can't function on wet tracks, so don't head here right after a downpour. Audience: All but young children; the queue-area message will be lost on them, and the speeds and other effects may prove frightening. No pregnant women or guests wearing back, neck, or leg braces. Minimum height: 40″. Rating:* ★★★

The Living Seas

Epcot is known for its fountains; the one outside The Living Seas, the first satellite pavilion on the western outer ring, flings surf in a never-ending wave against a rock garden beneath the stylized marquee. The pavilion itself is a favorite among children. Time and technology have caught up with the 5.7-million-gallon aquarium at the pavilion's core. Thrilling when it first opened, what was once revolutionary has now been equaled by top aquariums around the country. Still, the collection of sea life looks quite impressive when you circle the tank on the outside, even more so when you scuba dive within it or when you dine while admiring the sea life from the aquarium windows of the pavilion's Coral Reef restaurant. After the short Caribbean Coral Reef Ride, you may want to meander around the glass-walled tank at your leisure on an upper level, pointing out barracudas, stingrays, parrot fish, sea turtles, and even sharks.

Caribbean Coral Reef Ride. Think of this sea cab ride with a view of the big acrylic tank as just a shuttle to Sea Base Alpha, or up-front crowd control for the pavilion's interactive exhibits, and you won't be disappointed by its brevity. En route, in addition to spotting the aquarium's full-time denizens, you'll sometimes catch sight of a diver testing out the latest scuba equipment. Surrounded by a cloud of parrot fish, the diver may scatter Disney fish food—a mixture of dry dog food, chickens' laying pellets, amino-acid solution, and B-complex vitamins—or you may see him carefully place a head of lettuce within reach of a curious sea turtle. ☞ *Duration: 3 mins. Crowds: Large, all day long. Strategy: Go early, during the lunch rush, or late. Audience: All ages. Rating:* ★★

Sea Base Alpha. This typical Epcot playground, on two levels, contains six modules, each dedicated to specific subjects, such as ocean ecosystems, porpoises, and the endangered Florida manatee. Fully interactive, these contain films, touchy-feely sections, miniaquariums, and video quizzes. Unfortunately, Sea Base Alpha is accessible only via sea cab, so access can be difficult when it's busy. ☞ *Duration: 30 mins and up, depending on how long you play Diver Dan at the modules. Crowds: Large, all day long. Strategy: Stop in first thing in the morning, during lunch, or after 5. Audience: All ages. Rating:* ★★

The Land

Shaped like an intergalactic greenhouse, the enormous, skylighted Land pavilion dedicates 6 acres and a host of different attractions to everyone's favorite topic: food. You can easily spend two hours exploring here, more if you take one of the guided greenhouse tours available throughout the day.

Living with the Land. Piloted by an informative, overalls-clad guide, your canopied boat cruises through three biomes—rain forest, desert, and prairie ecological communities—and into an experimental greenhouse that demonstrates how food sources may be grown in the future, not only on the planet but also in outer space. Shrimp, sunshine bass, tilapia, and pacu— the piranha's vegetarian cousin—are raised in controlled aquacells, and tomatoes, peppers, and squash thrive in the Desert Farm area through a system of drip irrigation that delivers just the right amount of water and nutrients to their roots. Gardeners are usually interested in the section on integrated pest management, which relies on "good" insects like ladybugs to control more harmful predators. Many of the growing areas are actual experiments-in-progress, in which Disney and the U.S. Department of Agriculture have joined forces to produce, say, a sweeter pineapple or a faster-growing pepper. Interestingly, although the plants and fish in the greenhouse are all quite real—and are regularly harvested for use in The Land's restaurants—those in the biomes are artful fakes, manufactured by Disney elves out of flexible, lightweight plastic. The grass is made out of glass fibers that have been implanted in rubber mats. ☞ *Duration: 14 mins. Crowds: Moderate, all day. Strategy: The line moves fairly quickly, so go anytime. Use FASTPASS in the case of peak season crowds. Audience: Teens and adults. Rating:* ★★★

Food Rocks. In this rowdy little concert, recognizable rock-and-roll performers take the shape of favorite foods and sing about the joys of nutrition. There are performances by the Peach Boys, Chubby Cheddar, and Neil Moussaka, among others. *Duration: 20 mins. Crowds: A large theater absorbs them, no matter their size. Strategy: Go when the line at Living with the Land is too long. Audience: Children and parents who like classic rock. Rating:* ★★

The Circle of Life. Featuring three stars of *The Lion King*—Simba the lion, Timon the meerkat, and Pumbaa the waddling warthog—this film delivers a powerful message about protecting the world's environment for all living things. Part animation, part *National Geographic*–like film using spectacular 70-mm live-action footage, *Circle of Life* tells a fable about a "Hakuna Matata Lakeside Village" that Timon and Pumbaa are developing by clearing the African savanna. Simba cautions about mistreating the land by telling a story of a creature who occasionally forgets that everything is connected in the great Circle of Life. "That creature," he says, "is man." The lilting accompaniment, of course, is Tim Rice and Elton John's popular song, and the narration is provided by James Earl Jones. *Duration: 20 mins. Crowds: Moderate to large, all day. Strategy: Hit this first in the Land. Audience: Enlightening for children and adults; a nap opportunity for toddlers. Rating:* ★★

need a break? Talk about a self-contained ecosystem: the pavilion grows its own produce and houses the **Sunshine Season Food Fair,** a food court composed of a dozen or so stands—a soup-and-salad spot, bakery (with great jumbo-size cinnamon rolls and corn muffins before 11 AM), barbecue stand, sandwich counter, ice cream outlet, baked potato purveyor, and beverage house, which bolsters the usual soft drinks with milk shakes, buttermilk, vegetable juice, and exotic fruit nectars. Pause for a healthful snack. (Between noon and 2, lines are huge and tables are hard to come by.) The bakery's brownies are legendary, and Epcot staffers have been known to make a special trip to pick up some of its chocolate-chip cookies. Just remember that at this pavilion you must eat all your vegetables.

Imagination!

The theme here is the imagination and the fun that can be had when you let it loose. The leaping fountains outside make the point, as does the big attraction here, the 3-D film *Honey, I Shrunk the Audience.* The Journey into Your Imagination with Figment ride can be capped by a stroll through Image Works, a sort of interactive fun house devoted to music and art.

Fodor'sChoice **Honey, I Shrunk the Audience.** Don't miss this 3-D adventure about the futuristic "shrinking" technologies demonstrated in the hit films that starred Rick Moranis. Moranis reprises his role as Dr. Wayne Szalinski, who's about to receive the Inventor of the Year Award from the Imagination Institute. While Dr. Szalinski is demonstrating his latest shrinking machine, though, things go really, really wrong. Be prepared to laugh and scream your head off, courtesy of the special in-theater effects and 3-D film technology that are used ingeniously, from start to finish, to dramatize a hoot of a story. *Duration: 14 mins. Crowds: Large theater capacity should mean a relatively short wait, but the film's popularity can make for big crowds. Strategy: Go first thing in the morning or just before closing, or utilize the FASTPASS scheme. Audience: All but easily frightened children. For most, the humor quotient outweighs the few scary moments. Rating:* ★★★

Journey into Your Imagination with Figment. If this isn't your first trip to Disney, you may remember Figment, the fun-loving dragon and original host of the Journey to Imagination ride. When this attraction was updated for Disney's millennium celebration, Figment stepped out of his starring role, to the dismay of many. So Disney returned Figment to celebrity status and teamed him with Dr. Nigel Channing, the presenter of Dr. Szalinski's award in *Honey, I Shrunk the Audience*. The pair take you on a sensory adventure designed to engage your imagination through sound, illusion, gravity, dimension, and color. After the ride, you can check out Image Works, where several interactive displays allow you to further stretch your imagination. Here you can participate in games with Figment, and say "cheese" at the Incredible Picture Labs, where you can change your appearance, pose for a snapshot, and then send a photo of your new look back home. ☞ *Duration: 8 mins. Crowds: Although the ride is the newest at Epcot, lines move fairly quickly here. Strategy: Ride while waiting for your Honey, I Shrunk the Audience FASTPASS appointment. Audience: School-age children and adults. Preschoolers may be frightened by the brief period of darkness and the scanner at the end of the ride. Rating:* ★★

World Showcase

Nowhere but at Epcot can you explore a little corner of 11 countries in one day. As you stroll the 1⅓ mi around the 40-acre World Showcase Lagoon, you circumnavigate the globe according to Disney by experiencing the native food, entertainment, culture, and arts and crafts at pavilions representing 11 different countries in Europe, Asia, North Africa, and the Americas. The pavilion employees are from the countries they represent—Disney hires them to live and work for up to a year as part of its international college program. Several World Showcase pavilions include well-executed multimedia presentations that showcase a particular culture and people, and well-known landmarks have been re-created. Instead of rides, you have breathtaking films at the Canada, China, and France pavilions; several art exhibitions; and the chance to chat in the native language of the friendly foreign staff members. Each pavilion also has a designated Kidcot Fun Stop, open daily from 11 AM or noon until around 8 PM, where youngsters can try their hands at crafts projects—they might make a Moroccan fez or a Norwegian troll, for instance. Live entertainment is an integral part of the pavilions' presentations, and some of your finest moments here will be watching incredibly talented Chinese acrobats, singing along with a terrific band of Fab Four impersonators in the U.K. pavilion, or marveling at Imaginum, outside the France pavilion. Once known as the Living Statues, the group stuns passersby when its members suddenly change position and interact playfully with guests without breaking their statuesque demeanor. Dining is another favorite pastime at Epcot, and the World Showcase offers tempting tastes of the authentic cuisines of the countries that have pavilions.

The focal point of World Showcase is the American Adventure, directly opposite Spaceship Earth on the far side of the lagoon. The pavilions of other countries fan out from both sides, encircling the lagoon. Counterclockwise from World Showcase Plaza as you enter from Future World are Canada, the United Kingdom, France, Morocco, Japan, the American Adventure, Italy, Germany, China, Norway, and Mexico. The best times to visit are late April through May during the Epcot International Flower and Garden Festival and late October through mid-November during the Epcot International Food & Wine Festival.

Dotted with tiny islands (and fireworks staging platforms), the World Showcase Lagoon seems to represent the oceans between the countries whose pavilions encircle it. Throughout the day, ferries flit across the lagoon, delivering park guests to the docks near the Mexico, Germany, Morocco, and Canada pavilions. When night falls, the lagoon lights up as brilliant pyrotechnics explode overhead, lighted fountains dance above the surface, and colorful lasers beam at the crowds gathered for IllumiNations.

Fodor'sChoice **IllumiNations: Reflections of Earth.** This marvelous nighttime spectacular takes place over the lagoon's watery stage every night before closing. Be sure to stick around for the lasers, lights, fireworks, fountains, and music from every host nation that fill the air over the water. Although there's generally good viewing from all around the lagoon, some of the best spots are in front of the Italy pavilion, on the bridge between France and the United Kingdom, the promenade in front of Canada, and the bridge between China and Germany, which will give you a clear shot, unobstructed by trees. After the show, concealed loudspeakers play the theme music manipulated into salsa, polka, waltz, and even—believe it or not—Asian rhythms. ☞ *Duration: 13 mins. Crowds: Heavy. Strategy: Take your place 45 mins in advance. Audience: All ages. Rating:* ★★★

Canada

"Oh, it's just our Canadian outdoors," said a typically modest native guide upon being asked the model for the striking rocky chasm and tumbling waterfall that represent just one of the high points of Canada. The beautiful formal gardens do have an antecedent: Butchart Gardens, in Victoria, British Columbia. And so does the Hôtel du Canada, a French Gothic mansion with spires, turrets, and a mansard roof; anyone who's ever stayed at Québec's Château Frontenac or Ottawa's Château Laurier will recognize the imposing style favored by architects of Canadian railroad hotels. Like the size of the Rocky Mountains, the scale of the structures seems immense; unlike the real thing, it's managed with a trick called forced perspective, which exaggerates the smallness of the distant parts to make the entire thing look gigantic. Another bit of design legerdemain: the World Showcase Rockies are made of chicken wire and painted concrete mounted on a movable platform similar to a parade float. Ah, wilderness!

Canada also contains shops selling maple syrup, lumberjack shirts, and other trapper paraphernalia. Its restaurant, Le Cellier Steakhouse, is a great place to stop for a relaxing lunch.

O Canada! That's just what you'll say after seeing this CircleVision film's stunning opening shot—footage of the Royal Canadian Mounted Police surrounding you as they circle the screen. From there, you whoosh over waterfalls, venture through Montreal and Toronto, sneak up on bears and bison, mush behind a husky-pulled dogsled, and land pluck in the middle of a hockey game. This is a standing-only theater, with lean rails. ☞ *Duration: 17 mins. Crowds: Can be thick in late afternoon. Strategy: Go when World Showcase opens or in the evening. Audience: All ages, but no strollers permitted, and toddlers and small children can't see unless they're held aloft. Rating:* ★★★

United Kingdom

Never has it been so easy to cross the English Channel. A pastiche of there-will-always-be-an-England architecture, the United Kingdom rambles between the elegant mansions lining a London square to the bustling, half-timber shops of a village high street to the thatched-roof cottages from the countryside. (The thatch is made of plastic broom bristles in consideration of local fire regulations.) And of course there's a pair of the familiar red phone booths that were once found all over the United Kingdom but are now on their way to being relics. The pavilion has no single major attraction. Instead, you can wander through shops selling tea and tea accessories, Welsh handicrafts, Royal Doulton figurines, and woolens and tartans from Pringle of Scotland; the Magic of Wales sells delicate British china and collectibles. Outside, the strolling World Showcase Players coax audience members into participating in their definitely low-brow versions of Shakespeare. There's also a lovely garden and park with benches in the back that's easy to miss—relax and kick back to the tunes of the British Invasion, a band known for its on-target Beatles performances. Kids love to run through the hedge maze as the parents travel back in time to "Yesterday."

need a break? Revive yourself with a pint of the best—although you'll be hard-put to decide among the offerings—at the **Rose & Crown Pub,** which also offers traditional afternoon tea on the outdoor terrace. The adjacent dining room serves more substantial fare (priority seating reservation required). The terrace outside is one of the best spots to watch IllumiNations; arrive early.

France

You don't need the scaled-down model of the Eiffel Tower to tell you that you've arrived in France, specifically Paris. There's the poignant accordion music wafting out of concealed speakers, the trim sycamores pruned in the French style to develop signature knots at the end of each branch, and the delicious aromas surrounding the Boulangerie Pâtisserie bake shop. This is the Paris of dreams, a Paris of the years just before World War I, when solid mansard-roof mansions were crowned with iron filigree, when the least brick was drenched in romanticism. Here's a replica of the conservatory-like Les Halles—the iron-and-glass barrel-roof market that no longer exists in the City of Light; there's an arching footbridge, and all around, of course, there are shops. You can inspect artwork, Limoges porcelain, and crystal in the exquisite Plume et Palette; sample Guerlain perfume and cosmetics at La Signature; and acquire a bottle of Bouzy Rouge to wash it all down at Les Vins de France, where wine tastings are frequently held for a small charge. If you plan to dine at the beautifully remodeled Les Chefs de France, late lunch is a good plan.

Impressions de France. The intimate Palais du Cinema, inspired by the royal theater at Fontainebleau, screens this homage to the glories of the country. Shown on five screens spanning 200° in an air-conditioned, sit-down theater, the film takes you to vineyards at harvesttime, Paris on Bastille Day, the Alps, Versailles, Normandy's Mont-St-Michel, and the stunning châteaux of the Loire Valley. The musical accompaniment also hits high notes and sweeps you away with familiar segments from Offenbach, Debussy, and Saint-Saëns, all woven together by longtime Disney musician Buddy Baker. ☞ *Duration: 18 mins. Crowds: Considerable from World Showcase opening through late afternoon. Strategy: Come before noon or after dinner. Audience: Adults and children age 7 and up. Rating:* ★★★

need a break? The frequent lines at **Boulangerie Pâtisserie,** a small Parisian-style sidewalk cafe, are worth the wait. Have a creamy café au lait and an éclair, napoleon, or some other French pastry while enjoying the fountains and floral displays.

Morocco

You don't need a magic carpet to be transported into a different culture—just walk through the pointed arches of the Bab Boujouloud gate and you'll find yourself exploring the mysterious North African country of Morocco. The arches are ornamented with beautiful wood carvings and encrusted with intricate mosaics made of 9 tons of handmade, hand-cut tiles; 19 native artisans were sent to Epcot to install them and to create the dusty, stucco walls that seem to have withstood centuries of sandstorms. Look closely and you'll see that every tile has a small crack or some other imperfection, and no tile depicts a living creature—in deference to the Islamic belief that only Allah creates perfection and life.

Koutoubia Minaret, a replica of the prayer tower in Marrakesh, acts as Morocco's landmark. Traditional winding alleyways, each corner bursting with carpets, brasses, leather work, and other North African craftsmanship, lead to a beautifully tiled fountain and lush gardens. Check out the continually changing art and artifacts exhibit in the Gallery of Arts and History, watch native Moroccans weave rugs on looms, and entertain yourself examining the wares at such shops as Casablanca Carpets and The Brass Bazaar. The full-service restaurant, Marrakesh, is a highlight here if you enjoy eating couscous and roast lamb to the tune of a lithesome belly dancer. And the newest fast-food spot on the Epcot dining scene is Tangierine Café, with tasty Mediterranean specialties and freshly baked Moroccan bread.

Japan

A brilliant vermilion torii gate, based on Hiroshima Bay's much-photographed Itsukushima Shrine, frames the World Showcase Lagoon and stands as the striking emblem of Disney's serene version of Japan. Disney horticulturists deserve a hand for creating an authentic landscape: 90% of the plants they used are native to Japan. Rocks, pebbled streams, pools, and carefully pruned trees and shrubs complete the meticulous picture. At sunset, or during a rainy dusk, the twisted branches of the corkscrew willows frame a perfect Japanese view of the five-story winged pagoda that is the heart of the pavilion. Based on the 8th-century Horyuji Temple in Nara, the brilliant blue pagoda has five levels, symbolizing the five elements of Buddhist belief—earth, water, fire, wind, sky. As you wander along the twisting paths, listen for the wind chimes and the soothing clack of the water mill—Walt Disney World seems a million miles away.

The peace is occasionally interrupted by authentic performances on drums and gongs. Other entertainment is provided by demonstrations of traditional Japanese crafts, such as kite-making and the snipping of brown rice toffee into intricate shapes; these take place outdoors on the pavilion's plaza or in the Bijutsu-Kan Gallery, where there are also changing art exhibitions. Mitsukoshi Department Store, an immense three-centuries-old retail firm known as Japan's Sears Roebuck, is a favorite among Epcot shoppers and carries everything from T-shirts to kimonos and row upon row of Japanese dolls. A perfect souvenir is one of the many colorful silk, cotton, or polyester robes lining the front of the store. Diners are entertained by knife-juggling Japanese chefs at the Teppanyaki Dining Rooms.

American Adventure

In a Disney version of Philadelphia's Liberty Hall, the Imagineers prove that their kind of fantasy can beat reality hands down. The 110,000 bricks, made by hand from soft pink Georgia clay, sheathe the familiar structure, which acts as a beacon for those across Epcot's lagoon. And when those colored lights start flashing, rousing music explodes from loud-speakers, and the lasers zing between here and Spaceship Earth during the sound-and-light-and-fireworks IllumiNations show after dark, the patriotism in the air is palpable. The pavilion includes an all-American fast-food restaurant, a shop, lovely rose gardens, and an outdoor theater always booked with first-rate live entertainment.

The American Adventure Show. The pavilion's key attraction is this 100-yard dash through history, and you'll be primed for the lesson after reaching the main entry hall and hearing the stirring a cappella Voices of Liberty or the American Vybe, who sing gospel, swing, and jazz. Inside the theater, the main event begins to the accompaniment of "The Golden Dream," performed by the Philadelphia Symphony Orchestra. This show combines evocative sets, the world's largest rear-projection screen (72 ft wide), enormous movable stages, and 35 Audio-Animatronics players, which are some of the most lifelike ever created—Ben Franklin even climbs up stairs. Beginning with the arrival of the Pilgrims at Plymouth Rock and their grueling first winter, Ben Franklin and a wry, pipe-smoking Mark Twain narrate the episodes, both praiseworthy and shameful, that have shaped the American spirit. Disney detail is so painstaking that you never feel rushed, and, in fact, each speech and each scene seems polished like a little jewel. You feel the cold at Valley Forge and the triumph when Charles Lindbergh flies the Atlantic; are moved by Nez Perce chief Joseph's forced abdication of Native American ancestral lands and by women's rights campaigner Susan B. Anthony's speech; laugh with Will Rogers's aphorisms and learn about the pain of the Great Depression through an affecting radio broadcast by Franklin Delano Roosevelt. ☞ *Duration: 30 mins. Crowds: Large, but the theater is huge, so you can almost always get into the next show. Strategy: Check the entertainment schedule and arrive 10 mins before the Voices of Liberty or American Vybe are slated to perform. Grab a bench or a spot on the floor and enjoy the music before the show. Audience: All ages. Rating:* ★★★

America Gardens Theater. On the edge of the lagoon, directly opposite Disney's magnificent bit of colonial fakery, is this venue for concerts and shows—some that are of the "Yankee Doodle Dandy" variety and some that are hot tickets themed to Epcot events, such as the "Flower Power" concerts with '60s pop legends during the late-April-through-May International Flower and Garden Festival. This is also the spot for the annual yuletide Candlelight Processional—a not-to-be-missed event if you're at WDW during the holidays. The special Candlelight Dinner Package (available through Disney's dining reservations hot line) includes dinner in a select World Showcase restaurant, and preferred seating for the moving performance. ☞ *Crowds: Large during holiday performances and celebrity concerts. Strategy: Check the entertainment schedule and arrive 30 mins to 1 hr ahead of time for holiday and celebrity performances. Audience: Varies with performance.*

need a break? What else would you order at the counter-service **Liberty Inn** but apple pie and other all-American fare? If your youngsters want an ice cream sundae to eat before IllumiNations, this is the place to get it.

Italy

In WDW's Italy, the star is the architecture: reproductions of Venice's Piazza San Marco and Doge's Palace, accurate right down to the gold leaf on the ringlets of the angel perched 100 ft atop the campanile; the seawall stained with age, with barbershop-stripe poles to which two gondolas are tethered; and the Romanesque columns, Byzantine mosaics, Gothic arches, and stone walls that have all been carefully "antiqued" to look old. Mediterranean plants such as grapevines, kumquat, and olive trees add verisimilitude. Inside, shops sell Venetian beads and glasswork, leather purses and belts, olive oils, pastas, and Perugina cookies and chocolate kisses. At the always-hopping L'Originale Alfredo di Roma Ristorante, authentic fettuccine Alfredo and other Italian specialties provide a great carb high for all-day visitors who don't mind being serenaded table-side while they dine.

Germany

Germany, a make-believe village that distills the best folk architecture from all over that country, is so jovial that you practically expect the Seven Dwarfs to come "heigh-ho"-ing out to meet you. Instead, you'll hear the hourly chimes from the specially designed glockenspiel on the clock tower, musical toots and tweets from multitudinous cuckoo clocks, folk tunes from the spinning dolls and plush lambs sold at Der Teddy-bär, and the satisfied grunts of hungry visitors chowing down on hearty German cooking, which has improved mightily as part of Disney's dining renaissance. An oompah band performs up to four times a day in the Biergarten restaurant and in the courtyard. The Biergarten's wonderful buffet gives traditional German cuisine a modern twist: these include several sausage varieties, as well as sauerkraut, spaetzle, and roasted potatoes, rotisserie chicken, and German breads. There are also shops aplenty—more than in any other pavilion. The most irresistible are Die Weihnachts Ecke (The Christmas Corner), which sells nutcrackers and other traditional Christmas ornaments; Süssigkeiten, for irresistible butter cookies and animal crackers; and Volkskunst, with a folk-crafts collection that includes cuckoo clocks ranging from hummingbird scale to the size of an eagle.

need a break?

Bratwurst or goulash and cold beer from the **Sommerfest** cart, at the entrance of the Biergarten restaurant, makes a perfect quick and hearty lunch, while the soft pretzels and strudel are ever-popular snacks. There's not much seating, so you may have to eat on the run.

Saluting Africa–Outpost

It's not one of the 11 World Showcase pavilions, but as you stroll between Germany and China, you'll have to make a brief cultural shift when you encounter the Orisi Risi interactive drum circle, with its traditional African folklore performances. Village Traders sells African handicrafts and—you guessed it—souvenirs relating to *The Lion King*. Buy an ice cream or frozen yogurt at the Refreshment Outpost and enjoy the break at a table by the lagoon while the kids test their drumming skills on bongos or play beneath the cool mist set up to offer respite on hot, sunny days.

China

A shimmering red-and-gold, three-tier replica of Beijing's Temple of Heaven towers over a serene Chinese garden, an art gallery displaying treasures from the People's Republic, a spacious emporium devoted to Chinese goods, and two restaurants. The gardens, planted with a native Chinese tallow tree, water lilies, bamboo, and a 100-year-old weeping mulberry tree, is one of the most peaceful spots in the World Showcase. Piped-in traditional Chinese music flows gently over the peaceful hush of the gardens.

Wonders of China. Think of the Temple of Heaven as an especially fitting theater for a movie in which sensational panoramas of the land and

CloseUp

ILLUSIONS OF GRANDEUR

MUCH OF DISNEY WORLD'S breathtaking majesty comes from its architecture, and a little design trick called forced perspective, in which buildings appear taller than they actually are.

The best example of forced perspective is on Main Street in the Magic Kingdom. Look very carefully at the upper floors of the shops. Together, the second and third floors take up the same amount of space as the ground floor. The buildings start at normal scale at the base but then get imperceptibly smaller toward the top to simulate that cozy hometown feeling. Forced perspective is used in Cinderella's castle, too. Notice how it gets narrower toward the towers. This trick of the eye makes it look as if the spires are soaring into the clouds.

In the Animal Kingdom, architectural scale is suppressed to allow trees to overshadow the buildings. The aim is to relay a sense of humility in the face of nature's wonders. Building height is limited to just 30 ft, whereas trees can tower well above that. But the showcase of the park is the 145-ft Tree of Life, which looks like a skyscraper as it rises from the center of Animal Kingdom. The Tree of Life is a sculptural masterpiece, too. Its trunk is carved with the images of hundreds of animals, illustrating another important Disney design tenet: every structure must tell a story.

—*Ellen Parlapiano*

people are dramatically portrayed on a 360° CircleVision screen. This may be the best of the World Showcase films—the only drawback is that the theater has no chairs; lean rails are provided. ☞ *Duration: 19 mins. Crowds: Steady from World Showcase opening through late afternoon, but the theater's high capacity means you can usually get into the next show. Strategy: Go anytime. Audience: All ages, but no strollers permitted, and small children have to be held aloft to see. Rating:* ★★★

> **need a break?**
>
> **Lotus Blossom Café** has covered outdoor tables and serves egg rolls, sweet-and-sour anything, and not-too-exotic stir-fried dishes that you can wash down with cold Tsing Tao beer. The ginger ice cream is refreshing on a hot day.

Norway

Among the rough-hewn timbers and sharply pitched roofs here—softened and brightened by bloom-stuffed window boxes and figured shutters—are lots of smiling young Norwegians, all eager to speak English and show off their country. The pavilion complex contains a 14th-century, fortress-like castle that mimics Oslo's Akershus, cobbled streets, rocky waterfalls, and a stave church, modeled after one built in 1250, with wood dragons glaring from the eaves. The church houses an exhibit called "To the Ends of the Earth," which tells the story of two early 20th-century polar expeditions by using vintage artifacts. It all puts you in the mood for the pavilion's shops, which sell wood carvings, glass artwork, and beautifully embroidered woolen sweaters, a popular item despite Florida's heat. At the restaurant, Akershus, you can chow down on a traditional Norwegian *koldtbord* (buffet), a selection of hot and cold taste treats. The restaurant is the only one in the park where you can have breakfast with Disney princesses, including Sleeping Beauty, Belle, and Snow White. Book at least two or three months ahead, or check at Guest Relations for seats left by cancellations.

Maelstrom. In Norway's dandy boat ride, you pile into 16-passenger, dragon-headed longboats for a voyage through time that, despite its scary name and encounters with evil trolls, is actually more interesting than frightful. The journey begins in a 10th-century village, where a boat, much like the ones used by Eric the Red, is being readied for a Viking voyage. You glide steeply up through a mythical forest populated by trolls, who cause the boat to plunge backward down a mild waterfall, then cruise amid the grandeur of the Geiranger fjord, following which you experience a storm in the North Sea and, as the presence of oil rigs signals a return to the 20th century, end up in a peaceful coastal village. Disembarking, you proceed into a theater for a quick and delightful film about Norway's scenic wonders, culture, and people. ☞ *Duration: 10 mins. Crowds: Steady, with slow-moving lines from late morning through early evening. Strategy: Grab a FASTPASS appointment so you can return after lunch or dinner. Audience: All ages. Rating:* ★★

Age of the Viking Ship. Children adore this replica of a Viking ship, an interactive playground filled with ropes and climbing adventures from bow to stern. ☞ *Duration: As long as you want. Crowds: Not that bad. Strategy: Go anytime. Audience: Toddlers and elementary-school-age children. Rating:* ★★

need a break? You can order smoked salmon and other open-face sandwiches, plus Norwegian Ringnes beer at **Kringla Bakeri og Kafe.** The pastries here are worth the stop. Go early or late for speediest service and room to sit in the outdoor seating area.

Mexico

Housed in a spectacular Maya pyramid surrounded by dense tropical plantings and brilliant blossoms, Mexico contains the El Río del Tiempo boat ride, an exhibit of pre-Columbian art, a very popular restaurant, and, of course, a shopping plaza, where you can unload many, many pesos.

Modeled on the market in the town of Taxco, Plaza de los Amigos is well named: there are lots of friendly people—the women dressed in ruffled off-the-shoulder peasant blouses and bright skirts, the men in white shirts and dashing sashes—all eager to sell you trinkets from a cluster of canopied carts. The perimeter is rimmed with stores with tile roofs, wrought-iron balconies, and flower-filled window boxes. What to buy? Brightly colored paper blossoms, sombreros, baskets, pottery, leather goods, and colorful papier-mâché piñatas, which Epcot imports by the truckload.

El Río del Tiempo. True to its name, this attraction takes you on a trip down the River of Time. Your journey from the jungles of the Yucatán to modern-day Mexico City is enlivened by video images of feathered Toltec dancers; by garish Spanish-colonial Audio-Animatronics dancing puppets; and by film clips of cliff divers in Acapulco, speed boats in Manzanillo, and snorkeling around Isla Mujeres. ☞ *Duration: 9 mins. Crowds: Moderate, slow-moving lines from late morning through late afternoon. Strategy: Skip this one unless you have small children, who usually enjoy the novelty of a boat ride. Audience: All ages. Rating:* ★

Epcot A to Z

To research prices, get advice from other travelers, and book travel arrangements, visit www.fodors.com.

BABY CARE

Epcot has a **Baby Care Center** as peaceful as the one in the Magic Kingdom; it's near the Odyssey Restaurant in Future World. Furnished with rocking chairs, it has a low lighting level that makes it comfortable for nursing, and cast members have supplies such as formula, baby food, pacifiers, and disposable diapers for sale. Changing tables are available here, as well as in all women's rooms and some men's rooms. You can also buy disposable diapers near the park entrance at Baby Services. For stroller rentals ($7 single, $14 double; plus $1 refundable deposit), look for the special stands on the east side of the Entrance Plaza and at World Showcase's International Gateway.

CAMERAS & FILM

Disposable cameras are widely available, and you can get assistance with minor camera problems at the **Kodak Camera Center,** in the Entrance Plaza, and at **Cameras and Film,** at the Imagination! pavilion. Remember when you had your picture taken in front of Spaceship Earth when you entered the park? Pick up your photo at the **Kodak Camera Center** as you exit, or send someone from your group over to pick it up while you're waiting in line at Spaceship Earth.

For two-hour film developing, look for the **Photo Express** signs throughout the park: in Future World at the Kodak Camera Center as well as at Cameras and Film, and in World Showcase at Northwest Mercantile in Canada; World Traveler at International Gateway; Heritage Manor Gifts in the American Adventure; at the booth on the right as you enter Norway; and at Artesanias Mexicanas in Mexico. Drop your film in the container, and you can pick up your pictures at the Kodak Camera Center as you leave.

DINING

In World Showcase every pavilion sponsors at least one and often two or even three eateries. Where there's a choice, it's among a full-service restaurant with commensurately higher prices; a more affordable, ethnic fast-food spot; and carts and shops selling snacks ranging from French pastries to Japanese ices—whatever's appropriate to the pavilion. Lunch and dinner reservations are essential at the full-service restaurants; you can make them up to 60 days in advance by calling ☎ 407/939–3463 or going in person to the WorldKey terminals at the park (only on the day of the meal) or to the restaurants themselves when they open for lunch, usually at noon. Some of these are among Orlando's best dining options.

In Future World, a large fast-food emporium, **Electric Umbrella,** dominates the Innoventions' East Plaza area. The fare here is chicken sandwiches, burgers, and salads. At The Land's **Garden Grill,** you can eat solid American family-style lunch or dinner fare as the restaurant revolves, giving you an ever-changing view of each biome on the boat ride. Besides the Princess breakfast in Norway, this is the only Epcot restaurant that includes Disney character meet-and-greets during meals. The **Sunshine Season Food Fair** in The Land is a popular counter-service dining spot among Epcot regulars. Living Seas' **Coral Reef** serves excellent seafood in addition to chicken, steak, and special kids' entrées; one of its walls is made entirely of glass and looks directly into a 6-million-gallon aquarium full of interesting critters.

DISABILITIES & ACCESSIBILITY

Accessibility standards in this park are high. Many attractions and most restaurants and shops are fully wheelchair accessible. The *Guidebook for Guests with Disabilities* lays out services and facilities available and includes information about companion rest rooms and how to acquire Braille or audio guides and sign-language interpretation schedules for Epcot attractions. Assistive listening devices require a $25 deposit to amplify sound in many of the theater shows. Closed-captioning is available on TV monitors at attractions that have preshows.

ATTRACTIONS At Future World, to go on the **Spaceship Earth Ride,** you must be able to walk four steps and transfer to a vehicle; in the unusual case that emergency evacuation may be necessary, it's by way of stairs. Service animals should not be taken on this ride. Although much of the enchantment is in the visual details, the narration is interesting as well. The Epcot Discovery Center here is wheelchair accessible. **Innoventions** is completely wheelchair accessible. **Universe of Energy** is accessible to guests using standard wheelchairs and those who can transfer to them; especially because this is one of the attractions that has sound tracks amplified by rental personal translator units, it's slightly more interesting to those with hearing impairments than to those with visual impairments. **Wonders of Life,** including **Cranium Command,** *The Making of Me,* and "Goofy about Health" is totally wheelchair accessible, with special seating sections for guests using wheelchairs. Guests with visual impairments may wish to skip "Goofy about Health." To ride the turbulent **Body Wars,** you must transfer to a ride seat; if you lack upper-body strength, request extra shoulder restraints. Service animals are not allowed on this ride. At **Test Track,** one TV monitor in the preshow area is closed-captioned for people with hearing impairments. Visitors in wheelchairs are provided a special area where they can practice transferring into the ride vehicle before actually boarding the high-speed ride. **Mission: SPACE** also requires a transfer from wheelchair to seat and has an area where you can practice beforehand. In **Living Seas,** guests using wheelchairs typically bypass the three-minute ride—no loss—and move directly into the **Sea Base Alpha** and aquarium area, the best part of the pavilion. In **The Land,** *Circle of Life,* **Food Rocks,** and the greenhouse tour are completely wheelchair accessible. "Reflective captioning," in which captions are displayed at the bottom of glass panes mounted on stands, is available at the *Circle of Life.* If you can read lips, you'll enjoy the greenhouse tour. As for the **Living with the Land** boat ride, those using an oversize wheelchair or a scooter must transfer to a Disney chair. Boarding the **Journey into Your Imagination with Figment** ride requires guests to take three steps and step up into a ride vehicle. The theater that screens *Honey, I Shrunk the Audience* is completely accessible, although you must transfer to a theater seat to experience some of the special effects. The preshow area has one TV monitor that is closed-captioned. The hands-on activities of Image Works have always been wheelchair accessible and should continue to be; there's something to suit most tastes here. **Ice Station Cool** is not wheelchair accessible.

At World Showcase, most people stroll about, but there are also Friend-ship boats, which require those using oversize wheelchairs or scooters to transfer to Disney chairs; the **American Adventure, France, China,** and **Canada** are all wheelchair accessible; personal translator units amplify the sound tracks here. **Germany, Italy, Japan, Morocco,** and the **United Kingdom** all have live entertainment, most with strong aural as well as visual elements; the plaza areas where the shows are presented are wheelchair accessible. In **Norway,** you must be able to step down into and up out of a boat to ride the Maelstrom, and an emergency evacuation requires the use of stairs; service animals are not allowed. In **Mexico,** the El Río del Tiempo boat ride is accessible to guests using wheelchairs, but those using a scooter or oversize chair must transfer to a Disney model.

ENTERTAINMENT During IllumiNations, certain areas along the lagoon's edge at Showcase Plaza, the United Kingdom, and Italy are reserved for guests using wheelchairs. Arrive at least 45 minutes before showtime to stake out a spot.

RESTAURANTS & SHOPS With a few exceptions, all are wheelchair accessible. In both the Garden Grill and Living Seas' Coral Reef restaurant, only one level is wheelchair accessible.

WHEELCHAIR RENTALS Wheelchairs are available inside the Entrance Plaza on the left, to the right of the ticket booths at the Gift Stop, and at World Showcase's International Gateway. Standard models are available ($7; $1 deposit); you can also rent an electric scooter ($30; $10 deposit).

ENTERTAINMENT

Some of the most enjoyable entertainment takes place outside the pavilions and along the promenade. Live shows with actors, dancers, singers, mime routines, and demonstrations of folk arts and crafts are presented at varying times of day; get times in your Epcot Guide Map or at the WorldKey terminals at Guest Relations and Germany. Or look for signs posted at the pavilions. The enigmatic **Imaginum** (Living Statues) of France, the United Kingdom's **British Invasion,** Morocco's **MoRockin',** and China's incredible **Dragon Legend Acrobats** keep audiences coming back.

A group that calls itself the **JAMMitors** plays up a storm several days during the week (check Epcot entertainment schedule) at various Future World locations, using the tools of the janitorial trade—garbage cans, wastebaskets, brooms, mops, and dustpans. If you hear drumming from the vicinity of Japan, scurry on over to watch the traditional Japanese **Matsuriza** Taiko drummers in action.

FIRST AID

The park's First Aid Center, staffed by registered nurses, is in the Odyssey Center in Future World.

GETTING AROUND

It's a big place; a local joke suggests that Epcot is an acronym for "Every Person Comes Out Tired." But still, the most efficient way to get around is to walk. Just to vary things, you can cruise across the lagoon in one of the air-conditioned, 65-ft water taxis that depart every 12 minutes from World Showcase Plaza at the border of Future World. There are two docks: boats from the one on the left zip to the Germany pavilion, from the right to Morocco. You may have to stand in line for your turn to board, however.

If you think the huge distances involved may be a problem, start out by renting a stroller or wheelchair.

GUIDED TOURS

Reserve up to six weeks in advance for a behind-the-scenes tour, led by a knowledgeable Disney cast member. Don't forget to ask about tour discounts; some companies, such as American Express, may offer them. Several tours give close-up views of the phenomenal detail involved in the planning and maintenance of Epcot. All tours are open only to those 16 years of age and over (proof of age is required).

The newest tour is **The UnDISCOVERed Future World** ($49, plus park admission), which leaves at 9 AM Monday, Tuesday, Friday, and Saturday from the Guest Relations lobby just inside Epcot's main entrance. The four-hour behind-the-scenes walking tour covers all Future World pavilions, heading to corporate VIP lounges, the Epcot cast building, and the barge marina where Disney stores and maintains its IllumiNations show equipment. The three-hour **Hidden Treasures of World Showcase** ($59, plus park admission), beginning at 9 AM on Tuesday and Thursday, offers a look at the art, architecture, and traditions of the 11 nations represented. Take the three-hour **Gardens of the World Tour** ($59, plus park admission) to see the World Showcase's realistic replicas of exotic plantings up close and to get tips for adding landscape magic to your own garden. The tour runs on Tuesday and Thursday at 9 AM.

Behind the Seeds ($8 adults, $6 children ages 3–9, plus park admission) is a 60-minute guided tour of the greenhouses and aquacell areas in Future World's The Land pavilion. It covers the same topics as the Living with the Land boat ride but in much more detail—plus you have the chance to ask questions. Tours run every half hour from 11 to 4:30, and reservations are essential; they can be made on The Land's lower floor, in the corner opposite the boat ride entrance, behind the Green Thumb Emporium. This is a good activity for busy times of day.

If you want to get into the swim—and you have scuba open-water adult certification and can prove it—try Living Seas' **Epcot Divequest** ($140, park admission not required or included). Under the supervision of one of the Living Seas' master divers you can spend 2½ hours underwater in the mammoth aquarium. The tours take place daily at either 4:30 or 5:30. **Dolphins in Depth** ($150, neither park admission nor diving certification required) is an experience that encourages interaction with your favorite water friends. Tour officials meet you at the entrance at 9, where you'll be escorted to the Living Seas pavilion. Tours run Monday through Friday and last about 3½ hours; you'll still need to pay park admission if you want to remain after the tour.

▮ **Guided Tours** ☎ 407/939-8687.

LOCKERS
Lockers ($5; $2 deposit) are to the west of Spaceship Earth, outside the Entrance Plaza, and in the Bus Information Center by the bus parking lot. If what you need to store won't fit into the larger lockers, go to Guest Relations in the Entrance Plaza or at Earth Station.

LOST THINGS & PEOPLE
If you're worried about your children getting lost, get name tags for them at either Guest Relations or the Baby Care Center. Instruct them to speak to someone with a Disney name tag if you become separated. And if you do, immediately report your loss to any cast member and try not to panic; the staff here is experienced at reuniting families, and there are lost-children logbooks at Earth Station and the Baby Care Center. Earth Station also has a computerized Message Center, where you can leave notes for your traveling companions in any of the parks. For the Lost & Found, go to the west edge of the Entrance Plaza. After one day, all items are sent to the Main Lost & Found office.

▮ **Epcot Lost & Found** ☎ 407/560-7500. **Main Lost & Found** ✉ Magic Kingdom, Transportation and Ticket Center ☎ 407/824-4245.

MONEY MATTERS
For cash and currency exchange, go to the Guest Relations window. There are ATMs to the left of the park's main entrance; at the Disney Vaca-

tion Club kiosk on the walkway between Future World and the World Showcase; and at the American Adventure pavilion near the rest rooms.

PACKAGE PICKUP

Ask shop clerks to forward any large purchase you make to Guest Relations in the Entrance Plaza so that you won't have to carry it around all day. Allow three hours.

SHOPPING

At World Showcase, shopping is part of the entertainment—you should focus on gifts and souvenirs that might be hard to find in a typical boutique or department store. Some of the hottest items these days are the commemorative pins available throughout the park, especially in front of Spaceship Earth, at $6.50–$12.50 per pin. Disneyphiles love to collect and trade these special keepsakes: trading on the Internet has netted some collectors 10 times the original pin cost or more.

Some of the more exotic items to consider: nutcrackers at **Die Weinachts Ecke,** in Germany; Italian handbags, accessories, and collectibles at **Il Bel Cristallo,** in Italy; Guerlain perfume and cosmetics at **La Signature,** in France; English garden goods, including pots and potpourri, from the United Kingdom's **Magic of Wales;** kimonoed dolls at **Mitsukoshi,** in Japan; piñatas at **Plaza de los Amigos,** in Mexico; exotic clothing and jewelry at Morocco's **Tangier Traders;** and antiques and other collectibles at **Yong Feng Shangdian,** in China.

If your shopping time is limited, check out the two shops at the entrance to World Showcase. **Disney Traders** sells Disney-character dolls dressed in various national costumes as well as the requisite T-shirts and sweatshirts. Also sold here—and at some scattered kiosks throughout the park—is a great keepsake for youngsters: a World Showcase Passport ($9.95). At each pavilion, children can present their passports to be stamped—it's a great way to keep their interest up in this more adult area of Epcot. At **Port of Entry,** you'll find lots of merchandise for kids, including clothing and art kits.

Future World shopping won't tempt you to spend a lot of money unless you're heavily into the art of Disney animation. For the serious collector, the **Art of Disney** sells limited-edition figurines and cels (the sheets of celluloid on which cartoons are drawn). **Green Thumb Emporium,** a rare bright spot for acquisitive spirits in The Land pavilion, sells all sorts of kitchen- and garden-related knickknacks—from hydroponic plants to vegetable refrigerator magnets. If you want more standard Epcot-logo souvenirs, check out **Mouse Gear,** where you'll find more than 19,000 square ft of merchandise. You can pick up fitness gear, including sweats emblazoned with Disney characters exercising, at **Well & Goods Limited,** in the Wonders of Life. And at the **Test Track Shop,** near the attraction exit, model cars and racing merchandise abounds.

VISITOR INFORMATION

Guest Relations, in Innoventions East and at the park's main entrance, is the place to pick up schedules of live entertainment, park brochures, maps, and the like. Map racks are also at the park's International Gateway entrance between the U.K. and France pavilions, and most shops keep a stack handy. The **WDW Dine Telephones**—in the Guest Relations lobby at Innoventions East—can come in handy. Using the interactive kiosks, you can obtain detailed information about every pavilion, leave messages for companions, and get answers to almost all of your questions. International visitors also can pick up a map in French, German, Portuguese, Spanish, or Japanese.

DISNEY–MGM STUDIOS

When Walt Disney Company chairman Michael Eisner opened Disney–MGM Studios in May 1989, he welcomed attendees to "the Hollywood that never was and always will be." Attending the lavish, Hollywood-style opening were celebrities that included Bette Midler, Warren Beatty, and other Tinseltown icons. Unlike the first movie theme park— Universal Studios in southern California—Disney–MGM Studios combined Disney detail with MGM's motion-picture legacy and Walt Disney's own animated film classics. The park was designed to be a trip back in time to Hollywood's heyday, when Hedda Hopper, not tabloids, spread celebrity gossip and when the girl off the bus from Ohio could be the next Judy Garland. The result blends a theme park with fully functioning movie and television production capabilities, breathtaking rides with insightful tours, and nostalgia with high-tech wonders.

The rosy-hue view of the moviemaking business takes place in a dreamy stage set from the 1930s and '40s, amid sleek art moderne buildings in pastel colors, funky diners, kitschy decorations, and sculptured gardens populated by roving actors playing, well, roving actors, as well as casting directors, gossip columnists, and other colorful characters. Thanks to a rich library of film scores, the park is permeated with music, all familiar, all uplifting, all evoking the magic of the movies, and all constantly streaming from the camouflaged loudspeakers at a volume just right for humming along. The park icon, a 122-ft-high Sorcerer Mickey Hat, towers over Hollywood Boulevard. Unfortunately, the whimsical landmark blocks the view of the park's Chinese Theater, a more nostalgic introduction to old-time Hollywood. Watching over all from the park's backlot is the Earfful Tower, a 13-story water tower adorned with giant mouse ears.

Although most of the attractions are a draw for all ages, the park is really best for teenagers eager to experience the park's newest thrill rides and old enough to watch old movies on television and catch the cinematic references. Not quite as fantasy-oriented as the Magic Kingdom or as earnestly educational as Epcot, the Studios could almost be said to have attitude—not a lot, mind you, but enough to add a little sizzle to the steak.

The park is divided into sightseeing clusters. Hollywood Boulevard is the main artery to the heart of the park: the glistening red-and-gold, multiturreted replica of Graumann's Chinese Theater, now behind the mammoth Sorcerer Mickey Hat. Encircling it in a roughly counterclockwise fashion are Sunset Boulevard, where you'll find the Twilight Zone Tower of Terror, the amphitheater in which Fantasmic! is staged every night, and the Rock 'n' Roller Coaster; the Animation Courtyard, which houses the Magic of Disney Animation and *Voyage of the Little Mermaid*; Mickey Avenue, where you'll find *Who Wants to Be a Millionaire*—Play It! and the Studios Backlot Tour; the New York Street area, with Jim Henson's Muppet*Vision 3-D, *Honey, I Shrunk the Kids* Movie Set Adventure playground, and the Backlot Theater; and Echo Lake, which contains the Indiana Jones Epic Stunt Spectacular!, Star Tours, and Sounds Dangerous Starring Drew Carey.

The entire park is small enough—about 154 acres, and with only about 20 major attractions, as opposed to the more than 40 in the Magic Kingdom—that you should be able to cover it in a day. On nonpeak days, you might even be able to repeat a favorite ride. And even when the lines seem to stretch clear to Epcot, a little careful planning will allow you to see everything on one ticket.

Numbers in the margin correspond to points of interest on the Disney–MGM Studios map.

Hollywood Boulevard

With its palm trees, pastel buildings, and flashy neon, Hollywood Boulevard paints a rosy picture of Tinseltown in the 1930s. There's a sense of having walked right onto a movie set in the olden days, what with the art deco storefronts, strolling brass bands, and roving starlets and nefarious agents—actually costumed actors. These are frequently joined by characters from Disney movies new and old, who pose for pictures and sign autographs. *Beauty and the Beast*'s Belle is a favorite, as are Jafar, Princess Jasmine, and the Genie from *Aladdin,* the soldiers from *Toy Story,* and Esmeralda from *The Hunchback of Notre Dame.*

Hollywood Boulevard, like Main Street, has souvenir shops and memorabilia collections galore. Oscar's Classic Car Souvenirs & Super Service is crammed with fuel-pump bubble-gum machines, photos of antique cars, and other automotive knickknacks. At Sid Cahuenga's One-of-a-Kind antiques and curios store, you might find and acquire Meg Ryan's castoffs, Cher's vintage jewelry, or at least autographed stars' photos. Down the street at Cover Story, don the appropriate costume and have your picture put on the cover of a major magazine. At the end of the street, at the corner of Sunset Boulevard, you'll find loads of child-size character clothing at L.A. Prop Cinema Storage. Many will also appreciate this shop's collection of old Mickey Mouse Club black-and-white production stills.

> **need a break?** For a sweet burst of energy, snag a freshly baked chocolate-chip cookie, slice of pie, or even a sugar-free snack at **Starring Rolls Bakery,** near the Brown Derby. Or, if you're around for breakfast, try a croissant, turnover, or almost-authentic bagel.

❶ Great Movie Ride. At the end of Hollywood Boulevard just behind the Sorcerer Mickey Hat icon are the fire-engine-red pagodas of a replica of Graumann's Chinese Theater, which houses this attraction. Outside the theater are the concrete handprints and footprints of such stars as Bob Hope, Liza Minnelli, and Sally Field. What awaits inside is worthy of its elaborate exterior—the Imagineers pull out all the stops on this tour of great moments in film.

The lobby, really an ingenious way to spend time standing in line, slots you past such noteworthy artifacts as Dorothy's ruby slippers from *The Wizard of Oz,* a carousel horse from *Mary Poppins,* and the piano played by Sam in *Casablanca.* You then shuffle into the preshow area, an enormous screening room with continuously running clips from *Mary Poppins, Raiders of the Lost Ark, Singin' in the Rain, Fantasia, Footlight Parade,* and, of course, *Casablanca.* The line continues snaking through the preshow, which itself is so much fun that you almost regret missing favorite clips once the great red doors swing open and it's your turn to ride.

Disney cast members dressed in 1920s newsboy costumes usher you onto open trams waiting against the backdrop of the Hollywood Hills, and you're off on a tour of cinematic climaxes—with a little help from Audio-Animatronics, scrim, smoke, and Disney magic. First comes the world of musical entertainment with, among others, Gene Kelly clutching that immortal lamppost as he begins "Singin' in the Rain" and Mary Poppins with her umbrella and her sooty admirers reprising "Chim-Chim-Cher-ee." Soon, your car moves past amazing moving likenesses of James Cagney and John Wayne. The lights dim, and your

Best of the Park

Arrive well before the park opens. When it does, run, don't walk, right up Hollywood Boulevard, hang a right at Sunset Boulevard, and dash to the 13-story **Twilight Zone Tower of Terror.** You can make a FASTPASS appointment here. Next, head back to the Chinese Theater for the **Great Movie Ride.** It'll put you in the mood for a day at Disney–MGM like nothing else—and help you brush up on the songs pouring out of the hidden speakers. Return with your FASTPASS to ride Tower of Terror. Pick up your next FASTPASS now, this time for **Rock 'n' Roller Coaster Starring Aerosmith.** While you wait for your scheduled time, catch **Walt Disney: One Man's Dream** or, if you have small children, **Playhouse Disney—Live on Stage!** The **Disney–MGM Studios Backlot Tour** is another great option.

Grab a bite of early lunch at the **Sci-Fi Dine-In Theater,** where you can sit in a 1950s-era convertible and watch B-movie film clips. Then take in the **Magic of Disney Animation** before returning for your FASTPASS appointment at Rock 'n' Roller Coaster. Now, head over to either **Who Wants to Be a Millionaire—Play It!,** or the **Indiana Jones Epic Stunt Spectacular!** pavilion and grab another FASTPASS appointment. Then line up for **Sounds Dangerous Starring Drew Carey** or catch up with the **Disney–MGM Studios Backlot Tour** if you ran out of time before lunch. By now the time should have approached for your turn at Millionaire or Indiana Jones. If there's time to catch the **Disney Stars and Motor Cars** parade, it's worth a watch.

Afterward, dash over to **Star Tours,** where you should take a FASTPASS timed ticket unless the line is very short. Then turn the corner to **Jim Henson's Muppet*Vision 3-D.** If you can't see a line, nip in now. Or let the kids scramble around **Honey, I Shrunk the Kids Movie Set Adventure.**

Keep your Star Tours appointment, and then explore Sunset Boulevard, where the shops sell much of the same merchandise as those on Hollywood Boulevard but are less crowded. Grab a snack at the Anaheim Produce Company, and try to catch a late performance of **Beauty and the Beast—Live on Stage!** Finally, line up for a grand finale to cap the night with fireworks, lasers, fountains, and the cast of popular Disney characters—**Fantasmic!** Remember to turn at the gate for one last look at the Earfful Tower, its perky appendages outlined in gold lights.

On Rainy Days

If you must go on a rainy day, plan your day around the indoor attractions and utilize FASTPASS at the seven attractions at which it's available. Schedule ahead to enjoy a relaxing lunch at the Hollywood Brown Derby or a zany time in the '50s Prime Time Cafe, where a great cast of servers will help you forget all about the weather.

---

vehicle travels into either a gangland shoot-out with James Cagney snarling in *Public Enemy* or a western showdown in which a Disney-cast "Calamity Jane" tries to rob the Miners' and Cattlemen's Bank and hijack the tram. In both scenarios, the bad guys make off with your coach, and the adventure continues.

Nothing like a little time warp to bring justice. With pipes streaming fog and alarms whooping, the tram meets some of the slimier characters in *Alien*—look up for truly scary stuff—and then eases into the cobwebby, snake-ridden set of *Indiana Jones and the Temple of Doom,* where your hijacker attempts to steal an idol and gets his or her just desserts.

Each time you think you've witnessed the best scene, the tram moves into another set: Tarzan yodels and swings on a vine overhead; then Bogey toasts Bergman in front of the plane to Lisbon. The finale has hundreds of robotic Munchkins cheerily enjoining you to "Follow the Yellow Brick Road," despite the cackling imprecations by the Wicked Witch of the West, an Audio-Animatronics character so sophisticated you'll wonder if she's a live actor. Remember to check out Dorothy's tornado-tossed house—those on the right side of the tram can just spot the ruby slippers. The tram follows the Yellow Brick Road, and then there it is: Emerald City.

As icing on the cake, there's one more movie presentation with three screens all going at once to display yet more memorable moments, including great kisses ranging from Rhett Butler and Scarlett O'Hara's embrace to Roger and Jessica Rabbit's animated smooch. Then the lights come up, and the announcer calls you for the final scene: Exit Audience. ☞ *Duration: 22 mins. Crowds: Steady and large all day long; when the inside lines start spilling out the door, expect at least a 25-min wait. Strategy: Go first thing in the morning or at the end of the day. If the lines still look long, ask about the line's length before you slink away discouraged—Disney staffers often "stack" people up outside to clear up the crowds inside and to prepare for closing. Audience: All but young children, for whom it may be too intense. Rating:* ★★★

Disney Stars and Motor Cars. Disney–MGM Studios' glitzy daytime parade wends its way up Hollywood Boulevard in true Tinseltown style with a motorcade of characters from the park's many attractions and Disney's many films perched and draped across customized classic cars. Animated stars include Mickey Mouse, Minnie Mouse, Ariel, Mulan, Woody, Buzz Lightyear, and other Disney film celebrities. Also on view are Kermit and Miss Piggy, Luke Skywalker, and even the huggable Bear from the Big Blue House. ☞ *Duration: 20 mins. Crowds: Moderately heavy. Strategy: Find your piece of pavement at least 20 minutes before the parade begins. Audience: All ages. Rating:* ★★

Sunset Boulevard

This avenue pays tribute to famous Hollywood monuments, with facades derived from the Cathay Circle, the Beverly Wilshire Theatre, and other City of Angels landmarks.

As you turn onto Sunset Boulevard from Hollywood Boulevard, you'll run smack into Hollywood Junction Station, where reservations can be made for restaurants throughout the park. The nearby Legends of Hollywood brims with books, videos, and posters of classic films, and Once Upon a Time displays vintage character toys and sells assorted gift items, including housewares.

❷ *Beauty and the Beast*—Live on Stage! This wildly popular stage show takes place at the Theater of the Stars, a re-creation of the famed Hollywood Bowl. The long-running production is a lively, colorful, and well-done condensation of the animated film. As you arrive or depart, it's fun to check out handprints and footprints set in concrete of the television celebrities who've visited Disney–MGM Studios. ☞ *Duration: 30 mins. Crowds: Almost always. Strategy: Queue up at least 30 mins prior to*

When to Go

As at Epcot, it's best to go to Disney–MGM Studios early in the week, while most other people are rushing through Disney's Animal Kingdom and the Magic Kingdom.

Plan to arrive in the parking lot 30 minutes ahead of opening, so you can get to the entrance 15 minutes ahead.

When You're There

Pick up an entertainment map on your way into the park, and be sure to note where to meet the Disney characters if you have children in tow.

If you're interested in booking a Fantasmic! dinner package, check in at Guest Relations as soon as you enter the park.

Check the map for the occasional TV and film celebrity visitors, and plan your day around the celebrity motorcade if it's a star you don't want to miss.

Set up a rendezvous point and time at the start of the day, just in case you and your companions get separated. Three excellent spots are by the giant Sorcerer Mickey Hat icon in front of the Great Movie Ride, at the statue of Miss Piggy near the Muppets attraction, and on Mickey Avenue by the large Coke can that sprays water.

---

show time for good seats, especially with children. Performance days vary, so check ahead. Audience: All ages. Rating: ★★★

need a break? Grab lunch or a quick snack at one of the food stands along Sunset Boulevard. You can get a burger or hot dog at **Rosie's All-American Cafe,** a slice of pizza from **Catalina Eddie's,** or a fruit salad from the **Anaheim Produce Company.**

❸ Twilight Zone Tower of Terror. Ominously overlooking Sunset Boulevard is a 13-story structure that was once the Hollywood Tower Hotel, now deserted. You take an eerie stroll through an overrun, mist-enshrouded garden and then into the dimly lighted lobby. In the dust-covered library a bolt of lightning suddenly zaps a television set to life. Rod Serling appears, recounting the story of the hotel's demise and inviting you to enter the Twilight Zone. Then, it's onward to the boiler room, where you climb aboard the hotel's giant elevator ride. As you head upward past seemingly empty hallways, ghostly former residents appear in front of you. The Fifth Dimension awaits, where you travel forward past recognizable scenes from the popular TV series. Suddenly—faster than you can say "Where's Rod Serling?"—the creaking vehicle plunges downward in a terrifying, 130-ft free-fall drop and then, before you can catch your breath, shoots quickly up, down, up, and down all over again. No use trying to guess how many stomach-churning ups and downs you'll experience—Disney's ride engineers have upped the ride's fright factor by programming random drop variations into the attraction. It's a different thrill every time. As you recover from your final plunge, Serling warns, "The next time you check into a deserted hotel on the dark side of Hollywood, make sure you know what vacancy you'll be filling, or you'll

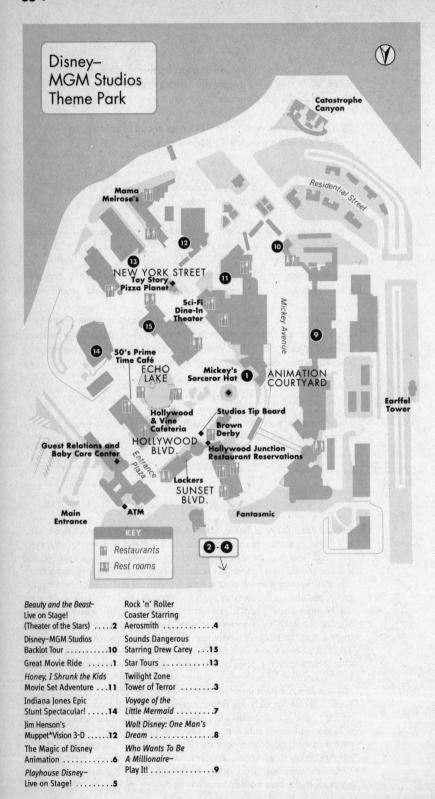

Disney–MGM Studios Theme Park

Catastrophe Canyon

Residential Street

Mama Melrose's

12

13 NEW YORK STREET
Toy Story Pizza Planet

10

11

Sci-Fi Dine-In Theater

15

Mickey Avenue

9

14 50's Prime Time Café

ECHO LAKE

Mickey's Sorceror Hat **1**

ANIMATION COURTYARD

Hollywood & Vine Cafeteria

Studios Tip Board

Brown Derby

HOLLYWOOD BLVD.

Hollywood Junction Restaurant Reservations

Guest Relations and Baby Care Center

Entrance Plaza

Lockers

SUNSET BLVD.

Earffel Tower

Main Entrance

ATM

Fantasmic

KEY
- Restaurants
- Rest rooms

2 · 4

be a permanent member of . . . the Twilight Zone!" ☞ *Duration: 10 mins. Crowds: Yes! Strategy: Get a FASTPASS reserved-time ticket. Otherwise, go early or wait until evening, when the crowds thin out. Audience: Older children and adults. No pregnant women or guests with heart, back, or neck problems. Minimum height: 40". Rating:* ★★★

4 **Rock 'n' Roller Coaster Starring Aerosmith.** Although this is an indoor roller
Fodor\$Choice coaster like Space Mountain in the Magic Kingdom, the similarity ends there. With its high-speed launch, multiple inversions, and loud rock music, it generates delighted screams from coaster junkies. The vehicles look like limos, and the track resembles the neck of an electric guitar that's been twisted; a hard-driving rock sound track by Aerosmith blasts from speakers mounted in each vehicle to accentuate the flips and turns. There's rock-and-roll memorabilia in the queue area, and Aerosmith stars in the preshow film. ☞ *Crowds: Huge. Strategy: Go early in the day. This is a definite FASTPASS candidate. Pick up your ticket first thing in the morning, and then head over to do the animation tour. Audience: Older children, teens, and adults. No guests with heart, back, or neck problems or motion sickness. Minimum height: 44". Rating:* ★★★

Fodor\$Choice **Fantasmic!** The Studios' after-dark show wows audiences of thousands with its 25 minutes of special effects and Disney characters. The omnipresent Mickey, in his Sorcerer's Apprentice costume, plays the embodiment of Good in the struggle against forces of Evil, personified by Disney villains and villainesses such as Cruella DeVil, Scar, and Maleficent. In some of the show's best moments, animated clips of images of these famous bad guys alternate with clips of Disney nice guys (and dolls), projected onto screens made of water—high-tech fountains surging high in the air. Disney being Disney, it's Good that emerges triumphant, amid a veritable tidal wave of water effects and flames, explosions, and fireworks worthy of a Stallone shoot-'em-up. The effects are so good that it's too bad the story doesn't rise to the same high level. If you don't think this will bother you, show up at the 6,500-seat Hollywood Hills Amphitheatre opposite the Twilight Zone Tower of Terror. Curtain time varies seasonally. Be sure to arrive up to an hour before start time (earlier is better); if this conflicts with your dinnertime, pick up fast food and bring it into the amphitheater. Where to sit? You get a better sense of the whole show if you're not too close, and you'll be able to exit most quickly if you take a seat near where you come in—the single way in is also the single nonemergency exit, and leaving the amphitheater is unbelievably tedious if you're on the left as you face the stage or up front. Besides, if you sit near the lagoon, spray from the fountains leaves droplets all over your glasses, if you wear them, and gives you a drenching that's not exactly pleasant when it's chilly. ☞ *Duration: 25 mins. Crowds: Heavy. Strategy: Arrive at least one hour early and sit toward the rear, near the entrance/exit. Audience: All ages. Rating:* ★★★

Animation Courtyard

As you exit Sunset Boulevard, veer right through the high-arched gateway to the Animation Courtyard. You're now at one end of Mickey Avenue, and straight ahead are the Magic of Disney Animation and *Voyage of the Little Mermaid*. At the far end of the avenue is the popular Disney–MGM Studios Backlot Tour.

5 *Playhouse Disney—Live on Stage!* The former Soundstage Restaurant now holds one of the best Walt Disney World shows for children. *Playhouse Disney—Live on Stage!* uses a perky host on a larger-than-life "storybook stage" to present stars of several popular Disney Channel shows. Preschoolers and even toddlers can sing and dance in the aisles as Bear

CloseUp

THE BIRTH OF WALT DISNEY WORLD

IT'D BE A GREAT QUESTION for Regis to ask: Florida was founded by (a) Juan Ponce de León, (b) Millard Fillmore, (c) Sonny Bono, or (d) Walt Disney. For travelers who can't fathom Florida without Walt Disney World, the final answer is "d"—in Central Florida at least. The theme park's arrival spawned a multibillion-dollar tourism industry that begat a population boom that begat new roads, malls, and schools that begat a whole new culture.

So how did it happen? Why did Walt pin his hopes on forlorn Florida ranchlands 3,000 mi from Disneyland? In the 1950s, Walt barely had enough money to open his theme park in California, and lacking the funds to buy a buffer zone, he couldn't prevent cheap hotels and tourist traps from setting up shop next door. This time he wanted land. And lots of it. Beginning in the early 1960s, Walt embarked on a supersecret four-year project: he traveled the nation in search of a location with access to a major population center, good highways, a steady climate, and, most important, cheap and abundant land. Locations were narrowed down, and in the end Orlando was it.

In May 1965, major land transactions were being recorded a few miles southwest of Orlando. By late June, the Orlando Sentinel reported that more than 27,000 acres had been sold so far. In October, the paper revealed that Walt was the mastermind behind the purchases. Walt and his brother Roy hastily arranged a press conference. Once Walt described the $400 million project and the few thousand jobs it would create, Florida's government quickly gave him permission to establish the autonomous Reedy Creek Improvement District. With this, he could write his own zoning restrictions and plan his own roads, bridges, hotels—even a residential community for his employees.

Walt played a hands-on role in the planning of Disney World, but just over a year a later, in December 1966, he died. As expected, his faithful brother, Roy, took control and spent the following five years supervising the construction of the Magic Kingdom. Fittingly, before the park opened on October 1, 1971, Roy

changed the name of his brother's park to "Walt" Disney World. Roy passed away three months after the park's opening, but by then WDW was hitting its stride. For the next decade, it became part of Florida's landscape. Families that once saw Orlando merely as a whistle-stop on the way to Miami now made their vacation base at WDW.

Behind the scenes, however, a few cracks began to appear in the facade. In its first decade, growth was stagnant. By 1982, when Epcot opened, construction cost overruns and low attendance created a 19% drop in profits. Meanwhile, the Disney Channel and Disney's film division were also sluggish. Eventually, in 1984, Michael Eisner came aboard as CEO and company chairman, along with Frank Wells as president and CFO. Their arrival got Disney out of the doldrums. Disney's unparalleled film catalog was brought out of storage with re-releases in theaters and on video. Jeffrey Katzenberg was put in charge of the Disney Studios, and with him came the release of "new classics" such as Aladdin, Beauty and the Beast, The Little Mermaid, and The Lion King.

In 1988 the Grand Floridian and Caribbean Beach resorts opened. The following year Disney–MGM Studios opened along with Typhoon Lagoon and Pleasure Island. Five resort hotels opened in the early 1990s. By 1997 Blizzard Beach, Disney's Wide World of Sports, and Downtown Disney West Side had opened; and by 1998 Disney's Animal Kingdom had come to life. Also arriving in this decade of growth were the planned community of Celebration, the Disney cruise lines, the book-publishing arm of Hyperion, and the purchase of Miramax Films and ABC television.

Walt Disney World continues to change and grow in the 21st century, constantly developing new attractions, such as Mickey's PhilharMagic and Mission: SPACE.

And it all started with a man who didn't have the cash to buy a little more land in Anaheim.

—Gary McKechnie

in the Big Blue House, Rolie Polie Olie, Pooh, and Stanley cha-cha-cha their way through positive life lessons. Who knew that personal grooming tips could be so much fun? ☞ *Duration: 25 mins. Crowds: Not a problem, but lines tend to be heavy in midafternoon. Strategy: Go first thing in the morning, when your child is most alert. Audience: Toddlers, preschoolers. Rating:* ★★★

⑥ The Magic of Disney Animation. This self-guided tour through the Disney animation process is one of the park's funniest and most engaging attractions. More than any other backstage tour, more than any other revelation of stunt secrets, this tour truly takes you inside the magic as you follow the many steps of animation. The animation studio is a satellite of Walt Disney's original California studio, and Disney's *Mulan* was produced here in its entirety, as were several Disney short films and portions of other popular Disney feature-length films.

Although you can move at your own pace, the staff tries to keep crowds to a minimum, so groups assemble in the lobby. Take the opportunity to check out the collection of drawings and cels, the clear celluloid sheets on which the characters were drawn for *Snow White, Fantasia,* and other Disney classics. Here, too, are the Academy Awards that Disney has won for its animated films.

From the lobby in the Animation Courtyard, you segue into the Disney Animation Theater for a hilarious eight-minute animated film in which Walter Cronkite and Robin Williams explain animation basics. It's a *Peter Pan* "sequel" called *Back to Neverland,* with Walter Cronkite as himself and his comic costar as a Lost Boy. The film was almost impossible to complete because the steadfast, avuncular Cronkite kept cracking up. (You might, too, if you suddenly discovered Tinkerbell in your jacket pocket.) Robin Williams discovers the potential range of animation: "Hey," he proclaims as he's redrawn into a familiar rodent, "I can be a corporate symbol!" Meanwhile, you learn about cel-making, layout artists, background artists, cleanup artists, sound effects, and more. You also get to meet an animation artist who explains these animation processes and answers any questions. From the theater, you follow walkways with windows overlooking the working animation studios, where you see Disney artists at their drafting tables doing everything you just learned about. Their desks are strewn with finished drawings of Simba, Scar, Aladdin, Genie, and other famous characters, and you can peer over their shoulders at soon-to-be-famous characters.

Meanwhile, Robin and Walter continue their banter on overhead monitors, explaining the processes as you saunter from the story room (where animators develop story lines), to the drawing boards (where ideas are transformed from sketch to colorful characters), to the cleanup room, the special effects area, and the special camera that transfers drawings to cels. To produce one 24-minute film, the 70-plus members of the animation team must create 34,650 drawings and add scenes from at least 300 background paintings. You also see animators working at computers, where they've made great strides in the last decade, animating complex scenes such as the wildebeest stampede in *The Lion King.*

The penultimate attraction on the tour is a continuously running video. "You believe the character *is* alive," confesses one of the animators who, as actors often do, identifies with his characters enough to take on their personalities. Watching a low-key, pleasant man become the evil Scar from *The Lion King* right before your eyes makes you wonder if pixie dust really is in the air.

Upon completion of the tour there's a valedictory quip from Robin Williams, and you head into the Disney Classics Theater for a presentation of the best moments from animated films. It's fascinating to see the evolution of the art from the bright colors and straightforward drawings in *Snow White* and *Pinocchio* to the rainbow hues and complex panoramas of *Beauty and the Beast, Aladdin, The Lion King, Pocahontas,* and *Tarzan*. Best of all, you know that here the characters will always live happily ever after. ☞ *Duration: Usually around 40 mins. Crowds: Steady all day. Strategy: Go in the morning or late afternoon, when you can get in with less waiting and still see the animators at work (they get in at 9, have lunch around noon, leave by 6, and are not always around on weekends). The smallest crowds gather at around 5. Audience: All but young children. Rating:* ★★★

❼ Voyage of the Little Mermaid. A boxy building on Mickey Avenue invites you to join Ariel, Sebastian, and the underwater gang in this stage show, which condenses the movie into a marathon presentation of the greatest hits. In an admirable effort at verisimilitude, a fine mist sprays the stage; if you're sitting in the front rows, expect to get spritzed. ☞ *Duration: 15 mins. Crowds: Perpetual. Strategy: If you decide not to ride the Rock 'n' Roller Coaster, go first thing in the morning, putting the FASTPASS to good use. Otherwise, wait until the stroller brigade's exodus after 5. Audience: All ages. Rating:* ★★

❽ Walt Disney: One Man's Dream. Next door to the Mermaid show, *One Man's Dream* is a photo, film, and audio tour through Walt's life. You get to peek at his Project X room, where many of his successes were born, and hear him tell much of his own story on tapes never before made public. If you qualify as a baby boomer, it's a real nostalgia trip to see Walt resurrected on film as his "Wonderful World of Color" intro splashes across the screen. And if you're into artifacts, there's plenty of Walt memorabilia to view as you absorb the history of this entertainment legend. ☞ *Duration: 20 mins. Crowds: Heavy. Strategy: Get your FASTPASS appointment to see Who Wants to Be a Millionaire—Play It!, then see this attraction while waiting. Audience: Ages 10 and up. Rating:* ★★

Mickey Avenue

A stroll down this street and you'll pass the soundstages that are used to produce some of today's television shows and motion pictures. On your left, there are several souvenir kiosks, as well as periodic streetside opportunities to mingle with character stars such as Buzz Lightyear, Woody, and pals Jessie and Bullseye from *Toy Story 2*. Check character schedules to be sure they're appearing.

❾ Who Wants to Be a Millionaire—Play It! Disney's popular live stage show on Soundstages 2 and 3 seats 600, all of whom have their own fastest-finger buttons and a chance at the hot seat next to the show's celebrity "Regis." Contestants don't vie for $1 million, but they do build points to get a shot at some parting prizes. Even kids can make it to the hot seat in this clever replica of the TV game show. Question categories range from Disney trivia (The animated TV series *Disney's Aladdin* stars all but which of the following characters: a. Aladdin, b. Jasmine, c. Iago, or d. Tarzan?) to geography (Havana is the capital of what country?). Everyone in the audience gets to play along with the contestant and accumulates points toward a potential shot at the hot seat. Instead of phoning a friend, you can phone a complete stranger (a theme-park visitor called to the phone by a Disney cast member stationed at one of two phones in the park). Disney pins, caps, and other prizes are awarded at graduated point levels, and big winners may get a trip to a taping of the syndicated show. ☞ *Duration: 30 mins. Crowds: Heavy. Strategy: Use FASTPASS. Audience: Ages 5 and up. Rating:* ★★★

⑩ Disney–MGM Studios Backlot Tour. The first stop on this tour, which you enter at the far end of Mickey Avenue, is an outdoor special-effects water tank. Here, two willing, if unwary, audience members don bright yellow slickers to play the skipper of the ill-fated SS *Miss Fortune* and the submarine commander Captain Duck, about to pilot his craft into battle. As the audience watches, the skipper nearly gets drowned in a thunderstorm, and the doughty Duck gets strafed, torpedoed, and doused with 400 gallons of water from a depth charge while a video camera records the scenario and plays it back with music and background.

Then it's time to queue up for the tram ride for the backlot tour. As you walk through the line, you're also touring a huge prop warehouse, which stores everything you could possibly imagine, from chairs to traffic lights to newspaper stands.

Board the tram for a tour of the backlot building blocks of movies: set design, costumes, props, lighting, and a standout movie set—Catastrophe Canyon. The tram's announcer swears that the film that's supposedly shooting in there is taking a break. But the next thing you know, the tram is bouncing up and down in a simulated earthquake, an oil tanker explodes in a mass of smoke and flame, and a water tower crashes to the ground, touching off a flash flood, which douses the tanker and threatens to drown the tram. Although the earthquake is more like a shimmy, the water and fire provoke genuine screams. As the tram pulls out, you see the backstage workings of the catastrophe: the canyon is actually a mammoth steel slide wrapped in copper-color concrete, and the 70,000 gallons of flood water—enough to fill 10 Olympic-size swimming pools—are recycled 100 times a day, or every 3½ minutes.

Let your heartbeat slow down as the tram takes another pass through the Big Apple. This time you're close enough to see that brownstones, marble, brick, and stained glass are actually expertly painted two-dimensional facades of fiberglass and Styrofoam. Grips can slide the Empire State and Chrysler buildings out of the way anytime. Note the large airplane that Walt Disney used to scout out what would be his Florida theme-park property.

Hop off the tram and walk through the American Film Institute Showcase, a display of movie and television memorabilia of the past and present. ☞ *Duration: 60 mins. Crowds: Steady through the afternoon, but lines seem to move quickly. Strategy: As you enter the tram, remember that people sitting on the left get wet. Go early; it closes at dusk. Audience: All but young children, who probably will be scared in Catastrophe Canyon. Rating:* ★★★

New York Street

It's well worth touring the sets here on foot—as long as crews aren't filming—so that you can check out the windows of shops and apartments, the taxicabs, and other details.

⑪ *Honey, I Shrunk the Kids* Movie Set Adventure. Let your youngsters run free in this playground based on the movie, where there are scenes of Lilliputian kids in a larger-than-life world. They can slide down a gigantic blade of grass, crawl through caves, climb a mushroom mountain, inhale the scent of a humongous plant (which will then spit water back in their faces), and dodge sprinklers set in resilient flooring made of ground-up tires. All the requisite playground equipment is present: net climbs, ball crawls, caves, and slides. Because the area is enclosed, there's often a line to get in—but attraction hosts don't fudge on capacity limits, which maintains a comfort zone for those inside. ☞ *Duration: Up to you. Crowds: Steady. Strategy: Come after you've done several shows or attractions and your children need to cut loose. Audience: Children and those who love them. Rating:* ★★★

⑫ Jim Henson's Muppet*Vision 3-D. You don't have to be a Miss Piggyphile to get a kick out of this combination 3-D movie and musical revue, although all the Muppet characters make appearances, including Miss Piggy in roles that include the Statue of Liberty. In the waiting area, Muppet movie posters advertise the world's most glamorous porker in *Star Chores* and *To Have and Have More,* and Kermit the Frog in an Arnold Schwarzenegger parody, *Kürmit the Amphibian,* who's "so mean, he's green." When the theater was constructed, special effects were built into the walls; the 3-D effects are coordinated with other sensory stimulation so you're never sure what's coming off the screen and what's being shot out of vents in the ceiling and walls. ☞ *Duration: Clever 10-min preshow, 20-min show. Crowds: Steady from morning through late afternoon. Strategy: Take advantage of your FASTPASS perk unless you encounter a short line. And don't worry—there are no bad seats. Audience: All ages. Rating:* ★★★

Echo Lake

Segue from New York Street into Echo Lake, an idealized California. In the center is the cool, blue lake of the same name, an oasis fringed with trees and benches and ringed with landmarks: pink-and-aqua restaurants trimmed in chrome, presenting sassy waitresses and black-and-white television sets at the tables; the shipshape Min and Bill's Dockside Diner, which offers snacks; and Gertie, a dinosaur that dispenses ice cream, Disney souvenirs, and the occasional puff of smoke in true magic-dragon fashion. Look for Gertie's giant footprints in the sidewalk. (Gertie, by the way, was the first animated animal to show emotion—an inspiration to the pre-Mickey Walt.) Here, too, you'll find two of the park's biggest attractions, the Indiana Jones Epic Stunt Spectacular! and Star Tours, and on the north side of the pond is Sounds Dangerous Starring Drew Carey.

⑬ Star Tours. Although the flight-simulator technology used for this ride was long ago surpassed on other thrill rides, most notably Universal Studios's *Back to the Future . . . The Ride,* this adventure (inspired by the *Star Wars* films) is still a pretty good trip. "May the force be with you," says the attendant on duty, "'cause I won't be!" Piloted by *Star Wars* characters R2D2 and C-3PO, the 40-passenger *StarSpeeder* that you board is supposed to take off on a routine flight to the moon of Endor. But with R2D2 at the helm, things quickly go awry: you shoot into deep space, dodge giant ice crystals and comet debris, innocently bumble into an intergalactic battle, and attempt to avoid laser-blasting fighters as you whiz through the canyons of some planetary city before coming to a heart-pounding halt. ☞ *Duration: 5 mins. Crowds: Can be substantial but occasionally are light. Lines swell periodically when the Indiana Jones Epic Stunt Spectacular! lets out. Strategy: To make sure you'll walk right on, go shortly before closing or first thing in the morning. Otherwise cruise on with the help of a FASTPASS timed ticket. When you line up to enter the simulation chamber, keep to the far left to sit up front and closer to the screen for the most realistic sensations (the ride is rougher in back but the sensations of motion less exhilarating). Audience: Star*

Wars fans, children and adults. No pregnant women, children under 3, or guests with heart, back, neck, or motion sickness problems; children under 7 must be accompanied by an adult. Rating: ★★★

need a
break?

Sweet tooths should be sure to save room for some soft-serve Ice Cream of Extinction at **Gertie's**, the ice-cream bar and snack shop inside the big green dinosaur on the shore of Echo Lake. Gertie's also makes nondairy frozen slushies.

⑭ **Indiana Jones Epic Stunt Spectacular!** If you haven't seen this show for a while, it's time to have another look. Disney's techno-wizards have pumped up the action with lighting, sound, and other technical enhancements. The rousing theme music from the Indiana Jones movies promises thrills that are delivered in this great show featuring the stunt choreography of veteran coordinator Glenn Randall, whose credits include *Raiders of the Lost Ark, Indiana Jones and the Temple of Doom, E.T.,* and *Jewel of the Nile*. Presented in a 2,200-seat amphitheater, the show starts with a series of near-death encounters in an ancient Maya temple. Clad in his signature fedora, Indy slides down a rope from the ceiling, dodges spears that shoot up from the floor, avoids getting chopped by booby-trapped idols, and snags a forbidden gemstone, setting off a gigantic boulder that threatens to render him two-dimensional.

It's hard to top that opener, but Randall and his pals do just that with the help of 10 audience participants. "Okay, I need some rowdy people," the casting director calls. While the lucky few demonstrate their rowdiness, behind them the set crew casually wheels off the entire temple: two people roll the boulder like a giant beach ball and replace it with a Cairo street, circa 1940. Nasty Ninja-Nazi stuntmen roll out a mat and bounce around performing flips and throws in the background. This is one of those times when it's better to be in the audience.

The scene they're working up to takes place on a busy Cairo street, down which saunter Indy and his redoubtable girlfriend, Marian Ravenwood, portrayed by a Karen Allen look-alike. She is kidnapped and tossed in a truck while Indy fights his way free with bullwhip and gun, and bad guys tumble from every corner and cornice. Motorcycles buzz around; the street becomes a shambles; and, as a stunning climax, the truck carrying Marian flips and bursts into flame.

The show's actors do a great job of explaining the stunts. You see how they're set up, watch the stars practice them in slow motion, and learn how cameras are camouflaged behind imitation rocks for trick shots. Only one stunt remains a secret: how do Indy and Marian escape the explosion? That's what keeps 'em coming back. ☞ *Duration: 30 mins. Crowds: Large, but the theater's high capacity means that everyone who wants to get in usually does. You can utilize your FASTPASS option here and avoid a 30- to 45-min wait to get a seat and walk right on in. Strategy: Go at night, when the idols' eyes glow red. If you sit up front, you can feel the heat when Marian's truck catches fire. Audience: All but young children. Rating:* ★★★

⑮ **Sounds Dangerous Starring Drew Carey.** A multifaceted demonstration of the use of movie sound effects, this show uses many of the gadgets created by sound master Jimmy MacDonald, who became the voice of Mickey Mouse during the 1940s and invented some 20,000 sound effects during his 45 years at Walt Disney Studios. Most qualify as gizmos—a metal sheet that, when rattled, sounds like thunder; a box of sand for footsteps on gravel; and other noises made from nails, straw, mud, leather, and other ordinary components. The premise of the show is that you will help Drew Carey, who portrays an undercover cop, find out who smuggled the diamonds from the snow globe. Then you don head-phones to listen to the many sounds that go into the production of a movie or television show. Because the entire show takes place in the dark, it's extremely frightening for young children.

The Sounds Dangerous postshow is a treat consisting of hands-on ex-hibits called **SoundWorks.** There are buttons that go "boing" and knobs you push to alter your voice. Earie Encounters lets you imitate flying-saucer sounds from the 1956 film *Forbidden Planet.* At Movie Mimics you can try your chords at dubbing Mickey Mouse, Roger Rabbit, and other Disney heroes. ☞ *Duration: 30-min show; the rest is up to you. Crowds: Steady. Strategy: Arrive 15 mins before show time. Audience: All but young, easily frightened children. Rating:* ★★

Disney–MGM Studios A to Z

To research prices, get advice from other travelers, and book travel ar-rangements, visit www.fodors.com.

BABY CARE

At the small **Baby Care Center,** you'll find facilities for nursing as well as formula, baby food, pacifiers, and disposable diapers for sale. There are changing tables here and in all women's rooms and some men's rooms. You can also buy disposable diapers in the Guest Relations building. **Oscar's,** just inside the entrance turnstiles and to the right, is the place for stroller rentals ($7 single, $14 double; plus $1 deposit).

CAMERAS & FILM

Walk through the aperture-shape door of the **Darkroom** on Hollywood Boulevard, where you can buy film and disposable cameras and get minor camera repairs. This is also the place to pick up pictures you want quickly. You can drop your film off here for one-hour developing or at any Photo Express container for two-hour developing. If you're stay-ing on-site, you can even have the pictures delivered to your hotel. Have your picture taken in front of the Chinese Theater, or with Mickey Mouse on Sunset Boulevard near the Brown Derby as an extra-special memento ($16.95 for an 8″×10″ photo).

DINING

FULL-SERVICE This park's full-service restaurants are so much fun that the magic con-
RESTAURANTS tinues—once you're inside, that is. Unfortunately, many diners never seem to want to leave their tables; after all, would you if you could watch television monitors airing '50s sitcoms while you chow down on veal-and-shiitake-mushroom meat loaf? Waits can be long.

To make priority seating reservations, call up to 60 days in advance, or stop in person at the restaurant or first thing in the morning at Holly-wood Junction Restaurant Reservations, just to the right of the Studios Tip Board, at the intersection of Hollywood and Sunset boulevards. There are three ways to book dinner packages that include the Fantasmic! after-dark show: in person at a Disney hotel, at the park's Guest Relations, and at Hollywood Junction.

With its staff in black tie and its airy, palm-fronded room positively ex-uding Hollywood glamour, the spacious **Brown Derby** is one of the nicest—and most expensive—places to eat in the park. The Cobb salad, salad greens enlivened by loads of tomato, bacon, turkey, egg, blue cheese, and avocado, was invented at the restaurant's Hollywood namesake. The dish is alive and well here, as you can see from the numerous or-ders being tossed table-side. The wine list is excellent, and you can count on creative chef specials. The butter comes in molds shaped like Mickey Mouse heads. If you request the Fantasmic! dinner package and make a reservation for no later than two hours before the start of the show, you can get priority seating for this big performance.

Spend a leisurely lunch at the **'50s Prime Time Café,** where video screens constantly show sitcoms, place mats pose television trivia quizzes, and waitresses play "Mom" with convincing enthusiasm, insisting that you clean your plate. The menu is what your own mom might have made were she a character on one of those video screens—meat loaf, broiled chicken, pot roast, hot roast beef sandwiches—all to be washed down with root beer floats and ice cream sodas. Don't go to Star Tours immediately afterward—the time warp has been known to be too much to endure after such a large meal.

To replace the energy you've no doubt depleted by miles of theme-park walking, you can load up on carbs at **Mama Melrose's Ristorante Italiano.** The menu has pasta, seafood, pizza baked in brick ovens, and several vegetarian entrées, including eggplant Parmesan. Ask for the Fantasmic! dinner package if you want priority seating for the show.

If you don't mind zombies leering at you while you slurp up chef salads, barbecue pork sandwiches, charbroiled sirloin, and Milky-Way-Out Milk Shakes, then head to **Sci-Fi Dine-In Theater,** a re-creation of a drive-in. All the tables are contained within candy-color '50s convertibles and face a large screen, on which a 45-minute reel of the best and worst of science-fiction trailers plays in a continuous loop. Only here would popcorn be considered an appropriate appetizer.

🎫 **Disney Reservation Center** ☎ 407/939–3463.

SELF-SERVICE RESTAURANTS The **ABC Commissary** has a refreshingly different fast-food menu that includes tabbouleh wraps, beef fajitas, and fish-and-chips. At the **Backlot Express,** in Echo Lake, you don't need a reservation to chow down on the burgers, fajitas, huge sandwiches, and chef salads.

A buffet of rotisserie meats and poultry, salads, seafood, and fresh pasta makes up the lunch fare at **Hollywood & Vine Cafeteria of the Stars.** Minnie, Goofy, Pluto, and Chip 'n' Dale put in appearances at breakfast and lunch character meals, where eggs, pancakes, French toast, and fritattas build energy for theme-park blitzing. There's a Hollywood theme to the place; characters and servers are just hoping to be discovered by some passing Hollywood screen agent, and the place is a real charmer—totally '50s and vaguely deco. In Echo Lake, **Min & Bill's Dockside Diner** is the spot for a dessert waffle or specialty shake. Step right up to the counter. The **Studio Catering Company,** near the Disney–MGM Studios Backlot Tour exit, can provide you with soft-serve ice cream treats before the next tour.

Toy Story Pizza Planet is for kids who need some amusement with their pizza—video games and other diversions allow parents to relax with a cappuccino or espresso while their children stay entertained.

DISABILITIES & ACCESSIBILITY
Almost everything in this park is wheelchair accessible.

ATTRACTIONS Studio attractions are wheelchair accessible, with certain restrictions on the Star Tours thrill ride and Twilight Zone Tower of Terror. Guests with hearing impairments can obtain a closed-captioning device for use with the monitors at preshow areas of some attractions.

To board the **Great Movie Ride,** on Hollywood Boulevard, you must transfer to a Disney wheelchair if you use an oversize model or a scooter;

the gunshot, explosion, and fire effects mean that service animals should not be taken on the rides.

To board Sunset Boulevard's **Twilight Zone Tower of Terror,** you must be able to walk unassisted to a seat on the ride and have full upper-body strength. The ride's free falls make it unsuitable for service animals. *Beauty and the Beast—Live on Stage!* at the Theater of the Stars is completely accessible to guests using wheelchairs. To ride the **Rock 'n' Roller Coaster Starring Aerosmith,** guests who use wheelchairs must transfer to a ride vehicle—an area in which to practice the transfer is available.

At Animation Courtyard, *Voyage of the Little Mermaid, Playhouse Disney—Live on Stage!,* and **The Magic of Disney Animation** are wheelchair accessible; all have preshow areas with TV monitors that are closed-captioned.

You can roll a wheelchair throughout the **Walt Disney: One Man's Dream** attraction, which features captioning in the theater. The **Disney–MGM Studios Backlot Tour** is wheelchair accessible, too. Guests with hearing impairments who lip-read should request a seat near the tour guide. The earthquake, fire, and water effects of the Catastrophe Canyon scene make the attraction inappropriate for some service animals. *Who Wants to Be a Millionaire—Play It!* is wheelchair accessible.

On New York Street, the *Honey, I Shrunk the Kids* Movie Set Adventure is barrier-free for most guests using wheelchairs, although the uneven surface may make maneuvering difficult. **Jim Henson's Muppet*Vision 3-D** is also completely wheelchair accessible. Those with hearing impairments may request a personal audio link that will amplify the sound here. A TV monitor in the preshow area is closed-captioned.

At Echo Lake, the **Indiana Jones Epic Stunt Spectacular!** is completely wheelchair accessible. Explosions and gunfire may make it inappropriate for service animals. **Star Tours,** a turbulent ride, is accessible by guests who can transfer to a ride seat; those lacking upper-body strength should request an extra shoulder restraint. Service animals should not ride. **Sounds Dangerous Starring Drew Carey** is completely wheelchair accessible. However, the entertainment value is derived from the different sound effects, so you may decide to skip this one if you have a hearing impairment.

ENTERTAINMENT Most live entertainment locations are completely wheelchair accessible. Certain sections of parade routes are always reserved for guests with disabilities. Tapings of television shows are wheelchair accessible, but none of the soundstages currently have sign-language interpreters. The noise and explosions in **Fantasmic!** may frighten service animals.

RESTAURANTS & SHOPS All restaurants and shops are fully wheelchair accessible, but there are no braille menus or sign-language interpreters.

WHEELCHAIR RENTALS **Oscar's Classic Car Souvenirs & Super Service,** to the right in the Entrance Plaza, has standard chairs ($7; $1 deposit) as well as motor-powered chairs ($30; $10 deposit). No electric scooters are available in this park. If your rental needs replacing, ask a host or hostess.

FIRST AID
First Aid is in the Entrance Plaza adjoining Guest Relations.

GETTING AROUND
Inside this park, distances are short and walking is the optimal way to get around.

GUIDED TOURS

No guided tours are available at Disney-MGM Studios.
☎ 407/939-8687.

LOCKERS

Lockers are alongside Oscar's Classic Car Souvenirs, to the right of the Entrance Plaza after you pass through the turnstiles. The cost is $5, with a $2 refundable key deposit.

LOST THINGS & PEOPLE

If you're worried about your children getting lost, get name tags for them at Guest Relations, and instruct them to go to a Disney staffer, anyone wearing a name tag, if they can't find you. If the worst happens, ask any cast member before you panic; logbooks of lost children's names are kept at Guest Relations.

Guest Relations also has a computerized Message Center, where notes can be left for traveling companions at this and other parks. Report any lost or found items at Guest Relations in the Entrance Plaza. Items lost for more than one day should be sought at the Main Lost & Found office.
Disney–MGM Studios Lost & Found ☎ 407/560-3720. **Main Lost & Found** ✉ Magic Kingdom, Transportation and Ticket Center ☎ 407/824-4245.

MONEY MATTERS

There's an ATM near the Production Information Window, outside the park's Entrance Plaza. Currency exchange is available at the Guest Relations window.

PACKAGE PICKUP

Ask the shop clerk to forward any large purchase you make to Guest Relations, in the Entrance Plaza, so you won't have to carry it around all day. Allow three hours for it to get there.

SHOPPING

Many Studios attractions, including those related to any of the wildly successful Disney films, have strategically positioned shops and push-carts that will have children clamoring for character merchandise. Genuine Indiana Jones bullwhips and fedoras are sold at the **Indiana Jones Adventure Outpost,** next to the stunt amphitheater. On your way out of Star Tours you're funneled through **Tatooine Traders,** which stocks Darth Vader and Wookie masks as well as other out-of-this-world paraphernalia—remember, Halloween is always just around the corner.

Other shops are not so obviously tied to the attraction you just visited. Budding animators can hone their talents with Paint-a-Cel, a kit with two picture cels ready to be illustrated. It's sold at the **Animation Gallery** in the Animation Building. Disney villains love the constant "ka-ching" at their own business, **The Beverly Sunset,** where villain and Fantasmic! clothing and accessories are sold next to a tempting collection of freshly made candies. **It's a Wonderful Shop,** tucked away in its own little corner in the New York Street area, is a great place to pick up very special Christmas decorations. For movie memorabilia, check out **Sid Cahuenga's One-of-a-Kind** shop, to the left as you enter the park. Alongside old movie posters, autographed pictures, and assorted, one-of-a-kind knickknacks are original costumes once worn by stars in feature movies. Avid readers should browse in **The Writer's Stop,** where, if you happen to hit it right, you might get a book signed by a celebrity author.

If finding just the right souvenir for someone back home is perplexing, several Disney–MGM Studios shops have some great picture frames—everyone can use another. **Legends of Hollywood** on Sunset Boulevard is brimming with kids' clothing, toys, and accessories themed to Pooh and the Hundred Acre Wood gang, and the **Sorcerer Hat Shop,** beneath the hat icon on Hollywood, is just the place to get your 100 Years of Magic pins, T-shirts, and other souvenirs.

VISITOR INFORMATION

The **Crossroads of the World** kiosk in the Entrance Plaza dispenses maps, entertainment schedules, brochures, and the like. You can pick up maps in languages that include French, German, Portuguese, Japanese and Spanish here. Take specific questions to **Guest Relations,** inside the turnstiles on the left side of the Entrance Plaza.

The Production Information Window, also in the Entrance Plaza, is the place to find out what's being taped when and how to get into the audience.

At the corner where Hollywood Boulevard intersects with Sunset Boulevard is the **Studios Tip Board,** a large board with constantly updated information about attractions' wait times—reliable except for those moments when everyone follows the "See It Now!" advice and the line immediately triples. Studio staffers are on hand.

📱 **Production Information Window** ☎ 407/560-4651.

DISNEY'S ANIMAL KINGDOM

Humankind's enduring love for animals is the inspiration for WDW's fourth theme park, Disney's Animal Kingdom. At 500 acres, the Animal Kingdom is the largest in area of all Disney theme parks worldwide and five times the size of the Magic Kingdom. So it gave Disney Imagineers plenty of scope for their creativity. The attraction explores the story of all animals—real, imaginary, and extinct. As you enter through the Oasis, exotic background music plays and you're surrounded by a green grotto, gentle waterfalls, and gardens alive with exotic birds, reptiles, and mammals. It's like a very good zoo that displays animals in their natural habitats—but unlike most zoos, which open in midmorning, this one opens early enough that you can do a lot of looking before its inhabitants settle down to snooze through the heat of the day.

But the Animal Kingdom is also equally an entertainment complex. Beyond the Oasis, the park thrives in true Disney fashion, showcasing careful re-creations of natural and man-made landscapes that recall exotic lands ranging from Thailand and India to southern Africa, in the present and long ago. You'll also find rides, some of Disney's finest musical shows, Disney-logo merchandise, knickknacks from around the world, eateries, and, of course, Disney characters—where else does the Lion King truly belong? Cast members come from all over the world, Kenya and South Africa as often as Kentucky and South Carolina; you see them here and there, at every turn, ready to answer your questions, and you never know what accent you'll hear when they open their mouths. That's part of the charm of the place. All this is augmented by an earnest educational undercurrent that is meant to foster a renewed appreciation for the animal kingdom.

The park is laid out very much like its oldest sibling, the Magic Kingdom. The hub of this wheel is the spectacular Tree of Life in the middle of Discovery Island. Radiating from Discovery Island's hub are several spokes—the other "lands," each with a distinct personality. The entrance is the Oasis, and to its right is DinoLand U.S.A. The northeast corner houses Asia; Africa is on the northwest side. South of Discovery

Best of the Park

Whatever you do, arrive early. Get to the parking lot a half hour before the official park opening. Make a beeline for **Kilimanjaro Safaris** and make your FASTPASS appointment. Then, stroll through **Pangani Forest Exploration Trail**, followed by a brief break at Tusker House for one of its huge hot cinnamon rolls. By now, it should be time to return to the Kilimanjaro Safaris. It should still be early enough that the animals will be frisky, and you'll see more critters than you typically would on a real African safari. Next, head over to the **Tree of Life—It's Tough to Be a Bug!** Don't bother with the FASTPASS here unless the line wait is longer than 45 minutes. The queue meanders along paths that encircle the Tree of Life and allows relaxed viewing of the tree's animal carvings as you get closer to the theater entrance.

Now zip over to **DINOSAUR** in DinoLand U.S.A. to pick up a timed FASTPASS ticket. Then try to grab a ride on **TriceraTop Spin** or **Primeval Whirl** before heading to **Restaurantosaurus** for a bite to eat. Kids love the food; parents, the music. Afterward, let the children explore the **Boneyard** while your food digests and they burn off some energy. By now, it should be time to return to DINOSAUR. Try to time your ride either before or just after the next performance of the *Tarzan Rocks!* stage show at the Theater in the Wild. Next, head over to Asia, where you can make another FASTPASS appointment for the **Kali River Rapids.** Don't forget to check the entertainment schedule so you know when to find your spot for **Mickey's Jammin' Jungle Parade.** Take in the next **Flights of Wonder** show and then check your FASTPASS time and see if you can now get *very* wet on the thrilling Kali River Rapids. Afterward, take a leisurely stroll along the **Maharajah Jungle Trek,** making sure to linger and watch the fascinating bats.

Do a half circle around Discovery Island and head on into Camp Minnie-Mickey, where you and the kids can have your pictures taken with—who else?—Mickey, Minnie, and several of their character friends. Then catch one of the two stage shows. Later, shop in Discovery Island and have any bulky purchases sent to package pickup so you don't lug them around. If time allows, take the train to **Rafiki's Planet Watch.**

If the wait's not too long, have dinner at the **Rainforest Café**; the surroundings alone are worth the visit.

On Rainy Days

The animals love a cool, light rain, so don't avoid this park in wet weather unless you're feeling wimpy. You're going to get wet on Kali River Rapids anyway!

Island, immediately west of the Oasis, is Camp Minnie-Mickey, a character-greeting and show area.

It's best to arrive at this park near opening time at 8 or 9 AM—that's when many of the animals are most likely to be active.

Numbers in the margin correspond to points of interest on the Disney's Animal Kingdom map.

1

The Oasis

This lush entrance garden makes you feel as if you've been plunked down in the middle of a rain forest. Cool mist, the aroma of flowers, and playful animals and colorful birds all exist within a miniature landscape of streams and grottoes, waterfalls, and glades fringed with banana leaves and jacaranda. On the finest Orlando mornings when the mists shroud the landscape, it's the scene-setter for the rest of your day. It's also the area to take care of essentials before entering the park. Here you'll find stroller and wheelchair rentals, Guest Relations, an ATM, and the ticket booths.

Discovery Island

Primarily the site of the Tree of Life, this land is encircled by Discovery River, which isn't an actual attraction but can be viewed from a bridge in Harambe. The island's whimsical architecture, with wood carvings hand made in Bali, adds plenty of charm and a touch of fantasy to this park hub. You'll find some great shops and some good counter-service eateries here, and the island is also the site of the daily Mickey's Jammin' Jungle Parade. Most of the visitor services that aren't in the Oasis are here, on the border with Harambe, including the Baby Care Center, First Aid Center, and Lost & Found.

❶ **Tree of Life—*It's Tough to Be a Bug!*** A monument to all Earth's creatures, the park's centerpiece is an imposing 14 stories high and 50 ft wide at its base. Its 100,000-plus leaves are several shades of green fabric, each carefully placed for a realistic effect. Carved into its thick trunk, gnarled roots, and soaring branches—some of which are supported by joints that allow them to sway in a strong wind—are nearly 350 intricate animal forms that include a baboon, a whale, a horse, the mighty lion, and even an ankylosaurus. Outside, paths tunnel underneath the roots as the fauna-encrusted trunk towers overhead. It's a rich and truly fascinating sight—the more you look the more you see. The path leads you inside the tree trunk to the star attraction of Discovery Island, where you get a bug's-eye view of life. The whimsical 3-D film adventure *It's Tough to Be a Bug!* is modeled vaguely on the animated film *A Bug's Life* from Disney and Pixar, the creators of *Toy Story.* Special film and theater effects spray you with "poison," zap you with a swatter, and even poke you with a stinger. It's all in good fun—and the surprise ending is too playful to give away. ☞ *Duration: 20 mins for show; as long as you like at the Tree of Life. Crowds: Not usually a problem unless it's peak season. Strategy: This show is now a FASTPASS mainstay, so you can pick up your reservation after you've done the Kilimanjaro Safaris. Audience: All ages, but the theater is dark and some effects may frighten young children. Rating:* ★★★

Mickey's Jammin' Jungle Parade. The parade takes off at 4 PM daily on the pathway around Discovery Island with a "characters on safari" theme. Rafiki in his adventure Rover, Goofy in a safari jeep, and Mickey in his "Bon Voyage" caravan join other popular characters each day for the festive daytime fanfare. Adding to the pomp are a batch of oversized puppets—snakes, giraffes, frogs, tigers, monkeys, and others—created by famed designer Michael Curry, known for the puppet costumes of *The Lion King* on Broadway. Throw in some fanciful "party animals" and animal rickshaws carrying VIPs or lucky park guests, and you've got another reason to strategize your day carefully. ☞ *Duration: 15 mins. Crowds: Moderately heavy. Strategy: To be sure you have a good van-*

FodorśChoice

When to Go
Wednesday is probably the best day to go, but you can expect big crowds all week long and especially weekends.

Go to bed early the night before, so you can arrive a half hour before park opening. As at the other parks, this is a good way to get a jump on the crowds. In fact, if you don't come early, you won't see the wild animals at their friskiest—as they were meant to be seen.

When You're There
Check the park's Tip Board for the latest information on lines just after crossing the bridge into Discovery Island.

Try to take a break in Discovery Island to enjoy the incredible architecture. The whimsical animal figures that adorn the shops and other buildings were carved by artisans in Bali specifically for this park.

Set up a rendezvous point and time at the start of the day, just in case you and your companions get separated. Some good places include the outdoor seating area of Tusker House restaurant in Africa, in front of DinoLand U.S.A.'s Boneyard, and at the turnstile of the *Festival of the Lion King* show.

1

---

tage point, grab curb space a half hour before the show begins. Audience: All ages. Rating: ★★

DinoLand U.S.A.

Just as it sounds, this is the place to come in contact with re-created prehistoric creatures, including the fear-inspiring Carnotaurus and the gentle Iguanadon. The landscaping includes live plants that have evolved over the last 65 million years. In collaboration with Chicago's Field Museum, Disney has added a complete, full-scale skeleton cast of Dino-Sue—also known as "Sue"—the 65-million-year-old Tyrannosaurus rex discovered near the Black Hills of South Dakota. After admiring "Sue," you can go on the thrilling DINOSAUR ride, amble along the Cretaceous Trail, play in the Boneyard, or take in the Tarzan Rocks! show at the Theater in the Wild. Kids will want to hitch a dino-ride on the TriceraTop Spin and on the Primeval Whirl family coaster, which has spinning "time machines." There's no need to dig for souvenirs at Chester and Hester's Dinosaur Treasures gift shop—all you need is your wallet.

❷ Boneyard. Youngsters can slide, bounce, slither, and stomp around this archaeological dig site–cum–playground, the finest play area in any of the four Disney parks. There are twisting short and long slides, climbing nets, caves, and a jeep to climb on. Stomp on the dino-footprints to make 'em roar. ☞ *Duration: Up to you and your children. Crowds: Can be heavy midmorning to early afternoon. Strategy: Let the kids burn off energy here while waiting for your DINOSAUR FASTPASS appointment, or head over late in the day when kids need a break to run free. Audience: Toddlers, school-age children and their families. Rating:* ★★★

❸ DINOSAUR. This wild adventure through time puts you face-to-face with huge dinosaurs who move and breathe with uncanny realism. When a carload of guests rouses a cantankerous carnotaurus from his Cretaceous slumber, it's show time. You travel back 65 million years on a fast-paced, twisting adventure and try to save the last living iguanodon as a massive asteroid hurtles toward Earth. Exciting Audio-Animatronics and special effects bring dinosaurs and the entire scene to life. ☞ *Duration: Not quite 4 mins. Crowds: Can get heavy midmorning. Strategy: Go first thing in the morning or at the end of the day, or use the FASTPASS. Audience: All ages except very young children, pregnant women, or guests with back, neck, or heart problems. Minimum height: 40″. Rating:* ★★★

④ Cretaceous Trail. Walk through a re-creation of a primeval forest containing some of the plant survivors from the dinosaur age, such as the monkey puzzle tree and ancient angiosperms. ☞ *Duration: Up to you. Crowds: Not a problem. Strategy: Stroll along here as you head toward Chester and Hester's for souvenirs or while you wait for the next Tarzan Rocks! show. Audience: All ages. Rating:* ★

⑤ TriceraTop Spin. Until now, there wasn't a true "kiddie ride" anywhere at Disney's Animal Kingdom. TriceraTop Spin is designed for playful little dinophiles, who ought to get a kick out of whirling around this ride's giant spinning toy top and dodging incoming comets in their dinomobiles. "Pop!" goes the top and out comes a grinning dinosaur as four passengers in each vehicle fly in a circle and maneuver up and down. ☞ *Duration: About 2 mins. Crowds: Heavy due to the ride's newness. Strategy: Ride early while everyone else heads for the safari, or queue up while waiting for your DINOSAUR FASTPASS appointment. Audience: Toddlers, school-age children and their families. Rating:* ★★

⑥ Primeval Whirl. This free-spinning, four-passenger "time machine" is DinoLand's newest attraction. On a track reminiscent of the boardwalk-style "Wild Mouse" coasters, your vehicle heads on a brief journey back in time, twisting, turning, and even venturing into the jaws of a dinosaur "skeleton." As you ride, crazy cartoon dinosaurs in shades of turquoise, orange, yellow, and purple pop up along the track bearing signs that warn "The End Is Near." More signs warn of "Meteors!" and suggest that you "Head for the Hills!"—coaster hills, that is. Halfway through the ride, your car seems to spin out of control and you take the next drop backward. The more weight there is in the vehicle, the more you spin. ☞ *Duration: About 2½ mins. Crowds: Heavy demand due to the ride's newness. Strategy: Kids may want to ride twice, so take your first spin early, then get a FASTPASS to return later if the wait is longer than 20 mins. Minimum height: 48″. Rating:* ★★★

⑦ Tarzan Rocks! This live musical stage show, based on the animated film, includes live acrobatics, extreme stunts, and a rock performance that showcase the buff jungle dude and his toned jungle honey. Costumes are great and the action nonstop. Don't miss it unless your time is limited and you haven't yet seen the superior *Festival of the Lion King*. ☞ *Duration: 30 mins. Crowds: Not a problem. Strategy: Arrive 15 mins before show time and grab an ice cream treat on the way—you can enjoy it in the theater as you wait for the curtain to rise. Audience: All ages. Rating:* ★★

Asia

Meant to resemble a rural village somewhere in Asia, this land is full of remarkable rain-forest scenery and ruins. Groupings of trees grow from a crumbling tiger shrine and two massive towers, one representing Thailand, the other Nepal. The towers are the habitat for two families of gibbons whose hooting fills the air at all hours of the day. While you're here, take the Maharajah Jungle Trek, see the Flights of Wonder bird show, and raft the Kali River Rapids.

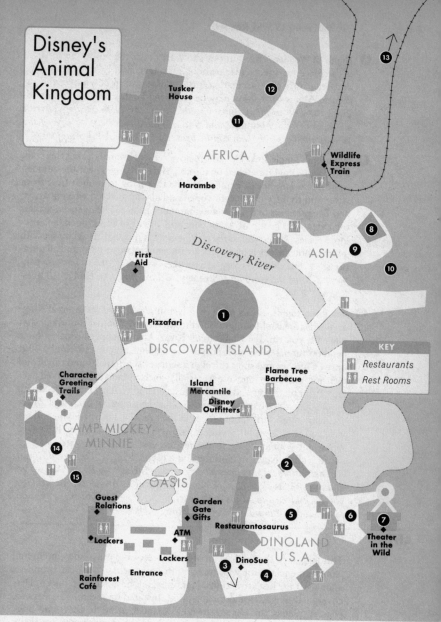

Disney's Animal Kingdom

Tusker House

12

11

AFRICA

Wildlife Express Train

13

◆ **Harambe**

Discovery River

First Aid

8

ASIA

9

10

1

Pizzafari

DISCOVERY ISLAND

Flame Tree Barbecue

KEY

🍴 *Restaurants*

🚻 *Rest Rooms*

Character Greeting Trails

Island Mercantile

Disney Outfitters

CAMP MICKEY-MINNIE

14

15

OASIS

2

Guest Relations

Garden Gate Gifts

5

6

7

Theater in the Wild

◆ **Lockers**

ATM

Restaurantosaurus

Lockers

3

◆ **DinoSue**

4

DINOLAND U.S.A.

Rainforest Café

Entrance

8 **Flights of Wonder.** This outdoor show area near the border with Africa is the place for spectacular demonstrations of skill by falcons, hawks, and other rare and fascinating birds, which swoop down over the audience. A new bird show may be replacing Flights of Wonder in mid-2003. ☞ *Duration: 30 mins. Crowds: Not a problem. Strategy: Arrive 15 mins before show time and find a shaded seat beneath one of the canvas awnings—the sun can be brutal. Audience: All. Rating:* ★★

9 **Maharajah Jungle Trek.** Get an up-close view of animals along this trail: a Komodo dragon perched on a rock; Malayan tapirs near the wooden footbridge; families of giant fruit bats that hang to munch fruit from wires and fly very close to the open and glass-protected viewing areas; and Bengal tigers in front of a maharajah's palace. The tigers have their own view of a group of Asian deer and a herd of black buck, an antelope species. At the end of the trek, you walk through an aviary set with a lotus pool. Disney interpreters are on hand to answer any and all questions. ☞ *Duration: As long as you like. Crowds: Not bad because people are constantly moving. Strategy: Go anytime. Audience: All ages. Rating:* ★★

10 **Kali River Rapids.** Asia's thrilling adventure ride is to the Animal Kingdom what Splash Mountain is to Frontierland. Aboard a round raft that seats 12, you run the Chakranadi River. After passing through a huge bamboo tunnel filled with jasmine-scented mist, your raft climbs 40 ft upriver, lurches and spins through a series of sharp twists and turns, and then approaches an immense waterfall, which curtains a giant carved tiger face. Past rain forests and temple ruins, you find yourself face-to-face with the denuded slope of a logged-out woodland burning out of control. There are many more thrills, but why spill the beans? Be warned: you will get wet, and there's an 80% chance you will get so soaked you'll have to wring out your clothing in the nearest rest room afterward, so plan ahead with a change of clothing and a plastic bag. ☞ *Duration: About 7 mins. Crowds: Long lines all day. Strategy: Use your FASTPASS, or go at day's end, as close to park closing as possible. Audience: All but very young children and adults with heart, back, or neck problems or motion sickness. Minimum height: 42″. Rating:* ★★★

Africa

This largest of the lands is an area of forests and grasslands, predominantly an enclave for wildlife from the continent. The focus is on live animals at the key attractions. Harambe, on the northern banks of Discovery River, is Africa's starting point. Inspired by several East African coastal villages, this Disney town has so much detail that it's mind-boggling to try to soak it all up. Signs on the apparently peeling stucco walls of the buildings are faded, as if bleached by the sun, and everything has a hot, dusty look. For souvenirs with both Disney and African themes, browse through the Mombasa Marketplace and Ziwani Traders. Safari apparel, decorative items for the home, and jewelry are on offer.

11 **Kilimanjaro Safaris.** A giant Imagineered baobab tree is the starting point *Fodor'sChoice* for this adventure into the up-country. Although re-creating an African safari in the United States (or even Florida, for that matter) may not be a new idea, this safari goes a step beyond merely allowing you to observe rhinos, hippos, antelope, wildebeests, giraffes, zebras, elephants, lions, and the like. There are illustrated game-spotting guides above the seats in the open-air safari vehicles, and as you lurch and bump over some 100 acres of savanna, forest, rivers, and rocky hills, you'll see most of these animals—sometimes so close you feel like you could reach out and touch them. It's easy to suspend belief here because the landscape is so effectively modeled and replenished by Disney horticulturists. This being a theme park, dangers lurk, in the form of ivory poachers, and it suddenly becomes your mission to save a group of elephants from would-be poachers. To get the most from your adventure, do this early in the day or in the late afternoon, when the animals are awake—humans aren't the only creatures that want to be napping inside on a hot Central Florida afternoon. ☞ *Duration: 20 mins. Crowds: Heavy in the morning. Strategy: Arrive in the park first thing in the morning—it's worth the trouble—and come straight here using the FASTPASS if necessary. If you arrive at the park late morning, save this for the end of the day, when it isn't so hot. You'll probably see about the same number of animals as in early morning. Audience: All ages—parents can hold small tykes and explain the poacher fantasy. Rating:* ★★★

⑫ **Pangani Forest Exploration Trail.** Calling this a nature walk doesn't really do it justice. A path winds through dense foliage, alongside streams, and past waterfalls. En route there are viewing points where you can stop and watch a beautiful rare okapi munching the vegetation, a family and a separate bachelor group of lowland gorillas, hippos (which you usually can see underwater), meerkats (a kind of mongoose), graceful gerenuk (an African antelope), exotic birds, and a bizarre colony of hairless mole rats. One habitat showcases colobus monkeys, mona monkeys, and an antelope species called the yellow-backed duiker. Interpreters are on hand at every viewing point to answer questions. ☞ *Duration: Up to you. Crowds: Heavy in the morning, but there's room for all, it seems. Strategy: Go while waiting for your safari FASTPASS; try to avoid going at the hottest time of day, when the gorillas like to nap. Audience: All ages. Rating:* ★★★

⑬ **Rafiki's Planet Watch.** Take the Wildlife Express steam train to this unique center of ecoawareness. Rafiki's, named for the wise baboon from The Lion King, is divided into three sections. At the Conservation Station, you can meet animal experts, enjoy interactive exhibits, learn about worldwide efforts to protect endangered species and their habitats, and find out ways to connect with conservation efforts in your own community. At the Habitat Habit! section, cotton-top tamarin monkeys play while you learn how to live with all Earth's animals. And you don't have to be a kid to enjoy the Affection Section, where young children and adults who are giving their inner child free rein get face-to-face with goats and other small critters. ☞ *Duration: 5-min ride; the rest is up to you. Crowds: Can get heavy midmorning. Strategy: Go in late afternoon if you've hit all key attractions. Audience: All ages. Rating:* ★★

Camp Minnie-Mickey

This Adirondack-style land is a meet-and-greet area where Disney characters gather for picture-taking and autographs. Mickey Mouse, Minnie, Daisy Duck, Goofy, and sometimes Brer Bear and Brer Rabbit, are the area's huggable, fun hosts. Live performances are staged at the Lion King Theater and Grandmother Willow's Grove.

⑭ *Festival of the Lion King.* If you think you've seen enough Lion King to last a lifetime, you're wrong unless you've seen this show. In an open-air theater-in-the-round, Disney presents a delightful tribal celebration of song, dance, and acrobatics that uses huge moving stages and floats. ☞ *Duration: 30 mins. Crowds: Not a problem. Strategy: Arrive 15 mins before show time. If you have a child who might want to go on stage, sit in one of the front rows to increase his or her chance of getting chosen. Audience: All ages. Rating:* ★★★

⓯ *Pocahontas and Her Forest Friends.* At Grandmother Willow's Grove, an actor portrays Pocahontas in this lesson on nature and how to preserve endangered species. Pocahontas works with an armadillo, a skunk, a boa constrictor, a red-tailed hawk, and other creatures. She also breaks out in song with "Just Around the River Bend." ☞ *Duration: 12 mins. Crowds: Not a problem. Strategy: May not be performed every day in low season; check entertainment guide map and arrive 15 mins before show time. Audience: All ages. Rating:* ★★

Disney's Animal Kingdom A to Z

To research prices, get advice from other travelers, and book travel arrangements, visit www.fodors.com.

BABY CARE

The **Baby Care Center** is in Discovery Island. You can buy disposable diapers, formula, baby food, and pacifiers. For stroller rentals ($7 single, $14 double; plus $1 deposit), go to Garden Gate Gifts, in the Oasis.

CAMERAS & FILM

Disposable cameras are widely available. For two-hour film developing, look for the Photo Express signs throughout the park. Photo pickup is at Garden Gate Gifts, in the Oasis.

DINING

Restaurants inside Disney's Animal Kingdom serve mostly fast food.

FULL-SERVICE RESTAURANT
You don't have to pay park admission to dine at the Rainforest Café, which has entrances both inside the park and at the gate. It's the only full-service eatery in the Animal Kingdom area. The restaurant serves a great sit-down breakfast, which can be a nice break midmorning if you've been here since an hour before opening. Make reservations by phone at least one day ahead and up to 60 days in advance or in person first thing in the morning.
🔲 **Disney Reservation Center** ☎ 407/939-3463.

SELF-SERVICE RESTAURANTS
At Discovery Island's **Flame Tree Barbecue** you can dig into ribs, brisket, and pulled pork with several sauce choices. There are also great vegetarian wraps. The tables, set beneath intricately carved wood pavilions, make great spots for a picnic.

On the other side of Discovery Island from Flame Tree Barbecue, **Pizzafari** serves individual pizzas (two young children—though not hungry teens—can easily share one), salads, and sandwiches. There's plenty of self-service seating in spacious rooms. The walls are painted with larger-than-life murals of animals in their natural habitats.

Restaurantosaurus, in DinoLand U.S.A., is the Animal Kingdom's hybrid of Disney and McDonald's fare. It's open for counter-service lunches and dinners. For breakfast, you can have the all-you-can-eat Donald's Prehistoric Breakfastosaurus buffet while being entertained by Disney characters. The theming is pure camp (literally and figuratively), and the food is sure to please the kids. They can even get a McDonald's Happy Meal (chicken nuggets only), with a special toy, different from what they get at home. Adults looking for healthful options will find a tasty dinner salad with grilled chicken.

Tusker House is a counter-service restaurant in Harambe unlike any fast-food eatery you've ever seen. The cinnamon buns served at breakfast are scrumptious—and huge. Chef Earl Penson's double-fried, African spiced chicken is a popular specialty—other favorites are the smoked turkey on focaccia and the vegetable sandwich. The large area inside is hung with colorful draperies of African cloth, and there's a charming patio out back. Listen carefully and you'll overhear the goings-on from the faux "guest house" upstairs—a nice Disney touch.

DISABILITIES & ACCESSIBILITY

ATTRACTIONS, RESTAURANT & SHOPS

All restaurant, shops, and attractions are completely wheelchair accessible, including the theater-in-the-round at Camp Minnie-Mickey and the Tree of Life theater showing *It's Tough to Be a Bug!*, which are also accessible to electric scooters. However, to fully experience all the bug movie's special effects, guests who use wheelchairs should transfer to one of the auditorium seats. Check the *Guidebook for Guests with Disabilities* for information about closed-captioning boxes for the monitor-equipped attractions such as the Tree of Life. Scripts and story lines for all attractions are available. Assistive listening devices ($25 refundable deposit) amplify sound in theaters.

In DinoLand U.S.A., you must transfer from your wheelchair to board the **DINOSAUR** thrill ride. Note that you will be jostled quite a bit on this twisting, turning, bumpy ride. **Primeval Whirl** requires a transfer, but **TriceraTop Spin** is wheelchair accessible. To board **Kali River Rapids** in Asia, you'll need to make transfer from your wheelchair to one of the ride rafts. If you're like most of the passengers who get soaked on this water ride, you will be soggy for hours unless you have a change of clothing handy. In Africa, you can roll your wheelchair on board the Wildlife Express train to **Rafiki's Planet Watch,** where you'll need it to traverse the path from the train stop to the station. The **Kilimanjaro Safaris** attraction is also wheelchair accessible. Service animals are allowed in most areas of the park; however, some areas are off-limits, including the Affection Section petting-zoo area of Rafiki's Planet Watch, the aviaries of **Pangani Forest Exploration Trail** and **Maharajah Jungle Trek,** and both the DINOSAUR and Kali River Rapids rides. Braille guides are available at Guest Relations, and Assistive Listening Devices (ALDs) are operating at most attractions—check with Guest Relations as you enter the park to pick up ALDs ($25 deposit), audiotape guides ($25 deposit), and braille guides ($25 deposit).

WHEELCHAIR RENTALS

Garden Gate Gifts, in the Oasis, rents wheelchairs ($7; $1 deposit) and electric scooters ($30; $10 deposit).

FIRST AID

The park's First Aid Center, staffed by registered nurses, is in Discovery Island.

GETTING AROUND

You get around mostly on foot here, although you must take a train to Rafiki's Planet Watch.

GUIDED TOURS

Backstage Safari takes an in-depth look at animal conservation every Monday, Wednesday, and Friday 8:15–11:15, stopping at the animal hospital and other behind-the-scenes areas. It's a great way to learn about animal behaviors and how handlers care for the critters in captivity, but don't expect to get up close to the animals on the park's savanna. Book ahead; you can make reservations up to a year in advance. Those in your party must all be at least 16 years old to participate and the cost is $65 plus park admission.

Wild by Design offers participants 14 and older insights into the creation of Disney's Animal Kingdom every Tuesday, Thursday, and Fri-

day, 8:30 to 11:30. The tour touches on the park's art, architecture, history, and agriculture, and reveals how stories of exotic lands are told at the park. You get a glimpse of behind-the-scenes buildings to see custodians taking care of the animals. A light Continental breakfast is served as part of the $58 tour price; park admission is required as well.
🎫 **Backstage Safari and Wild by Design** ☎ 407/939-8687.

LOCKERS
Lockers are in Guest Relations ($5; $2 key deposit).

LOST THINGS & PEOPLE
If you're worried about your children getting lost, get name tags for them at Discovery Island. Instruct them to speak to someone with a Disney name tag if you become separated. If you do, immediately report your loss to any cast member. Lost-children logbooks are at Discovery Island, which is also the location of the Lost & Found. To retrieve lost items after leaving the park, call Lost & Found on the same day, or call Main Lost & Found if more than a day has passed since you've lost the item.
🎫 **Lost & Found** ☎ 407/938-2785. **Main Lost & Found** ☎ 407/824-4245.

MONEY MATTERS
For cash and currency exchange, go to Guest Relations. There's an ATM in the Oasis to the right of the Entrance Plaza as you go into the park.

PACKAGE PICKUP
You can have shop clerks forward any large purchases to Garden Gate Gifts, on the right side of the Entrance Plaza in the Oasis, so that you won't have to carry them around all day. Allow three hours for the items to make the journey.

SHOPPING
Before you pass through the turnstiles on your way into the Animal Kingdom, stop at the **Outpost Shop,** where you'll find plush character animals dressed up in safari gear. The must-have here is a safari hat with Mouse ears.

Stores are scattered throughout the park, and **Harambe** village shops stock quite a selection of African imports and animal items—plush key chains, statues of various sizes and styles—as well as T-shirts, toys, and trinkets on various Disney and Animal Kingdom themes. Pick up extra film and disposable cameras at **Duka La Filimu,** in Harambe. Safari apparel, soapstone carvings, jewelry, and other items are across the street at **Mombasa Marketplace and Ziwani Traders.** At **Creature Comforts** (before you cross from Discovery Island to Harambe), you can get a Minnie Mouse headband with a safari-style bow, sunglasses, prince and princess costumes, and great kiddie togs. **Island Mercantile,** to the left as you enter Discovery Island, offers Animal Kingdom–logo goodies. **Disney Outfitters,** directly across from Island Mercantile and by the Tip Board, is another source of African-theme clothing and accessories.

VISITOR INFORMATION
Guest Relations, in the Oasis, is the place to pick up park maps and entertainment schedules and ask questions. Foreign visitors may want to stop here to get maps in five other languages besides English: French, German, Portuguese, Japanese, and Spanish.

TYPHOON LAGOON

Numbers in the margin correspond to points of interest on the Typhoon Lagoon map.

According to Disney legend, Typhoon Lagoon was created when the quaint, thatched-roof, lushly landscaped Placid Palms Resort was struck by a cataclysmic storm. It left a different world in its wake: surfboards sundered trees; once upright palms imitated the Leaning Tower of Pisa; a great buoy crashed through the roof of one building; a small boat was blown through the roof of another; and part of the original lagoon was cut off, trapping thousands of tropical fish—and a few sharks. Nothing, however, topped the fate of *Miss Tilly*, a shrimp boat from "Safen Sound, Florida," which was hurled high in the air and became impaled on Mt. Mayday, a magical volcano that periodically tries to dislodge *Miss Tilly* with huge geysers of water.

Ordinary folks, the legend continues, would have been crushed by such devastation. But the resourceful residents of Placid Palms were made of hardier stuff—and from the wreckage they created 56-acre Typhoon Lagoon, the self-proclaimed "world's ultimate water park."

Four times the size of now-closed River Country, Disney's first water park, Typhoon Lagoon offers a full day's worth of activities. You can bob along in 5-ft waves in a surf lagoon the size of two football fields, speed down arrow-straight water slides and around twisty storm slides, bump through rapids, go snorkeling, and, for a mellow break, float in inner tubes along the 2,100-ft Castaway Creek, rubberneck from specially constructed grandstands as human cannonballs are ejected from the storm slides, or merely hunker down in one of the many hammocks or lounge chairs and read a book. A children's area replicates adult rides on a smaller scale. It's Disney's version of a day at the beach—complete with friendly Disney lifeguards.

The layout is so simple that it's hard to get lost. The wave and swimming lagoon is at the center of the park; the waves break on the beaches closest to the entrance and are born in Mt. Mayday at the other end of the park. Castaway Creek encircles the lagoon. Anything requiring a gravitational plunge—storm slides, speed slides, and raft trips down rapids—starts around the summit of Mt. Mayday. Shark Reef and Ketchakiddie Creek flank the head of the lagoon, to Mt. Mayday's right and left, respectively, as you enter the park.

❶ Typhoon Lagoon. This is the heart of the park, a swimming area that spreads out over 2½ acres and contains almost 3 million gallons of clear, chlorinated water. It's scalloped by lots of little coves, bays, and inlets, all edged with white-sand beaches—spread over a base of white concrete, as body surfers soon discover when they try to slide into shore. Ouch! The main attraction is the waves. Twelve huge water-collection chambers hidden in Mt. Mayday dump their load with a resounding "whoosh" into trapdoors to create waves large enough for Typhoon Lagoon to host amateur and professional surfing championships. A piercing double hoot from *Miss Tilly* signals the start and finish of wave action: every 2 hours, for 1½ hours, 5-ft waves issue forth every 90 seconds; the next half hour is devoted to moderate bobbing waves. Even during the big-wave periods, however, the waters in Blustery Bay and Whitecap Cove are protected enough for timid swimmers. Surfers who don't want to risk a fickle ocean can surf here Tuesdays and Fridays before the park opens. Instruction and surfboard are included in the $125 cost, and the surfing experience lasts for 2½ hours. Reserve your waves by calling ☎ 407/939–7529.

② **Castaway Creek.** This circular, 15-ft-wide, 3-ft-deep waterway is every-one's water fantasy come true. Snag an inner tube and float along the creek that winds around the entire park, a wet version of the Magic King-dom's Walt Disney World Railroad. You pass through a rain forest that showers you with mist and spray, you slide through caves and grottos, you float by overhanging trees and flowering bushes, and you get dumped on at the Water Works, whose "broken" pipes the Typhoon Lagooners never got around to fixing. The current flows a gentle 2½ ft per second; it takes about 30 minutes to make a full circuit. Along the way there are exits where you can hop out and dry off or do something else—and then pick up another inner tube and jump right back in.

③ **Shark Reef.** If you felt like leaping onto the stage at the Studios' *Voyage of the Little Mermaid* or jumping into the tank at Epcot's Living Seas, make tracks for this 360,000-gallon snorkeling tank. The coral reef is artificial, but the 4,000 tropical fish—including black-and-white-striped sergeant majors, sargassum trigger fish, yellowtail damselfish, and ami-able nurse and bonnet-head sharks—are quite real. So are the southern stingrays that congregate in the warmer, shallower water by the entrance. To prevent algae growth, Shark Reef is kept at a brisk 72°F, which is about 15 degrees cooler than the rest of Typhoon Lagoon. A sunken tanker divides the reef; its portholes give landlubbers access to the un-derwater scene and let them go nose-to-nose with snorkelers. Go first thing in the morning or at the end of the day if you want to spend more time. During spring and summer, adults and children ages five and over can take a personal snorkeling lesson at $20 per half hour (plus an ad-ditional $15 per participant for each air tank). If your kids want to learn how to explore the depths of the ocean Disney style, sign them up at Guest Relations when you purchase your tickets.

④ **Humunga Kowabunga.** There's little time to scream, but you'll hear just such vociferous reactions as the survivors emerge from the catch pool opposite Shark Reef. The basic question is: want to get scared out of your wits in three seconds flat—and like it enough to go back for more? The two side-by-side Humunga Kowabunga speed slides rightly de-serve their acclaim among thrill lovers, as they drop more than 50 ft in a distance barely four times that amount. For nonmathematicians, that's very steep. Oh yes, and then you go through a cave. In the dark. The average speed is 30 mph; however, you can really fly if you lie flat on your back, cross your ankles, wrap your arms around your chest, and arch your back. Just remember to smile for the rubberneckers on the grandstand at the bottom. ☞ *Audience: Children under 48" are not al-lowed on this ride. No pregnant women or guests with heart, back, or neck problems or other physical limitations.*

⑤ **Storm Slides.** Each of these three body slides is about 300 ft long and snakes in and out of rock formations, through caves and tunnels, and under waterfalls, but each has a slightly different view and offers a twist. The one in the middle has the longest tunnel; the others' secrets you'll have to discover for yourself. Maximum speed is about 20 mph, and the trip takes about 30 seconds.

⑥ **Mt. Mayday.** What goes down can also go up—and up and up and up and up. "It's like climbing Mt. Everest," wailed one teenager about a climb that seems a lot steeper than this 85-ft peak would warrant. However, it's Mt. Everest with hibiscus flowers, a rope bridge, stepping-stones set in

Typhoon Lagoon

KEY
- Restaurants
- Rest rooms

Miss Tilly

6
7
5
4
8
9
3

Beach Area
Castaway Cove

Typhoon Tilly's

Low Tide Lou's

10

11

Rain Forest

Rain Forest

Typhoon Lagoon

1

2

Getaway Glen

Raft Rentals

Beach Area

Slurp's Up

High & Dry Towels

Castaway Creek

Singapore Sal's Saleable Salvage

Leaning Palms

First Aid

Entrance

plunging waters, and—remember that typhoon?—a broken canoe scattered over the rocks near the top. The view encompasses the entire park.

Lovers of white-water rafting will find Mayday Falls, Keelhaul Falls, and Gang Plank Falls at Mt. Mayday. These white-water raft rides in oversize inner tubes plunge down the mount's left side. Like the Storm Slides, they have caves, waterfalls, and intricate rock work, but with some extra elements.

❼ Mayday Falls. The 460-ft slide over Mayday Falls in blue inner tubes is the longest and generally acclaimed the bumpiest; it's a straight slide over the falls into a catchment, which gives you just enough time to catch your breath before the next plunge.

❽ Keelhaul Falls. This spiraling, 400-ft ride in yellow inner tubes seems way faster than the purported 10 mph.

❾ Gang Plank Falls. If you climb up Mt. Mayday for this ride, you'll go down in four-person, 6½-ft inner tubes that descend crazily through 300 ft of rapids.

❿ Ketchakiddie Creek. Typhoon Lagoon's children's area has slides, mini-rapids, squirting whales and seals, bouncing barrels, waterfalls, sprinklers, and all the other ingredients of a splash fiesta. The bubbling sand ponds, where youngsters can sit in what seems like an enormous whirlpool bath, are special favorites. ☞ *All adults must be accompanied by a child or children under 48" and vice versa.*

⓫ Bay Slides. These scaled-down versions of the Storm Slides are geared toward younger kids.

Strategies for Your Visit to Typhoon Lagoon

There's really only one problem with Typhoon Lagoon—it's a crowd pleaser. The closing of River Country in 2002 has added to the number of water-lovers visiting Typhoon Lagoon, and the presence of Blizzard Beach has shown no signs of eroding its popularity. In summer and on weekends, the park often reaches its capacity of 7,200 people by mid-morning. By this time Castaway Creek is a bank-to-bank carpet of tangled arms and legs; the Lagoon resembles the Times Square subway station at rush hour; and the waits for Humunga Kowabunga, the Storm Slides, and Shark Reef can top an hour. In that time, you could have driven to the Atlantic Ocean.

If you must visit in summer, go for a few hours during the dreamy late afternoon or when the weather clears up after a thundershower. Typically, rainstorms drive away the crowds, and lots of people simply don't come back. If you plan to make a whole day of it, avoid weekends—Typhoon Lagoon is big among locals as well as visitors. Instead, visit on a Monday or other weekday. Arrive 30 minutes before opening time so you can park, buy tickets, rent towels, and snag inner tubes before the hordes descend. Set up camp and hit the slides, white-water rides, and Shark Reef first. Then bobble along Castaway Creek and save the lagoon itself for later.

If you're visiting at a quiet time of year, go in the afternoon, when the water will have warmed up a bit. Do Castaway Creek first to get a sense of the park.

There are plenty of lounge chairs and a number of hammocks but definitely not enough beach umbrellas. If you crave shade, commandeer a spot in the grassy area around Getaway Glen on the left side of the park just past the raft-rental concession. If you like moving about, people-watching, and having sand in your face, go front and center at the surf pool. For your own patch of sand and some peace and quiet, head for the coves and inlets on the left side of the lagoon.

Typhoon Lagoon A to Z

To research prices, get advice from other travelers, and book travel arrangements, visit www.fodors.com.

DINING

Standard beach fare—burgers, dogs, chef salads, and, of course, ice cream and frozen yogurt—is what's cooking at **Leaning Palms**, to your left as you enter the park. **Let's Go Slurpin'**, a beach shack on the edge of Typhoon Lagoon, dispenses frozen margaritas as well as wine and beer. **Typhoon Tilly's Galley & Grog Shop**, on the right just south of Shark Reef, pours mostly sugary, nonalcoholic grog but also serves Davy Jones lager. Food carts with lemonade, soda, ices, and snow cones are scattered around the park.

DISABILITIES & ACCESSIBILITY

The park gets high ratings in the accessibility department. All paths that connect the different areas of Typhoon Lagoon are wheelchair accessible. Those who use a wheelchair and who can transfer to a raft or inner tube can also float in **Typhoon Lagoon** and on **Castaway Creek**. Wheelchairs are available in the entrance turnstile area and are free with ID.

DRESSING ROOMS & LOCKERS

There are men's and women's thatched-roof dressing rooms and two sizes of full-day lockers ($7 and $9, with $2 deposits for either) to the right of the entrance on your way into the park; a second, less-crowded set is near Typhoon Tilly's Galley & Grog Shop. The towels you can rent (for $1) at the stand to the right of the main entrance are a little skimpy; bring your own beach towel or buy one at Singapore Sal's if you like. The Typhoon Lagoon Imagineers thoughtfully placed rest rooms in every available nook and cranny. Most have showers and are much less crowded with clothes-changers than the main dressing rooms.

FIRST AID

The small First-Aid Stand, run by a registered nurse, is on your left as you enter the park, not far from the Leaning Palms food stand.

LOST THINGS & PEOPLE

Ask about your misplaced people and things at the Guest Relations window near the entrance turnstiles, to your left as you enter the park. Lost children are taken to High and Dry Towels.

PICNICKING

Picnicking is permitted, but you won't be allowed to bring in a cooler too large for one person to carry. Tables are set up at Getaway Glen and Castaway Cove, near Shark Reef. Bring a box lunch from your hotel or pick up provisions from the Goodings supermarket at the Crossroads shopping center (off SR 535), and you'll eat well without having to line up with the masses. Although you can find alcoholic beverages at Typhoon Lagoon, don't bring along your own or you'll be walking them back to the car. Glass containers are also prohibited.

SUPPLIES

The **rental-rafts concession,** the building with the boat sticking through the roof to the left of the entrance, past the Leaning Palms food concession, offers free inner tubes. You need to pick them up only for the lagoon; they're provided for Castaway Creek and all the white-water rides. You can borrow snorkels and masks at **Shark Reef.** Free life vests are available at **High and Dry Towels.** You may not bring your own equipment into Typhoon Lagoon.

Singapore Sal's, to the right of the main entrance (on the way into the park), is the place to buy sunscreen, hats, sunglasses, and other beach paraphernalia.

VISITOR INFORMATION

The staff at the **Guest Relations** window outside the entrance turnstiles, to your left, can answer many questions; a chalkboard inside gives water temperature and surfing information. During off-season, which encompasses October through April, the park is not open every day. Call WDW Information or check Disney's Web site for days of operation.

▣ **WDW Guest Information** ☎ 407/824-4321 ⊕ www.disneyworld.com.

BLIZZARD BEACH

With its oxymoronic name, Blizzard Beach promises the seemingly impossible—a seaside playground with an alpine theme. As with its older cousin, Typhoon Lagoon, the Disney Imagineers have created an entire legend to explain the park's origin: after a freak winter storm dropped snow over the western side of Walt Disney World, entrepreneurs decided to create Florida's first downhill ski resort. Saunalike temperatures soon returned. But just as the resort's operators were ready to close up shop, they spotted a playful alligator sliding down the "liquid ice" slopes. The realization that the melting snow had created the tallest, fastest, and most exhilarating water-filled ski and toboggan runs in the world gave birth to the ski resort–water park.

Disney Imagineers have gone all out here to create the paradox of a ski resort in the midst of a tropical lagoon. Lots of verbal puns and sight gags play with the snow-in-Florida motif. The park's centerpiece is Mt. Gushmore, with its 120-ft-high Summit Plummet, as well as other toboggan and water-sled runs with names such as Teamboat Springs, a white-water raft ride; Toboggan Racer; Slush Gusher; and Runoff Rapids. Between Mt. Gushmore's base and its summit, swim-skiers can also ride a chairlift converted from ski-resort to beach-resort use—with umbrellas and snow skis on their undersides. Devoted water-slide enthusiasts generally prefer Blizzard Beach to the other water parks.

Numbers in the margin correspond to points of interest on the Blizzard Beach map.

❾ Blizzard Beach Ski Patrol Training Camp. The preteens in your crowd may want to spend most of their time on the T-bar drop, bungee-cord slides, and culvert slides here. In addition, there's a chance to take on Mogul Mania, a wide-open area where you can jump from one slippery mogul to the next. The moguls really look more like baby icebergs bobbing in a swimming pool.

❹ Chair Lift. If you're waterlogged, take a ride from the beachfront base of Mt. Gushmore up over its face and on to the summit—and back down again.

⓫ Cross Country Creek. Just grab an inner tube, hop on, and circle the entire park on this creek during a leisurely 45-minute float. Along the way, you'll get doused with frigid water in an ice cave—wonderful on a steamy Florida day.

7 Downhill Double Dipper. These side-by-side racing slides are where future Olympic hopefuls 48″ and taller can compete against one another.

8 Melt Away Bay. The park's main pool is a 1-acre oasis that's constantly fed by "melting snow" waterfalls. The man-made waves are positively oceanlike. If you're not a strong swimmer, stay away from the far end of the pool, where the waves originate. You can get temporarily stuck in a pocket even if your head is still above water.

Mt. Gushmore. Slides off the top of this snowcapped peak at the center of the park include Runoff Rapids, Slush Gusher, Snow Stormers, Summit Plummet, Teamboat Springs, and Toboggan Racer.

10 Runoff Rapids. You have to steel your nerves to climb into an inner tube for these three twisting, turning flumes—even one that's in the dark. But once you're in, it's way more fun than scary.

2 Slush Gusher. This speed slide, which drops through a snow-banked mountain gully, is shorter and less severe than Summit Plummet but a real thriller nonetheless. ☞ *Minimum height: 48″.*

6 Snow Stormers. No water park would be complete without a fancy water slide, and Blizzard Beach has one—actually three flumes that descend from the top of Mt. Gushmore along a switchback course of ski-type slalom gates.

1 Summit Plummet. This is Mt. Gushmore's big gun, which Disney bills as "the world's tallest, fastest free-fall speed slide." From Summit Plummet's "ski jump" tower, it's a wild 55-mph plunge straight down to a splash landing at the base of the mountain. It looks almost like a straight vertical drop. If you're watching from the beach below, you can't hear the yells of the participants, but rest assured—they're screaming their heads off. ☞ *Minimum height: 48″.*

3 Teamboat Springs. Six-passenger rafts zip along in the world's longest family white-water raft ride. Since its original construction, it has doubled its speed of departure onto its twisting, 1,200-ft channel of rushing waterfalls. This is great for families—a good place for kids too big for Tike's Peak to test more grown-up waters.

12 Tike's Peak. Disney is never one to leave the little ones out of the fun, and this junior-size version of Blizzard Beach, set slightly apart from the rest of the park, has scaled-down elements of Mt. Gushmore.

5 Toboggan Racers. On this ride you slither down an eight-lane water slide over Mt. Gushmore's "snowy" slopes.

13 Winter Summerland. After a day in the sun, stop by this miniature golf course just outside the park, which carries out the Blizzard Beach theme.

Strategies for Your Visit to Blizzard Beach

Blizzard Beach is just as popular as Typhoon Lagoon—it's a toss-up as to which is more crowded. Your best bet is to get here early, before the gates fling open. Expect long lines at the Summit Plummet and other major attractions. If you go in summer, try to arrive in late afternoon, just after the daily thunderstorm. The air will be hot and humid, but you'll be cool as a cucumber because the hordes will have departed for indoor pursuits. If thrill rides aren't your top priority, though, there's always plenty of room in the wave pool at **Melt Away Bay.** A relaxing inner-tube ride on **Cross Country Creek** is a cool alternative as well.

Fodor'sChoice

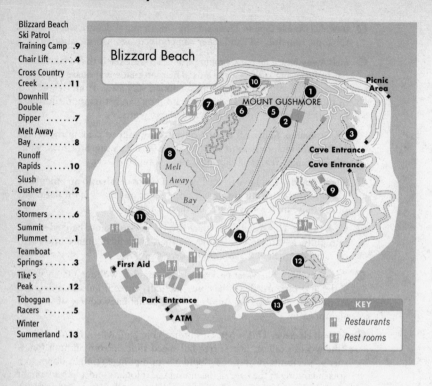

Blizzard Beach A to Z

To research prices, get advice from other travelers, and book travel arrangements, visit www.fodors.com.

DINING
Stands around the park sell ice cream, soft drinks, bottled water, and beer. **Lottawatta Lodge**—a North American ski lodge with a Caribbean accent—is the park's main emporium of fast food. Lines are long at peak feeding times.

Hot dogs, snow cones, and ice cream are on the menu at **Avalunch**. Beer, soft drinks, and bottled water can be purchased at the **Cooling Hut**. **Frostbite Freddie's** sells frozen drinks and spirits. The **Warming Hut** has Disney's famous roast turkey legs, hot dogs, and ice cream.

DISABILITIES & ACCESSIBILITY
Most paths are flat and level. If you use a wheelchair, you'll also be able to float in **Cross Country Creek**, provided you can transfer to a large inner tube. Other guests with limited mobility might also be able to use the inner tubes at some of the park's tamer slides. A limited number of wheelchairs are available near the park entrance and are free if you leave an ID.

DRESSING ROOMS & LOCKERS
Dressing rooms are in the Village area, just inside the main entrance. There are showers and rest rooms here as well. Lockers are strategically

located near the entrance, next to Snowless Joe's Rentals and near Tike's Peak, the children's area (more convenient if you have little swim-skiers in tow). At Snowless Joe's it costs $7 to rent a small locker, $9 for a large one; $2 deposit required. Only small lockers are available at Tike's Peak. Rest rooms are conveniently located throughout the park; there are facilities in the Village area near the entrance, in Lottawatta Lodge, at the Ski Patrol Training Camp, and just past the Melt Away Bay beach area. Towels are available for rent at Snowless Joe's ($1), but they're tiny. If you care, buy a proper beach towel in the Beach Haus or bring your own.

FIRST AID

The First-Aid Stand, overseen by a registered nurse, is in the Village, be-tween Lottawatta Lodge and the Beach Haus.

LOST THINGS & PEOPLE

Start your visit by naming a specific meeting place and time. Instruct your youngsters to let any lifeguard know if they get lost. If they do get lost, don't panic: head for Snowless Joe's, local lost-children central.

PICNICKING

Glass containers and bringing in your own alcoholic beverages are not allowed, but picnicking is, and several areas are good, most notably the terrace outside Lottawatta Lodge and its environs. Coolers must be small enough for one person to handle; otherwise, you won't be able to take them into the park.

SUPPLIES

Personal flotation devices, better known as life jackets, are available free to children and adults at **Snowless Joe's** (leave your ID with an atten-dant until you return them). You can't rent inner tubes here: they're pro-vided at the rides.

Sunglasses, sunscreen, bathing suits, waterproof disposable cameras, and other sundries are available at the **Beach Haus,** along with Blizzard Beach logo merchandise. Check out the ski equipment hanging from the ceil-ing. The **Sled Cart,** a kiosk-style shop, sells souvenirs, suntan lotion, and water toys.

VISITOR INFORMATION

Disney staffers at the Guest Relations window, to the left of the ticket booth as you enter the park, can answer most of your questions. Dur-ing the off-season months of October through April, the park isn't open every day. For the park's days of operation, contact the park directly.
 Blizzard Beach ☎ 407/824-4321 ⊕ www.disneyworld.com.

AND THERE'S MORE

DisneyQuest®

This five-story interactive indoor theme park in Downtown Disney West Side is a virtual kingdom of attractions and adventures in a single build-ing. Here Disney stories and characters come to life in a bold, interac-tive way—you not only partake in the magic, but you're immersed in it. It's a wonderful, unique place to cool off on a hot summer day or to sit out an afternoon thunderstorm. To avoid crowds, arrive when it opens, usually at 11:30 AM, but some days earlier (call to verify). Its location in the middle of an entertainment and shopping complex ensures crowds after dark. Plan to stay for at least four hours or longer to get the most of your one-time admission—The Cheesecake Factory Express restaurant is inside so you can have lunch or dinner and then get back to the virtual fun. Be warned: your kids won't want to leave. Bring along some aspirin just in case you develop a case of virtual overload.

You begin your journey at the Ventureport after exiting the elevator, here known as the Cybrolator. The Ventureport serves as a crossroads within the complex, and from there you can go on to enter any one of four distinct entertainment environments, or "zones": the Explore Zone, the Score Zone, the Create Zone, and the Replay Zone. One price gains you admission to the building and allows you entrance to all of the attractions, excluding prize play games. ⊠ *Downtown Disney, beginning at the intersection of Hotel Plaza Blvd. and Buena Vista Dr.* ☎ *407/828–4600* ⊕ *www.disneyworld.com* ✉ *$31, $25 children ages 3–9* ☉ *Sun.–Thurs. 11:30 AM–11 PM, Fri.–Sat. 11:30 AM–midnight.*

The Explore Zone
In this virtual adventureland, you're immersed in exotic and ancient locales. You can fly through the streets of Agrabah with the help of a virtual reality helmet on a hunt to release the genie on Aladdin's Magic Carpet Ride. Then take a Virtual Jungle Cruise down the roiling rapids of a prehistoric world and paddle (yes, *really* paddle) to adventure in the midst of volcanoes, carnivorous dinosaurs, and other Cretaceous threats. End your stay in this zone at Pirates of the Caribbean: Battle for Buccaneer Gold, where you and the gang must brave the high seas from the helm of your ship, sinking pirate ships and acquiring treasure.

The Score Zone
The Score Zone is where you can match wits and game-playing skills against the best. Battling supervillains takes more physical energy than you'd think as you fly, headset firmly intact, through a 3-D comic world in Ride the Comix. Escape evil aliens and rescue stranded colonists with your crew during Invasion! An Alien Encounter. Or hip-check your friends in a life-size Mighty Ducks Pinball Slam game.

The Create Zone
Let your creative juices flow in this studio of expression and invention. You can learn the secrets of Disney animation at the Animation Academy, where magic overload led one man who attended to propose to his girlfriend—she said yes! Create your own twisted masterpiece at Sid's Create-A-Toy, based on the popular animated film *Toy Story.* Make yourself over, and then morph your image to keep 'em laughing at the Magic Mirror. Or, at Living Easels, create a *living* painting. On a giant electronic screen you can choose from a number of objects, including, say, the Cinderella Castle; then you can add flowers, candy, funny faces, and other objects of your choosing. All of the above creative ventures are quite popular with the elementary-school crowd. The real thrills await at Cyberspace Mountain, where you can design your own roller coaster on a computer screen, then climb aboard a 360° pitch-and-roll simulator for the ride of your dreams. At Songmaker, produce your own hit in a sound booth equipped with a computer and audio system that helps incorporate all kinds of sounds into your recording (DisneyQuest claims there are 2 billion possible combinations of songs, lyrics, and musical styles). You can buy what you've created at the Create Zone counter.

The Replay Zone
The classic "prize play" machines are here, with futuristic twists. Play SkeeBall and Whack A Alien for 50¢ a pop by purchasing "play cards" of $5, $10, or $20, and earn tickets that are redeemable for prizes. Or sit with a partner in an asteroid cannon–equipped bumper car and blast others to make their cars do a 360° spin in Buzz Lightyear's AstroBlaster.

MAGIC ON THE HIGH SEAS

WITH DISNEY'S REACH **EXTENDING** all the way to the high seas on two cruise ships, the Disney Magic and the Disney Wonder, there's an alternative vacation for "sail" beyond the Orlando kingdom. Disney Cruise Line offers several excursions from Port Canaveral, Florida to eastern and western Caribbean destinations, with stops at a nice mix of ports and at Disney's own private island, Castaway Cay.

Aboard the Magic, Mickey's silhouette is on the funnels and Goofy clings to the stern. Styled like a classic liner, the ship sails on a seven-night eastern Caribbean cruise, stopping at St. Maarten and St. Thomas with excursions to St. John and Castaway Cay. On alternate weeks, the Magic follows a western Caribbean itinerary to ports of call in Key West, Grand Cayman, and Cozumel, with the grand finish at Castaway Cay.

The art nouveau–inspired Wonder is a three- or four-night Bahamian cruise, a popular option for first-time cruisers. Combine this ocean getaway with a stay at Walt Disney World Resort and you've signed up for a seven-night seamless land-and-sea vacation. You check in just once: your room key at your Disney resort hotel becomes both your boarding pass at Disney's terminal at Port Canaveral and the key to your stateroom. Seven-night sea cruises start at $829 for adults, $399 for children 3–12, and $119 for kids under 3; seven-night land-and-sea packages are $829 for adults, $399 for children 3–12, and $99 for kids under 3. Call ☎ 888/325–2500 or book on-line at www.disneycruise.com.

On both ships, several areas are set aside for just the grown-ups, including one of the three pools. Poolside games, wine tastings, and other activities are on the schedule daily. The ship's spa is a don't-miss for those who need some on-board pampering, but book as soon as you've checked in or risk missing the opportunity.

On both the Magic and the Wonder, there's nearly an entire deck reserved for kids only. The well-run Oceaneer Club

(both ships) is part of the cruise package, providing nonstop activities for kids ages 3–7, and giving parents the opportunity to enjoy some R&R. Kids ages 8–12 love the high-tech, game-filled Oceaneer Lab, and teens can chill out at Common Grounds, a coffeehouse-type place for music, big-screen TV, and meeting new friends. Baby-sitting is available at extra charge for children under 3 at Flounder's Reef Nursery.

Disney on-board dining is an experience in itself. At Animator's Palate (both ships), the color scheme goes from black-and-white to Technicolor as the meal progresses. Dining is slightly more formal at Lumiere's (Magic) and Triton's (Wonder). And the mood is casual-festive at the Caribbean-themed Parrot Cay (both ships). Disney schedules you for a different restaurant each night, so you sample all three. Your assigned wait staff travels with you. The intimate Palo (both ships), with its sweeping ocean view from one of the ship's highest points, is for adults only (reserve early—it's a hot ticket). Character breakfasts, champagne brunch, and high tea are options aboard the Magic. Tea with Wendy Darling of Peter Pan is offered to families and children. There's also a captain's gala cocktail party and dinner on the seven-night cruise.

Each night, lavish shows entertain families with tales of princesses, heroes, and pirates, with eye-popping special effects. On the Magic, the "Morty the Magnificent" shows include illusions that bring art and music to life; on both ships, "Who Wants to Be a Mouseketeer?" is a fun take-off of the popular TV show "Who Wants to Be a Millionaire." Each ship has a cinema showing Disney classics and first-run films, and there are nightclubs for grown-ups.

The Wonder calls at Nassau en route to Castaway Cay, where there are separate beaches for adults, families, and teens, as well as good snorkeling. Parents: enjoy some private time on the island while your well-tended kids forget you're even around. Then share some family time on the beach or in the water.

Cash in your winnings for candy, stuffed animals, mugs, T-shirts, and other prizes at the Midway on the Moon.

DisneyQuest A to Z

To research prices, get advice from other travelers, and book travel arrangements, visit www.fodors.com.

DISABILITIES & ACCESSIBILITY

DisneyQuest attractions all are wheelchair accessible, but most require transfer from wheelchair to the attraction itself, including the virtual thrill ride Cyberspace Mountain. You can, however, wheel right on to Pirates of the Caribbean: Battle for Buccaneer Gold, Aladdin's Magic Carpet Ride, and Mighty Ducks Pinball Slam. Wheelchairs can be rented ($7) at the Downtown Disney Guest Services locations at Downtown Disney West Side or Marketplace. Electronic wheelchairs cost $8 per hour or can be rented all day for $30 at the Marketplace location only. Guide dogs are permitted in all areas but are unable to ride several attractions.

DINING

At **Food Quest and Wonderland Café** you'll find varied soups, salads, sandwiches, pasta, pizza, and some of the best wraps around at this terrific eatery operated by The Cheesecake Factory Express. Desserts are worth the indulgence—cheesecake with strawberries, ice cream treats, and chocolate pastries will rev you up for more virtual game play. Surf Disney's limited-access Web at your table—there's a computer terminal in many of the booths. You don't need a reservation to eat here, but you do need to pay the price of admission.

VISITOR INFORMATION

Strollers are *not* permitted at DisneyQuest, which really doesn't provide much for very small children, though baby-changing stations are in both men's and women's rest rooms.

As you enter the building, children will receive a height check and, if they're at least 51″ tall, a wristband that allows access to all rides. The four attractions that have height requirements are Cyberspace Mountain (51″), Buzz Lightyear's Astro Blaster (51″), Mighty Ducks Pinball Slam (48″), and Pirates of the Caribbean: Battle for Buccaneer Gold (35″).

The Lost & Found is at the **Guest Services** window, film can be purchased at the Emporium, and cash is available at an ATM inside the House of Blues merchandise shop not far from the DisneyQuest entrance.

Lost children are first walked through the building accompanied by a security guard. If that method is not successful, then the children are taken to the manager's office to wait for their mom or dad.

Downtown Disney

Downtown Disney is really three entertainment areas in one, with attractions, theaters, nightclubs, shopping, and dining. First, there's **Downtown Disney West Side** with Cirque du Soleil and its breathtaking "La Nouba" performances five evenings a week; DisneyQuest; and the plush AMC movie theaters. A terrific lineup of shops and boutiques, including Guitar Gallery, Virgin Megastore, and the wonderful Hoypoloi fine art and jewelry gallery make for an interesting shopping excursion. Have lunch or dinner at House of Blues, Wolfgang Puck Café, Bongos Cuban Café, or Planet Hollywood.

Then, there's **Downtown Disney Pleasure Island,** which is primarily an evening entertainment complex geared toward adults (those under 18 are admitted if accompanied by an adult). Here you'll find destinations like the improv Comedy Warehouse and the richly decorated Adventurer's Club, where "club members" (actors) surprise you with their antics. At Motion, a DJ spins hip-hop music and other upbeat, modern sounds. Other clubs play jazz, rock and roll, disco, and alternative music.

Finally, there's **Downtown Disney Marketplace,** which has some of the wildest shops and restaurants in Walt Disney World Resort. Whatever you haven't found in the theme parks you'll probably find here. If you have kids, and even if you don't, you should visit World of Disney, the largest Disney-character store on the planet; and Once Upon a Toy, which had 16,000 square ft full of the latest theme-park editions of games and toys (check out the "it's a small world" Play-Doh set and Haunted Mansion CLUE), plus play castles, trains, plush critters, and even mini-monorail sets. The Lego Imagination Center sells LEGO sets of all sizes, but you don't have to buy for the children to play—there's a free outdoor LEGO building area with benches where parents can rest and watch. The Rainforest Cafe, the best themed eatery in town, is steps away.

Disney's Wide World of Sports

In the mid 1990s, seizing on the public's seemingly endless fascination with sports, Disney officials built an all-purpose, international sports complex—Disney's Wide World of Sports. Although the facilities aren't designed to provide a day's worth of entertainment, there are plenty of fun events and activities here for the sports enthusiast in your group.

It feels like a giant leap back in time as you approach the old-time Florida architecture that anchors this 200-acre manicured spread. For the bench warmers in your crowd, options include baseball at the Cracker Jack Stadium with the Atlanta Braves during spring training or the minor-league Orlando Rays from April through September; there are also dozens of championship events hosted by the Amateur Athletic Union (AAU) throughout the year. If you want to be part of the action, sign up for an interactive multiple-sports experience, which lets athletes of all ages test their mettle on the field. For more information and prices on all events, including the Braves games, call 407/939–4263 (GAME).

WALT DISNEY WORLD A TO Z

To research prices, get advice from other travelers, and book travel arrangements, visit www.fodors.com.

Admission

Visiting Walt Disney World is not cheap, especially if you have a child or two along. Everyone 10 and older pays adult price; reductions are available for children 3–9, and those under three are free. No discounted family tickets are available. Prices change often, so be sure to call for the most up-to-date information.

TICKETS & PASSES
In Disneyspeak, "ticket" refers to a single day's admission to the Magic Kingdom, Epcot, Disney–MGM Studios, or the Animal Kingdom. If you want to spend two or three days at WDW, you could buy a separate theme-park ticket each day or dole out more for a four-day Park Hopper Pass. A one-day ticket is good in the park for which you buy it only on the day you buy it; a Park Hopper, if not used for the full four days, can be saved and used on a return visit.

If you want to spend more than three days, you have several options. The **Park Hopper Passes** allow unlimited visits to the four parks on any four or five days, depending on the length of the pass, with any combination of parks on a day. The five-, six-, and seven-day **Park Hopper**

WALT DISNEY WORLD TIME-SAVERS

CAN YOU IMAGINE A TRIP to a major theme park without experiencing the wait? FASTPASS is a time-saving device that can enable you to experience multiple attractions in a single visit without spending all of your time waiting in line. Aside from this scheduling innovation, there are other simple ways to save time and get more out of your Walt Disney World experience.

–Visit during off-peak times. When crowds are sparse, so are the lines.

–Take your meals when everyone else is riding the rides and seeing the sites. A late lunch or early dinner will help you avoid peak lines.

–Arrive at the park about 30 minutes prior to opening so you can get a head start to the most popular attractions when everyone is first let in.

–Make your dining reservations and purchase your park tickets before you leave home.

–When park-hopping, use your own car to save time. There can be 30-minute waits for park-provided bus transportation. Your parking pass is good at any of the theme parks.

–If you stay at any Disney resort, you can gain early admission to the theme parks on certain days via the "Extra Magic Hour" program. Check at your resort or call the WDW information line to find out about park early admission days–it's a great way to see high-demand attractions before the masses get there.

PLUS includes unlimited visits to the four theme parks on any five, six, or seven days, plus visits to, respectively, two, three, or four of WDW's minor parks, including Blizzard Beach, Pleasure Island, and Typhoon Lagoon. If you don't use your admissions to the minor attractions on this visit, you can use them next time around—they don't expire (but are not transferable).

Although these passes don't represent a tremendous savings over the cost of one-day tickets, depending on the parks you plan to see and the number of days you have, they can save you money as well as time spent in line. Various **Annual Passes** are also available; if you plan to visit twice in a year, these are often a good deal.

Staying at Disney-owned resorts gets you additional options. **Ultimate Park Hopper** tickets are good from the time you arrive until midnight of the day you leave; pre-purchase them and you'll save $10–$22 off the regular price. Otherwise, buy them at the front desks of all resorts or in Guest Relations at the four theme parks. Prices, not including tax, are based on the number of room nights and range from $124 for a one-night, two-day pass ($100 for children 3–9) to $475 for 11 nights, 12 days ($348 for children 3–9). The pass is good for unlimited admission to all four theme parks, as well as unlimited admission to the two water parks, DisneyQuest, and Pleasure Island. In addition, **"E" Tickets** may be available at certain times of the year to those staying at Disney resorts for use on certain evenings during months that the Magic Kingdom closes early for everyone else. These tickets ($14 for adults; $12 for children 3–9) must be used in conjunction with a multiday ticket used that day. The number of E tickets is relatively few, you can ride the top rides over and over again, with nary a wait.

Imagine taking a trip to Disney and managing to avoid most of the lines. **FASTPASS** is your ticket to this terrific scenario, and it's included in regular park admission. You insert your theme-park ticket into a special FASTPASS turnstile. Out comes a FASTPASS ticket, complete with the time you should return to the attraction. In the meantime you're free to enjoy the other attractions in the park. At the appointed time you return to the attraction, head for the FASTPASS entrance, and proceed to the preshow or boarding area with little or no wait. It's important to note that you must use one FASTPASS ticket before trying to make your next FASTPASS appointment. At this writing, 24 attractions are using the system: Space Mountain, Splash Mountain, Big Thunder Mountain Railroad, the Haunted Mansion, The Many Adventures of Winnie the Pooh, Peter Pan's Flight, the Jungle Cruise, and Buzz Lightyear's Space Ranger Spin in the Magic Kingdom; at Epcot, Test Track, Living with the Land, *Honey, I Shrunk the Audience,* and Maelstrom in the Norway pavilion; in Animal Kingdom, Kali River Rapids, Kilimanjaro Safaris, Tree of Life—*It's Tough to Be a Bug,* DINOSAUR, and Primeval Whirl; and at Disney–MGM Studios, Twilight Zone Tower of Terror, Rock 'n' Roller Coaster Starring Aerosmith, *Voyage of the Little Mermaid,* Star Tours, Jim Henson's Muppet*Vision 3-D, *Who Wants to Be a Millionaire*—Play It!, and the Indiana Jones Epic Stunt Spectacular! Expect to find FASTPASS turnstiles at Mission: SPACE in Epcot and Mickey's PhilharMagic in the Magic Kingdom due to expected high-volume traffic.

Note that all Disney admission passes are nontransferable. The ID is your fingerprint. Although you slide your pass through the reader like people with single-day tickets, you also have to slip your finger into a special V-shape fingerprint reader before you'll be admitted.

PRICES
Disney changes its prices about once a year and without much notice. For that reason, you may save yourself a few bucks if you buy your WDW tickets or passes as soon as you know for sure you'll be going. At press time, WDW admission prices, including 6.5% tax, were as follows:

	ADULTS	CHILDREN
One-Day Ticket	$53.38	$44.73
Park Hopper		
Four days	$221.52	$177.86
Five days	$254.54	$204.48
Park Hopper PLUS		
Five days	$286.49	$230.04
Six days	$318.44	$255.60
Seven days	$350.39	$281.16
Blizzard Beach and Typhoon Lagoon	$33.02	$26.63
Pleasure Island (18 and up)	$21.25	
Disney's Wide World of Sports (does not include events)	$9.95	$7.47
DisneyQuest	$33.02	$26.63
Cirque du Soleil	$76.68–$87.33	$46.86–$52.19

PURCHASING TICKETS & PASSES
Tickets and passes to the Magic Kingdom, Epcot, the Studios, the Animal Kingdom, and the minor parks can be purchased at admission booths at the Transportation and Ticket Center in the Magic Kingdom (also

known as the TTC) and ticket booths in front of the other theme-park entrances, in all on-site resorts if you're a registered guest, at the Walt Disney World kiosk on the second floor of the main terminal at Orlando International Airport, and at various hotels and other sites around Orlando. American Express, Visa, and MasterCard are accepted, as are cash, personal checks with ID, and traveler's checks. Passes for five or more days are also available in many Disney Stores in malls throughout the country. Discounted tickets are available in varied locations. They're sold to members at many offices of the American Automobile Association, but check with your local office before you leave home. You can also get them from the Orlando Convention & Visitors' Bureau and from assorted visitor information stands not affiliated with the CVB. Note that some discounted tickets are available only if you agree to take a time-share tour—you may want to pass up the opportunity.

By purchasing tickets before you leave for Orlando, you get a jump on your first day while everyone else is lining up at Guest Services in the Disney hotels or at the theme-park ticket booths. You will, however, have to present yourself at Guest Services, near the parks' turnstiles, to have your pass processed—they'll record fingerprint information—so allow ample time when scheduling.

You can also buy your multiday tickets by mail or on-line. Allow four to six weeks for processing.

HAND STAMPS   If you want to leave any Disney park and return on the same day, be sure to have your hand stamped on the way out. You'll need both your ticket and the hand stamp to be readmitted.

🔗 **Orlando Convention & Visitors' Bureau** ✉ 8723 International Dr. ☎ 407/363–5871. **Ticket Mail Order Dept. Walt Disney World** 📮 Box 10000, Lake Buena Vista, FL 32830 🌐 www.disneyworld.com.

Arriving & Departing by Car

Walt Disney World has five exits off I–4. For the Magic Kingdom, Disney–MGM Studios, Disney's Animal Kingdom, Fort Wilderness, and the rest of the Magic Kingdom resort area, take the one marked **Magic Kingdom–U.S. 192 (Exit 64B)**. From here, it's a 4-mi drive along Disney's main entrance road to the toll gate, and another mile to the parking area; during peak vacation periods, be prepared for serious bumper-to-bumper traffic both on I–4 nearing the U.S. 192 exit and on U.S. 192 itself. A less-congested route to the theme parks and other WDW venues is via the exit marked **Epcot/Downtown Disney (Exit 67)**, 4 mi west of Exit 64.

Exit 65 will take you directly to Disney's Animal Kingdom and Wide World of Sports as well as the Animal Kingdom resort area via the Osceola Parkway.

For access to Downtown Disney (including the Marketplace, DisneyQuest, Pleasure Island, and West Side), as well as to Typhoon Lagoon, the Crossroads Shopping Center, and the establishments on Hotel Plaza Boulevard, get off at **Route 535–Lake Buena Vista (Exit 68)**.

The exit marked **Epcot–Downtown Disney (Exit 67)** is the one to use if you're bound for those destinations or for hotels in the Epcot and Downtown Disney resort areas; you can also get to Typhoon Lagoon and the Studios from here.

CAR CARE

The gas islands at the **Disney Car Care Center** near the Magic Kingdom are open daily until 90 minutes after the Magic Kingdom closes. You can also gas up on Buena Vista Drive near Disney's BoardWalk and in the Downtown Disney area across from Pleasure Island. Note that gas prices here are always more than 20¢ higher per gallon than off-property, so try to gas up several miles before you approach the Disney complex.

PARKING

Every theme park has a parking lot—and all are huge. Sections of the Magic Kingdom lot are named for Disney characters; Epcot's highlights modes of exploration; those at the Studios are named Stage, Music, Film, and Dance; and the Animal Kingdom's sound like Beanie Baby names—Unicorn, Butterfly, and so on. Although in theory Goofy 45 is unforgettable, by the end of the day, you'll be so goofy with eating and shopping and riding that you'll swear that you parked in Sleepy. When you board the tram, write down your location and keep it in a pocket. Trams make frequent trips between the parking area and the parks' turnstile areas. No valet parking is available for Walt Disney World theme parks.

Although valet parking is available at Downtown Disney, the congestion there is sometimes such that it may be faster to park in Siberia and walk. (Hint: arrive at Downtown Disney early in the evening—around 6 PM—and you'll get a much closer parking space; you'll also avoid long restaurant lines.) At Disney's BoardWalk, you park in the hotel lot, where valets are available as well.

FEES For each major theme-park lot, admission is $7 for cars, $8 for RVs and campers, and free to those staying at Walt Disney World resorts who have their room card with them. Save your receipt; if you want to visit another park the same day, you won't have to pay to park twice. Parking is always free at Typhoon Lagoon, Blizzard Beach, Downtown Disney, and Disney's BoardWalk. You can valet park at BoardWalk for $6.

Dining

Walt Disney World is full of places to snack and eat. The theme parks are chockablock with attractive, highly themed fast-food spots; all have not only fast food and cafeteria-style eateries but also full-service sit-down restaurants and, especially in Epcot's World Showcase, these eating-and-drinking spots are a big part of the show. On-site hotels offer still other options, including "buffeterias" as well as full-service restaurants.

This book does not describe and rate every eating spot. Best bets for quick snacks are described as "Need a Break?" in the theme-park sections of this chapter, and top options for meals are covered in the theme parks' Dining sections.

Fresh fruits, salads, steamed vegetables, and low-fat foods are more widely available than you might expect. In full-service restaurants, for instance, you can usually get skim milk, and many fast-food operations have low-fat milk. If you have special dietary requirements such as no sodium, kosher, or others—arrange meals 24 hours in advance by calling the Disney Reservation Center.

🗐 **Disney Reservation Center** ☎ 407/939-3463.

BEER, WINE & SPIRITS

The Magic Kingdom's no-liquor policy, a Walt Disney tradition that seems almost quaint in this day and age, does not extend to the rest of Walt

Disney World, and in fact, most restaurants and watering holes, particularly those in the on-site hotels, mix elaborate fantasy drinks based on fruit juices or flavored with liqueurs.

Disabilities & Accessibility

Attractions in all the Disney parks typically have both a visual element that makes them appealing without sound and an audio element that conveys the charm even without the visuals; many are accessible by guests using wheelchairs, and most are accessible by guests with some mobility. Guide dogs and service animals are permitted, unless a ride or special effect could spook or traumatize the animal.

At many rides and attractions, guest with mobility, hearing, and visual disabilities use accessible entrances; to find out where to enter or if you have specific questions, ask any host or hostess.

WDW's *Guidebook for Guests with Disabilities* details many specific challenges and identifies the special entrances. In addition, story notes, scripts, and song lyrics are covered in the *Guidebook for Guests with Hearing Impairments*. Both publications are available at the main visitor information locations in every park, along with **cassette tapes and portable players** that provide audio narration for most attractions (no charge, but refundable deposit required). There are also **wheelchair rentals** in every park.

Entertainment

Live entertainment adds texture to visits to the Disney theme parks and can often be a high point of the theme-park experience. Although the jokes may be occasionally silly, the humor broad, and the themes sometimes excessively wholesome, the level of professionalism is high and the energy of the performers unquestionable. Don't fail to pick up a performance schedule on your way into the theme parks, and keep the schedules in mind as you make your way around.

Getting Around

Walt Disney World has its own transportation system, including buses, trams, monorail trains, and boats, which can get you wherever you want to go. It's fairly simple once you get the hang of it. Officially, all charges for transportation are included in the price of your multiday ticket or are available for a small fee.

In general, allow up to an hour to travel between sites on Disney property. If you use your own car to get around, you might save the time you would have spent waiting for buses or making several stops before you reach your destination. On the other hand, using Disney transportation will save you parking fees and the walk through the parking lot at day's end.

BY BOAT

Motor launches connect WDW destinations on waterways. Specifically, they operate from the Epcot resorts—except the Caribbean Beach—to the Studios and Epcot; between Bay Lake and the Magic Kingdom; and also between Fort Wilderness, the Wilderness Lodge, and the Polynesian, Contemporary, and Grand Floridian resorts.

BY BUS

Buses provide direct service from every on-site resort to both major and minor theme parks, and express buses go directly between the major theme parks. You can go directly from or make connections at Downtown Disney, Epcot, and the Epcot resorts, including the Yacht and Beach Clubs, BoardWalk, the Caribbean Beach Resort, the Swan, and the Dolphin, as well as to Disney's Animal Kingdom and the Animal Kingdom resorts (the Animal Kingdom Lodge, the All-Star, and Coronado Springs resorts).

The buses to the Magic Kingdom all pass the Ticket and Transportation Center (TTC), so you avoid having to change to a monorail or boat to get to the turnstiles.

BY MONORAIL

The elevated monorail serves many important destinations. It has two loops: one linking the Magic Kingdom, TTC, and a handful of resorts (including the Contemporary, the Grand Floridian, and the Polynesian); and the other looping from the TTC directly to Epcot. Before this monorail line pulls into the station, the elevated track passes through Future World—Epcot's northern half—and circles the giant silver geosphere housing the Spaceship Earth ride to give you a preview of what you'll see.

BY TRAM

Trams operate from the parking lot to the entrance of each theme park. If you parked fairly close in, though, you may save time, especially at park closing time, by walking instead.

Hours

The monorail, launches, buses, and trams all operate from early in the morning until at least midnight, although hours are shorter during early closing periods. Check on the operating hours of the service you need if you plan to be out later than that.

Lost & Found

There are Lost & Found offices in the Magic Kingdom, at Epcot, in Disney–MGM Studios, and at Disney's Animal Kingdom. After one day, all items are sent to the Main Lost & Found office.

🄵 **Disney's Animal Kingdom** ☎ 407/938-2784. **Disney–MGM Studios Lost & Found** ☎ 407/560-3720. **Epcot Lost & Found** ☎ 407/560-7500. **Magic Kingdom Lost & Found** ✉ City Hall ☎ 407/824-4521. **Main Lost & Found** ✉ Magic Kingdom, Transportation and Ticket Center ☎ 407/824-4245.

Money Matters

The SunTrust branch in Lake Buena Vista is across the street from the Downtown Disney Marketplace (☎ 407/762–4786). Automatic teller machines are scattered throughout the Magic Kingdom, Epcot, the Studios, Animal Kingdom, and Downtown Disney. Currency exchange services are available at Guest Services in each major theme park.

Opening & Closing Times

MAJOR THEME PARKS

Operating hours for the Magic Kingdom, Epcot, the Studios, and Animal Kingdom vary throughout the year and change for school and legal holidays. In general, the longest days are during prime summer months and over the year-end holidays, when the Magic Kingdom may be open as late as 10 or 11, later on New Year's Eve; Epcot is open until 9 or 9:30 in the World Showcase area and at several Future World attractions, the Studios until 7. At other times, the Magic Kingdom closes around 6—but there are variations, so call ahead.

Animal Kingdom typically opens at 9 and closes at 5, though during holidays it may open at 8 and close at 6 or 7. Note that, in general, the Magic Kingdom, Epcot, and the Studios open at 9. (Epcot's World Showcase opens at 11). The parking lots open at least an hour before the parks do. If you arrive at the Magic Kingdom turnstiles before the official opening time, you can often breakfast in a restaurant on Main Street, which usually opens before the rest of the park, and be ready to dash to one of the popular attractions in other lands at Rope Drop, the Magic Kingdom's official opening time.

In the Magic Kingdom, there are occasional "E" ticket evenings, in which late entry is for Disney resort guests only.

WATER PARKS
Hours at Typhoon Lagoon and Blizzard Beach are 9 or 10 to 5 daily (until 7—occasionally 10—in summer).

Reservations

It's a good idea to plan and make reservations (Disney calls it "priority" seating) early for restaurants in Walt Disney World, including the heavily booked Epcot restaurants. Tours and gold tee times require reservations, too; tour booking information is given in the Guided Tours sections of the various theme parks' coverage.

🏛 **Disney Reservation Center** ☎ 407/939-3463. **Golf Reservations** ☎ 407/824-2270.

Strategies for Your Visit

The order in which you tour each of the Disney parks has everything to do with your priorities, the time of year you visit (which is in turn related to the opening and closing hours and the size of the crowds), the length of time you're staying in Walt Disney World, and whether you're staying on or off WDW property. The italicized "Crowds" and "Strategy" information that follows each attraction's review should help you draw up alternative plans. No matter where you go, you will have a smoother time if you follow certain basic rules.

- Plan to pull into the parking lot at least one-half hour ahead of the published opening times—so that you can check belongings into lockers, rent strollers, and otherwise take care of business before everyone else. When you go to any theme park except the Magic Kingdom, count on being at the entrance turnstiles before official opening time.

- See the three-star attractions either first thing in the morning, at the end of the day, or during a parade.

- Even with FASTPASS, you may end up in a line or two. If you have children who aren't quite ready to amuse themselves by people-watching, pack handheld games and other lightweight diversions to keep boredom at bay and avoid stressful blow-ups.

- Whenever possible when you're visiting the theme parks, eat in a restaurant that takes reservations, bring your own food discreetly (a big money- *and* time-saver), or have meals before or after mealtime rush hours (from 11 AM to 2 PM and again from 6 to 8 PM). Or leave the theme parks altogether for a meal in one of the hotels. If you're in the Magic Kingdom, for instance, it's simple and fairly quick to head over to the Polynesian, the Grand Floridian, or the Contemporary. Early meals are particularly advantageous; you'll be resting up and cooling off while the rest of the world is waiting in line; then while they're all waiting to order, you'll be walking right into many attractions.

- Spend afternoons watching high-capacity sit-down shows or catching live entertainment—or leave the theme parks entirely for a swim in your hotel pool. Don't forget to have your hand stamped on the way out.

- If you plan to take in Blizzard Beach or Typhoon Lagoon, go early in your visit (but not on a weekend). You may like it so much that you'll want to go again.

- If you have small children and a meal with the characters is in your plans, save it for the end of your trip, when your youngsters will have become accustomed to these large, sometimes startling figures.

- Familiarize yourself with all age and height restrictions. Ideally, you should measure young children ahead of time so they won't get excited about rides they're too short to experience. However, most rides have premeasured signs at the entrance to the queuing area, so even if you don't know how tall your child is, you won't have to wait in line before finding out.

- Call ahead to check on operating hours and parade times, which vary greatly throughout the year.

Visitor Information

For general WDW information, contact Guest Information or visit Guest Relations in any Disney resort. If you want to speak directly to someone at a specific Disney location, use the WDW Central Switchboard. To inquire about specific resort facilities or detailed park information, call the individual property via the switchboard. For accommodations and shows, call the Disney Reservation Center. One of the easiest ways to get Disney information is via the WDW Web site.
🏨 **Disney Reservation Center** ☎ 407/939-3463. **WDW Central Switchboard** ☎ 407/824-2222. **WDW Guest Information** ☎ 407/824-4321. **WDW Web site** ⊕ www.disneyworld.com.

UNIVERSAL ORLANDO® RESORT

2

Updated by
Gary
McKechnie

FROM THE OUTSET IT WAS A BATTLE between Disney–MGM Studios and Universal to attract film fans and production crews. Disney opened earlier and had the lead, but Universal used the extra time to tweak old rides, design new ones, and within a few years it had hit its stride to out-dazzle Disney. Next, they added CityWalk to compete with Disney's Pleasure Island and then opened themed hotels to transform themselves into a resort destination.

Borrowing a concept from Walt Disney World Resort (which encompasses theme parks and hotels), Universal refers to the conglomeration of Universal Studios Florida (the original movie theme park), Islands of Adventure (the second theme park), and CityWalk (the dining-shopping-nightclub complex) as *Universal Orlando*. Three hotels have opened—the Riviera-themed Portofino Bay, California Mission–styled Hard Rock Hotel, and the 1,000-room Royal Pacific Resort, a bow to the South Seas.

Bordered by residential neighborhoods and heavily trafficked International Drive, Universal Orlando is expansive yet surprisingly intimate. Two massive parking complexes (at 3.4 million square ft they're the largest on earth), easy walks to all attractions, and motor launches that cruise to the hotels keep the attractions accessible. Universal Orlando emphasizes "two parks, two days, one great adventure," but the presentation, creativity, and cutting-edge technology may bring you back for more. A recent drawback, albeit one that shouldn't prevent you from visiting, is a lax attitude toward park cleanliness, service, and employee appearance. A drop in tourist attendance and problems with its parent company seem to be showing on the park's surface.

On the positive side, new attractions are replacing ones which have run their course. The Funtastic World of Hanna-Barbera, Alfred Hitchcock: The Art of Making Movies, and Kongfrontation have been dropped in favor of updated Universal favorites Jimmy Neutron and Shrek. And when you want to forsake Universal's land-based action rides, an added attraction is a few blocks away. Wet 'n Wild (owned by Universal, but not officially part of Universal Orlando Resort) offers an afternoon of aquatic adrenaline and a convenient place to cool off.

UNIVERSAL STUDIOS FLORIDA

Disney does an extraordinary job when it comes to showmanship, which may be why Universal Studios has taken advantage of its distinctly non-Disney heritage to add attitude to its presentations. Universal Studios performers aren't above tossing in sometimes risque jokes and asides to get a cheap laugh.

Although this theme park caters to many different types of people, its primary appeal is to those who like loud, fast, high-energy attractions. If you want to calm down, there are quiet, shaded parks and a children's area where adults can enjoy a respite while the kids are ripping through assorted playlands at 100 mph. There are some, however, who miss the sort of connection that Disney forges with the public through its carefully developed history of singable songs and cuddly characters.

The park's 444 acres are a bewildering conglomeration of stage sets, shops, reproductions of New York and San Francisco, and anonymous soundstages housing themed attractions, as well as genuine moviemaking paraphernalia. On the map, these sets are neatly divided into six neighborhoods, which wrap themselves around a huge lagoon. The neighborhoods are **Production Central,** which spreads over the entire left side of the Plaza of the Stars; **New York,** with excellent street performances at 70 Delancey; the bicoastal **San Francisco/Amity; World Expo; Woody Woodpecker's KidZone;** and **Hollywood.**

Although it may look easy to navigate on a map, on foot a quick run through the park to hit the top rides first is difficult, since it involves a few long detours and some backtracking. If you need help, theme-park hosts are trained to provide more information than you thought you needed. Look to them for advice on moving around the park. Also keep in mind that some rides—and many restaurants—delay their openings until late morning, which may throw a kink in your perfectly laid-out plans.

In the off-season some rides and restaurants are shuttered: they're sometimes marked with misleading "reserved for special event" signs to keep people away. On busy days when everything's working right, the Universal Express system (which predates Disney's FASTPASS) can reserve you a place in a virtual line to get you on more rides faster. An important note: from using the Express system to staying at a Universal resort hotel to buying a VIP pass, do whatever you can to avoid waiting in line—it will improve your vacation considerably.

Although Universal Studios may seem like a mix of movie sets and an old-fashioned carnival (complete with cash-depleting midways to be avoided), the bottom line is that—despite the need for a spring cleaning of streets and stores and attitudes—the thrills and its informal approach make Universal Studios an entertaining respite from the sometimes synthetic worlds of entertainment you find elsewhere in Orlando.

Numbers in the margin correspond to points of interest on the Universal Studios map.

Production Central

Composed of six huge warehouses with working soundstages, this area also has added new attractions which should prove popular with kids. Follow Nickelodeon Way left from the Plaza of the Stars.

❶ Nickelodeon Studios. Much of the cable network's production has picked up and moved out west, although one show, *Slimetime Live,* is shot here for a few months each year. So what's the big attraction? Well, aside from the Slimetime Geyser in front of the studio, the show itself is a shorter version of the program that's taped for broadcast and the age limit is dropped so kids as young as 10 can participate (but all audience members need to be at least 7 years old). If you're here when the televised show is being taped, you have a chance to be selected as a contestant—provided that a mysterious scout happens to find you and the family and that you pass the audition. This long shot is made even longer by the mystery of Nick's production scheduling. ☞ *Duration: 20 mins. Crowds: Steady, long lines. Strategy: Skip it on a first-time visit or if no shows are taping. Audience: All ages, but especially grade-schoolers. Rating:* ★★

❷ Jimmy Neutron's Nicktoon Blast. Stepping into the void left by the departed Hanna-Barbera attraction, Jimmy has arrived with a similar virtual reality ride. The boy genius is joined by a large collection of Nickelodeon characters including SpongeBob SquarePants and Rugrats, as he demonstrates his latest invention (the powerful Mark IV rocket). Things go awry when evil egg-shaped aliens (from the Jimmy Neutron film, no less!) make off with the rocket and threaten to dominate the world. The ride features computer graphics and high-tech gizmos like programmable motion-based seats as you and your fellow travelers zip through the uni-

Best of the Park

If you want to attempt to see everything in one day, arrive early so that you can take care of business and see the fabled attractions before the park gets very crowded. Another way to increase your attraction quota is to ignore the faux Hollywood streets and the gift shops. During peak seasons, you can avoid long waits at major attractions with the highly recommended Universal Express pass. With it, you choose a time for a specific ride. In this way you can bypass the line and return later for a slight-wait or no-wait admission.

2

If you're one of the first people in the park and feel you have the stamina to circle the park twice to catch the A-list rides first and then pick up the B-list later, head to your right and start with *Terminator 2* **3-D**; then make tracks down the street to *Back to the Future* **. . . The Ride** while the lines are still at a minimum. As you continue counterclockwise, *Men in Black:* **Alien Attack** is next, followed by must-see *Jaws, Earthquake—***The Big One,** and, finally, back near the entrance, *Twister* **. . . Ride It Out.**

You've just circled the park, and chances are the crowds have arrived. Based on your preferences, you can backtrack to pick up other entertaining attractions like **Jimmy Neutron's Nicktoon Blast; Wild, Wild, Wild West Stunt Show; Animal Planet Live!;** and the **Universal Horror Make-Up Show.** The remaining rides and attractions are up to you. If the lines are short, all that remains are a tour of **Nickelodeon Studios,** the ride and show collection at *Woody Woodpecker's KidZone,* **Shrek 4-D,** and **Lucy: A Tribute.** It's been a full day. Go get some rest.

On Rainy Days

Unless it's the week after Christmas, rainy days mean that the crowd will be noticeably thinner. Universal is one of the area's best bets in rainy weather—the park is fully operational, and there are many places to take shelter from downpours. Only a few street shows are canceled during bad weather.

---

verse. ☞ *Duration: 8 mins. Crowds: Will likely be heaviest early in the day. Strategy: If you can talk your kids into waiting, come at the end of your visit. Audience: All ages. Rating:* ★★★

❸ **Shrek 4-D.** Mike Myers, Eddie Murphy, Cameron Diaz and John Lithgow reprise their vocal roles as the swamp-dwelling ogre, Shrek; his faithful chatterbox companion, Donkey; his bride, Princess Fiona; and the vengeful Lord Farquaad in a new animated saga. There is trouble in the Kingdom of Duloc as Shrek, Princess Fiona and Donkey leave for a honeymoon at enchanting Fairytale Falls. When the ghost of Lord Farquaad interrupts their honeymoon bliss, they—and you—are going to be in the center of an adventure marked by an aerial dogfight between fire-breathing dragons and a plunge down a 1,000-foot deadly waterfall. OgreVision glasses will bring the spectacle into sharper focus, and specially built seats will keep you on the edge of your seat during the 12-minute show. ☞ *Duration: 12 mins. Crowds: Likely to be heavy. Audience: All ages. Strategy and Rating: At press time, this ride had not yet opened.*

New York

This Universal take on the Big Apple recalls the original—right down to the cracked concrete and slightly stained cobblestones. Keep in mind that many of the sets you see are used in music videos and commercials. The **Blues Brothers Bluesmobile** regularly cruises the neighborhood, and musicians hop out to give scheduled performances at 70 Delancey. Adding a new and bizarre twist on music, dance, and the afterlife, **Extreme Ghostbusters: The Great Fright Way** is another scheduled street performance in which the Ghostbusters face down Beetlejuice, who turns them into a dreaded boy band. Now why didn't Andrew Lloyd Webber think of a show like this?

4 *Twister . . . Ride It Out.* This attraction accomplishes in two minutes what it took the highly contrived movie two long hours to do—and overall it's far more exciting. After enduring a slow line and a fairly boring lecture from the movie's stars about the destructive force of tornadoes, you're eventually ushered into a standing-room theater where a quiet country scene slowly transforms into a mighty scary make-believe windstorm. An ominous, five-story-high funnel cloud weaves in from the background to take center stage as 110 decibels of wind noise, crackling electrical lines, and shattered windows add to the confusion. A truck, signs, car, and cow are given frequent-flyer points as they sail across the stage; and even though you know you're in a building and more victims are waiting patiently outside, when the roof starts to fly away your first instinct is to head for the root cellar. Don't. Watch the whole thing and marvel at the special-effects masters who put this together—and tear it apart every few minutes. ☞ *Duration: 3 mins. Crowds: Expect very long lines. Strategy: You can use Universal Express here; otherwise, go first thing in the morning or at closing. Audience: All but young children, who may be frightened. Rating:* ★★★

5 **Revenge of the Mummy.** The Brendan Fraser film was seat-of-the-pants fun, and a new $40 million ride promises an unusual fusion of special effects that combine roller coaster technology, pyrotechnics, and some super-scary skeletal warriors into a spine-tingling journey through Egyptian burial chambers and passageways. The "psychological thrill ride" was designed in collaboration with *The Mummy* director Stephen Sommers. *At press time, Revenge of the Mummy was scheduled to replace the old Kongfrontation by spring 2004.*

San Francisco/Amity

This area combines two sets. One part is the wharves and warehouses of San Francisco's Embarcadero and Fisherman's Wharf districts, with cable-car tracks and the distinctive redbrick Ghirardelli chocolate factory; the other is the New England fishing village terrorized by Jaws.

6 **Beetlejuice's Graveyard Revue.** Whew! This is *some* show. In an amphitheater, a Transylvanian castle is the backdrop for Beetlejuice, who takes the stage and warms up the audience with his snappy lines, rude remarks, and sarcastic attitude. Then for some reason, which is hard or useless to remember, he introduces the stars of the show: Frankenstein's monster and his bride, the Werewolf, and Dracula. Thus begins a stage show never before seen on this planet. At some point, the monsters doff their traditional costumes in favor of glitzy and hip threads and sing the greatest hits of such diverse artists as Ricky Martin, Santana, Gloria Gaynor, and the Village People. Upping the weirdness factor, two Solid Gold–style dancers add sex appeal to the production. Despite a sense of pity for the performers (which once included *NSync's Joey Fatone

When to Go
Weekends are busiest here, with locals taking advantage of annual passes, although weekday traffic rises and falls depending on the season. Summers are usually crowded and hot and miserable all day, and the crowds return during Spring Break, the holidays, and special event dates such as Halloween Horror Nights.

Hours change with the seasons and the park, so be sure to call a few days before your visit to get current information. You can also get detailed info at www.universalorlando.com.

2

Hit the Ground Running
If you aren't a resort guest, arrive in the parking lot 45 minutes early and head for the biggest attractions first.

When entering the park, many people are attracted to the towering soundstages to their left. Head to your right (bypassing shops and restaurants) to avoid crowds, especially early in the day.

If you're overwhelmed by what to see and do, check with Guest Services, where Universal reps will create an itinerary for you based on your interests and available time. As you streamline your day down to exactly what you want to see, you'll find the free service may be worth a million bucks.

When You're There
Set up a rendezvous point and time early in the day, just in case you and your companions get separated. Good places are in front of the Lucy Tribute near the entrance, by the stage area across from Mel's Drive-In, and by the seating area of Beetlejuice's Graveyard Revue.

Be sure to write down your parking location.

Carry an AAA card? Show it and you'll receive 10 percent off food and merchandise purchases at selected gift shops and restaurants at both theme parks and CityWalk.

If you're traveling with small children, avoid backtracking. Universal is just too big. Expect them to get wet at Fievel's Playland and absolutely drenched at Curious George Goes to Town—bring a bathing suit or change of clothing. Look for a nearby locker where you can stash the spare clothes.

Head to the Front of the Line
Using a Universal Express pass is one of the best pieces of theme park intelligence you'll ever need to know. They're available during peak seasons to every guest at nearly every major ride and show. To obtain your pass, go to a well-marked kiosk near the entrance of the ride, make a reservation for a time later in the day, go out and enjoy a meal or other lesser attraction, and then return at the time stamped on your pass for priority admission to the ride. To be fair, you'll have to use the first pass before you're able to get, or use, a second one. Even better than a pass are the privileges you'll receive by staying at a Universal resort hotel. As a resort guest, your room key lets you bypass the crowds and go directly to the head of the line—a major time-saver.

Universal Studios

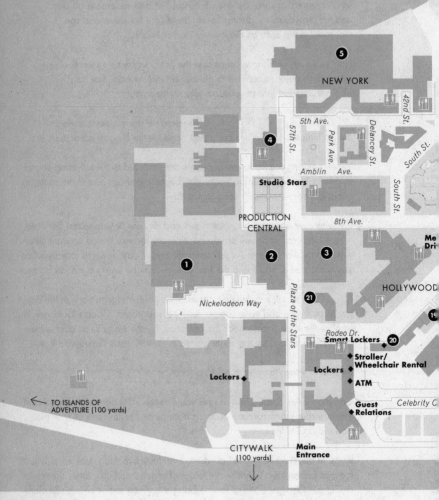

NEW YORK

5th Ave.

57th St.

42nd St.

Park Ave.

Delancey St.

South St.

South St.

Amblin Ave.

Studio Stars

PRODUCTION CENTRAL

8th Ave.

Me Dri

Nickelodeon Way

HOLLYWOOD

Plaza of the Stars

Rodeo Dr.
Smart Lockers

Lockers ◆

Lockers

◆ **Stroller/ Wheelchair Rental**

◆ **ATM**

Celebrity C

Guest ◆ Relations

← TO ISLANDS OF ADVENTURE (100 yards)

CITYWALK (100 yards) ↓

Main Entrance

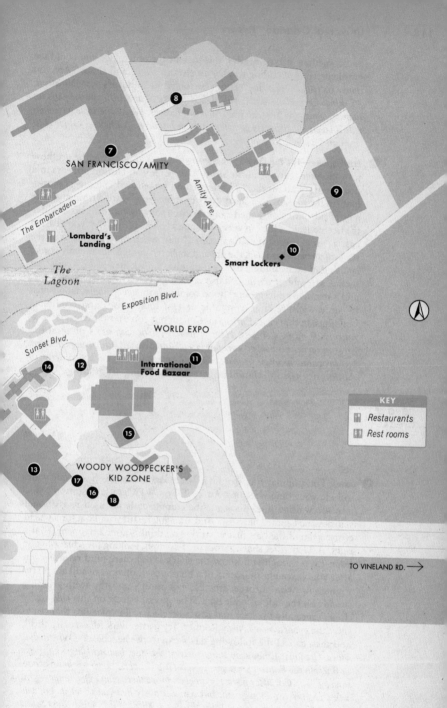

and comedian Wayne Brady), this may be the only place you could see Frankenstein pretending to play an electric guitar and shout "Are you ready to rock, Orlando?" Don't be fooled by imitators. ☞ *Duration: 25 mins. Crowds: Steady, but high capacity of amphitheater means no waiting. Strategy: You can use Universal Express here; otherwise, go when ride lines are at capacity or after dark on hot days. Audience: Older children and adults. Rating:* ★

❼ Earthquake—The Big One. Unless you volunteer as an extra, the preshow for onlookers can be a little slow. After Charlton Heston appears in a documentary about the 1973 movie and preselected volunteers participate in the making of a short disaster scene, you board a train and take a brief ride into a darkened San Francisco subway tunnel. This is where the heebie-jeebies kick in very, very quickly. The idea is that you've been cast as an extra for the "final scene," and when the train parks at the station, a few lights flash, the ground starts to shake, and suddenly you're smack dab in the middle of a two-minute, 8.3 Richter scale tremor that includes trembling earth, collapsing ceilings, blackouts, explosions, fire, and a massive underground flood coming from every angle. Don't miss it—unless you're claustrophobic or fear loud noises and crumbling buildings. In that case, *Earthquake* might put you over the edge. ☞ *Duration: 20 mins. Crowds: Heavy. Strategy: You can use Universal Express here; otherwise, go early or late. Audience: All but young children. No pregnant women or guests with heart, back, or neck problems or motion sickness. Minimum height: Without adult, 40". Rating:* ★★★

need a break? If you plan to have a full-service meal later inside (or outside) the park, a quick burger may be all you need to make it through the day. In San Francisco/Amity, **Richter's Burger Co.** lets you drop in and create your own burger or grilled chicken sandwich. Pretty quick, pretty convenient.

❽ Jaws. This popular ride around a 7-acre lagoon usually has a long wait, so bide your time watching Amity TV on WJWS, a fake station piped into the waiting line. Look for the commercials for used recreational vehicles and candied blowfish. And after you board your boat for a placid cruise around the bay, just what do you think's gonna happen? That's right. A 32-ft killer shark zeroes in at 20 mph, looking for a bite of your boat. Even though you know the shark is out there (and returns even after you've sought the safety of a boathouse), things can still get pretty frightening with surprise attacks, explosions, and the teeth-grinding sounds on the side of your boat. The special effects on this ride really shine, especially the heat and fire from electrical explosions that could singe the eyebrows off Andy Rooney. Try it after dark for an extra thrill, and then cancel the following day's trip to the beach. ☞ *Duration: 7 mins. Crowds: Lines stay long most of the day, but nothing like those at Back to the Future. Strategy: You can use Universal Express here; otherwise, go early or after dark for an even more terrifying experience—you can't see the attack as well, but can certainly hear and feel it. For the shortest lines, cast off for Jaws during a Wild, Wild, Wild West Stunt Show. Audience: All but young children, who will be frightened. No pregnant women or guests with heart, back, or neck problems or motion sickness. Rating:* ★★★

❾ Wild, Wild, Wild West Stunt Show. On the set of a frontier town, a mother and her two ne'er-do-well sons try to join Universal's professional stunt team; a setup for a live show filled with trapdoors, fistfights, bullwhips, bad gags, explosions, and shoot-outs. The quality of the stunts is matched only by the performers' lack of acting ability. Don't waste your time standing in line; there are plenty of seats and you should be able to walk right in after the majority of the crowd has entered. ☞ *Duration: 16 mins. Crowds: Large, but its 2,000-seat amphitheater means no waiting. Strategy: You can use Universal Express here; otherwise, go after dark, when the amphitheater is cooler. Note the splash zone near the well if you want to stay dry (or get wet). Audience: All ages. Rating:* ★★

World Expo

The far corner of the park contains Universal Studios' most popular attractions, *Back to the Future . . . The Ride,* and *Men in Black: Alien Attack.* These two make this the section to see for major thrills.

❿ **Men in Black: Alien Attack.** This star attraction is billed as the world's first "ride-through video game." The preshow provides the story line: to earn membership into MIB, you and your colleagues have to round up aliens who escaped when their shuttle crashed on Earth. A laser gun is mounted on your futuristic car, but unfortunately, since the gun's red laser dot is just a pinpoint, it's hard to see where you've shot. No one tells you exactly when, where, or what to shoot so you go through the attraction not knowing if you're successfully hitting targets—or having any fun. But you're already here so you might as well set off on a trip through dark New York streets, firing at aliens to rack up points. Keep in mind they can fire back at you and send your car spinning out of control. Be prepared to stomach the ending, when your car ends up swallowed by a 30-ft-high bug. To escape, you have to shoot your way out of the belly of the beast. Depending on your score, the ride ends with one of 35 endings, ranging from a hero's welcome to a loser's farewell. *Duration: 4½ mins. Crowds: Up to an hour in busy season. Strategy: You can use Universal Express here; otherwise, go during a Wild, Wild, Wild West Stunt Show, or first thing in the morning. Audience: Older children and adults. The spinning nature of the cars may cause dizziness, so use caution: no guests with heart, back, or neck problems or motion sickness. Rating:* ★★★

⓫ *Back to the Future . . . The Ride.* At heart, this is a motion simulator ride. Following a long wait you are seated in a cramped eight-passenger De-Lorean that takes off into a series of realistic past, present, and future scenes projected on a seven-story, one-of-a-kind Omnimax screen. Having no sense of perspective (or seat belts) makes this the rocking, rolling, pitching, and yawing equivalent of a hyperactive paint mixer. It is scary, jarring, and jolting. If you like your rides shaken, not stirred, this one'll be worth the wait—and the queasy feeling that'll follow you around afterward. ☞ *Duration: 5 mins. Crowds: Peak times between 11 and 3; and slightly less crowded first thing in the morning, when Twister siphons off the crowds. Strategy: You can use Universal Express here; otherwise, dash over when the gates open, or about a half hour afterward, or go later at night. Audience: Older children and adults. No pregnant women or guests with heart, back, or neck problems or motion sickness. Minimum height: 40". Rating:* ★★★

Woody Woodpecker's KidZone

Universal Studios has addressed the lack of a play area for preschoolers with this compilation of rides, attractions, shows, and places for kids to get sprayed, splashed, and soaked. It's a great place for children to burn out their last ounce of energy and give parents a much-needed break after nearly circling the park.

CloseUp

UNIVERSAL TECHS

ODDS ARE that while you're midway through a 100-ft spiral and G-forces are pushing your forehead through your feet, you won't be thinking about the technological soup of rotors and generators and gears it took to get you there. But every time you board a ride at Universal Studios or Islands of Adventures, what you experience is just the tip of a high-tech iceberg. Lasers, 3-D imaging, holograms, pulleys, motors, hydraulics, and supercharged power supplies are working like mad to ensure that, for a few minutes at least, you really think Poseidon is sparking lightning bolts or Spider-Man has joined you on a trip through New York.

Think of what your day would be like minus all this mechanical acumen. For instance, if you strapped yourself into the Incredible Hulk Coaster you'd just be sitting in a 32,000-pound lump of metal and plastic. But add four massive motors spinning fast enough to generate power to 220 smaller motors, and pretty soon you're whipping up enough force to throw this entire 32,000 pound vehicle (a mass equal to eight Mercedes-Benz cars) straight up a 150-ft track at a 30-degree incline, to rocket you from 0 to 40 mph in less than two seconds. If you want to experience a similar sensation, climb into an F-16 fighter attack jet and take it for a spin.

Less intense, but equally tricky, was creating a way to project a movie image onto a sheet of flowing water. At Poseidon's Fury, the 30-yard wide water screen flows in a steady sheet so guests can watch Poseidon on what may be the world's largest plasma screen.

At The Amazing Adventures of Spider-Man, 3-D effects, sensory drops, and virtual reality will fool you into believing you're actually being subjected to an assault of flaming pumpkins, careening garbage trucks, electric bolts, anti-gravity guns, swirling fog, frigid water, and an incredibly intense 400-ft, white-knuckle, scream-like-a-baby sensory drop. Yes, you'll believe this despite the fact that,

minutes earlier, you just walked into a 1.5-acre building in Orlando.

Each time you step inside a Universal attraction, there are more high-tech happenings going on behind the scenes . . . or right before your eyes:

The volume of air that rushes through Twister . . . Ride It Out could fill more than four full-size airborne blimps in ONE MINUTE. Its 110-decibel sound system uses 54 speakers cranking out 42,000 watts; enough wattage to power five average homes.

The motorcycle at Terminator 2 3-D is a custom-built Harley-Davidson "Fat Boy" that weighs 1,500 pounds. Its six T-70 soldiers stand eight feet tall and four feet wide.

At Back to the Future . . . The Ride, the elaborate, hand-designed and painted miniatures took two years to make and cost as much as a feature film. Twenty computers conduct 5,000 different cues to create the special ride and movie effects.

In E.T. The Adventure, there are 4,400 illuminated stars in the sky, 3,340 miniature city buildings, 250 cars on the street, and 140 street lights in the city. The ride utilizes 284 miles of electrical wiring, 250 miles of fiber optics, 68 show control computers, and 2,500 separate commands from those computers. Six thousand gallons of paint were used to cover the floor.

Earthquake—The Big One registers 8.3 on the Richter scale, releasing a slab of falling roadway that weighs 45,000 pounds. Nearly 65,000 gallons of water are released and recycled every six minutes.

Jaws's seven-acre lagoon contains five million gallons of water, 2,000 mi of wire, and 10,000 cubic yards of concrete reinforced with 7,500 tons of steel. The 32-ft steel and fiberglass shark weighs three-tons and swims at 20 ft per second with the thrust of a 727 jet engine.

12 Animal Planet Live! Animal shows are usually fun; this one is better than

most. An ark of animals is the star here, and the tricks (or *behaviors*) they perform are loosely based on shows from the cable network: *Emergency Vets, Planet's Funniest Animals,* and *The Jeff Corwin Experience.* A raccoon opens the show, Lassie makes a brief appearance, and is followed with an audience-participation segment in the clever, funny, and cute Dog Decathlon. Next, Gizmo the parrot from *Ace Ventura: Pet Detective* arrives to fly in front of a wind machine and blue screen, the televised image showing him soaring across a desert, a forest, and then in outer space. Very funny. In the grand finale Bailey the orangutan does some impressions (how an ape does Ricky Martin is a mystery), then there's an overpoweringly adorable chimpanzee, and finally there's a sneak peek at a boa constrictor, an entertaining show that shouldn't be missed. ☞ *Duration: 20 mins. Crowds: Can get crowded in peak times. Strategy: You can use Universal Express here; otherwise, go early for a good seat. Audience: All ages. Rating:* ★★★

13 E.T. Adventure. Steven Spielberg puts one of his most beloved creations on display at this large structure adjoining Fievel's Playland. To the hoarsely murmured mantra of "Home, home," you board bicycles mounted on a movable platform and fly 3 million light years from Earth (in reality just a few hundred yards), past a phalanx of policemen and FBI agents to reach E.T.'s home planet. Here the music follows the mood, and the strange sounds in E.T.'s world are as colorful as the characters, which climb on vines, play xylophones, and swing on branches in an alien Burning Man festival. Listen in at the end when E.T. offers you a personalized good-bye. ☞ *Duration: 5 mins. Crowds: Sometimes not bad, but can be heavy during busy seasons. Strategy: You can use Universal Express here; otherwise, go early. Audience: All ages. No guests with heart, back, or neck problems or motion sickness. Rating:* ★★★

14 AT&T at the Movies. You can usually tell what an attraction sponsored by a corporation will be like: it often turns out to be a boring commercial disguised as a supposedly fascinating presentation. This is no different. Here you'll find a few rooms of old microphones and recording devices and several computers, at which you can superimpose disguises on a picture of your face or hear your voice as it would sound on a Victrola. On the plus side, the air-conditioned rooms are a relief on a hot day. ☞ *Duration: Up to you. Crowds: Busy but usually not too crowded. Strategy: Go anytime. Audience: All ages. Rating:* ★

15 A Day in the Park with Barney. If you can't get enough of the big purple dinosaur, here he is again. After a long preshow starring "Miss Peek-a-Boo" (don't worry, she's rated G), parents tote their preschoolers into a theater filled with brilliantly colored trees, clouds, and stars. Within minutes, the kids go crazy as their beloved TV playmate (and Baby Bop) dance and sing though the clap-along, sing-along monster classics, including "Mr. Knickerbocker," "If You're Happy and You Know It," and (of course) "I Love You." Following the very pleasing show and a chance to meet Barney up close, you'll exit to a fairly elaborate play area featuring hands-on activities—a water harp, wood-pipe xylophone, and musical rocks—that propel the already excited kids to even greater heights. ☞ *Duration: 20 mins. Crowds: Room for all. Strategy: You can use Universal Express here; otherwise, arrive 10–15 mins early on crowded days for a good seat—up close and in the center. Audience: Young children. Rating:* ★★

16 Fievel's Playland. Another Spielberg movie spin-off, this playground's larger-than-life props and sets are designed to make everyone feel mouse-size. Boots, cans, and other ordinary objects disguise tunnel slides, water play areas, ball crawls, and a gigantic net-climb equipped with tubes, ladders, and rope bridges. A harmonica slide plays music when you slide along the openings, and a 200-ft water slide gives kids (and a parent if so desired) a chance to swoop down in Fievel's signature sardine can. It should keep the kids entertained for hours. The downside? You might have to build one of these for your backyard when you get home. ☞ *Duration: Up to your preschooler. Crowds: Not significant, although waits do develop for the water slide. Strategy: On hot days, go after supper. Audience: Toddlers, preschoolers, and their parents. Rating:* ★★

⑰ Woody Woodpecker's Nuthouse Coaster. Unlike the maniacal coasters that put you through zero-G rolls and inversions, this low-speed, mild thrill version (top speed 22 mph) makes it a safe bet for younger kids and action-phobic adults. (It's the same off-the-shelf design used on Islands of Adventures' Flying Unicorn and Goofy's Barnstormer at the Magic Kingdom.) The coaster races (a relative term) through a structure that looks like a gadget-filled factory; the coaster's cars look like shipping crates—some labeled "mixed nuts," others "salted nuts," and some tagged "certifiably nuts." Woody's Nuthouse has several ups and downs to reward you for the wait. ☞ *Duration: 1½ mins. Crowds: Heavy in midmorning and early afternoon, when the under-2 set is out in force. Strategy: Go at park closing, when most little ones have gone home. Audience: Young children and their parents. Rating:* ★★★

⑱ Curious George Goes to Town. The celebrated simian visits the Man with the Yellow Hat in a no-line, no-waiting alternative to other rides. The main town square has brightly colored building facades, and the plaza is an interactive aqua play area that adults avoid but kids are drawn to like fish to water. Yes, there's water, water everywhere, especially atop the clock tower, which periodically dumps a mighty huge 500 gallons down a roof and straight onto a screaming passel of preschoolers. Kids love the levers, valves, pumps, and hoses that gush at the rate of 200 gallons per minute: the better to spray, spritz, splash, and splatter themselves—and one another—with. At the head of the square, footprints lead to a dry play area, with a rope climb and a ball cage where youngsters can frolic among thousands of foam balls. Parents can get into the act, sit it out on nearby benches, or take a few minutes to buy souvenir towels to dry their waterlogged kids. ☞ *Duration: As long as you like. Crowds: Heavy in midmorning. Strategy: Go in late afternoon or early evening. Audience: Toddlers through preteens and their parents. Rating:* ★★★

Hollywood

Angling off to the right of Plaza of the Stars, Rodeo Drive forms the backbone of Hollywood.

⑲ Universal Horror Make-Up Show. On display in the fairly entertaining preshow area are the plaster face masks of Lon Chaney Jr., Burgess Meredith, and Jim Backus, as well as exhibits showing the methods early filmmakers used to create special-effects makeup. The real fun kicks off in the theater when a host brings out a "special-effects expert" to describe what goes into (and what oozes out of) some of the creepiest movie effects (corn syrup and food coloring makes for a dandy blood substitute, for example). The actors insert their own patter into their speeches, making the show a completely entertaining mix of movie secrets and comedy club timing. ☞ *Duration: 25 mins. Crowds: Not daunting. Strategy: You can use Universal Express here; otherwise, go in the afternoon or evening. Audience: All but young children, who may be frightened; older children eat up the blood-and-guts stories. Rating:* ★★★

FodorśChoice

㉒ Terminator 2 3-D. Arnold always says he'll be back, and he is, along with the popular film's other main characters, including a buff Linda Hamilton. Universal's show combines 3-D cinematography and digital composite computer graphics, and was directed by James *Titanic* Cameron (who also directed the first two Terminator movies). The skill shows. (Frame for frame, the 12-minute movie is the most expensive live-action film ever produced.) You've entered the headquarters of the futuristic consortium, Cyberdyne, and once you're inside the theater, a "community relations and media control" hostess greets your group and introduces their latest line of law-enforcing robots. Things go awry (of course), and the Schwarzenegger film, icy fog, live actors, gunfights, and a fantastically chilling grand finale keep the pace moving at 100 mph— although the 3-D effects seem few and far between. Kids may be scared silly and require some parental counseling, but if you can handle a few surprises, don't miss this one. ☞ *Duration: 21 minutes, with preshow. Crowds: Always. Strategy: You can use Universal Express here; otherwise, go first thing in the morning. Audience: All but very young children, who may be frightened. Rating:* ★★★

> **need a break?** In Hollywood, **Schwab's Pharmacy** is a recreation of the legendary drugstore where—studio publicists claim—Lana Turner was discovered. What you'll discover is a quick stop where you can order ice cream creations as well as hand-carved turkey and ham sandwiches.

㉑ Lucy: A Tribute. If you smile when you recall Lucy stomping grapes, practicing ballet, gobbling chocolates, or wailing when Ricky won't let her be in the show, then you need to stop here. This mini-museum (and major gift shop) pays tribute to Lucille Ball through scripts, props, costumes, awards, and clips from the comedian's estate. A challenging trivia quiz game has you trying to get Lucy, Ricky, Fred, and Ethel across country to Hollywood. It's a nice place to take a break and spend time with one of the funniest women of television. ☞ *Duration: About 15 mins. Crowds: Seldom a problem. Strategy: Save this for a peek on your way out or for a hot afternoon. Audience: Adults. Rating:* ★

Universal Studios A to Z

To research prices, get advice from other travelers, and book travel arrangements, visit www.fodors.com.

BABY CARE

There are diaper-changing tables in both men's and women's rest rooms. Nursing facilities are at two Health Services (a.k.a. First Aid) centers. One adjoins Louie's Italian Restaurant between San Francisco/Amity and New York; the other is by Guest Services, just inside Universal Studios' Main Entrance and to the right. No diapers are sold on the premises; instead, they're complimentary—to those with children in need—at Health Services.

Strollers are for rent just inside the Main Entrance to the left, next to the First Union National Bank (singles $9, doubles $15; no deposit required). No formula or baby food is sold in the park; the nearest sources are Kmart on Sand Lake Road, Walgreens on Kirkman Road, and Publix supermarkets on Sand Lake and Kirkman roads—each less than a half mile from Universal's gates.

BABY SWAP

Many rides have Baby Swap areas, so that one adult can watch a baby or toddler while the other enjoys the ride or show. The adults then change roles, and the former caretaker rides without having to wait in line all over again.

CAMERAS & FILM

Just inside the Universal Studios Main Entrance, at the **Lights, Camera, Action** shop in the Front Lot, you can find nearly everything you need to make your vacation picture perfect. The store sells disposable cameras and also rents walkie-talkies by the day ($15 for two) so that families can split up and still be in touch.

DINING

Most restaurants are on Plaza of the Stars and Hollywood Boulevard. Several accept "priority seating," which is not a reservation but an arrival time. You'll receive the first available seat after that particular time.

You can make arrangements up to 30 days in advance by calling or dropping by Guest Services when you arrive, or heading over to the restaurant in person.

FULL-SERVICE RESTAURANTS   San Francisco/Amity's **Lombard's Landing** is designed to resemble a warehouse from 19th-century San Francisco. The specialty is seafood (of course), including clams, shrimp, mussels, and catch of the day, but you can also get hamburgers, pastas, steak, and chicken.

Hidden in Production Central, **Finnegan's Bar & Grill** is an Ellis Island–era New York dining room serving shepherd's pie, Irish stew, fish and chips, and steaks. Guinness Harp and Bass ale are on tap, and there's a full liquor bar and live Irish folk music.

At the corner of Hollywood Boulevard and 8th Avenue—which turns into Sunset Boulevard along the bottom shore of the lagoon—is **Mel's Drive-In** (no reservations), a flashy '50s eatery with a menu and decorative muscle cars straight out of *American Graffiti*. For burgers and fries, this is one of the best choices in the park, and it comes complete with a roving doo-wop group. You're on vacation—go ahead and have that extra-thick shake. Mel's is also a great place to meet, in case you decide to go your separate ways in the park.

SELF-SERVICE RESTAURANTS   The **International Food Bazaar,** near *Back to the Future* . . . The Ride, is an efficient, multiethnic food court serving Italian (pizza, lasagna), American (fried chicken, meat loaf), Greek (gyros), and Chinese dishes (orange chicken, stir-fried beef) at affordable prices—usually $6–$7 an entrée). The Italian Caesar and Greek salads are especially welcome on a muggy day.

Production Central's **Classic Monsters Cafe** resembles a mad scientist's laboratory. The self-serve restaurant is open seasonally and offers wood-fired oven pizzas, pastas, chopped chef salads, four-cheese ravioli, and rotisserie chicken. Frankenstein's monster and other scary characters from vintage Universal films make the rounds of the tables as you eat. Be sure to check out the monster-meets-celebrity pictures at the entrance.

🎬 Classic Monsters Cafe ☎ 407/363-8769. Finnegan's Bar & Grill ☎ 407/363-8757. Guest Services ☎ 407/224-6350. Lombard's Landing ☎ 407/224-6400.

DISABILITIES & ACCESSIBILITY

At Universal, each attraction's sound track has appeal for those with visual impairments, and the sights interest those with hearing impairments.

In addition to being physically accommodating, the park has a professional staff that is quite helpful. At each park's Guest Services desk, you can pick up a Universal Rider's Guide which contains information for guests who require specific needs on rides, and offers details on interpreters, braille scripts, menus, and assisted devices. During orientation, all employees learn how to accommodate guests with disabilities, and you can occasionally spot staffers using wheelchairs. Additionally, power-assist buttons make it easier to get past heavy, hard-to-open doors; lap tables are provided for guests in shops; and already accessible bathroom facilities have niceties such as insulated under-sink pipes and companion rest rooms.

Many of the cobblestone streets now have paved paths, and photo spots have been modified for wheelchair accessibility. Various attractions have been retrofitted so that most can be boarded directly in a standard wheelchair; those using oversize vehicles or scooters must transfer to a standard model available at the ride's entrance—or into the ride vehicle itself.

ATTRACTIONS   **Animal Planet Live!,** the **Universal Horror Make-Up Show, Beetlejuice's Graveyard Revue,** the **Wild, Wild, Wild West Stunt Show,** *Twister* . . . **Ride It Out,** and *Terminator 2* **3-D** are all completely wheelchair-accessible, theater-style attractions. Good scripts and songs mean that even those with visual impairments can enjoy parts of all of these shows.

No motorized wheelchairs or electric convenience vehicles (EVCs) are permitted on any ride vehicle, at either park. To ride *E.T.* **Adventure,** you must transfer to the ride vehicle or use a standard-size wheelchair. Service animals are not permitted. There is some sudden tilting and accelerating, but even those with most types of heart, back, or neck problems can ride in E.T.'s orbs (the spaceships) instead of the flying bicycles. Those who use wheelchairs must transfer to the ride vehicles to experience **Woody Woodpecker's Nuthouse Coaster,** but most of **Curious George Goes to Town** is barrier-free.

If you use a standard-size wheelchair or can transfer to one or to the ride vehicle directly, you can board *Earthquake*—**The Big One,** *Jaws,* and *Men in Black* directly. Service animals should not ride, and neither should you if you find turbulence a problem. Note that guests with visual impairments as well as those using wheelchairs should cross San Francisco/Amity with care. The cobblestones are rough on wheelchair and stroller wheels.

The current **Nickelodeon Studios** tour is also completely accessible by guests using wheelchairs and enjoyable for guests with other disabilities. If you lip-read, ask to stay up front.

One vehicle in **Jimmy Neutron's Nicktoon Blast** is equipped with an access door that allows for standard-size wheelchairs, and two vehicles in the back of the attraction have closed caption screens. **Shrek 4-D** has eight handicap-equipped seats. Assisted listening devices are available at guest services.

Lucy: A Tribute is wheelchair accessible, but the TV-show excerpts shown on overhead screens are not closed-captioned. *Back to the Future* . . . **The Ride** is not accessible to people who use wheelchairs, nor are service animals permitted.

ENTERTAINMENT   There are special viewing areas at all of the outdoor shows.

RESTAURANTS   All restaurants are wheelchair accessible.

SERVICES   Many Universal Studios employees have had basic sign-language training; even some of the animated characters speak sign, but since many have only four fingers, it's an adapted version. Like Walt Disney World,

Universal supplements the visuals with a special guidebook containing story lines and scripts for the main attractions. The **"Studio Guide for Guests with Disabilities"** pinpoints special entrances available for those with disabilities; these routes often bypass the main line. You can get this and various booklets at Guest Services, just inside the Main Entrance and to the right. There's an **outgoing TTY** (Text Type Y) series hearing-impaired system on the counter in Guest Services.

WHEELCHAIR RENTALS Wheelchairs ($8) and electric wheelchairs ($40) can be rented in San Francisco/Amity and just inside the Main Entrance, next to the First Union National Bank. A driver's license or $50 deposit on a credit card is required for either, and advance reservations for the motorized wheelchairs are recommended. If the wheelchair breaks down, disappears, or otherwise needs replacing, speak to any shop attendant.

ENTERTAINMENT

If you're in Orlando at the right time of year, don't miss Universal's evening seasonal parties—most notably Mardi Gras (late February through early March), Fiesta Caliente (May), Rock the Universe (Christian music, September), the wildly popular Halloween Horror Nights (October), and Grinchmas (November/December). Except for Halloween and Rock the Universe, these festivals are included with park admission. They bring dazzling parades, live shows, and gastronomic delights. If a separate ticket is needed, then regular visitors are shooed out around 6 PM and need to have the event ticket to return when the gates reopen at 7 PM.

GUIDED TOURS

Universal has several variations on **VIP Tours,** which offer what's called "back-door admission" or, in plain English, the right to jump the line. It's the ultimate capitalist fantasy and worthwhile if you're in a hurry, if the day is crowded, and if you have the money to burn—from $120 for an individual five-hour VIP tour, including park admission, to $1,700 for an eight-hour tour for up to 15 people, again including park admission, but not including tax. You can see *Men in Black, Twister, Earthquake, Jaws, Terminator 2, Back to the Future,* and *E.T.,* but if there are other attractions you'd like to see or some you'd like to skip, your guide can suggest something else. The tours also offer extras and upgrades such as priority restaurant seating, bilingual guides, gift bags, and valet parking. Best of all, the guides can answer practically any question you can throw at them—they're masters of Universal trivia.

VIP Tours ☎ 407/363-8295.

HEALTH SERVICES/FIRST AID

Universal Studios' First Aid Centers are between New York and San Francisco (directly across from Beetlejuice's Graveyard Revue) and at the entrance between the bank and the Studio Audience Center.

HOURS

Universal Studios is open 365 days a year from 9 to 7, with hours as late as 10 during summer and holiday periods.

LOCKERS

Locker rental charges are $6 for small lockers and $9 for large ones per day. The high-priced lockers are clustered around the courtyard after you've cleared the turnstiles.

If you time it right, you may not need one because Universal also has "Smart Lockers" at major thrill rides, which are free for up to 90 minutes.

LOST THINGS & PEOPLE

If you lose an item, return to the last attraction or shop where you recall seeing it. If it's not there, then head to Guest Services. If you lose a person, there's only one place to look: head directly to Guest Services near the park entrance.

MONEY MATTERS

The First Union National Bank, just inside the Main Entrance on the right, cashes traveler's checks, makes cash advances on credit cards, and exchanges foreign currency. There's an ATM here linked to Plus, Honor, Cirrus, Visa, and MasterCard. A second ATM is in San Francisco/Amity near Lombard's Landing.

SHOPPING

Every ride and every attraction has its affiliated theme shop; in addition, Rodeo Drive and Hollywood Boulevard are pockmarked with money pits. It's important to remember that few attraction-specific souvenirs are sold outside of their own shop. So if you're struck by a movie- and ride-related pair of boxer shorts, seize the moment—and the shorts. Other choice souvenirs include Universal Studios' trademark movie clipboard, available at the **Universal Studio Store**; sepia prints of Richard Gere, Mel Gibson, and Marilyn Monroe from **Silver Screen Collectibles**; supercool Blues Brothers sunglasses from **Shaiken's Souvenirs**; plush animals, available at **Safari Outfitters, Ltd.**

Stop by Hollywood's **Brown Derby** for the perfect topper, from fedoras to bush hats from *Jurassic Park*.

VISITOR INFORMATION

Visit **Guest Services,** in the Front Lot to the right after you pass through the turnstiles, for brochures and maps in French, Spanish, Portuguese, Japanese, and German as well as English. The brochures also lay out the day's entertainment, tapings, and filmings. If you have questions prior to visiting, call Universal's main line or Guest Services.

Studio Information Boards in front of Studio Stars and Mel's Drive-In restaurants provide up-to-the-minute ride and show operating information—including the length of lines at the major attractions.

F Guest Services ☎ 407/224-6350. **Universal Main Line** ☎ 407/363-8000.

ISLANDS OF ADVENTURE

The creators of Islands of Adventure (IOA) brought theme park attractions to a new level. From Marvel Super Hero Island and Toon Lagoon to Seuss Landing, Jurassic Park, and the Lost Continent, almost everything is impressive, and the shows, attractions, and at times the rides can even out-Disney Disney.

But there are a few drawbacks: the park's layout can be difficult to grasp, and some rides and venues are still shuttered, empty, or lack a rousing ending. And you can fault the economy, slower tourist trade, or lax attitude, but similar to Universal Studios, there are parts of the park that need a good cleaning, some stores and venues and restaurants need to be re-opened or offer a reason why they're closed, and some employees need to take hint from Disney regarding service and show.

As you wander the park, you may not notice that each and every ride has a highly contrived story line, but you *will* notice that most have long queues that can stretch—get this—for more than half a mile! While you may feel long waits are a necessary evil of theme parks, you can use Universal Express to reserve a space in line and avoid unnecessary time killers.

Overall, despite some superficial glitches, Islands of Adventure has more than enough appeal for a day (or two) of fun. The park's five themed islands, connected by walkways, are arranged around a large central lagoon. The waterside is a good place to relax, either as a method to escape crowds or to recuperate from an adrenaline-surging coaster.

After passing the turnstiles, you've arrived at the Port of Entry plaza. This international bazaar brings together bits and pieces of architecture, landscaping, music, and wares from many lands: you may see Dutch windmills, Indonesian pedicabs, African masks, and Egyptian figurines. It's a visually stimulating area, and a massive archway inscribed with the notice THE ADVENTURE BEGINS seems accurate enough. There are bakeries and food carts and small restaurants where you are supposed to buy provisions for your journey—the first of many unnecessary story lines you're supposed to follow. Forgo the gift and food shops until later and head right into the park itself. You won't be disappointed.

Numbers in the margin correspond to points of interest on the Islands of Adventure map.

Marvel Super Hero Island

This island may return you to the halcyon days of yesteryear, when perhaps you were able to name every hero and villain in a Marvel comic book. The facades along Stanley Boulevard (named for Marvel's famed editor and co-creator Stan Lee) put you smack in the middle of these adventures, with cartoony colors and flourishes (stores are identified by signs like ARCADE and FOOD and ICE CREAM, for instance). Although the spiky, horrific tower of **Doctor Doom's Fearfall** makes it a focal point for the park, the **Amazing Adventures of Spider-Man** is the one to see. At various times Doctor Doom, Spider-Man, and the Incredible Hulk are available for photos, and sidewalk artists are on hand to paint your face like your favorite hero (or villain). Also dominating the scenery is the Hulk's own coaster, its track a vivid green. Along with a hard-driving rock sound track, the screams emanating from Doctor Doom's and from the Hulk Coaster set the mood for this sometimes pleasant, sometimes apocalyptic world.

❶ Fodor'sChoice **The Amazing Adventures of Spider-Man.** Even if you have never heard of Peter Parker or J. Jonah Jameson or have no clue what evil forces Spider-Man faces, the 4½ minutes spent in this building can make two hours standing in line worthwhile. Unlike any other ride at any theme park, this one combines moving vehicles, 3-D film, simulator technology, and special effects. Unless you use the Universal Express pass, expect a winding and torturous walk in line through the *Daily Bugle*'s offices. You learn that members of the Sinister Syndicate (Doctor Octopus [a.k.a. Doc Oc], Electro, Hobgoblin, Hydro Man, and deadly Scream) have used their Doomsday Anti-Gravity Gun to steal the Statue of Liberty. None of this matters, really, since once you board your car and don your 3-D glasses, you are instantly swept up into a weird cartoon battle. When Spider-Man lands on your car, you feel the bump; when Electro runs overhead, you hear his footsteps following you. You feel the sizzle of electricity, a frigid spray of water from Hydro Man, and the heat from a flaming pumpkin tossed by the Hobgoblin. No matter how many times you visit this attraction, you cringe when Doc Oc breaks through a brick wall, raises your car to the top of a skyscraper, and then releases you for a 400-ft sensory free fall to the pavement below. The bizarre angles and perspective at which scenes are shown are so disorienting, you really do feel as if you've entered a dimension that blurs the border between ride and reality. *Do not miss this one.* ☞ *Duration: 4½*

Best of the Park To see everything in Islands of Adventure, a full day is necessary, especially since the large number of thrill rides guarantees that long lines will greet you just about everywhere. To see the most without waiting, stay at a Universal resort hotel or arrive in the parking lot 45 minutes before the park's official opening. Also, take advantage of Universal Express ticketing.

2

This plan involves a lot of walking and retracing. It sounds crazy but it just . . . might . . . work. Unless you have preschoolers and need to see Seuss Landing first, take a left after the Port of Entry and head for the best and most popular attractions, starting with **The Amazing Adventures of Spider-Man.** Then double back to the **Incredible Hulk Coaster.** Skip Toon Lagoon in favor of the **Jurassic Park River Adventure.** In the Lost Continent next door, do **Dueling Dragons.** If it's showtime, next catch the **Eighth Voyage of Sindbad.** On the way back to Toon Lagoon, let the kids see either the **Jurassic Park Discovery Center** or **Camp Jurassic,** or both.

At Toon Lagoon, see **Dudley Do-Right's Ripsaw Falls** before or after the drenching at **Popeye & Bluto's Bilge-Rat Barges.** By now, if you're in luck, the young Dr. Seuss fans and their families will have left the park, so it's time to hit Seuss Landing. Go to **Cat in the Hat** first, then on to **One Fish, Two Fish, Red Fish, Blue Fish.** Make a stop at the **Green Eggs and Ham Cafe** to see how those green eggs are made, even if you're not ready to chow down. **Caro-Seuss-el** lets you be a kid again. Before you exit, walk through *If I Ran the Zoo.* The unusual animals here are definitely worth a look.

The remaining attractions are worthwhile if you've happened to arrive on a slow day and finish ahead of time: **Doctor Doom's Fearfall** and **Storm Force Accelatron** in Marvel Super Hero Island, the **Triceratops Discovery Trail** and **Pteranodon Flyers** at Jurassic Park, and **The Flying Unicorn** and **Poseidon's Fury** in the Lost Continent.

On Rainy Days Except during Christmas week, expect rainy days to be less crowded—even though the park is in full operation. (Coasters do run in the rain—although not in thunderstorms.) However, since most attractions are out in the open, you will get very wet.

---

mins. *Crowds: Usually inescapable unless you use Universal Express. Strategy: You can use Universal Express here; otherwise, go early in the day or at dusk. If you don't know much about Spider-Man's villains, check out the* WANTED *posters on the walls. Audience: All but timid young children; youngsters accustomed to action TV shows should be fine. No pregnant women or guests with heart, back, or neck problems. Minimum height: 40"; children under 48" must be accompanied by an adult. Rating:* ★★★

② **Doctor Doom's Fearfall.** Although the 200-ft-tall towers look really, really scary, the ride is really just pretty scary. After being strapped into a chair, you're hoisted almost to the top and then dropped to earth—with a moment of weightlessness courtesy of the brief pause at the peak. The process is then repeated with a little more force, making your plunge a little faster. Check the line, estimate your desire to be shot into the air, and your need to see a panoramic view of the Orlando skyline and Universal's parks. Leave loose items in the bins provided; no one else can reach them while you're on your trip. ☞ *Duration: 1 min. Crowds: Usually heavy all day. Strategy: You can use Universal Express here; otherwise, go later in the day, when crowds are thinner, but not on a full stomach. Audience: Older children and adults. No pregnant women or guests with heart, back, or neck problems or motion sickness. Minimum height: 52″. Rating:* ★

❸ Incredible Hulk Coaster. If you follow a clockwise tour of IOA, this is the first ride that'll catch your attention and probably the first you'll want to ride. The first third of the coaster is directly above the sidewalk and lagoon. You can watch as cars are spit out from a 150-ft catapult that propels them from 0 to 40 mph in less than two seconds. If that's enough to pique your interest, then enter and endure the queue (and the somewhat tedious artwork that explains how the superheros and villains got their powers). After you get on the coaster, prepare yourself for flesh-pressing G-forces that match those of an F-16 fighter. Things are enjoyable in a rough sort of way, since you are instantly whipped into an upside-down, zero-G position 110 ft above the ground. That's when you go into the roller coaster's traditional first dive—straight down toward the lagoon below at some 60 mph. Racing along the track, you then spin through seven rollovers in all and plunge into two deep, foggy subterranean enclosures. And just when you think it's over, it's not. It just keeps rolling along way after you've exhausted your supply of screams and shrieks. ☞ *Duration: 2¼ mins. Crowds: All the time. Strategy: You can use Universal Express here; otherwise, make a beeline either to this coaster or to Dueling Dragons as soon as you arrive in the park. The fog effects are most vivid first thing in the morning; darkness enhances the launch effect, since you can't see the light at the end of the tunnel. Front and rear seats give you almost entirely different experiences. The ride is fastest in the rear and has fine views, but is roughest on the sides; the front row, with its fabulous view of that green track racing into your face, is truly awesome—but you have to wait even longer for it. Audience: Coaster lovers. No pregnant women or guests with heart, back, or neck problems. Minimum height: 54″. Rating:* ★★★

❹ Storm Force Accelatron. This whirling ride is supposed to demonstrate the power of nature. Cartoon character Storm (of the X-Men) harnesses the power of weather to battle her archenemy Magneto (What?! A *story line?*) by having people like you board "Power Orbs." These containers convert human energy into electrical forces through the power of "cyclospin." Strip away the veneer, however, and what you've got is a mirror image of Disney World's twirling teacups. Definitely not a good idea if you have motion sickness or are prone to puking. ☞ *Duration: 2 mins. Crowds: Not a problem. Strategy: Go whenever—except after you've eaten. Audience: Older children and adults. No pregnant women or guests with heart, back, or neck problems. Minimum height: 54″. Rating:* ★★

Toon Lagoon

As you leave Marvel's world, there's no water to separate it from Toon Lagoon, just a change of pavement color and texture, midway games along the walkway, and primary colors turning to purple and fuchsia. Toon Lagoon's main street, Comic Strip Lane, makes use of cartoon characters that are instantly recognizable to anyone—anyone born before

When to Go
Aside from spring break, summer vacation, and holidays—which inevitably pack the park—crowds vary depending on the day, the season, and the weather. As at Universal Studios, Monday through Wednesday are busy. Crowds thin on Thursday and Friday and build up again on weekends, when locals join in the fun.

Call a day or two before your visit to get official park hours, and arrive in the parking lot 45 minutes early. See the biggest attractions first.

When You're There
Just in case you and your companions get separated, set up a rendezvous point and time at the start of the day. Don't pick an obvious and crowded location (such as the Jurassic Discovery Center), but a small restaurant or bridge between two islands.

Be sure to write down your parking location.

Have a filling snack around 10:30, lunch after 2, and dinner at 8 or later. Or lunch on the early side at a place that takes reservations, such as Thunder Falls Terrace or Mythos; then have dinner at 5. Be sure to make your reservations ahead of time or, at the very least, when you enter the park.

If you plan to ride the Dueling Dragons or the Incredible Hulk Coaster, wear shoes that are strapped firmly onto your feet—no flip-flops or heel-less sandals. If you wear glasses, consider bringing or wearing a sports strap to keep them firmly against your head when you're flung upside down. Neither coaster is so rough that you are certain to lose your glasses, but better safe than sorry. You should also leave loose change in one of the (temporarily free) lockers.

Head to the Front of the Line
Universal Express is available to all park guests at the more popular Islands of Adventure attractions. You check in at the ride entrance, are assigned a time, and then return later to bypass the line and ride within minutes. Those staying at a Universal resort can avoid Universal Express altogether and need only to show their room key to get to the front of the line of any attraction. If the attendance is unusually low, however, the Express system may be put on hold: the lines are already short.

2

1942, that is. Pert little Betty Boop, gangling Olive Oyl, muscle-bound Popeye, Krazy Kat, Mark Trail, Flash Gordon, Pogo, and Alley Oop are all here, as are the relatively more contemporary Dudley Do-Right, Rocky, Bullwinkle, Beetle Bailey, Cathy, and Hagar the Horrible. Either way, the colorful backdrop and chirpy music are as cheerful as Jurassic Park next door is portentous. There are squirting fountains for kids, hidden alcoves with photo ops (look for Aesop and Son) and great merchandise: a whole store is devoted to Rocky and Bullwinkle trinkets and a spate of clever Betty Boop items.

❺ **Dudley Do-Right's Ripsaw Falls.** Inspired by set-ups and a locale used on the popular 1960s animated pun-fest *Rocky and Bullwinkle*, this twist-

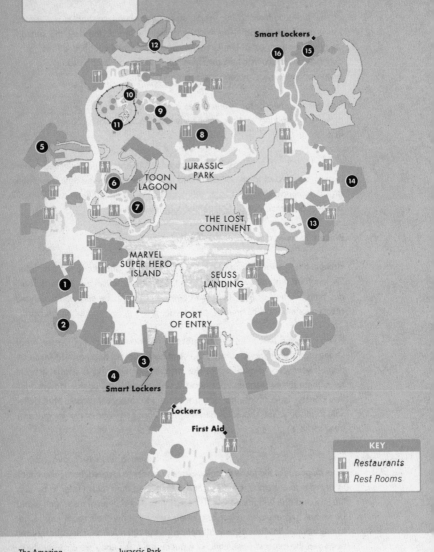

Islands of Adventure

Smart Lockers

JURASSIC PARK

TOON LAGOON

THE LOST CONTINENT

MARVEL SUPER HERO ISLAND

SEUSS LANDING

PORT OF ENTRY

Smart Lockers

Lockers

First Aid

KEY

🍴 *Restaurants*

🚻 *Rest Rooms*

ing, up-and-down flume ride is definitely wet and wild. You're supposed to help Dudley rescue Nell, his belle, from the evil and conniving Snidely Whiplash. By the time your mission is accomplished, you've dropped through the rooftop of a ramshackle dynamite shack and made an explosive dive 15 ft below water level into a 400,000-gallon lagoon, and you're not just damp—you're soaked to the skin. Actually, the final drop looks much scarier than it really is; the fact that the ride vehicles have no restraining devices at all is a clue to how low the danger quotient actually is here. You never know quite what's ahead—and you're definitely not expecting the big thrill when the time comes. If the weather is cold and you absolutely must stay dry, pick up a poncho at **Gasoline Alley,** opposite the entrance. ☞ *Crowds: Varies by season, but very heavy in the summer. Strategy: You can use Universal Express here; otherwise, go in late afternoon, when you're hot as can be, or at day's end, when you're ready to head back to your car. There's no seat where you can stay dry. Audience: All but the youngest children. No pregnant women or guests with heart, back, or neck problems. Minimum height: 44"; children under 48" must be accompanied by an adult. Rating:* ★★★

6 **Popeye & Bluto's Bilge-Rat Barges.** At times this river ride is quiet, but often it's a bumping, churning, twisting white-water raft ride that'll drench you and your fellow travelers. As with every ride at IOA, there's a story line here, but the real attraction is getting soaked, splashed, sprayed, or deluged. The degree of wetness varies, since your circular raft's spinning may or may not place you beneath torrents of water flooding from a shoreline water tower or streaming from water guns from an adjacent play area. Warning: there are no lockers here—IOA expects you to stow your stuff in a "waterproof" holder in the center of the raft. But it's not waterproof, it's waterlogged, and your stuff *will* get wet. ☞ *Duration: 5 mins. Crowds: Heavy all day. Strategy: You can use Universal Express here; otherwise, go first thing in the morning or about 1 hr before closing. Audience: All but young children. No pregnant women or guests with heart, back, or neck problems or motion sickness. Minimum height: 48"; children under 48" must be accompanied by an adult. Rating:* ★★★

7 **Me Ship, the Olive.** From bow to stern, dozens of participatory activities keep families busy as they climb around this boat moored on the edge of Toon Lagoon. Toddlers enjoy crawling in Swee' Pea's Playpen, and older children and their parents take aim at unsuspecting riders locked into the Bilge-Rat Barges. Primarily, this is designed for kids, with whistles, bells, and organs to trigger, as well as narrow tunnels to climb through and ladders to climb up. Check out the view of the park from the top of the ship. ☞ *Duration: As long as you wish. Crowds: Fairly heavy all day. Strategy: If you're with young children, go in the morning or around dinnertime. Audience: Young children. Rating:* ★★

Jurassic Park

Walking through the arched gates of Jurassic Park brings a distinct change in mood. The music is stirring and slightly ominous, the vegetation tropical and junglelike. All this plus the high-tension wires and warning signs do a great job of re-creating the Jurassic Park of Steven Spielberg's blockbuster movie—and its insipid sequels. The half-fun, half-frightening **Jurassic Park River Adventure** is the island's standout attraction, bringing to life key segments of the movie's climax.

8 **Jurassic Park Discovery Center.** If there's a scintilla of information your kids don't know about dinosaurs, they can learn it here. There are demonstration areas where a realistic raptor is being hatched and where you can see what you'd look like (or sound like) if you were a dino. In the Beasaurus area ("Be-a-Saurus"), you can look at the world from a dinosaur's point of view. There are numerous hands-on exhibits and a *Jeopardy!*-style quiz game where you can test your knowledge of dinosaur trivia. The casual restaurant upstairs is a nice place to take an air-conditioned break, and tables on the balcony overlook the lagoon. ☞ *Duration: As long as you like. Crowds: People mingle throughout, so that crowded feeling is almost extinct. Strategy: Go anytime. Audience: Older children and adults. Rating:* ★★

⑨ Triceratops Discovery Trail. This is an odd one. Supposedly, the attraction here is a walk through a safari camp, but obviously that's not much of an attraction. So you walk and walk and walk and eventually reach a large stable where there's a large triceratops. No, not a *real* triceratops but a 24-ft-long, 10-ft-high interactive robot that blinks and moves slightly when touched. There are actually three dinosaurs: on different days trails lead to a different dino. Trainers fill you in on the fake animal's family history, emotional state, and feeding habits. Kind of weird, really. ☞ *Duration: Up to you. Crowds: Minimal. Strategy: Go anytime. Audience: All ages. Rating:* ★

⑩ Camp Jurassic. Remember when you were a kid content with just a swing set and monkey bars? Well, those toys of the past have been replaced by fantastic play areas like this, which are interwoven with the island's theme. Though the camp is primarily for kids, some adults join in, racing along footpaths through the forests, slithering down slides, clambering over swinging bridges and across boiling streams, scrambling up net climbs and rock formations, and exploring mysterious caves full of faux lava. Keep an eye open for the dinosaur footprints; when you jump on them, a dinosaur roars somewhere (different footprints are associated with different roars). Watch out for the watery cross fire nearby—or join in the shooting yourself. ☞ *Duration: As long as you want. Crowds: Sometimes more, sometimes less. Strategy: Go anytime. Audience: One and all. Rating:* ★★

⑪ Pteranodon Flyers. These gondolas are eye-catching and can't help but tempt you to stand in line for a lift. The problem is that the wide, wing-spanned chairs provide a very slow, very low-capacity ride that'll eat up a lot of your park time. Do it only if you want a prehistoric-bird's-eye view of the *Jurassic Park* compound. ☞ *Duration: 2 mins. Crowds: Perpetual. Since the ride loads slowly, waits can last 1 hr or more. Strategy: Skip this on your first few visits. Audience: All ages. Children under 48″ must be accompanied by an adult. Rating:* ★

⑫ Jurassic Park River Adventure. Thanks to high-capacity rafts, the line for this water ride moves fairly quickly. You're about to take a peaceful cruise on a mysterious river past friendly, vegetarian dinosaurs. Of course, something has to go amiss or it wouldn't be much fun at all. A wrong turn is what it takes, and when you enter one of the research departments and see that it's overrun by spitting dinosaurs and razor-clawed raptors, things get plenty scary. This is all a buildup to the big finish: guarding the exit is a towering, roaring *T. Rex* with teeth the size of hams. By some strange quirk of fate, a convenient escape arrives via a tremendously steep and watery 85-ft plunge that'll start you screaming. Smile! This is when the souvenir photos are shot. ☞ *Duration: 6 mins. Crowds: Huge all day long. Strategy: You can use Universal Express here; otherwise, go early or late. Audience: All but young children, who may be frightened. No pregnant women or guests with heart, back, or neck problems. Minimum height: 42″. Rating:* ★★★

need a break? From **Thunder Falls Terrace,** which is open only in peak seasons, you can watch your fellow travelers make their harrowing plunge at the end of the Jurassic Park River Adventure. One terrace side, entirely glass, gives an optimal view. You can also sit outdoors next to the river's thundering waterfall.

Lost Continent

Ancient myths from around the world inspired this land. Just past a wooden bridge and huge mythical birds guarding the entrances, the trees are hung with weathered metal lanterns. From a distance comes the sound of booming thunder mixing with shimmering New Agey chimes and vaguely Celtic melodies. Farther along, things start to look like a sanitized version of a Renaissance Fair. Seers and fortune-tellers in a tent decorated with silken draperies and vintage Oriental carpets are on hand at **Mystics of the Seven Veils.** The gifted women read palms, tarot cards, and credit cards. **Tangles of Truth** sells ingenious puzzles. The **Dragon's Keep** carries Celtic jewelry along with stuffed dragons, toy swords in various sizes and materials, and perfectly dreadful fake rats, mice, and body parts. **Treasures of Poseidon** is stocked with shells and some baubles made from them, while a heavy drop hammer pounds out signs and symbols on classy $16.95 medallions at the interesting **Coin Mint.** In a courtyard outside the Sindbad show, a **Talking Fountain** offers flip responses to guest questions, such as "Is there a God?" Answer: "Yes. He's from Trenton and his name is Julio." Answers are followed by the fountain spraying unsuspecting guests.

13 Poseidon's Fury. Following a long walk through cool ruins guarded by the Colossus of Rhodes, a young archaeologist arrives to take you on a trek to find Poseidon's trident. Although each chamber you enter on your walk looks interesting, the fact that very little happens in most of them can wear down the entertainment quotient. To reach the final chamber, you walk through a tunnel of water which suggests being sucked into a whirlpool—hard to describe, hard to forget. Then when the wall disappears, you are watching a 180-degree movie screen on which actors playing Poseidon and his archenemy appear. Soon, they are shouting at each other and pointing at each other and triggering a memorable fireworks and waterworks extravaganza where roughly 350,000 gallons of water, 200 flame effects, massive crashing waves, thick columns of water, and scorching fireballs begin erupting all around you. Although the first fifteen minutes don't offer much, the finale is loud, powerful, and hyperactive. ☞ *Duration: 20 mins. Crowds: Heavy all the time. Strategy: You can use Universal Express here; otherwise, go at the end of the day. Stay to the left against the wall as you enter and position yourself opposite the podium in the center of the room. In each succeeding section of the presentation, get into the very first row, particularly if you aren't tall. Audience: Older children and adults. Rating: ★★*

14 Eighth Voyage of Sindbad. Stunt shows are almost always great fun, and Fodor'sChoice this one's no exception. Here's the easy-to-follow story line: Sindbad and his sidekick arrive in search of treasure, get distracted by the beautiful princess, and are threatened by a sorceress. The good guy spends the whole 25 nonstop minutes punching, climbing, kicking, diving, leaping, and Douglas Fairbanks–ing his way through the performance amid water explosions, flames, and pyrotechnics. Kids love the action, and women love Sindbad. The 1,700-seat theater can be a nice place to sit a spell and replenish your energy. ☞ *Duration: 25 mins. Crowds: Not a problem, due to size of the open-air auditorium. Strategy: You* *can use Universal Express here; otherwise, stake out seats about 15 mins prior to show time. Don't sit too close up front—you won't see the whole picture as well. Audience: Older children and adults. Rating: ★★★*

need a break? Pick up soft drinks at **Oasis Coolers** or head for the **Frozen Desert**—and be sure to check out the gleaming mosaic sign, with its gilded tiles, as you wait for your chance to order a swirled fruit-and-ice-cream sundae. **Fire-Eater's Grill** serves grilled gyros, chicken fingers, hot dogs, and spicy chicken "stingers."

⑮ Dueling Dragons. Since the cars of this ride are suspended from the track, your feet will be flying off into the wild blue yonder as you whip through corkscrews and loops and are flung upside-down and around. The twin coasters are on separate tracks so the thrill is in the near misses, which makes front-row seats a prized commodity (there's a separate, much longer line if you just *have* to ride in the lead car). Coaster weights are checked by a computer, which programs the cars to have near-misses as close as 12 inches apart. Top speed on the ride ranges 55–60 mph, with the Fire Dragon (red) offering more inversions and the Ice Dragon (blue) providing more cornering. Either way, take advantage of the small lockers (free for 45 minutes) in which you can stash your stuff: wallets, glasses, change, and, perhaps, an air-sickness bag. (NO HURLING caps are sold in the adjacent gift shop.) What you may remember most about this ride is that you have to walk *3,180 ft* (more than ½ mi) before you settled into a coaster. The creative team says the forced march is because the preshow queue through Merlinwood Forest and Merlinwood Castle tells the story of the knights who inspired the Fire and Ice coasters. Yeah, right. ☞ *Duration: 2¼ mins. Crowds: Perpetual. Strategy: You can use Universal Express here; otherwise, ride after dark, when most visitors are going home; or go early. For the most exciting ride, go for the rear car of the Fire Dragon or the front car of the Ice Dragon; be aware that the queues for the front car of both coasters are much longer. Audience: Older children with roller-coaster experience and adults with cast-iron stomachs. No pregnant women or guests with heart, back, or neck problems. Minimum height: 54". Rating: ★★★*

⑯ Flying Unicorn. If you made the mistake of putting your kid on Dueling Dragons, the antidote may be this child-size roller coaster. Following a walk through a wizard's workshop, the low-key thrill ride places kids on the back of a unicorn for a very, very brief ride through a mythical forest. This is the park's equivalent of Universal Studios' Woody Woodpecker coaster. ☞ *Duration: Less than a minute. Crowds: Moderate, but since the ride is so brief, lines move quickly. You can use Universal Express here if the lines are heavy. Audience: Kids under 7, with adults riding along for moral support. Minimum height: 36". Rating: ★★★*

need a break? If you're ready to toast your conquest of mortal fear, head straight across the plaza to the **Enchanted Oak Tavern**, ingeniously sprawled inside the huge base of a gnarled old oak tree. Chow down on barbecued chicken and ribs or corn on the cob, although the surroundings surpass the food's quality. In the adjacent Alchemy Bar, order a glass of the park's own Dragon Scale Ale.

Seuss Landing

This 10-acre island is the perfect tribute to Theodor Seuss Geisel, putting into three dimensions what had for a long time been seen only on the printed page. While adults recall why Dr. Seuss was their favorite author, kids are introduced to the Cat, Things One and Two, Horton, the Lorax, and the Grinch.

Visually, this is the most exciting parcel of real estate in America. From the topiary sculptures to the jumbo red-and-white-stripe hat near the entrance, the design is as whimsical as his books. Fencing is bent into curvy shapes, lampposts are lurching, and Seussian characters placed atop buildings seem to defy gravity. Everything, even the pavement, glows in lavenders, pinks, peaches, and oranges. Flowers in the planters echo the sherbet hues of the pavement. Stores such as **Cats, Hats & Things** and **Mulberry Store** stock Seuss books and wonderful Seussian souvenirs, from funny hats to Cat-top pencils and bold red-and-white-stripe coffee mugs. **Gertrude McFuzz's Fine-Feathered Finery** sells Seussian toppers. And when you're inspired to acquire a bit of two-dimensional Dr. Seuss, you can stop in to **Dr. Seuss' All the Books You Can Read.**

From the main avenue, you can follow the webbed footprints to **Sneetch Beach,** where the Sneetches are frolicking in the lagoon alongside a strand littered with their beach things; the Seussonic boom box even has its own sound track, complete with commercials. Look carefully in the sand and you can see where the Sneetches jumped the fence to get to the beach, fell flat on their faces, and finally started dragging their radio rather than carrying it. Nearby is the **Zax Bypass**—two Zaxes facing off because neither one will budge. And keep an eye peeled for the characters—the grouchy Grinch, Thing One and Thing Two, and even the Cat himself.

17 **The Cat in the Hat.** If you ever harbored a secret belief that a cat could actually come to your house to wreak havoc while your mom was out, then you get to live the experience here. After boarding a couch that soon spins, whirls, and rocks through the house, you roll past 18 scenes, 30 characters, and 130 effects that put you in the presence of the mischievous cat. He balances on a ball; hoists china on his umbrella; introduces Thing One and his wild sibling, Thing Two; and flies kites in the house while the voice of reason, the fish in the teapot, sounds the warning about the impending return of the family matriarch. This is high drama—and more fun than you should be allowed to have. ☞ *Crowds: Heavy. Strategy: You can use Universal Express here; otherwise, go early or near the end of the day, when the children go home. Audience: All ages. Children under 48" must be accompanied by an adult. Rating:* ★★★

18 **One Fish, Two Fish, Red Fish, Blue Fish.** Dr. Seuss put elephants in trees and green eggs and ham on trains, so it doesn't seem far-fetched that fish can circle "squirting posts" to a Jamaican beat. After a rather lengthy wait, climb into your fish, and as it spins, you (or your child) control its up-and-down motion. The key is to follow the lyrics of the special song—if you go down when the song tells you to go up, you may be drenched courtesy of the aforementioned "squirting post." Mighty silly, mighty fun. ☞ *Crowds: Thick all day. Strategy: You can use Universal Express here; otherwise, go very early or at the end of your visit when the tykes have left, so you can be a kid at heart. Otherwise, skip on your first visit. Audience: Young children. Children under 48" must be accompanied by an adult. Rating:* ★★

need a break? Grab a quick bite inside the **Circus McGurkus** fast-food eatery. Check out the walrus balancing on a whisker and the names on the booths: Tum-tummied Swumm, Rolf from the Ocean of Olf, the Remarkable Foon. Occasionally, a circus master–calliope player conducts a sing-along with the diners below.

⑲ If I Ran the Zoo. In this Seussian maze, kids can ditch the adults and have fun at their level. Here they encounter the trademarked fantasy creatures as they climb, jump, push buttons, and animate strange and wonderful animals. Park designers have learned that kids' basic needs include eating, sleeping, and getting splashed, so they've thoughtfully added interactive fountains. ☞ *Duration: Up to you and your young ones. Crowds: Probably heaviest early in the day. Strategy: If you can talk your kids into waiting, come at the end of your visit. Audience: Young children. Rating:* ★★★

⑳ Caro-Seuss-el. The centerpiece of Seuss Landing could have come straight from the pages of a Seuss book. Ordinary horse-centered merry-go-rounds may seem passé now that Universal has created this menagerie: the cowfish from *McElligot's Pool,* the elephant birds from *Horton Hatches the Egg,* and the Birthday Katroo from *Happy Birthday to You!*—an ark of imaginary animals. The 54 mounts are interactive: the animals' eyes blink and their tails wag when you get on. It's a cliché, but there's a good chance you'll feel like a kid again when you hop aboard one of these fantastic creatures. ☞ *Crowds: Lines move pretty well, so don't be intimidated. Strategy: You can use Universal Express here; otherwise, make this a special end to your day. Audience: All ages. Children under 48" must be accompanied by an adult. Rating:* ★★★

> **need a break?**
>
> Would you eat ice cream on a boat? Would you drink juice with a goat? Taste vanilla on a cone? Sip some grape juice all alone? Then there are places you must stop. Stop at **Hop on Pop Ice Cream Shop.** What do you say after **Moose Juice Goose Juice?** Say, thank you, thank you, Dr. Seuss.

Islands of Adventure A to Z

To research prices, get advice from other travelers, and book travel arrangements, visit www.fodors.com.

BABY CARE
There are diaper-changing tables in both men's and women's rest rooms, and nursing areas in the women's rest rooms; stroller rentals ($9 for singles, $15 for doubles) are at Guest Services, in the Port of Entry. Disposable diapers are available at no charge at Health Services, inside Guest Services (don't be greedy; these freebies are for emergencies). They are also for sale at De Fotos Expedition and the Universal Studios Islands of Adventure Trading Company in Port of Entry, the Marvel Alterniverse Store in Marvel Super Hero Island, Gasoline Alley in Toon Lagoon, and Mulberry Street in Seuss Landing.

BABY SWAP
All rides have Baby Swap areas, so that one parent or adult party member can watch a baby or toddler while the other enjoys the ride or show. The adults then do the Baby Swap, and the former caretaker rides without having to wait in line all over again.

CAMERAS & FILM
DeFotos is a camera shop in the Port of Entry on your right after the turnstiles.

DINING
Sit-down restaurants and fast-food eateries are scattered throughout Islands of Adventure. Several accept "priority seating," which is not a reservation but an arrival time that's issued—you receive the first available

seat after that particular time. To make arrangements up to 30 days in advance, just call Guest Services. You can also visit Guest Services or the restaurant in person when you arrive.

FULL-SERVICE
RESTAURANTS

The park's fancy mealtime option is the sophisticated and gorgeous **Mythos Restaurant,** in the Lost Continent. The menu is ambitious: crusted pork with sautéed greens and ripe plantains; mahi mahi pad thai; and a warm chocolate-banana cake. The second full-service restaurant is **Confisco's Grill,** near the lagoon at the intersection of Port of Entry and Seuss Landing. Meals include steaks, salads, sandwiches, soups, and pastas—and there's even a neat little pub. The **Thunder Falls Terrace,** in Jurassic Park, serves rotisserie chicken and ribs, although the restaurant may close when crowds are light.

SELF-SERVICE
RESTAURANTS

On Toon Lagoon, you can sample you-know-whats at **Blondie's Deli: Home of the Dagwood.** The jumbo sandwich that creates the restaurant's marquee is a hoot, and you can buy the real thing, by the inch, inside. At Seuss Landing's **Green Eggs and Ham Cafe,** traditional breakfast fare is also available. In Jurassic Park, you can have Caesar salad on a pizza crust, along with more traditional versions of the Italian specialty, at **Pizza Predatoria.** Check out the rapacious raptors on the sign.

📷 **Confisco's Grill** ☎ 407/224-9255 for reservations. **Guest Services** ☎ 407/224-6350. **Mythos Restaurant** ☎ 407/224-4534. **Thunder Falls Terrace** ☎ 407/224-4461.

DISABILITIES & ACCESSIBILITY

As at Universal Studios, Islands of Adventure has made an all-out effort not only to make the premises physically accessible for those with disabilities but also to lift barriers created through the attitudes of others. All employees attend workshops to remind them that people with disabilities are people first. And you can occasionally spot staffers using wheelchairs. Ask for the comprehensive *Guests with Disabilities* guidebook at Guest Services.

ATTRACTIONS

All attractions are completely accessible to guests who use wheelchairs with the exception of the **Incredible Hulk Coaster, Doctor Doom's Fearfall,** and **Dueling Dragons,** for which you must transfer from your chair to ride. Ask an attendant for assistance or directions to wheelchair access.

RESTAURANTS

All restaurants are wheelchair accessible.

SERVICES

Many employees have had basic sign-language training; even some of the animated characters speak sign, albeit sometimes an adapted version. You can pick up an "Adventure Guide for Rider Safety & Guests with Disabilities" booklet at Guest Services, just inside the Main Entrance and to your right as you enter the park. There's also an **outgoing TTY** (Text Type Y) series hearing-impaired system on the counter in Guest Services.

WHEELCHAIR
RENTALS

Rentals of regular and electric wheelchairs ($8 and $40, respectively) are handled at the Port of Entry to your left after the turnstiles. If the wheelchair breaks down, disappears, or otherwise needs replacing, speak to any shop attendant. If you need an electric wheelchair, make reservations in advance. Rentals require you leave either your driver's license or a $50 deposit (cash or credit card).

ENTERTAINMENT

Throughout the day there are character greetings and shows in each of the Islands. In Toon Lagoon, you may run into the **Toon Trolley,** which carries an assortment of Universal-related characters who disembark to sign autographs and pose for pictures. Adjacent to Ripsaw Falls, the Pandemonium Ampitheatre is usually dark, but does stage seasonal and/or special performances such as the skateboard and bicycle stunts of Extreme Adventures.

During the holidays, the **Grinchmas** celebration brings live shows and movie characters to Seuss Landing, and at Marvel Super Hero Island the **X-Men** make a guest appearance. During summer and holiday periods, when the park is open late, there's a big fireworks show that can be seen anywhere along the lagoon bordering the islands—the lagoon-side terrace of the Jurassic Park Discovery Center has a fairly unimpeded view.

GUIDED TOURS

Like Universal Studios, Islands of Adventure has VIP tours, which offer what's called "back-door admission"—you go straight to the head of the line. It's worthwhile if you're in a hurry, if the day is crowded, and if you have the money—prices begin around $120 for an individual five-hour VIP tour including park admission, and go up to $1,700 for an eight-hour tour for up to 15 people, again including park admission. If you can't get enough of being pampered, there's also a two-day, two-park tour for $3,000 for up to 15 people. For details, call VIP Tours. **⚡ VIP Tours** ☎ 407/363-8295.

HEALTH SERVICES/FIRST AID

There are two First Aid Centers at Islands of Adventure: one at the front entrance inside Guest Services, and the main center near Poseidon's Fury in the Lost Continent.

HOURS

Islands of Adventure is open 365 days a year, from 9 to 7, with hours extended to 10 during summer and holiday periods.

LOCKERS

The $6-a-day lockers are across from Guest Services at the entrance. There are also various Smart Lockers, which are free for roughly the first hour (and $2 per hour afterward), scattered strategically throughout the park—notably at Dueling Dragons, the Incredible Hulk Coaster, and Jurassic Park River Adventure. Stash backpacks and cameras here while you're being drenched or going through the spin cycle.

LOST THINGS & PEOPLE

If you've misplaced a possession, return to the last attraction where you had it. If it's not there, head to Guest Services in the Port of Entry. If you lose your children or others, head directly to Guest Services.

MONEY MATTERS

There's an ATM outside the turnstiles to your right leading into the Port of Entry, as well as one near Dueling Dragons in the Lost Continent.

SHOPPING

Be sure to check out the various theme shops and their treasures, ranging from a stuffed Cat in the Hat to a *Jurassic Park* dinosaur and a Blondie mug. In Toon Lagoon, you can pick up a poncho at **Gasoline Alley**, along with clever blank books and cartoon-character hats and wigs that recall Daisy Mae and others.

Wossamotta U., which is generally open just in summer, is a good source for Bullwinkle stuffed animals and clothing. The **Dinostore** in Jurassic Park has a *Tyrannosaurus rex* that looks as if he's hatching from an egg, along with all manner of educational dino toys. The **Comics Shop** stocks Spider-Man memorabilia and toys. In the **Shop of Wonders** in the Lost

Continent, Merlin wanna-bes can buy things to make magic of their own. And the **Universal Studios Islands of Adventure Trading Company** store, in the Port of Entry, stocks just about every kind of souvenir you saw elsewhere in the park.

VISITOR INFORMATION

Guest Services is located just before the turnstiles on your right before you enter the park. Step through the turnstiles and you'll find a rack of brochures and maps in French, Spanish, Portuguese, Japanese, and German, as well as English. If you have questions prior to visiting, call Universal's main line or Guest Services.

Studio Information Boards are found at the Port of Entry in front of the Lagoon (where the circular walk around the park splits). The information boards are posted with up-to-the-minute ride and show operating information—including the length of lines at the major attractions.
Guest Services ☎ 407/224-6350. **Universal Main Line** ☎ 407/363-8000.

UNIVERSAL CITYWALK

CityWalk is Universal's answer to Downtown Disney. Like Disney, they've gathered themed retail stores and kiosks, restaurants, and nightclubs and placed them in one spot—here they're right at the entrance to both Universal Studios Florida and Islands of Adventure. CityWalk attracts a mix of conventioneers, vacationers, and what seems to be Orlando's entire youth market. You may be too anxious to stop on your way into the parks and too tired to linger on your way out, but at some point on your vacation you may drop by for a drink at Jimmy Buffett's Margaritaville, a meal at Emeril's, a concert at Hard Rock Live, or a souvenir from one of several gift stores. Visiting the stores and restaurants is free, as is parking after 6 PM. The only price you'll have to pay is a cover charge for the nightclubs, or you can invest in the more sensible $9.49 one price–all clubs Party Pass admission.

WET 'N WILD

The world's first water park, Wet 'n Wild opened in 1977 and quickly became known as the place for thrilling water slides. Although it's now far from alone, Wet 'n Wild is still the nation's most popular water park thanks to its ability to create more heart-stopping water slides, rides, and tubing adventures than its competitors. There are a complete water playground for kids, numerous high-energy slides for adults, a lazy river ride, and some quiet sandy beaches on which you can stretch out and get a tan.

After skimming down a super-speedy water slide, it may be time for a break. You can bring a cooler or stop for lunch at one of several food courts and find a picnic spot at various pavilions near the lakeside beach, pools, and attractions. Pools are heated in cooler weather, and Wet 'n Wild is one of the few water parks in the country to be open year-round.

A few words of advice: if your bare feet aren't used to it, the rough and hot surface of the sidewalks and sandpaperlike pool bottoms can do a number on your soles. Bring a pair of wading slippers when you're walking around, but be ready to carry them as you're plunging down a slide. Also, the lines here are Disney-esque. Once you think you're almost there, you'll discover there's another level or two to go. Be ready to be patient. Finally, eat some high-energy food. A day here involves nearly nonstop walking, swimming, and climbing.

If you're not a strong swimmer, don't worry. Ride entrances are marked with warnings to let you know which ones are safe for you, there are plenty of low-key attractions available, and during peak season as many as 400 lifeguards are on duty daily.

Black Hole. One of the most popular attractions here, this two-person tube ride (solo travelers share a lift with a stranger) starts in the bright light of day and suddenly plunges into a curvaceous 500-ft-long pitch-black tube illuminated only by a guiding, glowing line. The lack of light makes the spinning, twisting, 1,000-gallon-a-minute torrent more fun, and you'll likely be screaming your head off as you zip into curves and up the enclosed watery banked turns. *Minimum height: 36", 48" without an adult.*

Blue Niagara. For a real thrill head to the top of this giant, six-story-tall slide. Twin tubes wrap around each other like snakes. Inside is a rushing waterfall. Since the tubes are roughly horizontal, you have the luxury of keeping your eyes open and watching the action unfold as you're shot through the curves. With two tubes, the line usually moves fairly quickly. *Minimum height: 36", 48" without an adult.*

Bomb Bay. Lines move quickly here, but not because the capacity is great. It's because a lot of kids chicken out once they reach the top. If you challenge yourself to the ultimate free fall, here's what happens: you step inside a large enclosed cylinder mounted above a nearly vertical drop. The attendant looks through the glass door to make sure your arms and legs are crossed (thereby hindering water-based wedgies), and then punches a button to release the trap door. Like a bomb dropping out of a plane, you free-fall for 76 ft and then skim down the long, steep slide. The force of the water on your feet, legs, and back can be substantial, rivaling the emotional toll it took to do it in the first place. *Minimum height: 36", 48" without an adult.*

Bubba Tub. Because up to four people can take this ride together, this is one of the park's most popular attractions. After scaling the platform, a huge inner tube is waiting to accommodate your group. From the top of the six-story slide it flows over the edge and starts an up-and-down, triple-dip, roller-coaster ride that splashes down into a watery pool. *Minimum height: 36", 48" without an adult.*

Bubble Up. After catching sight of this enormous, wet beach ball about 12-ft tall, many kids race right over to try to climb to the top and then slide back down. Surrounding the ball is a wading pool, a respite between attempts to scale the watery mountain.

Der Stuka. Adjacent to Bomb Bay is a steep slide that offers a similar thrill, but without the trap door drop. *Der Stuka,* "steep hill" in German, is hard to beat for sheer exhilaration. After climbing the winding six-story platform, you sit down on a horizontal slide, nudge yourself forward a few inches, and then gravity takes over. You're hurtling down a slippery, 250-ft-long speed slide that'll tax your back and test the security of your bathing suit. This one's a real scream. *Minimum height: 36", 48" without an adult.*

The Flyer. Another good ride for families, this four-person toboggan carries you into switchback curves and down suddenly steep drops. The turns are similar to those on a real toboggan run. *Minimum height: 36", 48" without an adult.*

Hydra Fighter. Attached by a bungee cord to several towers are several two-person seats—each with a fire hose mounted on the front. Sitting

Dress the Part

Be sensible when choosing your bathing suit. You can't wear cutoffs or anything that has rivets, metal buttons, or zippers.

If you have a pair of wading slippers, wear them. Your feet will feel the burn from the hard sidewalks and rough surfaces.

Keep money, keys, and other valuables in a locker. They could get lost on the super slides. If you wear prescription sunglasses, you can bring them on the rides; just take them off and clutch them tightly before you take the plunge.

While You're There

Bring a towel, but leave it behind when you ride. You'll dry off by the time you reach the next attraction.

Wear sunblock. The higher the SPF, the better protection it offers. Remember that you can get a sunburn even on a cloudy day.

---

back-to-back, you and your partner alternate between firing the hoses. The springy cord you're on starts to hoist you up and then from side to side. The stronger the stream of water, the higher and faster you go in all directions (and the farther you fall). Try to avoid sharing a seat with a chubby guy—it kills the bounce. Between getting everyone situated, letting them ride, and getting them unloaded, this one can mean a long wait. *Minimum height: 36", 48" without an adult.*

Kids' Park. Designed for children under 48", Kids' Park is like a day at the beach. There's a kid-size sand castle to play in, and a 5-ft-tall bucket that dumps 250 gallons of water every few minutes onto a seashell-decorated awning, where it splashes off to spray all and sundry. In the center is a pool surrounded by miniaturized versions of the more popular grown-up attractions and rides. Children overjoyed when they play with a garden hose will go absolutely nuts when they see that they can slide, splash, squirt, and swim on rides here. Tables and chairs go fast, with many families here for nearly their whole visit.

Knee Ski. A molasses-slow line marks the entrance to this attraction. A moving cable with ski ropes attached encircles a large lake. After donning protective headgear and a life vest, you kneel on a knee board or try to balance yourself on a wakeboard, grab a ski rope, and are given the opportunity to circumnavigate the lake. The ½-mi ride includes five turns: roughly 75 percent of the riders wipe out after turn number one, and 90 are gone by turn two. Only the agile and athletic few make it the distance. Hint: if you wipe out before turn one, you get to go back and try again. *Minimum height: 36", 48" without an adult.*

Lazy River. Had enough? Then settle into an inner tube for a peaceful trip down a gently moving stream. Bask in the sun as you drift by colorful flowers and tropical greenery. It's a nice break when your body just can't handle any more 45-degree drops.

Mach 5. After grabbing a soft foam board, you scale a few steps and arrive at one of three water slides. Conventional wisdom says that lane B is the best, but it's possible all three are the same. Riding on your belly, you zip through some great twists, feel the sensation of hitting the high banks, and then splash down in a flood of water. Mucho fun. *Minimum height: 36", 48" without an adult.*

The Storm. At the top of the tower, two tubes carry a torrent of water. Climb in the tube, shove off in the midst of a tidal wave, and the slow, curving arc takes you around and around until you reach a 30-ft diameter bowl. Now you spin around again like soap suds whirling around a sink drain. After angular momentum has had its fun, you drop through a hole in the bottom of the bowl into a small pool. After you get your bearings and find the surface, you may be tempted to climb up and do it again. *Minimum height: 36", 48" without an adult.*

Surf Lagoon. This 17,000-square-ft lagoon is as close to a beach as you'll get in the park, which explains why it's generally packed. Also known as the Wave Pool, it's just past the turnstiles. Every so often, the lagoon is buffeted by 4-ft-high waves, which elicit screams of delight from kids. Likewise, adults are thrilled to find that the money they spent on the kid's floats, surfboards, and inner tubes was worth it.

The Surge. The title overstates the thrill of this ride, although it borders on exhilarating. Up to five passengers can fit in this giant raft: once you've gone over the lip of the first drop, there's no turning back. The raft zips down five stories while twisting and turning through a series of steeply banked curves and beneath waterfalls. If you or your kids are too nervous for rides like Bomb Bay or the Black Hole, then this is probably a safe bet. *Minimum height: 36", 48" without an adult.*

The Wild One. Open seasonally (usually April through September), this is a large, two-person inner tube that's towed around the lake. The ease of staying afloat is countered by the challenge of hanging on when you cross the boat's wake. *Minimum height: 36", 48" without an adult.*

Strategies for Your Visit to Wet 'n Wild

Wet 'n Wild is a must-stop spot for families. It can be very crowded, especially when the weather is hot. Peak months are June through August, slowing down most from December to February. The park fills up as the day progresses. If you want to try to avoid the hordes, get here in the morning a half hour before opening hours, or come on a cloudy day. In the summer, come before or after the daily afternoon thunderstorms. Be prepared for long lines at the most popular rides, such as the Hydra Fighter and Bubba Tub.

On the surface, there doesn't seem to be much reason to go to this park when it's gray and drizzly, but as a Wet 'n Wild spokeswoman observes, "This is a water park. If you aren't coming here to get wet, why are you here?" OK. If you do come on a day that rains, it will likely be a quick summer afternoon shower that will close attractions and clear pools only until the thunder and lightning pass within 30 minutes or so. If it looks like a soggy, thorough, all-day rain, skip it.

Wet 'n Wild A to Z

To research prices, get advice from other travelers, and book travel arrangements, visit www.fodors.com.

ADMISSION

Admission is $31.95 for adults and $25.95 for children ages three to nine (plus 6.5% sales tax). The price is dropped by ten bucks roughly three to four hours before the park closes. Since closing times vary, call in advance to find out when the discount begins. For information about the Orlando FlexTicket, a combination ticket for all of the Universal Studios parks, *see* Discounts *in* Universal Orlando A to Z.

DINING
The food courts aim to cover most types of fast food. For hamburgers, hot dogs, vegetarian burgers, salads, and sub sandwiches, head to the **Surf Grill. Bubba's BBQ & Chicken** specializes in lightly smoked ribs and chicken, fried chicken strips, subs, and barbecued beef sandwiches. **Pizza & Subs** is the place to go for calzones, spaghetti, and deep-dish pizzas. When you just want something cool, you can't beat the sundaes and ice cream cones at **Cookies & Cones.** For an unusual treat, try the funnel cakes or chilly Dippin' Dots, bite-size bits of ice cream in a candy coating, at **Sidewalk Sweets.**

DISABILITIES & ACCESSIBILITY
Slides are accessible via stairway towers, which must be climbed. Guests with limited mobility might be able to bob about on a raft in **Surf Lagoon** or tube down the **Lazy River.** Many of the paths are flat and easily accessible in a wheelchair; however, no rides accommodate people using wheelchairs, and wheelchair rentals are not available.

FACILITIES
Don't think the expenses stop with parking and admission. If you came without a towel, you can rent one for $2 with a $2 deposit. Mighty small lockers, $5 with a $2 deposit, are near the entrance and at handy locations throughout the park. Tubes for the Wave Pool cost $4 with a $2 deposit. To save you $2, a combination of all three goes for nine bucks and requires a $4 deposit.

There are dressing rooms (with lockers), showers, and rest rooms to the left just after the main entrance. Additional dressing rooms, showers, and rest rooms are near the Bubble Up ride.

HEALTH SERVICES/FIRST AID
The First Aid Stand is between Surf Grill and Pizza & Subs.

HOURS
Wet 'n Wild is open 365 days a year, from 10 to 5, with hours extending from 9 AM to 9 PM in the summer. Call for exact hours during holiday periods.

LOST THINGS & PEOPLE
If you plan to split up, be sure everyone knows where and when you plan to meet. Lifeguards look out for kids who might be lost. If they spot one, they'll take the child to Guest Services, which will page the parent or guardian. The Lost & Found is at Guest Services, to the left just after you walk through the entrance to Wet 'n Wild.

MONEY MATTERS
The single ATM is located at the rental facility, which is just inside the entrance and slightly to the right as you enter the park.

PARKING
Parking is $6 for cars, $7 for RVs.

PICNICKING
You are welcome to picnic and to bring coolers with food into the park. However, glass containers and alcoholic beverages are not permitted.

There are many picnic areas scattered around Wet 'n Wild, in both covered and open areas.

SUPPLIES
Personal flotation devices, also known as life jackets, are provided by the staff. If you are looking for sunscreen, sunglasses, bathing suits, camera film, and other necessities, stop in the **Breakers Beach Shop** near the park entrance.

VISITOR INFORMATION
Wet 'n Wild has a **Guest Services** desk to the left as you enter the park.
🚩 General Information **Wet 'n Wild** ☎ 407/351-3200 recorded information; 407/351-1800 park operations.

UNIVERSAL ORLANDO A TO Z

To research prices, get advice from other travelers, and book travel arrangements, visit www.fodors.com.

Admission

One-day one-park tickets for Universal Studios or Islands of Adventure cost $52.95 for adults, and $43.41 for children three to nine, including tax. Multiday **Escape Passes** sell for $100.65 for adults and $86.87 for children for two days, two parks, and this ticket option offers a third day free as well as admission to CityWalk clubs. Tickets do not have to be used on consecutive days, but must be used within seven days of your first visit. You can get tickets in advance by mail through Ticketmaster or by contacting Universal Studios Vacations.

HAND STAMPS If you want to leave the park and come back the same day, have your hand stamped when you leave, and show your hand and your Studio Pass (ticket) when you return.
🚩 **Ticketmaster** ☎ 800/745-5000. **Universal Studios Vacations** ☎ 888/322-5537.

DISCOUNTS
If you buy tickets at the Orlando/Orange County Convention & Visitors Bureau, you save about $4 per adult ticket ($3 on children's prices). American Automobile Association members get 10% off, sometimes more, at AAA offices.

The **Orlando FlexTicket** is similar to Walt Disney World's pass system. The four-park version gets you into Universal Studios, Islands of Adventure, Wet 'n Wild, and SeaWorld—all for $180.15 for adults, and $143.05 children ages three to nine. The five-park version ($215.46 and $175.12) buys unlimited admission to all of the above plus a safari through Busch Gardens. Both the four-park and five-park FlexTickets are good for 14 days.
🚩 **Orlando/Orange County Convention & Visitors Bureau** ✉ 8723 International Dr. ☎ 407/363-5871.

Arriving & Departing by Car

Traveling east on I–4 (from WDW and the Tampa area), get off at Universal Boulevard (Exit 75A). Then take a left onto Universal Boulevard and follow the signs.

Traveling west on I–4 (from the Daytona and Jacksonville areas), take Universal Boulevard (Exit 74B). Turn right onto Hollywood Way and follow the signs.

UNIVERSAL ORLANDO TIME SAVERS

UNIVERSAL ORLANDO isn't nearly the size of the Walt Disney World resort, so navigating it is much easier. There are some ways to reduce wait time even further.

If you want to get to the best rides faster, skip the gargantuan parking garage and follow the signs to valet parking. For $14—about twice the price of regular parking—you'll be in a lot just a few steps from the entrance to CityWalk and have a head start in reaching Universal Studios and Islands of Adventure, as well.

If you're toting a baby around with you, check out the Baby Swap areas. Although you won't be able to ride with your spouse, one parent can enter the attraction, take a spin, and then return to take care of the baby while the other parent rides without having to wait in line again.

When you stay at one of Universal's resort hotels (Portofino Bay, Hard Rock Hotel, Royal Pacific), you receive early admission to the parks, priority seating at some restaurants, and the option of an unlimited-access ticket.

Do what you can to get into Universal Orlando's theme parks early—as early as 8 AM. Seriously. Seeing the park with about 100 other people is far better than seeing it with thousands. You can do in a few hours what could otherwise take an entire day. Plus, it's cooler in the morning: you can always leave and come back later if you get tired.

CAR CARE

A Hess gas station is conveniently located at the Turkey Lake Road entrance. If you need a battery jump in the parking garage, raise your hood and speak to the nearest employee.

PARKING

Universal's single parking garage complex, which serves both theme parks and CityWalk, is one of the world's largest car parks. Because your vehicle is covered, it's not so sweltering at the end of the day even when it's hot. The cost is $8 for cars, $10 for campers. Valet parking is available for $14.

Visitor Information

🎫 Universal Orlando ✉ 1000 Universal Studios Plaza, Orlando 32819-7610 ☎ 407/363-8000 or 888/331-9108 🌐 www.universalorlando.com

SEAWORLD ORLANDO AND BUSCH GARDENS

3

FODOR'S CHOICE

Myombe Reserve, in Busch Gardens

Pets Ahoy, in SeaWorld

Rhino Rally, in Busch Gardens

Sea Lion and Otter Stadium, in SeaWorld

Shamu Rocks America, in SeaWorld

Updated by
Gary
McKechnie

IN CENTRAL FLORIDA, two other parks—SeaWorld Orlando and Busch Gardens—vie for the tourists (and money) not already pledged to Disney or Universal. For entertainment value and location, perhaps the best choice is SeaWorld. Just 10 minutes from both Universal and Disney, it is designed for animal lovers and anyone who favors a slower-paced park. The legendary animal and dolphin-theme presentations, as well as high-energy circus stage shows, ski displays, and the addition of two thrill coasters make this a must-see.

SeaWorld's highly publicized "add-on" attraction, Discovery Cove, is also worth considering. At this laid-back oasis, you can pose with (as opposed to swim with) a dolphin. There's plenty of time to relax on a tropical beach, and when you leave you get a pass good for seven days' admission to the SeaWorld park.

Busch Gardens is roughly 90 minutes from Orlando. Once this just seemed a useful place to stash the brewing family's collection of exotic animals and birds while tending to the real business of making and selling beer. In the end, the call of the wild proved so strong that the brewery became a sidekick to Busch Gardens' Africa-themed park and zoo. Busch Gardens is now a major zoological and thrill-ride park. If you've already counted on a Gulf Coast beach excursion, then the Tampa park is well worth a side trip.

As this book went to press, Cypress Gardens, Florida's original amusement park, closed its doors for the last time after over sixty years of entertaining visitors with its unique combination of a botanical garden, amusement park, and waterskiing show. Though its days as a tourist attraction seemed finally over, the fate of the 200 acres of land and gardens that composed the park remained undecided at press time.

SEAWORLD ORLANDO

There's a whole lot more to SeaWorld than Shamu, the "stage name" used for its mammoth killer-whale mascots. Sure, you can be splashed by the whales, stroke a stingray, see manatees face-to-snout, learn to love an eel, and be spat at by a walrus. But as the world's largest marine adventure park, SeaWorld celebrates all the mammals, birds, fish, and reptiles that live in the ocean and its tributaries.

Every attraction is designed to showcase the beauty of the marine world and to demonstrate ways that humans can protect its waters and wildlife. The presentations come across as thoughtful reminders of humanity's responsibility to safeguard the environment. Best of all, SeaWorld's use of humor plays a major role in this education.

The park rivals Disney properties for sparkling cleanliness, courteous staff, and attention to detail. Because there are more exhibits and shows than rides, you can go at your own pace without that hurry-up-and-wait feeling. And despite the park's size (200 acres), touring it can actually be calming.

First-timers may be slightly confused by the lack of distinct "lands" here—SeaWorld's performance venues, attractions, and activities surround a 17-acre lake, and the artful landscaping, curving paths, and concealing greenery sometimes lead to wrong turns. But armed with a map that lists show times, it's easy to plan a chronological approach that flows easily from one show and attraction to the next and allows enough time for rest stops and meal breaks.

Numbers in the margin correspond to points of interest on the SeaWorld map.

1 Dolphin Nursery. In a large pool, dolphin moms and babies (with birth dates posted on signs) play and leap and splash. You can't get close enough to pet or feed them, so you'll have to be content peering from several feet away and asking the host questions during a regular Q and A session. Here's a popular answer: No, you can't take one home. *☞ Crowds: Not a problem. Strategy: Go during a Shamu show so the kids can be up front. Audience: All ages. Rating:* ★★

2 Tropical Reef. A good place to get out of the sun or rain, this indoor walk-through attraction contains 30 small aquariums filled with weird, ugly, and/or beautiful tropical fish, eels, worms, and crustaceans. The fish lay camouflaged on the bottom, dig holes, glow in the dark, or float lazily and stare at you through the glass. Clear and concise printed descriptions reveal interesting facts about each tank's inhabitants, leading to comments such as, "Hey, cool, look at this one!" or "Hey, let's go get some sushi." *☞ Crowds: Not usually a problem. Strategy: Go at the end of the day—because it's near the entrance, most people stop here on their way in. Audience: All ages. Rating:* ★★

3 Turtle Point. At this re-creation of a small beach and lagoon, many of the sea turtles basking in the sun or drifting in the water were rescued from predators or fishing nets. Injuries make it impossible for these lumbering beauties to return to the wild. A kiosk is filled with sea turtle info, and an educator is usually on hand to answer questions. Well worth a brief look. *☞ Crowds: Sporadically crowded, but generally enough space for all to get a good view. Strategy: Go anytime. Audience: All ages. Rating:* ★★

4 Stingray Lagoon. In a broad, shallow pool, dozens of stingrays are close enough to touch, as evidenced by the many outstretched hands surrounding the rim. Smelts (small sardinelike fish) are available for $3 a tray at nearby concession stands. They are a delicacy for the rays, and when they flap up for lunch you can feed them and stroke their velvety skin. Even though they still have their stingers they won't hurt you; they just want food. This is one of the most rewarding experiences for everyone, and the animals are obligingly hungry all day. Look for the nursery pool with its baby rays. *☞ Crowds: Can make it hard to get to the animals during busy seasons. Strategy: Walk by if it's crowded, but return before dusk, when the smelt concession stand closes. Audience: All ages. Rating:* ★★★

5 Key West at SeaWorld. This laid-back, 5-acre area is modeled after Key West, Florida's southernmost outpost, where the sunsets are spectacular and the mood is festive. There are no distinct "lands" within Sea-World, but Key West at SeaWorld comes close, containing individual shows and attractions within its loosely defined borders. If you liked the stingrays, then look for the huge pool that holds a few dozen Atlantic bottlenose dolphins—they're hungry, too. Each evening, Sea-World re-creates the real Key West's Sunset Celebration as children get their faces painted and have their pictures taken with a larger-than-human-size Shamu or Dolly Dolphin. A reggae beat gets things grooving, and even the dolphins seem to join the party. It's a fun place to end the day and a nice prelude to the nighttime Shamu show on the other side of the park. *☞ Crowds: Can get thick. Strategy: To get a good seat, attend a late Shamu show and hit Key West on your way out of the park or before the crowds thicken for the Sunset Celebration. Audience: All ages. Rating:* ★★★

6 Key West Dolphin Stadium. In this thoroughly enjoyable show, bottlenose dolphins and a couple of Pseudorca whales (cousin to the killers) wave,

Best of the Park

Although there's room for all at the stadiums, the other attractions—especially Penguin Encounter and Key West at SeaWorld—can get unpleasantly crowded, and there may be lines at Wild Arctic, Shark Encounter, and Journey to Atlantis.

After passing the turnstiles, go straight ahead to the information desk for a park map and schedule of the day's shows. In this courtyard, take a moment to review show times and plan your day. With luck, you can set up a clockwise tour of the park by seeing the show at **Key West Dolphin Stadium,** and then visiting no-line attractions like **Turtle Point, Stingray Lagoon,** and **Dolphin Cove.** While you're in the neighborhood, allow time to see **Manatees.**

A few feet away are the park's two roller coasters, **Kraken** and **Journey to Atlantis.** Chances are there'll be a line so you'll have to decide if you want to stay or return once the crowds have thinned. **Penguin Encounter** is a good next stop, followed by a chance to visit and feed the sea lions at **Pacific Point Preserve.** Remember to keep track of the time so you can find a good seat at the **Sea Lion & Otter Stadium.** If you've built up an appetite by now, you may want to hit one of the three nearby places for quick bites: **Chicken 'n' Biscuit,** the **Waterfront Sandwich Grill,** or the **Dockside Smokehouse.**

Shark Encounter is the next upcoming popular attraction, followed by the arcades, games, and playground of **Shamu's Happy Harbor.** Check the show schedules again to take in a performance at **Shamu Stadium** and stick around afterward to visit the **Wild Arctic.**

You've now seen most of the attractions, and you'll likely have time to see the **Dolphin Nursery** and **Tropical Reef** before heading back to **Key West at SeaWorld** for the Sunset Celebration. If your feet are still friendly, you may consider a cross-park hike back to **Shamu Stadium** for the *Shamu Rocks America* show.

On Rainy Days

Although SeaWorld gives the impression of open-air roominess, nearly a third of the attractions are actually indoors, and many others are shielded from the elements by canopies, cantilevered roofs, or tautly stretched tarpaulins. Rides that may close during a thunderstorm include Journey to Atlantis, Kraken, Sky Tower, Ski Show, Shamu's Happy Harbor, and the Paddle Boats. If you're unprepared for a cloudburst, pick up a poncho at one of the ubiquitous concession stands, and dive right in.

---

leap, and do back flips as the crowd oohs and aahs. In one sequence, a trainer rides on one of their backs and then gets torpedoed into the air. Sure, these acts are a staple of marine parks, but there seems to be more entertainment in this 20-minute show than in a week of prime-time television. Make plans to get here early for a few reasons: a Jimmy Buffett–style crooner plays some soothing songs; and if you ask an attendant, your child may be chosen to help the trainer conduct a dolphin behavior (what used to be called a "trick"). ☞ *Duration: 20 mins. Crowds:*

You can always get in. Strategy: Sit in the first four rows if you want to get splashed. Audience: All ages. Rating: ★★★

❼ Manatees: The Last Generation? If you don't have time to explore Florida's springs in search of manatees in the wild, then don't miss the chance to see this. The lumbering, whiskered manatees, which look like a cross between walruses and air bags, were brought here after near-fatal brushes with motorboats. Tramping down a clear tunnel beneath the naturalistic, 3½-acre lagoon, you enter Manatee Theater, where a film describes the lives of these gentle giants and the ways in which humans threaten the species' survival. In Manatee Habitat, a 300,000-gallon tank with a 126-ft seamless acrylic viewing panel, you can look in on the lettuce-chomping mammals as well as native fish, including tarpon, gar, and snook. Keep an eye out for mama manatees and their nursing calves. ☞ *Crowds: Since the area is fairly large, that "crowded" feeling is nonexistent. Strategy: Go during a Shamu show and not right after a dolphin show. Audience: All ages. Rating:* ★★★

❽ Journey to Atlantis. SeaWorld's first entry in Florida's escalating "coaster wars" combines elements of a high-speed water ride and roller coaster with lavish special effects. There are frequent twists, turns, and short, shallow dives but few hair-raising plunges except for the first, which sends you nearly 60 ft into the main harbor (plan on getting soaked to the skin), and the final drop, a 60-ft nosedive into S-shape, bobsledlike curves. Like most other attractions, this has a story line that doesn't really matter, but here it is: the lost continent of Atlantis has risen in the harbor of a quaint Greek fishing village, and you board a rickety Greek fishing boat to explore it. Once you're inside, an ominous current tugs at your boat, and an old fisherman offers a golden sea horse (actually Hermes—the messenger of the gods—in disguise!) to protect you from the evil Sirens. That's it. The wild, watery battle between Hermes and Allura (queen of the Sirens) is all a ploy to crank up effects using liquid crystal display technology, lasers, and holographic illusions. ☞ *Duration: 6 mins. Crowds: Large. Strategy: Make a beeline here first thing in the morning or go about an hr before closing; going at night is definitely awesome, and the wait, if there is one, will be cooler. Audience: Older children and adults; definitely not for the faint of heart or for anyone with a fear of dark, enclosed spaces. Minimum height: 42".* *Rating:* ★★★

❾ Kraken. SeaWorld rolled out its second coaster with a different approach and story line. Big draws for coaster enthusiasts are the seven inversions and moments of weightlessness. Folks around these parts claim this is the tallest (149 ft) and fastest (up to 65 mph) and only floorless coaster. *Duration: 6 mins. Crowds: Expect lines. Strategy: Get to the park when it opens and head straight to Kraken. Audience: Older children and adults. Minimum height: 54".* *Rating:* ★★★

❿ Penguin Encounter. In a large white building between Key West Dolphin Stadium and Sea Lion & Otter Stadium, 17 species of penguin scoot around a refrigerated re-creation of Antarctica. They're as cute as can be, waddling across icy promontories and plopping into frigid waters to display their aquatic skills. You watch an average day in their world through the thick, see-through walls. A moving walkway rolls you past at a slow pace, but you can also step off to an area where you can stand and marvel at these tuxedo-clad creatures as they dive into 45°F (7°C) water and are showered with three tons of snow a day. A similar viewing area for puffins and murres (a kind of seabird) is just as entertaining. ☞ *Duration: Stay as long as you like. Crowds: Sometimes gridlocked despite the moving walkway nudging visitors past the glassed-in habitat. Strategy: Go while the dolphin and sea lion shows are on, and be-*

When to Go

Friday, Saturday, and Sunday are usually busier than the rest of the week, except during weeks that include Easter, July 4, and Christmas, when every day is equally busy.

As you get closer to the park, tune your car radio to 1540 AM for all the latest SeaWorld information.

Dress the Part

Wear comfortable sneakers—no heels or open sandals—since you may get your feet wet on the water rides.

Pack a bathing suit or dry clothes for yourself and your children, since sooner or later, everyone is soaked. (The culprits: Shamu's Happy Harbor, the up-close rows in the Shamu show, and Journey to Atlantis.)

While You're There

If you prefer to take your own food, remove all plastic straws and lids before you arrive—they can harm fish and birds.

Budget ahead for food for the animals—feeding time is a major part of Sea-World charm. A small carton of fish is usually $3.

Try to arrive early for Shamu shows, which generally fill to capacity on even the slowest days. Prepare to get wet in the "splash zone" down front.

---

fore you've gotten soaked at Journey to Atlantis, or you'll feel as icy as the penguins' environment. *Audience: All ages. Rating:* ★★

⑪ **SeaWorld Theater—*Pets Ahoy.*** Between Penguin Encounter and the central lagoon, SeaWorld Theater is the venue for the lively and highly entertaining *Pets Ahoy*. A dozen dogs, 18 cats, and an assortment of ducks, doves, parrots, and a pig (nearly all rescued from the local animal shelter) are the stars here. The show builds and builds to a fun—and funny—finale. Stick around after the show and you'll have a chance to shake paws with the stars. ☞ *Duration: 20–25 mins. Crowds: Can be substantial on busy days. Strategy: Gauge the crowds and get there early if necessary. Audience: All ages. Rating:* ★★★

Fodor'sChoice

⑫ **Sea Lion & Otter Stadium.** Inside the sister to Key West Dolphin Stadium, a wildly inventive, multilevel pirate ship forms the set for *Clyde and Seamore Take Pirate Island*. SeaWorld's celebrated sea lions, otters, and walruses prevail over pirate treachery in this swashbuckler of a saga. Arrive early to catch the preshow—the mime is definitely one of the best you'll ever see. ☞ *Duration: 40 mins, including the 15-min preshow. Crowds: No problem. Strategy: Sit toward the center for the best view, and don't miss the show's opening minutes. Audience: All ages. Rating:* ★★★

Fodor'sChoice

⑬ **Pacific Point Preserve.** A nonstop chorus of "aarrrps" and "yawps" leads you to the 2½-acre home for California sea lions and harbor and fur seals. This naturalistic expanse of beaches, waves, and huge outcroppings of upturned rock was designed to duplicate the rocky northern Pacific coast. You can stroll around the edge of the surf zone, a favorite hangout for fun-loving pinnipeds, and peep at their underwater activities through the Plexiglas wall at one side of the tank. Buy some smelts and

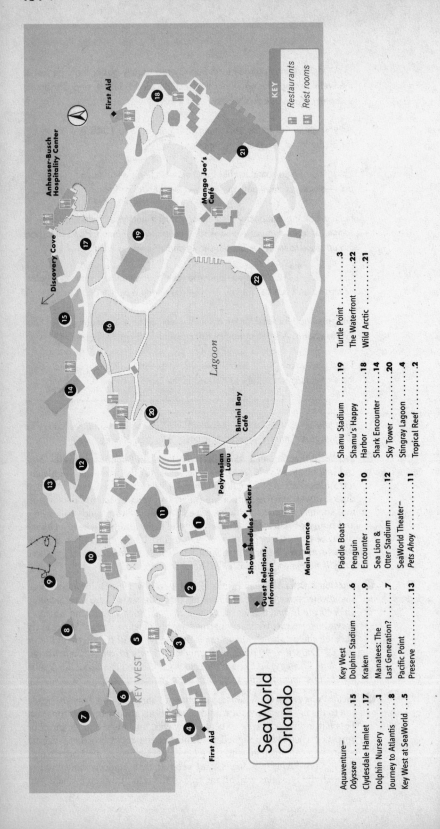

SeaWorld Orlando

First Aid

Anheuser-Busch
Hospitality Center

Discovery Cove

Mango Joe's
Café

Lagoon

Bimini Bay
Café

Polynesian
Luau

Guest Relations,
Information

Show Schedules
Lockers

Main Entrance

KEY WEST

First Aid

KEY
Restaurants
Rest rooms

watch the sea lions sing for their supper from close up. ☞ *Crowds: Not a problem. Strategy: Go anytime. Audience: All ages. Rating:* ★★★

⑭ **Shark Encounter.** Within this large, innocuous white structure are some thoroughly creepy critters: eels, barracuda, sharks, and poisonous fish. Each animal is profiled via a video screen and educational posters. Then you walk through a series of four Plexiglas tubes, surrounded by tanks containing the world's largest collection of such animals—a half dozen species of shark alone in some 300,000 gallons of water. The entrance to the attraction has changed to make room for **Sharks Underwater Grill,** where diners can order fresh fish and Floribbean cuisine while watching their entrées' cousins. ☞ *Duration: Plan to spend 20 mins. Crowds: Most significant when adjacent sea lion show gets out. Strategy: Go during the sea lion show. Audience: All ages. Rating:* ★★★

⑮ **Aquaventure–Odyssea** is the follow-up to the long-running and successful show *Cirque de la Mer*, featuring Peruvian silent comic Cesar Aedo. At press time, Aedo was adding more extravagant and ethereal presentations of fire-juggling, gymnastics, and mime. Presented in the large, air-conditioned Nautilus Theater, this is a good place to stop and sit a spell. ☞ *Duration: 30 mins. Audience: All ages. Crowds, Strategy, Rating: At press time, this show had not yet opened.*

⑯ **Paddle Boats.** A separate fee of $6 is required for a 30-minute cruise aboard these flamingo-shape watercraft. You provide the pedal power as you traverse a portion of the broad lagoon. ☞ *Duration: 30 mins. Crowds: Fairly light. Strategy: Skip it on a first trip; try it on your free 2nd day. Audience: All ages. Rating:* ★★

⑰ **Clydesdale Hamlet.** At its core, this is a walk around the stable where the hulking Clydesdale horses are kept, and a look at the clean corral where they get a chance to romp and play. A statue of an mighty stallion—which kids are encouraged to climb upon—makes a good theme-park photo opportunity. ☞ *Duration: You'll probably stay between 10 and 15 mins. Crowds: Very light. Strategy: Go anytime. Audience: All ages. Rating:* ★

⑱ **Shamu's Happy Harbor.** If you want to take a break while your kids exhaust the last ounce of energy their little bodies possess, bring them here. This sprawling, towering, 3-acre outdoor play area has places to crawl, climb, explore, bounce, and get wet. There's also a four-story net climb and adjacent arcade with midway games. Youngsters go wild for the tent with an air-mattress floor, pipes to crawl through, and "ball rooms," one for toddlers and one for grade-schoolers, with thousands of plastic balls to wade through. With big sailing ships to explore and water to play in and around, Happy Harbor is spacious and airy. ☞ *Crowds: Often a challenge. Strategy: Don't go first thing in the morning or you'll never drag your child away; but if you go midafternoon, expect plenty of hubbub. Bring a towel to dry them off. Audience: Toddlers through grade-schoolers. Rating:* ★★★

⑲ **Shamu Stadium.** Starring Shamu, SeaWorld's orca mascot, this stadium is the site of *The Shamu Adventure*, the most popular show in the park hands down. The preshow, including video footage of orcas in the wild and a bald eagle in flight, introduces several daily performances of the whales' fantastic flips, jumps, and other acrobatic antics. In the funkier nighttime *Shamu Rocks America*, the famous orca jumps to music and the patriotic show is not to be missed. Careful: in the "splash zone," Shamu uses his weight and massive fluke to flood the front rows. Wherever you sit, arrive early to get the seat of your choice. ☞ *Duration: 30 mins.*

FodorsChoice

Crowds: Sometimes a problem. Strategy: Go 45 mins early for the early afternoon show. Close-up encounters through the Plexiglas walls are not to be missed, so trot on down. Audience: All ages. Rating: ★★★

20 Sky Tower. The focal point of the park is this 400-ft-tall tower, the main mast for a revolving double-decker platform. During the six-minute rotating round-trip up and down, you'll get the inside scoop on the park's history, its attractions, and surrounding sights. There's a separate $3 admission for this one. ☞ *Crowds: Fairly light. Strategy: Look for a line and go if there's none. Audience: All ages. Rating:* ★★

21 Wild Arctic. This pseudo–ice station is a flight-simulator helicopter ride leading to rooms with interactive, educational displays. If your stomach can handle the rolls and pitches of a virtual helicopter, it makes for scary, enjoyable fun. Afterward, there are above- and below-water viewing stations where you can watch beluga whales blowing bubble rings, polar bears padding around with their toys, and groaning walruses trying to hoist themselves onto a thick shelf of ice. ☞ *Crowds: Expect a wait during peak season, (spring break, summer, and all holidays). Strategy: Go early, late, or during a Shamu show. You can skip the simulated helicopter ride if you just want to see the mammals. Audience: All ages. Minimum height for motion option: 42″. Rating:* ★★★

22 The Waterfront. Realizing that they had long neglected the potential of a large section of lakefront property, SeaWorld unveiled a new stretch of promenade near the Atlantis Bayside Stadium in May 2003. The Waterfront includes shops, eateries, kiosks, and street performers. ☞ *Duration: As long as you like. Audience: Should appeal to everyone. Crowds, Strategy, and Rating: At press time, this attraction was not yet open.*

> **need a break?** End your visit with a sweets detour at **Cypress Bakery, Polar Parlor Ice Cream Shop,** or **Sweet Sailin' Confections**; their delectable treats are hard to pass up.

Discovery Cove

Making a quantum leap from the traditional theme park, SeaWorld took a chance when it opened Discovery Cove, a 32-acre limited-admission park where a maximum of 1,000 people each day enter an extraordinary environment: a re-creation of the Caribbean complete with coral reefs, sandy beach, margaritas, and dolphins.

Here's how it works: after entering a huge thatched-roof tiki building, you register and are given a time to swim with the dolphins, the highlight of your Discovery Cove day. You're issued a photo ID that allows you to charge drinks during the day, and that's all you need to worry about. With your admission, everything else is inclusive.

Even if you're aware of the neighboring interstate highway, you can't help feeling that you've entered a tropical oasis. Once inside, you are awash in rocky lagoons surrounded by lush landscaping, intricate coral reefs, and underwater ruins. The pool where snorkeling lessons are taught has cascading waterfalls, and white beaches are fringed with thatched huts, cabanas, and hammocks. Exciting encounters of animal species from the Bahamas, Tahiti, and Micronesia are part of the experience. A free-flight aviary is aflutter with exotic birds, which you reach by swimming in a river and then beneath a waterfall.

Although $219 per person may seem steep, if you skip the dolphin swim it's only $119 in summer and as low as $109 in fall. Then when you consider that a dolphin swim in the Florida Keys runs approximately $125, and SeaWorld throws in a complimentary seven-day admission to its park (usually $52.95 a day), it starts looking like a bargain. Here's an alphabetized approach to what you'll see.

Aviary. The entrance to this 12,000-square-ft birdhouse is a kick. To get here, swim under one of two waterfalls. When you enter, you'll arrive in a small bird sanctuary filled with more than 250 darting hummingbirds, small finches, and honeycreepers which you can feed by hand. In the large bird sanctuary, you'll spy emus, toucans, and red-legged seriema.

Beaches. So popular are the sugar-white beaches that Discovery Cove expanded the strand in 2002 to provide more beachfront, lockers, and rest rooms. Lined with swaying palms, tropical foliage, and quaint thatched huts, this is where you claim your own private spot in the sand with shady umbrellas, hammocks, lounges, or beach chairs. Since the park's biggest selling feature is limited guest capacity, the most seductive aspect is staking out your private stretch of sand and leaving the real world behind.

Coral Reef. Snorkelers follow tropical fish through this habitat, although their colors and numbers aren't as striking as on a real coral reef. The sudden presence of large, graceful rays, however, is an undeniable thrill. Swimmers can also snorkel beside an artificial sunken ship, peering through a glass partition at the barracudas and sharks.

Dolphin Lagoon. This highlight of a Discovery Cove day has its good and bad points. On the plus side, following a training session beneath a cabana, you enter the water and "interact" for roughly 25 minutes with one of 25 dolphins in a chilly deepwater lagoon surrounded by sandy beaches and lush tropical landscaping. SeaWorld trainers teach you about animal behaviors, and you discover the hand signals used to communicate with them. The downside is that your image of swimming and cavorting with the dolphin is probably mistaken. Your one-on-one time with them is extremely limited, and the actual "swimming with," rather than the "interacting," lasts a few minutes at most.

The rest of the time is spent treading water and posing for pictures with a dolphin. Following the session, you're corralled into a kiosk to spend a half hour staring at computer screens featuring your just-snapped images. You're prodded and urged to spend $15 for the cheapest souvenir photo and another $15 for the souvenir frame and then to spend more for other photo configurations. It's a cheap commercial and not the best way to end the experience. Even nonswimmers and children over six can handle this dolphin "interaction," courtesy of a flotation vest everyone must wear. ☞ *Duration: 45–60 mins.*

Ray Lagoon. This is where you can wade and play with dozens of southern and cow-nosed rays. Don't be afraid—they've had their barbs removed. Often, several rays get together and make continuous loops of the pool, so if you stay in one spot they'll continue to glide past you—well within arm's reach.

Tropical River. The Tropical River meanders its way throughout most of Discovery Cove. River swimmers float lazily through different environments—a sunny beach; a dense, tropical rain forest; an Amazon-like river; a tropical fishing village; an underwater cave; and the aviary. The only drawback here is that the bottom of the river is like the bottom of a pool and the redundancy of the scenery along the way makes it a little boring after a while.

Discovery Cove A to Z

To research prices, get advice from other travelers, and book travel arrangements, visit www.fodors.com.

ADMISSION

If you're committed to visiting Discovery Cove, make reservations well in advance—attendance is limited to 1,000 people a day. Tickets are $219 per person with the dolphin swim, with prices dropping to $119 if you choose to forsake the swim. Either fee includes unlimited access to all swim and snorkeling areas and the free-flight aviary; a full meal; use of a mask, snorkel, swim vest, towel, locker, and other amenities; parking; and a pass for seven days of unlimited, come-and-go-as-you-please admission to SeaWorld Orlando.

GUIDED TOURS

Introduced in 2002, Discovery Cove's **Trainer for a Day** program allows up to 12 guests a day to work side by side and behind the scenes with animal experts and interact with dolphins, birds, sloths, anteaters, sharks, rays and tropical fish. Whether they have an in-water training experience with a dolphin, pamper a pygmy falcon, feed tropical fish, or play with an anteater, participants have the hands-on opportunity to train and care for these unique animals. You'll receive a reserved dolphin swim, an enhanced dolphin interaction and training encounter, and a chance to feed and take care of exotic birds in the aviary. Plus, you have behind-the-scenes access for feedings in the coral reef, small-mammal playtime and training, animal food preparation and record review, and behavioral training class. You'll walk away with a lot of memories as well as a souvenir shirt, dolphin book, and waterproof camera. Be sure about this one. It costs $399 (plus 6% tax), but it does include the regular admission price.

HOURS

Discovery Cove hours are daily 9–5:30.

RESERVATIONS

Reservations for Discovery Cove can be made by calling ☎ 877/434–7268, daily 9–8. Additional information can be found at www.discoverycove.com.

OTHER TIPS

- The masks Discovery Cove provide don't accommodate glasses, so wear contacts or a prescription mask if you can.

- If it becomes an all-day thunder and lightning rainstorm on your reserved day, attempts will be made to reschedule your visit when you're in town. If not, you have to settle for a refund.

- The earlier you make your reservations, the more latitude you have in selecting the time you want to swim (or interact) with the dolphins.

SeaWorld Orlando A to Z

To research prices, get advice from other travelers, and book travel arrangements, visit www.fodors.com.

ADMISSION

TICKETS At press time, regular one-day tickets to SeaWorld cost $55.33 for adults, and $45.74 for children three to nine, including tax. For a 10% discount, purchase your tickets on-line at www.seaworld.com.

DISCOUNTS   Complimentary "2nd Day Fun" passes are occasionally handed out near the park's entrance and exit. The nontransferable tickets, valid for seven days, are good for a second day's free admission, which can effectively cut this major cost in half. Make sure your entire party is together when arranging the following day's admission.

The Orlando FlexTicket, which covers SeaWorld, other Busch parks, and the Universal parks, is similar to Walt Disney World's pass system. The four-park versions allow you 14 consecutive days of unlimited admission to Universal Orlando parks, Wet 'n Wild, and SeaWorld ($180.15 adults, $143.05 children three to nine) and five-park versions that allow you 14 consecutive days of unlimited admission to all of the above as well as Busch Gardens Tampa ($215.46 and $175.12). SeaWorld–Busch Gardens combination Value Tickets, which include one day at each park, cost $85.95 for adults and $72.95 for children three to nine, with tax included.

ARRIVING & DEPARTING BY CAR

SeaWorld is just off the intersection of I–4 and the Beeline Expressway, 10 minutes south of downtown Orlando and 15 minutes from Orlando International Airport. Of all the Central Florida theme parks, it's the easiest to find. If you're heading west on I–4 (toward Disney), take Exit 72 onto the Bee Line Expressway (a.k.a. Highway 528) and take the first exit onto International Drive and follow signs a short distance to the parking lot. Heading east, take Exit 71.

PARKING   Parking costs $7 per car, RV, or camper. Preferred parking, which costs $10, allows you to park in the six rows closest to the front gate.

BABY CARE

Diaper-changing tables are in or near most women's rest rooms and in the men's rest room at the front entrance, near Shamu's Emporium. You can buy diapers at machines in all changing areas and at Shamu's Emporium. A special area for nursing is alongside the women's rest room at Friends of the Wild gift shop, equidistant from SeaWorld Theater, Penguin Encounter, and Sea Lion & Otter Stadium.

No formula or baby food is sold on the premises; the nearest sources are a five-minute drive away at Gooding's Supermarket on International Drive, Publix supermarket and Eckerd Drug on Central Florida Parkway, and Kmart on Turkey Lake Road. Strollers can be rented at the Information Center for $10 for a single, $16 for a double, with a $2 refundable deposit.

CAMERAS & FILM

Disposable cameras are for sale on the premises, as are film and blank videotapes.

DINING

Burgers, barbecue, and the other theme park offerings are available at restaurants and concessions throughout the park. Two restaurants are especially good lunch choices. **Mango Joe's Café** serves fajitas, steak, fish, and chicken sandwiches, and salads; **Bimini Bay Café** is a full-service restaurant. At dinnertime, Mango Joe's closes down, and the luau takes over Bimini Bay, leaving a choice of the **Anheuser-Busch Hospitality Center**, the **Buccaneer Smokehouse**, and **Mama Stella's Italian Kitchen.**

DINNER SHOW   During the **Aloha! Polynesian Luau Dinner and Show,** an Anheuser-Busch family version of a 1960s-era beach movie, scantily clad dancers bring lei-draped platters of roast pig, mahimahi, piña coladas, and carrot cake and cookies to the tables. The food here is not the draw—the entertaining two-hour show's nonstop sense of fun more than makes up for anything else that might be lacking.

Reservations, which are required, may be made the same day either at the luau reservations counter in the entrance's information center or by calling SeaWorld. For advanced reservations, call ☎ 800/327–2424 Ext. 2559. The cost is $40.23 for adults, $29.63 for children 8–12, and $17.97 for kids 3–7, which includes unlimited nonalcoholic drinks and one cocktail for adults. Although the restaurant at which it's held, Bimini Bay Café, is inside the park, you don't have to pay park admission to attend just the feast.

FULL-SERVICE
RESTAURANT

Sharks Underwater, near Shark Encounter, is an upscale restaurant which specializes in fresh fish and Floribbean cuisine such as Caribbean seafood pasta with spiced shrimp, scallops, and fish; oak grilled filet mignon topped with jerk seasoning; and pork medallions topped with a black bean sauce. Wash it all down with a drink from from the full beer, wine, and liquor bar. Reached through an underwater grotto, the restaurant has clear walls revealing the sand tiger, sandbar, nurse, black nose, and Atlantic black tip sharks that fill the 660,000-gallon aquarium. Call ahead for priority seating, ☎ 407/351–3600, or visit the host stand at the restaurant.

Backstage at Shamu Stadium, **Dine With Shamu** offers a chance to sample a buffet meal (salads, pasta, seafood, beef, and chicken entrées, and desserts) before meeting with a trainer who will share information about the training of the whales and animals that are hovering nearby. In season, there are two seatings each afternoon, in slower seasons just one. About 200 guests can be accommodated per seating, at $28 for adults and $16 for children ages 3–9. Reservations can be made at the information counter at the front of the park or by calling ☎ 407/351–3600 (press 3).

SELF-SERVICE
RESTAURANTS

Just far enough away from the Clydesdale stables, the light and airy **Anheuser-Busch Hospitality Center** combines cafeteria-style service with a bar serving Anheuser-Busch beverages (Michelob, Budweiser, O'Doul's) and soft drinks. Learn how to brew your own beer at the free half-hour A.B. Beer School, every hour. Hot tip: those 21 and over can also score two free beers here.

At tropical-hued **Mango Joe's Café,** a cafeteria near Shamu Stadium, you can find fresh fajitas, hefty salads, and a delicious key lime pie. Many of the umbrella-shaded tables are right on the lake, and offer a calming place to dine. **Buccaneer Smokehouse** serves up barbecued chicken and ribs. **Chicken 'n' Biscuit** has chicken salads and crispy chicken dinners with all the trimmings. **Mama Stella's Italian Kitchen** is a good place for pizza, spaghetti, and salads. **Waterfront Sandwich Grill** carves its sandwich fillings to order and also sells big, juicy hamburgers.

🚻 **Visitor Information** SeaWorld Orlando ☎ 407/351–3600 or 800/327–2424 ⊕ www.seaworld.org.

DISABILITIES & ACCESSIBILITY

ATTRACTIONS

With wide sidewalks and gentle inclines to the seats at shows, SeaWorld may be the most accessible park in Florida. **Key West Dolphin Stadium, Sea Lion & Otter Stadium, SeaWorld Theater,** and **Shamu Stadium** all provide reserved seating areas that are accessible and have entry via sloping ramps. The stadium shows usually fill to capacity, so plan to arrive 30–45 minutes before each show, 45–60 minutes in peak seasons.

At Shamu Stadium, the reserved seating area is inside the splash zone, so if you don't want to get soaking wet, get a host or hostess to recommend another place to sit.

Penguin Encounter, Shark Encounter, Tropical Reef, and **Journey to Atlantis** are all wheelchair accessible. To ride the moving-sidewalk viewing areas in Penguin Encounter, Shark Encounter, and Journey to Atlantis, you must transfer to a standard wheelchair, available in the boarding area, if you do not already use one. Tropical Reef and Penguin Encounter have minimal entertainment value for guests with visual impairments, but being hearing impaired does not detract from enjoying them. To ride **Kraken** you must transfer to the ride vehicles.

Shamu's Happy Harbor has some activities that are accessible to children using wheelchairs, including many of the games in the midway. Most of the other attractions are geared toward those who can climb, crawl, or slide.

RESTAURANTS & SHOPS
Restaurants are accessible, but drinking straws are not provided here out of concern for the safety of the animals. Shops are level, but many are so packed with merchandise that maneuvering in a wheelchair can be a challenge.

SERVICES
There are outgoing TTY (Text Type Y) series hearing-impaired systems at Bimini Bay Café and across from Key West Dolphin Stadium. Sign-language interpreters for guided tours are available with advance notice.

WHEELCHAIR RENTALS
Both standard ($8) and electric wheelchairs ($32) are available at Sea-World.

GUIDED TOURS
Following the lead of Disney and Universal, SeaWorld has created many backstage tours. The shortest is the $6.95 **Let's Talk Training** course held at Sea Lion & Otter stadium Monday through Thursday. For an all too brief 25 minutes, you're shown how SeaWorld's animals are taught to perform.

There are three hour-long educational tours to choose from, including **Polar Expedition,** which gives you a close-up view of polar bears and penguins. The **Predators!** tour teaches about the care of the Shark Encounter sharks, and **To the Rescue** takes a look at such rescued animals as manatees and turtles. All cost $8.95 for adults and $7.95 for children, and leave every 30 minutes until 3 PM. Register at the guided tour center to the left of the Guest Relations information center at the park entrance.

At nearly six hours, **Adventure Express** includes lunch, reserved seating for two at shows, and the knowledge of an educator assigned to the group. The guided tour is limited to 16 people and costs $75 per adult and $70 for children, on top of park admission. There's free fish to feed the animals, backstage access to the penguins, and instant admission to Kraken, Journey to Atlantis, and Wild Arctic. You can make reservations in person through the Guided Tour Counter or by phone.

The **False Killer Whale Interactive Program** is the long name of a tour that finds you learning about and working with pseudorcas, the smaller version of Shamu. For two hours those 13 and older can go behind the scenes, stepping into waist-deep water with the long, sleek gray and white mammals. You then can play with, pet, command, and feed the 1,300-pound creatures. The $200 fee includes lunch, wetsuit, admission to Sea-World, and a souvenir T-shirt and photo. The tours are limited to four or fewer participants per session. The **Animal Care Experience** is an eight-hour class at which you work side by side with a SeaWorld caretaker, helping care for the manatees, dolphins, walruses, beluga whales, and seals. At the Manatee Rehab Center, you may even have the chance to bottle-feed a baby manatee. If you have $389 worth of animal love in your heart and are prepared to start caring at 6:30 AM, then this one's for you. The price include lunch and admission to the park as well as a souvenir photo and T-shirt.

The latest tour offering, **Sharks Deep Dive** is based on the real-life shark dives adventurers do in exotic locations. Here, guests ten and older will don a SeaWorld wetsuit and either snorkel or scuba dive in an authentic shark cage as it is drawn through a 125-ft-long underwater habitat teeming with an array of more than 50 sharks, including sand tigers, sand bars, Atlantic and Pacific black tips, nurse, sawfish, as well as hundreds of tropical fish. It costs $150 to scuba (you'll need proof of certification), or $125 to snorkel—but the price also includes two-day park admission, a commemorative T-shirt and a shark information booklet.

If you're serious about seeing how trainers work with animals, you can join the **Trainer for a Day Program** (TDP; $389), held daily in two tours with a maximum of just three people each. Each tour shadows a SeaWorld trainer for the day, making for a behind-the-scenes look at their responsibilities. The course includes the diet preparation and feeding of the animals, and show preparation and training sessions at all three training areas—Shamu Stadium, Sea Lion & Otter Stadium, and the Key West Dolphin Stadium. The tours begin at 9 AM and end at 4 PM; lunch and admission to the park is included. At the end of the day, you walk away with a "Trainer for a Day" T-shirt, a souvenir photo, a waterproof disposable camera, and any pictures you chose to take. Register in advance with the Education Reservation Office.

🛈 Fees & Schedules **Education Reservation Office** ☎ 407/370-1382. **Behind-The-Scenes Tour Counter** ☎ 800/406-2244.

HEALTH SERVICES/FIRST AID

First Aid Centers, staffed by registered nurses, are behind Stingray Lagoon and near Shamu's Happy Harbor. In case of an emergency ask any SeaWorld employee to contact Security.

HOURS

SeaWorld opens daily at 9 AM, but closing hours vary between 6 PM, sometimes 7 PM, and, during the holidays, as late as 11 PM. To be safe, call in advance for park hours.

LOCKERS

Coin-operated lockers are available inside the park entrance and to the right as you enter, next to Shamu's Emporium. There are also lockers throughout the park and, conveniently, by the wild coaster, Kraken. The cost ranges between $1 and $1.50, depending on size.

LOST THINGS & PEOPLE

Go to the Information Center, just inside the park entrance, to report or look for lost children. The Center also operates as the park's Lost & Found.

All employees who see lost-looking children take them to the Information Center. A parkwide paging system also helps reunite parents with kids.

MONEY MATTERS

An ATM linked to various bank and credit-card networks is at the exit gate, but five others are around the park—mostly near shops, restaurants, and rest rooms. Foreign currency can be exchanged at the Special Services window at the Main Gate (daily 10–3).

PACKAGE PICKUP

Purchases made anywhere in the park can be sent to Package Pickup, in Shamu's Emporium, on request. Allow an hour for your purchases to make it there.

PET CARE CENTER

A pet care center near the Main Entrance accommodates dogs, cats, hamsters, and whatever other creatures you may have brought. Dogs must be walked at least once during the day. If you have a cat, bring a litter box. For meals, you're expected to bring food for your pet, but SeaWorld will spring for the water. The cost is $6 per day.

SHOPPING

The brave soul who can pass up a plush Shamu is rare indeed—not in the least because the dolls are available all over the park.

The **Friends of the Wild** shop near Penguin Encounter carries various items, including tropical fish earrings and hair ornaments. Get a special souvenir photo at **Keyhole Photo,** near Shamu's Emporium. Key chains, mugs, and frames can be made with your picture while you wait, or you can pick them up at the end of the day. At **Manatee Cove,** near the manatee exhibit, proceeds from the stuffed Shamus, soft manatees, and other toys go to benefit a manatee preservation organization. If you've left the park before realizing that your Aunt Betsy simply must have a Shamu slicker, visit **Shamu's Emporium,** just outside the entrance.

VISITOR INFORMATION

The **Main Information Center** is just inside the park, near the entrance. A large board nearby lists all show times.

Tourist Information **SeaWorld Orlando** ✉ 7007 SeaWorld Dr., Orlando 32821 ☎ 407/351-3600 or 800/327-2424 ⊕ www.seaworld.com.

BUSCH GARDENS

After you've endured an overdose of urban density, you can drive through Tampa to reach an exotic thrill ride–adventure–botanical garden. Busch Gardens manages to be the land-based equivalent of Sea-World—it's quiet and calming, but it's also entertaining, intriguing, and wild.

The dozen areas are loosely themed to recall turn-of-the-20th-century Africa. Scattered throughout are rides (including some thrilling roller coasters), water attractions, a sky ride, and shops galore. And throughout the whole park are some stunning animals to admire and learn about.

The main entrance takes you through Morocco. Walking counterclockwise from the main entrance along the winding paths, you encounter Myombe Reserve, Nairobi, Timbuktu, the Congo, Stanleyville, Land of the Dragons, and the Bird Gardens. Take a sharp right from Myombe Reserve and Nairobi to get to the Crown Colony, Egypt, Edge of Africa, and the Serengeti Plain. Although it's not as easy to navigate as the "hub-and-wheel" design of Disney's Magic Kingdom, each area has its own distinctive architectural style as well as regional music pumped through carefully camouflaged loudspeakers.

Despite the proliferation of rides, animals are the cornerstone of Busch Gardens' appeal. More than 2,700 birds, mammals, and reptiles inhabit its 335 acres; the aviary houses some 600 rare birds; and about 500 African big-game animals roam uncaged on the 70-acre Serengeti Plain.

Aside from steam trains, there's no mass transit here. Exploring these far-flung lands requires strong legs and a comfortable pair of walking shoes. There's little of the crowd and bustle of the Disney parks here, however, so relax and enjoy the beauty of nature spiced up by an occasional adrenaline-pumping adventure.

Numbers in the margin correspond to points of interest on the Busch Gardens map.

Morocco

Busch Gardens' main entrance leads you through the gates of a tiled and turreted Moroccan fort and into a land of swirling colors, striped awnings, and exotic music. Before you go too far, be sure to pick up a park map. On the back of the map you'll find a handy listing of park information, entertainment and show times, tours, animal exhibits, and dining.

Morocco itself contains two eateries, the Zagora Café and Sultan's Sweets, and there are numerous souvenir stands arranged in a replica of an open-air "souk," or marketplace. To the left are lockers as well as the open-air Marrakesh Theater stage for the *Moroccan Roll* musical revue. Throughout this area, Middle Eastern music peals, brightly colored wool tassels droop overhead, brass urns glimmer, bangles shimmer, veils waft in the wind, and mouthwatering smells float from the bakery.

❶ Sultan's Tent. From the entrance, the path to the right rolls past the shops and bazaars until, adjacent to the Zagora Café, you'll find a raised platform hung with multicolor-striped curtains. At various times of the day (show times are posted next to the tent), a snake charmer appears and snuggles up to a python, wrapping it around her arms, waist, and neck. Just to the right, a lagoon is filled with some mighty hefty alligators. ☞ *Crowds: Not a problem. Strategy: Pause to take in the surroundings before entering. Audience: All ages. Rating:* ★

❷ Moroccan Palace Theater. Across from the alligator lagoon is a stunning palace. Inside, awnings, minarets, cupolas, columns, trees, and vines turn the theater into a Moroccan bazaar. The show held here, "World Rhythms on Ice," alternates between sublime and jaw-droppingly weird. Skaters salute the world through costumes, music, and dances reflecting several nations and continents. Africa finds the skaters and extremely creative puppets in animal costumes and native dress. This is followed by an unusual tribute to England during which Beatles music is played over pictures of King George III, all followed by skaters wearing mod Carnaby Street threads spinning to "Jumpin' Jack Flash." The salute to Japan includes sexy costumes and a break from skating as an acrobat spins tables and vases on her feet. After several other scenes of varying quality, everything is wrapped up with an overblown crescendo of patriotic American standards. All in all, it's 20 minutes of great entertainment packed into a 37-minute show. ☞ *Duration: 37 mins. Crowd: Sizable, but there's always enough room. Strategy: Shows 4 times daily, 6 in high season; check schedules posted outside. Arrive 30 mins before show time if you'd like to get a good seat. Audience: All ages. Rating:* ★★

Best of the Park

Figuring out the most efficient way to visit Busch Gardens is only slightly less complicated than planning a safari. Pick up a list of shows at the entrance gate and loosely schedule your day around them; they make welcome breaks in a full day on your feet. Must-see shows feature the birds, elephants, and ice skaters. If you're a coaster enthusiast, after passing right on through Morocco, head directly for **Gwazi.** If not, then head for the **Myombe Reserve.** Upon exiting you'll be in Nairobi, where you should make tracks for **Rhino Rally,** which will get real crowded real quick. Afterward, you can breeze through the **Elephant Display, Animal Nursery,** and **Curiosity Caverns** en route to Egypt and **Montu.** After the coaster, stop by **Tut's Tomb** before taking a well-deserved break at the British Colonial–themed Crown Colony restaurant.

You've now covered about half the park, and you can take a round-trip **Skyride** or walk through the **Edge of Africa** before hoofing it over to the Congo. Ride the **Congo River Rapids, Kumba,** the **Tanganyika Tidal Wave,** and, if you wish, the slower **Stanley Falls Log Flume Ride.** Now that you're soaked to the bone, head through the **Land of the Dragons** (stopping if you have kids) and then to the **Lory Landing** aviary. If your timing's right, you can step right up for the performance at the **Bird Show Theater.** Follow the path to the free beer at the **Hospitality House.** If you skipped **Gwazi** earlier, head back toward Morocco and catch it now and then take in the last ice-show performance of the day at the **Moroccan Palace Theater.** It's a nice way to end your visit, and you can hit the Moroccan souk on your way out.

On Rainy Days

The Skyride may close temporarily because of lightning or high winds, but otherwise inclement weather generally means business as usual in the park. However, you will get wet, and because the animals seek shelter (as you probably will want to), your experience may not be as rich as it would be when the sun is out.

Crown Colony

Crown Colony, at the far right side of the park, is here to disguise a transportation and hospitality center, contain a stable of Clydesdale horses, and serve as a transition into Egypt. The Skyride Station here is the entryway for an aerial trip to the Congo and back.

❸ Show Jumping Hall of Fame. One of the Busch daughters is a successful equestrian rider, hence this permanent exhibit devoted to jumping and racing horses. Pictures, trophies, saddles, and decorations help tell the story of famous equestrians and their horses. ☞ *Duration: As long as you like. Crowds: Seldom a problem. Strategy: Skip it the first time, unless you have time to kill at the end of the day. Audience: All ages. Rating:* ★★

❹ Clydesdale Hamlet. The usual batch of oversize beasts galumphs around a corral and stables; a particularly patient horse is periodically led out for photographs, much to the delight of kids and their parents. If your daughter is obsessed with *National Velvet,* and most other things equine, take her to the Show Jumping Hall of Fame next door. ☞ *Crowds: Very light. Strategy: Go anytime. Audience: All ages. Rating:* ★

Skyride. This elevated tour places you five stories above Timbuktu and the Serengeti Plain. Departing from the Skyride Station in Crown Colony, you can disembark at the Congo station (which places you close to Kumba) or continue on for a round-trip. The Skyride gives you a great overview, so you can plan your pedestrian approach to the park. If the weather's bad, this service may be closed. ☞ *Duration: Round-trip 7 mins. Crowds: Can get heavy in midday. Strategy: Ride in the morning or toward park closing time. Audience: All ages. Rating:* ★★★

Egypt

Dominating this section of the park is the awesome roller coaster known as Montu. There are also plenty of shops, midway games to take your money, and an interesting tour through a replica of the tomb of King Tutankhamen ("Tut" to his friends).

❺ Akbar's Adventure Tours. Martin Short is Akbar, the "world's greatest tour guide," and to help keep his failing business afloat he takes you on a trip aboard a virtual flying carpet across Egypt. The flight has all the requisite bounces, drops, twists, and turns. Don't plan your trip around this ride; occasionally it's closed to be utilized as a back entrance gate during special ticket promotions and holiday events. ☞ *Duration: 5 mins. Crowds: Lines are almost nonexistent. Strategy: Go anytime. Audience: All but young children. No guests with motion sickness or heart, neck, or back problems. Rating:* ★★

❻ Tut's Tomb. The entrance (adjacent to a wide-open bazaar) may be hard to spot, but this recreation of Howard Carter's 1922 discovery and excavation of the boy king's tomb is dead on. Like the real thing, the ceilings are low and confining, and an outer chamber contains perfect replicas of the beautiful objects and golden animals buried with Tut. When you enter the actual tomb, the outer sarcophagus is raised so you can view the mummy and iconic golden mask. Exit into the gift shop and buy some recreations of the items you just saw. ☞ *Duration: 10 mins. Crowds: Lines are almost nonexistent. Strategy: Go anytime. Audience: Everyone. Rating:* ★★

❼ Montu. Arriving at Montu is like walking on the set of *Cleopatra*. The towering walls are carved with the likenesses of Egyptian emperors and animals. The snaking 4,000-ft-long roller coaster is a gut-wrenching thrill ride. As is true of its cousin Kumba, the mere sound and sheer size of Montu are intimidating, but take the chance if you want to brag about it later. ☞ *Duration: 3 mins. Crowds: Lines can get long on busy days. Strategy: Go early in the morning or late in the day. Most of the time, settle in for a wait that will be worth it. Audience: Older children and adults. No guests with motion sickness or heart, neck, or back problems. Minimum height: 54". Rating:* ★★★

Edge of Africa

On the southern edge of the Serengeti Plain, this 15-acre walk-through area showcases hippos, baboons, crocodiles, and various species of fish. In addition, there are an African village, supposedly vacated by a Masai tribe that had been overtaken by lions and hyenas, and a safari encampment with giraffes and zebras, as well as habitats for meerkats (a kind of African mongoose) and vultures.

When to Go

Credit a huge number of local annual pass holders for making Fridays through Saturdays the most crowded times at the park. In summertime, however, it's hot enough that even the local crowd lightens up.

Because animals nap through most of the day, the bulk of the action occurs first thing in the morning and in late afternoon. Arrive early and try to see them during the first hour if possible.

Dress the Part

Know how to spot a theme-park novice? Look at their shoes. High heels and cowboy boots are signs of first-timers. Don't make that mistake here. At 350 acres, the park is more than three times the size of the Magic Kingdom.

Busch Gardens charges $5 for ponchos for water rides and 25¢ to give others riding the water rides a quick squirt. Water rides will get you wet—very wet—and you'll get quite cold on winter and overcast days.

If you carry a backpack, get ready to pay $1 to stow it in a locker each time you go on a coaster. There are lockers adjacent to the Moroccan Palace Theater at the entrance, as well as lockers outside most flume rides and coasters.

While You're There

As soon as you arrive in the park, set up a specific rendezvous location and time in case you and your companions get separated. Good spots to meet are in front of the Moroccan Palace Theater, at the entrance to any of the train stations, by the Clydesdale Hamlet, at the Edge of Africa Welcome Center, or at a park bench in Land of the Dragons.

A large sign at the entrance lists each day's performance schedule, which is also printed on a handout. Show times are also posted next to the individual stages and theaters.

If kids and parents want to go their separate ways, you can rent Motorola radios to stay in touch. They're $10 (plus a $100 deposit).

If you want to snap loved ones in midride, look for photo-staging spots at Congo River Rapids, Kumba, and the Tanganyika Tidal Wave.

---

❽ Edge of Africa. Set off on a self-guided tour down a winding path and you'll reach caves where lions rest behind (hopefully) unbreakable glass. Throughout the area, you are quite close to lions, giraffes, hyenas, impalas, antelope, and baboons. A real treat is stopping by the submerged acrylic windows to watch lumbering multi-ton hippos race gently underwater—a very odd, dreamlike visual. Animal lovers may want to invest in the half-hour-long Edge of Africa **Serengeti Safari**, which puts you and up to 19 others on the veldt in an open-air flatbed truck. During this up-close and personal encounter, the guides are very informa-

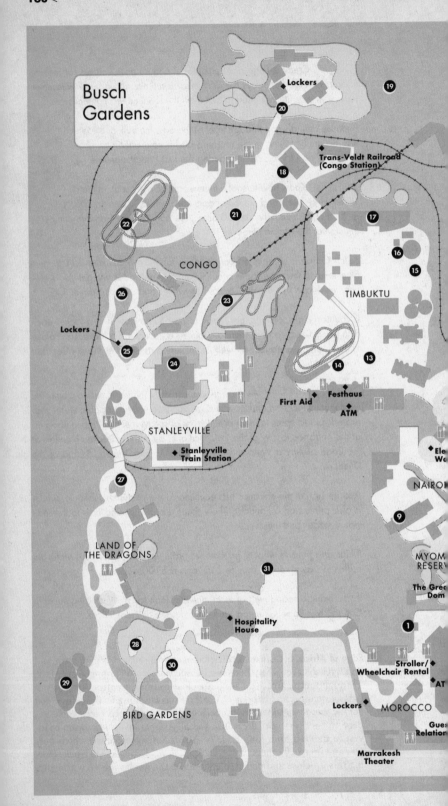

Busch
Gardens

Lockers

19

20

Trans-Veldt Railroad
(Congo Station)

18

21

17

16

22

CONGO

15

TIMBUKTU

26

23

Lockers

25

13

14

24

First Aid   Festhaus
ATM

STANLEYVILLE

Ele
Wa

Stanleyville
Train Station

NAIRO

27

9

LAND OF
THE DRAGONS

MYOM
RESERV

31

The Gre
Dom

Hospitality
House

1

28

30

Stroller/
Wheelchair Rental

29

AT

BIRD GARDENS

Lockers   MOROCCO

Gues
Relation

Marrakesh
Theater

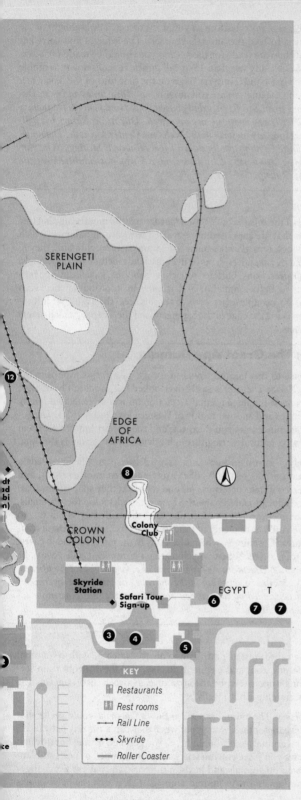

SERENGETI
PLAIN

EDGE
OF
AFRICA

CROWN
COLONY

Colony
Club

Skyride
Station

Safari Tour
Sign-up

EGYPT   T

KEY

🍽 *Restaurants*

🚻 *Rest rooms*

—▪— *Rail Line*

•◆•◆• *Skyride*

▬▬▬ *Roller Coaster*

tive, fielding as many questions as you want to ask. The highlight of the trip is getting to feed the animals yourself. The giraffes and ostriches and cape buffalo are ready for food—and you should be ready for a perfect photo, especially when an 18-ft-tall giraffe reaches down to nibble leaves from your hand. Hint: try to go on the first tour of the day, when it's cooler and the animals are still moving. ☞ *Tour times and cost: Departures vary from 2 to 6 times daily based on season. Call for frequency. Cost is $29.99; reservations are required. Duration: Safari tour 30 mins; stay as long as you wish in the Welcome Center. Crowds: The wide-open Welcome Center usually doesn't feel crowded. Strategy: The earlier the better. Audience: Children under 5 are not admitted on the Safari Tour. Rating:* ★★★

Serengeti Plain

This is one of the must-sees at Busch Gardens: 500 animals running free on 70 acres that are supposed to re-create their natural habitats (which turn out to look remarkably similar to Florida pastureland). Still, they're not confined by cages. Residents of the grasslands include zebras, camels, impalas, giraffes, lions, buffalo, ostriches, baboons, gazelles, Cape buffalo, kudus (a heftier impala), and rhinos. In addition to the Safari Tour, there are a couple other ways to see this area: the Trans-Veldt Railroad, which skirts the edge of the Serengeti; and the Skyride, which grants an aerial view.

Myombe Reserve: The Great Ape Domain

Fodor'sChoice   The entrance to this luxuriant walk-through rain forest (opposite the Moroccan Palace Theater) is easily overlooked but shouldn't be missed. The park's most-heralded animal attraction houses an extended family of chimpanzees and another family of Western lowland gorillas. The gorillas are magnificent as you'd expect, and the opportunity to see them in a somewhat natural setting through a wide viewing area is thrilling.

Guides make scheduled appearances to disperse gorilla knowledge, sharing that gorillas rest 40% of the day and feed another 30%, and that they enjoy a treat of termite mound tops that they snap off and eat. Plaques and educational signage also help you understand these animals. The gorillas seem to like the soft hay near the wide bay windows, so chances are you'll have plenty of time to share face time with these stunning creatures. The chimps, which often stay in the tall grass and in caves, can be harder to see. When you do catch a glimpse, it will always be entertaining. ☞ *Duration: As long as you like. Crowds: Not significant. Strategy: Visit either first thing in the morning or late in the afternoon; both are close to feeding time, when both apes and chimps are more active. Audience: All ages. Rating:* ★★★

Nairobi

Myombe's rain-forested path leads you to Nairobi, with its animal nursery, petting zoo, and elephant display, and the Nairobi train station—a gingerbread clapboard structure. Nairobi also contains the highly entertaining Rhino Rally.

❾ **Animal Nursery.** The animal experts at Busch Gardens would prefer that the mothers care for their young, but when they can't, the tiny baby birds, reptiles, and animals are brought here. You can't go inside, but through the windows you'll see convalescing animals wrapped in nests of blankets. With 2,700 animals and birds in the park, the patient list changes daily—from newborns to injured animals. Just watch the baby koalas or featherless infant cockatoos and the cuteness factor is off the charts. ☞ *Duration: As long as you like. Crowds: Not a problem. Strategy: Visit anytime. Audience: All ages. Rating:* ★★

🔟 **Elephant Display.** A big attraction in Nairobi is this open enclosure where roughly a dozen Asian elephants walk and sway and graze. There's a swimming pool where older elephants and their offspring snort, swim, and clean off before tossing dust on their backs to prevent sunburn. Throughout the day, some elephants troop over to the Elephant Wash area where a caretaker keeps them cool with sprays from a garden house. ☞ *Duration: As long as you like. Crowds: Can be significant for the Elephant Wash, but you can usually see. Strategy: Go anytime. Audience: All ages. Rating:* ★★

⓫ **Curiosity Caverns.** This walk-through exhibit takes you through caves filled with snakes and bats and rats. Living in small but comfortable environments are a green tree python, rat snakes, a boa constrictor, and a reticulated python that has no trouble reaching a branch 10 ft off the ground. The lighting here is dark and mysterious: all the better for watching the fruit bats and vampire bats hanging from branches and stalactites. It may be more than just the coolness of the cave giving you chills. ☞ *Duration: Up to you. Crowds: Light, and it moves smoothly. Audience: All ages. Strategy: Go anytime. Rating:* ★★★

⓬ **Rhino Rally.** Even on very slow days it can take a long time to earn a seat
Fodor'sChoice in one of the 17-passenger Land Rovers that zip through the veldt. Similar to Disney's Jungle Cruise, this attraction stars fast-talking drivers and lots of bad gags. A guest is chosen to be each expedition's race rally navigator; he or she helps direct the driver up steep hills and into deep rivers, bringing the truck very close to white rhinos, antelope, crocodiles, Cape buffalo, warthogs, and other exotic animals. The thrills and laughs don't stop at the water's edge, since the scary grand finale finds your vehicle entering a raging and turbulent river. Aside from the wait, this is a perfect ride. ☞ *Duration: 8 mins. Crowds: Significant. Strategy: Very early or very late. Audience: All ages, but may be scary for younger kids. Rating:* ★★★

Trans-Veldt Railroad. The Kenya Kanteen outdoor café is a good place to watch and listen for the arrival of this faithful copy of an East African steam locomotive. It arrives here at the Nairobi Train Station. With room for 400, the train will likely have a seat for you. The train chugs around the Serengeti Plain and then circumnavigates the park in a 2½-mi journey, with stops near the Congo River Rapids and in Stanleyville. If you're taking pictures, try to sit on the left side of the benches: it's closer to the veldt. If the animals are scarce and you want to save some time, just get a taste of the train and disembark at the first stop, in the Congo. ☞ *Duration: 20 mins. round-trip; it's about 10 mins to the Congo Train Station and another 5–6 mins to Stanleyville. Crowds: Steady, but you almost always find a seat. Strategy: Since it comes only every 20 mins, watch the mother elephants dunking the little ones in the elephant pool until you hear the whistle; then dash for the station. Audience: All ages. Rating:* ★★

Timbuktu

Outside Timbuktu are the gates of a towering white mud fort. Inside is a collection of kid-size rides, arcades, and midway games.

⓭ **Sandstorm.** Why ride this spinning and pitching and revolving machine? Because it's the "number one ride for making guests throw up," says a Busch Gardens staffer. It doesn't look all that menacing, but the constant rotation of both your seat and the arm to which it's attached does the trick. ☞ *Duration: 2½ mins. Crowds: Not a problem. Strategy: Go anytime. Audience: Older children and adults. No guests with motion sickness or heart, neck, or back problems. Rating:* ★★

⑭ Scorpion. Compared with Montu and Kumba, this looming 1,805-ft steel roller coaster looks like child's play. But the beast is twisted into a gigantic 360° hoop with a 65-ft drop and reaches a maximum speed of 50 mph. Far scarier than it looks. ☞ *Duration: 2 mins. Crowds: Lines can build at midday in busy periods. Strategy: Go early or late. Audience: Older children and adults. No guests with motion sickness or heart, neck, or back problems. Minimum height: 42". Rating:* ★★

⑮ Phoenix. Similar to the pendulumlike pirate ships at traveling fairs, this towering structure offers increasingly elevated crescent swings back and forth, higher and higher, until the whole thing swoops sickeningly over the top. Bon voyage! ☞ *Duration: 2 mins. Crowds: Lines can build at midday in busy periods. Strategy: Go early or late. Audience: Older children and adults. No guests with motion sickness or heart, neck, or back problems. Minimum height: 48". Rating:* ★★

⑯ Crazy Camel. This hopped-up carousel resembles a Mexican hat, with cars careening up and over bumps on the brim. Brightly painted camels dance alongside the traditional horses. Nearby, you can pay a few bucks to win a cheap prize at a dozen midway games. Rhino Rings, fishing with a magnet, popping a frog onto a lily pad, swatting multiple King Tuts . . . it's all here, a cash-sucking profusion of chance. ☞ *Crowds: Can get heavy in midafternoon. Strategy: Do the ride in early morning. Audience: All ages. Rating:* ★★★

⑰ R.L. Stine's Haunted Lighthouse. Brand-spankin' new at press time, this show premiered in mid-2003 at the site of the former dolphin stadium. The 3-D film was written exclusively for the attraction by the children's horror author. The film features veteran actors Christopher Lloyd, Michael McKean, and Lea Thompson, but the real star may be the spectrum of sensory surprises that will immerse the audience in the movie. Synchronized special effects include blasts of air, sprays of water, buzzers, and surround sound in every seat. ☞ *Duration, Crowds, Strategy, Audience, Rating: At press time, this ride was not yet open.*

Congo

Unlike the open, dusty plains of the Serengeti and Nairobi, Congo and Stanleyville next door are delightfully shaded by lush plantings and lofty, leafy trees, under whose branches nestle African fetish statues and piles of expedition-supply boxes.

A few huts scattered throughout contain snakes in wire boxes and inquisitive parrots perched in cages. Keepers are on hand to explain their behavior and hold them for you to stroke. One end of the Skyride and a stop on the Trans-Veldt Railroad can also be found here. Hysterical shrieks often emanate from the area's several thrill rides, reminding you that the visitors, if not the natives, are perpetually restless.

⑱ Ubanga-Banga Bumper Cars. Aptly named, this popular attraction has a carnival allure, and young kids, along with big kids who have never grown up, love them. If it's been years since you've sat behind the wheel of a bumper car, you may be surprised that they're not quite as fast as the ones you recall from your youth—but they're still immensely fun. ☞ *Duration: About 4 mins. Crowds: Never significant enough to cause* *a wait except in midafternoon during busy periods. Strategy: Go anytime, but don't wait if there's a line. Audience: Older children and adults. Rating:* ★★

⑲ Kumba. The counterpart to Egypt's Montu, this is nearly 4,000 ft of twisting turquoise steel. The cars speed up to 60 mph as they race through three popular coaster maneuvers: a "diving loop" that plunges you from 110 ft; a camelback, with a 360° spiral and three seconds of weightlessness; and the world's largest loop, with a height of 108 ft. That's in addition to spirals, cobra rolls, and a corkscrew in the dark. When it's all over, you'll be holding your spinning head and walking away on wobbly knees. If you like coasters, don't miss this. ☞ *Duration: 3 mins. Crowds: Often. Strategy: Go as soon as the park opens. Audience: Older children and adults. No guests with motion sickness or heart, neck, or back problems. Minimum height: 54". Rating:* ★★★

⑳ Congo River Rapids. People who love the pitching and plunging and soaking of water rides rate this as one of the best. Twelve people sit in an inner tube–like raft and set sail for a bumper-car ride on a stream. As you go bumping and bucketing through nearly ¼ mi of rapids and waterfalls and then through a dark cave, watch for surges of splashing water from the river, as well as the sadistic observers firing water cannons from the banks. The adjacent gift shop sells $5 ponchos that should keep you relatively dry. ☞ *Duration: 5 mins. Crowds: There's usually a line. Strategy: Go early to avoid waits and have the best time. Audience: Older children and adults. No guests with motion sickness or heart, neck, or back problems. Children under 42" must be accompanied by an adult. Rating:* ★★★

㉑ Claw Island (Bengal tigers). Somehow all the hoopla at the park doesn't seem to bother the lazy Bengal and albino tigers. There are several observation points from the sidewalks and courtyards that encircle the island and moat. If you want to see the cats when they're most active, come in early morning or late afternoon. The shady benches overlooking the island are a pleasant place to recuperate before hitting the next ride. ☞ *Crowds: Nonexistent. Strategy: Go in the early morning, when the animals are awake. Audience: All ages. Rating:* ★★★

㉒ Python. When this ride premiered in the late 1970s, it was a cutting-edge coaster. Today you'll be amazed that it only lasts just over a minute and is absent of the series of twists newer coasters offer. Passengers are hurled through two hoops at 50 mph on the 1,250-ft track of this steel roller coaster. Thrilling, but it takes a backseat to its wilder siblings. This may be a good test coaster for kids. ☞ *Duration: 70 seconds. Crowds: Significant only in busy seasons. Strategy: Go early or late during holiday periods. Audience: Older children and adults. No guests with motion sickness or heart, neck, or back problems. Children must be accompanied by an adult. Minimum height: 48". Rating:* ★★

Stanleyville

Named for a city in Zaire now known as Kisangani, this area is very much akin to the Congo in flavor. Here, too, you're surrounded by lush tropical vegetation and animals native to that part of Africa—as well as the requisite rides and stores selling handcrafts. Yet another train station—a twin of Nairobi's—is near the orangutans' island behind the Stanleyville Theater.

㉓ Stanley Falls Log Flume Ride. Although somewhat dated, the Log Flume is still very popular because of its 40-ft drop. The creaking creek ride is a little slow, but at least you're certain to get wet. ☞ *Duration: 3½ mins. Crowds: Significant, with lines even on average days. Strategy: Ride early in the morning or in the evening. Audience: Older children and adults. Minimum height: 42″. Rating:* ★★

㉔ Stanleyville Theatre. This show venue changes its acts every one to six months to keep things current. Busch Gardens' talent scouts have gone as far as China, France, and Morocco to recruit first-class shows, which often consist of acrobats, jugglers, and other circus-style acts. A listing of the current performance is displayed at the entrance and on park brochures. Not only is the open-air theater a cool place to retreat, the beauty of these shows will remind you that Busch's best offerings aren't always from a tap or on a track. ☞ *Duration: 30 mins. Crowds: Theater can get crowded. Strategy: Arrive at least 15–20 mins prior to show time. Audience: All ages. Rating:* ★★★

㉕ Tanganyika Tidal Wave. There are two ways to get covered in water here. During the ride itself, a 55-ft drop sends you into a splash pool. And then there's the viewing bridge at the bottom of the drop, where a recording of Tchaikovsky's *1812 Overture* heralds the next wave. Either huddle behind the Plexiglas shelter on the bridge or skitter off—fast. ☞ *Duration: 6 mins. Crowds: Significant, with lines even on average days. Strategy: Ride early in the morning or in the evening. Audience: Older children and adults. Minimum height: 42″. Rating:* ★★★

㉖ Orchid Canyon. Often overlooked, this quiet and lovely 100-yard walk winds around 200-odd cascading orchids and bromeliads native to South Africa, the Philippines, and South America. Lemurs, rhinoceroses, elands, and orangutans peacefully snooze away in spacious enclosures accessorized with rocks, trees, and, for the orangutans, gymnastic equipment. ☞ *Duration: As long as you like. Crowds: Not a problem. Strategy: Go anytime. Audience: All ages. Rating:* ★★

Land of the Dragons

This cluster of kid-size attractions is one of the best children's areas in any theme park. Rope climbs and bouncing walkways fill the three-story Tree House at the center, and there are miniature carousels, Ferris wheels, and cars that preschoolers can "drive." Several times daily, conservation specialists arrive to tell animal stories, sometimes bringing live animals as props. It's wonderfully colorful and cheerful, and some local season-ticket holders are known to spend hours here. ☞ *Crowds: Can peak when parents need a break. Strategy: Wait until later in the day, or you may never get your youngsters away; or go at midday for a respite from the heat. Audience: Young children. Rating:* ★★★

Bird Gardens

Following the path from Stanleyville, past the orangutans, and onto the bridge over the train tracks brings you here. Bird Gardens has a sterling children's playground and more than 1,800 exotic birds from 350 species. The flock of vivid Caribbean flamingos is one of the largest in captivity; the hundred or so birds, which also include a paler breed from Chile, are fed beta-carotene supplements to maintain their color.

㉗ Lory Landing. The multicolor birds from Indonesia and the South Pacific fly freely beneath two sprawling live oaks just over the ramp from Stanleyville. For $1 you can feed the lories Lorikeet Nectar, a juice mixed just for them. Most birds will land on a shoulder or outstretched hand to take a sip. A trainer is usually on hand to answer questions. ☞ *Duration: As long as you like. Crowds: Not a problem. Strategy:*

Go in the morning, when the birds will be hungriest. Audience: All ages. Rating: ★★★

28 **Flamingo Island.** Whether they're strutting, preening, standing on one leg, or bobbing for food, the sight of around 100 flamingos en masse is striking. ☞ *Duration: As long as you like. Crowds: Not a problem. Strategy: Go early or late to see birds at their most active. Audience: All ages. Rating:* ★★

29 **Aviary.** Nearly 200 species of birds, including macaws and egrets, flutter freely among the trees and walk along the ground of this lushly landscaped walk-through cage. ☞ *Duration: As long as you like. Crowds: Not a problem. Strategy: Go early or late to see birds at their most active. Audience: All ages. Rating:* ★★

30 **Bird Show Theater.** *For the Birds,* performed at this open amphitheater just behind Flamingo Island, brings together macaws, condors, and eagles. Bird enthusiasts rate this show as one of the best, due to the interesting stunts and the variety of birds on display. You can have your photo taken with one of the squawking stars at the adjacent posing area just after each show. ☞ *Duration: 30 mins. Crowds: Sometimes significant during holiday periods. Strategy: Arrive 15 mins before show time in busy seasons. Audience: All ages. Rating:* ★★

31 **Gwazi.** Even up close, this wooden roller coaster looks like a shaky stack of toothpicks. The clattering of the cars on the rails and the clanking of the chains on the gears makes this a nostalgic thrill. Your confidence is tested early and often: Gwazi goes much faster and falls far longer than you'd expect from an "old-fashioned" ride. Two trains on separate tracks depart the station in unison and then hurtle toward each other in an apparent headlong collision no fewer than six times. Although the cars' individual speeds are roughly 50 mph, staffers love to point out that the "fly-by" speed makes it seem more like 100. Add to this a 90-ft drop, and there's every reason to scream your lungs out. Modeled after Coney Island's Cyclone, Gwazi attracts those who know the original, as well as families drawn by the lack of inversions. ☞ *Crowds: Expect heavy lines all day: its location near the entrance helps keep it busy. Strategy: Ride early or late. Leave your possessions with a nonrider or in lockers at the bottom of the ride. Audience: Older children and adults. No guests with motion sickness or heart, neck, or back problems. Minimum height: 48". Rating:* ★★★

Busch Gardens A to Z

To research prices, get advice from other travelers, and book travel arrangements, visit www.fodors.com.

ADMISSION

TICKETS At press time, adults pay $53.44 and children three to nine pay $43.81, including tax. It's possible you won't see everything during your visit, so you may want to take advantage of the $10.95 next-day admission offer: popular with people whose flights don't leave until late the following afternoon. Those tickets, which need to be purchased on the first day of your visit, are on sale at Guest Services near the entrance.

Realizing that an international slate of visitors may not always find Florida's weather conducive to touring the park, Busch Gardens makes a very generous offer with its **Foul Weather Guarantee.** If you seriously think that it's too hot, cold, muggy, humid, rainy, whatever, go to the Courtesy Center to see whether they'll credit you for a free return visit. This applies whether it's the beginning or the end of the day.

DISCOUNTS Special pricing and discounts appear and disappear with great frequency. Before buying a one-day ticket, check for current offers posted at the entrance. The combination Busch Gardens–SeaWorld value tickets allow you to spend one day in each park. The price with tax is $85.95 for adults and $72.95 for children three to nine. If you arrive between January and April, ask about the Fun Card: for the cost of a full-price one-day admission, you receive free admission to the park for a full year.

The Orlando FlexTicket, which includes Busch Gardens as an afterthought, is available here, but only in its five-park version. The cost with tax is $215.46 for adults and $175.12 for children three to nine. The pass is good for 14 days of unlimited admission to Busch Gardens, Universal Orlando parks, Wet 'n Wild, and SeaWorld.

ARRIVING & DEPARTING BY CAR
Busch Gardens is at the corner of Busch Boulevard and 40th Street, 8 mi northeast of downtown Tampa, 2 mi east of I–275, and 2 mi west of I–75. It'll take you an hour and 15 minutes to drive the 81 mi from Orlando on I–4. From Orlando, travel west on I–4, then north on I–75 to Fowler Avenue (Exit 265). This is also the exit for the University of South Florida. Bear left on the exit ramp, and it'll lead you onto Fowler Avenue. Head west on Fowler Avenue to McKinley Avenue. (McKinley Avenue is the first light past the main entrance to the university.) Turn left on McKinley. Go south on McKinley to parking and the main entrance to the park. If you're already in Tampa and taking the much easier I–275, look for Busch Boulevard at Exit 33 and follow it east 2 mi to the park.

CAR CARE If you have car trouble, raise your hood and the parking patrol will assist you.

PARKING The cost for parking is $7 for motorcycles, cars, trucks, and campers. For $10 you can pay for preferred parking closer to the front gates.

BABY CARE
Nursing facilities and diaper-changing tables are in Land of the Dragons; only the women's rest rooms also have changing tables. Stroller rentals are available at Stroller and Wheelchair Rental in Morocco ($6 for singles, $10 for doubles, including $1 deposit; doubles resemble safari trucks!).

Disposable diapers are sold at Stroller and Wheelchair Rental. Baby food and formula are sold at the Food Lion on 50th Street and Busch Boulevard. Go down a little farther, to 56th Street, to find a Kmart (on Busch Boulevard itself) as well as a Publix and a Kash 'N' Karry, which are on 56th Street, left off Busch Boulevard.

CAMERAS & FILM
Disposable cameras are for sale at **Safari Foto**, near the main entrance, as well as at other stores throughout the park.

DINING
Most meals revolve around beef routinely washed down with Anheuser-Busch products. Budweiser, Bud Light, Michelob, and the nonalcoholic O'Doul's are sold throughout the park. Ice cream and popcorn stands are numerous.

snorkel you left in the Keys: $12
cell phone you lost in South Beach nightclub: $99
flip-flops you forgot in Orlando: $16

replacing your card anywhere:
priceless

For everything from card replacement to cash advances
to locating the nearest ATM, call 1-800-MasterCard.

there are some things money can't buy.
for everything else there's MasterCard."

Find America *with a Compass*

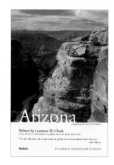

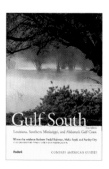

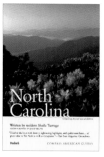

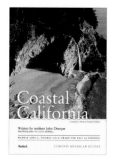

Written by local authors and illustrated throughout
with spectacular color images, Compass American
Guides reveal the character and culture of more than
40 of America's most fascinating destinations. Perfect
for residents who want to explore their own backyards
and for visitors who want an insider's perspective
on the history, heritage, and all there is to see and do.

Fodor's COMPASS AMERICAN GUIDES

At bookstores everywhere.

FULL-SERVICE RESTAURANTS

Crown Colony is the fanciest place in the park. Although the first floor is a counter-service restaurant with fast food (sandwiches, salad platters, pizza, etc.), the second floor is done up to resemble an outpost of the British empire, with portraits of top-hatted sahibs, polo mallets, and nicely faded Oriental carpets.

Reasonably priced entrées include steak, chicken, and pasta dishes served in white-tablecloth splendor by proper waiters and waitresses, with huge windows and a great view of the African Veldt as a free appetizer and relaxer. The change in altitude affects the price only a little. Unfortunately, the number of window tables is limited, so have lunch before noon and dinner around 4:30 to be sure of getting one without waiting. When the park closes early, seating may end around 4, although this varies.

The **Hospitality House,** in Bird Gardens, provides free whistle-wetting drafts (beer limit: two; age limit: 21). After a full day at Busch Gardens, you'll probably need it. You can also order a salad, pizza, or delicious deli sandwich served on fresh-baked bread. With peacocks, flowers, and a flowing river, it's a pleasant place to calm down.

SELF-SERVICE RESTAURANTS

The **Bazaar Café** offers hearty barbecued beef sandwiches. The **Stanleyville Smokehouse** serves slow-cooked chicken, beef, and ribs with corn on the cob and all the trimmings.

Just beyond the entrance is Morocco's **Zagora Café,** an enormous open-air dining area with a North African flair. The several food court–style restaurants serve basic burgers, fajitas, and turkey sandwiches. In pleasant weather, you can't beat it.

DISABILITIES & ACCESSIBILITY

To many wheelchair users, the Busch Gardens experience is represented less by the wild rides than by the animals, which are on display at almost every turn. However, almost all the rides are accessible by guests who can transfer into the ride vehicles.

ATTRACTIONS

All attractions are wheelchair accessible in Morocco, Myombe Reserve, and Nairobi. **Akbar's Adventure Tours** is completely wheelchair accessible. To play in Land of the Dragons, children must be able to leave their wheelchairs, although there's an adjoining wheelchair-accessible playground to the side.

You must leave your wheelchair to board vehicles at **Montu** in Egypt; **Congo River Rapids, Ubanga-Banga Bumper Cars,** and **Python** in Congo; **Stanley Falls** and **Tanganyika Tidal Wave** in Stanleyville; **Crazy Camel, Phoenix, Sandstorm,** and **Scorpion** in Timbuktu; and **Gwazi** in Bird Gardens. For these, you must also be able to hold lap bars or railings, as well as sit upright and absorb sudden and dramatic movements.

Transferring out of a wheelchair is also required for the **Congo kiddie rides,** including the bumper cars.

RESTAURANTS & SHOPS

All shops and restaurants in Busch Gardens are wheelchair accessible.

SERVICES

The park publishes a leaflet describing each attraction's accessibility. It's available at Guest Relations.

WHEELCHAIR RENTALS

At **Stroller and Wheelchair Rental** in Morocco, you can rent standard chairs ($5; $1 deposit) and motorized wheelchairs ($25; $5 deposit). If your rented wheelchair disappears and needs replacing, ask for a replacement in any gift shop.

GUIDED TOURS

The **Serengeti Safari** (☎ 813/987–5212) leaves Edge of Africa five times a day on a 30-minute tour of the Serengeti Plain. Excursions are available on a first-come, first-served basis, so reservations are strongly recommended ($29.99). The animals are more active earlier in the day, with the first tour leaving at 11:15. Inquire at the Edge of Africa gift shop for availability.

HEALTH SERVICES/FIRST AID

If you need urgent medical assistance, see a host or hostess. Otherwise, the primary First Aid location is in Timbuktu, with a second location at the Skyride Station in Crown Colony.

HOURS

The park is open daily from 9:30 to 6, except in summer and some holidays, when hours are extended.

LOCKERS

Lockers are available in the Moroccan village; in Stanleyville, near the Tanganyika Tidal Wave; and in the Congo, at the Kumba and Congo River Rapids rides. The cost is $1. There are change machines near the lockers.

LOST THINGS & PEOPLE

Guest Relations, at the main entrance, handles Lost & Found. For lost companions, go to Security or speak to any of the security personnel, who wear white shirts, badges, and hats.

MONEY MATTERS

There are two ATMs—one just outside the main entrance and the other in Timbuktu. For currency exchange, go to the Guest Relations window near the main entrance in Morocco.

PACKAGE PICKUP

If you'd rather not lug around your purchases all day, have them sent from any store in the park to **Sahara Traders,** in the Moroccan village area near the entrance. You can pick them up on your way out. The service is free; allow an hour for delivery.

SHOPPING

There are three must-have stuffed animals on the Central Florida theme-park circuit, and two of them are here (SeaWorld's plush killer whales are the other). Cuddly gorillas are available at **J. R.'s Gorilla Hut,** just outside Myombe Reserve, along with a delightfully long-limbed chimpanzee whose Velcro palms attach in an everlasting hug. White-tiger puppets are sold at the **Stanleyville Bazaar.**

Plenty of pseudo-African schlock—along with some authentic imported treasures—is also available. Craftspeople fashion their wares outside, and some interesting handcrafted items are available for sale. It's a good place to look for the perfect birthday trinket or Yuletide stocking stuffer, perhaps a set of carved wooden zoo animals or brilliantly colored, elephant-shape napkin rings.

The stock in Stanleyville's **Air Africa** is similar to that of the Stanleyville Bazaar. **Continental Curios** in Morocco is the stop for inexpensive bangles, moderately priced brass, and exorbitantly priced Moroccan leather, not to mention a rainbow of gauze veils in which to swathe your own little Salome.

If you leave the park without purchasing that beautiful bird key ring and want to run back for one, ask about one of the 30-minute **shopping passes,** available for a deposit equaling the price of admission.

VISITOR INFORMATION
On-site park information is available at Morocco's **Guest Relations,** near the main entrance, in Morocco. Here you can find out if there are any tapings of *Jack Hanna's Animal Adventures* in the park that day.
🖪 Tourist Information **Busch Gardens** ⬛ Box 9158, Tampa 33674 ☎ 813/987–5082 or 888/800–5447 ⊕ www.buschgardens.com.

AWAY FROM THE THEME PARKS

4

FODOR'S CHOICE

Bok Tower Gardens, in Lake Wales

Charles Hosmer Morse Museum, in Winter Park

Green Meadows Farm, in Kissimmee

Orlando Science Center, in downtown Orlando

Wekiwa Springs State Park, in Apopka

HIGHLY RECOMMENDED

Scenic Boat Tour, in Winter Park

Splendid China, in Kissimmee

Trainland International, in the I-Drive Area

Water Mania, in Kissimmee

WonderWorks, in the I-Drive Area

Updated by
Jennie Hess

WHEN YOU'RE READY TO PUT SOME DISTANCE between you and Mickey, you'll find that Orlando and the surrounding Central Florida area offer much more than theme parks. Nature buffs like to escape to the Ocala National Forest or the Audubon's Center for Birds of Prey, just north of Orlando in Maitland. Art devotees head for Winter Park and Rollins College's Cornell Fine Arts Museum or the Charles Hosmer Morse Museum of American Art and its stunning collection of Tiffany glass. New Agers flock to the town of Cassadaga, where more than half the residents are psychics, mediums, and healers. Attraction lovers seek out the additional rides and shows, such as WonderWorks and the Orlando Science Center. Indeed, you can discover an abundance of sights that are equally enjoyable and often less crowded and less expensive than those at the theme parks.

Take this opportunity to explore one or more of the many attractions throughout Central Florida. But don't make the mistake of darting into a museum in one neighborhood and beelining it to a great park in another or you could spend all your time in the car. These towns are spread out over quite a wide area, so check the map before you start.

Just to the southeast of Walt Disney World is the sprawling town of Kissimmee, which has a few sights of its own. Another group of things to do is clustered to the northeast of WDW, on International Drive, halfway to Orlando. Downtown Orlando has a combination of skyscrapers, quiet parks and gardens, museums, theaters, coffeehouses, art exhibits, shops, and restaurants. Northeast of downtown is Winter Park, a quiet college town with old oak trees, several fine museums, sidewalk cafés, and boutique shopping. Just north is Maitland, where there's a bird sanctuary and an art center.

Farther afield lie local and state parks, zoos, lakes, and the Ocala National Forest. So choose what you like, and linger for a while.

Numbers in the margin correspond to points of interest on the Away from the Theme Parks map.

ORLANDO & ENVIRONS

Kissimmee

10 mi southeast of WDW; take I–4 Exit 64A.

Although Kissimmee is primarily known as the gateway to Walt Disney World, its non-WDW attractions just might tickle your fancy.

❶ Long before Walt Disney World, there was **Gatorland.** This campy attraction south of Orlando on U.S. 441 has endured since 1949 without much change, despite competition from the major parks. Through the monstrous aqua gator-jaw doorway await thrills and chills in the form of thousands of alligators and crocodiles, swimming and basking in the Florida sun. There's also a small zoo that houses many other reptiles and mammals, and an aviary where a bird might land on your shoulder. A free train ride provides an overview of the park, taking you through an alligator breeding marsh and a natural swamp setting where you can spot gators, birds, and turtles. A three-story observation tower overlooks the breeding marsh, swamped with gator grunts, especially come sundown during mating season.

For a glimpse of 37 giant rare and deadly crocodiles, check out the exhibit called **Jungle Crocs of the World.** Don't miss the **Gator Jumparoo Show,** in which gators leap out of the water for their food. The most

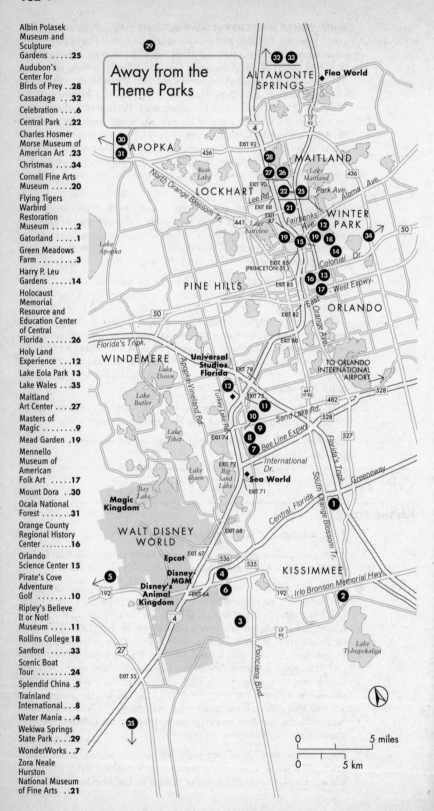

Away from the Theme Parks

thrilling is the first one in the morning, when the gators are hungriest. There's also a **Gator Wrestlin' Show,** and although there's no doubt who's going to win the match, it's still fun to see the handlers take on those tough guys with the beady eyes. In the educational **Snakes of Florida Show,** high drama is provided by the 30–40 rattlesnakes that fill the pit around the speaker. This is a real Florida experience, and you walk out through those aqua gator jaws knowing the difference between a gator and a croc. ✉ *14501 S. Orange Blossom Trail, between Orlando and Kissimmee* ☎ *407/855–5496 or 800/393–5297* ⊕ *www.gatorland.com* ☛ *$21.15 adults, $10.55 children 3–12 (discount coupons online)* ⊗ *Daily 9 AM–6 PM.*

❷ Old war birds never die—they just become attractions at the **Flying Tigers Warbird Restoration Museum.** The working aircraft restoration facility is nicknamed Bombertown USA because most of the planes here are bombers. Once they're operational they're usually flown away by private collectors, but the museum also houses a permanent collection of about 40 vintage planes in its hangar, with a few big ones out on the tarmac. Tour guides are full of facts and personality and have an infectious passion for the planes. From U.S. 192, turn south on North Hoagland Boulevard, a.k.a. Airport Road. ✉ *231 N. Hoagland Blvd.* ☎ *407/933–1942* ⊕ *www.warbirdmuseum.com* ☛ *$9 adults, $8 children 8–12, children 7 and under free* ⊗ *Mon.–Sat. 9–5:30, Sun. 9–5.*

❸ Friendly farmhands keep things moving on the two-hour guided tour

Fodor'sChoice of **Green Meadows Farm**—a 40-acre property with almost 300 animals. There's little chance to get bored and no waiting in line because tours are always starting. Everyone can milk the fat mama cow, and chickens and geese are turned loose in their yard to run and squawk while city slickers try to catch them. Children take a quick pony ride, and everyone gets jostled about on the old-fashioned hayride. Youngsters come away saying, "I milked a cow, caught a chicken, petted a pig, and fed a goat." Take U.S. 192 for 3 mi east of I–4 to South Poinciana Boulevard; turn right and drive 5 mi. ✉ *1368 S. Poinciana Blvd.* ☎ *407/846–0770* ⊕ *www.greenmeadowsfarm.com* ☛ *$17 ages 2 and up* ⊗ *Daily 9:30–5:30 (last tour begins at 4 PM).*

★ ❹ **Water Mania** has all the requisite rides and slides without Walt Disney World's aesthetics. However, it's the only water park around to have **Wipe Out,** a surfing simulator, where you grab a body board and ride a continuous wave form. The giant Pirate Ship in the **Rain Forest,** one of two children's play areas, is equipped with water slides and water cannons. The **Abyss** is an enclosed tube slide through which you twist and turn on a one- or two-person raft through 380 ft of deep-blue darkness. At this 36-acre park there are also a sandy beach, go-carts, a picnic area, snack bars, gift shops, and periodic concerts, which can be enjoyed while floating in an inner tube. Its 18-hole miniature golf course won't win any local prizes, considering the competition, but it does give you another way to pass the time while you're out of the water. It's 1½ mi from Walt Disney World, and from I–4 it's ¼ mi east. Be sure to call for exact opening and closing times, which can vary due to weather. Also call for unadvertised special rates during certain off-season times. ✉ *6073 W. Irlo Bronson Memorial Hwy.* ☎ *407/239–8448, 407/396–2626, or 800/527–3092* ⊕ *www.watermania-florida.com* ☛ *$19.95 adults, $16.95 ages 3–9; parking $5* ⊗ *Mid-Mar.–Sept., daily 10–5; Oct., Wed.–Sat. 10–5.*

★ ❺ More open-air museum than activity-filled theme park in the Mickey Mouse tradition, **Splendid China** is of most interest to older teens and adults. Here, in this 76-acre park, you can stroll among painstakingly re-created versions of China's greatest landmarks and watch artisans demonstrate traditional Chinese woodworking, weaving, and other crafts while tinkling meditative music plays in the background. It took $100 million and 120 Chinese craftspeople working for two years using, whenever possible, historically accurate building materials and techniques to create the 60-plus replicas. Both man-made structures and natural phenomena are represented—some life-size, others greatly reduced in scale. (The bricks in the Great Wall, for example, are only 2 inches long.) The emphasis is on tradition over technology. In the heat of the Florida summer, it's best to arrive at opening to tour the park, take a midday break, and return for the evening show.

The park map numbers exhibits counterclockwise, but if you travel clockwise, you finish with the most impressive sights. Although the ½-mi-long **Great Wall** cannot begin to replicate the size of the 1,500-mi-long original, it's nevertheless amazing—containing 6.5 million tiny bricks that were mortared into place by hand. Other exhibits of note include the **Imperial Palace,** the centerpiece of Beijing's famed Forbidden City; the **Leshan Buddha,** a 35-ft re-creation of the largest man-made statue in the world; and the **Temple of Heaven,** a striking, blue-tile structure where the emperor, as high priest of his people, would spend time in fasting and prayer. Tuesday through Sunday, the Golden Peacock Theater presents a 90-minute live show, **Mysterious Kingdom of the Orient.** Besides the star attractions, Splendid China also has reproductions of Chinese temples, pagodas, and grottoes filled with religious statuary. Each display is accompanied by a short written explanation, a recorded message, or both. To reach the park, take I–4 Exit 64B and continue west on U.S. 192 approximately 3 mi, past all the Disney exits. Stay in the far-left lane and look for the dragon. ⊠ *3000 Splendid China Blvd.* ☎ *407/ 397–8800 recording; 407/396–7111; 800/244–6226* ⊕ *www. floridasplendidchina.com* ✉ *$28.88 adults, $18.18 children 5–12, admission includes all attractions and 90-min live show at 6; $16 adults, $10.65 children 5–12, includes 90-min live show only; parking and Chinatown free* ☉ *Daily 9:30–7, later in peak seasons; Chinatown shops and restaurants until 7 and later in peak seasons.*

Celebration

❻ *6 mi south of Epcot; take I–4 to Exit 64A and follow the "Celebration" signs.*

This Disney-created community, named Celebration, in which every blade of grass in every lawn is just right, reminds some locals of something out of the 1970s film *The Stepford Wives.* But Celebration, which draws on vernacular architecture from all over the United States and was based on ideas from some of America's top architects and planners, offers a great retreat from the theme parks and from the garish reality of the U.S. 192 tourist strip just 1 mi to the east. The shell of it is as faux as Main Street, U.S.A., but as the town evolves, you see signs that real life is being lived here—and a good life it is. Celebration is a real town, complete with its own hospital and school system. Houses and apartments, which are built to conform to a strict set of design guidelines, spread out from the compact and charming downtown area, which wraps around the edge of a lake. The town is so perfect it could be a movie set, and it's a delightful place to spend a morning or afternoon. Sidewalks are built for strolling, restaurants have outdoor seating with lake views, and inviting shops beckon. After a walk around the lake, take your youngsters over to the huge interactive fountain, and have fun getting sopping wet. Starting the Friday after Thanksgiving Day and continuing through New Year's Eve, honest-to-goodness snow sprinkles softly down over Main Street for several hours every night, to the absolute delight of children of all ages. Search www.celebrationfl.com for event listings or call 407/566–2200.

International Drive Area

7 mi northeast of WDW; take I–4 Exit 74 or 75 unless otherwise noted.

A short drive northeast of WDW are a number of attractions that children adore; unfortunately, some may put wear and tear on parents.

★ **7** Just up the street, the Ripley's Believe It or Not! building seems to be sinking into the ground, but true to Orlando tradition, the newer attraction, **WonderWorks**, one-ups the competition: it's sinking into the ground at a precarious angle and upside down. If the strange sight of a topsy-turvy facade complete with upended palm trees and simulated FedEx box doesn't catch your attention, the swirling "dust" and piped-out creaking sounds will. Inside, the upside-down theme continues only as far as the lobby. After that, it's a playground of 100 interactive experiences, some incorporating virtual reality. Some are educational (similar to those at a science museum) and others just pure entertainment. Experience an earthquake or a hurricane, swim with sharks, play laser tag in the largest laser-tag arena in the world, design and ride your own awesome roller coaster, or even play basketball with a 7-ft opponent. ✉ *9067 International Dr.* ☎ *407/352–8655* ⊕ *www.wonderworksonline. com* 🖃 *$16.95 adults, $12.95 children 4–12; packages include laser tag and Magical Dinner Show (see online coupons)* ☉ *Daily 9 AM–midnight.*

★ **8** **Trainland International** is just what the conductor ordered for the train enthusiast young or old. The museum has one of the nation's largest indoor G-gauge layouts (with tiny tracks only 1¾ inches wide), and you can see scale-model Aristocraft, LGB, USA, and Bachman locomotives pulling 14 continuously operating trains through a vast wonderland of spaces: forests, farmland, cities, and mountainous wilderness. It's quite a sight to watch the trains barely miss one another as they emerge from one of the 32 underground tunnels, cross one of the 24 bridges, or round a curve and switch onto a new track. Visitors can join in an indoor–outdoor scavenger hunt to look for items hidden in the scenery; winners are entered in a monthly random drawing to receive a model train set or a $100 gift certificate to the store. Don't leave without hopping on the diesel train that takes you for a ride through the outdoor gardens. ✉ *8990 International Dr.* ☎ *407/363–9002* ⊕ *www. trolleyandtrainmuseum.com* 🖃 *$4 adults, $3 children 3–12. Train ride is $2 for adults and $1 for children* ☉ *Daily 10 AM–7 PM.*

9 Children of all ages delight in the world-class shows at **Masters of Magic**. This is not your typical birthday party magic show, but rather a Las Vegas–like spectacle choreographed by internationally acclaimed Master Magician Typhoon Lou. Each 90-minute performance has state-of-the-art digital surround-sound grand illusions, and dazzling special effects that rival today's newest movies. ✉ *8815 International Dr.* ☎ *407/352–3456* ⊕ *www.mastersofmagic.net* 🖃 *$24.95 adults, $17.95 children 4–12; or dinner package with pizza and beverage $29.95 adults, $19.95 children 4–12* ☉ *Wed.–Sun., shows at 6:30 and 9:15 PM.*

10 You can play the crème de la crème of miniature golf at the two **Pirate's Cove Adventure Golf** locations. Each site has two 18-hole courses that wind around artificial mountains, through caves, and into lush foliage. The beginner's course is called Captain Kidd's Adventure; a more difficult game can be played on Blackbeard's Challenge. The courses are opposite Mercado Mediterranean Village and in the Crossroads of Lake Buena Vista shopping plaza. ✉ *8501 International Dr.* ☎ *407/352–7378* ✉ *Crossroads Center, I–4 Exit 68* ☎ *407/827–1242* ✉ *At International Drive course: $9.50 adults, $8.45 children 4–12; at Crossroads course $9 adults, $7.94 children 4–12* ☉ *Daily 9 AM–11:30 PM on I-Drive and 9 AM–11 at Crossroads.*

⓫ **Ripley's Believe It or Not! Museum** challenges the imagination. A 10-ft-square section of the Berlin Wall. A pain and torture chamber. A Rolls-Royce constructed entirely of matchsticks. A 26'×20' portrait of van Gogh made from 3,000 postcards. These and almost 200 other oddities speak for themselves in this museum-cum-attraction in the heart of tourist territory on International Drive. The building itself is designed to appear as if it's sliding into one of Florida's notorious sinkholes. Give yourself an hour or two to soak up the weirdness here, but remember, this is a looking, not touching, experience, which may drive antsy youngsters—and their parents—crazy. The museum is ¼ mi south of Sand Lake Road. ✉ *8201 International Dr.* ☎ *407/363–4418 or 800/998–4418* ⊕ *www.ripleysorlando.com* ✉ *$15.95 adults, $10.95 children 4–12* ☉ *Daily 9 AM–1 AM.*

⓬ The **Holy Land Experience,** a project of a Baptist minister who was raised Jewish, is a 14-acre Christian theme park modeled after the ancient city of Jerusalem as it is imagined to have appeared between 1450 BC and AD 66. You can visit a first-century street market and bargain with the vendors (played by actors), and see the Qumran Vaces and the Holy Temple. Shofars, menorahs, and gifts imported from Israel are for sale; Goliath Burgers feed the hungry. There are no rides. ✉ *4655 Vineland Rd., I–4 east to Exit 78, turn left onto Conroy Rd. and then right onto Vineland Rd.* ☎ *407/367–2065 or 866/872–4659* ✉ *$29.75 adults, $19.75 children 6–12; parking $3* ☉ *Mon.–Thurs. 9–5, Fri.–Sat. 9–6, Sun. noon–6; closed Thanksgiving and Christmas.*

Downtown Orlando

15 mi northeast of WDW; take I–4 Exit 82C or 83A eastbound, or Exit 85 for Loch Haven Park sights.

Downtown Orlando is a dynamic community that's constantly growing and changing. Here are many high-rise buildings, interesting museums, sporting events, nightspots, and restaurants. Numerous parks, many of which surround lakes, provide pleasant relief from the tall office buildings. Just a few steps away from downtown's tourist centers are delightful residential neighborhoods with brick-paved streets and live oaks dripping with Spanish moss.

⓭ In the heart of downtown is **Lake Eola Park,** with its signature fountain in the center. The park represents an inner-city victory over decay. Established in 1892, the now family-friendly park experienced a series of ups and downs that left it very run-down by the late 1970s. With the support of determined citizens, the park gradually underwent a renovation that restored the fountain and added a wide brick walkway around the lake. The security here is such that families with young children use the well-lighted playground in the evening and downtown residents toss bread to the ducks, swans, and birds and walk their dogs late at night in safety. The **Walt Disney Amphitheater,** perched on the lake, is a dramatic site for the annual Shakespeare Festival (April and May) as well as for weekend concerts and other events. The most fun to be had in the park is a ride in a swan-shape pedal boat, one of which frequent Walt Disney World visitor Michael Jackson is reputed to have ordered for his personal use at his ranch. The view at dusk, as the fountain lights up in all its colors and the sun sets behind Orlando's ever-growing skyline, is spectacular. ⊠ *Robinson St. and Rosalind Ave.* ☎ *407/246–2827 park; 407/839–8899 swan boats* ⊠ *Boat rental $7.50 per half hr, maximum 3 people per boat; children under 10 must be with an adult* ☉ *Park daily 6 AM–midnight; swan boats weekdays 10–6, weekends 10–8; café weekdays 10–8, weekends 10–9.*

⑭ The **Harry P. Leu Gardens,** a few miles outside of downtown on the former lakefront estate of a citrus entrepreneur, are a quiet respite from the artificial world of the theme parks. On the grounds' 50 acres is a collection of historical blooms, many varieties of which were established before 1900. You can see ancient oaks, a 50-ft floral clock, an orchid conservatory, and one of the largest camellia collections in eastern North America (in bloom October–March). **Mary Jane's Rose Garden,** named after Leu's wife, is filled with more than 1,000 bushes; it's the largest formal rose garden south of Atlanta. The simple 19th-century **Leu House Museum,** once the Leu family home, preserves the furnishings and appointments of a well-to-do, turn-of-the-20th-century Florida family. ⊠ *1920 N. Forest Ave.* ☎ *407/246–2620* ⊠ *$4 adults, $1 children in kindergarten through 12th grade* ☉ *Garden daily 9–5; guided house tours daily on the hr and half hr 10–3:30.*

⑮ With all the high-tech glitz and imagined worlds of the theme parks, is it worth visiting the reality-based **Orlando Science Center**? Absolutely. The action-packed, 207,000-square-ft, four-level building is the perfect antidote to long lines and overwhelming gimmickry. The 12 themed display halls house a multitude of exciting hands-on exhibits covering mechanics; electricity and magnetism; math; health and fitness; nature; the solar system; and light, lasers, and optics. Walk through an enormous open mouth (literally) and take a journey through the human body (figuratively). Raise a suspended VW bug with the help of a lever, and learn about physics while you're showing off (you don't need to tell the children it's educational if you don't want to). The **Dr. Phillips Cine-Dome,** a movie theater with a giant eight-story screen, offers large-format IWERKS films (Ub Iwerks was an associate of Walt Disney's in the early days), as well as planetarium programs and, on weekends, laser light shows. In addition, the **Darden Adventure Theater** is home to the center's in-house performance troupe, the Einstein Players. ⊠ *777 E. Princeton St.* ☎ *407/514–2000 or 888/672–4386* ⊕ *www.osc.org* ⊠ *Exhibits and Darden Adventure Theater $10 adults, $7.50 children 3–11; CineDome films or planetarium only, $7 adults, $5 children; Double Combo (all exhibits plus 2 CineDome films) $16 adults, $13.50 children; Combo (all exhibits plus 1 Cinedome film) $13 adults, $10.50 children; parking $3.50* ☉ *Tues.–Thurs. 9–5, Fri.–Sat. 9–9, Sun. noon–5; Mon. 9–5 Memorial Day–mid-Aug. and on school holidays.*

⑯ The **Orange County Regional History Center** takes you on a journey back in time to discover how Florida's Paleo-Indians hunted and fished the land; what the Sunshine State was like when Spaniards first arrived in the New World; and how life in Florida was different when citrus was king. Visit a cracker cabin from the late 1800s, complete with Spanish moss–stuffed mattresses, mosquito netting over the beds, and a room where game was preserved pre-refrigeration. Seminole Indian displays include interactive screens, and tin-can tourist camps of the early 1900s preview Florida's destiny as a future vacation mecca. ⊠ *65 E. Central Blvd.* ☎ *407/836–8500 or 800/965–2030* ⊕ *www.thehistorycenter.org* ⊠ *$7 adults, $3.50 children 3–12* ☉ *Mon.–Sat. 10–5, Sun. noon–5.*

FodorśChoice

⑰ The **Mennello Museum of American Folk Art** is one of the few museums in the United States devoted to folk art and the only one in Florida. It contains the nation's most extensive permanent collection of Earl Cunningham paintings as well as works by many other self-taught artists. At the **Museum Shop** you can purchase folk art books, toys, and unusual gifts. ⊠ *900 E. Princeton St.* ☎ *407/246–4278* ⊕ *www.mennellomuseum.com* ☞ *$4 adults, children under 12 free* ⊙ *Tues.–Sat. 11–5, Sun. noon–5; closed major holidays.*

Winter Park

20 mi northeast of WDW; take I–4 Exit 87 and head east 3 mi on Fairbanks Ave.

This peaceful, upscale community may be just north of the hustle and bustle of Orlando, but it feels miles away. You can spend a pleasant day here shopping, eating, visiting museums, and taking in the scenery along Park Avenue. When you want a rest, look for a bench in the shady Central Park. Away from the avenue, stroll beneath the moss-covered trees that form a canopy over brick streets, and cruise the area's lakes on pontoon boats to see wildlife and the old estates that surround canal-linked lakes.

⑱ **Rollins College,** a private liberal arts school, is in the heart of Winter Park's downtown. Among the school's alums is Mister (Fred) Rogers—yes, this was once his neighborhood. Anthony Perkins also attended. The grounds include the **Knowles Memorial Chapel,** built in 1932, and the **Annie Russell Theatre,** a 1931 building that's often the venue for local theatrical productions. ⊠ *1000 Holt Ave.* ☎ *407/646–2000; 407/646–2145 theater box office* ⊕ *www.rollins.edu.*

⑲ The 55 acres in the unusual park, **Mead Garden,** have been intentionally left to grow as a natural preserve. Walkers and runners are attracted to the trails that wind around the creek, and a boardwalk provides a better view of the delicate wetlands. ⊠ *1300 S. Denning Ave.* ☎ *407/599–3334* ☞ *Free* ⊙ *Daily 8–sunset.*

⑳ On the Rollins College campus, the **Cornell Fine Arts Museum** is the oldest collection of art in Florida, with the first paintings acquired in 1896. It houses more than 6,000 objects, including 19th- and 20th-century American and European paintings, decorative arts, and sculpture. Artists represented include William Merritt Chase, Childe Hassam, and Louis Comfort Tiffany. In addition, special exhibitions are scheduled throughout the year. Outside the museum, a small but charming garden overlooks Lake Virginia. ⊠ *Rollins College, end of Holt Ave.* ☎ *407/646–2526* ⊕ *www.rollins.edu/cfam* ☞ *Free* ⊙ *Tues.–Fri. 10–5, weekends 1–5.*

㉑ The **Zora Neale Hurston National Museum of Fine Arts** showcases creative works by artists of African descent. The museum holds five six-week-long exhibits each year, with one reserved for promising, up-and-coming artists. The museum is named after former local resident Zora Neale Hurston (1891–1960), a writer, folklorist, and anthropologist best known for her novel *Their Eyes Were Watching God.* ⊠ *227 E. Kennedy Blvd., Eatonville* ☎ *407/647–3307* ☞ *Donations accepted* ⊙ *Weekdays 9–4.*

In the center of town is **Park Avenue,** an inviting brick street with chic boutiques, cozy cafés, restaurants serving a variety of cuisines, and hidden alleyways that lead to peaceful nooks and crannies as well as more restaurants and shops. An invasion of stores such as Ann Taylor,

Williams-Sonoma, Chico's, Peterbrooke Chocolatier, Douglas Cosmetics, and Restoration Hardware keeps the avenue busy with shoppers.

㉒ **Central Park** is Winter Park's gathering place. This lovely green space has a stage and gazebo, which are often the scene of concerts. If you don't want to browse in the shops across the street, a walk through the park is a delightful alternative. ⊠ *Park Ave.* ☉ *Sunrise–sunset.*

The world's most comprehensive collection of the works of Louis Comfort Tiffany, including immense stained-glass windows, lamps, water-

㉓ colors, and desk sets, is at the **Charles Hosmer Morse Museum of American Art.** The museum's constant draws include exhibits on the Tiffany Long Island mansion, Laurelton Hall, and the 800-square-ft Tiffany Chapel, originally built for the 1893 world's fair in Chicago. It took craftsmen 2½ years to painstakingly reassemble the chapel here. Also displayed at the museum are collections of paintings by 19th- and 20th-century American artists, and jewelry and pottery, including a fine display of Rookwood vases. ⊠ *445 N. Park Ave.* ☎ *407/645–5311* ⊕ *www. morsemuseum.org* ⊠ *$3 adults, $1 students, children under 12 free; Sept.–May, Fri. free 4–8* ☉ *Tues.–Sat. 9:30–4, Sun. 1–4; Sept.–May, Fri. until 8.*

FodorśChoice

★ **㉔** From the dock at the end of Morse Avenue, you can depart for the **Scenic Boat Tour,** a Winter Park tradition that's been in continuous operation for more than 60 years. The relaxing, narrated one-hour pontoon boat tour, which leaves hourly, cruises by 12 mi of Winter Park's opulent lakeside estates and travels across three lakes. ⊠ *312 E. Morse Blvd.* ☎ *407/ 644–4056* ⊕ *www.scenicboattours.com* ⊠ *$8 adults, $4 children 2–11* ☉ *Daily 10–4.*

Stroll along on a guided tour through lush gardens showcasing the graceful sculptures created by internationally known sculptor Albin Po-

㉕ lasek (1879–1965) at the **Albin Polasek Museum and Sculpture Gardens.** The late artist's home, studio, galleries, and private chapel are centered on 3 acres of exquisitely tended lawns, colorful flower beds, and tropical foliage. Paths and walkways lead past classical life-size, figurative sculptures and whimsical mythological pieces. Inside the museum are works by Hawthorne, Chase, Mucha, and Saint-Gaudens. ⊠ *633 Osceola Ave.* ☎ *407/647–6294* ⊕ *www.polasek.org* ⊠ *$4 adults, $2 students ages 13 and up with student ID, children under 12 free* ☉ *Tues.–Sat. 10–4, Sun. 1–4* ☉ *Closed July and Aug.*

Maitland

25 mi northeast of WDW; take I–4 Exit 90A, then Maitland Blvd. east, and turn right (south) on Maitland Ave.

An Orlando suburb with an interesting mix, Maitland is home to both the Florida Save the Manatee Society and one of Central Florida's larger office parks. A number of spectacular homes grace the shores of this town's various lakes, and there's a bird sanctuary and an art center there as well.

㉖ The **Holocaust Memorial Resource and Education Center of Central Florida** chronicles major events of the Holocaust. Exhibits are arranged in chronological order and include a large number of photographs and audiovisual presentations. The museum also contains a library and archives. ⊠ *851 N. Maitland Ave.* ☎ *407/628–0555* ⊕ *www.holocaustedu.org* ⊠ *Free, but donations welcome* ☉ *Mon.–Thurs. 9–4, Fri. 9–1, Sun. 1–4.*

㉗ It's local lore that the historic **Maitland Art Center,** near Lake Sybelia, is inhabited by the spirit of its architect-painter founder, André Smith. He began constructing his studio retreat in 1937, and the grounds and 23 buildings themselves are works of art. The seemingly infinite reliefs and other details on all the structures reflect Smith's fascination with Maya and Aztec influences and further account for the mystical aura. An outdoor chapel is a favorite spot for weddings, and romantic gardens blend harmoniously with the natural surroundings. Inside, galleries display an extensive collection of Smith's work as well as changing exhibits by local, regional, and national artists. Take Maitland Avenue ¾ mi south of Maitland Boulevard; turn right on Packwood Avenue. ⊠ *231 W. Packwood Ave.* ☎ *407–539–2181* ⊕ *www.maitartctr.org* ✎ *Donations welcome* ☉ *Weekdays 9–4:30, weekends noon–4:30.*

❷❽ More than 20 bird species, including hawks, eagles, owls, falcons, and vultures, make their home at the **Audubon's Center for Birds of Prey.** This wildlife rehabilitation center has viewing windows into its medical exam labs, a self-guided conservation tour with interactive exhibits, and walkways through the wetlands. There's an earnestness to this newly expanded working facility on Lake Sybelia in Maitland, which takes in more than 600 injured wild birds of prey each year. Fewer than half the birds are able to return to the wild; permanently injured birds continue to live at the center and can be seen in the aviaries along the pathways and sitting on outdoor perches. The center also tracks eagles and occasionally sets up a closed-circuit monitor to observe a nest, so visitors can watch a genuine nature show. There's a nice spot to picnic here, too. From Maitland Avenue, turn right on U.S. 17–92, right on Kennedy Boulevard, and right on Audubon Way. ⊠ *1101 Audubon Way* ☎ *407/644–0190* ⊕ *www.adoptabird.org* ✎ *$5 adults, $4 children 3–12* ☉ *Tues.–Sun. 10–4.*

SIDE TRIPS FROM ORLANDO

When you feel like venturing farther afield, hop in your car and within an hour or two you can be where you can celebrate Christmas year-round, canoe down a river, meet with a psychic, feed farm animals at a small zoo, or walk in a beautiful park. The areas below are arranged in a roughly clockwise fashion starting northwest of Orlando.

Apopka

13 mi northwest of Orlando and 28 mi north of WDW.

Orange groves used to cover this part of Florida, but housing developments continue to replace one grove after another. East of Apopka is a state park with pristine waterways and scenic drives through longleaf-pine forests.

❷❾ Where the tannin-stained Wekiva River meets the crystal-clear Wekiwa
FodorsChoice headspring, there's a curious and visible exchange—like strong tea infusing water. Wekiva is a Creek Indian word meaning "flowing water;" wekiwa means "spring of water." **Wekiwa Springs State Park** sprawls around this area on 6,400 acres. The parkland is well suited to camping, hiking, and picnicking; the spring to swimming; and the river to canoeing and fishing. Canoe trips can range from a simple hour-long paddle around the lagoon to observe a colony of water turtles to a full-day excursion through the less-congested parts of the river that haven't changed much since the area was inhabited by the Timacuan Indians. Take I–4 Exit 94 (Longwood) and turn left on Route 434. Go 1¼ mi to Wekiwa Springs Road; turn right and go 4½ mi to the entrance, on the right. ⊠ *1800 Wekiva Circle* ☎ *407/884–2009* ⊕ *www.myflorida.com* ✎ *$4 per vehicle* ☉ *Daily 8–sunset.*

en route
As you drive northwest on U.S. 441, you head into aptly named Lake County, an area renowned for its pristine water and excellent fishing. Watch the flat countryside, thick with scrub pines, take on a gentle roll through citrus groves and pastures surrounded by live oaks.

Mount Dora

30 *35 mi northwest of Orlando and 50 mi north of WDW; take U.S. 441 (Orange Blossom Trail in Orlando) north or take I–4 to Exit 92, then Rte. 436 west to U.S. 441, and follow the signs.*

The unspoiled Lake Harris chain of lakes surrounds remote Mount Dora, an artsy valley community with a slow and easy pace, a rich history, New England–style charm, and excellent antiquing. Although the town's population is less than 8,000, there's plenty of excitement here, especially in fall and winter. The first weekend in February is the annual Mount Dora Art Festival, which opens Central Florida's spring art-fair season. Attracting more than 200,000 people over a three-day period, it's one of the region's major outdoor events. During the year, there's a sailing regatta (April), a bicycle festival (October), a crafts fair (October), and many other happenings.

Take a walk down **Donnelly Street.** The yellow Queen Anne–style mansion is **Donnelly House** (✉ 515 Donnelly St.), an 1893 architectural gem. Notice the details on the leaded-glass windows. Built in the 1920s, what was once known as the Dora Hotel is now **The Renaissance** (✉ 413 Donnelly St.), a shopping arcade with restaurants and an Icelandic pub.

If you walk along **5th Avenue,** you'll pass a number of charming restaurants and gift and antiques shops. The **Park Bench Restaurant** (✉ 116 E. 5th Ave. ☎ 352/383–7004) is the perfect spot for a late soup-and-salad lunch or an early dinner of fresh seafood, steaks, or pasta. Skip over to **Uncle Al's Time Capsule** (✉ 140 E. 4th Ave. ☎ 352/383–1958), where you can sift through some terrific Hollywood memorabilia and collectibles.

Gilbert Park has a public dock and boat-launching ramp, a playground, and a large picnic pavilion with grills. ✉ *Tremain St. and Liberty Ave.* ◷ *Daily 7:30–1 hr after sunset.*

Stop in for tea or something stronger at the **Lakeside Inn** (✉ 100 N. Alexander St. ☎ 352/383–4104), a country inn built in 1883. A stroll around the lakefront grounds makes you feel as if you've stepped out of the pages of *The Great Gatsby*; there's even a croquet court.

A historic train depot serves as the offices of the **Mount Dora Chamber of Commerce.** Stop in and pick up a self-guided tour map that tells you everything you need to know—from historic landmarks to restaurants. Don't forget to ask about the trolley tour schedule. ✉ *341 Alexander St., at 3rd Ave.* ☎ *352/383–2165* ⊕ *www.mountdora.com* ◷ *Weekdays 9–5, Sat. 10–4; after hrs, maps on display at kiosk.*

The **Orlando and Mount Dora Railway** offers several scenic rail excursions that originate in Orlando and nearby towns with Mount Dora as a destination. For a shorter ride while in Mount Dora, check to see if a tour is available on the Dora Doodlebug vintage motor car or, if you're visiting in December, on The Polar Express "round trip to the North Pole." ✉ *Alexander St. and 3rd Ave.* ☎ *352/735–4667* ⊕ *www.mtdoratrain. com* ✉ *Orlando to Mount Dora round trip, $27 adults, $17 children 4–12; Dora Doodlebug, $12 adults, $8 children 4–12.*

Palm Island Park, on the shores of Lake Dora and within walking distance of downtown, gives nature lovers a close-up view of Florida's wildlife and foliage. Take a stroll along the boardwalks and watch out for herons, raccoons, otters, and even an alligator or two. You also see pond cypress, bald cypress, and many varieties of palm. Fishing in the lake is permitted, and well-placed picnic tables offer pleasant stops to enjoy a meal. ⊠ *1 Liberty Ave.* ⊘ *Daily 7:30–1 hr after sunset.*

Ocala National Forest

③ *60 mi northwest of WDW; take I–4 east to Exit 92, and head west on Rte. 436 to U.S. 441, which you take north to Rte. 19 north.*

Between the Oklawaha and the St. Johns rivers lies the 366,000-acre Ocala National Forest. Clear streams wind through tall stands of pine or hardwoods. This spot is known for its canoeing, hiking, swimming, and camping, and for its invigorating springs. Here you can walk beneath tall pine trees and canoe down meandering streams and across placid lakes. Stop in at the **Ocala National Forest Visitor Center** (⊠ 45621 Rte. 19, Altoona ☎ 352/669–7495) for general park information. The center is open daily 9–5.

There are a number of developed recreation sites in the forest, including **Alexander Springs** (☎ 352/669–3522). This park is favored by the locals in the summer for its cold, fresh water. After hiking down to its small beach, swim out, preferably with a snorkel and fins, to the steep drop-off at the head of the spring, where the water rushes out from rock formations below. It's not unusual to see alligators sitting on the bank opposite the sandy beach—remember that they're still wild, can move very fast, and should not be provoked. Notice that the natives leave the water before sundown—feeding time! To get to Alexander Springs from the Ocala National Forest Visitor Center at Altoona, go north on Route 19 and turn right on Route 445. The entrance is on the left.

Cassadaga

② *35 mi northeast of Orlando and 50 mi northeast of WDW; take I–4 to Exit 114 (Cassadaga and Lake Helen), turn left on Rte. 472, then right on Martin Luther King Parkway, then right again on Cassadaga Road (Rte. 4139), and continue 1½ mi.*

This tiny town is headquarters of the **Southern Cassadaga Spiritualist Camp Meeting Association,** now on the National Register of Historic Places. More than half of this community's 350 residents are psychics, mediums, and healers, which makes it the nation's largest such community. Pick up a brochure at the **Information Center** (⊠ Andrew Jackson Davis Building, 1112 Stevens St. ☎ 386/228–2880 ⊕ www.cassadaga.org) in the center of town, which describes the town's history and its philosophy of spiritualism. The pamphlet also lists certified mediums and their locations; you can book a full hour of consultation or opt for a mini 15-minute meeting. It's suggested that the best way to find a medium who's right for you is to walk or drive through this rustic, five-block by five-block neighborhood and see if you can find a house that's giving off the right energy. Then call ahead to schedule an appointment.

Church services are held at **Colby Memorial Temple,** and visitors are welcome. Spiritualist services are nonsensational, meditative gatherings, with the most unconventional aspect being the "message" portion, during which certified mediums deliver specific messages to attendees from spirits in the beyond. ⊠ *1112 Stevens St.* ☎ *386/228–3171* ⊘ *Services Sun. 10:30–11:45* AM *and Wed. 7:30–9*PM.

This community rich in spirit doesn't offer much to the material world, except the modest **Cassadaga Spiritualist Camp Bookstore and Information Center.** People here are friendly and wholesome and accustomed to curiosity seekers, but they do request respect. ⊠ *1112 Stevens St.* ☎ *386/ 228–2880* ☉ *Mon.–Sat. 10–5:30, Sun. noon–5:30.*

Sanford

㉝ *22 mi north of Orlando and 37 mi northeast of WDW; take I–4 to Exit 104.*

This growing community on the shores of Lake Monroe has attracted a number of Orlandoans seeking a respite from the burgeoning urban sprawl. A small collection of antiques stores, secondhand shops, and galleries, which date from the 1880s to the 1920s, is found in buildings along 1st Street.

A visit to the **Central Florida Zoological Park** is likely to disappoint if you're expecting a grand metro zoo. However, this is a respectable display representing more than 100 species of animals, tucked under pine trees, and, like the city of Orlando, it continues to grow. The elephant exhibit is popular, as are the tortoises and the exotic and native snakes housed in the herpetarium. The zoo is becoming specialized in exotic cats, including servals, caracals, and cheetahs, and there's an aviary that houses American bald eagles that have been grounded owing to injury. Children love the **Animal Adventure,** which has domestic and farm animals to pet and feed. Take I–4 Exit 104, and drive 1 mi east on U.S. 17–92 to the entrance, on the right. ⊠ *3755 N.W. U.S. 17–92* ☎ *407/323–4450* ⊕ *www.centralfloridazoo.org* ☜ *$8 adults, $4 children 3–12; Thurs. 9–10 half price* ☉ *Daily 9–5, pony rides weekends 10–4.*

Christmas

㉞ *33 mi northeast from WDW; 18 mi east of Orlando on Rte. 50 (Colonial Dr.).*

There really is a Santa Claus in this tiny hamlet. Locals zipping to the beach or en route to Kennedy Space Center, on the coast near Cocoa Beach, can miss this town if they blink. But they flock here during December to have their holiday missives postmarked at the local post office. The headquarters of the Tosohatchee State Preserve, with more than 28,000 acres of woodlands, are also here.

If the children have been cooped up in the car for a while, the **Fort Christmas Historical Park, Fort, and Museum** is a great place for them to let off steam. There's a large play area and picnic area, plus a restored 1837 fort, built as a supply depot and to house soldiers during the Second Seminole War. Inside the fort is a museum that details Florida pioneer life in the mid-19th century. There are also seven pioneer homes that have been restored and are furnished in the style of the early 1800s and a sugar cane mill. During the week the fort is often brimming with local schoolchildren who visit on Florida-history field trips. ⊠ *2 mi north of Rte. 50 on Rte. 420, Ft. Christmas Rd.* ☎ *407/568–4149* ⊕ *www. onetgov.net* ☜ *Free* ☉ *Park daily 8–8 (8–6 in winter), Fort and Museum Tues.–Sat. 10–5, Sun. 1–5; call for guided-tour schedule.*

Hop on a boat and take a thrilling ride through a real Florida swamp teeming with alligators. At **Jungle Adventures** pontoon boats bring you face-to-face with these slithery reptiles in their natural habitat. At daily wildlife shows you can see the rare and endangered Florida panther, the Florida black bear, alligators, and various snakes. There are also daily alligator feeding demonstrations. ⊠ *17 mi east of Orlando on Rte. 50* ☎ *407/568–2885 or 877/424–2867* ⊕ *www.jungleadventures.com* 🖃 *$16 adults, $8.50 children 3–11 (online coupon)* ⊘ *Daily 9:30–5:30.*

The **Orlando Wetlands Park** showcases the first large-scale man-made wetlands in Florida to be created and maintained with highly treated, reclaimed water, and it provides a habitat for native wildlife. Created in 1987, the park is home to more than 170 species of birds, plus otters, foxes, deer, turtles, snakes, and alligators. There are a 2-mi bird viewing trail, many shorter trails that lead to good bird and wildlife viewing places, and a lake. More than 18 mi of trails are open for hiking and biking, but the woodland trails are off-limits for bikes. Don't expect to find a snack bar or crowds of people here. Unlike most other Central Florida attractions, this one is basically a showcase for nature. From Route 50, go 2⅓ mi north on Route 420 (Ft. Christmas Road), turn east on Wheeler Road, and drive 1½ mi east. ⊠ *25155 Wheeler Rd.* ☎ *407/568–1706* 🖃 *Free* ⊘ *Jan. 21–Sept. 30, daily sunrise–sunset.*

Lake Wales

③⑤ *57 mi southwest of Orlando; 42 mi southwest of WDW.*

If, after several days at the theme parks, you find that you're in need of a back-to-nature fix, head south along U.S. 27. Along the way, you see what's left of Central Florida's citrus groves (quite a lot of them remain) as well as a few RV parks, but the big bonus is getting away from the congestion of the city. If you just can't bear a day without a theme park, stop in at nearby Cypress Gardens.

FodorśChoice   **Bok Tower Gardens** is an appealing sanctuary of plants, flowers, trees, and wildlife that's overlooked by most visitors, but it's definitely worth a trip. Shady paths meander through pine forests in this peaceful world of silvery moats, mockingbirds and swans, blooming thickets, and hidden sundials. You'll be able to boast that you stood on the highest measured point on Florida's peninsula, a colossal 298 ft above sea level. The majestic, 200-ft Bok Tower is constructed of coquina—from seashells—and pink, white, and gray marble. The tower houses a carillon with 57 bronze bells that ring every half hour after 10 AM. Each day at 3 PM there's a 45-minute live recital, which may include early American folk songs, Appalachian tunes, Irish ballads, or Latin hymns. There are also moonlight recitals.

The landscape was designed in 1928 by Frederick Law Olmsted Jr., son of the planner of New York's Central Park. The grounds include the 20-room, Mediterranean Revival–style **Pinewood Estate**, built in 1930. Take I–4 to Exit 55, and head south on U.S. 27 for about 23 miles. Proceed past Eagle Ridge Mall, then turn left after two traffic lights onto Mountain Lake Cut Off Road and follow signs. ⊠ *1151 Tower Blvd., Lake Wales* ☎ *863/676–1408* ⊕ *www.boktower.org* 🖃 *$6 adults, $2 children 5–12, free Sat. 8–9; Pinewood Estate, $5 suggested donation* ⊘ *Daily 8–6; Pinewood Estate tours Oct.–May 15, daily at 11 and 1:30.*

WHERE TO EAT

FODOR'S CHOICE

Anthony's Pizzeria, in Thornton Park

La Fontanella Da Nino, in Thornton Park

Le Coq au Vin, in Central Orlando

Les Chefs de France, in Walt Disney World

Little Saigon, in Central Orlando

Cinderella's Royal Table, in Walt Disney World

Spoodles, in Walt Disney World

Victoria and Albert's, in Walt Disney World

HIGHLY RECOMMENDED

Alfonso's Pizza & More, in College Park

Artist Point, in Walt Disney World

Bistro de Paris, in Walt Disney World

Bonefish Grill, in the Sand Lake Road Area

California Grill, in Walt Disney World

Delfino Riviera, in Universal Orlando

Emeril's, in Universal Orlando

Enzo's on the Lake, in Longwood

L'Originale Alfredo di Roma, in Walt Disney World

Manuel's on the 28th, in Downtown Orlando

Numero Uno, in Central Orlando

Panera Bread, around Orlando

Rainforest Café, in Walt Disney World

Restaurant Akershus, in Walt Disney World

Vito's Chop House, in the I-Drive Area

White Wolf Café, in Central Orlando

Wolfgang Puck Café, in Walt Disney World

Revised by
Rowland
Stiteler

FABULOUS CUISINE IS AVAILABLE throughout Walt Disney World—and all over Orlando—and it's getting progressively easier to find it. Now it's almost as easy to find a salade niçoise as it is to find an order of fries. That's the good news.

The bad news is that, at least in tourist areas, the restaurant marketing people seem to be calling the shots. And they have made a couple of decisions. First, they think that you want to eat in a restaurant connected to a celebrity. The marketing wizards also seem to have decreed that all newcomers must have themes, especially those on tourist strips such as Kissimmee's Irlo Bronson Highway and Orlando's International Drive.

All the same, if you persevere, you can actually find original, one-of-a-kind eateries in Orlando. Fresh, imaginative local restaurants have emerged in sections of the downtown and Thornton Park neighborhoods, driven by the mass influx of white-collar workers making their homes in the Central Orlando district. The restaurants there tend to be urbane and not driven by tourism—you'll dine among the locals. Another good dining area has emerged in the Winter Park Village retail complex in the suburb just north of the downtown area.

WALT DISNEY WORLD RESORT AREA

Meals with Disney Characters

At these breakfasts, brunches, and dinners staged in hotel and theme-park restaurants all over Walt Disney World, kids can snuggle up to all the best-loved Disney characters. Sometimes the food is served buffet style; sometimes it's served to you banquet style. The cast of characters, times, and prices change frequently (although locations of performances remain fairly constant), so be sure to call ahead.

Reservations are often required, and some meals can fill up more than 60 days in advance. However, you can also book by phone on the same day you plan to dine, and it never hurts to double-check the character lineup before you leave for the meal. If you have your heart set on a specific meal, make your reservations when you book your trip—up to six months in advance. Smoking is not permitted.

Breakfast

Main Street, U.S.A.'s **Crystal Palace Buffet** (☎ 407/939–3463 ☒ $16.99 adults, $8.99 children 3–11) has breakfast with Winnie the Pooh and friends daily from 8:05 to 10:30 AM. At Disney–MGM Studios, Minnie, Chip 'n' Dale, and Goofy are on hand 8–11 daily at **Hollywood & Vine** (☎ 407/939–3463 ☒ $16.99 adults, $8.99 children 3–11).

At Disney's Beach Club, characters are on hand at the **Cape May Café** (☎ 407/939–3463 ☒ $16.99 adults, $8.99 children 3–11) 7:30–11 daily. At the Contemporary Resort, **Chef Mickey's** (☎ 407/939–3463 ☒ $16.99 adults, $8.99 children 3–11) has a no-holds-barred buffet 7–11:15 daily. The Polynesian Resort's **'Ohana** (☎ 407/939–3463 ☒ $16.99 adults, $8.99 children 3–11) serves breakfast with Mickey and his friends daily 7:30–11. At the Wyndham Palace Suite Resort and Spa at Walt Disney World Resort, you can drop in Sunday 8–11 for a character meal at the **Watercress Restaurant** (☎ 407/827–2727 ☒ $19.95 adults, $10.95 children under 11).

BY RESERVATION
ONLY

The Princess Storybook Breakfasts with Snow White, Sleeping Beauty, and at least three other princesses are held at Epcot Center in **Restaurant Akershus** (☎ 407/939–3463 ☒ $19.99 adults, $9.99 children 3–11) in the Norway Pavilion from 8:30–10:30 daily. Donald Duck and his

Dinner Shows

Dinner shows are popular in Orlando, although the meal is not usually as memorable as the entertainment. Walt Disney World has several table-side extravaganzas, among them the perennially sold-out Hoop-Dee-Doo Revue at the Fort Wilderness Campground area. If you can't score a reservation for the Disney hoop-along, check out the shows like Arabian Nights Dinner Theater in Kissimmee or the Pirate's Dinner Adventure on International Drive.

Dress

Because tourism is king around Orlando, casual dress is the rule. Very few restaurants require jackets or other dress-up attire for men, and many that once did are lightening up. Except in the priciest establishments, you can wear very casual clothing. In the reviews, dress is mentioned only when men are required to wear a jacket.

Reservations

Reservations are always a good idea in a market where the phrase "Bus drivers eat free" may as well be emblazoned on the city's coat of arms. Many area restaurants accept what's known in these parts as requests for "priority seating"—they make no commitments to honor the time you both agree on, but will try to seat you next. Still others don't take reservations at all.

If you plan to tackle one of these no-reservations spots, you can minimize your wait by using the same off-hours strategy that works in the theme parks: lunch at 11 AM and dinner before 5 PM. And if you must eat during peak hours, plan to arrive well before you think you'll want to eat, have a snack before you leave home, and bring a good paperback—you're in for a wait.

For restaurants within Walt Disney World, reservations are especially easy to make, thanks to its central reservations lines (☎ 407/939–3463 or 407/560–7277). And, although you can't make reservations on-line at the Disney Web site, www.disney.go.com/Disneyworld, you can certainly get a world of information about dining options throughout Disney, like the hours, price range, and specialties of all Disney eateries. Universal Orlando, which has become a major player in the culinary wars, also has its own reservation line (☎ 407/224–9255) and a diner-friendly Web site, www.universalorlando.com.

In reviews, reservations are mentioned only when they're essential or not accepted. Unless otherwise noted, the restaurants listed are open daily for lunch and dinner.

WHAT IT COSTS				
	$$$$	$$$	$$	$	¢
AT DINNER	over $30	$22–$30	$15–$22	$8–$15	under $8

Prices are per person for a main course.

friends are at "Donald's Breakfastosaurus" 8:10–10:40 daily at the **Restaurantosaurus** (☎ 407/939–3463 ✉ $16.99 adults, $8.99 children 3–11), in Disney's Animal Kingdom. Mary Poppins presides at **1900 Park Fare Restaurant** (☎ 407/824–2383 ✉ $16.99 adults, $9.99 children 3–11) in the Grand Floridian 7:30–11:30 daily. Cinderella herself hosts Magic Kingdom breakfasts 8:05–10 daily at **Cinderella's Royal Table** (☎ 407/939–3463 ✉ $19.99 adults, $9.99 children 3–11).

FodorsChoice

Lunch

WDW offers only three daily character lunches, but all have relatively long time windows. The **Crystal Palace Buffet** (☎ 407/939–3463 ✉ $17.99 adults, $9.99 children 3–11) on Main Street U.S.A. offers food plus Winnie the Pooh, Tigger, and Eeyore 11:10–2:30. At the **Garden Grill** (☎ 407/939–3463 ✉ $19.99 adults, $9.99 children 3–11) in Future World's The Land pavilion, Mickey, Pluto, and Chip 'n' Dale join diners 12–3:50. **Hollywood & Vine** (☎ 407/939–3463 ✉ $17.99 adults, $9.99 children 3–11), at the Disney–MGM Studios, serves lunch with Minnie, Goofy, Chip 'n' Dale, and Pluto 11:10–2:30.

Afternoon Tea

At the **Grand Floridian Resort** (☎ 407/939–3463 ✉ $24.99) afternoon tea, Alice and the Wonderland characters preside weekdays 1:30–2:30. With the cast's help, children can bake their own cupcakes and then eat them at the tea party. Open only to children 3–10; all participants must be potty-trained.

Dinner

All character dinners require reservations. Minnie Mouse and friends (which in this case does not include Mickey) make an evening appearance at the Liberty Square **Liberty Tree Tavern** (☎ 407/939–3463 ✉ $21.99 adults, $9.99 children 3–11); dinner is served at 8:40 daily. Farmer Mickey appears at Future World's **Garden Grill** (☎ 407/939–3463 ✉ $21.99 adults, $9.99 children 3–11) 4–8 daily. Winnie the Pooh and friends appear at a nightly buffet 4–8:45 at the **Crystal Palace Buffet** (☎ 407/939–3463 ✉ $21.99 adults, $9.99 children 3–11) on Main Street, U.S.A.

Every night at 8 (7 in winter), near Fort Wilderness's Meadow Trading Post, there is a **Character Campfire** (☎ 407/824–2727) with a free sing-along. There are usually around five characters there, with Chip 'n' Dale frequent attendees.

Winnie the Pooh and friends are at the Grand Floridian's **1900 Park Fare Restaurant** (☎ 407/939–3463 ✉ $23.99 adults, $10.99 children 3–11), for a buffet served 5–8:40 daily. The Contemporary Resort hosts a wildly popular dinner starring the head honcho himself at **Chef Mickey's** (☎ 407/939–3463 ✉ $23.99 adults, $10.99 children 3–11), 5–9:15 daily. At the Walt Disney World Swan, you can dine with *Lion King* characters Monday and Friday 5:30–10 at **Gulliver's Grill** (☎ 407/934–1609). Gulliver's hosts Goofy and Pluto the other five nights of the week. Meals are à la carte—an adult dinner runs $18–$30 and a child's meal $4–$10. The same restaurant is called Garden Grove during breakfast and lunch.

Magic Kingdom

American/Casual

$–$$ ✕ **Cinderella's Royal Table.** Because Cinderella and her sisters make regular appearances at this eatery, book reservations 60 days in advance. The menu ranges from prime rib to barbecued chicken breast. If your kids don't feel up to anything as substantial as a balanced meal, there are cheeseburgers, chicken tenders, or cheese dog rolls for $4.99 a pop. Strawberry shortcake is the best bet for dessert; your kids may yearn for a fruit smoothie in a Cinderella glass. ⊠ *Cinderella Castle* ☎ *407/ 939–3463* ⌕ *Reservations essential* ▭ *AE, MC, V.*

$–$$ ✕ **Crystal Palace.** Named for the big glass atrium surrounding the restaurant, the Crystal Palace is a great escape in summer, when the air-conditioning is turned down near meat-locker level. The buffet-style meal includes upscale mass-meal items, from prime rib to peel-and-eat shrimp, with pasta, fresh-baked breads, and ice cream sundaes part of the package (dinner price is $19.95 for adults). There's also a kids-only buffet with macaroni and cheese, hot dogs, and pizza for $9.95 per child. ⊠ *Main Street, U.S.A.* ☎ *407/939–3463* ▭ *AE, MC, V.*

$–$$ ✕ **Liberty Tree Tavern.** This "tavern" is dry, but it's a prime spot on the parade route, so you can catch a good meal while you wait. Colonial-period comfort food like roast turkey, honey-cured Virginia ham, and beef brisket is a mainstay here, and you can sample all of the choices at the fixed-price, family-style meals, ranging from $9.99 for children at lunch to $20.99 for adults at dinner. A favorite is the Benedict Arnold Sandwich—corned beef and Swiss on molasses bread. And if you want something really hearty, go for the New England pot roast, in a wine and mushroom sauce and served with mashed potatoes. ⊠ *Liberty Square* ☎ *407/824–6461* ▭ *AE, MC, V.*

Italian

$$–$$$ ✕ **Tony's Town Square Restaurant.** Inspired by the animated classic *Lady and the Tramp,* Tony's offers everything from spaghetti and meatballs to more creative fare such as wood-oven pizza and a very decent chicken cacciatore. The good food here makes a great way to pass the time while you're waiting for one of the big Main Street parades. The restaurant's recommended breakfast fare includes a tasty Italian frittata and a bacon, egg, and cheese calzone. ⊠ *Main Street, U.S.A., Liberty Square* ☎ *407/ 939–3463* ▭ *AE, MC, V.*

Magic Kingdom Resort Area

Restaurants are in the Contemporary, Polynesian, and Grand Floridian hotels and the rustic Wilderness Lodge. To get to the area, take Exit 62, 64B, or 67 off I–4.

American/Casual

$$–$$$ ✕ **Whispering Canyon Cafe.** No whispering goes on here. The servers, dressed as cowboys and cowgirls, deliver corny jokes and other talk designed to keep things jovial at this family-style restaurant, where huge stacks of pancakes and big servings of spare ribs are the orders of the day. The $22 all-you-can-eat barbecue dinner includes pork ribs, beef brisket, smoked sausage, and smoked turkey. This option is a good bargain, considering that a rib plate alone would cost you $19. For dessert, kids love "Worms in the Dirt," a concoction of chocolate cake and chocolate pudding, with gummy worms mixed in. ⊠ *Wilderness Lodge* ☎ *407/939–3463* ▭ *AE, MC, V.*

$–$$$ ✕ **Chef Mickey's.** Since Mickey, Minnie, and Goofy preside at virtually every meal, this is not the place for a quiet bite. The buffet includes eggs and pancakes for breakfast and thick, oven-roasted prime rib, pasta, and mashed potatoes and gravy for lunch or dinner. (The Parmesan mashed potatoes are great, but you can opt for plain mashed spuds if you prefer.) If you don't like buffets, you can order kid-driven dishes like macaroni and cheese, hot dogs, and pizza for lunch and dinner. The

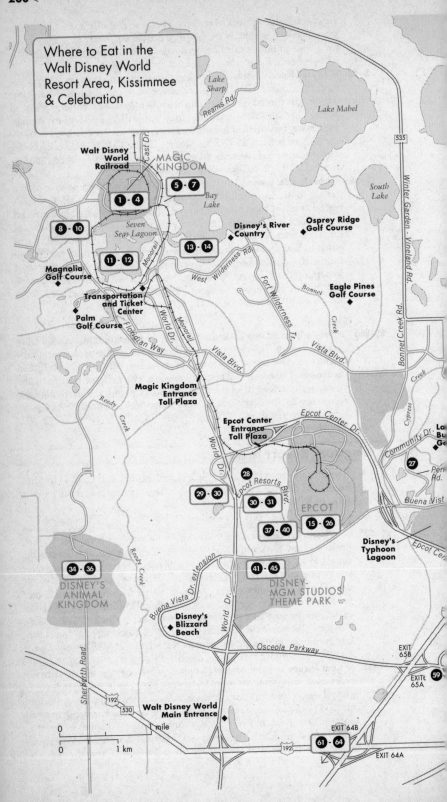

Where to Eat in the Walt Disney World Resort Area, Kissimmee & Celebration

Lake Sheen

Big Sand Lake

Pocket Lake

Lake Ruby

Lake Ave.

ORLANDO INT'L AIRPORT

Old Vineland Cir.

Grand Cypress Blvd

Buena Vista Dr.

Bronson Rd.

Hotel Plaza Blvd

Palm Pkwy.

Vineland Ave.

Lake
Buena Vista
Golf Course

Lake Buena Vista

Little Lake Bryan

Lake Bryan

EXIT 68

Peninsular Rd.

Vista Dr.

EXIT 67B

EXIT 67A

International Dr.

International Dr. South

International Dr.

Central Florida Greeneway

Osceola Parkway

TO ORLANDO

TO CELEBRATION

53   55   56   54   57   58   60   46 - 52

435   535   4   536   535   417   192

Walt Disney World Resort Area ▼

Artist Point **13**
Biergarten **15**
Big River Grille & Brewing Co. . . .**37**
Bistro de Paris **16**
Boma **34**
Bongos Cuban Café . . .**46**
California Grill **5**
Chef Mickey's **6**
Cinderella's Royal Table **1**
Citricos **8**
Concourse Steak House **7**
Coral Reef Restaurant **17**
Crystal Palace **2**
ESPN Sports Club **38**
'50s Prime Time Cafe **41**
Flying Fish **39**
Fulton's Crab House . . .**47**
Gulliver's Grill at Garden Grove **31**
Hollywood & Vine **42**
Hollywood Brown Derby **43**
House of Blues **48**
Kimonos **32**
Kona Cafe **11**
Le Cellier Steakhouse **18**
Les Chefs de France . . .**19**
Liberty Tree Tavern **3**
L'Originale Alfredo di Roma Ristorante **20**
Mama Melrose's Ristorante Italiano **44**
Marrakesh **21**
Mitsukoshi **22**
Narcoosee's **9**
Nine Dragons Restaurant **23**
'Ohana **12**
Olivia's Café **27**
Palio **33**
Planet Hollywood **49**
Portobello Yacht Club **50**
Rainforest Café (Animal Kingdom) **35**
Rainforest Café (Downtown Disney) . . .**51**
Restaurant Akershus . . .**24**
Restaurantosaurus **36**
Rose & Crown **25**
San Angel Inn **26**
Sci-Fi Dine-In Theater Restaurant **45**

Shula's Steak House . . .**29**
Spoodles **40**
Tony's Town Square Restaurant **4**
Tubbi's Buffeteria **30**
Victoria and Albert's **10**
Whispering Canyon Cafe **14**
Wolfgang Puck Café **52**
Yachtsman Steakhouse **28**

Lake Buena Vista, Celebration, Kissimmee ▼

Arthur's 27 . . . .**54**
Café d' Antonio **61**
Celebration Town Tavern/Bostonian **62**
Chevy's **55**
Columbia Restaurant **64**
Hawk's Landing **58**
La Coquina **53**
Landry's Seafood House **57**
Market Street Café **63**
Old Hickory Steak House **59**
Pebbles **56**
Romano's Macaroni Grill **60**

all-you-can-eat dessert bar includes ice cream sundaes. ☒ *Contemporary Resort* ☎ *407/939–3463* ▭ *AE, MC, V.*

Contemporary

$$$$
Fodor'sChoice
✕ **Victoria and Albert's.** At this Disney fantasy, the servers work in man-woman pairs, reciting specials in tandem. It's one of the plushest fine-dining experiences in Florida: a regal meal in a lavish, Victorian-style room. The seven-course, prix-fixe menu ($85; wine is an additional $42) changes daily. Appetizers might include veal sweetbreads or artichokes in a mushroom-based sauce; entrées may be seared boar tenderloin with corn and herb spaetzle or grilled beef fillet with a Vidalia onion risotto. There are two seatings, at 5:45 and 9. In July and August, there's usually just one seating—at 6:30. Chef's table dinner event is $115–$162 (with wine pairing) per person. ☒ *Grand Floridian* ☎ *407/ 939–3463* ✍ *Reservations essential* 🏛 *Jacket required* ▭ *AE, MC, V* ⊙ *No lunch.*

$$$–$$$$
✕ **Cítricos.** Although the name implies that you might be eating lots of local citrus-flavored specialties, you won't find them here, aside from drinks like a "Citropolitan" martini, infused with lemon and lime liqueur, and an orange chocolate mousse for dessert. Standout entrées include paprika-and-honey–marinated pork tenderloin with smoked eggplant dip and roasted duck breast with sweet-and-sour pomegranate glaze. The wine list, one of Disney's most extensive, includes vintages from around the world. Many are available by the glass. ☒ *Grand Floridian* ☎ *407/939–3463* ▭ *AE, MC, V.*

★ **$$–$$$$**
✕ **California Grill.** The view of the surrounding Disney parks from this rooftop restaurant is as stunning as the food, and you can watch the nightly Magic Kingdom fireworks from the patio. Start with the brick-oven flatbread with grilled duck sausage or the *unagi* (eel) sushi. Try the pan-seared golden tilefish with wild mushroom risotto and red wine reduction for a main course. Good dessert choices include the orange crepes with Grand Marnier custard, raspberries and blackberry coulis and the warm apple tart with caramel ice cream and Myer's Rum caramel sauce. ☒ *Contemporary Resort* ☎ *407/939–3463* ▭ *AE, MC, V.*

★ **$$$**
✕ **Artist Point.** If you're not a guest at the Wilderness Lodge, a meal here is worth it just to see the giant totem poles and huge rock fireplace in the lobby. Cedar-plank salmon is the specialty here, and there are always some unusual offerings on the menu like grilled buffalo sirloin with sweet potato–hazelnut gratin and sweet onion jam. For dessert, try the wild berry cobbler or an apple-rhubarb tartlet with vanilla ice cream. There's a good northwestern U.S. wine list. ☒ *Wilderness Lodge* ☎ *407/ 939–3463* ✍ *Reservations essential* ▭ *AE, MC, V.*

$–$$$
✕ **Kona Cafe.** Desserts get a lot of emphasis at this eclectic restaurant, with choices ranging from a tasty tangerine crème brûlée to a smooth banana mousse. Best of the entrées are macadamia-crusted mahimahi and pan-Asian pasta (noodles, chicken, and vegetables stir-fried and served in a sauce of ginger, lemon grass, and soy sauce). The barbecue pork sandwich, with a special mango sauce, makes it a standout for lunch. As the name of the place hints, coffee is a specialty, too. ☒ *Polynesian Resort* ☎ *407/939–3463* ▭ *AE, MC, V.*

Polynesian

$$$
✕ **'Ohana.** The only option here is an all-you-can-eat fixed-price meal ($23.95 for adults, $9.99 for kids) of grilled pork, beef, chicken, or salmon, which are sliced directly onto your plate from the mammoth skewer they were grilled on. The chef performs in front of an 18-ft fire pit, grilling the meats as flames shoot up to sear in the flavors and entertain the diners. Special desserts include the coconut snowball and the chocolate Chan-

tilly cake with butterscotch icing. ⊠ *Polynesian Resort* ☎ *407/939–3463* ▭ *AE, MC, V.*

Seafood

$$$–$$$$ ✕ **Narcoosee's.** A salute to small-town Florida, the menu here emphasizes seafood, including panfried grouper, grilled shrimp, and crab with potato cakes. Good entrées include Narcoosee's grilled pork tenderloin with smoky, cheesy grits and black pepper cream and the seared jumbo scallops with herb polenta and caviar butter sauce. For dessert, there's a delicious praline cheesecake. The dining room overlooks the Seven Seas Lagoon and is a great place to catch the Electric Water Pageant at night. ⊠ *Grand Floridian Resort* ☎ *407/939–3463* ▭ *AE, MC, V.*

Steak

$–$$$ ✕ **Concourse Steak House.** If you've always liked that trademark monorail that runs from the Magic Kingdom into the Contemporary Resort, you might want to have a meal here, set as it is one story below the train (the tracks run above). The place isn't as noisy as it might seem. Steaks include a succulent prime rib. Among the other entrées are mango-glazed barbecued pork ribs, oak wood–roasted chicken, herb-crusted salmon with red potatoes, and pan-seared tuna. For dessert, try the crème brûlée or the marbled cheesecake. ⊠ *Contemporary Resort* ☎ *407/939–3463* ▭ *AE, MC, V.*

Epcot

Epcot's World Showcase offers some of the finest dining in Orlando. But you have to pay Epcot admission to eat in these establishments; the top-of-the-line places, such as those in the French, Italian, and Japanese pavilions, can be expensive; and reservations are often hard to come by. On the other hand, most of the restaurants have a limited-selection children's menu with dramatically lower prices.

Dress is informal—no one expects you to go all the way back to your hotel to tidy up. And if you have unruly youngsters in tow, you probably won't be alone. Kosher and vegetarian meals are available on request. And Epcot offers another noshing bonus—walk-up kiosks are everywhere, dispensing everything from Mexican tacos to French crepes to a Canadian snack called beavertails—sweet whole-wheat waffles shaped like the tail of a beaver and covered with tasty toppings.

Reservations

All restaurants, unless otherwise noted, are open for both lunch and dinner daily. For both meals, reservations are a must. At Epcot, there are two ways of making reservations: call the central reservations lines (☎ 407/939–3463 or 407/560–7277) or go to the restaurant directly and sign up.

Be flexible about your mealtimes. For the more popular establishments, it is much easier to get a reservation for lunch than for dinner, to get lunch reservations before noon, and to get dinner reservations for seatings before 6 and after 8. And it's always worth stopping by the restaurant during the day in hopes of a cancellation.

No matter how you book, show up a bit early to be sure of getting your table. You can pay with cash; charge with American Express, MasterCard, or Visa; or, if you're a guest at a hotel on Disney property, charge the tab to your room.

Canadian

$$–$$$ ✕ **Le Cellier Steakhouse.** With the best Canadian wine cellar in the state, this charming eatery, with stone arches and dark-wood paneling, has a good selection of Canadian beer as well. Aged beef is king, although many steaks appear only on the dinner menu. If you are a carnivore, go for the herb-crusted prime rib. Even though the menu changes periodically, they've always got the maple-ginger–glazed Canadian salmon—it's too much in demand to ever be taken off the menu. Canadian fruit cobbler is the best choice for a sweet; the Canadian Club chocolate cake comes in a close second. ⊠ *Canada* ▱ *AE, MC, V.*

Chinese

$–$$$$ ✕ **Nine Dragons Restaurant.** Though a showcase for all regions of Chinese cooking, including Szechuan and Hunan, the majority of the menu is Cantonese, from an excellent *moo goo gai pan* (a stir-fried chicken and vegetable dish) and sweet-and-sour pork to lobster. Other good choices are the "Imperial Pine Cone Fish"—a crispy whole (deboned) snapper topped with sweet-and-sour sauce, and the Cantonese roast duckling. For a fiery hot treat, try the fried squid with Szechuan peppercorn sauce. The distinctive building has a curved, yellow-tile roof with ornate carvings inspired by the Forbidden City. ⊠ *China* ▱ *AE, MC, V.*

English

$–$$ ✕ **Rose & Crown.** If you are an Anglophile and you love a good, thick beer, this is the place to soak up both the suds and the British street culture. (You can even go for the ale and beer sampler, five 4-ounce glasses for $8.25.) "Wenches" serve up traditional English fare—fish-and-chips, meat pies, Yorkshire pudding, and the ever-popular "bangers and mash," English sausage over mashed potatoes. You can also sample cottage pie—ground beef and carrots topped with mashed potatoes and cheddar cheese. For dessert, try the chocolate mousse parfait. The terrace has a splendid view of IllumiNations. ⊠ *United Kingdom* ▱ *AE, MC, V.*

French

★ $$$$ ✕ **Bistro de Paris.** The great secret in the France pavilion—and, indeed, in all of Epcot—is the Bistro de Paris, upstairs from Les Chefs de France. The sophisticated menu changes regularly and reflects the cutting edge of French cooking; representative dishes include lobster fricassee, roast duck with cherry brandy sauce, and roast rack of venison. Grand Mariner soufflé, which has become a cliche at some restaurants, is a triumph here. Come late, ask for a window seat, and plan to linger to watch the nightly Epcot light show. Moderately priced French wines are available by the glass. ⊠ *France* ▱ *AE, MC, V.*

$$–$$$$ ✕ **Les Chefs de France.** What some consider the best restaurant at Disney was created by three of France's most famous chefs: Paul Bocuse, Fodor'sChoice ney was created by three of France's most famous chefs: Paul Bocuse, Gaston Lenôtre, and Roger Vergé. Classic escargots, a good starter, are prepared in a casserole with garlic butter; you might follow up with seared grouper on vegetable julienne with sorrel cream sauce or *marmite du pecheur parfumée au safran* (traditional Mediterranean seafood casserole of grouper, scallops and shrimp flavored with saffron, served with garlic sauce); and end with crepes *au chocolat.* The nearby Boulangerie Patisserie, run by the same team, offers limited selections, including great desserts, to go. ⊠ *France* ▱ *AE, MC, V.*

German

$–$$ ✕ **Biergarten.** Oktoberfest runs 365 days a year here. The cheerful, sometimes raucous, crowds are what you would expect in a place with an oompah band. Waitresses in Bavarian garb serve *breseln,* hot German pretzels, which are made fresh daily on the premises. Other classic German fare in the one-price all-you-can-eat buffet ($18.99 for adults, $7.99 for kids ages 3–11) are sauerbraten, bratwurst, chicken schnitzel, as well as a good apple strudel and Black Forest cake. Patrons pound pitchers of all kinds of beer and wine on the long communal tables—even when the yodelers, singers, and dancers aren't egging them on. ⊠ *Germany* ▭ *AE, MC, V.*

Italian

★ **$$–$$$$** ✕ **L'Originale Alfredo di Roma Ristorante.** Waiters skip around singing arias, a show in itself. Their voices and the restaurant's namesake dish, made with mountains of butter, account for its popularity. The classic dish—fettuccine with cream, butter, and loads of freshly grated Parmesan cheese—was invented by Alfredo de Lelio. (Disney and de Lelio's descendants both had a hand in creating this restaurant). Besides the excellent pasta, try the *zuppa di pesce con fettuccine,* which sounds like the most expensive soup in Florida, but is actually a pasta dish, with fettuccine and fresh fish including grouper, scallops, mussels, shrimp, and calamari in a white wine, garlic and tomato broth. Dessert offerings include the ricotta cheesecake and a credible cannoli. Dinner is prix fixe ($30). ⊠ *Italy* ▭ *AE, MC, V.*

Japanese

$$–$$$$ ✕ **Mitsukoshi.** Three restaurants are enclosed in this complex, which overlooks tranquil gardens. Yakitori House, a gussied-up fast-food stand in a small pavilion, is modeled after a tea house in Kyoto's Katsura Summer Palace. At the Tempura Kiku, diners watch the chefs prepare sushi, sashimi, and tempura (batter-dipped deep-fried shrimp, scallops, and vegetables). In the five Teppanyaki dining rooms, chefs frenetically chop vegetables, meat, and fish and stir-fry them at the grills set into the communal tables. The Matsu No Ma Lounge, more serene than the restaurants, has a great view of the World Showcase Lagoon. ⊠ *Japan* ▭ *AE, MC, V.*

Mexican

$$ ✕ **San Angel Inn.** In the dark, grottolike main dining room, a deep purple, dimly lit mural of a night scene in Central Mexico seems to envelop the diners. San Angel is a popular respite for the weary, especially when the humidity outside makes Central Florida feel like equatorial Africa. At dinner, guitars and marimbas fills the air. Try the authentic *mole poblano* (chicken simmered in a rich sauce of chilies, green tomatoes, ground tortillas, cocoa, cumin, and 11 other spices). ⊠ *Mexico* ▭ *AE, MC, V.*

Moroccan

$$–$$$ ✕ **Marrakesh.** Chef Abrache Lahcen of Morocco presents the best cooking of his homeland in this ornate eatery, which looks like something from the set of *Casablanca.* Try the couscous, served with vegetables, or *bastilla,* an appetizer made with layers of chicken or lamb in a thin pastry redolent of almonds, saffron, and cinnamon. A good way to try a bit of everything is the Marrakesh Feast ($27.75 per person), which includes chicken bastilla and beef *brewat* (minced beef in a layered pastry dusted with cinnamon and powdered sugar), plus vegetable couscous and assorted Moroccan pastries; or better still, upgrade to the Royal Feast ($30 per person) which includes everything in the Marrakesh Feast, plus crepes for dessert. ⊠ *Morocco* ▭ *AE, MC, V.*

Scandinavian

★ **$$** ✕ **Restaurant Akershus.** The Norwegian buffet at this restaurant is as extensive as you'll find on this side of the Atlantic. Appetizers usually include herring, prepared several ways, and cold seafood, including *gravlax* (cured salmon served with mustard sauce) or *fiskepudding* (a seafood mousse with herb dressing). Pick up cold salads and meats on your next trip to the buffet line, and on your last foray, fill up on hot lamb, veal, or venison. Make sure you try some *lefse,* a wonderful flatbread made from potatoes and wheat. The à la carte desserts include cloudberries, a delicate tundra fruit that tastes like a raspberry. ⊠ *Norway* ☱ *AE, MC, V.*

Seafood

$$–$$$$ ✕ **Coral Reef Restaurant.** Part of the attraction here is the view of the giant Living Seas aquarium: the three-tiered seating area gives every diner a good view. Edible attractions include pan-seared salmon fillet with garlic pesto mash and Caribbean lobster, roasted with sautéed zucchini and shallots, braised potato, garlic, and butter (admittedly, a shade on the pricey side at $42). A great appetizer: mussels simmered in tomato broth with roasted garlic, leeks, and chives. If you want to be able to tell the folks back home you tried alligator, the lunch menu includes grilled alligator sausage in a creole vinaigrette. ⊠ *The Living Seas* ☱ *AE, MC, V.*

Epcot Resort Area

The hotels and nightlife complexes clustered around Epcot, Disney's BoardWalk, and the Yacht and Beach Club hold many good restaurants. To get to the area, take I–4 and use Exit 64B or 67.

American/Casual

$$–$$$ ✕ **Big River Grille & Brewing Co.** Strange but good brews, like Pale Rocket Red Ale, Wowzers Wheat, and Tilt, abound here. You can dine inside among the giant copper brewing tanks, or sip your suds outside on the lake-view patio. The menu emphasizes red meat, with baby-back ribs, barbecue pork, and a house-special steak called a "Drunken Ribeye," but there's also a worthwhile grilled Atlantic salmon fillet with dill butter. The grilled meat loaf is served with gravy and cheddar cheese–mashed potatoes. ⊠ *Disney's BoardWalk* ☎ 407/560–0253 ☱ *AE, MC, V.*

$–$$ ✕ **ESPN Sports Club.** Not only can you watch sports on big-screen TV here, but you can periodically see ESPN programs being taped in the club itself and be part of the audience of sports radio talk shows. Food ranges from an outstanding half-pound burger to a 10-ounce sirloin and grilled chicken and shrimp in penne pasta, topped with marinara sauce. For dessert, how about a "Superbowl Sundae"? It sets you back $15, but it's easily enough for two people. If your sweet tooth is not quite that big, there's an excellent, New York–style cheesecake. This place is open quite late by Disney standards—until 2 AM on Friday and Saturday. ⊠ *Disney's BoardWalk* ☎ 407/939–5100 ☱ *AE, MC, V.*

¢ ✕ **Tubbi's Buffeteria.** This buffet in the Walt Disney World Dolphin would be forgettable were it not for its hours—Tubbi's serves up hot food around the clock. The menu includes sandwiches, pizza, and two daily blue-plate specials, like meat loaf or barbecued chicken. Also on hand are nonfood necessities like laundry detergent and disposable diapers: there if you need them at 3 AM. Breakfast, including a worthy omelet, is served from 6 to 11:30 AM. ⊠ *Walt Disney World Dolphin* ☎ 407/934–4000 ☱ *AE, MC, V.*

Contemporary

$–$$$$ ✕ **Gulliver's Grill at Garden Grove.** The legend is that this eatery was founded by Peter Miles Gulliver, a direct descendant of the Jonathan Swift character. Eat among tall palms and lush greenery inside a giant greenhouse. The menu includes grilled filet mignon and lobster tail, barbecued pork ribs, wood-oven pizza, burgers and peanut butter and jelly sandwiches for the kids. Catch the *Legend of the Lion King* characters on Mondays and Fridays, and Goofy and Pluto the rest of the week. ⊠ *Walt Disney World Swan* ☎ 407/934–3000 ⊕ *www.swandolphin. com* ⌕ *Reservations essential* ☱ *AE, D, DC, MC, V* ⊙ *No lunch.*

Italian

$–$$$$ ✕**Palio.** You can find some of the classic upscale Italian dishes here, like saltimbocca (veal with prosciutto), chicken alla marsala (in a wine sauce), osso buco (veal shanks), and a great chicken cacciatore (in a tangy tomato sauce). There's a good pizza from the restaurant's wood-fired oven, and the house specialty—veal scaloppine with marsala wine sauce makes a great dinner choice. Standout desserts include amaretto and sour cream cheesecake and the house tiramisu. Strolling minstrels are on hand to entertain. ⊠ *Walt Disney World Swan* ☎ *407/934–3000* ⊕ *www. swandolphin.com* ▤ *AE, MC, V.*

Japanese

$$ ✕**Kimonos.** Knife-wielding sushi chefs prepare world-class sushi and sashimi but also excellent beef teriyaki and other Japanese treats good for a full dinner or just a snack. The steamed dumplings, stuffed with pork, are quite good, as is the Japanese spin on a soft-shell crab. One of the best bets here is the sushi–sashimi combination, which gives you a generous amount of both for the price. ⊠ *Walt Disney World Swan* ☎*407/934–3000* ⊕*www.swandolphin.com* ▤*AE, D, DC, MC, V* ✆*No lunch.*

Mediterranean

$$–$$$
Fodor'sChoice ✕**Spoodles.** The international tapas-style menu here draws on the best foods of the Mediterranean, from tuna with sun-dried tomato couscous to Italian fettuccine with rich Parmesan cream sauce. Oak-fired flatbreads with such toppings as roasted peppers make stellar appetizers. Best desserts include Marco Polo cake—a moist chocolate-filled layer cake—and pumpkin coconut flan. Can't decide? The dessert sampler lets you taste everything on the dessert cart. The children's menu includes macaroni and cheese and pepperoni pizza. There's a walk-up pizza window, if you prefer to stroll the boardwalk and snack. ⊠ *Disney's BoardWalk* ☎ *407/939–3463* ▤ *AE, MC, V.*

Seafood

$$–$$$ ✕**Flying Fish.** One of Disney's better restaurants, this fish house's best dishes include the potato-wrapped Florida red snapper served with leek–fennel fondue and the handmade triple-cheese ravioli with sweet red pepper sauce. The "peeky toe" crab cakes with ancho-chile rémoulade is an appetizer that never leaves the frequently changing menu—try them and you will see why. Save room for the Lava Cake, chocolate cake served warm with a liquid chocolate center and topped with pomegranate ice cream. ⊠ *Disney's BoardWalk* ☎ *407/939–2359* ▤ *AE, MC, V.*

Steak

$$$–$$$$ ✕**Shula's Steak House.** The hardwood floors, dark-wood paneling, and pictures of former Miami Dolphins coach Don Shula make this restaurant resemble an annex of the NFL Hall of Fame. Among the best selections are the porterhouse and prime rib. Finish the 48-ounce porterhouse and you get a football with your picture on it, but it's not an easy task to eat three pounds of red meat at one sitting unless you are a polar bear. If you're not a carnivore, go for the Norwegian salmon, the Florida snapper, or the huge (up to 4 pounds) Maine lobster. Save room for the seven-layer chocolate cake. ⊠ *Walt Disney World Dolphin* ☎ *407/934–1362* ▤ *AE, D, DC, MC, V* ✆ *No lunch.*

$$–$$$$ ✕**Yachtsman Steakhouse.** Aged beef, the attraction at this steak house in the ultra-polished Yacht and Beach Club, can be seen mellowing in the glassed-in butcher shop near the entryway. The slow-roasted prime rib is superb, as are the barbecued baby-back ribs, so tender you can eat them with just a fork. The tasty surf and turf is an 8-ounce filet mignon and a 6-ounce lobster tail. For dessert, try the tasty Jack Daniels cake: chocolate mousse flavored with the Tennessee whiskey. ⊠ *Yacht and Beach Club* ☎ 407/939–3463 ⊟ *AE, MC, V* ⊘ *No lunch.*

Disney–MGM Studios

The Studios tend to offer more casual American cuisine than the other parks. In other words, it's cheeseburger city. However, there are also some good, imaginative offerings.

American

$–$$ ✕ **'50s Prime Time Cafe.** Who says you can't go home again? If you grew up in middle America in the 1950s, just step inside. While *I Love Lucy* and *The Donna Reed Show* play on a television screen, you can feast on meat loaf, pot roast, or fried chicken, all served on a Formica tabletop. At $13, the meat loaf is one of the best inexpensive dinners in any Orlando theme park. Follow it up with chocolate cake or a thick milk shake— available in chocolate, strawberry, vanilla, even peanut butter and jelly. Just like Mother, the menu admonishes, "Don't put your elbows on the table!" ⊠ *Disney–MGM Studios* ☎ 407/939–3463 ⊟ *AE, MC, V.*

American/Casual

$–$$ ✕ **Hollywood & Vine.** This restaurant is designed for those who like lots of food and lots of choices. You can have everything from frittatas to fried rice at the same meal. Even though the buffet ($20 for adults; $10 for children ages 3–11) is all-you-can-eat at a relatively low price, it does offer some upscale entrées like smoked salmon, sage-rubbed rotisserie chicken, and oven-roasted pork. There are plenty of kids' favorites, such as mac and cheese, hot dogs, and fried chicken, and with good reason: Minnie, Chip 'n' Dale, and Goofy are on hand at breakfast and lunch daily. Priority seating reservations are a must. ⊠ *Disney–MGM Studios* ☎ 407/939–3463 ⊟ *AE, MC, V.*

$–$$ ✕ **Sci-Fi Dine-In Theater Restaurant.** At this faux drive-in, you can sit in fake cars and watch trailers from classics like *Attack of the Fifty-Foot Woman* and *Teenagers from Outer Space* while you munch burgers and fries and other drive-in goodies. The menu is not limited to items like the $11 cheeseburger, however; try the smoked prime rib sandwich, the pan-seared tuna over a bed of noodles with a wild berry cilantro sauce, or the applewood-smoked pork-loin sandwich. The milk shakes are delicious. All told, this place is a tad more entertaining than the old drive-ins. ⊠ *Disney–MGM Studios* ☎ 407/939–3463 ⊟ *AE, MC, V.*

Contemporary

$–$$ ✕ **Hollywood Brown Derby.** At this reproduction of the famous 1940s Hollywood restaurant, the walls are lined with movie-star caricatures, just like in Tinseltown. The house specialty is the Cobb salad, which by legend was invented by Brown Derby founder Robert Cobb; the salad consists of a lettuce base with bacon, blue cheese, tomatoes, chopped egg, and avocado tossed table-side. The rest of the menu is more up-to-date, with offerings such as rock shrimp quesadillas with cilantro cream and skillet-fired polenta-dusted grouper. The best dessert choice is the chocolate banana cake served with buttery rum ice cream and candied hazelnuts. ⊠ *Disney–MGM Studios* ☎ 407/939–3463 ⊟ *AE, MC, V.*

Italian

$$ ✕ **Mama Melrose's Ristorante Italiano.** Casual Italian dining in what looks like an old warehouse is what you'll find here. The menu ranges from oak-grilled salmon with sun-dried tomato pesto to veal osso bucco with risotto Milanese. Wood-fired flatbreads with hearty toppings such as chicken and Italian cheeses make great starters; the sangria, available

by the carafe for $16.50, flows generously. Baked cappuccino, a custard with a sugar glaze, is the way to go for dessert. Kids' choices include a good burger and a $5 pizza. ⊠ *Disney–MGM Studios* ☎ *407/939–3463* ⊟ *AE, MC, V.*

Disney's Animal Kingdom

American/Casual

★ **$–$$** ✕ **Rainforest Café.** Since the Café resembles the one in Downtown Disney Marketplace, complete with the long lines for lunch and dinner, go early or late if you can. Choices include "Eyes of the Ocelot," a hearty meat loaf topped with sautéed mushrooms; and "Mojo Bones," tender ribs with barbecue sauce. The coconut bread pudding with apricot filling and whipped cream is great. Breakfast, from steak and eggs to excellent French toast, is served beginning at 7:30. ⊠ *Disney's Animal Kingdom* ☎ *407/938–9100 or 407/939–3463* ⊕ *www.rainforestcafe.com* ⊟ *AE, D, DC, MC, V.*

¢ ✕ **Restaurantosaurus.** This diner is Restaurantosaurus for breakfast and then, shortly before noon, it becomes a McDonald's. Come in the morning, when a group of college archaeology students sets up camp during a dig. You can catch the "college students," along with Donald Duck and others, at the daily character breakfast ($16.99 adults, $8.99 children 3–11), which is a massive buffet affair (with everything from pancakes to omelets). Reservations for this are essential. Lunch and dinner brings straightforward McDonald's fare, with worthwhile peanut butter brownies for dessert. ⊠ *Disney's Animal Kingdom* ☎ *407/939–3463* ⊟ *AE, D, DC, MC, V.*

Contemporary

$–$$$ ✕ **Boma.** Boma takes Western-style ingredients and prepares them with an African twist. The dozen or so walk-up cooking stations have such entrées as grilled salmon with a tamarind barbecue sauce and pepper steak with couscous. The zebra bones dessert is just chocolate mousse covered with white chocolate and striped with dark chocolate. All meals are prix fixe ($24 for adults; $10 for children 3–11). The South African wine list is outstanding. Priority seating reservations are essential if you are not a guest at the hotel. ⊠ *Disney's Animal Kingdom Lodge* ☎ *407/939–3463* ⊟ *AE, D, DC, MC, V* ⌂ *Reservations essential* ⊗ *No lunch.*

Downtown Disney/Lake Buena Vista Area

Downtown Disney has three sections: the Marketplace, a small shopping-and-dining area; Pleasure Island, a nightlife complex with a hefty admission after dark; and, close by, Disney's West Side, another group of hipper-than-hip entertainment, dining, and shopping spots. The edge of Disney property is about a block away.

Just on the other side of the highway that marks the border is a group of many restaurants and hotels, both freestanding and in small malls. This is the Lake Buena Vista area. There are some wonderful mealtime options here, along with a great Gooding's supermarket. To get to the Lake Buena Vista–Downtown Disney area, take I–4 Exit 68.

American/Casual

$$ ✕ **Olivia's Café.** This is like a meal at Grandma's—provided she lives south of the Mason-Dixon line. The menu ranges from fried shrimp and grilled grouper to fried chicken with mashed potatoes and gravy. Two meat options stand out—slow-roasted prime rib and oven-roasted pork loin with egg noodles and sautéed cabbage. For dessert try the white-chocolate key lime cheesecake. The indoor palms and rough wood walls resemble those of an old Key West house, but the inside is just pleasant: not that special. The outdoor seating, which overlooks a waterway, is attractive any time that midsummer's heat is not bearing down. ⊠ *Old Key West Resort* ☎ *407/939–3463* ⊟ *AE, D, DC, MC, V.*

$–$$ ✕ **Planet Hollywood.** Patrons still flock to see the movie memorabilia assembled by celebrity owners Schwarzenegger, Stallone, Willis, and restaurateur Robert Earl. The wait has been abated by a system that allows you to sign in, take a number, and get an assigned time window to return and eat. The place covers 20,000 square ft if you count the indoor waterfall. On offer are sandwiches and tasty burgers as well as grilled specialties including steak, salmon, ribs, and pork chops. You can also indulge in unusual pastas and salads. Among the better offerings is the creole pizza with shrimp, chicken, and Cajun sausage. ⊠ *Downtown Disney West Side, at entrance to Pleasure Island* ☎ *407/827–7827* ⊕ *www.planethollywood.com* ⌁ *Reservations not accepted* ⊟ *AE, D, DC, MC, V.*

★ **$–$$** ✕ **Rainforest Café.** People start queuing up half an hour before the 10:30 AM opening of this 30,000-square-ft jungle fantasy in Downtown Disney's Marketplace, drawn as much by the gimmicks (man-made rainstorms, volcano eruptions) as the menu. But the food, a mix of American fare with imaginative names, is nevertheless worthwhile. Top choices include "Eyes of the Ocelot," a nice meat loaf topped with sautéed mushrooms; and "Mojo Bones," tender ribs with barbecue sauce. Best dessert: "Tortoise" Pie—actually chocolate espresso ice cream and Oreo cookies. ⊠ *Downtown Disney Marketplace* ☎ *407/827–8500 or 407/939–3463* ⊕ *www.rainforestcafe.com* ⊟ *AE, D, DC, MC, V.*

Cajun/Creole

$–$$$ ✕ **House of Blues.** From the outside, House of Blues resembles an old factory; the inside looks like an old church, complete with angelic frescoes. In any case, the southern cooking is truly righteous. Best bets are catfish, Cajun meatloaf, and Louisiana crawfish and shrimp étouffée, as well as the "Elwood" sandwich—blackened chicken with chili garlic mayonnaise and sour cream. The place gets noisy when the live music plays (11 PM–2 AM); lunches can be almost serene. The Sunday Gospel Brunch ($30 adults, $15 children 4–12) is a feast worth its price tag. ⊠ *Downtown Disney West Side* ☎ *407/934–2583* ⊟ *AE, D, MC, V.*

Contemporary

★ **$$–$$$$** ✕ **Wolfgang Puck Café.** There are lots of choices here, from wood-oven pizza at the informal Puck Express to five-course meals at the upstairs, formal dining room, where there's also a sushi bar and an informal café. Must-tries at Express include the pizzas, with toppings such as grilled chicken or salmon, and various inspired pastas, which have sauces sublimely laced with chunks of lobster, salmon, or chicken. The dining room always offers a worthy fresh ravioli and a Puck trademark—Wiener schnitzel. Special five-course prix-fixe dinners ($100 with wine, $65 without) require 24-hour notice. ⊠ *Downtown Disney West Side* ☎ *407/938–9653* ⊕ *www.wolfgangpuck.com* ⊟ *AE, MC, V.*

$–$$ ✕ **Pebbles.** This is California cuisine, dude, with a Florida touch that adds grouper and other regional favorites to the mix. In addition to the Crossroads original, there are now four other locations. Good entrées include angel-hair pasta smothered with smoked duck, scallops, and Asian spices, and the Mediterranean salad, with the obligatory sun-dried tomatoes. The Caesar salad, tossed table-side, is delicious. Burgers covered with excellent cheeses are also served, and the wine list is thoughtful and reasonably priced. ⊠ *Crossroads of Lake Buena Vista, 12551 SR 535, Lake Buena Vista* ☎ *407/827–1111* ⊠ *17 W. Church St., Downtown Orlando* ☎ *407/839–0892* ⊠ *2516 Aloma Ave., Winter*

Park ☎ 407/678–7001 ✉ *2110 Rte. 434, Longwood* ☎ *407/774–7111* 🌐 *www.pebblesworldwide.com* ⚑ *Reservations not accepted* ▤ *AE, D, DC, MC, V.*

Continental

$$$$ ✕ **Arthur's 27.** The haute cuisine here comes with a world-class view from the 27th floor of the Wyndham Palace Resort, overlooking all of Disney World. Entrées include an excellent grilled veal loin and a consistently well-prepared tenderloin of beef. There are also more exotic choices, such as roasted rack of elk or loin of rabbit. Best dessert is the stellar Grand Marnier soufflé. There are also prix-fixe options: $68 for five courses, $62 for four. ✉ *Wyndham Palace Resort & Spa, 1900 Buena Vista Dr., I–4 Exit 68, Lake Buena Vista* ☎ 407/827–3450 🌐 *www.wyndham.com/hotels/MCOPV/main.wnt* ⚑ *Reservations essential* ▤ *AE, D, DC, MC, V.*

Cuban

$$–$$$ ✕ **Bongos Cuban Café.** Singer Gloria Estefan's Cuban eatery is inside a two-story building shaped like a pineapple. Hot-pressed Cuban sandwiches, black bean soup, deep-fried plantain chips, and beans and rice are mainstays on the menu for the lunch crowd. One of the best entrées is *La Habana*: lobster, shrimp, scallops, calamari, clams, and mussels in a piquant creole sauce. Other worthwhile offerings include *arroz con pollo* (rice with chicken), *El Hatuey* (skirt steak), tasty ham croquettes, and *boliche asado*, an expertly prepared Cuban pot roast. There's live Latin music on Friday and Saturday. ✉ *Downtown Disney West Side* ☎ 407/828–0999 🌐 *www.bongoscubancafe.com* ⚑ *Reservations not accepted* ▤ *AE, D, DC, MC, V.*

French

$$$–$$$$ ✕ **La Coquina.** This restaurant, just outside Disney property, bills itself as French with an Asian influence, and if you sample the veal tenderloin with sake-glazed prawns, you'll approve of its methods. Come for Sunday brunch, when the generous selection of goodies makes the price ($49.95 adults, $24.95 kids) almost seem like a bargain. In an unusual touch, during brunch your waiter takes you into the kitchen, where you pick out what you want and watch the chef cook it to order. For a closer look at the chef in action, ask the manager about sitting at the special chef's table in the kitchen. ✉ *Hyatt Regency Grand Cypress, 1 Grand Cypress Blvd.* ☎ 407/239–1234 🌐 *www.hyattgrandcypress.com* ▤ *AE, D, DC, MC, V.*

Italian

$$$–$$$$ ✕ **Portobello Yacht Club.** The northern Italian cuisine here is uniformly good. The *spaghettini alla Portobello* (with scallops, clams, and Alaskan king crab) is outstanding; other fine pasta options include the linguine with Manila clams in a white wine sauce and the *rigatoni alla Calabrese*, with sausage, mushrooms, tomatoes, and black olives. There's always a fresh-catch special, as well as tasty wood-oven pizza. ✉ *Pleasure Island* ☎ 407/934–8888 ▤ *AE, MC, V.*

Seafood

$$$–$$$$ ✕ **Fulton's Crab House.** Set in a faux riverboat docked in a lagoon between Pleasure Island and the Marketplace, this fish house offers fine, if expensive, dining. The signature seafood is flown in daily. Dungeness crab from the Atlantic banks, Alaskan king crab, Florida stone crab: it's all fresh. For a real crustacean feast, try the crab and lobster for two, which includes three pounds of Alaskan king crab and snow crab, plus a 1¼-pound lobster, for $31.95 a head. The sublime cappuccino ice cream cake is $13, but one order is easily enough for two. ✉ *Downtown Disney Marketplace* ☎ 407/934–2628 ▤ *AE, MC, V.*

$–$$ ✕ **Landry's Seafood House.** Set in a fake warehouse building—popular architecture in Central Florida—this branch of a nationwide chain delivers good seafood at reasonable prices. The food is first-rate, especially Cajun dishes like the fresh-caught fish Pontchartrain, a broiled fish with slightly spicy seasoning and a creamy white-wine sauce that's topped with a lump of crabmeat. Good appetizers include bacon-wrapped shrimp en brochette with seafood stuffing, jack cheese, and jalapeño peppers, as well as excellent jumbo lump crab cakes. A $15 seafood platter lets you sample crab fingers, fried oysters, and shrimp. ⊠ *8800 Vineland Ave., Rte. 535 Lake Buena Vista* ☎ *407/827–6466* ⊕ *www.landrysseafood.com* ⊟ *AE, D, DC, MC, V.*

Steak

$$–$$$$ ✕ **Hawk's Landing.** If you have lunch at this golf clubhouse, you can see virtually the entire back nine. The beef is a step up from what you'd find at a typical clubhouse. The signature dish is a 16-ounce, boneless rib eye for $28; the thick, juicy veal chop is well worth the $29. Maryland-style crab cakes with key lime tartar sauce make an excellent appetizer, as do the pan-roasted mussels with lemon butter and garlic chips. For dessert, try a classic key lime pie. ⊠ *Orlando World Center Marriott, 8701 World Center Dr., I–4 Exit 67, Southwest Orlando* ☎ *407/238–8829* ⚓ *Reservations essential* ⊟ *AE, D, DC, MC, V.*

Tex-Mex

$ ✕ **Chevy's.** True, the ersatz cantina motif here looks like that of every other Mexican place in every suburb you've ever seen. But the food is a shocker: it's quite good. Try the hot tamales, made with a fresh cornmeal shell and filled with chicken, pork, or beef. The menu, making use of some gringo creativity, includes chicken with Dijon mustard wrapped in a tortilla and a huge burrito made with pork and beef barbecue and black beans. If you're up for a mucho grande feast from the grill, try the plato gordo that is heaped with Baja-style ribs (grilled with a tangy sauce), grilled chicken breast, seasoned jumbo shrimp, skirt steak and grilled garden fresh vegetables. For dessert, look for the good flan and cream pies. ⊠ *12547 Rte. 535, Lake Buena Vista* ☎ *407/827–1052* ⊠ *277 W. Hwy. 436, Altamonte Springs* ☎ *407/869–5559* ⊠ *2809 W. Vine St., Kissimmee* ☎ *407/847–2244* ⊕ *www.chevys.com* ⊟ *AE, MC, V.*

UNIVERSAL ORLANDO RESORT AREA

With more than a dozen restaurants and the world's largest Hard Rock Cafe, Universal Orlando's CityWalk is a culinary force. At Islands of Adventure, each of the six lands has between two and six eateries—not all of them strictly burgers-and-fries affairs. Universal has done a good job of providing information and access to these eateries, with a special **reservation and information line** (☎ 407/224–9255 ⊕ www. universalorlando.com) and a Web site that includes menus for many of the restaurants.

To get to Universal, take I–4 Exit 75A from eastbound lanes, Exit 74B when you're westbound.

Meals with Universal Characters

Universal Studios offers meals with its characters, specifically Scooby-Doo, Woody Woodpecker, and Curious George, although the line up is not nearly as extensive as what is offered at Disney World.

Dinner

Currently, all character meals at Universal are dinners served at the theme park's three, on-property hotels and are by reservation only. Characters appearing at the following restaurants vary, so please call the restaurant in advance to see which of the following will be appearing: Shaggy, Scooby-Doo, Woody Woodpecker, and Curious George. Reservations can be made at the **character meal reservation line** (☎ 407/503–3463).

The meals, times, and prices are: Royal Pacific Resort in the **Islands Dining Room** (✉ $24.50 adults, $9.75 children 12 and under), Mon.–Tues. from 6:30 to 9:30 PM; Portofino Bay Hotel in the **Trattoria del Porto** (✉ $19.95 adults; $9.75 children 12 and under), Fri. from 6:30 to 9:30; and at the Hard Rock Hotel in the **Sunset Grill** (✉ guests dine off the regular restaurant menu, with a price range of $6–$20), Sat. from 6:30 to 9:30.

Islands of Adventure

Islands of Adventure, where it's as easy to get a glass of Merlot and a croissant as it is to get a burger and fries, offers a few culinary adventures as well. There are only a couple of full-service, sit-down restaurants in the park, but the offerings at several of the cafeteria-style eateries are pretty creative and tasty, too.

American

$–$$$ ✕ **Confisco Grille.** You could walk right past this Mediterranean eatery, but if you want a good meal and sit-down service, don't pass by too quickly. The menu changes often, but typical entrées include pan-seared pork medallions with roasted garlic and red peppers, baked cod with spinach and mashed potatoes, and Thai noodles with chicken, shrimp, tofu, and bean sprouts. Save room for desserts like chocolate-banana bread pudding or crème brûlée. ✉ *6000 Universal Blvd., Port of Entry section at Universal Studios Islands of Adventure* ☎ 407/224–9255 ▤ AE, D, MC, V ⊙ *No lunch.*

American/Casual

¢ ✕ **Green Eggs and Ham Cafe.** This Dr. Seuss–inspired spot is the only place in Orlando where the eggs are intentionally green. The eggs (tinted with food coloring) are in an egg and ham sandwich, the most popular item at this walk-up, outdoor eatery, which looks like a hallucinatory McDonald's. There's also a fairly tasty "green" garden salad, as well as some other conventional fare, including a normal cheeseburger, fries, and "frings," a type of onion ring. ✉ *6000 Universal Blvd., Seuss Landing section at Universal Studios Islands of Adventure* ☎ 407/224–9255 ▤ AE, D, MC, V.

Contemporary

$–$$$ ✕ **Mythos.** The name sounds Greek, but the dishes are eclectic. The menu, which changes frequently, usually includes standouts like meat loaf, roast pork tenderloin, and assorted kinds of wood-fired pizzas. Among the creative desserts is a fine pumpkin cheesecake. But the building itself is enough to grab your attention. It looks like a giant rock formation from the outside and a huge cave (albeit one with plush upholstered seating) from the inside. Mythos also has a waterfront view of the big lagoon in the center of the theme park. ✉ *6000 Universal Blvd., Lost Continent at Universal Studios Islands of Adventure* ☎ 407/224–9255 ▤ AE, D, MC, V.

CityWalk

American/Casual

$–$$$ ✕ **Motown Café Orlando.** This music shrine is primarily a nightclub. At night, when there's a $5 cover charge, it's jumping with the sounds that made Motown Records an American music legend. By day, though, it's

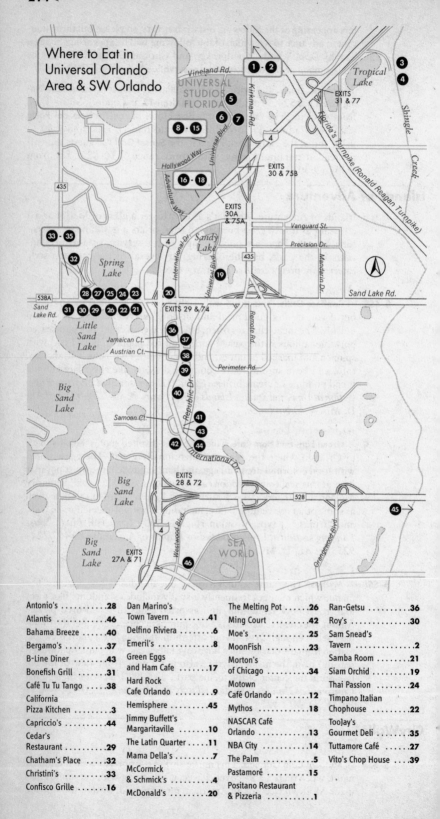

Where to Eat in Universal Orlando Area & SW Orlando

a quiet, uncrowded place to grab a good meal. The eclectic menu ranges from the vaguely Asian "Jackson 5" pot stickers to Smokey's ribs. Some offerings defy categorization, like the fried chicken and Belgian waffles combo. Best piece of soul memorabilia: the 28-ft Motown "record," billed as the world's largest, suspended from the ceiling. ⊠ *6000 Universal Blvd., at Universal Orlando's CityWalk* ☎ *407/224–3663* ⊡ *$5 cover charge after 9* PM ⊟ *AE, D, MC, V.*

$–$$ ✕ **Hard Rock Cafe Orlando.** Built to resemble Rome's Coliseum, this 800-seat restaurant is the largest of the 100-odd Hard Rocks in the world, but getting a seat at lunch can still require a long wait. The music is always loud and the walls are filled with rock memorabilia. Appetizers range from spring rolls to boneless chicken tenders. The most popular menu item is still the $8.49 burger, with the baby-back ribs and the home-made-style meat loaf both strong contenders. The best dessert is the $5 chocolate chip cookie (it's big), which is covered with ice cream. ⊠ *6000 Universal Blvd., at Universal Orlando's CityWalk* ☎ *407/224–3663 or 407/351–7625* ⊕ *www.hardrockcafe.com* ⟿ *Reservations not accepted* ⊟ *AE, D, DC, MC, V.*

$–$$ ✕ **Jimmy Buffett's Margaritaville.** Parrot-heads can probably name the top two menu items before they even walk in the door. You've got your cheeseburger, featured in the song "Cheeseburger in Paradise," and, of course, your Ultimate Margarita. The rest of the menu is an eclectic mix of quesadillas, chowder, and crab cakes, a tasty fried fish platter, stone-crab claws, and a pretty decent steak. Worthy dessert choices include the Last Mango in Paradise cheesecake, the key lime pie, and a tasty chocolate bread pudding. ⊠ *6000 Universal Blvd., at Universal Orlando's CityWalk* ☎ *407/224–2155* ⊟ *AE, D, MC, V.*

$–$$ ✕ **NASCAR Café Orlando.** If you are a racing fanatic, this is your place. If the memorabilia on the walls is not enough for you, a couple of actual race cars hang from the ceiling. The food is better than you might think: highlights include a good chicken mushroom soup (with grilled chicken and shiitake mushrooms); the remarkably ungreasy popcorn shrimp; the Thunder Road burger, with melted pimento cheese and sautéed onions; and a decent chicken potpie. Aside from the white chocolate cheesecake, desserts are largely forgettable. ⊠ *6000 Universal Blvd., at Universal Orlando's CityWalk* ☎ *407/224–3663* ⊕ *www. nascarcafe.com* ⊟ *AE, D, MC, V.*

$–$$ ✕ **NBA City.** The NBA memorabilia and video games are great, but the food is actually the real draw here. Best choices include the barbecued chicken quesadilla and a 12-ounce pork chop glazed with maple-mustard sauce. The brick-oven pizzas include an unusual BLT variety. And the milk shake is worth every bit of its $5 price tag. The big-screen TVs, which naturally broadcast nonstop basketball action, probably won't surprise you, but the relatively quiet bar upstairs, with elegant blond-wood furniture, probably will. ⊠ *6000 Universal Blvd., at Universal Orlando's CityWalk* ☎ *407/363–5919* ⊕ *www.nbacity.com* ⊟ *AE, D, MC, V.*

Contemporary

★ $$$–$$$$ ✕ **Emeril's.** The popular eatery is a culinary shrine to Emeril Lagasse, the famous Food Network chef who occasionally appears here. The menu changes frequently, but you can always count on New Orleans treats like andouille sausage, shrimp, and red beans appearing in some form or fashion. Entrées may include rack of lamb with a creole mustard crust and citrus-glazed duck with walnut-pear chutney. The wood-baked pizza, topped with exotic mushrooms, is stellar. Desserts, including bread pudding and a chocolate Grand Marnier soufflé (which must be ordered 30 minutes in advance), are also notable. ⊠ *6000 Universal Blvd., at Universal Orlando's CityWalk* ☎ *407/224–2424* ⊕ *www.emerils.com* ⟿ *Reservations essential* ⊟ *AE, D, MC, V.*

Italian

$–$$ ✕ **Pastamoré.** Since it doesn't have name appeal like its neighbor, Emeril's, Pastamoré is something of a CityWalk sleeper. But this could be the best uncrowded restaurant at Universal, with wood-fired pizza, fresh pasta, and Italian beer and wines. Especially notable are the huge Italian sandwiches, with ingredients like marinated chicken, peppers, and sun-dried tomatoes, as well as a good tiramisu. In an unusual touch, you can also come here for Italian breakfast breads—the place opens at 8 AM. The breakfast pizza, topped with sausage and eggs, will make you glad you didn't opt for a McMuffin. ⌧ *6000 Universal Blvd., at Universal Orlando's CityWalk* ☎ *407/224–3663* ▤ *AE, D, MC, V.*

Latin

$$–$$$ ✕ **The Latin Quarter.** This grottolike restaurant and club, with domed ceilings and stone walls, is one of those jumping-by-night, dormant-by-day spots, but the food is good all the time. Cuisines from 21 Latin nations are on the menu, as is a wide selection of South American beers. Good entrée choices include *churrasco* (skirt steak), *puerco asado* (roasted pork), *pollo rostistado* (slow-roasted chicken), and an outstanding fried snapper with tomato salsa. Most main dishes come with black beans and rice. Best bets for dessert: the crepes and the mango and guava cheesecakes. ⌧ *6000 Universal Blvd., at Universal Orlando's CityWalk* ☎ *407/224–3663* ⊕ *www.thelatinquarter.com* ▤ *AE, D, MC, V.*

Portofino Bay Hotel

Italian

★ $$–$$$$ ✕ **Delfino Riviera.** This lavish restaurant, a stunning copy of one in Portofino, Italy, has high-beam ceilings, stone columns, and marble floors. The architecture is not the only awe-inspiring part of the formula—so is the cuisine. One of the best dishes is risotto *Al Frutti Di Mare* with cararoli rice, shrimp, squid, clams, and mussels, mixed with white wine, garlic, and tomatoes. A strong second is the *Filetto Col Vegetali*, grilled aged prime beef tenderloin, Italian eggplant, oven-dried tomatoes and roasted garlic with red wine and rosemary oil. For dessert try the chef's spin on a cannoli, which is stuffed with apples and pine nuts in a sweet ricotta base. ⌧ *5601 Universal Blvd.* ☎ *407/503–1000* ▤ *AE, D, DC, MC, V* ⊗ *No lunch.*

$$–$$$ ✕ **Mama Della's.** The premise here is that Mama Della is a middle-aged Italian housewife who has opened up her home as a restaurant. "Mama" is always on hand (there are several of them, working in shifts), strolling among the tables and making small talk. The food, which is served family style, is no fantasy—it's excellent. The menu has Italian traditions like chicken cacciatore, veal parmigiana, and spaghetti with sirloin meatballs or bolognese sauce, and all of the pastas are made in-house. The quality of the food experience starts with hot garlic bread and continues through the dessert course; the tiramisu and the Italian chocolate torte both make sure bets. ⌧ *5601 Universal Blvd.* ☎ *407/503–1000* ▤ *AE, D, DC, MC, V* ⊗ *Closed Mon. No lunch.*

Hard Rock Hotel

Steak

$$–$$$$ ✕ **The Palm.** With its dark-wood interior and hundreds of framed celebrity caricatures, this restaurant resembles its famed New York City namesake. Steaks are the reason to dine here, but most are available only at dinner. The steak fillet cooked on a hot stone is a specialty, as is the Double Steak, a 36-ounce New York strip for two (or one extreme carnivore). There are several veal dishes on the menu, along with a 3-pound

Nova Scotia lobster, broiled crab cakes, and a good linguine with white clam sauce. ✉ *1000 Universal Studios Plaza* ☎ *407/503–7256* ⊕ *www.thepalm.com* ▭ *AE, D, DC, MC, V* ✆ *No lunch weekends.*

KISSIMMEE

Although Orlando is the focus of most theme-park visitors, Kissimmee is actually closer to Walt Disney World. To visit the area, follow I–4 to Exit 64A. Allow about 15 or 20 minutes to travel from WDW, or about 30 minutes from I-Drive.

Italian

$–$$ ✕ **Romano's Macaroni Grill.** You may have a location of this prolific chain in your hometown, and the three popular Orlando branches deliver a known quantity—good but not great cuisine. It's friendly, it's casual, and it's comfortable. The scallopini, made with chicken instead of the traditional veal, is topped with artichokes and capers and served with angel-hair pasta. House wines are brought to the table in gallon bottles—you serve yourself and then report how many glasses you had. Your kids can pass the time doodling with crayons on the white-paper table covering. ✉ *5320 W. Irlo Bronson Memorial Hwy., Kissimmee* ☎ *407/396–6155* ✉ *884 W. Rte. 436, Altamonte Springs* ☎ *407/682–2577* ✉ *12148 S. Apopka–Vineland Rd., Lake Buena Vista* ☎ *407/239–6676* ▭ *AE, D, DC, MC, V.*

Steak

$$$$ ✕ **Old Hickory Steak House** If paying $40 for a steak (and an extra $7 for a side of fries) then dining inside a barn seems a bit surreal, remember that this is Orlando. The barn, like many of the unusual eateries in the Orlando area, is a faux building, a movie-set kind of edifice designed for effect. Dine on the deck adjacent to the barn and you will overlook the hotel's faux Everglades, where electronic alligators cavort with fiberglass frogs. The experience is designed to entertain, and does; the food at the steak house is worth the roughly $50 a person you'll spend for dinner if you eschew alcohol. In addition to the corn-feed angus beef, there's a tenderloin of American buffalo for $39. ✉ *Gaylord Palms Resort, 6000 W. Osceola Pkwy. I–4 Exit 65, Kissimmee* ☎ *407/586–0000* ▭ *AE, DC, MC, V* ⊕ *www.gaylordhotels.com* ✆ *No lunch.*

CELEBRATION

If this small town with Victorian-style homes and perfectly manicured lawns reminds you a bit of Main Street, U.S.A., in the Magic Kingdom, it should. The utopian residential community was created by Disney, with all the Disney attention to detail. Every view of every street is warm and pleasant, though the best are out the windows of the town's four restaurants, all of which face a pastoral (if man-made) lake. There's even an interactive fountain in the small park near the lake, giving kids a great place to splash. To get here take I–4 to Exit 64A and follow the "Celebration" signs.

American/Casual

$–$$$$ ✕ **Celebration Town Tavern/Bostonian.** This New England–cuisine eatery has a split personality. Half is the casual Celebration Town Tavern with sandwiches and less expensive fare; the other half is the slightly more formal Bostonian, with dishes like prime rib and fresh, two-pound Maine lobster. Both halves are open for lunch and dinner, and you can order the larger-portioned entrées from the Bostonian menu in the Tavern. You'll find standouts such as Manhattan and New England clam chowder, as well as a good selection of sandwiches at the Tavern, although you can choose from heaping platters of fried Ipswich clams, fried oysters, or Florida stone crabs served in season (spring) at the Bostonian. There are great New England crab cakes and, of course, Boston cream pie. ⊠ *721 Front St., Celebration* ☎ *407/566–2526* ☲ *AE, D, MC, V.*

$–$$ ✕ **Market Street Café.** Looking like a 1950s classic, this informal diner's menu ranges from the house-special baked-potato omelet (served until 4:30 PM) to chicken Alfredo and prime rib. One appetizer, the cheese quesadilla, is large enough to make a meal. Standout entrées include the pot roast and meat loaf. In addition to a hearty version of the quintessential American hamburger, there's also a salmon burger and a veggie burger for the cholesterol-wary. The excellent house-made potato chips come with a blue cheese sauce. ⊠ *701 Front St., Celebration* ☎ *407/566–1144* ⌂ *Reservations not accepted* ☲ *AE, D, MC, V.*

Italian

$–$$$ ✕ **Café d' Antonio.** The wood-burning oven and grill are worked pretty hard here, and the mountains of hardwood used in the open kitchen flavor the best of the menu—the pizza, the grilled fish and chicken, the steaks and chops, even the lasagna. Standouts include salmon from the grill and veal chops cooked in cognac. For dessert, try the hazelnut chocolate cake or the ricotta cheesecake. Italian vintages dominate the wine list. Like the rest of Celebration's restaurants, there's an awning-covered terrace overlooking the lagoon. ⊠ *691 Front St., Celebration* ☎ *407/566–2233* ⊕ *www.antoniosonline.com* ☲ *AE, D, MC, V.*

Latin

$$–$$$ ✕ **Columbia Restaurant.** Celebration's branch of this statewide, family-owned Latin chain is generally as good as the original in Tampa. Zero in on the paella—either *à la Valenciana,* with clams, shrimp, scallops, chicken, pork, and calamari mixed into tasty yellow rice; or the all-seafood *marinara,* which also includes lobster. A good lighter dish is the Atlantic *merluza,* a delicate white fish rolled in bread crumbs, then grilled and topped with lemon butter, parsley, and diced eggs. Desserts include key lime pie and a good Cuban flan. ⊠ *649 Front St., Celebration* ☎ *407/ 566–1505* ⊕ *www.columbiarestaurant.com* ☲ *AE, D, DC, MC, V.*

ORLANDO

International Drive

A number of restaurants are scattered among the hotels that line manicured International Drive. Many are branches of chains, from fast-food spots to theme coffee shops and up. The food is sometimes quite good. To get to the area, take I–4 Exit 72 or 74A. Count on it taking about half an hour from the Kissimmee area or from WDW property.

American/Casual

$–$$$ ✕ **B-Line Diner.** As you might expect from its hotel location, this slick, 1950s-style diner with red vinyl counter seats is not exactly cheap, but the salads, sandwiches, and griddle foods are tops. The greatest combo ever—a thick, juicy burger served with fries and a wonderful milk shake—is done beautifully. It's open 24 hours. ⊠ *Peabody Orlando, 9801 International Dr., I-Drive Area* ☎ *407/352–4000* ⊕ *www. peabodyorlando.com* ☲ *AE, D, DC, MC, V.*

$–$$$ ✕ **Dan Marino's Town Tavern.** Part of a Florida sports bar chain begun by the Miami Dolphins quarterback, the Tavern mixes burgers and steaks with some sophisticated surprises, including seared tuna. ⊠ *Pointe*Orlando, 9101 International Dr., I-Drive Area* ☎ *407/363– 1013* ⊕ *www.danmarinostowntavern.com* ☲ *AE, MC.*

Caribbean

$–$$$ ✕ **Bahama Breeze.** Even though the lineage is corporate, the menu here is creative and tasty. The casual fun and the Caribbean cooking draw a crowd: so be prepared for a wait. Meanwhile, you can sip piña coladas and other West Indian delights on a big wooden porch. The food is worth the wait. Start with *tostones con pollo* (plantain chips topped with chicken and cheese), followed by coconut curry chicken or paella. ⊠ *8849 International Dr., I-Drive Area* ☎ *407/248–2499* ⊠ *8735 Vineland Ave., I-4 Exit 68, I-Drive Area* ☎ *407/938–9010* ⊕ *www.bahamabreeze.com* ⚅ *Reservations not accepted* ⊟ *AE, D, DC, MC.*

Chinese

$–$$$$ ✕ **Ming Court.** A walled courtyard and serene pond make you forget you're on International Drive. The extensive menu includes simple chicken Szechuan, plum-blossom boneless duck, and aged filet mignon grilled in a spicy Szechuan sauce. The flourless chocolate cake, certainly not Asian, has been a popular standard for years. Ming Court is within walking distance of the Orange County Convention Center and can be quite busy at lunchtime. ⊠ *9188 International Dr., I-Drive Area* ☎ *407/351–9988* ⊕ *www.ming-court.com* ⊟ *AE, D, DC, MC, V.*

Contemporary

$$–$$$ ✕ **Café Tu Tu Tango.** The food here resembles tapas—everything is appetizer-sized. The eclectic menu is fitting for a restaurant on International Drive. If you want a compendium of cuisines at one go, try the Cajun chicken egg rolls with blackened chicken, Greek goat cheese, creole mustard, and tomato salsa. The restaurant is supposedly a crazy artist's loft; artists paint at easels while diners sip drinks like Matisse Margaritas. Although nothing costs more than $8, it's not hard to spend $50 for lunch for two. ⊠ *8625 International Dr., I-Drive Area* ☎ *407/248–2222* ⊕ *www.cafetututango.com* ⚅ *Reservations not accepted* ⊟ *AE, D, DC, MC, V.*

Fast Food

¢ ✕ **McDonald's.** Despite the billboard's claim, this is the *second*-largest McDonald's in the world, after the one on Arbat Street in Moscow. But this burger joint certainly has more frills than any other. How many other McDonald's have a place to buy airline tickets . . . or socks? (They're required in the huge indoor playground.) There's also a theater with musicians and magicians and a gift shop brimming with T-shirts (and socks). Dining rooms include the tiki bar–style Sunset Terrace; the Maui Room, with a 600-gallon saltwater aquarium; or the Rock and Roll Room, featuring '50s memorabilia and a jukebox. ⊠ *6875 Sand Lake Rd., I-Drive Area* ☎ *407/351–2185* ⚅ *Reservations not accepted* ⊟ *AE, DC, MC, V.*

Italian

$$$–$$$$ ✕ **Bergamo's.** If you like Broadway show tunes with your spaghetti and opera with your osso bucco, then head here for the booming voices as well as the good food, both of which are provided by servers in satin vests. Management does not rely on the entertainment alone to fill seats: the food is very worthwhile. Try the roast duck ravioli in marsala cream sauce; linguine pescatore with lobster, shrimp, clams, and mussels; or a big veal T-bone in olive-anchovy butter. Save room for a chocolate, flourless hazelnut torte. ⊠ *8445 International Dr., I-4 Exit 75A or 75B, I-Drive Area* ☎ *407/352–3805* ⊕ *www.bergamos.com* ⊟ *AE, D, DC, MC, V* ☉ *No lunch.*

$$–$$$$ ✕ **Capriccio's.** From the marble-top tables in this Italian restaurant, you can view the open kitchen and the wood-burning pizza ovens, which turn out whole-wheat-flour pies ranging from pizza *margherita* (with sun-dried tomatoes and smoked mozzarella, fontina, provolone, and Parmesan cheeses) to pizza *blanca* (with mozzarella, goat cheese, and fresh thyme). For dessert, sample the imported-from-Italy ladyfingers with amaretto sauce. ⊠ *Peabody Orlando, 9801 International Dr., I-Drive Area* ☎ *407/352–4000* ⊟ *AE, DC, MC, V* ☺ *Closed Mon.*

Japanese

$$–$$$$ ✕ **Ran-Getsu.** The surroundings are a Disney-style version of Asia, but the food is fresh and carefully prepared, much of it table-side. Unless you're alone, you can have your meal Japanese-style at the low tables overlooking a carp-filled pond and decorative gardens. You may wish to try the sukiyaki, *shabu-shabu* (thinly sliced beef and vegetables cooked table-side in a simmering broth), or the *kushiyaki* (grilled skewers of shrimp, beef, chicken, and scallops). If you feel adventurous, try the deep-fried alligator tail, glazed in a ginger-soy sauce. ⊠ *8400 International Dr., I-Drive Area* ☎ *407/345–0044* ⊟ *AE, DC, MC, V* ☺ *No lunch.*

Seafood

$$$–$$$$ ✕ **Atlantis.** A harpist plays in this dining room, which is outfitted with frescoes, dark-wood paneling, and plush green carpet. The waiters even bring forth the entrées on silver-dome trays. Go for one of the various lobster dishes or the grilled fish, such as yellowfin tuna and salmon. There are also worthy red-meat dishes, including roast loin of lamb, and the obligatory surf-and-turf combo—in this case a sirloin served with lobster and pesto sauce. Desserts include some fine soufflés, which must be ordered 30 minutes in advance. ⊠ *Renaissance Orlando Resort, 6677 Sea Harbor Dr., I-Drive Area* ☎ *407/351–5555* ⊕ *www. atlantisorlando.com* ⊟ *AE, MC, V* ☺ *No lunch.*

Steak

★ $–$$$$ ✕ **Vito's Chop House.** There's a reason they keep the blinds closed most of the time: it's for the wines' sake. The dining room doubles as the cellar, with hundreds of bottles stacked in every nook and cranny. The steaks and the wood-grilled pork chops di Vito are superb. If you don't mind laying out $94.95 for Vito's Ultimate Surf 'n' Turf, you can feast on a 50-ounce porterhouse and a 1½-pound lobster (which feed at least two people). Worthwhile desserts include Grilled Peach di Vito, an excellent key lime pie, and Italian wedding cake. Finish your meal by enjoying a fine cigar along with a glass of aged cognac, armagnac, or grappa in the lounge. ⊠ *8633 International Dr., I-Drive Area* ☎ *407/354–2467* ⊟ *AE, D, DC, MC, V* ⊕ *www.vitoschophouse.com* ⌒ *Reservations essential* ☺ *No lunch.*

Thai

$–$$ ✕ **Siam Orchid.** One of Orlando's more elegant Asian restaurants occupies a gorgeous structure a bit off International Drive. Waitresses, who wear costumes from Thailand, serve authentic fare such as Siam wings, a chicken wing stuffed to look like a drumstick, and *pla rad prik,* a whole, deep-fried fish covered with a sauce flavored with red chilies, bell peppers, and garlic. Pad thai dishes come in a variety of choices: beef, pork, seafood, and vegetable. If you like it spicy, remember to say "Thai hot," but be sure you mean it. ⊠ *7575 Universal Blvd., I-Drive Area* ☎ *407/351–0821* ⊟ *AE, DC, MC, V.*

Southwestern Orlando

This is the part of the city nearest the main Disney tourism area, a mere five minutes or so northeast of International Drive or Universal Orlando. Because the neighborhood has many expensive homes, with high incomes to match, it's where you'll find some of the city's more upscale stores and restaurants. Over the past few years, one of the most significant dining sectors in Orlando has sprung up along Sand Lake Road, Exit 74A, just about a mile west of crowded International Drive where the quality of the average restaurant is not up to par with the eateries on Sand Lake.

Contemporary

\$\$–\$\$\$\$ ✕ **Chatham's Place.** In Florida, grouper is about as ubiquitous as Coca-Cola, but to discover its full potential, try the rendition here: it's sautéed in pecan butter and flavored with cayenne. It's one of the best dishes in Orlando. A close second is the pan-roasted rack of lamb flavored with rosemary. The most popular appetizer is the Maryland-style crab cakes, but the New Orleans–style shrimp brochette is also noteworthy. The chef does wonders with desserts like pecan–macadamia nut pie. Take I–4 Exit 74A. ⊠ *7575 Dr. Phillips Blvd., Southwest Orlando* ☎ *407/345–2992* ⊕ *www.splace.com* ⊟ *AE, D, DC, MC, V.*

\$\$–\$\$\$ ✕ **The Melting Pot.** This fondue restaurant keeps you busy while you eat—you'll be doing part of the cooking. Diners sit and dip morsels ranging from lobster tails to sirloin slices into hot liquids in stainless steel pots built into the center of the table. The lineup also includes the traditional cheese fondues along with chocolate fondue for dessert. ⊠ *7549 W. Sand Lake Rd., I–4 Exit 74A, Sand Lake Road Area* ☎ *407/903–1100* ⊟ *AE, D, DC, MC, V.*

\$\$–\$\$\$ ✕ **Sam Snead's Tavern.** This lively grill is a tribute to the late golf champion Sam Snead. The wood-paneled walls are chockablock with pictures and memorabilia of his illustrious career. The menu includes hamburgers, grilled chicken, veal chops, and fish. The Caesar salad is excellent, as are the barbecued spare ribs. A Chocolate Sack sounds weird but isn't—it's pound cake, ice cream, strawberries, and whipped cream packed into what looks like a paper bag made of chocolate, and it's much too much for one person. The Downtown location on East Pine has a sidewalk seating area. ⊠ *2461 S. Hiawassee Rd., Southwest Orlando* ☎ *407/295–9999* ⊠ *301 E. Pine St., Downtown Orlando* ☎ *407/999–0109* ⊟ *AE, D, DC, MC, V.*

Delis

¢–\$ ✕ **TooJay's Gourmet Deli.** This place is worth the visit just for the pastries, especially the *rugalach,* traditional Jewish cookies that have fruit or chocolate rolled into the dough. A versatile family dining spot as well as a kosher deli, TooJay's has classic sandwiches including turkey Reubens, Italian subs, and corned beef and pastrami smeared with chopped liver. Breakfast is also served throughout the day. The lunch and dinner menus include such comfort food as pot roast, matzo ball soup, lasagna, and shepherd's pie. The decor, brick and knotty pine walls, is pleasant if not memorable. ⊠ *7600 Dr. Phillips Blvd., Dr. Phillips Marketplace, Sand Lake Road Area* ☎ *407/355–0340* ⊠ *515 E. Altamonte Dr., Palm Springs Shopping Center, Altamonte Springs* ☎ *407/ 830–1770* ⊠ *2400 E. Colonial Dr., Colonial Market Plaza, Downtown Orlando* ☎ *407/894–1718* ⌲ *Reservations not accepted* ⊟ *AE, D, DC, MC, V.*

Hawaiian

\$\$–\$\$\$ ✕ **Roy's.** Chef Roy Yamaguchi has more or less perfected his own cuisine type—Hawaiian fusion, replete with lots of tropical fruit–based sauces and lots of imagination. The menu changes daily, but typical dishes include treats like citrus-marinated shrimp in a sushi roll salad with ginger-pineapple-chili vinaigrette or cilantro-seared Hawaiian Monchong (fish) with toasted-coconut black plum butter sauce. Frequently served desserts include black plum upside-down cake and coconut-crusted, fried cheesecake. If your tastes prefer to remain on the mainland, go for classics like a wood-fired, homemade-style meat loaf and warm apple crumb pie with vanilla bean ice cream. ✉ *7760 W. Sand Lake Rd., I–4 Exit 74A, Sand Lake Road Area* ☎ *407/352–4844* 🖃 *AE, D, DC, MC, V.*

Italian

$$$–$$$$ ✕ **Christini's.** Locals, visitors, and Disney execs gladly pay the price at Christini's, one of the city's best places for northern Italian. Owner Chris Christini is on hand nightly to make sure that everything is perfect. Try the pasta with lobster, shrimp, and clams or the huge veal chops, seasoned with fresh sage. The multicourse dinner often takes a couple of hours or more, but if you like Italian minstrels at your table, this place should please you. Take I–4 Exit 74A. ✉ *7600 Dr. Phillips Blvd., Dr. Phillips Marketplace, Sand Lake Road Area* ☎ *407/345–8770* ⊕ *www. christinis.com* 🖃 *AE, D, DC, MC, V.*

$$–$$$$ ✕ **Antonio's.** This pleasant trattoria, which has an outdoor terrace, has great service, welcoming surroundings, and a good chef with both the skill and the authority to give the place an individuality. Tasty creations include veal scaloppine in a lemon-flavored sauce, fresh-grilled salmon on a bed of sautéed spinach and risotto *frutti di mare,* with shrimp, scallops, clams, and mussels. Daily specials of fish (like Florida grouper) and red meat are always available. ✉ *7559 W. Sand Lake Rd., I–4 Exit 75A, Sand Lake Road Area* ⊕ *www.antoniosonline.com* ☎ *407/363–9191* 🖃 *AE, D, DC, MC, V* ☉ *Closed Sun. No lunch on Sat.*

$–$$$ ✕ **Positano Restaurant & Pizzeria.** This far-west-of-downtown restaurant has a split personality that allows it to conform to your mood—one side is a bustling family-style pizza parlor; the other is a more formal dining room, with white linen tablecloths. Although you can't order pizza in the dining room, you can get anything on the menu in the pizzeria, which serves some of the best New York–style pies in Central Florida. Try the unusual, piquant *ziti aum* (mozzarella, Parmesan, eggplant, and basil in a tomato sauce). The tiramisu is excellent. ✉ *Good Homes Plaza, 8995 W. Colonial Dr., Southwest Orlando* ☎ *407/291–0602* 🖃 *AE, D, DC, MC, V.*

$–$$$ ✕ **Timpano Italian Chophouse.** In this celebration of the America of the '50s and '60s, you may feel transported to Vegas when you hear the piano player and vocalist—and sometimes the waiters—belt out Sinatra and Wayne Newton chestnuts. American beef definitely gets its due here, but that doesn't cancel out any of the Italian flair. Along with the 18-ounce New York strip and the 16-ounce center-cut pork chops, there are credible versions of saltimbocca (braised veal and prosciutto in a white-wine sauce) and chicken marsala. Other Italian touches include a good minestrone soup; sides of pasta are available with any main course. ✉ *7488 W. Sand Lake Rd., I–4 Exit 75A, Sand Lake Road Area* ☎ *407/248–0429* 🖃 *AE, D, DC, MC, V.*

$–$$ ✕ **Tuttamore Café.** Small and unpretentious, this café can't match its neighbors in terms of decor, but the food is good and the prices are easy on your budget. Treat yourself to lobster ravioli with vodka sauce for a reasonable $12.25 or feast on a salami, mozzarella, tomato, and eggplant sandwich for $7.50. Some of the desserts, like the $6 slice of truffle cheesecake, are pricey but worth it. ✉ *7555 W. Sand Lake Rd., I–4 Exit 74A, Southwest Orlando* ☎ *407/352–2033* ✍ *Reservations not accepted* 🖃 *AE, D, DC, MC, V.*

$ ✕ **California Pizza Kitchen.** The now ubiquitous CPK often has a waiting line at the Mall at Millenia location, but the wait is worth it. The specialty is individual-size pizza, served on a plate with toppings ranging from Jamaican jerk chicken to spicy Italian peppers. Pasta dishes also offer unusual ingredients like Cajun Jambalaya and Kung Pao chicken. Appetizers range from tortilla spring rolls to hummus with pita bread. ✉ *4200 Conroy Rd., Mall at Millenia, Southwest Orlando* ☎ *407/248–7887* ✉ *8001 Orange Blossom Trail, Florida Mall* ☎ *407/854–5741* ⊕ *www.cpk.com* ▭ *AE, D, DC, MC, V.*

Mexican

¢ ✗ **Moe's.** Based on the names chosen for the menu entries, the Moe in this equation could almost be the guy who cavorted on film with Larry and Curly. There's an "Ugly Naked Guy" taco and other offerings called "The Other Lewinsky" and "Joey Bag of Donuts." But the food is more sublime than the nomenclature. The Ugly Naked Guy, for instance, is a vegetarian taco with guacamole and a side of red beans for $2.29. Try a "Full Monty" (taco with beans and choice of grilled chicken, steak, or tofu) and "Triple Lindy" burrito (with meat, cheese, beans, and salsa) and you're still well south of $10 for the price of your meal. ✉ *7541D W. Sand Lake Rd., I–4 Exit 74A, Sand Lake Road Area* ☎ *407/264–9903* ✉ *847 S. Orlando Ave., Winter Park* ☎ *407/629–4500* ⊕ *www.moes.com* ⚠ *Reservations not accepted* ▭ *AE, D, MC, V.*

Middle Eastern

$$–$$$ ✗ **Cedar's Restaurant.** Set in a small strip shopping center that's become part of a restaurant row, this family-owned, Lebanese eatery includes Middle Eastern standards like shish kebob, falafel, and hummus as well as tasty daily specials. One of the best of the latter is the fish *tajine*, grilled fish in a sauce of sesame paste, sautéed onions, pine nuts, and cilantro. You may also want to try sautéed or grilled quail with a cilantro and garlic sauce. A tad more formal than the average Orlando-area Middle Eastern restaurant, Cedar's has tables with white linen tablecloths and diners who tend to go for resort casual attire. ✉ *7732 W. Sand Lake Rd., I–4 Exit 75A, Sand Lake Road Area* ☎ *407/351–6000* ▭ *AE, D, DC, MC, V.*

Latin

$$–$$$$ ✗ **Samba Room.** Although owned by the same company that operates the TGI Friday's chain, this big, vibrant restaurant is a good version of an "authentic" Latin experience. You may agree once you've heard the bongos and tasted the paella. To sample the extensive menu, go for the *bocaditas* (small plates) offerings, which include mango barbecued ribs with plantain fries and grilled mussels with a coconut sour-orange sauce. A standout on the main course menu is the Argentinian-style skirt steak. For dessert, try the coconut crème brûlée and the green apple and banana cobbler. ✉ *7468 W. Sand Lake Rd., I–4 Exit 75A, Sand Lake Road Area* ☎ *407/226–0550* ▭ *AE, D, MC, V.*

Seafood

$$–$$$$ ✗ **MoonFish.** The big waterfall on the sign on the front of the building will grab your attention, but once you get inside, you'll find the gimmickry gives way to solid cuisine, served in a serene space with dark-wood paneling and white tablecloths on the tables. Specialties range from grilled Caribbean green back lobster tail to Alaskan red king crab, and Florida stone crab in season (spring). The restaurant also specializes in aged beef (which you can view in a big refrigerator cabinet as you walk in the door). And there's a good sushi bar, with selections ranging from the ubiquitous yellowtail tuna to octopus, squid, and eel. ✉ *7525 W. Sand Lake Rd., I–4 Exit 74A, Sand Lake Road Area* ☎ *407/363–7262* ⊕ *www.fishfusion.com* ▭ *AE, D, DC, MC, V.*

$–$$$ ✗ **McCormick & Schmick's.** Dark-wood paneling, white starched tablecloths, and private dining booths behind green curtains and leaded-glass windows give this place a touch of class, although dress is resort casual. The menu changes daily, but there are always more than 30 varieties of fish—

from Hawaiian albacore tuna to Yukon River salmon to Key West red snapper—on hand in the kitchen. All are typically available in some form on the menu, or grilled with lemon butter by request. Typical standout entrées from the dinner menu include Nantucket Bay scallops with white wine sauce and the always-available 14-ounce New York strip steak. Extensive, but expensive, wine list. ⊠ *4200 Conroy Rd., Mall at Millenia, Southwest Orlando* ☎ *407/226–6515* ▤ *AE, D, DC MC, V.*

★ **$-$$** ✕ **Bonefish Grill.** After polishing its culinary act in the Tampa Bay area, this Florida-based seafood chain has moved into the Orlando market with a casually elegant eatery that offers standout dishes like grouper piccata, rock shrimp fettucine diablo, and a house specialty, Lily's chicken—fire-roasted chicken topped with goat cheese, spinach, artichokes, and a lemon-basil sauce. For the record, there's no bonefish on the menu. It's a gamefish, caught for sport in the Florida Keys, which is not edible. ⊠ *7830 Sand Lake Rd., I–4 Exit 74A, Sand Lake Road Area* ☎ *407/355–7707* ⊕ *www.bonefishgrill.com* ▤ *AE, D, DC MC, V* ⊘ *No lunch.*

Steak

$$-$$$$ ✕ **Morton's of Chicago.** Center stage in the kitchen is a huge broiler, kept at 900°F to sear in the flavor of the porterhouses, sirloins, T-bones, and other cuts of aged beef. Morton's looks like a sophisticated private club, and youngsters with mouse caps are not common among the clientele. It's not unusual for checks to hit $65 a head, but if beef is your passion, this is the place. The wine list has about 500 vintages from around the world. Take I–4 Exit 74A. ⊠ *Dr. Phillips Marketplace, 7600 Dr. Phillips Blvd., Suite 132, Sand Lake Road Area* ☎ *407/248–3485* ⊕ *www.mortons.com* ▤ *AE, DC, MC, V.*

Thai

$-$$$ ✕ **Thai Passion.** The atmosphere is serene and exudes a southeast Asian feeling, a minor miracle considering that the restaurant is in a strip mall on a busy thoroughfare. Dinners sit at low, hardwood tables and sample such traditional Thai tidbits as satay (marinated beef or chicken strips) and tender spring rolls. Curry dishes are excellent here, especially the Panaeng curry, a red curry with chicken, beef, or lamb. Traditional Thai noodle dishes like pad thai are also worth your attention. ⊠ *7533 W. Sand Lake Rd., I–4 Exit 74A, Sand Lake Road Area* ☎ *407/313–9999* ▤ *AE, D, DC, MC, V* ⊘ *No lunch Sat. or Sun.*

Downtown Orlando

Downtown Orlando, north of Walt Disney World and slightly north of the International Drive area, is a thriving business district with a tourist fringe in the form of Church Street Station. Restaurants mainly serve weekday workers, sports fans attending events in the nearby arena, and tourists who head for the station area to party hearty. However, a burst of development in the downtown area has spurred a lot of activity in the past few years, and after-hours is no longer the time they roll up the sidewalks.

If you want to see the city when it's markedly less tourist-oriented and frenetic, especially at night, downtown Orlando is worth the 15- to 25-mi drive from the heart of Disney. If you go during the day, wait until after morning rush hour. To get here take Exit 84 off I–4 if you're heading westbound, Exit 83A if eastbound, unless otherwise noted.

Contemporary

★ **$$$-$$$$** ✕ **Manuel's on the 28th.** Restaurants with great views don't always have much more than that to offer, but this lofty spot on the 28th floor is also a culinary landmark. The menu changes regularly, but there's always a representative sampling of fish, Angus beef, pork, and duck. Dinner offerings may include sea scallops covered in macadamia nuts, Black Angus filet mignon, and even wild boar loin marinated in coconut milk. For dessert, try the baked apples wrapped in pastry, beggar's-purse style, which come with caramel sauce. ⊠ *Bank of America building, 390 N. Orange Ave., Suite 2800, Downtown Orlando* ☎ *407/246–6580* ⊕ *www.manuelsonthe28th.com* ⊟ *AE, D, DC, MC, V* ⊗ *Closed Sun.–Mon. No lunch.*

$$–$$$$ ✕ **The Boheme Restaurant.** The company that operates Manuel's on the 28th also runs the Boheme. No panorama here, but the food is every bit as adventurous. On offer are such dishes as fennel-seared Atlantic salmon with artichoke and wild mushroom barigoule and noisettes of Parmesan-crusted veal. Corn-fed Angus beef is always on the menu: try the pepper steak. At breakfast, the French toast with a triple sec–strawberry glaze is an excellent way to awaken your palate. The Sunday brunch here is a worthwhile experience: you can get prime rib and sushi as well as omelets. ⊠ *Westin Grand Bohemian, 325 S. Orange Ave., Downtown Orlando* ☎ *407/313–9000* ⊕ *www.grandbohemianhotel.com* ⊟ *AE, D, DC, MC, V* ⚲ *Reservations essential for dinner.*

$$–$$$ ✕ **Concha Me Crazy.** If the name of this sparkling downtown eatery makes you think that it should be contained within Disney property, it's because the place is a product of Johnny Rivers, a former head chef at Disney, who clearly believes Orlando restaurants need silly names. The food is serious business, however. Sure, there's great conch chowder and black bean soup, but other good offerings include peanut-crusted grouper with ginger soy sauce, fire-roasted chicken with cinnamon sweet potatoes, and a great filet mignon with brandy mushroom sauce. There's a big aquarium indoors; outside there's a fine sidewalk seating area. ⊠ *Embassy Suites Hotel, 191 E. Pine St., Downtown Orlando* ☎ *407/ 246–0011* ⊟ *AE, D, DC, MC, V.*

$–$$ ✕ **Harvey's Bistro.** A loyal business crowd peoples this clubby café at lunch. It also attracts a nighttime following by staying open until 11 on weekends. On the upscale menu, which has a good mix of bistro and comfort foods, escargot is the top starter. Pasta favorites include chicken Stroganoff, duck and shrimp in Asian peanut sauce on linguine, and salmon with lobster Alfredo sauce. If you're a red-meat fan, rejoice. Harvey's has a good pot roast, a pan-seared tenderloin, and meatloaf baked in parchment. ⊠ *Bank of America building, 390 N. Orange Ave., Downtown Orlando* ☎ *407/246–6560* ⊕ *www.culinaryconceptsinc. com* ⊟ *AE, D, DC, MC, V* ⊗ *Closed Sun. No lunch Sat.*

French

$$–$$$$ ✕ **Le Provence Bistro Français.** This charming, two-story restaurant in the heart of downtown does a fine imitation of an out-of-the-way bistro in Paris's Left Bank—as long as you don't spot the palm trees out the window. For lunch try the salade niçoise, made with fresh grilled tuna, French string beans, and hard-boiled eggs; or the cassoulet *toulousain,* a hearty mixture of white beans, lamb, pork, and sausage. At dinner you can choose among a six-course prix-fixe menu, a less pricey four-course version, or à la carte options. The bistro doesn't always answer the phone during dinner. ⊠ *50 E. Pine St., Downtown Orlando* ☎ *407/843–1320* ⊟ *AE, DC, MC, V* ⊗ *Closed Sun. No lunch Sat.*

Japanese

$$–$$$$ ✕ **Amura.** A quiet respite from the vibrant—and loud—bars around it, Amura, Japanese for "Asian village," is comfortable sophisticated. There's an extensive list of about 40 sushi choices, from aoyagi (round clams) to yellowtail tuna, as well as tempura-fried shrimp or vegetables.

To get a taste of it all, try the Tokyo special plate—with chicken teriyaki, ginger pork, salmon teriyaki, California roll, and tempura-fried veggies. The Mexican roll, with avocado, shrimp, and jalapeño peppers, makes for an unusual appetizer. The Sand Lake Road location has a big, performance-style dining room, where the tables all surround grills and the chef cooks while you watch. ⊠ *55 W. Church St., Downtown Orlando* ☎ *407/316–8500* ⊠ *7786 W. Sand Lake Rd., I–4 Exit 74A, Southwest Orlando* ☎ *407/370–0007* ⊟ *AE, D, DC, MC, V* ⊘ *No lunch Sun.*

Tex-Mex

¢–$ ✕ **Tijuana Flats.** At this fine little downtown cantina, you'll find a wild, weird assortment of bottled hot sauces from around the world. You can buy a bottle of Blair's Sudden Death or Sgt. Pepper's Tejas Tears for $7, or simply opt for the fiery house brand, free with your meal. Two-fisted burritos, plate-covering chimichangas, and four-alarm chili are the things to get here. Mexican beers and $7.50 pitchers of Dos Equis flow freely. The sidewalk seating area faces the Orange County Historical Center and a pleasant little park. ⊠ *50 E. Central Blvd., Downtown Orlando* ☎ *407/839–0007* ⊟ *AE, D, DC, MC, V.*

Central Orlando

The center of Orlando shows what the town as a whole was like before it became a big theme park. Quiet streets are lined with huge oaks covered with Spanish moss. Museums and galleries are along main thoroughfares, as are dozens of tiny lakes, where herons, egrets, and, yes, alligators, peacefully coexist with human city dwellers. This is quintessential urban Florida.

The restaurants in this area, a good half hour from the Disney tourism area via I–4, tend to have more of their own sense of character and style than the eateries going full tilt for your dollars in Kissimmee or on International Drive.

American/Casual

★ $–$$ ✕ **White Wolf Café.** A perfect fit for Orlando's small but vibrant antiques and art-gallery district, this urbane bistro offers a fine menu and a good sidewalk café area. A great appetizer is the *lavosh* (Mediterranean-style cracker bread) topped with artichoke hearts, sun-dried tomatoes, and mozzarella. Entrées usually include a deep-dish lasagna; there's also an excellent lasagna variation that's made with French bread rather than with pasta. For dessert, try the chocolate hazelnut torte or a chocolate chip truffle cookie. There's live music on Friday and Saturday nights. ⊠ *1829 N. Orange Ave., Central Orlando* ☎ *407/895–5590* ⊕ *www.whitewolfcafe.com* ⊟ *AE, MC, V.*

★ ¢ ✕ **Panera Bread.** Standard upscale urban snacks like bagels, fresh-baked pastries, and cafe latte are the mainstays here, although you can grab a hearty and inexpensive meal like a hot Cuban pork sandwich and a bowl of bean soup and still have change left from a $10 bill. Fresh-baked breads include everything from sourdough to focaccia with basil pesto or Asiago cheese baked in the dough. With 10 locations in Orlando, this place is almost as ubiquitous as McDonald's, with the Lake Eola and Mall at Millenia locations being standouts, and almost all offering outdoor seating sections. ⊠ *227 N. Eola Dr., Thornton Park* ☎ *407/481–1060* ⊠ *4200 Conroy Rd., Mall at Millenia, Southwest Orlando* ☎ *407/248–0811* ⊠ *118 W. Fairbanks, Winter Park* ☎ *407/645–3939* ⊠ *296 E. Michigan St., Central Orlando* ☎ *407/481–9880* ⊠ *696 E. Altamonte Dr., Altamonte Springs* ☎ *407/332–7600* ⊠ *1210 International Pkwy., Lake Mary* ☎ *407/804–8340* ⊠ *11472 University Blvd., East Orlando* ☎ *407/273–4411* ⊠ *473 N. Alafaya Trail, Waterford Lakes*

Where to Eat in Central Orlando & Outlying Towns

☎ 407/737–3011 ✉ *West Town Corners; 200 S. State Rd. 434* ☎ *407/ 831–3741* ✉ *Fashion Square Mall; 3462 E. Colonial Dr.* ☎ *407/228– 2874* ✉ *7826 W. Sand Lake Rd., Sand Lake Road Area* ☎ *407/226– 6992* ▤ *AE, MC, V.*

Barbecue

¢–$ ✕ **Wildfires Bar n' Grill.** Inside a former auto repair shop and gas station, Wildfires is the latest addition to the trendy dining district growing in Thornton Park, just east of downtown and near Lake Eola. St. Louis ribs, rubbed with spices and slowly roasted, are the specialty here. The ribs are both spicy and tender, and you can get a half-rack and couple of sides, like pasta salad and barbecued beans, for $10. Another good choice is the chicken, rib, and pork sampler plate ($14). If you're not a red-meat person, try the wood-grilled salmon with cilantro-lime vinaigrette. ✉ *700 E. Washington St., Thornton Park* ☎ *407/ 872–8665* ▤ *MC, V.*

Chinese

¢–$ ✕ **Forbidden City.** The Hunan-style food, served inside what was once a gas station, is terrific. Start with the diced chicken with pine nuts wrapped in icy lettuce cups. It's a delightful mix of hot and cold. The sesame chicken goes well with bright-green broccoli in a subtle garlic sauce. The traditional 10-ingredient lo mein is full of fresh shrimp, chicken, beef, and pork. ✉ *5370 W. Colonial Dr., Central Orlando* ☎ *407/ 293–5803* ✉ *948 N. Mills Ave., Downtown Orlando* ☎ *407/894– 5005* ▤ *MC, V* ☻ *Closed Sun. No lunch Sat.*

Contemporary

$–$$$ ✕ **HUE.** On the ground floor of a condo high-rise on the edge of Lake Eola, this place takes its name from a self-created acronym: Hip Urban Environment. While it may not be quite as cool as its press clippings, the food is both good and eclectic, with offerings ranging from succulent fried oysters to tasty crab cakes to a good filet mignon, served with Portobello polenta. Unfortunately, the large outdoor dining area overlooks the street and not the lake. ✉ *629 E. Central Blvd., Thornton Park* ☎ *407/849–1800* 🖷 *407/872–3348* ⌕ *Reservations not accepted* ▤ *AE, D, DC, MC, V.*

Cuban

★ $–$$$ ✕ **Numero Uno.** To the followers of this long-popular Latin restaurant, the name is accurate. Downtowners have been filling the place up at lunch for years. It bills itself as "the home of paella," and that's probably the best choice. If you have a good appetite and you either called to order ahead or can spare the 75-minute wait, then try the paella Valenciana, made with yellow rice, sausage, chicken, fish, and Spanish spices and served with a side order of plantains. Otherwise, you can go for traditional Cuban fare like shredded flank steak or arroz con pollo. Take I–4 Exit 81A or 81B. ✉ *2499 S. Orange Ave., Central Orlando* ☎ *407/841– 3840* ▤ *AE, D, DC, MC, V.*

French

$$–$$$$
Fodor'sChoice ✕ **Le Coq au Vin.** Chef-owner Louis Perrotte is something of a culinary god in Orlando, but he doesn't let it go to his head. He operates a modest little kitchen in a small house in south Orlando. Perrotte's homey eatery is usually filled with locals who appreciate the lovely traditional French fare: homemade chicken liver pâté, fresh trout with champagne sauce, and Long Island duck with green peppercorns. The menu changes seasonally to insure the freshest ingredients for house specialties. But the house namesake dish is always available and always excellent. For dessert, try the Grand Mariner soufflé. ✉ *4800 S. Orange Ave., Central Orlando* ☎ *407/851–6980* ▤ *AE, DC, MC, V* ☻ *Closed Mon.*

Greek

$–$$ ✕ **The Athenian.** This unpretentious little place serves up some great Greek cooking at reasonable prices. Don't miss the classic *moussaka* (eggplant, potatoes, and meat sauce, topped with sour cream). For a cross section of Hellenic cookery, go for the Athenian combo, with *dolmades* (stuffed grape leaves), moussaka, gyro, and *tsatsiki* (yogurt-based) sauce, all for $13, or try the octopus and *spanakopita* (spinach pie) combo for the same price. The sidewalk café section is pleasant. ✉ *2918 N. Orange Ave., Central Orlando* ☎ *407/898–2151* ▣ *AE, MC, V.*

Italian

$–$$ ✕ **Gargi's Italian Restaurant.** In the area just north of downtown filled with antique shops and overlooking Lake Ivanhoe is a great mom-and-pop Italian restaurant with fine pasta. If you crave old-fashioned spaghetti and meatballs, lasagna, or manicotti made with sauces that have been simmering all day, this storefront hole-in-the-wall is the place. If you want more than basic pasta, try the veal marsala or the tasty linguine with shrimp, peppers, and marinara. Take I-4 Exit 84. ✉ *1421 N. Orange Ave., Central Orlando* ☎ *407/894–7907* ▣ *AE, MC, V* ☞ *Beer and wine only* ☉ *Closed Sun.*

$–$$ ✕ **La Fontanella Da Nino.** A courtyard seating area with a lovely fountain makes a great spot to enjoy a glass of pinot grigio or chardonnay, along with what the menu calls *stuzzichini*, a Neapolitan phrase that means "something to nibble on." The *peperoni saltati* (roasted peppers sautéed with garlic, black olives, and capers) is a good choice, as is the *melenzane all griglia* (grilled marinated eggplant). A standout entrée is *pollo Scarpariello* (pasta with chicken, grilled sausage, and mushrooms in a cream sauce). ✉ *900 E. Washington St., Thornton Park* ☎ *407/425–0033* ▣ *AE, MC, V* ☉ *No lunch Sun.*

Fodor'sChoice

$–$$ ✕ **Tiramisu Cafe.** As the name implies, this is a great place to pop in for a quick Italian dessert and a cup of cappuccino. But this small bistro on the edge of Lake Ivanhoe in Orlando's antiques and gallery district offers a lot more, including a sidewalk seating area and some great light Italian cooking. Focaccia pizzas—individual servings on crusts of Italian flatbread—are among the better choices, as are the Italian soups, smoked and grilled fish selections, and focaccia sandwiches, especially the smoked salmon with capers and onions. Take I-4 Exit 84. ✉ *399 Ivanhoe Blvd., at Orange Ave., Central Orlando* ☎ *407/228–0303* ▣ *AE, MC, V* ☉ *Closed Sun.*

★ ¢–$ ✕ **Alfonso's Pizza & More.** This is a strong contender for the best pizza in Orlando (in the non–wood-fired-oven division). Since it's just across the street from a high school, things get frenzied at lunch. The hand-tossed pizza's toppings range from pepperoni to pineapple—but the calzones and some of the pasta dishes, such as fettuccine Alfredo, are quite worthy as well. There are also subs and salads for lighter fare. The secret to the superior pizza is simple: the dough and all the sauces are made from scratch daily. Take I-4 Exit 84 to the College Park neighborhood area. ✉ *3231 Edgewater Dr., College Park* ☎ *407/872–7324* ▣ *MC, V.*

¢–$ ✕ **Anthony's Pizzeria.** This neighborhood spot in Thornton Park is well known to locals for its deep-dish pizza, but the pasta is worthy in its own right—and correctly priced for those on a budget. Try the sausage and peppers in marinara sauce with your choice of spaghetti, ziti, or linguine. If you're in a hurry, go for the pizza by the slice, ranging from $1.65 for plain cheese to $3.95 for a slice of the Anthony's Extravaganza, with cheese, pepperoni, sausage, green peppers, onions, mushrooms, and sliced meatballs. ✉ *100 N. Summerlin, Thornton Park* ☎ *407/648-0009* ▣ *MC, V.*

Fodor'sChoice

Japanese

$$–$$$ ✕ **Shari Sushi Lounge.** Resplendent with chrome and glass, this trendy eatery has more of the atmosphere of a fast-lane singles bar than of an Oriental oasis, but the items from the kitchen—fresh sushi and daily fresh fish entrées—acquit the place well as a legit dining establishment. Start with the tako (not taco) salad, with octopus, cucumber, enoki mushrooms, mandarin oranges, and spicy kim chee sauce. ⊠ *621 E. Central, Thornton Park* ☎ *407/420–9420* ⊟ *AE, D, DC, MC, V.*

Mexican

¢ ✕ **Baja Burrito Kitchen.** Because of the excellent fish tacos as well as a specialty called the LA Burrito (grilled chicken or steak, plus guacamole and jack cheese), Baja Burrito calls itself a "Cal-Mex" palace. However, the mainstays of the menu—like a huge, $6 burrito filled with chicken or steak, pinto beans, guacamole, and sour cream—will be familiar to denizens of the American heartland. It's not fancy, but it won't drain your wallet. ⊠ *2716 E. Colonial, Central Orlando* ☎ *407/895–6112* ⊠ *931 N. State Rd. 434, Altamonte Springs* ☎ *407/788–2252* ⌂ *Reservations not accepted* ⊟ *AE, D, MC, V.*

Seafood

$$–$$$ ✕ **Straub's Fine Seafood.** With items like escargots for $6—less than the price of a burger in Kissimmee—Straub's proves that the farther you drive from Disney, the less you pay. Owner Robert Straub, a fishmonger of many years, prepares a fine mesquite-grilled Atlantic salmon with béarnaise on the side. He fillets all his own fish and won't serve anything he can't get fresh. The Captain's platter, with lobster and mesquite-grilled shrimp, is a great choice. The menu states the calorie count and fat content of every fish item, but for the coconut-banana cream pie you just don't want to know. ⊠ *5101 E. Colonial Dr., Central Orlando* ☎ *407/273–9330* ⊠ *512 E. Altamonte Dr., Altamonte Springs* ☎ *407/831–2250* ⊟ *AE, D, DC, MC, V.*

Steak

$$$–$$$$ ✕ **Del Frisco.** Locals like this quiet, uncomplicated steak house. Del Frisco delivers carefully prepared, corn-fed beef and attentive service. When your steak arrives, the waiter asks you to cut into it and check that it was cooked as you ordered it. The menu is simple: T-bones, porterhouses, filets mignons, and such seafood as Maine lobster, Alaskan crab, and a good lobster bisque. Bread is baked daily at the restaurant, and the bread pudding, with a Jack Daniels sauce, is worth a try. There's a piano bar next to the dining room. ⊠ *729 Lee Rd., Central Orlando* ☎ *407/645–4443* ⊟ *AE, D, DC, MC, V* ⊘ *Closed Sun. No lunch.*

$$–$$$ ✕ **Linda's La Cantina.** Beef is serious business here. As the menu says, management "cannot be responsible for steaks cooked medium-well and well done." Despite that stuffy-sounding caveat, this down-home steakhouse has been a favorite among locals since the Eisenhower administration. The menu is short and to the point, including about a dozen steaks and just enough ancillary items to fill up a page. Among the best is the La Cantina large T-bone—more beef than most can handle, for $22. With every entrée you get a heaping order of spaghetti (which isn't particularly noteworthy) or a baked potato. ⊠ *4721 E. Colonial Dr., Central Orlando* ☎ *407/894–4491* ⊕ *www.lindaslacantina.com* ⊟ *AE, D, MC, V.*

Vietnamese

¢ ✕ **Little Saigon.** This local favorite is one of the best of Orlando's ethnic restaurants. Sample the summer rolls (spring-roll filling in a soft wrapper) with peanut sauce, or excellent Vietnamese crepes, filled with shredded pork and noodles. Then move on to the grilled pork and egg, served atop rice noodles, or the traditional soup, filled with noodles, rice, vegetables, and your choice of either chicken or seafood; ask to have extra meat in the soup if you're hungry, and be sure they bring you the mint and bean sprouts to sprinkle in. ✉ *1106 E. Colonial Dr., Central Orlando* ☎ *407/423–8539* ▤ *MC, V* ☞ *Beer and wine only.*

Orlando International Airport

Eclectic

$$–$$$ ✕ **Hemisphere.** The view competes with the food on the ninth floor of the Hyatt Regency Orlando International hotel. Although Hemisphere overlooks a major runway, you don't get any jet noise, just a nice air show. Entrées change frequently, but often include selections such as miso-glazed sea bass on soba noodles, tamarind barbecue glazed filet mignon with fingerling potatoes, and grilled swordfish with truffle-scented mashed potatoes. Desserts change daily, but there's always a good tiramisu. ✉ *Hyatt Regency Orlando International Airport, Orlando International Airport Area* ☎ *407/825–1234 Ext. 1900* ▤ *AE, DC, MC, V* ☻ *No lunch.*

OUTLYING TOWNS

Winter Park

Winter Park is a charming suburb on the northern end of Orlando, 25 minutes from Disney. It's affluent, understated, and sophisticated—and can be pleasurable when you need a break from the theme parks. To get into the area, follow I–4 to Exit 87.

American Casual

$ ✕ **Briarpatch Restaurant & Ice Cream Parlor.** With a faux country store facade, this small eatery makes quite a contrast to its neighbors—upscale stores such as Gucci. But it makes a great place to catch a hearty and inexpensive meal before shopping 'til you drop. Standouts include pesto-crusted salmon with bowtie pasta and old fashioned liver and onions with mashed potatoes. Good breakfast choices include Belgian waffles and raisin bread French toast and freshly made scones. About 30 flavors of ice cream are available to help cool off on those long strolls down Park Avenue. ✉ *252 Park Ave. N., Winter Park* ☎ *407/628–8651* ⌨ *Reservations not accepted* ▤ *AE, D, DC, MC, V.*

Chinese

$–$$ ✕ **P. F. Chang's.** Two huge, faux-stone, Ming dynasty–style statues of horses stand guard outside this Chinese restaurant, which is a bit like a California wine bar. There's a lengthy wine list, for instance, and very un-Asian desserts such as chocolate macadamia-nut pie and fruit tortes. Standout entrées include the Cantonese duck, Chang's spicy chicken, and lemon scallops. The house appetizer, Soothing Lettuce Wraps, consists of lettuce leaves in which you wrap an assortment of stir-fried meats and vegetables. The Mall at Millenia location has an outdoor dining area. ✉ *423 N. Orlando Ave., U.S. 17–92, Winter Park* ☎ *407/622–0188* ✉ *4200 Conroy Rd., Mall at Millenia, Southwest Orlando* ⊕ *www.pfchangs.com* ☎ *407/345–2888* ▤ *AE, MC, V.*

Contemporary

$–$$$ ✕ **Cheesecake Factory.** Here's a place to go for more than 30 varieties of the namesake treat, from passion fruit piña colada to chocolate raspberry truffle. If you just don't like cheesecake, try the excellent apple dumplings. But this big restaurant also offers many full-meal options, from baby-back ribs to wood-oven pizza to herb-crusted fillet of salmon to Thai chicken pasta. Great appetizers include avocado and sun-dried tomato egg rolls and bruschetta topped with chopped tomato, garlic, basil, and olive oil. ⊠ *520 N. Orlando Ave., Winter Park* ☎ *407/644–4220* ⊠ *4200 Conroy Rd., Mall at Millenia, Southwest Orlando* ☎ *407/226–0333* ⊕ *www.thecheesecakefactory.com* ♧ *Reservations not accepted* ▤ *AE, D, DC, MC, V.*

$–$$$ ✕ **Houston's.** This Atlanta-based chain seized a prime spot on big Lake Killarney, with a spectacular view. As you watch the egrets and herons on the lake, you can savor some meaty fare. The fancy wood-grilled burger acquits itself well, but there's nothing like the steaks, wood-grilled or pan-seared to your specifications. The grilled fish entrées, such as tuna and salmon, offer tasty alternatives. Of the excellent soups, the New Orleans–style red beans and rice is the best. The patio makes a great place for a drink around sunset. ⊠ *215 S. Orlando Ave., U.S. 17–92, Winter Park* ☎ *407/740–4005* ⊕ *www.houstons.com* ♧ *Reservations not accepted* ▤ *AE, MC, V.*

$ ✕ **Dexter's.** The good wine list and imaginative menu tend to attract quite a crowd of locals. Dexter's has its own wine label and publishes a monthly newsletter for those who appreciate a good varietal. The best entrées include chicken tortilla pie, a stack of cheese-laden tortillas that looks like a spaceship, and Cajun-spiced shrimp served with garlic bucatini. There's often live music on Thursday night. The East Washington location is in gentrified Thornton Park, just east of downtown Orlando; you may be the only out-of-towner here. ⊠ *558 W. New England Ave., Winter Park* ☎ *407/629–1150* ⊠ *808 E. Washington St., Orlando* ☎ *407/648–2777* ⊕ *www.dexwine.com* ♧ *Reservations not accepted* ▤ *AE, D, DC, MC, V.*

Continental

$$–$$$ ✕ **Park Plaza Gardens.** Sitting at the sidewalk café and bar is like sitting on the main street of the quintessential American small town. But the locals know the real gem is hidden inside—a smallish (seats about 30) atrium with live ficus trees, a brick floor, and brick walls that give the place a Vieux Carré feel. The menu is not exceptionally creative, but the crispy chicken Oscar with béarnaise and blue crab topping or the herb-seared New York strip makes a worthy reason to soak up the dining room's fine atmosphere. Sunday brunch frequently includes live jazz. ⊠ *319 Park Ave. S, Winter Park* ☎ *407/645–2475* ⊕ *www.parkplazagardens.com* ▤ *AE, D, DC, MC, V.*

Italian

$$–$$$ ✕ **Brio Tuscan Grille.** Head to this trendy restaurant for wood-grilled pizzas and oak-grilled steaks, lamb chops, veal scallopini, and even lobster. "Chicken under the Brick" is a whole chicken breast, slow-roasted under a weight. It's served with a tasty, mushroom-laden wine sauce. A good appetizer choice is the *brio bruschetta*, a wood-baked flatbread covered with shrimp scampi, mozzarella, and roasted peppers. The dining room's Italian archways are elegant, but the sidewalk tables are also a good option. ⊠ *480 N. Orlando Ave., Winter Park* ☎ *407/622–5611* ⊠ *4200 Conroy Rd., Mall at Millenia, Southwest Orlando* ☎ *407/351–8909* ⊕ *www.bestitalianusa.com* ▤ *AE, MC, V.*

¢–$$ ✕ **Pannullo's.** The view of the tidy little downtown park across the street rivals the quality of the Italian cuisine when you dine in the sidewalk seating section. But when the rain or the heat drives you indoors, you've still got the consistently great cooking at this place, which includes an excellent chicken or veal piccata and a compelling veal-stuffed tortellini with artichokes and roasted red peppers in a creamy marinara sauce. Pizza-by-the-slice starts at $2.25 if you are in a hurry or on a budget. ⊠ *216 Park Ave. S, Winter Park* ☎ *407/629–7279* ▤ *AE, D, DC, MC, V.*

Japanese

$$–$$$ ✕ **Seito Sushi.** Tucked into a corner of the Winter Park Village, this pleasant eatery combines two great elements: sushi and sidewalk dining. Order a Japanese beer (or some hot sake) and sample the raw fish offerings, including the signature Seito roll, composed of tuna, whitefish, salmon, and crabmeat in a cucumber skin. If you want something exotic, try the "octopus salad," an octopus sushi plate. There's also plenty of inspired cooked cuisine, including baked green mussels, an excellent salmon teriyaki, and even a good New York strip steak. Top off your meal with some red bean ice cream or fried bananas. ⊠ *510 N. Orlando Ave., Winter Park* ☎ *407/644–5050* ▤ *AE, MC, V.*

Seafood

$$–$$$$ ✕ **Black Fin.** Representative offerings at this fish-focused restaurant include Canadian halibut with a Parmesan crust, oak-grilled yellowfin tuna, and Ponce Inlet mahimahi. In addition to the rotating seafood selections, there are such standards as broiled Caribbean lobster, Alaskan king crab, and a lobster and filet mignon combo. Don't overlook the large selection of fresh oyster appetizers prepared on the half shell including Florentine, broussard, or spicy hot. Save room for the carrot cake. The interior feels like an old mansion, even though Black Fin is inside a modern shopping complex. ⊠ *460 N. Orlando Ave., Winter Park* ☎ *407/691–4653* ⊕ *www.blackfinseafood.com* ▤ *AE, D, DC, MC, V.*

Maitland

Not quite as far from Disney as the northernmost Orlando suburbs, this town, 25 minutes from Disney and 5 mi north of downtown Orlando, is still more like reality than you can find on I-Drive. And like most Orlando residential areas, it's dotted with serene lakes shaded by stately oaks and has worthwhile shopping and dining as well. To get into the area, follow I–4 to Exit 90.

Italian

$$–$$$$ ✕ **Antonio's La Fiamma.** The wood-burning grill and oven do more than give the place a delightful smell. They're used to turn out great grilled fish dishes, delicious pizzas, and homemade bread. Try the *zuppa di pesce*, made with plenty of shrimp, scallops, and langostino, and well worth its $23 price tag, or the equally compelling *pollo all'aglio e rosmarin,* which is chicken basted with fresh rosemary, garlic, and olive oil, and then roasted over a wood-burning rotisserie. For a quick bite, the deli-style version downstairs has many of the same menu items. ⊠ *611 S. Orlando Ave., U.S. 17–92, Maitland* ☎ *407/645–5523* ⊕ *www. antoniosonline.com* ▤ *AE, MC, V* ◷ *Closed Sun.*

Altamonte Springs

This suburb is a good 45 minutes (30 mi) from Disney, but it has one thing making it worth the drive—the inverse relationship between prices and proximity to the Magic Kingdom. And it's not just the restaurants; everything from a gallon of gas to a pair of sunglasses costs significantly less in Altamonte than in, say, Kissimmee. To get to the area, follow I–4 to Exit 92.

Tex-Mex

¢–$ ✕ **Amigo's.** Tex-Mex restaurants come and go in Central Florida, but Amigo's, a local chain run by a family of transplanted Texans, is consistently in the top tier. They start with good basics, like refried beans that would play well in San Antonio. Go for the Santa Fe dinner, so big it almost takes a burro to bring it to your table; you can sample tamales, enchiladas, *chiles rellenos* (fried, stuffed peppers), and those wonderful refried beans. Lighter fare includes spinach enchiladas. ⊠ *120 N. West-monte, Altamonte Springs* ☎ *407/774–4334* ⊠ *494 N. Semoran, Winter Park* ☎ *407/657–8111* ⊠ *25 W. Church St., Downtown, Orlando* ☎ *407/999–4885* ⊠ *6036 S. Orange Blossom Trail, South Orlando, Orlando* ☎ *407/857–3144* ⊠ *4250 Alafaya Trail, Oviedo* ☎ *407/ 359–1333* ⌕ *Reservations not accepted* ☰ *AE, MC, V.*

Longwood

A northern suburb 45 minutes from Disney, Longwood is a long way from the tourism treadmill. The community has some worthy restaurants as well. To get into the area, follow I–4 to Exit 94.

Italian

★ $$–$$$ ✕ **Enzo's on the Lake.** This is one of Orlando's foodies' favorite restaurants, even though it's on a tacky stretch of highway filled with used-car lots. Enzo Perlini, the Roman charmer who owns the place, has turned a rather ordinary lakefront house into an Italian villa. It's worth the trip, about 45 minutes from WDW, to sample the antipasti. Mussels in the shell, with a broth of tomatoes, olive oil, and garlic, make a great appetizer. The *bucatini à la Enzo* (sautéed bacon, mushrooms, and peas served over long hollow noodles) is very popular. ⊠ *1130 S. U.S. 17–92, Longwood* ☎ *407/834–9872* ⊕ *www.enzos.com* ☰ *AE, DC, MC, V* ⊙ *Closed Sun.*

Lake Wales

A tiny hamlet about an hour southwest of Walt Disney World, Lake Wales offers no particular reason to visit, except for its lush orange groves, a calming attraction (Cypress Gardens), and one outstanding restaurant. To get into the area, follow I–4 to Exit 55 and U.S. 27 south.

Continental

$$$$ ✕ **Chalet Suzanne.** If you are on your way south, or are visiting Bok Tower Gardens, consider making time for a good meal at this family-owned country inn. Many devotees come for the traditional dinner—all lunch and dinner meals are prix-fixe affairs—or for a sophisticated breakfast of eggs Benedict or Swedish pancakes with lingonberries. The best meal, if you are on a budget, is lunch. The house signature Chicken Suzanne (baked and carefully basted) is tender and worth the dinner price of $59, but it's just as tasty at lunch for $32. ⊠ *3800 Chalet Suzanne Dr., I–4 Exit 55, Lake Wales* ☎ *863/676–6011* ☰ *AE, DC, MC, V* ⊕ *www. chaletsuzanne.com* ⊙ *Closed Mon. June–Aug.*

WHERE TO STAY

FODOR'S CHOICE

Animal Kingdom Lodge, in Walt Disney World

BoardWalk Inn and Villas, in Walt Disney World

Gaylord Palms Resort, in Kissimmee

Grand Floridian Resort & Spa, in Walt Disney World

Hyatt Regency Grand Cypress Resort, near Lake Buena Vista

Ritz-Carlton Orlando Grande Lakes, in Southwestern Orlando

Royal Pacific Resort, in Universal Studios

Studio Plus Orlando, near Universal Studios

Wilderness Lodge, in Walt Disney World

HIGHLY RECOMMENDED

The Courtyard at Lake Lucerne, in Downtown Orlando

Caribbean Beach Resort, in Walt Disney World

Eō Inn & Urban Spa, in Thornton Park

Four Points Hotel, in Downtown Orlando

JW Marriott Orlando Grande Lakes, in Southwestern Orlando

Peabody Orlando, on International Drive

PerriHouse Bed & Breakfast Inn, in Lake Buena Vista

Radisson Resort Parkway, in Kissimmee

Walt Disney World Dolphin, in Lake Buena Vista

Wyndham Palace Resort & Spa, in Downtown Disney

Yacht and Beach Club Resorts, in Walt Disney World

Updated by
Rowland
Stiteler

ONCE UPON A TIME, SIMPLY BEING in the midst of the world's largest concentration of theme parks was enough of a selling point to make most Orlando hotels thrive. But somewhere along the way, as the room inventory topped 120,000 (more hotel rooms than New York City or Los Angeles), the competition became so intense that hotels needed to become attractions unto themselves. Hoteliers learned that you've got to have a bit of showbiz to bring 'em in, so the choices here are anything but ordinary. Orlando may not be Las Vegas, but its hotels are definitely big, fancy, and, in some cases, leaning toward gaudy.

The idea in Orlando is for a hotel to entertain you as much as provide lodging. The Gaylord Palms Resort, with a 4-acre glass-covered atrium, has its own version of the Everglades inside, plus a re-creation of old St. Augustine, a mini–Key West, and a 60-ft sailboat that houses a bar on an indoor waterway. Besides showy lobbies, restaurants, and pool areas, most of the larger hotels also have their own in-house children's clubs, many of which provide clown shows, magic shows, and other forms of live entertainment. It's as if the owners expect you to never leave the hotel during your entire vacation.

Most of the bigger, glitzier hotels have room rates comensurate with their huge construction and maintenance budgets, but many other hotels maintain moderate and inexpensive rates. Because of the sheer number of properties in the Orlando area, you will find choices in every price range. One trend is the proliferation of all-suites properties, many with relatively low rates. Virtually all these suites have in-room kitchens, making them a great option for families on a budget. These properties can be found in the newer sections of International Drive; along Palm Parkway, just east of State Road 535, I–4 Exit 68; and north of Universal Orlando, off Kirkman Road, I–4 Exit 75A.

Your first big decision, however, will probably be whether to stay within WDW or outside the property. Clearly, Disney is a major player in the Orlando hotel market, with more than 27,000 rooms, about a quarter of all hotel rooms in the metro area. If you're coming to Orlando for only a few days and are interested solely in the Magic Kingdom, Epcot, and other Disney attractions, then hotels in Walt Disney World Resort— whether or not they're actually owned by Disney—are definitely the most convenient. The on-site hotels were built with families in mind. Older children can use the transportation system on their own without inviting trouble. Younger children get a thrill from knowing that they're actually staying in Walt Disney World.

If you're planning to visit attractions other than WDW or if the Disney resorts seem too rich for your blood, then staying off-site holds a number of advantages. You enjoy more peace and quiet and may have easier access to Orlando, SeaWorld, and Universal Studios, and you're almost certain to save money. To help you find your perfect room, we've reviewed hundreds of offerings throughout the main hotel hubs both in and surrounding Walt Disney World.

DISNEY-OWNED HOTELS IN WALT DISNEY WORLD® RESORT

With a wide selection of price ranges available, most lodging decisions come down to what area of Walt Disney World Resort or what style of hotel strikes your fancy. Resort hotels predominate, but there are also campsites, trailers, and kitchen-equipped suites and villas. These accommodations are clustered in four different areas: the Magic Kingdom

6

When considering where to stay, give careful thought to the kind of vacation you want, what you want to see during your visit, and how long your trip will last. If you're traveling with children, ask if they stay free with you and if the hotel has children's programs. Finally, don't overlook time spent in transit; if you're not staying at a property in or near Walt Disney World, you may use up a few hours a day sitting in traffic.

One rule of thumb in selecting a hotel—assuming you plan far enough in advance—is to request a brochure or check out the hotel's Web site. If there are lots of pictures of, say, Walt Disney World and no pictures of the hotel, chances are that the hotel is bare-bones. Places that don't renovate regularly often try to use proximity to Disney as their sole selling point.

Staying in WDW
If you stay in WDW, you can put aside your car keys, because Disney buses and monorails are efficient enough to make it possible to visit one park in the morning and another after lunch, with a Park Hopper pass. You have the freedom to return to your hotel for R&R when the crowds are thickest, and if it turns out that half the family wants to spend the afternoon in one of the parks and the other half wants to float around Typhoon Lagoon, it's not a problem.

Rooms in the more expensive Disney-owned properties are large enough to accommodate up to five, and villas sleep six or seven. All room have cable TV with the Disney Channel and a daily events channel.

If you're an on-site guest at a Disney hotel, you are guaranteed entry to parks even when they have reached capacity, as the Magic Kingdom, Disney–MGM Studios, Blizzard Beach, and Typhoon Lagoon sometimes do. And depending on the time of year, Walt Disney World parks often open an hour earlier for Disney hotel guests than for the general public. There are other conveniences, too. You can charge most meals and purchases throughout Walt Disney World to your Disney-owned hotel room. And if you golf, keep in mind that Disney guests get first choice of tee times at the golf courses and can reserve them up to 30 days in advance.

Staying Around Orlando
The hotels closest to Walt Disney World Resort are clustered in a few principal areas: along International Drive within Orlando city limits; the U.S. 192 area, which includes the town limits of Kissimmee, where hotels tend to be small and cheap; and in the Downtown Disney–Lake Buena Vista area around Walt Disney World's northernmost entrance, just off I–4 Exit 68. Nearly every hotel in these areas provides frequent transportation to and from Walt Disney World Resort. In addition, there are some noteworthy, if far-flung, options in the suburbs and in the Greater Orlando area. Because the city isn't very large, even apparently distant properties are seldom more than 45 minutes' drive from Disney toll plazas, as long as traffic is running smoothly. If you're willing to make the commute, you'll probably save a bundle. Whereas accommodations at the Hilton on Hotel Plaza Boulevard, near Downtown Disney, cost upwards of $200 a

night in season, another Hilton about 45 minutes away in Altamonte Springs has rates that start $60 lower. Other costs, such as gas and restaurants, are also lower in the northeast suburbs. One suburban caveat: traffic on I–4 in Orlando experiences typical freeway gridlock during morning (7–9) and evening (4–6) rush hours—unless you are extremely patient, you should try to avoid the interstate during these times.

Reservations

Reserve your hotel several months in advance—as much as a year ahead if you want to snag the best rooms during high season. All on-site accommodations that are owned by Disney may be booked through the **Walt Disney World Central Reservations Office** (⌂ Box 10100, Suite 300, Lake Buena Vista 32830 ☎ 407/934–7639 ⊕ www.disneyworld.com). People with disabilities can call **WDW Special Request Reservations** (☎ 407/939–7807) to get information or book rooms at any of the on-site Disney properties. Rooms at most non-Disney chain hotels can be reserved by calling either the hotel itself or the toll-free number for the entire chain. Be sure to tell the reservations clerk exactly what you are looking for—location, price range, the number of people in your party, and the dates of your visit. When you book a room, be sure to mention whether you have a disability or are traveling with children and whether you prefer a certain type of bed or have any other concerns. If possible, stay flexible about dates; many hotels and attractions offer seasonal discounts of up to 40%. You may need to pay a deposit for your first night's stay within three weeks of making your reservation. At many hotels you can get a refund if you cancel at least five days before your scheduled arrival. However, individual hotel policies vary, and some properties may require up to 15 days' notice for a full refund. Check before booking.

If neither the WDW Central Reservations Office nor the off-site hotels have space on your preferred dates, look into packages from American Express, Delta, or other operators, which have been allotted whole blocks of rooms. In addition, because there are always cancellations, it's worth trying at the last minute; for same-day bookings, call the property directly. Packages, including airfare, cruises, car rentals, and hotels both on and off Disney property, can be arranged through your travel agent or **Walt Disney Travel Co.** (✉ 7100 Municipal Dr., Orlando 32819 ☎ 407/828–3232 ⊕ www.disneyworld.com).

Prices

The lodgings we list are the top selections of their type in each category. Rates are lowest from early January to mid-February, from late-April to mid-June, and from mid-August to the third week in December; low rates often remain in place longer at non-Disney properties. Hotels in the Lake Buena Vista area and off International Drive are less expensive than those on Walt Disney World or Universal Studios property. Always call several places—availability and special deals can often drive room rates at a $$$$ hotel down into the $$ range—and don't forget to ask if you're eligible for a discount. Many hotels offer special rates for members of, for example, the American Automobile Association (AAA) or the American Association of Retired Persons (AARP). Don't overlook the savings to be gained from preparing your own breakfast and maybe a few other meals as well, which you can do if you choose a room or suite with a kitchenette or kitchen. In listings, we always name the facilities that are available, but we don't specify whether they cost extra. When pricing accommodations, always ask what's included and what entails an additional charge.

WHAT IT COSTS					
	$$$$	**$$$**	**$$**	**$**	**¢**
DOUBLE ROOMS	over $220	$160–$220	$110–$160	$70–$110	under $70

Price categories reflect the range between the least and most expensive standard double rooms in non-holiday high season, based on the European Plan (with no meals) unless otherwise noted. City and state taxes (10%–12%) are extra.

resort area has ritzy hotels, all of which lie on the Magic Kingdom monorail route and are only minutes away from the park. Fort Wilderness Resort and Campground, with trailers and RV and tent sites, is just southeast of the Magic Kingdom. The Epcot resort area, south of the park, includes the luxurious Yacht and Beach Club resorts and villas, as well as the popular Caribbean Beach Resort, Coronado Springs Resort, and BoardWalk Inn and Villas. The Downtown Disney–Lake Buena Vista resort area, east of Epcot, is near Pleasure Island and the Downtown Disney shopping and entertainment complex. Accommodations include two midprice resorts with an Old South theme. The fourth resort area comprises two budget-priced hotel complexes: All-Star Village, in the park's southwest corner not far from U.S. 192, and the Pop Century Resort, on Osceola Parkway.

Magic Kingdom Area

Take I–4 Exit 62, 64B, or 65.

$$$$ ☒ **Contemporary Resort.** Looking like an intergalactic docking bay, this 15-story, flat-topped pyramid bustles from dawn to after midnight. Upper floors of the main tower (where rooms are more expensive) offer a great view of all the day and night activities in and around the Magic Kingdom. Rooms have a modern look, with lamps that look like they might have come from the Sharper Image, and those facing the Magic Kingdom have a great view of the evening fireworks show. Restaurants include the character-meal palace Chef Mickey's, the laid-back Concourse Steak House, and the top-floor and top-rated California Grill. ☎ 407/824-1000 🖷 407/824-3539 ➾ *1,008 rooms, 36 suites* ♨ *3 restaurants, snack bar, room service, in-room data ports, in-room safes, some refrigerators, cable TV, golf privileges, 3 pools, wading pool, 6 tennis courts, health club, hair salon, indoor and outdoor hot tubs, massage, beach, boating, marina, waterskiing, shuffleboard, volleyball, 2 lobby lounges, shops, baby-sitting, children's programs (ages 4–12), playground, laundry facilities, laundry service, concierge, concierge floor, business services, convention center, meeting rooms, no-smoking rooms* ▤ *AE, D, DC, MC, V.*

$$$$ ☒ **Grand Floridian Resort & Spa.** This Victorian-style property on the shores
Fodor'sChoice of the Seven Seas Lagoon has a red gabled roof, delicate gingerbread, rambling verandas, and brick chimneys. Rooms have ornate hardwood furniture and fancy-print carpeting. Add a dinner or two at Victoria and Albert's, or Cítricos, and you'll probably spend more in a weekend here than on an average mortgage payment, but you'll have the memory of the best Disney offers. The Grand Floridian is what Disney considers its flagship resort—no other has better amenities or higher rates. ☎ 407/824-3000 🖷 407/824-3186 ➾ *900 rooms, 90 suites* ♨ *5 restaurants, snack bar, room service, in-room data ports, in-room safes, cable TV, golf privileges, 2 tennis courts, 3 pools, hair salon, health club, massage, spa, beach, boating, marina, croquet, shuffleboard, volleyball, wading pool, waterskiing, 4 lounges, video game room, baby-sitting, children's*

programs (ages 4–12), playground, laundry facilities, laundry service, concierge, concierge floor, business services, convention center, meeting rooms, no-smoking rooms ⊟ AE, D, DC, MC, V.

$$$$ ▢ **Polynesian Resort.** If it weren't for the kids in Mickey Mouse caps, you might think you were in Fiji. A three-story tropical atrium fills the lobby. Orchids bloom alongside coconut palms and banana trees, and water cascades from volcanic rock fountains. A mainstay here is the evening luau (Wednesday through Sunday), in which Polynesian dancers perform before a feast with Hawaiian-style roast pork. Rooms sleep five, since they all have two queen-size beds and a daybed. Lagoon-view rooms—which overlook the Electrical Water Pageant—are the most peaceful and the priciest. Most rooms have a balcony or patio. ☎ 407/824–2000 ⊟ 407/824–3174 ⇩ 853 rooms, 5 suites ⚭ 3 restaurants, snack bar, room service, in-room data ports, in-room safes, cable TV, golf privileges, 2 pools, wading pool, health club, hair salon, massage, beach, boating, shuffleboard, volleyball, bar, lobby lounge, video game room, baby-sitting, children's programs (ages 4–12), playground, laundry facilities, laundry service, concierge, concierge floors, business services, no-smoking rooms ⊟ AE, D, DC, MC, V.

$$$$ ▢ **Fort Wilderness Resort Cabins.** If you're seeking a calm spot amid the theme-park storm, you need go no farther than these 700 acres of scrubby pine, tiny streams, and peaceful canals on the shore of subtropical Bay Lake, about a mile from the Wilderness Lodge. This is about as relaxed as it gets in Walt Disney World. Sports facilities abound, bike trails are popular, and there's a marina where you can rent a sailboat. In the old days people stayed here when the rest of moderately priced Orlando was booked up, but now people are calling months in advance and requesting the same Wilderness Cabin they had last year. These perfectly comfortable accommodations put the relaxed friendliness of Fort Wilderness within reach of families who haven't brought their own RV and don't want to camp out. The larger cabins can accommodate four grown-ups and two youngsters; the bedroom has a double bed and a bunk bed, and the living room has a double sleeper sofa or Murphy bed. ☎ 407/824–2900 ⊟ 407/824–3508 ⇩ 408 cabins ⚭ Cafeteria, grocery, snack bar, cable TV, in-room VCRs, 2 tennis courts, 2 pools, beach, boating, bicycles, basketball, horseback riding, shuffleboard, volleyball, laundry facilities, baby-sitting, playground, no-smoking rooms ⊟ AE, D, DC, MC, V.

$$$$ ▢ **Wilderness Lodge.** The architects outdid themselves with this seven-
FodorśChoice story hotel, modeled after the turn-of-the-20th-century lodges out west. The five-story lobby, supported by towering tree trunks, has an 82-ft-high, three-sided fireplace made of rocks from the Grand Canyon and lit by enormous tepee-shape chandeliers. Two 55-ft-tall hand-carved totem poles complete the illusion. Rooms have leather chairs, patchwork quilts, and cowboy art. Each has a balcony or a patio. The hotel's showstopper is its Fire Rock Geyser, a faux Old Faithful, near the large pool, which begins as a hot spring in the lobby. ☎ 407/824–3200 ⊟ 407/824–3232 ⇩ 728 rooms, 31 suites ⚭ 2 restaurants, room service, in-room data ports, in-room cable TV with movies, pool, wading pool, beach, boating, bicycles, 2 lobby lounges, baby-sitting, children's programs (ages 4–12), laundry facilities, laundry service, concierge, concierge floor, no-smoking rooms ⊟ AE, D, DC, MC, V.

⚠ **Fort Wilderness Resort Campground.** Bringing a tent or RV is one of the cheapest ways to stay on WDW property, especially considering that sites accommodate up to 10. Tent sites with water and electricity are real bargains. RV sites cost more but are equipped with electric, water, and sewage hookups as well as outdoor charcoal grills and picnic tables. Campground guests have full use of the recreational facilities and services available to Fort Wilderness cabin guests, such as horseback riding and tennis. The campgrounds are the only place in WDW where your pet can stay with you, for a $5 daily fee. ☎ 407/824–2900 📠 407/824–3508 ➷ *307 tent sites (90 with full hookups), 386 trailer sites with full hookups* ⌫ *$58–$73* ⚷ *Flush toilets, full hook-ups, dump station, drinking water, guest laundry, showers, food service, grills, picnic tables, electricity, public telephone, playground, 2 pools* ▭ *AE, D, DC, MC, V.*

Epcot Area

Take I–4 Exit 64B or 65.

$$$$ 🏠 **Beach Club Villas.** Everything you could ever want in a vacation home, each villa has a separate living room, kitchen, and one or two bedrooms, except the studios, which are more like hotel rooms. Interiors are soft yellow and green with white iron bedsteads. Private balconies on the upper levels or porches at street level ensure that you can enjoy your morning cup of coffee in the sun with a view of the lake. The villas opened in summer 2002 for time-sharing, but many are available on a per-night rental basis. You'll have access to all the facilities of the adjacent Yacht and Beach Club resorts, including Stormalong Bay. ☎ 407/934–8000 📠 407/934–3850 ➷ *208 villas* ⚷ *Restaurant, snack bar, room service, in-room data ports, in-room safes, cable TV with movies, golf privileges, 2 tennis courts, 3 pools, hair salon, gym, health club, massage, sauna, beach, boating, croquet, volleyball, 3 lobby lounges, video game room, baby-sitting, laundry service, concierge, business services, convention center, no-smoking rooms* ▭ *AE, D, DC, MC, V.*

$$$$ 🏠 **BoardWalk Inn and Villas.** A beautiful re-creation of Victorian-era Atlantic City, WDW's smallest deluxe hotel is the crowning jewel of the

Fodor's Choice BoardWalk complex. WDW's architectural master, Robert A. M. Stern, designed this inn to mimic 19th-century New England building styles. Rooms have floral-print bedspreads and blue-and-white painted furniture. A 200-ft water slide in the form of a classic wooden roller coaster cascades into the pool area. The proximity to the BoardWalk dining and entertainment area is no small benefit: it's where you'll find the popular ESPN Sports Club and some of Disney's better restaurants. ☎ 407/939–5100 *inn;* 407/939–6200 *villas* 📠 407/939–5150 ➷ *370 rooms, 19 suites, 526 villas* ⚷ *3 restaurants, room service, in-room data ports, in-room safes, tennis court, pool, gym, croquet, lobby lounge, nightclub, video game room, baby-sitting, children's programs (ages 4–12), laundry facilities, laundry service, concierge, business services, convention center, no-smoking rooms* ▭ *AE, D, DC, MC, V.*

★ **$$$$** 🏠 **Yacht and Beach Club Resorts.** Straight out of a Cape Cod summer, these properties on Seven Seas Lagoon are coastal-style inns on a grand Disney scale. The five-story Yacht Club has hardwood floors, a lobby full of gleaming brass and polished leather, an oyster-gray clapboard facade, and evergreen landscaping; there's even a lighthouse on its pier. Rooms have white-and-blue naval flags on the bedspreads and a small ship's wheel on the headboard. At the Beach Club, a croquet lawn and cabana-

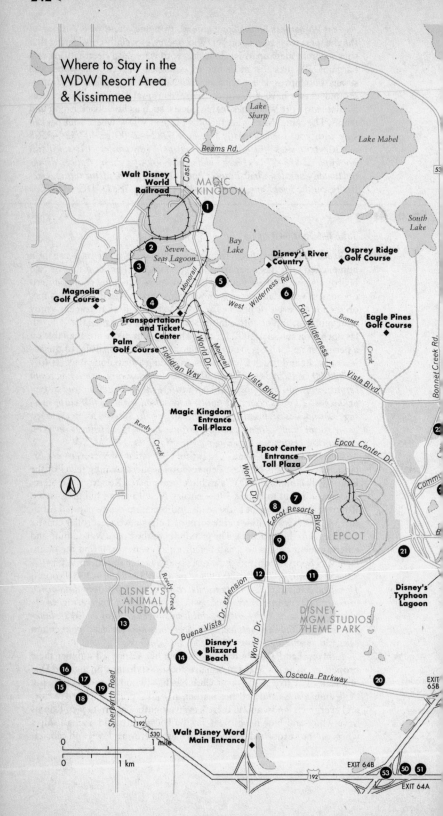

Where to Stay in the
WDW Resort Area
& Kissimmee

Reams Rd.

Cast Dr.

Walt Disney World Railroad

MAGIC KINGDOM

1

Lake Sharp

Lake Mabel

2

Seven Seas Lagoon

3

Bay Lake

South Lake

Disney's River Country

Osprey Ridge Golf Course

5

6

Magnolia Golf Course

West Wilderness Rd.

Fort Wilderness Tr.

Bonnet

Eagle Pines Golf Course

4

Transportation and Ticket Center

Monorail

Palm Golf Course

Floridian Way

Monorail

World Dr.

Vista Blvd.

Vista Blvd.

Bonnet Creek Rd.

Magic Kingdom Entrance Toll Plaza

Reedy Creek

Epcot Center Entrance Toll Plaza

Epcot Center Dr.

World Dr.

8 **7**

Epcot Resorts Blvd.

EPCOT

9

10

21

12

11

Disney's Typhoon Lagoon

DISNEY'S ANIMAL KINGDOM

Reedy Creek

Buena Vista Dr. extension

World Dr.

DISNEY-MGM STUDIOS THEME PARK

13

Disney's Blizzard Beach

14

Osceola Parkway

20

EXIT 65B

16

15 **17** **19**

18

Sherberth Road

192

530

Walt Disney Word Main Entrance

0   1 mile

0   1 km

EXIT 64B

53 **50** **51**

192

EXIT 64A

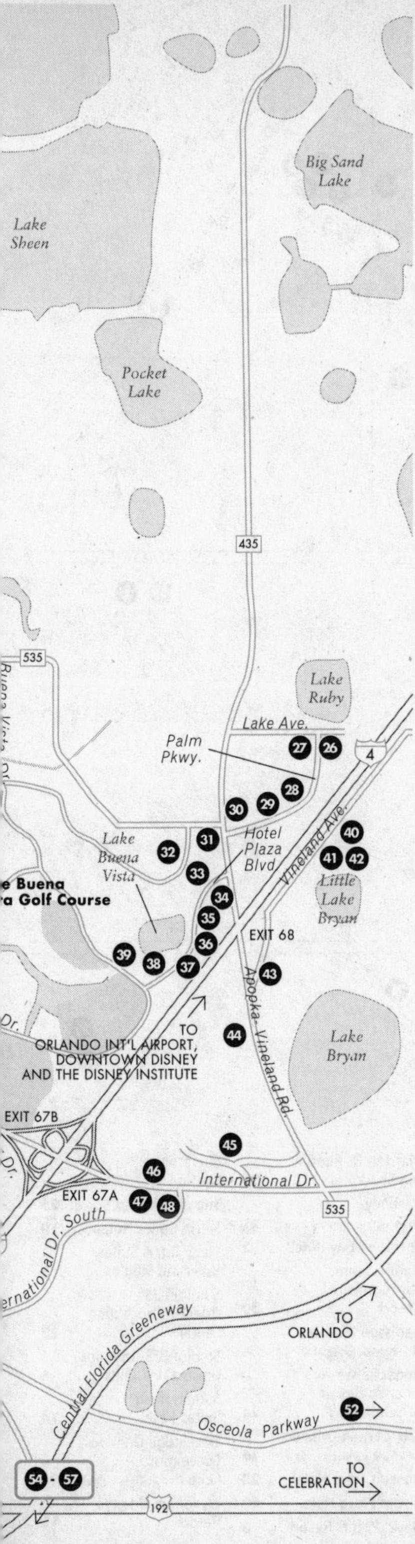

Big Sand Lake
Lake Sheen
Pocket Lake
435
535
Lake Ruby
Lake Ave.
Palm Pkwy.
4
Vineland Ave.
Hotel Plaza Blvd
Lake Buena Vista
e Buena
a Golf Course
Little Lake Bryan
EXIT 68
Apopka-Vineland Rd.
Lake Bryan
TO ORLANDO INT'L AIRPORT, DOWNTOWN DISNEY AND THE DISNEY INSTITUTE
EXIT 67B
International Dr.
EXIT 67A
535
International Dr. South
Central Florida Greeneway
TO ORLANDO
Osceola Parkway
TO CELEBRATION
192
26
27
28
29
30
31
32
33
34
35
36
37
38
39
40
41
42
43
44
45
46
47
48
52
54 - 57

Disney Hotels

All-Star Sports, All-Star Music and All-Star Movies Resorts 14
Animal Kingdom Lodge 13
Beach Club Villas 7
BoardWalk Inn and Villas 11
Caribbean Beach Resort 21
Contemporary Resort 1
Coronado Springs Resort 12
Fort Wilderness Resort and Campground 6
Grand Floridian Resort & Spa 3
Old Key West Resort 22
Polynesian Resort 4
Pop Century Resort 20
Port Orleans Resort–French Quarter 23
Port Orleans Resort–Riverside 24
Walt Disney World Dolphin 9
Walt Disney World Swan 10
Wilderness Lodge 5
Yacht and Beach Club Resorts 8

Other Hotels

AmeriSuites Lake Buena Vista South 52
Best Western Central Florida 54
Best Western Lake Buena Vista Resort Hotel 33
Buena Vista Suites 46
Caribe Royale Resort Suites & Villas 47
Celebration Hotel 53
Chalet Suzanne 55
Country Inn & Suites by Carlson 31
Coutryard by Marriott at Lake Buena Vista 40
Courtyard by Marriott at WDW Resort 36
DoubleTree Guest Suites in the WDW Resort 34
DoubleTree Resort Orlando Maingate 17
Embassy Suites Hotel Lake Buena Vista 26
Fairfield Inn at Lake Buena Vista 41
Gaylord Palms Resort 49
Grosvenor Resort 38
Hampton Inn Orlando Maingate South 56
Hawthorn & Suites Resort Lake Buena Vista 29
Hilton at WDW Resort 37
Holiday Inn Express, Davenport 57
Holiday Inn Family Suites Resort 48
Holiday Inn Hotel & Suites Main Gate East 16
Holiday Inn Maingate West 19
Holiday Inn SunSpree Resort Lake Buena Vista 43
Homewood Suites Resort Lake Buena Vista 28
Hyatt Orlando Hotel . . . 50
Hyatt Regency Grand Cypress Resort 32
La Quinta Inn Lakeside 15
Marriott Residence Inn 27
Marriott's Orlando World Center 45
PerriHouse Bed & Breakfast Inn 25
Quality Suites Maingate East 18
Radisson Resort Parkway 51
Royal Plaza 35
Shades of Green 2
Sheraton Safari Hotel . . 30
Sheraton Vistana Resort 44
SpringHillSuites at Lake Buena Vista 42
Wyndham Palace Resort & Spa in the WDW Resort 39

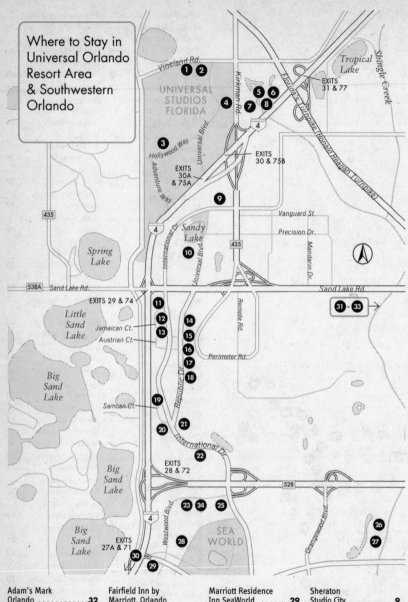

Where to Stay in
Universal Orlando
Resort Area
& Southwestern
Orlando

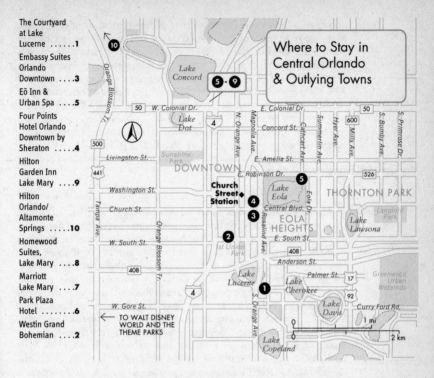

Where to Stay in Central Orlando & Outlying Towns

dotted, white-sand beach set the scene. Stormalong Bay, a 3-acre water park with water slides and whirlpools, is part of this Club. ☎ 407/934–8000 Beach Club; 407/934–7000 Yacht Club 🏢 407/934–3850 Beach Club; 407/934–3450 Yacht Club 🖥 1,213 rooms, 112 suites 🍴 4 restaurants, snack bar, room service, in-room data ports, in-room safes, cable TV with movies, golf privileges, 2 tennis courts, 3 pools, hair salon, gym, health club, massage, sauna, beach, boating, croquet, volleyball, 3 lobby lounges, video game room, baby-sitting, laundry service, concierge, business services, convention center, no-smoking rooms 🚭 AE, D, DC, MC, V.

★ $$–$$$ 🏨 **Caribbean Beach Resort.** Awash in dizzying Caribbean colors, this hotel complex was the first of Disney's moderately priced accommodations. Six palm-studded "villages" share 45-acre Barefoot Bay and its white-sand beach. A promenade circles the lake and bridges over it connect to a 1-acre path-crossed play area called Parrot Cay. The Old Port Royale complex, decorated with pirates' cannons, tropical birds, and statues, has a food court, tropical lounge, and pool with waterfalls and a big water slide. Rooms are done in soft pastel colors like turquoise and peach, with white wood furniture. ☎ 407/934–3400 🏢 407/934–3288 🖥 2,112 rooms 🍴 Restaurant, food court, in-room data ports, in-room safes, cable TV with movies, golf privileges, 7 pools, wading pool, hot tub, beach, boating, bicycles, lobby lounge, baby-sitting, playground, video game room, laundry facilities, laundry service, no-smoking rooms 🚭 AE, D, DC, MC, V.

$$–$$$ 🏨 **Coronado Springs Resort.** This moderately priced hotel on yet another Disney-made lake serves two constituencies. Because of its on-property convention center, it's popular with business groups. But family vaca-

tioners come for its casual southwestern architecture; its wonderful, lively, Mexican-style Pepper Market food court; and its elaborate swimming pool complex, which has a Maya pyramid with a big water slide. There's a full-service health club, but if you like jogging, walking, or biking you're in the right place—a sidewalk circles the property's 15-acre lake. ☎ 407/939–1000 🖷 407/939–1001 🛏 1,967 rooms ♨ 2 restaurants, food court, room service, in-room data ports, in-room safes, cable TV with movies, golf privileges, 4 pools, hair salon, health club, boating, bicycles, bar, video game room, baby-sitting, laundry service, business services, convention center, no-smoking rooms ▤ AE, D, DC, MC, V.

Animal Kingdom Area

Take I–4 Exit 64B.

$$$$ 🖭 **Animal Kingdom Lodge.** Giraffes, zebras, and other African wildlife
Fodor'sChoice roam three 11-acre savannas separated by wings of this grand hotel. The atrium lobby exudes African style, from the inlaid carvings on the hardwood floors to the massive faux-thatched roof almost 100 ft above. Cultural ambassadors, natives of Africa, give talks about their homelands, the animals, and the artwork on display; in the evening, they tell folk stories around the fire circle on the Arusha Rock terrace. All of the somewhat tentlike rooms (with drapes descending from the ceiling) have a bit of African art, including carved headboards and watercolors, penand-ink, or other kinds of original African prints. Every room looks out on one of the savannas, and most also have balconies. ☎ 407/934–7639 🖷 407/934–7629 🛏 1,293 rooms ♨ 3 restaurants, in-room data ports, in-room safes, cable TV with movies, golf privileges, 2 pools, health club, spa, bar, lobby lounge, baby-sitting, children's programs (ages 4–12), playground, laundry facilities, laundry service, no-smoking rooms ▤ AE, D, DC, MC, V.

Downtown Disney Area

Take I–4 Exit 64B or 68.

$$$$ 🖭 **Old Key West Resort.** A red-and-white lighthouse helps you find your way through this marina-style resort. Freestanding villas resemble turn-of-the-20th-century Key West houses, with white clapboard siding and private balconies that overlook the waterways winding through the grounds. The one-, two-, or three-bedroom houses have whirlpools in the master bedrooms, full-size kitchens, full-size washers and dryers, and outdoor patios. The 2,265-square-ft three-bedroom grand villas accommodate up to 12 adults—so grab some friends. ☎ 407/827–7700 🖷 407/827–7710 🛏 704 units ♨ Restaurant, in-room data ports, in-room safes, cable TV with movies, snack bar, golf privileges, 3 tennis courts, 4 pools, health club, spa, boating, bicycles, basketball, shuffleboard, lobby lounge, video game room, baby-sitting, playground, laundry facilities, laundry service, no-smoking rooms ▤ AE, D, DC, MC, V.

$$–$$$ 🖭 **Port Orleans Resort–French Quarter.** This vision of New Orleans has ornate row houses with vine-covered balconies, clustered around squares planted with magnolias. Lamp-lighted sidewalks are named for French Quarter thoroughfares. The rooms themselves are fairly standard. The food court serves such Crescent City specialties as jambalaya and beignets. Doubloon Lagoon, one of Disney's most exotic pools, includes a clever "sea serpent" water slide that swallows swimmers and then spits them into the water. ☎ 407/934–5000 🖷 407/934–5353 🛏 1,008 rooms ♨ Restaurant, food court, in-room safes, in-room data ports, cable TV with video games, golf privileges, pool, wading pool, hot tub, boating, *bicycles, croquet, lobby lounge, baby-sitting, laundry facilities, laundry service, concierge, no-smoking rooms* ⊟ *AE, D, DC, MC, V.*

$$-$$$ 🏨 **Port Orleans Resort–Riverside.** Disney's Imagineers drew inspiration from the Old South for this sprawling resort. Buildings look like plantation-style mansions and rustic bayou dwellings. Rooms accommodate up to four in two double beds. Elegantly decorated, they have wooden armoires and gleaming brass faucets; a few rooms have king-size beds. The registration area looks like a steamboat interior, and the 3½-acre, old-fashioned swimming-hole complex called Ol' Man Island has a pool with slides, rope swings, and a nearby play area. ☎ 407/934–6000 🖷 407/934–5777 ⟿ *2,048 rooms* ♧ *Restaurant, in-room data ports, in-room safes, cable TV with movies, snack bar, golf privileges, 3 tennis courts, 4 pools, health club, spa, boating, bicycles, basketball, shuffleboard, lobby lounge, video game room, baby-sitting, playground, laundry facilities, laundry service, no-smoking rooms* ⊟ *AE, D, DC, MC, V.*

All-Star Village & Pop Century Resort

Take I–4 Exit 64B.

$–$$ 🏨 **All-Star Sports, All-Star Music, and All-Star Movies Resorts.** These Disney economy resorts depict five sports themes, five music themes, and movie themes from *Fantasia, 101 Dalmatians,* and *The Mighty Ducks* to *The Love Bug.* Stairwells shaped like giant bongos frame Calypso, whereas in the Sports resort, 30-ft tennis rackets strike balls the size of small cars, and in the Movies resort, giant icons like *Toy Story*'s Buzz Lightyear frame each building. Each room has two double beds, a closet rod, an armoire, and a desk. The All-Star resorts are as economically priced as most any hotel in Orlando. The food courts sell standard fast food. ☎ 407/939–5000 *Sports;* 407/939–6000 *Music;* 407/939–7000 *Movies* 🖷 407/939–7333 *Sports;* 407/939–7222 *Music;* 407/939–7111 *Movies* ⟿ *1,920 rooms at each* ♧ *3 food courts, room service, 6 pools, in-room data ports, in-room safes, cable TV with movies, 3 bars, video game rooms, baby-sitting, playground, laundry facilities, laundry service, Internet, no-smoking rooms* ⊟ *AE, D, DC, MC, V.*

$–$$ 🏨 **Pop Century Resort.** Following the success of the moderately priced, gargantuan All-Star Resorts, this massive budget-hotel megaplex is set to open sometime in 2004. Three-story-tall juke boxes and bowling pins herald its arrival, and the pop-culture theme continues with huge sculptures of yo-yos and Big Wheel tricycles scattered about the grounds. Brightly colored rooms are functional for families, with two double beds or one king. A big food court, cafeteria-style eatery, and room-delivery pizza service offer reasonably priced food. ☎ 407/934–7639 ⟿ *2,880 rooms* ♧ *Food court, room service, in-room data ports, in-room safes, cable TV with movies, 2 pools, hair salon, health club, bicycles, bar, video game room, baby-sitting, laundry service, no-smoking rooms* ⊟ *AE, D, DC, MC, V.*

OTHER HOTELS IN & NEAR WALT DISNEY WORLD RESORT

Although not operated by the Disney organization, the Swan and the Dolphin just outside Epcot, the military's Shades of Green Resort near the Magic Kingdom, and the seven hotels along Hotel Plaza Boulevard near Downtown Disney call themselves "official" Walt Disney World hotels. While the Swan, Dolphin, and Shades of Green have the special privileges of on-site Disney hotels, such as free transportation to and from the parks and early park entry, the Downtown Disney resorts have their own systems to shuttle hotel guests to the parks.

Magic Kingdom Area

Take I–4 Exit 64B or 67.

¢–$ 🏨 **Shades of Green on Walt Disney World Resort.** Operated by the U.S. Armed Forces Recreation Center, the resort is available only to vacationing active-duty and retired personnel from the armed forces, as well as reserves, National Guard, and active civilian employees of the Department of Defense. Rates vary with your rank, but are significantly less than rates at Disney hotels open to the general public. While the resort is closed for renovations until December 2003, you may be able to stay at the Contemporary Resort for reduced rates. Contact Shades of Green for more information. ⊠ *1950 W. Magnolia Palm Dr., Lake Buena Vista 32830-2789* ☎ *407/824–3600 or 888/593–2242* 🖷 *407/824–3665* ⊕ *www.shadesofgreen.org* ⚄ *2 restaurants, room service, in-room data ports, in-room safes, cable TV with movies and video games, golf privileges, 2 outdoor tennis courts, 2 pools, wading pool health club, 2 bars, baby-sitting, children's programs (ages 4–12), laundry facilities, laundry service, no-smoking rooms* ▭ *AE, D, MC, V.*

Epcot Area

Take I–4 Exit 64B or 65.

★ $$$$ 🏨 **Walt Disney World Dolphin.** The Dolphin and Swan completed a massive renovation and expansion of their already-huge convention center in late 2002, but don't worry, none of Michael Graves's architecture was changed. Outside, a pair of 56-ft-tall sea creatures bookend the 25-story glass pyramid of a building. The fabric-draped lobby inside resembles a giant sultan's tent. All rooms have either two queen beds or one king and bright, beach-inspired bedspreads and drapes. Extensive children's programs include Camp Dolphin summer camp and the five-hour Dolphin Dinner Club. Grotto Pool has a big water slide. ⊠ *1500 Epcot Resorts Blvd., Lake Buena Vista 32830-2653* ☎ *407/934–4000 or 800/227–1500* 🖷 *407/934–4884* ⊕ *www.swandolphin.com* ⇥ *1,509 rooms, 136 suites* ⚄ *9 restaurants, room service, in-room data ports, in-room safes, cable TV with movies and video games, 4 tennis outdoor courts, 5 pools, wading pool, gym, massage, spa, beach, boating, 3 lobby lounges, video game room, baby-sitting, children's programs (ages 4–12), concierge, concierge floor, business services, convention center, no-smoking rooms* ▭ *AE, D, MC, V.*

$$$$ 🏨 **Walt Disney World Swan.** Facing the Dolphin across Crescent Lake, the Swan is another example of the postmodern "Learning from Las Vegas" school of entertainment architecture characteristic of Michael Graves. Two 46-ft swans grace the rooftop of this coral-and-aquamarine hotel, connected to the Dolphin by a covered causeway. Guest rooms are quirkily decorated with floral and geometric patterns, pineapples painted on furniture, and exotic bird-shape lamps. Every room has two queen beds or one king, two phone lines (one data port), and a coffeemaker; some have balconies. ⊠ *1200 Epcot Resorts Blvd., Lake Buena Vista 32830* ☎ *407/934–3000 or 800/248–7926* 🖷 *407/934–4499* ⊕ *www.swandolphin.com* ⇥ *750 rooms, 55 suites* ⚄ *6 restaurants, room service, in-room data ports, in-room safes, cable TV with movies and video games, 4 outdoor tennis courts, 5 pools, wading pool, gym, massage, spa, beach, boating, 2 lobby lounges, video game room, baby-sitting, children's programs (ages 4–12), concierge, concierge floor, business services, convention center, no-smoking rooms* ▭ *AE, DC, MC, V.*

Downtown Disney Area

Take I–4 Exit 68.

A number of non-Disney-owned resorts are clustered on Disney property not far from Downtown Disney, and several more sprawling, high-quality resorts are just outside the park's northernmost entrance.

As a rule, the bigger the resort and the more extensive the facilities, the more you can expect to pay. All hotels on Hotel Plaza Boulevard are within walking distance of Downtown Disney Marketplace though most offer shuttle service anyway. One hotel may emphasize one recreational activity more than another, so your ultimate decision may depend on how much time you plan to spend at your hotel and which of your strokes—your drive or your backhand—requires the most attention.

★ $$$ **Wyndham Palace Resort & Spa in the WDW Resort.** This luxury hotel gets kudos as much for its on-site charms (such as a huge health spa) as for its location—100 yards from the Wolfgang Puck's in Downtown Disney. All rooms have balconies or patios, as well as high-speed Internet access. At the Top of the Palace, the club-bar on the 27th floor, guests receive a free glass of champagne at sunset to accompany the wonderful view of the sun sinking into the Disney complex. Book reservations early if you want a meal at the rooftop restaurant, Arthur's 27. ⊠ *1900 Buena Vista Dr., Downtown Disney 32830* ☎ *407/827–2727 or 800/327–2990* 🖷 *407/827–6034* ⊕ *www.wyndham.com* ⇨ *1,014 rooms, 209 suites* ⚘ *4 restaurants, patisserie, snack bar, room service, in-room data ports, in-room safes, cable TV with movies, tennis courts, 2 pools, wading pool, health club, hot tub, massage, spa, volleyball, 4 lobby lounges, video game room, baby-sitting, children's programs (ages 4–12), playground, laundry facilities, laundry service, business services, convention center, no smoking rooms* 🗀 *AE, D, DC, MC, V.*

$$ **DoubleTree Guest Suites in the WDW Resort.** The lavender-and-pink exterior looks strange, but the interior is another story. Comfortable one- and two-bedroom suites are decorated in tasteful hues, with gray carpeting and blond-wood furniture. Each bedroom has either a king bed or two doubles. Units come with a TV in each room and another (black-and-white) in the bathroom, plus a wet bar and coffeemaker. The smallish lobby has a charming feature—a small aviary with birds from South America and Africa. There's a special "registration desk" for kids, where they can get coloring books and balloons. ⊠ *2305 Hotel Plaza Blvd., Downtown Disney 32830* ☎ *407/934–1000 or 800/222–8733* 🖷 *407/934–1015* ⊕ *www.doubletree.com* ⇨ *229 units* ⚘ *Restaurant, microwaves, refrigerators, room service, in-room data ports, in-room safes, cable TV with movies, golf privileges, 2 tennis courts, pool, wading pool, gym, hot tub, 2 bars, laundry facilities, laundry service, business services, no-smoking rooms* 🗀 *AE, DC, MC, V.*

$$ **Hilton at WDW Resort.** It's not palatial, but this Hilton is still a fine, upscale hotel that's only a five-minute walk from Downtown Disney Marketplace. An ingeniously designed waterfall tumbles off the covered entrance and into a stone fountain surrounded by palm trees. Although not huge, rooms are upbeat, cozy, and contemporary, and many on the upper floors have great views of Downtown Disney. The evening seafood-tasting buffet in the lobby will tempt you to step into the on-site restaurant, Finn's. You also get the privilege to enter Disney parks one hour before they open. ⊠ *1751 Hotel Plaza Blvd., Downtown Disney 32830* ☎ *407/827–4000; 800/782–4414 reservations* 🖷 *407/827–6369* ⊕ *www.hilton-wdw.com* ⇨ *814 rooms, 27 suites* ⚘ *6 restaurants, room service, in-room data ports, in-room safes, cable TV with movies, 3 pools,*

health club, outdoor hot tub, lobby lounge, baby-sitting, children's programs (ages 3–12), laundry facilities, laundry service, business services, meeting rooms, no-smoking rooms ⊟ *AE, DC, MC, V.*

$$ 🏨 **Royal Plaza.** Built in the '70s, the casual and lively Royal Plaza keeps its look up-to-date and attractive. Each earth-tone room, though not extravagant, has a terrace or balcony, and some have hot tubs. Ask for a room overlooking the pool. Families like the Royal Plaza because of its moderate rates and proximity to Downtown Disney, and golfers appreciate the advance reservation privileges at five nearby courses. Children 12 and under eat free with parents at the hotel restaurant. ⊠ *1905 Hotel Plaza Blvd., Downtown Disney 32830* ☎ *407/828–2828 or 800/248–7890* 🖶 *407/828–8046* ⊕ *www.royalplaza.com* 🛏 *394 rooms, 21 suites* ⎔ *Restaurant, grill, room service, in-room data ports, in-room safes, some in-room hot tubs, cable TV with movies, golf privileges, 4 outdoor tennis courts, pool, hot tub, sauna, 2 bars, baby-sitting, laundry service, convention center, meeting rooms, no-smoking rooms* ⊟ *AE, D, DC, MC, V.*

$–$$ 🏨 **Grosvenor Resort.** This pink high-rise across from Downtown Disney is nondescript on the outside but quite pleasant on the inside. Blond-wood furniture and rose carpeting make the rooms homey, and those in the tower have a great view of Downtown Disney. Public areas are decorated in an easy-going Caribbean style. The restaurant Baskervilles hosts a Saturday murder-mystery dinner show. A free shuttle takes you to all Disney theme parks. ⊠ *1850 Hotel Plaza Blvd., Downtown Disney 32830* ☎ *407/828–4444 or 800/624–4109* 🖶 *407/828–8192* ⊕ *www.grosvenorresort.com* 🛏 *626 rooms, 5 suites* ⎔ *3 restaurants, room service, in-room data ports, in-room safes, cable TV with movies, refrigerators, in-room VCRs, 2 tennis courts, 2 pools, wading pool, hot tub, basketball, volleyball, lobby lounge, video game room, baby-sitting, playground, laundry service, business services, meeting rooms, no-smoking rooms* ⊟ *AE, DC, MC, V.*

$–$$ 🏨 **Courtyard by Marriott at WDW Resort.** In the tranquil 14-story atrium, accented with gazebos, white-tile trim, and tropical gardens, you can enjoy a well-prepared breakfast under white umbrellas. By evening, activity has shifted to the Tipsy Parrot, the hotel's welcoming bar. Rooms are attractive but not necessarily *Architectural Digest* material, with green carpets, rose-colored couches, and floral print bedspreads. ⊠ *1805 Hotel Plaza Blvd., Downtown Disney 32830* ☎ *407/828–8888 or 800/223–9930* 🖶 *407/827–4623* ⊕ *www.courtyardorlando.com* 🛏 *323 rooms* ⎔ *Restaurant, in-room data ports, in-room safes, data ports, cable TV with movies, 2 pools, wading pool, gym, outdoor hot tub, lobby lounge, playground, laundry facilities, laundry service, business services, no-smoking rooms* ⊟ *AE, DC, MC, V.*

$–$$ 🏨 **Best Western Lake Buena Vista Resort Hotel.** This 18-story property was completely renovated and redecorated in 2002. An attractive mural of Florida wildlife and landscapes graces the lobby, though the view of a jungle-like wetland out the windows of the atrium restaurant is more compelling. Most rooms have private, furnished balconies with spectacular views of nightly Disney firework shows. Disney shuttles are available, but you can walk to Downtown Disney in 10 minutes or less. ⊠ *2000 Hotel Plaza Blvd., Downtown Disney 32830* ☎ *407/828–2424 or 800/348–3765* 🖶 *407/828–8933* ⊕ *www.orlandoresorthotel.com* 🛏 *325 rooms* ⎔ *Restaurant, room service, in-room data ports, cable TV with movies, snack bar, pool, wading pool, lobby lounge, playground, laundry facilities, laundry service, business services, meeting rooms, no-smoking rooms* ⊟ *AE, D, DC, MC, V.*

Lake Buena Vista Area

Many people choose to stay in one of the resorts a bit farther east of Downtown Disney because, though equally grand, they tend to be less expensive that those right on Hotel Plaza Boulevard. If you're willing to take a five-minute drive or shuttle ride, you might save as much as 35% off your room tab.

Perennially popular with families are the all-suites properties, many with in-room kitchens, just east of Lake Buena Vista Drive. Furthermore, the 1,100-room Marriott Village at Lake Buena Vista, across I–4 from Downtown Disney, has made a splash in hotel-laden Orlando with its utter comprehensiveness. The gated, secure village has three hotels, a multi-restaurant complex, a video-rental store, a 24-hour convenience store, and a Hertz rental-car station. There's also an on-property Disney booking station, staffed by a Disney employee who can answer questions and make suggestions.

$$$$
Fodor'sChoice
Hyatt Regency Grand Cypress Resort. Spread over 1,500 acres just outside Disney's north entrance in Orlando, this spectacular resort offers virtually every amenity you could wish for—even a 45-acre nature preserve. Golf facilities, including a high-tech golf school, are first-class. The huge, 800,000-gallon pool resembles an enormous grotto, has a 45-ft water slide, and is fed by 12 waterfalls. There's also a small lake, with a nice little white-sand beach, adjacent to the pool area. A striking 18-story atrium is filled with tropical plants, ancient Chinese sculptures, and tropical birds. Accommodations are divided between the Hyatt Regency Grand Cypress and the **Villas of Grand Cypress** (⊠ 1 N. Jacaranda Dr., Lake Buena Vista Area 32836 ☎ 407/239–1234 or 800/835–7377), with 146 villas. Although pricey, the resort provides tremendous value. All rooms, decorated with rattan furniture, have a private balcony, with standard rooms overlooking the Lake Buena Vista area and slightly more expensive rooms overlooking the pool. Villas have fireplaces and whirlpool baths. ⊠ *1 Grand Cypress Blvd., Lake Buena Vista Area 32836* ☎ *407/239–1234 or 800/233–1234* ⊟ *407/239–3800* ⊕ *www.hyattgrandcypress.com* ⋧ *750 rooms* ⌂ *5 restaurants, room service, in-room data ports, in-room safes, cable TV with movies, two 18-hole and one 9-hole golf courses, 12 tennis courts, 2 pools, health club, 4 hot tubs, massage, spa, boating, bicycles, croquet, horseback riding, 4 lobby lounges, baby-sitting, children's programs (ages 5–12), laundry service, business services, convention center, meeting rooms, no-smoking rooms* ⊟ *AE, D, DC, MC, V.*

$$$$
Marriott's Orlando World Center. At 2,000 rooms, this is one of the largest hotels in Orlando, and one very popular with conventions. All rooms have patios or balconies, and the lineup of amenities and facilities seems endless—there's even on-site photo processing. One of the pools here is the largest in Florida. Upscale villas—the Royal Palms, Imperial Palms, and Sabal Palms—are available for daily and weekly rentals. The hotel's Hawk's Landing Steakhouse and Grille is among the better beef-centric restaurants in the Disney area. ⊠ *8701 World Center Dr., I–4 Exit 65, Lake Buena Vista Area 32821* ☎ *407/239–4200 or 800/228–9290* ⊟ *407/238–8777* ⊕ *www.marriotthotels.com* ⋧ *2,000 rooms, 98 suites, 259 villas* ⌂ *6 restaurants, ice cream parlor, room service, in-room data ports, cable TV with movies, 4 pools (1 indoor), wading pool, hair salon, health club, 4 hot tubs, 2 lobby lounges, baby-sitting, children's programs (ages 4–12), laundry facilities, laundry service, business services, convention center, no-smoking rooms* ⊟ *AE, D, DC, MC, V.*

$$–$$$
Caribe Royale Resort Suites & Villas. This big pink palace of a hotel, with flowing palm trees and massive, man-made waterfalls, wouldn't look out of place in Vegas. Huge ballrooms attract corporate confer-

ences, but there are key family-friendly ingredients, too: free transportation to Walt Disney World (10 minutes away), and a huge children's recreation area, including a big pool with a 65-ft water slide. The complimentary hot-breakfast buffet offers an extensive selection of stick-to-your-ribs dishes, ranging from sausage and eggs to French toast. The suites all have wet bars and a coffeemaker; many have an in-room hot tub. Take I–4 Exit 67. ⊠ *8101 World Center Dr., Lake Buena Vista Area 32821* ☏ *407/238–8000 or 800/823–8300* 🖷 *407/238–8088* ⊕ *www.cariberoyale.com* ⇄ *1,218 suites, 120 villas* ⌂ *3 restaurants, room service, in-room data ports, microwaves, refrigerators, cable TV with movies, 2 tennis courts, pool, wading pool, lobby lounge, laundry facilities, laundry service, concierge, business services, convention center, no-smoking rooms* ▭ *AE, D, DC, MC, V* ⦿ *BP.*

$$–$$$ 🏨 **Sheraton Vistana Resort.** Consider this peaceful resort, just across I–4 from Downtown Disney, if you're interested in tennis. Its clay and all-weather courts can be used without an extra charge, and private or semiprivate lessons are available for a fee. It's also a good bet if your family is large or you're traveling with friends. Spread over 135 landscaped acres, the spacious, tastefully decorated villas and town houses come in one- and two-bedroom versions with a living room, a full kitchen (with range, dishwasher, coffeemaker, and blender), and mini-laundry with a washer and dryer. ⊠ *8800 Vistana Center Dr., Lake Buena Vista 32821* ☏ *407/239–3100 or 800/208–0003* 🖷 *407/239–3111* ⊕ *www.vistana. com* ⇄ *1,700 units* ⌂ *2 restaurants, grocery, in-room data ports, in-room safes, kitchens, microwaves, refrigerators, cable TV with movies, miniature golf, 13 tennis courts, 7 pools, 5 wading pools, health club, 7 hot tubs, basketball, shuffleboard, lobby lounge, baby-sitting, children's programs (ages 4–12), business services, meeting rooms, no-smoking rooms* ▭ *AE, D, DC, MC, V.*

$–$$$ 🏨 **Holiday Inn SunSpree Resort Lake Buena Vista.** This place is as kid-oriented as it gets. The little ones have their own registration desk, and there's usually a costumed clown to hand out balloons and such. Off the lobby you'll find the CyberArcade; a small theater where clowns perform weekends at 7 PM; and a buffet restaurant where kids accompanied by adults eat free at their own little picnic tables. Families love the Kid-suites, playhouse-style rooms within a larger room. ⊠ *13351 Rte. 535, Lake Buena Vista 32821* ☏ *407/239–4500 or 800/366–6299* 🖷 *407/ 239–7713* ⊕ *www.kidsuites.com* ⇄ *507 rooms* ⌂ *Restaurant, grocery, in-room data ports, in-room safes, microwaves, refrigerators, cable TV with movies and video games, pool, wading pool, gym, 2 hot tubs, basketball, Ping-Pong, bar, lobby lounge, theater, video game room, children's programs (ages 4–12), playground, laundry facilities, laundry service, business services, no-smoking rooms* ▭ *AE, D, DC, MC, V.*

$$ 🏨 **Buena Vista Suites.** In this all-suites property, you get a bedroom, a separate living room with a fold-out sofa bed, two TVs, two phones, and a small kitchen area with a coffeemaker. King suites have a single king bed and a whirlpool bath. The hotel serves a complimentary full-breakfast buffet daily and provides complimentary shuttle transportation to the Walt Disney World theme parks. ⊠ *8203 World Center Dr., Lake Buena Vista Area 32821* ☏ *407/239–8588 or 800/537–7737* 🖷 *407/239–1401* ⊕ *www.buenavistasuites.com* ⇄ *280 suites* ⌂ *Restaurant, room service, in-room data ports, in-room safes, microwaves, refrigerators, cable TV with movies, outdoor pool, wading pool, hot tub, 2 tennis courts, gym, laundry facilities, car rental, no-smoking rooms* ▭ *AE, D, DC, MC, V* ⦿ *BP.*

$$ 🏨 **Embassy Suites Hotel Lake Buena Vista.** Some locals are shocked by the wild turquoise, pink, and peach facade (clearly visible from I–4, it's something of a local landmark), but the Embassy Suites resort is an attractive option for other reasons. It's just 1 mi from Walt Disney World, 3 mi from SeaWorld, and 7 mi from Universal Orlando. Each suite has a separate living room and two TVs. The central atrium lobby, loaded with tropical vegetation and soothed by the sounds of a rushing fountain, is a great place to enjoy the complimentary full breakfast and evening cocktails. ✉ *8100 Lake Ave., Lake Buena Vista 32836* ☎ *407/239–1144, 800/257–8483, or 800/362–2779* 🖷 *407/239–1718* ⊕ *www.embassysuitesorlando. com* 🛏 *330 suites* ♿ *Restaurant, room service, in-room data ports, in-room safes, cable TV with movies, tennis court, indoor-outdoor pool, wading pool, gym, hot tub, basketball, shuffleboard, volleyball, lobby lounge, baby-sitting, children's programs (ages 4–12), playground, business services, meeting room, no-smoking rooms* ▭ *AE, D, DC, MC, V* ⊙ *BP.*

$$ 🏨 **Holiday Inn Family Suites Resort.** This all-suites, family-oriented hotel is convenient to all of the WDW parks. A railroad theme runs through all seven kinds of units, and the lobby and restaurant are decorated with railroad murals and memorabilia. A tram that looks like a train ferries visitors from the main building to the various hotel units. The fitness suites have a workout room with a recumbent cycle, an abdominal bench, and free weights, and the cinema suites have an entertainment room with a 60″ TV, VCR, and double recliner-couch. Two-bedroom kids' suites offer a brightly decorated children's room with bunk beds, 20″ TV with VCR, and a Nintendo 64 unit. ✉ *14500 Continental Gateway, I–4 Exit 67, Lake Buena Vista Area, 32821* ☎ *407/387–5437 or 877/387–5437* 🖷 *407/387–1489* ⊕ *www.hifamilysuites.com* 🛏 *800 suites* ♿ *3 restaurants, ice cream parlor, room service, in-room data ports, in-room safes, cable TV with movies, 2 pools, hair salon, health club, 2 hot tubs, 2 lobby lounges, baby-sitting, children's programs (ages 4–12), laundry facilities, laundry service, business service, no-smoking rooms* ▭ *AE, D, DC, MC, V.*

$$ 🏨 **Homewood Suites Resort Lake Buena Vista.** The suites here are pleasant if not enormous, and both the prices and location make this a great home-base for a family vacation. Each suite has a full kitchen, complete with dishes. Downtown Disney Marketplace is about 1 mi away, and at least a dozen other restaurants and a Publix supermarket are ½ mi away. The suites sleep up to six if you fold out the couch-bed in the living room. In addition to a daily buffet breakfast, snacks are laid out for a "social hour" Monday through Thursday 5–7 PM. ✉ *8200 Palm Pkwy., Lake Buena Vista 32836* ☎ *407/465–8200 or 800/225–5466* 🖷 *407/465–0200* ⊕ *www.homewoodsuiteslbv.com* 🛏 *123 suites* ♿ *In-room data ports, in-room safes, kitchens, microwaves, refrigerators, cable TV with movies, gym, hot tub, pool. wading pool, basketball, playground, laundry facilities, laundry services, business services, meeting room, no-smoking rooms* ▭ *AE, D, DC, MC, V* ⊙ *CP.*

$$ 🏨 **Marriott Residence Inn.** Billing itself as a Caribbean-style oasis, with lush palms and an outdoor waterfall near the swimming pool, this all-suites hotel's most compelling features are a bit more pragmatic: every room has a full kitchen with a stove and dishwasher, and there's an on-site convenience store. (A supermarket is a few blocks down Palm Parkway.) Pleasant suites include a separate living room/kitchen and bedrooms. Two-bedroom suites have two bathrooms. The recreation area has both a kids' pool and a putting green. ✉ *11450 Marbella Palms Ct., Lake Buena Vista 32836* ☎ *407/465–0075* 🖷 *407/465–0050* ⊕ *www.residenceinn. com* 🛏 *210 suites* ♿ *In-room data ports, in-room safes, kitchenettes, microwaves, refrigerators, cable TV with movies, putting green, pool, wading pool, gym, hot tub, basketball, playground, laundry facilities, laundry service, business services, no-smoking rooms* ▭ *AE, D, DC, MC, V.*

$$ 🏨 **Sheraton Safari Hotel.** This little piece of Nairobi in the hotel district adjacent to Downtown Disney is a bona fide success. From the pool's jungle motif to the bamboo enclosures around the lobby pay phones, this place is a trip. Although there are some leopard-skin-print furniture coverings and wild animal portraits on the walls, the guests are relatively sedate. Suites include kitchenettes with microwaves, and six deluxe suites have full kitchens. Watch your kids slide down the giant water slide in the pool area while you sip drinks at the poolside Zanzibar. ✉ *12205 Apopka Vineland Rd., Lake Buena Vista Area, Orlando 32836* ☎ *407/ 239–0444 or 800/423–3297* 🖷 *407/239–4566* ⊕ *www.sheratonsafari.com* 🛏 *496 rooms, 96 suites* ⚬ *Restaurant, room service, in-room data ports, in-room safes, some kitchenettes, some microwaves, some refrigerators, cable TV with movies, pool, health club, hot tub, lobby lounge, business services, meeting room, no-smoking rooms* ☱ *AE, D, DC, MC, V.*

$–$$ ▦ **Country Inn & Suites by Carlson.** The signature lobby fireplace looks a little ridiculous in an Orlando hotel, but the in-room amenities and the proximity to Downtown Disney (½ mi away) make this place a good bet for either families or couples. For $120 you can book what the hotel calls a one-bedroom "Country Kids Suite," with two beds, two TVs (one of which is hooked up for video games), a refrigerator, and a microwave. There's no full-service restaurant, but the hotel is next door to two restaurants and within walking distance of a dozen others. Shuttle service to the Disney parks is provided. ✉ *12191 S. Apopka Vineland Rd., Lake Buena Vista Area 32836* ☎ *407/239–1115 or 800/456–4000* 🖷 *407/239–8882* ⊕ *www.countryinns.com* 🛏 *170 rooms, 50 suites* ⚬ *In-room data ports, in-room safes, refrigerators, microwaves, cable TV with movies, pool, wading pool, gym, hot tub, laundry facilities, no-smoking rooms* ☱ *AE, D, DC, MC, V* ⊺⊘⊺ *CP.*

$–$$ ▦ **Courtyard by Marriott at Lake Buena Vista.** With refrigerators in every room and hot tubs in some, this tidy hotel offers lots of perks for the price. Rooms are decorated with yellow floral patterns and blond-wood furniture, and they include coffeemakers, work desks, and Web TV. The indoor-outdoor pool area has a bar with seating in the pool. ✉ *8623 Vineland Ave., Marriott Village 32821* ☎ *407/938–9001 or 877/682– 8552* 🖷 *407/938–9002* ⊕ *www.marriottvillage.com* 🛏 *312 rooms* ⚬ *Restaurant, room service, in-room data ports, in-room safes, some in-room hot tubs, microwaves, refrigerators, cable TV with movies and video games, pool, gym, bar, children's programs (ages 4–12), laundry facilities, laundry service, business services, meeting rooms, no-smoking rooms* ☱ *AE, D, DC, MC, V* ⊺⊘⊺ *CP.*

★ $–$$ ▦ **PerriHouse Bed & Breakfast Inn.** An eight-room bed-and-breakfast inside a serene bird sanctuary is a unique lodging experience in fast-lane Orlando. The PerriHouse offers you a chance to split your time between sightseeing and spending quiet moments bird-watching: the 13-acre sanctuary has observation paths, a pond, a feeding station, and a small birdhouse museum. About 200 trees and more than 1,500 bushes have been planted, making it attractive to bobwhites, downy woodpeckers, red-tail hawks, and the occasional bald eagle. The rooms are larger than average, and some have four-poster beds and fireplaces. ✉ *10417 Vista Oak Ct., Lake Buena Vista 32836* ☎ *407/876–4830 or 800/780–4830* 🖷 *407/876–0241* ⊕ *www.perrihouse.com* 🛏 *8 rooms* ⚬ *In-room data ports, in-room safes, cable TV, golf privileges, pool, hot tub* ☱ *AE, D, DC, MC, V* ⊺⊘⊺ *CP.*

$–$$ ▦ **SpringHillSuites at Lake Buena Vista.** Each suite here has separate sleeping and dining areas. The kitchenettes have microwaves, and the rooms offer work areas with high-speed Internet hookups. Marriott Village amenities, such as numerous restaurants and shops, plus transportation to area attractions, make your stay that much more enjoyable. ✉ *8623 Vineland Ave., Marriott Village 32821* ☎ *407/938–9001 or 877/682– 8552* 🖷 *407/938–9002* ⊕ *www.marriottvillage.com* 🛏 *400 suites*

⚓ *Restaurant, room service, in-room data ports, in-room safes, kitchenettes, microwaves, refrigerators, cable TV with movies and video games, pool, gym, bar, children's programs (ages 4–12), laundry facilities, laundry service, business services, meeting rooms, no-smoking rooms* ▭ *AE, D, DC, MC, V* ⫙ *CP.*

$ ▦ **Fairfield Inn at Lake Buena Vista.** Geared for business travelers and families on a budget, these rooms are just as bright and pleasant as what you find in the SpringHill Suites or Courtyard by Marriott, if not quite as amenity-laden. There's a pool bar and grill and a complimentary Continental breakfast buffet. ⊠ *8623 Vineland Ave., Marriott Village 32821* ☏ *407/938–9001 or 877/682–8552* 🖷 *407/938–9002* ⊕ *www. marriottvillage.com* ⇋ *388 rooms* ⚓ *Restaurant, room service, in-room data ports, in-room safes, microwaves, refrigerators, cable TV with movies and video games, pool, gym, bar, children's programs (ages 4–12), laundry facilities, laundry service, business services, meeting rooms, no-smoking rooms* ▭ *AE, D, DC, MC, V* ⫙ *CP.*

$ ▦ **Hawthorn Suites Resort Lake Buena Vista.** The free-breakfast bar becomes just a bar during the social hour from Monday through Thursday, 5 to 7 PM, but if you'd rather go out, Downtown Disney is just 1 mi away. Every suite at the Hawthorn has a separate bedroom/living room and a full kitchen, including a dishwasher, so you can even stay in and cook. ⊠ *8303 Palm Pkwy., Lake Buena Vista 32836* ☏ *407/ 597–5000 or 800/269–8303* 🖷 *407/597–6000* ⊕ *www. hawthornsuiteslbv.com* ⇋ *120 suites* ⚓ *In-room data ports, in-room safes, kitchens, microwaves, refrigerators, cable TV, pool, wading pool, exercise equipment, hot tub, basketball, playground, laundry facilities, business services, no-smoking rooms* ▭ *AE, D, DC, MC, V* ⫙ *CP.*

UNIVERSAL ORLANDO RESORT AREA

Take I–4 Exit 74B or 75A, unless otherwise noted.

Universal Orlando's on-site hotels were built in a little luxury enclave that has everything you need, so you never have to leave Universal property. In minutes, you can walk from any hotel to CityWalk, Universal's dining and entertainment district, or take a ferry that cruises the adjacent man-made river. If you need a mundane item such as a new toothbrush, there's plenty of shopping just across the street from Universal on Kirkman Road.

A significant perk for staying at one of these properties is that your hotel key lets you go directly to the head of the line for most Universal Orlando attractions. Other special services at some hotels include a "Did You Forget?" closet that offers everything from kid's strollers to dog leashes to computer accessories.

If the on-property Universal hotels are a bit pricey for your budget, don't worry, a burgeoning hotel district with almost a dozen name-brand hotels has sprung up across Kirkman Road, offering convenient accommodations and some room rates less than $50 a night. While these off-property hotels don't offer perks like head-of-the-line privileges inside the park, you'll probably be smiling when you see your hotel bill.

$$$$ ▦ **Portofino Bay Hotel.** Built to resemble the Italian Riviera town of Portofino, this hotel complex puts on a Feast of St. Gennaro (the patron saint of Naples) each September and holds monthly Italian wine tastings. There's even a boccie ball court, possibly the only one in Florida. Large, plush rooms are done in cream and white with down comforters. Other nice touches include gelato machines around the massive pool, a wood-fired pizzeria, and two great Italian restaurants—Mama Della's and

Delfino Riviera. ⊠ *5601 Universal Blvd., Universal Studios 32819* ☎ *407/503–1000 or 888/322–5541* ⊕ *www.loewshotels.com* ➭ *699 rooms, 51 suites* ⟁ *3 restaurants, pizzeria, room service, in-room data ports, in-room fax, in-room safes, cable TV with movies, in-room VCRs, 3 pools, health club, massage, spa, boccie, bar, baby-sitting, children's programs (ages 4–14), playground, laundry service, business services, convention center, no-smoking rooms* ▭ *AE, D, DC, MC, V.*

$$$
Fodor'sChoice

🖼 **Royal Pacific Resort.** The hotel entrance—a footbridge across a tropical stream—sets the tone for the South Pacific theme of this hotel, which is on 53 acres planted with tropical shrubs and trees, most of them palms. The resort's focal point is a 12,000-square-ft, lagoon-style swimming pool (Orlando's largest) with its own sand beach. Indonesian wood carvings decorate the walls everywhere, even in the rooms; and Emeril Lagasse's newest Orlando restaurant, Tchoup Chop, brings in crowds. ⊠ *6300 Hollywood Way, Universal Studios 32819* ☎ *407/503–3000* 🖷 *407/503–3010* ⊕ *www.loewshotels.com* ➭ *1,000 rooms, 113 suites* ⟁ *3 restaurants, room service, in-room data ports, in-room safes, cable TV with movies, minibars, in-room VCRs, putting green, pool, wading pool, health club, hot tub, massage, sauna, steam room, 2 bars, lobby lounge, children's programs (ages 4–14), laundry facilities, laundry service, concierge floor, business services, convention center, some pets allowed, no-smoking rooms* ▭ *AE, DC, MC, V.*

$$–$$$

🖼 **Hard Rock Hotel.** Although it's not quite as plush as Portofino Bay, the price tag isn't quite as high either, and the appealing, comfortable lodging is close to all Universal attractions. Inside the California mission–style building, you'll find lots of rock-music memorabilia, including the slip Madonna wore in her "Like a Prayer" video. Rooms have white walls and black-and-white photos of pop icons. Stay in a suite and you'll get a stereo system with CD player, big-screen TV, wet bar, fax, and possibly a cute, kid-friendly room-within-a-room. ⊠ *1000 Universal Studios Plaza, Universal Studios 32819* ☎ *407/503–7625 or 800/232–7827* 🖷 *407/503–7655* ⊕ *www.loewshotels.com* ➭ *621 rooms, 29 suites* ⟁ *3 restaurants, room service, in-room data ports, in-room safes, cable TV with movies and VCRs, refrigerators, 2 pools, health club, 3 bars, video game room, baby-sitting, children's programs (ages 4–14), laundry service, business services, meeting rooms, some pets allowed, no-smoking rooms* ▭ *AE, D, DC, MC, V.*

$–$$

🖼 **Holiday Inn Hotel & Suites Orlando/Universal.** Staying at this hotel directly across the street from Universal Orlando could eliminate your need for a rental car if Universal, SeaWorld, Wet 'n Wild, and International Drive are your only planned vacation stops. There's a shuttle to all four, though you can easily walk to Universal. Rooms come with coffeemakers, hair dryers, irons, and ironing boards; one- and two-bedroom suites also have refrigerators, microwaves, dishwashers, and tableware. The on-property restaurant is a T.G.I. Friday's. ⊠ *5905 S. Kirkman Rd., I–4 Exit 75B, Universal Studios Area 32819* ☎ *407/351–3333 or 800/327–1364* 🖷 *407/351–3527* ⊕ *www.hiuniversal.com* ➭ *390 rooms, 120 suites* ⟁ *Restaurant, room service, in-room data ports, in-room safes, cable TV with movies, some microwaves, some refrigerators, pool, health club, lounge, baby-sitting, laundry service, meeting rooms, some pets allowed, no-smoking rooms* ▭ *AE, D, DC, MC, V.*

$–$$

🖼 **Radisson Hotel Universal Orlando.** When it opened in the mid-1970s, this was the largest convention hotel between Miami and Atlanta. It's still a hotbed of business-trippers, but it also attracts plenty of pleasure-seekers since it's right at the Universal Orlando entrance. Don't worry about noisy conventioneers—the meeting and convention facilities are completely isolated from the guest towers. If you happen to be at the hotel on business, the hotel has a teleconferencing center from which you can originate live video links with points all over the world. ✉ *5780 Major Blvd., I–4 Exit 75B, Universal Studios Area 32819* ☎ *407/351–1000 or 800/327–2110* 🖷 *407/363–0106* ⊕ *www.radisson.com* ↩ *742 rooms, 15 suites* ⚓ *Restaurant, room service, in-room safes, in-room data ports, cable TV, golf privileges, pool, wading pool, gym, hot tub, lobby lounge, baby-sitting, playground, dry cleaning, laundry facilities, business services, convention center, meeting rooms, no-smoking rooms* 🖃 *AE, D, DC, MC, V.*

$ 🏨 **Sleep Inn & Suites Universal Studios.** This 11-story, 196-room hotel, opened in 2000, is the largest in the Sleep Inn chain. Rooms have two double beds or one king, and suites add full kitchens and a sofa that folds out into a double bed. In every room, baths have large, walk-in showers. Universal's entrance is two blocks away, and restaurants and shopping are also within walking distance. ✉ *5605 Major Blvd., Universal Studios Area 32819* ☎ *407/363–1333* 🖷 *407/363–4510* ⊕ *www.choicehotels.com* ↩ *196 rooms, 40 suites* ⚓ *In-room data ports, in-room safes, kitchens, microwaves, refrigerators, cable TV with movies and video games, pool, gym, video game room, laundry facilities, laundry service, business services, meeting rooms, no-smoking rooms* 🖃 *AE, D, DC, MC, V* ⏚ *CP.*

¢ 🏨 **Extended Stay America Orlando/Universal Studios.** The brick exterior with Victorian-style architectural touches makes the place look like a dorm at a small-town college, but the amenities inside are far more extensive than what you probably had at your alma mater. Each efficiency studio has a full kitchen with microwave. There's no on-site gym, but a Bally's fitness center is a short walk away, and the neighborhood has lots of entertainment and dining options. Take Exit 75B off I–4. ✉ *5615 Major Blvd., Universal Studios Area 32819* ☎ *407/313–2000 or 800/951–7829* 🖷 *407/313–2010* ⊕ *www.suburbanhotels.com* ↩ *150 suites* ⚓ *In-room data ports, in-room safes, cable TV, pool, playground, laundry facilities, business services, no-smoking rooms* 🖃 *AE, D, DC, MC, V.*

¢ 🏨 **Studio Plus Orlando/Universal Studios.** This is no luxury resort, but the *FodorsChoice* rooms are spacious, tidy, and pleasant. What's more, every suite has a full kitchen, so you can save money on meals if you enjoy cooking. Each suite also has a work table with data-ports on the phones, a queen-size bed, and a sofa that folds out into a double bed. Two blocks from Universal, the hotel is in a central neighborhood replete with shopping and dining choices. ✉ *5610 Vineland Rd., Universal Studios Area 32819* ☎ *407/370–4428 or 800/398–7829* 🖷 *407/370–9456* ⊕ *www.extstay.com* ↩ *84 suites* ⚓ *In-room data ports, kitchens, microwaves, refrigerators, cable TV, pool, gym, laundry facilities, no-smoking rooms* 🖃 *AE, D, DC, MC, V.*

KISSIMMEE

Take I–4 Exit 64A, unless otherwise noted.

If you're looking for anything remotely quaint, charming, or sophisticated, move on. With a few exceptions (namely, the flashy Gaylord Palms Resort), the U.S. 192 strip—a.k.a. the Irlo Bronson Memorial Highway—is a neon-and-plastic theme park crammed with mom-and-pop motels, bargain-basement hotels, cheap restaurants, fast-food spots, nickel-and-dime attractions, overpriced gas stations, and minimarts where a small bottle of aspirin costs $8.

But if all you want is a decent room with perhaps a few extras for a manageable price, this is Wonderland. Room rates start at $29 a night in the older hotels if you can cut the right deal. Most cost $40–$80 a night, depending on facilities and proximity to Walt Disney World.

Among the chain hotels—Best Western, Comfort Inn, Econo Lodge, Holiday Inn, Radisson, Sheraton, Travelodge, and so on—are a pride of family-owned properties, many of which are run by recent immigrants. One caveat: the word "maingate" is a vast exaggeration in most hotel names. It's a good 6 mi from Kissimmee's "maingate" hotel area, around Lake Cecile, to the legitimate main gate of any WDW park, although the "maingate west" area is only about 2 mi from WDW.

Whatever your hotel choice, you will find basic rooms, grounds, and public spaces that vary little from one establishment to the next. Keep in mind that the newer the property, the more comfortable your surroundings. Of course, the greater the distance from Walt Disney World, the lower the room rates. A few additional minutes' drive may save you a significant amount of money, so shop around. And if you wait until arrival to find a place, don't be bashful about asking to see the rooms. It's a buyer's market.

$$$ ⊠ **Gaylord Palms Resort.** With a huge atrium that re-creates such Florida
Fodor'sChoice landmarks as the Everglades, Key West, and old St. Augustine under a 4-acre glass roof, this massive property, 5 mi from WDW, is Orlando's most elaborate hotel. The five dramatic atrium restaurants include Sunset Sam's Fish Camp, perched on a 60-ft fishing boat docked on the hotel's indoor ocean, and the Old Hickory Steak House in an old warehouse overlooking the alligator-ridden Everglades. Rooms carry on the Florida themes with colorful, tropical decorations. With extensive children's programs, two pool areas, and a huge spa, the hotel connives to make you never want to leave. ⊠ *6000 Osceola Pkwy., I-4 Exit 65, Kissimmee, 34746* ☎ *407/586-0000* 🖷 *407/586-1999* ⊕ *www.gaylordpalms.com* ⇨ *1,406 rooms, 86 suites* ⚄ *6 restaurants, in-room data ports, in-room safes, cable TV with movies, golf privileges, 2 pools, gym, hot tub, massage, spa, 2 bars, lobby lounge, children's programs (ages 4–12), laundry service, business services, convention center, meeting rooms, no-smoking rooms* ☰ *AE, D, DC, MC, V.*

$$ ⊠ **Celebration Hotel.** Like everything in the fantasy-driven, Disney-created town of Celebration, this 115-room hotel borrows from the best of the 19th and 21st centuries. The lobby resembles that of the grand Victorian-era hotels, with hardwood floors and decorative millwork on the walls and ceilings. Room may look as if they date from the early 1900s, but each has a 25″ TV, two phone lines, high-speed Internet access port, and a six-channel stereo sound system. Even though it's less than 1 mi south of the U.S. 192 tourist strip in Kissimmee, the hotel's surroundings are serene. ⊠ *700 Bloom St., Celebration 34747* ☎ *407/566-6000 or 888/472-6312* 🖷 *407/566-1844* ⊕ *www.celebrationhotel. com* ⇨ *115 rooms* ⚄ *2 restaurants, in-room data ports, cable TV with movies, golf privileges, pool, health club, hot tub, lobby lounge, laundry service, no-smoking rooms* ☰ *AE, D, DC, MC, V.*

$$ ⊠ **DoubleTree Resort Orlando Maingate.** The red-tile-and-stucco villas and palm-studded grounds are attractive, but the brochure stretches a point when it says the resort has the charm of a small village in the Spanish region of Andalusia. Nevertheless, the spacious accommodations are noteworthy. Each of the one-, two-, or three-bedroom units has a living and dining area, a kitchen, and two TVs; the three-bedroom villa has 1,200 square ft of living space and sleeps up to eight comfortably. A wonderful small touch: the "welcome" chocolate-chip cookies. ⊠ *4787 W. Irlo Bronson Hwy., Kissimmee, 34746* ☎ *407/397-0555 or 800/222-8733* 🖷 *407/397-0553* ⊕ *www.doubletree.com* ⇨ *150 villas* ⚄ *Restaurant, room service, grocery, in-room data ports, in-room safes, cable TV with movies, tennis court, pool, wading pool, health club, hot tub, lobby lounge, laundry facilities, no-smoking rooms* ☰ *AE, D, DC, MC, V.*

$$ 🖬 **Hyatt Orlando Hotel.** At this gigantic hotel, 10 two-story buildings surround four "courts" on 54 acres: it would look like a college campus were the buildings not pink. Each court has its own heated pool, hot tub, park, and playground. The rooms are spacious with bright floral bedspreads, but otherwise are not memorable. The mall-like lobby has numerous shops and restaurants, and it's a five-minute drive from Disney's main gate. Guests get membership privileges at the Falcon's Fire and Celebration golf courses, both five minutes away. ⊠ *6375 W. Irlo Bronson Memorial Hwy., Kissimmee 34747* ☎ *407/396–1234 or 800/233–1234* 🖷 *407/396–5090* ⊕ *www.hyatt.com* ⟿ *922 rooms, 29 suites* ♻ *3 restaurants, room service, in-room data ports, in-room safes, cable TV with movies, golf privileges, 3 tennis courts, 4 pools, gym, hair salon, 4 hot tubs, bar, lobby lounge, sports bar, shops, playground, laundry facilities, laundry service, business services, meeting rooms, no-smoking rooms* ⊟ *AE, D, DC, MC, V.*

★ $$ 🖬 **Radisson Resort Parkway.** This bright, spacious Radisson may offer the best deal in the neighborhood: an attractive location amid 1½ acres of lush tropical foliage, with good facilities and competitive prices. A free shuttle makes 10-minute trips to Disney. Children age 10 and younger eat for free in the hotel restaurants, when accompanied by an adult who orders a meal. Other on-site refueling options include Starbucks, Krispy Kreme, and Pizza Hut. Generously proportioned rooms are decorated with blond-wood furniture and vibrant multicolor bedspreads and curtains. Rooms with the best view and light face the pool, which has a 40-ft water slide and wide, gentle waterfall. Off the lobby is a lively sports bar with an 11′×6′ TV. ⊠ *2900 Parkway Blvd., Kissimmee 34746* ☎ *407/396–7000 or 800/634–4774* 🖷 *407/396–6792* ⊕ *www.radissonparkway.com* ⟿ *712 rooms, 8 suites* ♻ *Restaurant, snack bar, in-room data ports, cable TV with movies, 2 tennis courts, 2 pools, wading pool, gym, 2 hot tubs, sauna, volleyball, lobby lounge, sports bar, laundry facilities, laundry service, business services, meeting rooms, no-smoking rooms* ⊟ *AE, D, DC, MC, V.*

$–$$ 🖬 **Holiday Inn Maingate West.** Precious few Orlando hotels allow furry friends, requiring that you put them in a kennel such as those at WDW, if you bring them at all. But this hotel allows a pet to stay in your room if you pay $25 and put up another $50 as a refundable deposit. The hotel also has some Kidsuites, in which kids get their own room with bunk beds, Nintendo-equipped TV, a CD player, and other toys. The Kidsuites also include a refrigerator, microwave, coffeemaker, and queen-size bed for the adults. ⊠ *7601 Black Lake Rd., 2 mi west of I–4, Kissimmee 34747* ☎ *407/396–1100 or 800/365–6935* 🖷 *407/396–0689* ⊕ *www.enjoyfloridahotels.com* ⟿ *248 rooms, 30 suites* ♻ *Restaurant, room service, in-room data ports, in-room safes, some microwaves, some refrigerators, cable TV with movies, pool, gym, volleyball, lobby lounge, laundry facilities, laundry service, some pets allowed (fee), no-smoking rooms* ⊟ *AE, D, DC, MC, V.*

$–$$ 🖬 **Quality Suites Maingate East.** Here's an excellent option for a large family or group of friends. The spacious suites, designed to sleep 6 or 10, come with one or two bedrooms (two double beds in each) and a living room with a pull-out couch. All suites have a dishwasher, microwave, and refrigerator. In addition to the complimentary Continental breakfast, free beer and wine are served afternoons at the poolside bar. A free shuttle takes you to WDW, Universal Studios, and SeaWorld. ⊠ *5876 W. Irlo Bronson Memorial Hwy., Kissimmee 34746* ☎ *407/396–8040 or 800/848–4148* 🖷 *407/396–6766* ⊕ *www.qualitysuites.com* ⟿ *225 suites* ♻ *Restaurant, in-room data ports, kitchenettes, microwaves, refrigerators, cable TV with movies, pool, wading pool, hot tub, bar, lobby lounge, playground, laundry service, business services, no-smoking rooms* ⊟ *AE, D, DC, MC, V* ⏁ *CP.*

$ ◫ **AmeriSuites Lake Buena Vista South.** A stay here gets you into the adjacent Caribbean-themed outdoor recreation complex for free. The complex includes an 18-hole miniature golf course and three outdoor pools, one with a waterslide. Complimentary Continental breakfast is served daily, and there's free scheduled shuttle service to WDW, Universal Studios, SeaWorld, Wet 'n Wild, and the Lake Buena Vista Factory Stores. The brightly colored, tropical-style suites have separate bedrooms and living rooms with kitchenettes and king-size sofa-beds. ⊠ *4991 Calypso Cay Way, Kissimmee 34746* ☎ *407/997–1300 or 800/833–1516* 🖷 *407/997–1301* ⊕ *www.amerisuites.com* ⇨ *151 suites* ⌂ *In-room data ports, in-room safes, kitchenttes, microwaves, refrigerators, cable TV with movies, pool, gym, laundry service, meeting rooms, no-smoking rooms* ▭ *AE, D, DC, MC, V* ⏆ *BP.*

$ ◫ **La Quinta Inn Lakeside.** Fifteen, two-story, balconied buildings make up this 27-acre hotel complex. A small man-made lake offers pedal boating, and four outdoor tennis courts are available on a first-come, first-serve basis. Rooms are done in green and pink, and they come with two double beds or one king. Children's activities involve arts and crafts, movies, or miniature golf in a comfortable play area. Kids under 11 eat free at all meals with at least one paying adult. ⊠ *7769 W. Irlo Bronson Memorial Hwy., 2 mi west of I–4, Kissimmee 34747* ☎ *407/396–2222 or 800/848–0801* 🖷 *407/239–2650* ⊕ *www.laquinta.com* ⇨ *651 rooms* ⌂ *2 restaurants, room service, in-room safes, refrigerators, cable TV with movies, miniature golf, 4 tennis courts, 3 pools, wading pool, gym, boating, fishing, lobby lounge, children's programs (ages 4–12), playground, laundry facilities, laundry service, no-smoking rooms* ▭ *AE, D, DC, MC, V.*

¢–$ ◫ **Holiday Inn Hotel & Suites Main Gate East.** Within walking distance of the Old Town shopping and entertainment complex, and 3 mi from WDW, this hotel is popular with families. Kidsuites include a special room for kids, with bunk beds, separate TVs and video games. All rooms have kitchenettes and VCRs. Free scheduled transportation to Disney World's four theme parks is available. ⊠ *5678 W. Irlo Bronson Memorial Hwy., Kissimmee 34746* ☎ *407/396–4488, 800/366–5437, or 800/465–4329* 🖷 *407/396–1296* ⊕ *www.familyfunhotel.com* ⇨ *614 rooms, 110 suites* ⌂ *Restaurant, food court, grocery, room service, kitchenettes, cable TV with video games, in-room VCRs, 2 tennis courts, 2 pools, wading pool, 2 hot tubs, basketball, volleyball, bar, video game room, children's programs (ages 3–12), playground, dry cleaning, laundry facilities, meeting rooms, no-smoking rooms* ▭ *AE, D, DC, MC, V.*

ORLANDO

International Drive

Take I–4 Exit 72, 74A, or 75A, unless otherwise noted.

The sprawl of newish hotels, restaurants, shopping malls, and dozens of small attractions known as International Drive—"I-Drive" to locals—makes a convenient base for visits to Walt Disney World, Universal, and other attractions in the Orlando area. Parallel to I–4, this four-lane boulevard stretches from Universal Orlando in the north all the way to Kissimmee in the south. Each part of I-Drive has its own personality. The southern end is classier, and south of SeaWorld there's still, amazingly, quite a lot of wide-open space just waiting for new hotels and restaurants to open up. The concentration of cheaper restaurants, fast-food joints, T-shirt shops increases as you go north; Universal Orlando is in this area, but remains a self-contained enclave.

I-Drive's popularity makes it a crowded place to drive in any season. Try to avoid the morning (7–9 AM) and evening (4–6 PM) rush hours. If you're planning a day visiting I-Drive attractions, consider riding the I–Ride Trolley, which travels the length of I-Drive from Florida's Turnpike to the outlet center on Vineland Avenue, stopping at Wet 'n Wild and SeaWorld.

★ **$$$$** ▦ **Peabody Orlando.** Every day at 11 AM, the celebrated Peabody ducks exit a private elevator and waddle across the lobby to the marble fountain where they pass the day, basking in their fame. At 5, they repeat the ritual in reverse. Built by the owners of the landmark Peabody Hotel in Memphis, this 27-story structure looks like three high-rise offices from afar, but don't be put off by the austerity. The interior is handsome and impressive, with gilt and marble halls. Some of the oversize upper-floor rooms have panoramic views of WDW. You can leave your cares behind at the spa or the wellness center, which has medical staff. By 2006 the hotel plans to add 1,700 rooms and be connected to the Orange County Convention Center via an enclosed walkway. ⊠ *9801 International Dr., I-Drive Area 32819* ☎ *407/352–4000 or 800/732–2639* 🖷 *407/351–9177* ⊕ *www.peabodyorlando.com* 🛏 *891 rooms* ♿ *3 restaurants, room service, in-room data ports, in-room safes, cable TV with movies, golf privileges, 4 tennis courts, pool, wading pool, health club, hot tub, massage, spa, 2 lobby lounges, baby-sitting, concierge, business services, convention center, no-smoking rooms* 🖃 *AE, D, DC, MC, V.*

$$$$ ▦ **Rosen Centre Hotel.** This 24-story palace is adjacent to the Orange County Convention Center and within easy walking distance of some of International Drive's newer attractions, like the Pointe*Orlando shopping and entertainment center and Ripley's Believe It or Not! There's a massive pool area surrounded by tropical vegetation and a couple of good restaurants, including the Everglades Room and Cafe Gauguin, where you can admire a big Gauguin-inspired mural while you eat. Universal Orlando ticket and shuttle services are available here. ⊠ *9840 International Dr., I-Drive Area 32819* ☎ *407/996–9480 or 800/ 204–7234* 🖷 *407/996–3169* ⊕ *www.rosencentre.com* 🛏 *1,334 rooms, 80 suites* ♿ *3 restaurants, pizzeria, room service, pool, health club, hot tub, massage, lobby lounge, laundry service, business services, convention center, no-smoking rooms* 🖃 *AE, D, DC, MC, V.*

$$$ ▦ **Embassy Suites Hotel International Drive South.** This all-suites hotel has an expansive Mediterranean-style lobby with marble floors, pillars, hanging lamps, and old-fashioned ceiling fans. The atrium is alive with tropical gardens full of fountains and palm trees. Elsewhere, ceramic tile walkways and brick arches complement the tropical mood. The hotel offers a good number of little extras, like a health club with a fine steam room, free shuttle service to all four Disney parks and Universal Orlando, and a free hot breakfast and nightly beverages. ⊠ *8978 International Dr., I-Drive Area 32819* ☎ *407/352–1400 or 800/433–7275* 🖷 *407/ 363–1120* ⊕ *www.embassysuitesorlando.com* 🛏 *244 suites* ♿ *Restaurant, in-room data ports, in-room safes, cable TV with movies, 2 pools (1 indoor), health club, hot tub, sauna, steam room, lobby lounge, business services, meeting rooms, no-smoking rooms* 🖃 *AE, D, DC, MC, V* 🍴| *BP.*

$$–$$$ ▦ **Embassy Suites International Drive/Jamaican Court.** The concept of an all-suites hotel that serves a free buffet breakfast and complimentary cocktails, pioneered by the Embassy Suites chain, has proved very popular in Orlando. This particular hotel has a central atrium with a lounge where a player piano sets the mood. Each suite has a bedroom and separate living room with a wet bar, pullout sofa, and two TVs—all for a better price than that of many single rooms in the area. Two-room suites can sleep six. ⊠ *8250 Jamaican Ct., I-Drive Area 32819* ☎ *407/345–8250 or 800/327–9797* ⊟ *407/352–1463* ⊕ *www.embassysuites.com* ↩ *246 suites* ⚴ *Room service, in-room safes, in-room data ports, refrigerators, cable TV with movies, indoor-outdoor pool, gym, hot tub, sauna, steam room, lobby lounge, baby-sitting, business services, meeting rooms, car rental, no-smoking rooms* ⊟ *AE, D, DC, MC, V* ⦿ *BP.*

$$–$$$ 🏨 **Sheraton World.** On 28 acres just south of the Orange County Convention Center, this 17-story hotel welcomes families as well as conventioneers. It's roughly midway between the airport and WDW, less than a mile from SeaWorld, and a five-minute shuttle ride from Universal Orlando. Rooms and suites have bright red carpeting and purple-accent couches and drapes. ⊠ *10100 International Dr., I-Drive Area 32821* ☎ *407/352–1100 or 800/327–0363* ⊟ *407/352–3679* ⊕ *www. sheratonworld.com* ↩ *1,102 rooms, 68 suites* ⚴ *3 restaurants, room service, in-room data ports, in-room safes, cable TV with movies, miniature golf, 3 pools, health club, hot tub, massage, lobby lounge, laundry service, business services, convention center, meeting rooms, car rental, no-smoking rooms* ⊟ *AE, D, DC, MC, V.*

$$–$$$ 🏨 **Wyndham Orlando Resort.** The Wyndham has a children's entertainment center, an upscale shopping court, and best of all, a prime location—you could almost throw a baseball from the hotel's driveway and have it land inside the Universal Orlando complex. If you choose the Family Fun Suites option, the youngsters get a separate room with bunk beds. This is one of the few hotels in Orlando that allows pets (with a $50, non-refundable fee). ⊠ *8001 International Dr., I-Drive Area 32819* ☎ *407/351–2420 or 800/996–3426* ⊟ *407/351–5016* ⊕ *www.wyndham. com* ↩ *1,064 rooms* ⚴ *4 restaurants, room service, in-room data ports, in-room safes, refrigerators, cable TV with movies, 4 tennis courts, 3 pools, health club, hot tub, lobby lounge, shops, laundry service, business services, convention center, car rental, some pets allowed (fee), no-smoking rooms* ⊟ *AE, D, DC, MC, V.*

$$ 🏨 **Renaissance Orlando Resort at SeaWorld.** The hotel's 10-story atrium is full of waterfalls, goldfish ponds, and palm trees; as you shoot skyward in sleek, glass elevators, look for the exotic birds—on loan from SeaWorld across the street—twittering in the large, hand-carved, gilded Venetian aviary. Rooms have more floor space than the average Central-Florida hotel plus nice touches like high-speed Internet connections, speakers, and two-line phones. Atlantis, the formal restaurant, is something of an undiscovered gem, serving Mediterranean cuisine. ⊠ *6677 Sea Harbor Dr., I-Drive Area 32821* ☎ *407/351–5555 or 800/ 468–3571* ⊟ *407/351–4618* ⊕ *www.renaissancehotels.com* ↩ *778 rooms* ⚴ *5 restaurants, room service, in-room data ports, cable TV with movies, golf privileges, 4 tennis courts, pool, wading pool, hair salon, health club, hot tub, massage, sauna, volleyball, 3 lounges, baby-sitting, laundry service, concierge, business services, convention center, no-smoking rooms* ⊟ *AE, D, DC, MC, V.*

$$ 🏨 **Summerfield Suites Hotel.** Parents can use that trump-card disciplinary option: "Go to your room!" at this hotel. Sleeping from four to eight people, the one- and two-bedroom units at the all-suites Summerfield are a great option for families. Two-bedroom units, the most popular, have fully equipped kitchens, plus a living room with TV and VCR, and another TV in one bedroom. Plush landscaping make the place seem secluded even though it's on International Drive. ⊠ *8480 International Dr., I-4 Exit 74A, I-Drive Area 32819* ☎ *407/352–2400 or 800/830– 4964* ⊟ *407/352–4631* ⊕ *www.summerfield-orlando.com* ↩ *146 suites* ⚴ *Grocery, in-room data ports, in-room safes, kitchens, microwaves, refrigerators, cable TV with movies, pool, wading pool, gym, hot tub, lobby lounge, laundry facilities, laundry service, video game*

room, business services, meeting rooms, no-smoking rooms ⊟ AE, D,
DC, MC, V.

$–$$ 🏨 **Enclave Suites at Orlando.** With three 10-story buildings surrounding
an office, restaurant, and recreation area, this all-suites lodging is less
a hotel than a condominium complex. Here, what you would spend for
a normal room in a fancy hotel gets you a complete apartment, with a
living room, a full kitchen, two bedrooms, and small terraces with a view
of a nearby lake. Studios with one bed are also available. There's free
transportation to SeaWorld, Wet 'n Wild, and Universal Orlando, but
Wet 'n Wild is an easy walk. ⊠ 6165 Carrier Dr., I-Drive Area 32819
☎ 407/351–1155 or 800/457–0077 🖷 407/351–2001 ⊕ www.
enclavesuites.com ➯ 352 suites ⟁ Grocery, in-room data ports, in-room
safes, kitchens, microwaves, refrigerators, cable TV with movies, tennis court, 3 pools (1 indoor), 2 wading pools, gym, hot tub, playground,
laundry facilities, laundry service, meeting rooms, no-smoking rooms
⊟ AE, D, DC, MC, V.

$–$$ 🏨 **La Quinta Inn & Suites Orlando Convention Center.** A half mile south of
the Orange County Convention Center, this family-oriented hotel is in
the heart of the more upscale part of International Drive. The hotel has
the added convenience of a front entrance on Universal Boulevard, the
relatively undiscovered thoroughfare a block east of I-Drive. Despite the
proximity to the tourist strip, things are still serene here. The king
rooms and suites have refrigerators and microwaves; and, although
there's no restaurant, the hotel provides a complimentary Continental
breakfast daily, and there are a half dozen eateries nearby. ⊠ 8504 Universal Blvd., I–4 Exit 74A, I-Drive Area 32819 ☎ 407/345–1365
🖷 407/345–5586 ⊕ www.laquinta.com ➯ 170 rooms, 15 suites ⟁ In-
room data ports, in-room safes, some microwaves, some refrigerators,
room TV with movies, pool, gym, outdoor hot tub, bar, video game room,
laundry facilities, laundry services, business services, meeting rooms, some
pets allowed; no-smoking rooms ⊟ AE, D, DC, MC, V.

$–$$ 🏨 **Marriott Residence Inn SeaWorld International Center.** The longish name
hints at all the markets the hotel is attempting to tap. SeaWorld, International Drive, and the Orange County Convention Center, all within
a 2-mi radius, are served by hotel shuttles. Suites have data-port phones,
work desks, and full kitchens. Even the least expensive units can sleep
five people. The recreation area around the pool is like a summer camp,
with a basketball court, playground equipment, picnic tables, and gas
grills. Get a firm grip on directions if you are driving. The hotel is adjacent to I–4, but it's 2 mi from the interstate via two expressways, including Beeline Expressway, and four turns. ⊠ 11000 Westwood Blvd.,
I–4 Exit 72, I-Drive Area 32821 ☎ 407/313–3600 🖷 407/313–3631
⊕ www.residenceinnseaworld.com ➯ 350 suites ⟁ Restaurant, ice
cream parlor, pizzeria, in-room data ports, in-room safes, kitchens,
cable TV with movies, pool, wading pool, exercise equipment, gym, outdoor hot tub, basketball, bar, playground, laundry facilities, laundry service, business services, meeting rooms, no-smoking rooms ⊟ AE, D,
DC, MC, V ⊮ BP.

$–$$ 🏨 **Quality Suites Parc Corniche Resort.** A good bet for golf enthusiasts,
the suites-only resort is framed by a Joe Lee–designed course. Each of
the one- and two-bedroom suites, which are full of pastels and tropical
patterns, has a kitchen complete with dishes and a dishwasher, plus a
patio or balcony with golf-course views. The largest accommodations,
with two bedrooms and two baths, can sleep up to six. A complimentary full buffet breakfast is served daily, and SeaWorld is only a few blocks
away. ⊠ 6300 Parc Corniche Dr., I-Drive Area 32821 ☎ 407/239–7100
or 800/446–2721 🖷 407/239–8501 ⊕ www.parccorniche.com ➯ 210
suites ⟁ Restaurant, room service, picnic area, cable TV with movies,

18-hole golf course, pool, wading pool, hot tub, baby-sitting, play-ground, laundry facilities, laundry service, business services, no-smok-ing rooms ⊟ *AE, D, DC, MC, V* ⦿ *BP.*

$–$$ ⊡ **Rosen Plaza Hotel.** Harris Rosen, the largest independent hotel owner in the Orlando market, loves to offer bargains, and you can find one here. This is essentially a convention hotel, although leisure travelers like the prime location and the long list of amenities. Rooms are simple but large, with two queen-size beds. Two upscale restaurants, Jack's Place and Café Matisse, offer great steaks and a great buffet, respectively, but the best food option is the pizza at Rossini's. ⊠ *9700 International Dr., I-Drive Area 32819* ☎ *407/352–9700 or 800/627–8258* ᛒ *407/352–9710* ⊕ *www.rosenplaza.com* ⇱ *810 rooms* ⌕ *2 restaurants, coffee shop, ice cream parlor, pizzeria, room service, in-room data ports, in-room safes, cable TV, pool, hot tub, bar, lobby lounge, nightclub, baby-sitting, video game room, laundry facilities, laundry service, business services, meet-ing rooms, no-smoking rooms* ⊟ *AE, D, DC, MC, V.*

$–$$ ⊡ **Sheraton Studio City.** Atop this Sheraton is a giant silver globe suit-able for Times Square on New Year's Eve. But the interior has a Hol-lywood theme, with movie posters and black-and-white art-deco touches throughout the public spaces and rooms, most of which have two queen beds. The 20th floor has plush luxury suites for those ready to spring for a good view of Universal Studios, directly across I–4. Free shuttles go to the major theme parks and shopping malls. ⊠ *5905 Interna-tional Dr., I-Drive Area 32819* ☎ *407/351–2100 or 800/327–1366* ᛒ *407/345–5249* ⊕ *www.grandthemehotels.com* ⇱ *302 rooms* ⌕ *Restaurant, room service, in-room data ports, in-room safes, cable TV with movies and video games, pool, wading pool, hair salon, hot tub, bar, lobby lounge, video game room, laundry service, concierge, busi-ness services, no-smoking rooms* ⊟ *AE, D, DC, MC, V.*

$–$$ ⊡ **Sierra Suites Hotel.** The two Orlando locations of this all-suites hotel chain are designed for the business traveler: personal voice mail, two phone lines, speakerphone, and a good-size work table in each room. But the benefit for families is that you get a lot for your money. There's a full kitchen, including dishwasher, cookware, and silverware—every-thing you need to avoid restaurant tabs for as long as you like. The earth-tone color scheme is warm if not memorable, and the suites have two queen- or one king-size bed, plus a sofa bed. Although neither Sierra has a restaurant, lots of eateries are within walking distance of both. ⊠ *8750 Universal Blvd., I–4 Exit 74A, I-Drive Area 32819* ☎ *407/903–1500 or 800/473–4772* ᛒ *407/903–1555* ⊕ *www.sierrasuites.com* ⇱ *137 suites* ⌕ *In-room safes, kitchens, cable TV with movies, pool, outdoor hot tub, gym, laundry facilities, laundry service; no-smoking rooms* ⊠ *8100 Palm Pkwy., I–4 Exit 68, 32836* ☎ *407/239–4300 or 800/473–4772* ᛒ *407/239–4446* ⇱ *125 suites* ⌕ *In-room safes, kitchens, cable TV with movies, pool, outdoor hot tub, gym, laundry facilities, laundry service, no-smoking rooms* ⊟ *AE, D, DC, MC, V.*

$ ⊡ **The DoubleTree Castle.** You won't really think you're in a castle at this midprice hotel, although the tall gold-and-silver-color spires, medieval-style mosaics, arched doorways, and U.K. tourists may make you feel like reading Harry Potter. Take your book to either the rooftop terrace or the inviting courtyard, which has a big, round swimming pool. Café Tu Tu Tango, one of the better restaurants in this part of Orlando, has a zesty, small-dish, multi-cultural menu. ⊠ *8629 International Dr., I-Drive Area 32819* ☎ *407/345–1511 or 800/952–2785* ᛒ *407/248–8181* ⊕ *www.doubletreecastle.com* ⇱ *216 rooms* ⌕ *2 restaurants, room service, in-room data ports, in-room safes, minibars, refrigerators, cable TV with movies, pool, gym, hot tub, lobby lounge, video game room, laundry service, no-smoking rooms* ⊟ *AE, D, DC, MC, V.*

$ ▣ **Fairfield Inn by Marriott, Orlando International Drive.** This understated, few-frills, three-story hotel—the Marriott corporation's answer to the Motel 6 and Econo Lodge chains—is a natural for single travelers or small families on a tight budget. It's squeezed between International Drive and I–4, and although it doesn't have the amenities of top-of-the-line Marriott properties, there are nice perks such as complimentary coffee and tea, and free local phone calls. Fitness buffs can walk to the nearby YMCA. ⊠ *8342 Jamaican Ct., I-Drive Area 32819* 🕾🕾 *407/363–1944* 🕾 *800/228–2800* ⊕ *www.fairfieldinn.com* 🛏 *134 rooms* ⟋ *In-room data ports, in-room safes, room TVs with movies, pool, business services, no-smoking rooms* ☰ *AE, D, DC, MC, V.*

$ ▣ **Holiday Inn Hotel & Suites Orlando Convention Center/International Drive Area.** About a mile from the Orange County Convention Center, this is a great headquarters for vacationing families. All rooms have refrigerators and microwaves, and suites have full kitchens with dishwashers. The hotel is one block from the Mercado shopping and dining complex at the heart of International Drive, and it's within walking distance of two-thirds of the attractions on I-Drive. Shuttles run to Universal Orlando, SeaWorld, and Wet 'n Wild, all within 2 mi. ⊠ *8214 Universal Blvd., I-4 Exit 74A, I-Drive Area 32819* 🕾 *407/581–9001* 🖷 *407/581–9002* ⊕ *www.holidayinnconvention.com* 🛏 *150 rooms, 35 suites* ⟋ *Restaurant, in-room data ports, in-room safes, microwaves, refrigerators, cable TV with movies, 2 pools, gym, outdoor hot tub, bar, video game room, laundry facilities, laundry services, business services, meeting rooms, no-smoking rooms* ☰ *AE, D, DC, MC, V.*

$ ▣ **Travelodge Orlando Convention Center.** If you don't want a room with just the bare essentials yet don't have the budget for luxury, this three-story motel is a find. The rooms are comfy if not spectacular; all have two double beds. Children 17 and under stay free in their parents' room (with a maximum of four people per room). The hotel is ¼ mi from Sea-World. Free scheduled transportation is provided to SeaWorld, Universal Studios, and Disney World. ⊠ *6263 Westwood Blvd., I-Drive Area 32821* 🕾 *407/345–8000 or 800/346–1551* 🖷 *407/345–1508* ⊕ *www.travelodge.com* 🛏 *144 rooms* ⟋ *Restaurant, in-room data ports, in-room safes, room TV with movies, 2 pools, exercise equipment, bar, video game room, laundry facilities, laundry services, business services, no-smoking rooms* ☰ *AE, DC, MC, V.*

¢ ▣ **Studio Plus Orlando Convention Center.** Tucked behind a pine forest, this small, all-suites property feels remote but SeaWorld, the Orange County Convention Center, and Pointe*Orlando are all within a 1-mi drive. Amenities are minimal, and the pool area is smallish, but this is a great place to save on your vacation budget. Weekly rates start as low as $255. ⊠ *6443 Westwood Blvd., I-4 Exit 72, I-Drive Area 32821* 🕾 *407/351–1982* 🖷 *407/351–1719* ⊕ *www.extstay.com* 🛏 *13 suites* ⟋ *In-room data ports, in-room safes, kitchens, cable TV, pool, exercise equipment, laundry facilities, business services, no-smoking rooms* ☰ *AE, D, DC, MC, V.*

Southwestern Orlando

The southwest quadrant of Orlando, which includes and surpasses Universal Studios and International Drive, has burgeoned with development since the mid-1990s, with several hotels built within a few miles of I-Drive.

$$$$ ▣ **Ritz-Carlton Orlando Grande Lakes.** Orlando had more than 110,000

Fodor's Choice   hotel rooms before it had a single Ritz-Carlton, but Marriott International, Inc., the parent company of Ritz-Carlton, decided to make up for its absence when it began construction on this particularly extravagant Ritz. In addition to having Wolfgang Puck's Spago restaurant (one of only three in the United States), the hotel also has a waterpark complex that resembles a more upscale version of Wet 'n Wild. The hotel caters to the convention crowd, but also to families, with extensive children's programs. An enclosed hallway connects the Ritz-Carlton to a JW Marriott Hotel, and the two share some amenities, including a huge spa. ⊠ *3000 Central Florida Pkwy. Southwestern Orlando 32837* ☎ *407/529–2255* ▣ *407/529–2240* ⊕ *www.grandelakes.com* ⤺ *584 rooms, 66 suites* ♨ *6 restaurants, room service, in-room data ports, cable TV with movies, 18-hole golf course, 2 pools, wading pool, indoor and outdoor hot tubs, health club, spa, 2 bars, lobby lounge, children's programs (ages 4–12), laundry service, concierge, concierge floor, business services, meeting rooms, no-smoking rooms* ▤ *AE, D, DC, MC, V.*

$$$–$$$$ ▥ **JW Marriott Orlando Grande Lakes.** With more than 70,000 square ft of meeting space, this hotel caters to a convention clientele. But because the hotel is part of a lush resort that includes a European-style spa and a Greg Norman–designed golf course, it also is an appealing place for tourists with a flexible budget. Rooms, at 420 square ft, are on the large side, and most have balconies that overlook the resort's huge pool complex, the spa building, and beyond those, the golf course. Wander down a long connector hallway to the adjoining Ritz-Carlton, where you can use your room charge card in the restaurants and shops. ⊠ *3000 Central Florida Pkwy., Southwestern Orlando 32837* ☎ *407/529–2255* ▣ *407/529–2240* ⊕ *www.grandelakes.com* ⤺ *1,000 rooms, 57 suites* ♨ *4 restaurants, room service, in-room data ports, cable TV with movies, 18-hole golf course, 2 pools, wading pool, indoor and outdoor hot tubs, health club, spa, 2 bars, lobby lounge, laundry service, concierge, concierge floor, business services, meeting rooms, no-smoking rooms* ▤ *AE, D, DC, MC, V.*

Central Orlando

Downtown Orlando, north of Walt Disney World and slightly north of the International Drive area, is a thriving business district with a tourist fringe in the form of Church Street Station. Central Orlando, the area stretching a couple of miles out from downtown in all directions, also offers a number of worthwhile hotels. To get there take Exit 83B off I–4 westbound, Exit 84 off I–4 eastbound.

$$$–$$$$ ▦ **Westin Grand Bohemian.** This European-style property is downtown Orlando's only luxury hotel. Opposite city hall, the Grand Bohemian showcases more than 100 pieces of art—including an Imperial Grand Bösendorfer piano, one of only two in the world, which sits in a posh ground-floor lounge. Rooms are more sedate, despite red and purple curtains. All rooms have three phones and interactive television, and the suites have a fax machine–computer printer as well. Off the main lobby are a Starbucks and an art gallery. ⊠ *325 S. Orange Ave., Downtown Orlando 32801* ☎ *407/313–9000 or 888/472–6312* ▣ *407/313–9001* ⊕ *www.grandbohemianhotel.com* ⤺ *250 rooms, 36 suites* ♨ *Restaurant, bar, room service, in-room data ports, cable TV with movies, pool, gym, concierge, concierge floor, business services, meeting rooms, parking (fee), no-smoking rooms* ▤ *AE, D, MC, V.*

★ $$–$$$ ▦ **The Courtyard at Lake Lucerne.** This group of four B&Bs, all next door to each other, is almost under an expressway bridge at the southwestern edge of downtown. The beautifully restored Victorian houses surround a lush, palm-lined courtyard. There's no noise from the expressway, and as you sit on the porch of one of the mansions, it's easy to imagine yourself back in the time when citrus ruled, and the few tourists who came to the area arrived at the old railroad station on Church Street, six blocks away. Rooms have hardwood floors, Persian rugs, and antique furniture. ✉ *21 N. Lucerne Circle E., 32801* ☎ *407/648–5188* 🖷 *407/246–1368* ⊕ *www.orlandohistoricinn.com* ➥ *15 rooms, 14 suites* ⌂ *In-room data ports, cable TV, meeting room, no-smoking rooms* ▤ *MC, V* ⭤ *CP.*

★ **$$–$$$** 🖼 **Eō Inn & Urban Spa.** The entrance to this boutique hotel is at the rear of the building, behind Panera Bread, the bakery and restaurant that occupies the ground floor. Consequently, this charming three-story hotel in a 1923 building is somewhat of an undiscovered gem. The spa, which offers many services from Swedish massage to beauty treatments, does a brisk business on its own, but hotel guests can always get an appointment. Rooms have black-and-white photographs on the walls and thick down comforters on the beds, as well as high-speed Internet connections. Best of all, Lake Eola, with its 1-mi walking path, is across the street—treat yourself to a king suite overlooking the lake. Thornton Park restaurants and night spots are within easy walking distance. ✉ *227 N. Eola Dr., off E. Robinson St., Thornton Park 32801* ☎ *407/481–8485 or 888/481–8488* 🖷 *407/481–8495* ⊕ *www.eoinn.com* ➥ *17 rooms* ⌂ *In-room data ports, in-room safes, cable TV with movies, indoor and outdoor hot tubs, massage, sauna, spa, laundry service, no-smoking rooms* ▤ *AE, D, DC, MC, V.*

$$ 🖼 **Embassy Suites Orlando Downtown.** Although designed for business travelers, this downtown all-suites property, which opened in 2001, has nice touches for vacationers, too. All suites have two TVs—one in each room. Many suites overlook nearby Lake Eola, and the hotel is a short walk from a half dozen sidewalk cafés, including the on-site Concha Me Crazy, a zesty Caribbean-style eatery. The seven-story, indoor atrium gives the hotel a classy touch. ✉ *191 E. Pine St., Downtown Orlando 32801* ☎ *407/841–1000 or 800/609–3339* 🖷 *407/841–0010* ⊕ *www.embassyorlandodowntown.com* ➥ *167 suites* ⌂ *Restaurant, in-room data ports, in-room safes, refrigerators, cable TV with movies, pool, gym, outdoor hot tub, lobby lounge, laundry service, business services, meeting rooms, no-smoking rooms* ▤ *AE, D, DC, MC, V* ⭤ *BP.*

★ **$$** 🖼 **Four Points Hotel Orlando Downtown by Sheraton.** Across the street from Lake Eola, this downtown oasis is a pleasant place to get away from the tourism district's mayhem, and it's within an easy walk of a lot of good eateries, both downtown and in nearby Thornton Park. The exterior's gold-leaf domes give it a distinctive European look. Many of the suites have splendid lake views. ✉ *151 Washington Ave., Downtown Orlando 33801* ☎ *407/841–3220 or 800/325–3535* 🖷 *407/648–4758* ⊕ *www.fourpoints. com* ➥ *203 rooms, 48 suites* ⌂ *Restaurant, room service, in-room data ports, some refrigerators, some minibars, cable TV with movies, pool, health club, 2 bars, laundry service, concierge, concierge floor, business services, meeting rooms; no-smoking rooms* ▤ *AE, D, MC, V.*

Orlando International Airport

The area around the airport, especially the neighborhood just north of the Beeline Expressway, has become hotel city over the past few years, with virtually every big-name hotel you can think of, including plenty of family-style choices, such as suites with kitchens. All the hotels listed include free airport shuttle service.

$$–$$$ 🖼 **Hyatt Regency Orlando International Airport.** If you have to catch an early morning flight, this hotel, inside the main terminal complex, is a good option. Counting the time you spend waiting for the elevator, your room is just a five-minute walk from the nearest airline ticket counter. Rooms have views of either the runways or a 10-story-tall terminal atrium, and the terminal-side rooms all have balconies. Hemisphere, the hotel's upscale restaurant on the 9th floor, offers a seasonal "worldly eclectic" menu and a spectacular view of the airport runways. An in-house health club and swimming pool provide places to unwind. ✉ *9300 Airport Blvd., Orlando International Airport Area 32827* ☎ *407/825–1234 or 800/ 233–1234* 🖷 *407/856–1672* ⊕ *www.orlandoairport.hyatt.com* ⋑ *446 rooms* ⟐ *2 restaurants, room service, in-room data ports, cable TV with movies, pool, hot tub, health club, laundry service, business services, meeting rooms, no-smoking rooms* ⊟ *AE, D, DC, MC, V.*

$–$$ 🏨 **Adam's Mark Orlando.** About 5 mi from the airport gates, this hotel is between Orlando International and International Drive. And if you like to shop in nontourist-driven stores, there's a real bonus here: the hotel is connected to one of Orlando's biggest shopping centers, the upscale Florida Mall. The hotel feels quite upscale, too, with polished marble floors, fountains in the lobby, and a good in-house restaurant, Le Jardin. Typical rooms have either two queen beds or a king and a fold-out sofa; microwaves and refrigerators are available for a small fee. ✉ *1500 Sand Lake Rd., at S. Orange Blossom Trail, Orlando International Airport Area 32809* ☎ *407/859–1500 or 800/444–2326* 🖷 *407/855–1585* ⊕ *www.adamsmark. com* ⋑ *510 rooms* ⟐ *Restaurant, room service, in-room data ports, cable TV, pool, health club, hot tub, laundry service, business services, meeting rooms, no-smoking rooms* ⊟ *AE, D, DC, MC, V.*

¢–$ 🏨 **AmeriSuites Orlando Airport Northeast and Northwest.** These two hotels (one on each side of State Road 436, north of the airport) offer suites with separate bedrooms and living room/kitchen areas. With red carpeting, gold drapes, an overstuffed couch and lounge chair, and of course, a coffeemaker, the living area has the warm feeling of the quintessential American home. The best factor is that you can pay for a suite and get change back from a $100 bill, even in high season. ✉ *7500 Augusta National Dr., Orlando International Airport Area 32822* ☎ *407/240–3939* 🖷 *407/240–3920* ⊕ *www.amerisuites.com* ⋑ *128 suites* ⟐ *In-room data ports, in-room safes, microwaves, refrigerators, cable TV with movies, pool, gym, hot tub, laundry facilities, laundry service, meeting rooms, no-smoking rooms* ✉ *5435 Forbes Place, Orlando International Airport Area 32822* ☎ *407/816–7800* 🖷 *407/816– 0050* ⊕ *www.amerisuites.com* ⋑ *135 suites* ⟐ *In-room data ports, in-room safes, microwaves, refrigerators, cable TV with movies, pool, gym, hot tub, laundry facilities, laundry service, meeting rooms, no-smoking rooms* ⊟ *AE, D, DC, MC, V* ⦿ *BP.*

OUTLYING TOWNS

Travel farther afield and you can get more comforts and facilities for the money, and maybe even some genuine Orlando charm—of the cozy country-inn variety.

Altamonte Springs

Take I–4 Exit 92.

Staying among the suburban developments, office parks, and shopping malls of Altamonte Springs may not be as glamorous as dwelling with the Disney characters, but accommodations in this suburb, 45 minutes' drive from the theme parks, cost on average about 35% less than comparable lodgings elsewhere in the Orlando area. If you have a yen to visit Daytona Beach, you can get there in about 45 minutes, too. In addition, the area is convenient to Enzo's on the Lake, one of Orlando's best restaurants, as well as to the jumbo Altamonte Mall. One warning: much of the metro-area population lives in this northeastern sector and works in central Orlando. I–4 rush hours can be a big problem.

$ ▣ **Hilton Orlando/Altamonte Springs.** Although the emphasis at this eight-story, concrete-and-glass tower is on the business traveler, the hotel's quiet elegance is a plus for everyone who stays here. The comfortable rooms are decorated with dark-green florals and prints. This hotel also has two floors of one- and two-bedroom suites and individual rooms with concierge service. Everyone is welcome to a free Continental breakfast and another great bonus—free milk and cookies at the end of each day. ⊠ *350 S. Northlake Blvd., 32715* ☎ *407/830–1985 or 800/445–8667* 🖶 *407/331–2911* ⊕ *www.hilton.com* 🛏 *322 rooms, 5 suites* ⚒ *Restaurant, room service, in-room data ports, in-room safes, cable TV with movies, pool, gym, outdoor hot tub, lobby lounge, laundry facilities, laundry service, concierge, concierge floor, business services, meeting rooms, no-smoking rooms* ▭ *AE, D, DC, MC, V* ¶❘ *CP.*

Davenport

Take I–4 Exit 55.

The beauty of Davenport is that virtually no one in Orlando has ever heard of it, even though it's only 13 mi southwest of Walt Disney World's main gate. The relative obscurity of this town makes it a bargain oasis. You'll save 30% or more at Davenport hotels, which surround I–4 at Exit 55 and Baseball City, the big stadium complex there, compared with the same hotel chains on International Drive. Both areas are about the same distance from WDW but in opposite directions.

$ **Hampton Inn Orlando Maingate South.** They've taken some poetic (or marketing) license with the name here. For the record, the hotel is 27 mi from Orlando and there is no "Maingate South" for WDW. Disney's main entrance is just 13 mi away, however, and the hotel offers good bargains and access to attractions west of Orlando, like Cypress Gardens and Fantasy of Flight. Rooms are bright and pleasant—some come with DVD players—and you get a free Continental breakfast and local phone calls. ⊠ *44117 U.S. 27 N, 33897* ☎ *863/420–9898 or 888/ 213–4012* 🖶 *863/420–9797* ⊕ *www.hamptoninn.com* 🛏 *83 rooms* ⚒ *In-room data ports, cable TV, pool, exercise equipment, outdoor hot tub, laundry facilities, meeting room, no-smoking rooms* ▭ *AE, D, DC, MC, V* ¶❘ *CP.*

¢–$ **Best Western Central Florida.** The hotel is nothing extraordinary, but offers a nice, palm-lined courtyard with a swimming pool and outdoor hot tub. The guest rooms, with pink and blue floral pattern bedspreads and blue carpets, are pleasant if not palatial. There's no restaurant, but a Bob Evans Family Restaurant is just across the parking lot, and there's a free Continental breakfast in a small dining area adjacent to the lobby. There's a free shuttle bus to Walt Disney World, plus shuttles to SeaWorld and Universal Orlando for a small fee. ⊠ *2425 Frontage Rd., 33837* ☎ *863/424–2596 or 800/424–1880* 🖶 *863/420–8717* ⊕ *www. bestwestern.com* 🛏 *113 rooms* ⚒ *In-room data ports, cable TV, pool, outdoor hot tub, laundry facilities, no-smoking rooms* ▭ *AE, D, DC, MC, V* ¶❘ *CP.*

¢–$ **Holiday Inn Express Disney South.** Large burgundy-accented rooms and suites at this tidy hotel have irons, ironing boards, and hairdryers, but no coffeemakers. There's no on-site restaurant, but a free Continental breakfast buffet is set up in a small dining area near the lobby, and several chain restaurants are nearby. Suites include microwaves and refrigerators. ⊠ *5225 US Hwy 27 N, 33837* ☎ *863/424–2120 or 800/ 225–3351* 🖶 *863/424–5317* ⊕ *www.hiexpress.com* 🛏 *104 rooms* ⚒ *In-room data ports, some microwaves, some refrigerators, cable TV,* *pool, outdoor hot tub, laundry facilities, meeting room, no-smoking rooms* ⊟ *AE, D, DC, MC, V* ⦿ *CP.*

Lake Mary

Take I–4 Exit 98C.

You may choose Lake Mary for the same reason the American Automobile Association moved its national headquarters here—it's close to Orlando, but just far enough away from the theme park areas to be removed from the maddening crowds. If you love the outdoors, you'll appreciate Lake Mary's proximity to the Orlando area's most treasured natural resource, Wekiva Springs State Park. Daytona Beach is an easy one-hour drive away.

$$ **Marriott Lake Mary.** Opened in summer 2002, this stylish, 10-story hotel markets itself to business travelers, but its location on the north side of Lake Mary gives it a strategic location for tourists as well. It's roughly equidistant between Disney World and Daytona Beach, with either being about 40 mi away. The hotel offers a European-style flair, with a chic Continental eatery, Bistro 1501, on the ground floor. All rooms have work desks and high-speed Internet access. ⊠ *1501 International Pkwy., 32746* ☎ *407/995–1100 or 888/236–2427* 🖷 *407/995–1150* ⊕ *www. marriott.com* ⇨ *299 rooms, 5 suites* ⚘ *Restaurant, room service, in-room data ports, in-room safes, cable TV with movies, pool, gym, outdoor hot tub, bar, laundry facilities, laundry service, concierge, concierge floor, business services, no-smoking rooms* ⊟ *AE, D, DC, MC, V.*

$–$$ **Hilton Garden Inn Lake Mary.** Free HBO, kitchenettes, and hot tubs in the suites are a few of this hotel's extras. If you don't want to cook, you can take your youngsters to the nearest Chuck E. Cheese's, about a mile away off Rinehart Road. Lake Mary is the quintessential upscale suburb, and you'll find plenty of shops and restaurants in the area. Wekiva Springs State Park is a 20-minute drive away. ⊠ *705 Currency Circle, 32746* ☎ *407/531–9900 or 800/445–8667* 🖷 *407/531–1144* ⊕ *www.hilton. com* ⇨ *123 rooms* ⚘ *Grocery, in-room data ports, in-room safes, some in-room hot tubs, microwaves, refrigerators, cable TV with movies, pool, health club, outdoor hot tub, bar, laundry facilities, laundry service, business services, no-smoking rooms* ⊟ *AE, D, DC, MC, V.*

$–$$ **Homewood Suites.** Part of a Hilton-owned chain, this all-suites hotel targets business travelers, but offers some great amenities that benefit families. Each suite has two TVs and a full kitchen. If you don't care to cook, there's a free full breakfast every day. You are also welcome to complimentary drinks during an evening social hour Monday through Thursday. T.G.I. Friday's and several other chain eateries are within a five-minute walk. ⊠ *755 Currency Circle, 32746* ☎ *407/805–9111 or 800/225–5466* 🖷 *407/805–0236* ⊕ *www.homewood-suites.com* ⇨ *112 suites* ⚘ *Restaurant, room service, in-room data ports, in-room safes, cable TV with movies, pool, gym, outdoor hot tub, bar, laundry facilities, laundry service, concierge, concierge floor, business services, no-smoking rooms* ⊟ *AE, D, DC, MC, V* ⦿ *BP.*

Lake Wales

Take I–4 Exit 55 and U.S. 27 S.

South of greater Orlando, this town is a good base for people visiting Bok Tower Gardens or for those on their way to or from South Florida. It's within about 45 minutes of the parks.

$$$–$$$$ **Chalet Suzanne.** This quiet, family-owned country inn, a world away from the world of Disney, was constructed in the 1930s, and subsequent updates have not taken away its original architectural charm. Although painted tropical pink and aqua, the buildings otherwise resemble a Swiss village. Some of the lovely antiques-dotted guest rooms have original tile baths, whereas others have whirlpools. The best overlook a lake or garden. But perhaps the biggest treat is a meal in the inn's elegant restaurant, where a six-course dinner is the house specialty. ⊠ *3800 Chalet Suzanne Dr., 33859* ☎ *863/676–6011 or 800/433–6011* 🖨 *863/676– 1814* ⊕ *www.chaletsuzanne.com* ⇨ *30 rooms* ⚭ *Restaurant, cable TV, pool, lake, badminton, croquet, volleyball, bar, no-smoking rooms* 🚍 *AE, D, DC, MC, V* ⧖*◎⧗ BP.*

Winter Park

Take I–4 Exit 87 or 88.

Winter Park, a small college town and greater Orlando's poshest and best-established neighborhood, is full of chichi shops and restaurants. If its heart is the main thoroughfare of Park Avenue, then its soul must be Central Park, an inviting greensward dotted with huge trees hung with Spanish moss. It feels a million miles away from the tourist track, but it's just a short drive from the major attractions.

$–$$ ▦ **Park Plaza Hotel.** Small and intimate, this 1922 establishment feels almost like a private home. Best accommodations are front garden suites with a living room, which opens onto a long balcony usually abloom with impatiens and bougainvillea. Balconies are so covered with shrubs and ferns that they are somewhat private, inspiring more than a few romantic interludes, a member of management confided. There's not much for kids here, but for adults, a half-dozen sidewalk cafés are within a block, and the Charles Hosmer Morse Museum of Art is within two blocks. ⊠ *307 Park Ave. S, 32789* ☎ *407/647–1072 or 800/228– 7220* 🖨 *407/647–4081* ⊕ *www.parkplazahotel.com* ⇨ *27 rooms* ⚭ *Restaurant, room service, cable TV, lobby lounge, laundry service, no-smoking rooms; no kids under 5* 🚍 *AE, DC, MC, V.*

SHOPPING

FODOR'S CHOICE

Belz Factory Outlet World, in the I-Drive Area
Downtown Disney, in Walt Disney World
Outdoor World, in the I-Drive Area

HIGHLY RECOMMENDED

Florida Mall, in the I-Drive Area
Mall at Millenia, in the I-Drive Area
Park Avenue, in Winter Park
Renninger's Twin Markets, in Mount Dora

Updated by
Gary
McKechnie

SHOPPING IS PART OF THE ENTERTAINMENT at Walt Disney World and throughout the Greater Orlando area. There's something in every price range in virtually every store. Shop-till-you-drop types will be delighted to know that Orlando is packed with malls—and every year there are larger and more elaborate ones. It's nearly impossible to step outside your hotel room without seeing a mall or a sign advertising one. City planners hope that by 2024, there will be a mall for every man, woman, and child in Orlando. So whatever your shopping interests—stuffed toys, blue jeans, flea-market finds—the area provides a great opportunity to do a lifetime of shopping in a few days. Most stores accept traveler's checks, major credit cards, and as much cash as you can leave behind.

WALT DISNEY WORLD RESORT

Naturally, you can find your recommended daily allowance of Disney trinkets in every park. And do you think it's a coincidence that Disney merchandisers route guest exits directly into a gift shop? Not a chance. Beyond the obvious Disney film tie-ins, there are more unusual items to be found, such as the Western-style gifts at the Magic Kingdom's Frontier Trading Post. Outside the parks, there's even more shopping, offering a wealth of wonderfully themed Disney products in categories from sporting goods to artwork to clothing to jewelry. Most Disney stores will hold your merchandise and deliver it free to your room—provided you're staying at a Disney resort. If you return home and realize that you've forgotten a critical souvenir, call WDW's Merchandise Mail Order service at 407/363–6200.

Downtown Disney

Fodor'sChoice The largest concentration of stores on Disney property is found in Downtown Disney. This three-in-one shopping and entertainment complex comprises the Marketplace, West Side, and Pleasure Island, which is known primarily for its clubs.

Marketplace

For pure shopping pleasure, this pleasant complex of lakeside shops (hours generally 9:30 AM–11 PM) is the best bet at Downtown Disney. Although you can find treasures such as animal-theme gifts at the Rainforest Cafe, the most fun is walking around the shopping village, following the sidewalks that curve around the lake and into quiet alcoves. When you need to rest your feet, just dine at a sidewalk café or sit back with a cup of coffee or tea beside the lagoon. The various stores offer a nice blend of chocolates, housewares, artwork, scrapbooks, garden accents, swimwear, silver, gold, cut crystal, games, sporting goods and apparel, and Christmas decorations. If you happen to be out of cash, the Marketplace has instant Disney credit applications next to each register. How convenient.

LEGO Imagination Center. An impressive backdrop of large and elaborate LEGO sculptures and piles of colorful LEGO pieces wait for children and their parents to build toy kitties, cars, or cold fusion chambers. ☎407/828–0065.

Once Upon A Toy. The 16,000-square-ft store arrived in 2002 with a new Disney partner, Hasbro. A whole lotta stuff here, highlighted by Hasbro toys marked with Disney logos and characters. Could life get any better? ☎ 407/934–7775.

World of Disney. For Disney fans, this is *the* Disney superstore. It pushes you into sensory overload with nearly a half-million Disney items from

Tinkerbell wings to Tigger hats. Of course, there's also an artistic side to Disney which you'll see in elegant watches, limited-edition artwork, and stylish furniture pieces with a Disney twist. ☏ *407/828–1451.*

West Side

The West Side is generally a wide promenade bordered by an intriguing mix of shops and restaurants. There are also gift shops attached to **Cirque du Soleil, DisneyQuest,** the **House of Blues,** and **Planet Hollywood.**

Guitar Gallery. This git-box shop sells videos, music books, accessories, guitars, guitars, and more guitars, ranging in price from $89 to $17,000. Keep an eye open for the guitar heroes who drop in prior to gigs at the neighboring House of Blues. If you miss your favorite musician, the clerks have had the stars sign oversize guitar picks, which they display throughout the store. ☏ *407/827–0118.*

Magic Masters. This small shop is arguably the most popular one here. As the magician on duty performs close-up card tricks and sleight of hand, an enraptured audience packs the shop for the free show. After the trick is finished, the sales pitch begins with a promise that (if you buy) they'll teach you how to do that particular feat of prestidigitation before you leave. ☏ *407/827–5900.*

Magnetron. As the name implies, this place sells magnets—some 20,000 of them. So what's the big attraction? Well, they light up, change color, glow in the dark, and come in every shape, size, color, and pop culture character (check out magneto-Elvis). ☏ *407/827–0108.*

Sosa Family Cigar Company. Cigars are kicking ash at this family-owned business. A fella's usually rolling stogies by hand in the front window and there's even a humidor room filled with see-gars. Smoking! ☏ *407/ 827–0114.*

Starabilia's. If you're comfortable paying a few hundred simoleons for a framed, autographed picture of the cast of your favorite '70s sitcom, stop by Starabilia's. Although prices for the memorabilia run high—shoppers have paid from $195 for a Pee-Wee Herman autograph to $250,000 for a Hofner bass signed by The Beatles—you can't lose any money window-shopping, and the turnover of items means the inventory's always entertaining. ☏ *407/827–0104.*

Virgin Megastore. At 49,000 square ft, this enormous store has a selection as large as its prices. You can find better deals elsewhere, but not every record store has around 150,000 music titles, more than 300 listening stations, a full-service café, a 10,000-square-ft book department, and tens of thousands of DVD, software, and video titles. ☏ *407/828–0222.*

There are several smaller, yet still enjoyable, shops along the West Side pedestrian mall. If you need a boost of sugar, the **Candy Cauldron** is filled with chocolate, fudge, hard candy, and other similarly wholesome foods. **Celebrity Eyeworks** carries designer sunglasses as well as replicas of glasses worn by celebrities in popular (as well as forgettable) films of the last few decades. **Mickey's Groove** has hip lamps, posters, greeting cards, and souvenirs inspired by the rodent. **Hoypolloi** adds art to the mix, with beautifully creative sculptures in various media—glass, wood, clay, and metals.

UNIVERSAL ORLANDO RESORT

CityWalk

To spice up the mix of CityWalk's entertainment and nightlife, Universal added stores geared to trendy teens and middle-age conventioneers who can't go back home without a little something. Most stores are tucked between buildings on your left and right when you exit the moving walkway that rolls in from the parking garages, and a few are hidden upstairs. Hours vary but are generally 11 AM–11 PM, closing at midnight on weekends. You can call the shops directly or get complete theme-park, nightlife, and shopping information from **Universal Orlando** (☎ 407/363–8000 ⊕ www.citywalkorlando.com).

All Star Collectibles. Some sports collectors will buy anything signed, thrown, hit, or scratched by their favorite players. That's where All Star comes in. This place appeals to sports junkies with its one-of-a-kind items and paraphernalia that professional autograph hounds hound athletes into signing. If you follow Florida sports, the state's college and professional teams are well represented. ☎ *407/224–2380.*

Cigarz. When the children are still running 100 mph but the din of Universal has worn you adults down, duck upstairs to smoke a hand-rolled cigar and sip a coffee, cordial, or single-malt scotch. Cigarz is open daily from 11 AM to 2 AM. ☎ *407/370–2999.*

Dapy. If you can't locate a lava lamp at your local mall, you can find one here—as well as novelty clocks and other trendy items that display a European flair. ☎ *407/224–2411.*

Elegant Illusions. Still can't tell whether your wedding ring is a cubic zirconia or a 48-carat diamond? Then you won't mind shopping here, where the faux jewelry has creative and nostalgic designs. ☎ *407/224–2347.*

Endangered Species. Merchandise is designed to raise awareness of endangered species, ecosystems, and cultures worldwide. Another draw are periodic appearances by artists, authors, and educators who discuss issues regarding the preservation of the planet. The store sells stuffed animals and T-shirts, prints, and figurines—all with an animal theme. ☎ *407/224–2310.*

Fossil. This shop has hundreds of hip watches, such as the futuristic, limited-edition Brain watch, which can save messages and memos, and other more retro designs. There are also leather goods, apparel, and sunglasses. ☎ *407/226–1705.*

Fresh Produce Sportswear. The idea is to take the color and designs of produce and use them to create bright, comfortable styles for men, women, and children. The style is casual resort wear, all 100% cotton. ☎ *407/363–9363.*

Glow! Borrowing on the magnetic appeal of Downtown Disney's Magnetron (all magnets), Glow! sells everything that shines, glows, reflects, or illuminates, from apparel to home decor. ☎ *407/224–2401.*

Jimmy Buffett's Margaritaville. If you absolutely *must* buy a Jimmy Buffett souvenir and can't make it to Key West, this is the next best thing. You can stock up on JB T-shirts, books, toy guitars, margarita glasses, sunglasses, picture frames, license plates, key chains, and theme hats (cheeseburger, parrot, and toucan). ☎ *407/224–2144.*

Quiet Flight. Florida has managed to turn a natural detriment (small waves) into an asset—Florida's Cocoa Beach is the "Small Wave Capital of the World." This explains Quiet Flight, where surf- and beachwear and accessories either will confirm that you're over the hill or will motivate you to take up the sport. The store opens earlier than most, at 8:30 AM. ☎ 407/224–2126.

Silver. This shop has a great interior—it's designed like the 1930s ship *The Normandie*—and swing music on the speakers creates an art deco–era feeling. The store has an impressive line of silver jewelry and accessories such as watches, handbags, earrings, bracelets, necklaces, rings, candlesticks, and picture frames. ☎ 407/224–2300.

Universal Studios Store. The mother lode of Universal icons can be found here, next to Pastamore. Items are branded with recognizable images from TV, theater, and classic films: monsters, Woody Woodpecker, Babe, Curious George, Jurassic Park, Hercules . . . you want 'em, they got 'em. ☎ 407/224–2207.

THE ORLANDO AREA

Factory Outlets

The International Drive area is filled with factory outlet stores, most on the northeast end. These outlets are clumped together in expansive malls or scattered along the drive, and much of the merchandise is ostensibly discounted 20%–75%. You can find just about anything, some of it top quality, but be advised: retailers have learned that they can fool shoppers into believing they must be getting a deal because they're at a stripped-down outlet store. Actually, prices may be the same as or higher than those at other locations.

Fodor'sChoice **Belz Factory Outlet World.** With more than 200,000 square ft of shopping action, this is the area's largest collection of outlet stores—more than 170—in two malls and four nearby annexes. The malls include such stores as Maidenform, Danskin, Jonathan Logan, Calvin Klein, Van Heusen, Burlington Brands, Bugle Boy, Gap, OshKosh, Bally Shoes, Bass Shoes, DKNY, Fossil, Big Dog, Guess, Polo, Etienne Aigner, Tommy Hilfiger, and Banister. Especially popular are the outlets for athletic shoes: Converse, Reebok, Foot Locker, and Nike. There are also good buys in housewares and linens in such outlets as Pfaltzgraff, Corning/Revere, Mikasa, and Fitz & Floyd. Don't worry about carting home breakable or cumbersome items; these stores will ship your purchases anywhere in the United States by UPS. Although the mall isn't fancy, it's clean and pleasant, attracting shoppers from South America, Japan, and across the USA. Mall 2 offers a carousel for children and an adequate food court. The information booth sells discount tickets to all the non-Disney theme parks. ⊠ 5401 W. Oak Ridge Rd., at northern tip of International Dr. ☎ 407/354–0126 or 407/352–9611 ⊕ www.belz.com ☉ Mon.–Sat. 10–9, Sun. 10–6.

Lake Buena Vista Factory Stores. Although there's scant curb appeal, there is a nice gathering of standard outlet stores. The center is roughly 2 mi south of I–4 and includes Reebok, Nine West, Big Dog, Sony, Liz Claiborne, Wrangler, Disney's Character Corner, American Tourister, Murano, Sony/JVC, Tommy Hilfiger, Ralph Lauren, Jockey, Casio, OshKosh, Fossil, and the area's only Old Navy Outlet. Take Exit 68 at I–4. ⊠ 15591 State Rd. 535, 1 mi north of Hwy. 192 ☎ 407/238–9301 ⊕ www.lbvfs.com ☉ Mon.–Sat. 10–9, Sun. 10–6.

Orlando Premium Outlet. This outlet capitalizes on its proximity to Disney (it's at the confluence of I–4, Highway 535, and International Drive). It can be tricky to reach—you have to take I–4 Exit 68 at Highway 535, head a few blocks east and find the very subtle entrance to Little Lake Bryan Road (it parallels I–4). Parking is plentiful and the center's design makes this almost an "open air" market, so walking can be pleasing on a nice day. Swing by here if you think you can actually get a bargain on Nike, Timberland, Polo, Ralph Lauren, Adidas, Giorgio Armani (he runs a "General Store"), Burberry, Tommy Hilfiger, Dockers, Reebok, Versace, Guess?, Bebe, Mikasa, Max Mara, Nautica, Calvin Klein, and 110 other hip offerings. Take a break in the food court or the pleasant outdoor plaza. The outlet's extended hours offer a good excuse to skip the Disney nightlife and keep on shopping. ✉ *8200 Vineland Rd.* ☎ *407/238–7787* ⊕ *www.premiumoutlets.com* ⊙ *Mon.–Sat. 10–10, Sun. 10–9.*

FodorsChoice **Outdoor World.** The very large and very nice megastore carries goods and provisions for every aspect of outdoor life. In a sparkling 150,000-square-ft western-style lodge accented by antler door handles, fishing ponds, deer tracks in the concrete, and a massive stone fireplace, the store packs in countless fishing boats, RVs, tents, rifles, deep-sea fishing gear, freshwater fishing tackle, scuba equipment, fly-tying materials (classes are offered, too), a pro shop, outdoor clothing, Uncle Buck's Cabin (a restaurant and snack bar), and a shooting gallery. If you're an outdoor enthusiast, this is a must-see. ✉ *5156 International Dr.* ☎ *407/563–5200* ⊕ *www.basspro.com* ⊙ *Mon.–Sat. 9 AM–10 PM, Sun. 10 AM–7 PM.*

Sports Dominator. The huge, multilevel Sports Dominator could probably equip all the players of Major League Baseball and the NFL, NBA, and NHL combined. Each sport receives its own section, crowding the floor with soccer balls, golf clubs, catcher's mitts, jerseys, bows, and a few thousand more sports items. The prices may not be less than anywhere else, but the selection is a winner. A second store, in Kissimmee, serves those staying closer to Disney. ✉ *6464 International Dr.* ☎ *407/354–2100* ✉ *7550 W. Irlo Bronson Hwy., Kissimmee* ☎ *407/397–4700* ⊕ *www.sportsdominator.com* ⊙ *Daily 9 AM–10 PM.*

Flea Markets

Flea World. It's a long traffic-choked haul from the attractions area (about 30 mi northeast), but Flea World claims to be America's largest flea market under one roof. It sells predominately new merchandise—everything from car tires, Ginsu knives, and pet tarantulas to gourmet coffee, biker clothes, darts, NASCAR souvenirs, rugs, books, incense, leather lingerie, and beaded evening gowns. It's also a great place to buy cheap Florida and Mickey Mouse T-shirts. In one building, fifty antiques and collectibles dealers cater to people who can pass up the combination digital ruler and egg timer for some authentic good old junque and collectibles. A free newspaper, distributed at the parking lot entrance, contains a map and directory. Children are entertained at Fun World next door, which offers two unusual miniature golf courses, arcade games, go-carts, bumper cars, bumper boats, children's rides, and batting cages. Flea World is 3 mi east of I–4 Exit 98 on Lake Mary Blvd., then 1 mi south on U.S. 17–92. ✉ *U.S. 17–92, Sanford* ☎ *407/321–1792* ⊕ *www.fleaworld.com* ✆ *Free* ⊙ *Fri.–Sun. 9–6.*

192 Flea Market Outlet. With 400 booths, this market is about one-quarter the size of Sanford's Flea World, but it's much more convenient to the major Orlando attractions (about 10 mi away in Kissimmee) and is open daily. The all-new merchandise includes "tons of items": toys, lug-

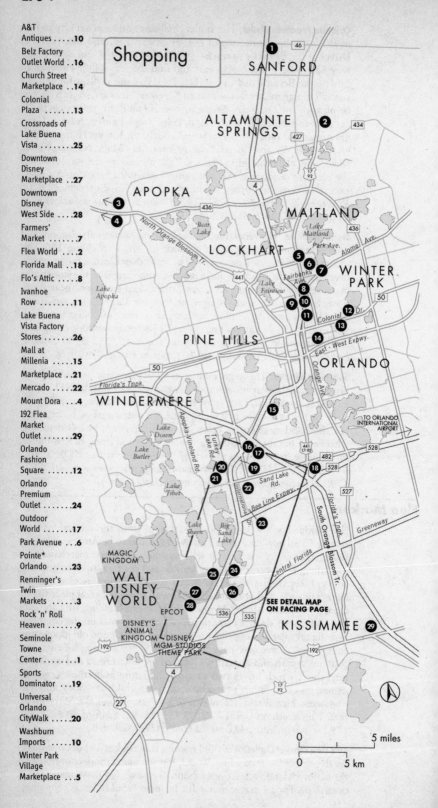

Shopping

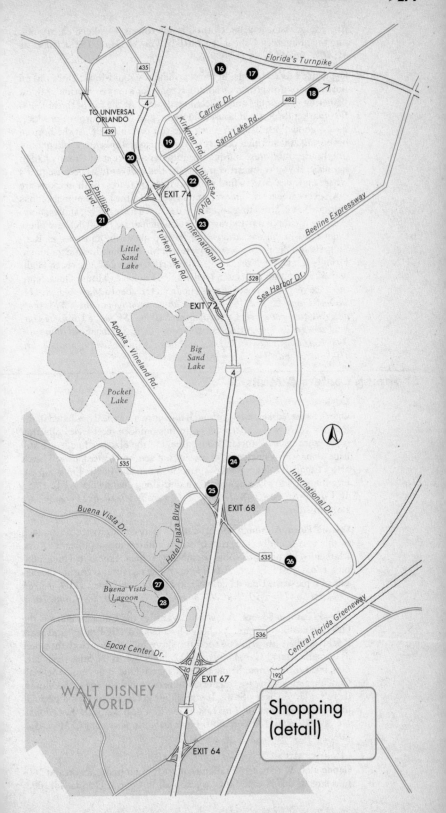

Shopping
(detail)

gage, sunglasses, jewelry, clothes, beach towels, sneakers, electronics, and the obligatory T-shirts. ⊠ *4301 W. Vine St., Hwy. 192, Kissimmee* ☎ *407/396–4555* ⊙ *Daily 9–6.*

★ **Renninger's Twin Markets.** In the charming town of Mount Dora (30 mi northwest of downtown Orlando), Renninger's may be Florida's largest gathering of antiques and collectibles dealers. At the top of the hill, 400 flea-market dealers sell household items, garage-sale surplus, produce, baked goods, pets, and anything else you can think of. At the bottom of the hill, 200 antiques dealers set up shop to sell ephemera, old phonographs, deco fixtures, antique furniture, and other stuff Granny had in her attic. If you're smart, you'll hit the flea market first, because that's where antiques dealers find many of their treasures. Both markets are open every weekend, but on certain weekends, the antiques market has Antique Fairs, attracting about 500 dealers. The really big shows, however, are the three-day Extravaganzas, which draw 1,400 dealers. These events can be all-day affairs; otherwise, spend the morning at Renninger's and then move on to downtown Mount Dora in time for lunch. From I–4, take the Florida Turnpike north to Exit 267A to reach Highway 429 east and, 8 mi later, Highway 441 north to Mount Dora. Summers are very slow, the pace picks up from October to May. ⊠ *U.S. 441, Mount Dora* ☎ *352/383–8393* ⊕ *www.renningers.com* ✉ *Markets and Antiques Fairs free; Extravaganzas $10 Fri., $5 Sat., $3 Sun.* ⊙ *Markets, weekends 9–5; Antiques Fairs, Mar.–Oct., 3rd weekend of month, 9–5; Extravaganzas Nov., Jan., and Feb., 3rd weekend of month, Fri. 10–5, weekends 9–5.*

Shopping Centers & Malls

Downtown Orlando

Church Street Marketplace. Although downtown's appeal has faded in the last few years, a few folks still go to this outdoor mall-style collection of restaurants and stores. Brookstone and the Sharper Image are still here, along with a smattering of jewelry, hot dog, and coffee kiosks. There's also a Cigarz, Hooters, Friday's American Bar, and Jungle Jim's. For entertainment, Howl at the Moon is a sing-along dueling piano bar. ⊠ *55 W. Church St.* ☎ *407/841–8000* ⊙ *Generally 10–10, but hrs may vary store-to-store.*

Colonial Plaza. Although you have to navigate dense city traffic to reach it, this user-friendly collection of stores and restaurants includes Ross, Marshalls, Barnes and Noble, SteinMart, Staples, Linens 'n Things, Babies 'R' Us, Just for Feet, and Old Navy. The restaurants feature the cuisine of some of the United Nations' most popular countries. ⊠ *2400-2788 Colonial Dr., Hwy. 50* ☎ *407/894–3601* ⊙ *Mon.–Sat. 10–9, Sun. 10–6.*

Orlando Fashion Square. A few blocks east of the Colonial Plaza is the Orlando Fashion Square. Anchored by a Dillard's, JCPenney, and Sears Roebuck, there are also 165 specialty shops including such chain stores as Camelot Music, Gap, Lerner, and Lechters. Wicks 'N' Sticks sells candles; local entrepreneur Selma serves delicious (and eponymous) Selma's Cookies; and, just in case you missed something at the home of the Mouse, there's a large Disney Store. If you didn't get lunch, there's a popular food court. The mall is 3 mi east of I–4 Exit 83B. ⊠ *3201 E. Colonial Dr.* ☎ *407/896–1131* ⊕ *www.orlandofashionsquare.com* ⊙ *Mon.–Sat. 10–9, Sun. 11–6.*

International Drive Area, Orlando

★ **Florida Mall.** With nearly 2 million square ft of shopping action and 260-plus stores, this is easily the largest mall in Central Florida. In 2002, they added to the appeal by opening the area's first Nordstrom and Lord & Taylor stores. In addition, its full slate of anchor stores and specialty shops includes Burdines, Sears Roebuck, JCPenney, Dillard's, Saks Fifth Avenue, Restoration Hardware, J. Crew, Pottery Barn, Brooks Brothers, Cutter & Buck, Harry & David Gourmet Foods, Swarovski, Mystique, seven theaters, a 17-restaurant food court, as well as sit-down restaurants Ruby Tuesday, California Cafe, Paradise Bakery, and a Pebbles Cafe in Saks. Stroller and wheelchair rentals are available, along with concierge services and, because the mall attracts crowds of Brazilian and Puerto Rican tourists, foreign language assistance. The mall is minutes from the Orlando International Airport and 4½ mi east of I–4 and International Drive at the corner of Sand Lake Road and South Orange Blossom Trail. ⊠ *8001 S. Orange Blossom Trail* ☎ *407/851-6255* ⊕ *www.shopsimon.com* ◷ *Mon.–Sat. 10–9:30, Sun. 11–6.*

★ **Mall at Millenia.** The biggest arrival in Orlando's retail wars is the 1.2 million square ft. Mall at Millenia. A few minutes northwest of Universal Orlando, they've upped the ante with several stores which are exclusive to the area, including their three anchors; Neiman Marcus, Bloomingdale's and Macy's. Restaurants including P. F. Chang's, The Cheesecake Factory, Panera Bread, and the California Pizza Kitchen may lure you to dine even if you don't shop—but you will, thanks to standouts like Orlando's only Apple Store, plus Gucci, Brookstone, Crate & Barrel, Burberry, Pottery Barn for Kids, Futuretronics, Cartier, Tiffany, and about 170 neighbors. Swing by Bang & Olufsen, where cutting-edge stereo and video gear will make your latest electronics purchase look like an eight-track player. The retro-nouveau design of the mall's furnishings incorporates 250-million-year-old fossilized tile as well as a dozen LED screens suspended in the mall rotunda broadcasting entertainment and fashion shows. The food court offers sustenance from Cajun to sushi and dozens of tastes in between, and a currency exchange counter is handy for international guests (who make up a third of the mall's shoppers). Other hotel-like services include a concierge selling area attraction tickets, a post office, and valet parking ($5). Across the street, there's a Home Depot and a Home Depot Expo—a classy design center with some extraordinary home furnishings. Easy to reach, take Exit 78 off I–4. ⊠ *4200 S. Conway Road* ☎ *407/363–3555* ⊕ *www.mallatmillenia.com* ◷ *Mon.–Sat. 10–9:30, Sun. 11–7.*

Marketplace. Convenient for visitors staying on or near International Drive, the Marketplace (not to be confused with Disney's Marketplace) provides all the basic necessities in one spot. Stores include a pharmacy, post office, one-hour film processor, stationery store, bakery, dry cleaner, hair salon, optical shop, natural-food grocery, and 24-hour supermarket. Also in the Marketplace are three popular restaurants: Christini's, Enzo's, and the Phoenician. Take the I–4 Sand Lake Road exit (Exit 74AB) and head west. ⊠ *7600 Dr. Phillips Blvd.* ☎ *no phone* ◷ *Hrs vary.*

Mercado. This is a Mediterranean-style entertainment-retail center for bus tours and tourists meandering along International Drive. It's home to specialty shops and an international food court, and live entertainment offered at various times throughout the day. That said, a dwindling number of shops makes this one a toss up. ⊠ *8445 International Dr.* ☎ *407/345–9337* ⊕ *www.themercado.com* ◷ *Daily 10 AM–11 PM.*

Pointe*Orlando. Strategically located within walking distance of the Peabody Orlando and Orange County Convention Center, this is perhaps the most impressive retail center along the I-Drive corridor. In addition to WonderWorks and the enormous Muvico Pointe 21 theater, the massive complex, houses 70 specialty shops, including A/X Armani

Exchange, Abercrombie & Fitch, Foot Locker Superstore, Chico's, Denim Place, Gap, Tommy Hilfiger, Victoria's Secret, Dan Marino's Town Tavern, Hooters, Monty's Conch Harbor, and Johnny Rockets. There are also a few dozen pushcart vendors selling hair ribbons, sunglasses, and other small items. The focal point, however, is the mighty impressive F. A. O. Schwarz, the legendary store with every toy you can imagine—75% of them exclusive to F. A. O. Considering you have to pay to park ($2 for 15 minutes–2 hours, $5 daily), the nearby ATM is more than convenient. ☒ *9101 International Dr.* ☎ *407/248–2838* ⊕ *www. pointeorlandofl.com* ⊙ *Sun.–Thurs. 10–10, Fri.–Sat. 10 AM–11 PM.*

Lake Buena Vista

Crossroads of Lake Buena Vista. Directly across from the main entrance to Walt Disney World, 11 restaurants and more than 25 shops cater primarily to tourists. Upscale and casual shops are geared to sun and surf, electronics, and children, but the necessities, such as the 24-hour **Gooding's supermarket** (☎ 407/827–1200), post office, bank, and cleaners, are also here. You can find the usual franchised restaurants as well as some local spots, such as the casual Pebbles. While you shop, your offspring can entertain themselves at Pirate's Cove Adventure Golf. To reach it, head out the Disney entrance/exit of Lake Buena Vista or take I–4 to Exit 68. ☒ *12545–12551 Rte. 535* ⊙ *Stores daily 10–10; restaurant hrs vary.*

Northern Suburbs

Seminole Towne Center. This mall answers the shopping needs of Orlando's burgeoning northern suburbs. About 30 mi northeast of downtown Orlando, the mall is anchored by Dillard's, Sears Roebuck, JCPenney, Burdines, and Parisian, and contains more than 120 retailers. For something tropical, try A Shop Called Mango, owned by singer Jimmy Buffett. And just in case you missed something in the theme parks, there's a branch of the Disney Store here. Strollers and wheelchairs are available for rent. There's a pretty good food court, too. About five minutes east on Highway 46, downtown Sanford has a nice—if sporadic—mix of antiques shops. The mall is ¼ mi east of I–4 (Exit 101C) and south of Route 46. ☒ *200 Towne Center Circle, Sanford* ☎ *407/323–2262* ⊕ *www.shopsimon.com* ⊙ *Mon.–Sat. 10–9, Sun. noon–6.*

Winter Park Village Marketplace. Just a few miles north of Orlando in fashionable Winter Park is this hopping spot, with a nice mix of shops and restaurants and a 20-screen movie theater. Evenings are particularly active with young professional types coming by for stores such as Borders, Pier One, Wolf Camera, Chamberlin's natural foods market, Owen Allen (creative furniture), Ann Taylor, Hallmark, and Kidz Quest, or to grab a bite at P. F. Chang's, Brio Tuscan Grille, or Johnny Rockets. From I–4, take Exit 88 (Lee Road) and head east 2 mi to Route 17–92, then turn right (south)—the Village is ¼ mi on your left. ☒ *500 N. Orlando Ave., Winter Park* ⊕ *www.shopwinterparkvillage.com* ⊙ *Mon.–Sat. 10–9, Sun. noon–6.*

Shopping Districts

Orlando's Antiques Row

Orlando has a small antiques row north of downtown on North Orange Avenue. At present, some shops are battling increased rents and the incursion of medical offices flowing in from the nearby hospital. Still, there are enough vintage clothing stores, baseball card shops, and funky furniture and import stores to make it worth a visit if you're in the neighborhood or are en route to dinner on Winter Park's Park Avenue. Get off I–4 at Exit 85, take Princeton Avenue east to North Orange Avenue, and turn right.

A&T Antiques. They pride themselves on having the area's largest selection of antiques. Keep in mind that here antiques will be primarily European and country pine furniture and decorative pieces. ⊠ *1620 N. Orange Ave.* ☎ *407/896–9831* ⊘ *Weekdays 9–6, Sat. 10–5.*

Flo's Attic. The wonderful neighborhood store sells furniture, pottery, china, jewelry, and other treasures. There's lots of stuff to sort through. ⊠ *1800 N. Orange Ave.* ☎ *407/895–1800* ⊘ *Daily 9–5.*

Ivanhoe Row. Several blocks south is a group of shops that sell delightful (but pricey) antiques. The Fly Fisherman specializes in accoutrements for the angler. Swanson's Antiques carries a fine selection of 19th- and 20th-century furniture and bric-a-brac. Fredlund Wildlife Gallery offers paintings and sculptures of various members of the animal kingdom. Other shops include the William Moseley Gallery (19th-century oil paintings), Tim's Wine Market (hundreds of labels), Jarboe (upscale women's fashions), and Christopher Jude (upscale men's clothing). After antiquing, cross the street and take a stroll in the beautiful park surrounding the lake. ⊠ *1211–1231 N. Orange Ave., at Virginia Dr.* ☎ *407/898–6050* ⊘ *Weekdays 10–6, Sat. 10–5.*

Washburn Imports. Next door to A&T Antiques, this shop is loaded with funky furniture and home accent pieces from faraway destinations. Prices are fair and the mix appears better than at many import stores. ⊠ *1616 N. Orange Ave.* ☎ *407/228–4403* ⊘ *Daily 11–6.*

need a break? The **White Wolf Café** (⊠ 1829 N. Orange Ave. ☎ 407/895–5590) is a happening sidewalk eatery, attracting weekend shoppers and evening locals who dine at sidewalk tables and then stroll among the neighboring shops. Specialties include a lunch entrée of a chicken breast, goat cheese, walnuts, and dried cranberries on a field of mixed greens.

Rock 'n' Roll Heaven. If you're wondering where old vinyl records have gone, they're at Rock 'n' Roll Heaven. Crammed with rare albums, 45s, rock paraphernalia, board games, and sheet music, the shop is a fun spot for the curious and a must-see for collectors. The Ehmen brothers are devoted to the genre and take pride in selling only mint-condition records—although they also sell funkified dance discs in a side room. ⊠ *1814 N. Orange Ave.* ☎ *407/896–1952* ⊘ *Mon.–Sat. 10–7:30; call ahead for Sun. hrs.*

Mount Dora

Founded by homesteaders in 1874, this charming little town has 19th-century stores, houses, and bed-and-breakfasts tucked into rolling hills that overlook Lake Dora. The New England–style village is recognized as the antiques capital of Florida and is also called "Festival City" for its art, antiques, and crafts shows that take place nearly every weekend in fall, winter, and spring. There are dozens of crafts shops, boutiques, galleries, and antiques shops here—and more opening nearly every day. The intersection of 5th Avenue and Donnelly Street is the hub, and shops spread out from there in every direction. Among the standouts are Uncle Al's Time Capsule (collectibles and autographed celeb photos), Piglet's Pantry (fancy pet food and toys), Yesterday, Today and Tomorrow (surprisingly chic ladies' fashions), and Dickens-Reed (a cozy village bookstore and coffee shop).

When you're finished shopping, you can get a bite at any of Mount Dora's varied eating establishments, from the tea and scones at the Windsor Rose Tea Room to the creative cuisine of the Goblin Market. Look for

Shiraz bistro, which serves tasty urban cuisine—it's hidden upstairs in a retail complex. Mount Dora is west of U.S. 441 on Old U.S. 441 or Route 44B. Contact the **Chamber of Commerce** (☎ 352/383–2165 ⊕ www. mountdora.com) for more information.

Winter Park

★ In the more than 100 years since rich northern families started building grand estates in this swank Orlando suburb, **Park Avenue** has become a favorite for tony shopping. Although longtime residents complain that the avenue is beginning to resemble a mall—as local one-of-a-kind stores are replaced by chains—visitors are usually charmed by this posh shopping district, with its tiny courtyards ringed by chic restaurants (perfect for people-watching), galleries, bookstores, and other little shops.

For shoppers and nonshoppers alike the real fun of Park Avenue is exploring the little nooks and crannies that divert you from the main drag. Between Welbourne and Morse avenues, around the corner from Barnie's Coffee, you find Greeneda Court. A walk to the back reveals a delightful fountain and wrought-iron tables and chairs where you can sit and relax with a cappuccino from Barnie's. Of course, the antiques store hidden there could keep you on your feet. In the middle of the next block, wedged in between Victorian Joy (No. 316), a children's boutique with designer clothing, and the Rune Stone, a European toy store that adults enjoy as much as the kids, is the Hidden Garden Shops, which houses Pooh's Corner, a delightful children's bookstore specializing in hard-to-find titles. Also look for Wood, Stone and Steel, which carries culinary tools and tabletop items. Scott Laurent Gallery showcases the works of more than 150 Central Florida artists and artisans, including paintings, original jewelry, original and limited-edition framed art, sculpture, art glass, fountains, and decorative gifts. Elsewhere you can find a Caswell-Massey Express, Crabtree & Evelyn, Talbot's Petites, Asiantiques, Williams-Sonoma, Thomas Kinkade Gallery, and the mighty cool Restoration Hardware and Home Elements. The third weekend in March brings the **Winter Park Sidewalk Art Festival** (☎ 407/672–6390); more than 40 years after its debut, it still attracts thousands of art aficionados and a few hundred of America's better artists. ⊠ *Park Ave. between Fairbanks and Canton Aves.* ◷ *Most shops Mon.–Sat. 10–5, some also Sun. noon–5.*

Farmers' Market. If you happen to be in town on Saturday morning, you might want to walk over to the Farmer's Market, next to the downtown train depot, two blocks west of Park Avenue. This market shows the real community behind the upper-crust facade. Friends and neighbors gather to shop for fresh fruits and vegetables, breads and pastas, fish, sausage, herbs and spices, and colorful fresh flowers and tropical plants. Early risers nibble on tangerines, oranges, avocados, and strawberries or drop by for a breakfast of pastries, bagels, rolls, or crepes served with a cup of hot chocolate, espresso, or spiced tea. ⊠ *New England and New York Aves.* ☎ *407/599–3358* ◷ *Sat. 7–1.*

SPORTS AND THE OUTDOORS

FODOR'S CHOICE

Disney's Wide World of Sports Complex

Grand Cypress Equestrian Center, near Lake Buena Vista

Osprey Ridge Golf Course, in Walt Disney World

Sky Venture, off International Drive

Wekiva River, in Apopka

The Winter Summerland Miniature Golf Course, in Walt Disney World

HIGHLY RECOMMENDED

The Aiguille Rock Climbing Center, in Longwood

Bay Lake Fishing Trips, in Walt Disney World

Champions Gate Golf Club, near Kissimmee

The Orlando Magic, in dowtown Orlando

The Richard Petty Driving Experience at the Walt Disney World Speedway

The West Orange Bike Trail, from Oakland to Apopka

Wyndham Palace Resort & Spa Health Club, in Lake Buena Vista

Updated by
Rowland
Stiteler

THERE'S MORE TO AN ACTIVE ORLANDO experience than walking 10 mi a day in the theme parks. Warm Florida weather encourages plenty of activity in myriad parks, pools, lakes, and rivers, plus golf, tennis, and did anyone mention Disney's Wide World of Sports? As many residents will tell you, there's nothing that can quite compare to an afternoon paddling down a Florida river, watching the alligators splash into the water and the snowy egrets glide among the palm trees.

Orlando is definitely the place to visit if you want to be outside, and you can find just about every outdoor sport here—unless it involves a ski lift. There are plenty of tennis courts and more than 130 golf courses, staffed by nearly three dozen PGA pros, in a 40-mi radius. Some of the world's best-known golfing champions—huge names such as Arnold Palmer and Tiger Woods—have homes in the Orlando area. Anglers soak up the Orlando sun on the dozens of small lakes, and the metropolitan area has as many big-league professional bass fishermen as big-league baseball stars and PGA golf luminaries. Predictably, boating is popular, on the hundreds of lakes and on the scores of backcountry rivers fed by clear, warm springs.

As a professional sports town, Orlando holds a hot ticket. The Orlando Magic basketball team is big time, and baseball fans have plenty of minor-league action to enjoy. The International Hockey League franchise, the Orlando Solar Bears, has a rabid fan base, and the Walt Disney World Speedway is the home of the Indy 200 and the Richard Petty Driving Experience. At Disney's Wide World of Sports, you can watch or you can play. The complex hosts participatory and tournament-type events in more than 25 individual and team sports, including basketball, softball, and track-and-field; and it serves as the spring-training home of the Atlanta Braves.

But not everything in Orlando is wholesome, Disney-style family fun. Wagering a wad of cash at the jai-alai fronton or the dog track is guaranteed to wipe the refrain from "It's a Small World" right out of your head. Most of the tracks and frontons now have closed-circuit TV links with major horse-racing tracks, so you can bet on the ponies and then watch the race on a big-screen TV. And even if you bet and lose steadily, you won't necessarily spend more than you would at most Disney attractions—that is, depending on how much you wager.

Auto Racing

★ **The Richard Petty Driving Experience** allows you to ride in or even drive a NASCAR-style stock car on a real racetrack. Depending on what you're willing to spend—prices range from $95 to $1,270—you can do everything from being a passenger for three laps on the 1-mi track to taking 1½ days of lessons, culminating in your very own solo behind the wheel. The Richard Petty organization has a second Central Florida location at the Daytona International Speedway, but it involves riding in the car with an experienced race-car driver rather than driving a car yourself. ⊠ *Walt Disney World Speedway* ☎ *800/237–3889* ⊕ *www.1800bepetty.com.*

Baseball

Watching a minor-league game or a major-league spring-training game in a small ballpark can take you back to a time when going to a game didn't mean bringing binoculars or watching the big screen to see what was happening. Minor-league teams play April through September, and spring training lasts only a few weeks, usually February through March. It can be a thrill to watch stars of the big leagues up close in spring-training games while you, and they, enjoy a spring break before getting back to work. Tickets to the minors usually run $3–$6, and spring-training seats, except for the Braves, cost $8–$10.

Minor League

The Orlando Rays are the Tampa Bay Devil Rays' Class AA Southern League affiliate. They play 70 home games April through August. Tickets are $5–$8. ⊠ *Disney's Wide World of Sports Stadium, 700 W. Victory Way, Kissimmee* ☎ *407/939–4263* ⊕ *www.orlandorays.com.*

Major League Spring Training

For dates and more information about spring training, get a copy of the free **Florida Spring Training Guide.** For a copy, contact the **Florida Sports Foundation** (⊠ 2964 Wellington Circle N, Tallahassee 32308 ☎ 850/488–8347), which publishes the guide each February.

The Atlanta Braves hold spring training and exhibition baseball games with other major-league teams during February and March. Tickets are $11.50–$19, and are available through Ticketmaster or at the stadium box office. The Braves offer an instructional training season for rookie prospects in September and October. ⊠ *Disney's Wide World of Sports Stadium, 700 W. Victory Way, Kissimmee* ☎ *407/939–4263; 407/839–3900 Ticketmaster* ⊕ *atlanta.braves.mlb.com.*

The Houston Astros (⊠ Osceola County Stadium, 1000 Bill Beck Blvd., Kissimmee ☎ 407/933–5500) have spring training 18 mi south of Orlando. Ticket prices are $9–$14.

Basketball

★ **The Orlando Magic** has driven the city to new heights of hoop fanaticism. Tickets, which run $10–$150, are so hard to get that your best bet for seeing a game might be a sports bar. ⊠ *TD Waterhouse Centre, 600 W. Amelia St., Downtown Orlando, 2 blocks west of I–4 Exit 41* ☎ *407/839–3900 Ticketmaster; 407/896–2442 season tickets* ⊕ *www.nba.com/magic.*

Biking

Walt Disney World

The most scenic biking in Orlando is on Walt Disney World property, along roads that take you past forests, lakes, golf courses, wooded campgrounds, and resort villas. Most rental locations have children's bikes with training wheels and bikes with baby seats, in addition to regular adult bikes. Disney's lawyers are always watching out for liability problems, so management asks that you wear helmets, which are free with all bike rentals.

Theoretically, bike rentals are only for those lodging on WDW property; in practice, rental outfits usually check I.D.'s only in busy seasons. Bikes must be used, however, only in the area in which you rent them. You must be 18 or older to rent a bike at all Disney locations.

You can rent bikes for $7.55 per hour at the **Barefoot Bay Marina** (☎ 407/934–2850), open daily from 10 to 5. Rentals at **Coronado Springs Resort** (☎ 407/939–1000), near Disney–MGM Studios, are $8 per hour or $22 per day. The resort's odd collection of rental bikes includes a two-seat surrey bike (a four-wheel bike designed to look like an old-fashioned carriage), which rents for $18 per half hour, and a four-seat surrey bike that rents for $22 per half hour. At **Fort Wilderness Bike Barn** (☎ 407/824–2742), bicycles rent for $8 per hour and $21 per day. At the **BoardWalk Resort** (☎ 407/939–6486; 407/560–8754 surrey bikes), near Disney–MGM Studios, two types of bikes are offered at two separate kiosks. Surrey bikes cost $18, $20, and $23 per half hour, depending on the size of the bike. Regular bicycles are $7 per hour.

Orlando Area

For years, Orlando had no bike trails to speak of and a tough stand on riding bikes on sidewalks. But things have changed. The city now has two good bike trails, created from former railroad lines, part of the nationwide Rails to Trails network. Information about Orlando bike trails can be obtained from the **Orlando City Transportation Planning Bureau** (☎ 407/246–2775).

★ **The West Orange Trail,** the longest bike trail in the Orlando area, runs some 20 mi through western Orlando and the neighboring towns of Winter Garden and Apopka. **Clarcona Horseman's Park** (⊠ 3535 Damon Rd., Apopka ☎407/654–1108) is the best place to access the West Orange Trail. See www.floridagreenwaysandtrails.com for more information. You can rent bikes and rollerblades at **West Orange Trail Bikes & Blades** (⊠ 17914 State Rd. 438, Winter Garden ☎ 407/877–0600).

The Cady Way Trail connects eastern Orlando with the well-manicured enclave suburb of Winter Park. The pleasant trail is only 3½ mi long, with water fountains and shaded seating along the route. The best access point is the parking lot at the west end of the trail, immediately adjacent to the east side of the Orlando Fashion Square Mall (3201 E. Colonial Dr., about 3 mi east of I–4 Exit 83B). You can also enter the trail on its east end, at Cady Way Park (1300 S. Denning Ave.).

The Clermont–Lake County region is where most cyclists prefer to ride. Since it's out in the boonies, there isn't much traffic. Orange groves are great scenery, and some hills afford challenges.

The Rollins College area in Winter Park is the place to pedal for views of lakes, tree-lined streets, and grand old-money homes.

Dog Racing

The Sanford Orlando Kennel Club has dog racing and betting, as well as South Florida horse racing simulcasts and betting. The club is open November through April, and has races at 7:30 PM Monday through Saturday and matinees on Monday, Wednesday, and Saturday at 12:30. Admission is $1, and $2 for the clubhouse. ⊠ *301 Dog Track Rd., Longwood* ☎ 407/831–1600.

Fishing

Central Florida freshwater lakes and rivers teem with all kinds of fish, especially largemouth black bass but also perch, catfish, sunfish, and pike.

Licenses

To fish in most Florida waters (but not at Walt Disney World) anglers over 16 need a fishing license, available at bait-and-tackle shops, fishing camps, most sporting-goods stores, and Wal-Marts and Kmarts. Some of these locations may not sell saltwater licenses, or they may serve non-Florida residents only; call ahead to be on the safe side. Freshwater or saltwater licenses are each $17 for seven days and $32 for one year. For Florida residents, a freshwater or saltwater license is $13.50 each, or $27 for both. Residents over 65 need no license. Information on obtaining fishing licenses is available from the **Florida Game & Fish Commission** (☎ 850/488–3641).

Walt Disney World

★ **Bay Lake Fishing Trips** (☎ 407/939–7529) offers two-hour fishing excursions on regularly stocked Bay Lake and Seven Seas Lagoon. Departing from the Fort Wilderness, Wilderness Lodge, Contemporary, Polynesian, and Grand Floridian resort marinas, trips include boat, equipment, and a guide for up to five anglers. These organized outings are the only way you're allowed to fish on the lakes, which are brimming with fish. Reservations are required. Yacht and Beach Club guests and Boardwalk Hotel guests can book a similar fishing excursion on Crescent Lake for the same fee as the Bay Lake trip. Two-hour trips, which depart daily at 7, 10, and 1:30, are $180–$210, plus $80 for each additional hour. Shinners (live bait) are available for $15 per dozen.

On **Captain Jack's Guided Bass Tours** (☎ 407/828–2204), bass specialists go along for the two-hour fishing expeditions on Lake Buena Vista. Anglers depart from the Downtown Disney Marketplace marina at 6:30 AM, 9 AM, 1:30 PM, and 3:25 PM. Trips for groups of 2 to 5 people cost $180–$195. Per-person admission, available only for the 9 AM trip, is $80.

The Fort Wilderness Bike Barn (☎ 407/824–2742), open daily 8–6, rents poles and tackle for fishing in the canals around the Port Orleans–Riverside (formerly Dixie Landings) and Port Orleans resorts and at Fort Wilderness Resort and Campground. Fishing without a guide is permitted in these areas. A cane pole with tackle is $4 per hour and $9 per day; rod and reel with tackle is $5 per hour and $9.50 per day. You must be at least 18 to rent a rod and reel. Policy stipulates that rod users must be 12 years old, though this is not strictly enforced.

Kids-Only Fishing Trips (☎ 407/939–7529), for ages 5–12 are led by adult Disney staff members who drive the boats and serve as guides. One-hour excursions set out Monday through Friday at 10 AM and are $30 per child.

Ol' Man Island Fishing Hole (✉ Port Orleans–Riverside ☎ 407/934–5409) has fishing off a dock. Catch-and-release is encouraged, but you can have your fish packed in ice to take home—you have to clean them yourself. Cane poles and bait are $4 per hour; a rod and reel is $8 per hour and can be shared by the whole family. You must rent your equipment here to use the dock. Two-hour excursions in a boat with a driver are $80 per person, and include rod, reel, and bait. The Fishing Hole is open daily 7–3, and reservations are required.

Sassagoula River Fishing Trips (✉ Port Orleans–Riverside ☎ 407/939–7529) include guide, rod, bait, and soft drinks. Trips are two hours long, $80 per person, and leave daily at 7 AM and 10 AM. Up to five anglers are allowed per boat. You must reserve in advance.

Orlando Area

Top Central Florida fishing waters include Lake Kissimmee, the Butler and Conway chains of lakes, and Lake Tohopekaliga—a Native American name that means "Sleeping Tiger." (Locals call it Lake Toho.) The lake got its centuries-old name because it becomes incredibly rough during thunderstorms and has sent more than a few fishermen to a watery grave. Be careful in summer when you see storm clouds. Your best chance for trophy fish is between November and April on Toho or Kissimmee. For good creels, the best producer is usually the Butler area, which has the additional advantage of its scenery—lots of live oaks and cypresses, plus the occasional osprey or bald eagle. Toho and Kissimmee are also good for largemouth bass and crappie. The Butler chain yields largemouth, some pickerel, and the occasional huge catfish. Services range from equipment and boat rental to full-day trips with guides and guarantees.

A number of excellent fishing camps in the form of lakeside campgrounds draw a more outdoorsy crowd than you'll find elsewhere in the area.

East Lake Fish Camp (✉ 3705 Big Bass Rd., Kissimmee ☎ 407/348–2040), on East Lake Tohopekaliga, has a restaurant and country store, sells live bait and propane, and rents boats. You can also take a ride on an airboat. The camp has 286 RV sites that rent at $20 per night for two people. Cabins are $56 a night for two people and $5 a night for each additional person with a limit of five per cabin. Try to reserve one of the 24 cabins at least two weeks in advance in winter and spring.

Lake Toho Resort (✉ 4715 Kissimmee Park Rd., St. Cloud ☎ 407/892–8795), on West Lake Tohopekaliga, has 319 RV sites. Most of the full hookups are booked year-round, but electrical and water hookups are usually available, as are live bait, food, and drinks. The RV sites are $20 per night and $210 per month, plus electricity.

Richardson's Fish Camp (✉ 1550 Scotty's Rd., Kissimmee ☎ 407/846–6540), on West Lake Tohopekaliga, has 11 cabins with kitchenettes, 16 RV sites, six tent sites, boat slips, and a bait shop. The RV sites are $25 per night, tent sites are about $20, and cabins are $44 for one bedroom, about $68 for two bedrooms, and $79 for three bedrooms.

Guides fish out of the area's fishing camps, and you can usually make arrangements to hire them through the camp office. Rates vary, but for two people a good price is $150 for a half day and $225 for a full day. Many area guides are part-timers who fish on weekends or take a day off from their full-time job.

All Florida Fishing (✉ 4500 Joe Overstreet Rd., Kenansville 34739 ☎ 407/436–1966 or 800/347–4007 ⊕ www.all-florida-fishing.com) takes you on half- and full-day trips to go after the big bass that make the Kissimmee chain of lakes southeast of Disney ideal for sportfishing. Captain Rob Murchie also leads full-day saltwater fishing expeditions in the Indian River Lagoon and Atlantic, an hour's drive to the east, in pursuit of tarpon and other game fish. Half-day, freshwater trips are $200; full-day trips are $300. Saltwater trips (full day only) are $350. Prices are for one to two people. A third participant can join the group for $50. You can buy your license and bait here.

Pro Bass Guide Service (✉ 398 Grove Ct., Apopka 34787 ☎ 407/877–9676 or 800/771–9676 ⊕ www.probassguideservice.com), run by Captain Paul Solomon, has been in business for more than 20 years and provides boat, tackle, transportation, soft drinks, and ice for bass fishing on local lakes. Live bait is available for an extra charge. Prices per person start at $150 for a half day and $250 for a full day. Each additional adult is $50, and children under six go free.

Bass Challenger Guide (BCG) (✉ 195 Heather Lane Dr., Deltona 32738 ☎ 407/273–8045 or 800/241–5314 ⊕ www.basschallenger.com) takes you out in Ranger boats and equips you with tackle, license, bait, and ice. Transportation can be arranged between fishing spots and local hotels. Bass is the only quarry. Half-day trips for one or two people begin at $200; full-day trips begin at $300. You can buy your license and bait here. If you want a multi-day trip or need nearby accommodations, Captain Eddie Bussard may book you a room at a local hotel for $55 a night.

Football

The Orlando Predators play in the indoor Arena Football League. Teams have only eight players, each of whom holds both offensive and defensive positions. Games are held May through August, and tickets are

$7.50–$45, with special season "Dream Seats," rarely available, that put you front row, midfield, for $960–$1,200 per person. ⊠ *TD Waterhouse Centre, 600 W. Amelia St., Orlando* ☎ *407/648–4444; 407/872–7362 season ticket information.*

Golf

Sunny weather practically year-round makes Central Florida a golfer's haven, and there are about 130 golf courses within a 45-minute drive of Orlando International Airport. Most of Florida is extremely flat, but many of the courses listed here have man-made hills that make them more challenging. Many resort hotels let nonguests use their golf facilities. Some country clubs are affiliated with particular hotels, and their guests can play at preferred rates. If you're staying near a course you'd like to use, call and inquire. Because hotels have become so attuned to the popularity of golf, many that don't even have golf courses nearby have golf privileges or discounts at courses around town. Check with your hotel about what it offers before you set out on your own.

In general, even public courses have dress codes—most courses would just as soon see you stark naked as wearing a tank top, for instance—so call to find out the specifics at each, and be sure to reserve tee times in advance. The yardages quoted are those from the blue tees. Greens fees usually vary by season, but the highest and lowest figures are provided, and virtually all include mandatory cart rental, except for the few 9-hole walking courses.

Golfpac (⬚ Box 162366, Altamonte Springs 32716-2366 ☎ 407/260–2288 or 800/327–0878 ⊕ www.golfpactravel.com) packages golf vacations and prearranges tee times at more than 60 courses around Orlando. Rates vary based on hotel and course, and at least 60 to 90 days' advance notice is recommended to set up a vacation.

Walt Disney World

Where else would you find a sand trap shaped like the head of a well-known mouse? Walt Disney World has 99 holes of golf on five championship courses—all on the PGA Tour route—plus a 9-hole walking course. Eagle Pines and Osprey Ridge are the newcomers, flanking the Bonnet Creek Golf Club just east of Fort Wilderness. WDW's original courses, the Palm and the Magnolia, flank the Shades of Green Resort to the west and the Lake Buena Vista course near Downtown Disney's Marketplace. All courses are full-service facilities, and include a driving range, pro shop, locker room, snack bar–restaurant, and PGA-staffed teaching and training program. Disney offers a special perk to any guest at a WDW hotel who checks in specifically to play golf: free cab fare for you and your clubs between the hotel and the course you play. (It saves you from having to lug your clubs onto a hotel shuttle bus.) Ask at the front desk when you check into the hotel.

GREENS FEES   There are lots of variables here, with prices ranging from $20 for a youngster 17 or under to play 9 holes at Oak Trail walking course, to an adult nonhotel guest paying $179 to play 18 holes at one of Disney's newer courses in peak season. Disney guests get a break of $5 per round of golf, with rates ranging from $129 for a Disney hotel guest at the Lake Buena Vista course to $179 for a day visitor playing the Osprey Ridge course. All offer a twilight discount rate, $60–$80, which goes into effect at 2 PM from October 27 to February 28 and at 3 PM from April 1 to October 26. The 9-hole, par-36 Oak Trial course is best for those on a budget, with a year-round rate of $20 for golfers 17 and under and $36 golfers 18 and older. Rates at all courses except Oak Trail include an electric golf cart. No electric carts are allowed at Oak Trail, and a pull cart for your bag is $6. If you've got the stamina and desire to play the same course twice in the same day, you can do so for half price the second time around, but you can't reserve that option in advance, and this "Re-Play Option," as Disney calls it, is subject to availability.

TEE TIMES & RESERVATIONS
Tee times are available from 6:45 AM until dark daily. You can book them up to 90 days in advance if you're staying at a WDW-owned hotel, 30 days ahead if you're staying elsewhere from May to December, and four days in advance from January to April. For tee times and private lessons at any course, call **Walt Disney World Golf & Recreation Reservations** (☎ 407/939–4653).

GOLF INSTRUCTION
One-on-one instruction from PGA-accredited professionals is available at any Disney course. A 30-minute lesson is $50 for adults and $30 for youngsters 17 and under. Call the Walt Disney World Golf & Recreation Reservations to book a lesson.

COURSES
Eagle Pines, one of the newer Walt Disney World courses, was designed by golf-course architect Pete Dye. Greens are small and rolling, and fairways are lined with pines and punctuated by challenging bunkers. ⊠ *Bonnet View Golf Club* ⅄ *6,772 yards. Par: 72. USGA rating: 72.3. 18 holes.*

The Lake Buena Vista course winds among Downtown Disney–area town houses and villas. Greens are narrow, and hitting straight is important because errant balls risk ending up in someone's bedroom. ⊠ *Lake Buena Vista Dr.* ⅄ *6,819 yards. Par: 72. USGA rating: 72.7. 18 holes.*

The Magnolia, played by the pros in the Disney/Oldsmobile Golf Classic, is long but forgiving, with extra-wide fairways. ⊠ *Shades of Green, 1950 W. Magnolia-Palm Dr.* ⅄ *7,190 yards. Par: 72. USGA rating: 73.9. 18 holes.*

Oak Trail is a walking course designed to be fun for the entire family. It was designed by Ron Garl and is noted for its small, undulating greens. ⊠ *Shades of Green, 1950 W. Magnolia-Palm Dr.* ⅄ *2,913 yards. Par: 36. 9 holes.*

Fodor'sChoice
Osprey Ridge, sculpted from some of the still-forested portions of the huge WDW acreage, was transformed into a relaxing tour in the hands of designer Tom Fazio. However, tees and greens as much as 20 ft above the fairways keep competitive players from getting too comfortable. ⊠ *Bonnet Creek Golf Club, 3451 Golf View Dr.* ⅄ *7,101 yards. Par: 72. USGA rating: 73.9. 18 holes.*

The Palm, one of WDW's original courses, has been confounding the pros as part of the annual Disney/Oldsmobile Golf Classic for years. It's not as long as the Magnolia, or as wide, and there are more trees. And don't go near the water! ⊠ *Shades of Green, 1950 W. Magnolia-Palm Dr.* ⅄ *6,957 yards. Par: 72. USGA rating: 73. 18 holes.*

Orlando Area

Greens fees at most non-Disney courses fluctuate with the season. A twilight discount applies after 2 PM in busy seasons and after 3 PM during the rest of the year; the discount is usually half off the normal rate. Because golf is so incredibly popular around Orlando, courses raise their rates regularly.

Arnold Palmer's Bay Hill Club course is only open to those who have been invited by a member or who book lodging at the club's 64-room hotel. But with double-occupancy rates for rooms overlooking the course—

including a round of golf—running as low as $189 per person a night in summer, many consider staying at the club a real bargain. The course is the site of the annual Nestlé Invitational, and its par-4 18th hole is considered one of the toughest on the PGA tour. ✉ *9000 Bay Hill Rd., Orlando* ☎ *407/876–2429 or 888/422–9445* ⊕ *www.bayhill.com* ⅄ *7,207 yards. Par: 72. USGA rating: 75.1. 18 holes; 3,409 yards. Par: 36. 9 holes* ⛳ *Greens fees included in room rates; $189 single, $305 double* ☞ *Restaurant, private lessons, club rental.*

Barnett Park Golf Practice Facility, besides having an attractive course, has a great asset: it's free. All a golfer has to do is show up to use the net-enclosed driving range (with 10 pads), the three chipping holes with grass and sand surroundings, and the 9-hole putting green. As a special bonus, children ages 7–13 can spend time with a pro at no charge from 3 to 4:30 PM on Wednesdays. ✉ *4801 W. Colonial Dr., Orlando* ☎ *407/836–6248* ⛳ *Free.*

The Celebration Golf Club course—in addition to its great pedigree (it was designed by Robert Trent Jones Jr. and Sr.)—has the same thing going for it that the Disney-created town of Celebration, Florida, has: it's just 1 mi off the U.S. 192 tourist strip and a 10-minute drive from Walt Disney World, yet it is lovely and wooded, and as serene and bucolic as any spot in Florida. In addition to the 18-hole course, driving range, and three-hole junior course, the club includes a quaint, tin-roof clubhouse with a pro shop and restaurant, flanked by a tall, wooden windmill that is a local landmark. The club offers golf packages, which include lodging at the nearby Celebration Hotel. ✉ *701 Golf Park Dr., Celebration* ☎ *407/566–4653* ⊕ *www.celebrationgolf.com* ⅄ *6,783 yards. Par: 72. USGA rating: 73. 18 holes* ⛳ *Greens fees $45–$130, depending on time of year, time of day you play, whether you're a Florida resident, and whether you're a Celebration resident; daily discount rates begin at 2 PM* ☞ *Restaurant, pro shop, private lessons, club rental.*

★ **Champions Gate Golf Club,** which offers the David Leadbetter Golf Academy on its property, has courses designed by Greg Norman. The club is less than 10 mi from Walt Disney World at Exit 24 on I-4. The two courses offer distinct styles; the 7,406-yard International has the feel of the best British Isles courses, whereas the 7,048-yard National course is designed in the style of the better domestic courses, with a number of par-3 holes with unusual bunkers. ✉ *1400 Masters Blvd., Champions Gate* ☎ *407/787–4653; 888/558–9301; 888/633–5323 Ext. 23. Leadbetter Academy* ⊕ *www.championsgategolf.com* ⅄ *International: 7,406 yards. Par: 72. USGA rating: 73.7. 18 holes. National: 7,048 yards. Par: 72. USGA rating: 72.0. 18 holes* ⛳ *Greens fees $59–$130, depending on time of year and time of day you play. Golf lessons at Leadbetter Academy are $225 per hr and $1,500 per day for private lessons; group lessons are $150 for 3 hrs; a 3-day mini-school is $975; a 3-day complete school is $3,000* ☞ *Pro shop, golf school, private lessons, club rental.*

Cypress Creek Country Club is a demanding course with 16 water holes and lots of trees. ✉ *5353 Vineland Rd., Orlando* ☎ *407/351–2187* ⊕ *www.cypresscreekcc.com* ⅄ *7,014 yards. Par: 72. USGA rating: 73.6. 18 holes* ⛳ *Greens fees $40–$70* ☞ *Tee times 7 days in advance. Restaurants, private lessons, club rental, putting green.*

Diamond Players Club Clermont bills itself as "Florida's Mountain Golf Course" because it involves altitude changes of 190 ft, with its highest point at 250 ft above sea level—the Alps by Florida standards. Water plays into 7 of the 18 holes. A 30-minute drive west of Orlando, the Clermont area gives you a good look at Florida at a less frenetic pace.

✉ 2601 Diamond Club Dr., Clermont ☎ 352/243–0411 ⊕ *www.dpcgolf.com* 🏌 *6,911 yards. Par: 71. USGA rating: 73.7. 18 holes* 🏷 *Greens fees $37–$65 Florida residents, $60–$70 nonresidents* ☞ *Restaurant, private lessons, club rental, lockers, driving range, putting green.*

Falcon's Fire Golf Club, designed by golf-course architect Rees Jones, has strategically placed fairway bunkers that demand accuracy off the tee. This club is just off the Irlo Bronson Highway and is one of the most convenient to the hotels in the so-called "Maingate" area. ✉ *3200 Seralago Blvd., Kissimmee* ☎ 407/239–5445 ⊕ *www.falconsfire.com* 🏌 *6,901 yards. Par: 72. USGA rating: 73.8. 18 holes* 🏷 *Greens fees $110–$130, $70 after 2 PM, $40 after 4 PM* ☞ *Tee times 8–60 days in advance. Restaurants, private and group lessons, club rental, lockers, driving range, putting green.*

Faldo Golf Institute by Marriott is the team effort of world-famous golf pro Nick Faldo and Marriott Corp. An extensive-curriculum golf school and 9-hole golf course occupy the grounds of the corporation's biggest time-share complex, Marriott's Grande Vista. Here you can do anything from taking a one-hour, $125 lesson with a Faldo-trained pro (although not with the great Faldo himself, of course) to immersing yourself in a three-day extravaganza ($795–$999) in which you learn more about golf technique than most nonfanatics would care to know. Other instruction packages start as low as $475. Among the high-tech teaching methods at the school is the Faldo Swing Studio, in which instructors tape you doing your initial, unrefined swing; analyze the tape; and then teach you how to reform your physical skills the Faldo Way. The course, designed by Ron Garl, is geared to make you use every club in your bag—and perhaps a few you may elect to buy in the pro shop. As with virtually everything else in Florida, prices go up in peak seasonal months, but there's always a group discount at the Faldo Institute, even for groups as small as two people. ✉ *Marriott Grande Vista, 12001 Avenida Verde, Orlando 32821* ☎ 407/903–6295 ⊕ *www.gofaldo.com* 🏌 *2,308 yards. Par: 32. 9 holes.*

Hawk's Landing Golf Course, originally designed by Joe Lee, was extensively upgraded with a Robert E. Cupp III design in 2000. The course includes 16 water holes, lots of sand, and exotic landscaping. ✉ *Orlando World Center Marriott, 8701 World Center Dr., Orlando 32821* ☎ 407/238–8660 ⊕ *www.golfhawkslanding.com* 🏌 *6,307 yards. Par: 71. USGA rating: 73.2. 18 holes* 🏷 *Greens fees $65–$165* ☞ *Tee times 7 days in advance for public, 90 days in advance for World Center guests. Restaurants, private and group lessons, club and shoe rental.*

Hunter's Creek Golf Course, designed by Lloyd Clifton, has large greens and 14 water holes. ✉ *14401 Sports Club Way, Orlando 32837* ☎ 407/240–4653 🏌 *7,432 yards. Par: 72. USGA rating: 76.1. 18 holes* 🏷 *Greens fees $35–$75* ☞ *Tee times 3 days in advance. Snack bar, private lessons, club rental.*

MetroWest Country Club has a rolling Robert Trent Jones Sr. course, with few trees but lots of sand. ✉ *2100 S. Hiawassee Rd., Orlando 32835* ☎ 407/299–1099 ⊕ *www.metrowestgolf.com* 🏌 *7,051 yards. Par: 72. USGA rating: 74.1. 18 holes* 🏷 *Greens fees $59–$85 residents, $69–$115 nonresidents* ☞ *Tee times 7 days in advance. Restaurant (lunch only), private and group lessons, club rental.*

The Orange Lake Resort & Country Club, about five minutes from Walt Disney World's main entrance, has three 9-hole courses, all very similar. Distances aren't long, but fairways are very narrow, and there's a great deal of water, making the course difficult. The fourth course, Legends, was designed by Arnold Palmer. Standard practice is to play two of the three 9-hole courses, the Orange, Lake, and Cypress courses, in combination for a single round of golf, yielding the same experience as playing a single, par-72 course. ⊠ *8505 W. Irlo Bronson Memorial Hwy., Kissimmee 34747* ☎ *407/239–0000 or 800/877–6522* ⅃. *Lake/Orange: 6,531 yards. Par: 72. USGA rating: 72.2. 18 holes. Orange/Cypress: 6,670 yards. Par: 72. USGA rating: 72.6. 18 holes. Cypress/Lake: 6,571 yards. Par: 72. USGA rating: 72.3. 18 holes. Legends: 7,074 yards. Par: 72. USGA rating: 74.3* ☒ *Greens fees $22–$90 for guests of the resort; $31–$135 nonguests* ☞ *Tee times 2 days in advance. Restaurant, private and group lessons, club rental, driving range, putting green.*

Timacuan Golf and Country Club has a two-part course designed by Ron Garl. Part I, the front nine, is open, with lots of sand. Part II, the back nine, is heavily wooded. You can reserve tee times via e-mail on the club Web site. ⊠ *550 Timacuan Blvd., Lake Mary 32746* ☎ *407/321–0010* ⊕ *www.golftimacuan.com* ⅃. *6,915 yards. Par: 71. USGA rating: 73.2. 18 holes* ☒ *Greens fees $44–$94* ☞ *Tee times 5 days in advance. Restaurant, club rental, driving range, putting green.*

The Winter Park Municipal Golf Club, opened in 1914, is an inexpensive 9-hole course with a low-key approach (their five carts are reserved for players with disabilities, for instance). It has narrow fairways and a cozy clubhouse where you can buy everything from a 50¢ candy bar to a $200 golf bag. ⊠ *761 Old England Ave., Winter Park 32789* ☎ *407/623–3339* ⅃. *2,400 yards. Par: 35. USGA rating: 64.5. 9 holes* ☒ *Greens fees $10, or $16.25 to play the course twice* ☞ *Wed.–Thurs. 8:45–10* AM *members only. Club rental, putting green.*

Health Clubs

Admission prices listed are per person per day, unless otherwise noted. For massage and most other special services, admission is free.

Walt Disney World

Although most of the Walt Disney World health clubs accept only guests of Walt Disney World hotels—and some accept only guests of that particular hotel—it's not difficult to find a hotel fitness center or spa that is open to the public. In fact, the number of hotels adding public spas grows each year. Because massage therapy schools are turning out hundreds of graduates every year in Orlando, competition has increased, and getting rubbed the right way has become more and more of a bargain. Some hotel spas have even (gasp!) lowered their rates (minimally) for an hour of massage.

Body by Jake, at the Dolphin, has step and water aerobics classes, hand weights, treadmills, stationary bikes, personal training, massage, a sauna, and a hot tub. ⊠ *Walt Disney World Dolphin* ⊕ *www. swandolphin.com* ☎ *407/934–4264* ☒ *Free for Dolphin guests, $11 nonguests. Swedish massage: $55 for 25 min, $80 for 50 min, and $135 for 75 min; deep massage: $65 for 25 min, $90 for 50 min, $140 for 75 min* ☉ *Daily 6* AM*–9* PM.

The Grand Floridian Spa and Health Club has Cybex and cardiovascular equipment, treadmills, stair steppers, free weights, personal training, massage, saunas, steam rooms, hot tubs, body treatments, and facials. Youth services called "My First" treatments, for ages 4–12, are offered at the spa. Couples rooms are available for massage. Spa packages are available. ⊠ *Grand Floridian* ☎ *407/824–2332* ☒ *$18 per day; $30 per per-*

son or $40 per family up to 5 members for length of stay. Massage: $57 for 25 min, $103 for 50 min, $147 for 80 min. Add aromatherapy to any massage for $15 ☉ Daily 6 AM–9 PM.

Muscles and Bustles Health Club has Cybex equipment, circuit training, tanning, massage, and steam rooms. ⊠ BoardWalk Inn and Villas ☎ 407/939–2370 🖅 $15 per day; $25 per person or $45 per family for length of stay. Massage: $50 for 25 min, $75 for 50 min, $125 for 75 min ☉ Daily 6 AM–9 PM.

Old Key West Resort Exercise Room, open only to Disney resort guests, has Nautilus equipment, free weights, and massage. ⊠ Old Key West Resort ☎ 407/827–7700 🖅 Free. Massage: $35 for 30 min, $65 for 60 min ☉ Daily 6:30 AM–midnight.

The Olympiad Fitness Center, open to all Disney guests, has Nautilus and hand weights, stair climbers, stationary bikes, cross-country ski machines, treadmills, a dry sauna, and a tanning bed. Massages are offered at the club or in your room. ⊠ Contemporary Resort ☎ 407/824–3410 🖅 $15 per day; $25 per person or $45 per family for length of stay. Massage: $50 for 25 min, $75 for 50 min, $125 for 75 min; for in-room rate add $40 to all. Add aromatherapy to any massage for $15 ☉ Daily 6 AM–7 PM.

Ship Shape Health Club has Nautilus, cardiovascular equipment, and free weights, plus massage, a sauna, a spa, and a steam room. All-day admission is free with the purchase of a massage. ⊠ Yacht and Beach Club Resorts ☎ 407/934–3256 🖅 $15 per day; $25 per person or $45 per family for length of stay. Massage: $50 for 25 min, $75 for 55 min, $125 for 75 min. Add $15 to any massage for aromatherapy or deep tissue massage ☉ Daily 6 AM–7 PM.

★ The **Wyndham Palace Resort & Spa Health Club** has the entire spectrum of fitness equipment, including Nautilus machines, weights, stair climbers, stationary bikes, and treadmills. There's also a lap pool, hot tub, dry sauna, and steam bath. Massages and 60 other health and beauty therapies are offered in the full-service spa, the largest in the Disney area. If you want to get your body treated with seaweed, mud, mustard, or other astounding liquids or semisolids, this is the place. ⊠ 1900 Buena Vista Dr., Lake Buena Vista ☎ 407/827–2727 🖅 $11 hotel guests; $20 nonguests, free with purchase of massage or spa treatment. Massage: $62 for 25 min, $85–$95 for 50 min, $130–$145 for 80 min ☉ Spa daily 8–7, massage daily 8–8.

Orlando Area

To find out what's hot in exercise facilities when you visit, the best bet is to ask at your hotel, because clubs outside WDW come and go. The local YMCAs, however, are longtime favorites. Most have a single-visit fee of $10–$12, and you don't have to be a Y member. To find the YMCA nearest to where you're staying, phone the **Metropolitan YMCA office** (☎ 407/896–9220).

The Downtown YMCA Family Center has Nautilus and Cybex machines, free weights, racquetball, a half-Olympic-size pool, two gyms, and aerobics classes. It's an older property, but the weight-room facilities have been revamped. For prospective members, the first two visits are free. ⊠ 433 N. Mills Ave., Orlando ☎ 407/896–6901 🖅 $12; 5 free visits per month for YMCA members from outside Orlando ☉ Weekdays 5 AM–9:30 PM, Sat. 8–6, Sun. noon–6.

The International Drive YMCA is definitely more posh than the average Y. It has Nautilus, free weights, racquetball, two swimming pools (one

Olympic-size), and a diving well. Members can call ahead to reserve racquetball courts. ✉ *8422 International Dr., Orlando* ☎ *407/363–1911* ✉ *$10; 3 free visits per month for YMCA members outside Orlando* ⊙ *Weekdays 6 AM–9 PM, Sat. 8–5, Sun. noon–4.*

Horseback Riding

Walt Disney World

Fort Wilderness Resort and Campground (✉ Fort Wilderness Resort ☎ 407/824–2832) offers tame trail rides through backwoods. Children must be at least nine to ride, and adults must weigh less than 250 pounds. Trail rides are $32 for 45 minutes; hours of operation vary by season. You must check in 30 minutes prior to your ride, and reservations are essential. Both horseback riding and the campground are open to nonguests.

Orlando Area

Fodor'sChoice **Grand Cypress Equestrian Center** gives private lessons in hunt seat, jumping, combined training, dressage, and Western riding. Supervised novice and advanced group trail rides are available daily 8:30 to 5. Trail rides are $45 per hour for novice, $100 per hour for advanced. Private lessons are $55 per half hour and $100 per hour. Call at least a week ahead for reservations in winter and spring. ✉ *Hyatt Regency Grand Cypress Resort, 1 Equestrian Dr., Lake Buena Vista Area* ☎ *407/239–4608.*

Horse World Riding Stables, open daily 9 to 5, has basic and longer, more advanced nature-trail tours along beautifully wooded trails near Kissimmee. Pony rides are also available, and the stables area has picnic tables, farm animals you can pet, and a pond to fish in. Trail rides are $34 for basic, $39 for intermediate, and $49 for advanced. Pony rides for children under six are $6. Reservations a day in advance are recommended for the advanced trails. ✉ *3705 S. Poinciana Blvd., Kissimmee* ☎ *407/847–4343.*

Rock Springs Stable. A slice of semitropical Florida outside the immediate environs of WDW has horseback getaways along trails in the Rock Springs State Reserve near the Wekiva River. Florida black bear roam wild in this area—the high chain-link fences along State Road 41 are there to keep the bears from getting hit by cars. Have no fear, the bears present no threat, especially to people on horseback. Trail rides are $22 per hour, and are available Wednesday to Sunday, 8–5. The stable is easy to find, but has no street address, so it's best to call ahead and ask for directions. ✉ *State Road 41, 8 mi east of I–4 (Mount Dora exit), Sorrento* ☎ *352/735–6266.*

Ice Hockey

The Orlando Seals don't play in the top-notch National Hockey League, and they don't bring the likes of the Boston Bruins to town. But the Seals do compete in the feisty Atlantic Coast Hockey League, facing teams from Florida cities, like Jacksonville and St. Petersburg, and other cities, like Macon, Georgia, and Knoxville, Tennessee. Single-game seats go for $10–$50. All home games are played at the TD Waterhouse Centre. ✉ *TD Waterhouse Centre, 600 W. Amelia St., Downtown Orlando* ✉ *Tickets: 33 E. Robinson St., Orlando* ☎ *407/999–7887* 🖶 *407/423–2374* ⊕ *www.orlandoseals.com.*

Jai Alai

Orlando-Seminole Jai-Alai (✉ 6405 S. U.S. 17–92, Fern Park ☎ 407/331–9191), about 20 minutes north of Orlando off I–4 Exit 48, offers South

Florida horse racing simulcasts and betting in addition to jai alai at the fronton. Admission is $1, and $2–$5 for reserved seating. Simulcast races are Monday through Saturday noon–9 PM and Sunday noon–7:30 PM. Specific times vary, so call ahead for a schedule.

Miniature Golf

The Fantasia Gardens Miniature Golf Course (☎ 407/560–4870) is heavily themed in imagery from Disney's *Fantasia*. It is adjacent to the Swan and Dolphin Resort complex and the Winter Summerland Mini-Golf Course and is near the Disney–MGM Studios. Games are $9.67 for adults, $7.78 for children ages 3–9, and there's a 50% discount for the second consecutive round played, which is also valid at the Winter Summerland course.

Fodor'sChoice **The Winter Summerland Miniature Golf Course** (☎ 407/560–7161), with everything from sand castles to snowbanks, is allegedly where Santa and his elves spend their summer vacation. The course is close to Disney's Animal Kingdom and the Coronado Springs and All-Star resorts. Adults play for $10.35 and children ages 3 to 9 play for $8.50. A 50% discount on the second consecutive round played can be used here or at Fantasia Gardens.

Rock Climbing

★ **The Aiguille Rock Climbing Center,** has the only cliffs in the Orlando area—on 6,500 square ft of rock-studded walls. Climbers can reach a height of 45 ft, and different areas of the indoor, air-conditioned facility are set up to provide varying levels of challenges for varying skill levels. For safety, all climbers are tethered to a rope controlled by someone on the ground level. ⊠ *999 Charles St., Longwood* ☎ *407/332–1430* ⊕ *www.climborlando.com* ⊠ *Day passes $15 adults, $10 children under 12; $6 equipment rental, which includes proper shoes and harness; $30 per hr for rock climbing instruction, reservation required* ⊗ *Weekdays 10–10, Sat. 10 AM–midnight, Sun. noon–7.*

Running

Walt Disney World

Walt Disney World has several scenic running trails. Pick up maps at any Disney resort. Early in the morning all the roads are fairly uncrowded and make for good running. The roads that snake through Downtown Disney resorts are pleasant, as are the cart paths on the golf courses.

At the **Caribbean Beach Resort** (☎ 407/934–3400), there's a 1½-mi running promenade around Barefoot Bay. **Fort Wilderness Campground** (☎ 407/824–2900) has a 2½-mi running course with plenty of fresh air and woods, as well as numerous exercise stations along the way.

Orlando Area

Orlando has two excellent bike trails, the West Orange Trail and the Cady Way Trail, which are also good for running. Rural Orlando has some unbelievable hiking trails with long, densely wooded, nonrocky stretches that are tremendous for running, and often you can run for half an hour and not see any other living being—except wild game.

Turkey Lake Park, about 4 mi from Disney, has a 3-mi biking trail that's popular with runners. Several wooded hiking trails also make for a good run. The park closes at 5 PM, and fees are $2 for adults and $1 for children ages 3–12. ⊠ *3401 S. Hiawassee Rd., Orlando* ☎ *407/299–5581.*

The Rollins College area, in Winter Park, has paths along the shady streets and around the lakes, where you can breathe in fresh air and the aroma of old money.

The Orlando Runners Club meets every Sunday at 7 AM in Central Park (corner of Park Avenue and Welbourne Boulevard) for 6-, 10-, and 11-mi jaunts. The Track Shack, a sporting goods store open weekdays 10–7 and Saturdays 10–5, has details. *c/o Track Shack* ⊠ *1104 N. Mills Ave.* ☎ *407/898–1313.*

The Tosohatchee State Reserve runs through a huge pine forest and around the edges of a virgin cypress swamp. You can spot deer, all sorts of wild fowl—including an occasional eagle—and possibly some wild hogs or black bear along the miles of wilderness trails. The park's entrance fee is $2 per car. ⊠ *3365 Taylor Creek Rd., Christmas* ☎ *407/568–5893.*

Orlando Wilderness Park, managed by the Orlando Parks and Recreation Department, is off U.S. 50, just north of the town of Christmas. The park is a conservation success story. The 4-mi walking-jogging-biking trail circles a wetlands area that's actually used to clean Orlando wastewater. Don't worry, there's no foul smell—but there are fowl, plenty of them. Bird-watchers consider this one of the best spots in the state. An additional 5-mi trail that links up to the primary trail takes you to the banks of the St. Johns River. Park admission is free. ⊠ *Wheeler Rd., at State Rd. 420, Christmas* ☎ *407/246–2288.*

Skateboarding

Vans Skatepark—for those hip enough to know that a bowl is not something from which you consume soup but a giant, concrete skate course—is a 61,000-square-ft skatepark with a great indoor bowl. The park has a 31,000-square-ft, plywood indoor street course, a 11,000-square-ft, concrete indoor street course, a snack bar, and a viewing area. Skaters must be over 18 or have a parent or guardian sign a release form. Mandatory protective gear is for rent here. Two hours of skating is $7 for members and $15 for nonmembers. ⊠ *5220 International Dr., Orlando* ☎ *407/351–3881.*

Sky Diving & Parasailing

Sammy Duvall's Water Sports Centre (⊠ Disney's Contemporary Resort ☎ 407/939–7529) offers parasailing on Bay Lake in addition to water sports. Flights, $85 per outing, reach a height of 450 ft and last 7–10 minutes. Individual participants must weigh at least 100 pounds, but youngsters may go aloft accompanied by an adult. Tandem flights are $135.

Fodor$Choice **Sky Venture**, a 120-mph vertical-lift wind tunnel, allows you to experience everything sky divers enjoy, all within an air blast that reaches only 12 ft. The experience starts with sky-diving instruction, after which you suit up and hit the wind tunnel, where you soar like a bird under the watchful eye of your instructor. While you are "falling" on the wind stream, you even experience what divers called "ground rush," because you are surrounded by a video depiction of a real sky dive. The experience is so realistic that sky-diving clubs come to Sky Venture to hone their skills. Famous people who have tried this include George Bush Sr. There's no minimum (or maximum) age requirement, but you must be 250 pounds or less and at least 4 ft tall. You can purchase a video of your jump for $16. ⊠ *6805 Visitors Circle, I-Drive Area Orlando* ☎ *407/903–1150* ⊕ *www.skyventure.com* ✇ *$38.50 per jump for adults, $33.50 for children 12 and under; $600 per hr, $300 per ½ hr* ☉ *Weekdays noon–midnight, weekends 2–midnight.*

Soccer

Disney's Wide World of Sports Complex (☎ 407/828–3267), among its cornucopia of events, presents soccer matches and tournaments, including the annual Disney Soccer Classic, an October match that attracts men's and women's teams from around the world.

Sporting Clays

TM Ranch Shotgun Sports, on an 11,000-acre family-owned ranch near the Orlando International Airport, has year-round sporting clays—an increasingly popular activity in which you use shotguns to shoot targets, which include clay discs launched into the air in patterns that mimic the flight of wild game birds. Part of the appeal of a sporting-clays course is its natural backdrop, and the TM Ranch course—surrounded by pine, cypress, and palmettos—measures up. Expert marksmanship instruction is available at the Remington Shooting School, which operates on the property in winter. The facility has a pro shop, catered barbecue lunches, a meeting pavilion that can handle groups of up to 500 people, and a camping area with 90 RV hook-ups. A round of 50 clay shots is $25, a round of 100 is $43, gun rental is $10, and ammunition is $6 per box. TM Ranch also has a package deal with the Orlando Renaissance Hotel–Airport, in which you get a night at the hotel and 100 rounds of clay shots at the ranch for as little as $140. ⊠ *15520 TM Ranch Rd., Orlando 32832* ☎ *407/737–3788.*

Tennis

Walt Disney World

You can play tennis at any number of Disney hotels, and you may find the courts a pleasant respite from the milling throngs in the parks. All have lights and are open 7 AM to 8 PM, unless otherwise noted, and most have lockers and rental rackets for $3 to $5 a day. There seems to be a long-term plan to move from hard courts to clay. Most courts are open to all players—court staff can opt to turn away nonguests when things get busy, but that doesn't often happen. The tennis pros are employees of Peter Burwash, Inc., a national company that has been giving tennis lessons at Disney for as long as it's been offering them, and they will travel to any Disney resort to give lessons.

The Contemporary Resort, with its sprawl of six clay courts, is the center of Disney's tennis program. It has two backboards and an automatic ball machine. Reservations are available up to 24 hours in advance, and there's an arrange-a-game service. ☎ *407/939–7529 reservations* ✉ *Free; lessons $70 per hr for individual and $40 per hr for group of two* ☉ *Daily 7–7.*

Fort Wilderness Resort and Campground has two tennis courts in the middle of a field. They're popular with youngsters, and if you hate players who are too free about letting their balls stray to their neighbors' court, this is not the place for you. There are no court reservations and instruction is not available. ⊠ *3520 N. Fort Wilderness Trail* ☎ *407/824–2742* ✉ *Free* ☉ *Daily 8–6.*

The Grand Floridian has two clay courts that attract a somewhat serious-minded tennis crowd. Court reservations are available up to 24 hours in advance. ☎ *407/939–7529* ✉ *Free* ☉ *Daily 8–8.*

The Yacht and Beach Club Resorts have two blacktop tennis courts. Court reservations are not required. Equipment is available at the towel window at no charge. ☎ *407/934–3256* ✉ *Free* ☉ *Daily 7 AM–10 PM.*

Orlando Area

Lake Cane Tennis Center has 13 lighted hard courts. Six pros provide private and group lessons. ✉ *5108 Turkey Lake Rd., Orlando* ☎ *407/352–4913* 💲 *$3 per hr weekdays during day, $5 per hr weekends and weekday evenings after 5, $40 per hr and $21 per ½ hr private lessons* ☉ *Weekdays 8 AM–10 PM, weekends 7 AM–8:30 PM.*

Orange Lake Country Club has, in addition to its golf courses, seven lighted, all-weather hard tennis courts. It's five minutes from Walt Disney World's main entrance. Court reservations are necessary. ✉ *8505 W. Irlo Bronson Memorial Hwy., Kissimmee* ☎ *407/239–0000 or 800/877–6522* 💲 *Free for guests, $5 per hr nonguests, $60 per hr for private lessons, $10 per ½ hr for group clinics, $2 per hr and $5 per day racket rental* ☉ *Daily dawn–11 PM.*

The Orlando Tennis Center has 16 lighted tennis courts—nine HarTru and seven asphalt—two outdoor racquetball courts, and three teaching tennis pros. Call in advance for court availability. Normal rates are slightly cheaper for Orlando residents with proper I.D. ✉ *649 W. Livingston St., Orlando* ☎ *407/246–2162* 💲 *$6 per 1½ hr for tennis on HarTru and $4 per 1½ hr on asphalt, $2 per hr for racquetball, $35 per hr and $18 per ½ hr for private lessons, $7 group lessons* ☉ *Weekdays 8 AM–10 PM, weekends 8–6.*

Red Bug Park has 16 lighted hard tennis courts and eight outdoor covered four-wall racquetball courts. Court reservations are available up to 24 hours in advance. ✉ *3600 Red Bug Lake Rd., Casselberry* ☎ *407/695–7113* 💲 *$2 per hr before 5 and $4 per hr after 5 for tennis; $4 per hr for racquetball; $34–$40 per hr for private lessons, plus court fee* ☉ *Daily 8 AM–10 PM.*

Sanlando Park has 25 lighted hard tennis courts and eight covered, fan-cooled racquetball courts. Call for court reservations by 9:30 AM one day in advance. ✉ *401 W. Highland St., Altamonte Springs* ☎ *407/869–5966* 💲 *$2 per hr before 5 and $4 per hr after 5 for tennis; $4 per hr for racquetball; $40 per hr for private lesson with head pro, $34 per hr and $16 per ½ hr for private lesson with assistant pro* ☉ *Daily 8 AM–10 PM.*

Walt Disney World Sports

Fodor'sChoice **Disney's Wide World of Sports Complex** is proof that Disney doesn't do anything unless it does it in a big way. The huge complex contains a 7,500-seat baseball stadium—housed in a giant stucco structure that from the outside looks like a Moroccan palace—a 5,000-seat field house, and a number of fan-oriented commercial ventures such as the Official All-Star Cafe and shops that sell clothing and other items sanctioned by Major League Baseball, the NBA, and the NFL. During spring training, the perennially great Atlanta Braves play here, and the minor-league Orlando Rays have games during the regular season. But that's just the tip of the iceberg. The complex hosts all manners of individual and team competitions, including big-ticket tennis tournaments. In all, some 30 spectator sports are represented among the annual events presented, including Harlem Globetrotters basketball games, baseball fantasy camps held in conjunction with the Braves at the beginning of spring training each year, and track events ranging from the Walt Disney World Marathon to dozens of annual Amateur Athletic Union (AAU) championships. The complex offers softball, basketball, and other games for group events ranging from family reunions to corporate picnics. ✉ *Osceola Pkwy.* ☎ *407/828–3267 events information* ⊕ *dwws.disney.go.com/wideworldofsports.*

A key source for sports information on all things Disney is the **Sports Information and Reservations Hotline** (☎ 407/939–7529 ⊕ www. disneyworld.disney.go.com).

Water Sports

Walt Disney World

Boating is big at Disney, and it has the largest fleet of for-rent pleasure craft in the nation. There are marinas at the Caribbean Beach Resort, Contemporary Resort, Downtown Disney Marketplace, Fort Wilderness Resort and Campground, Grand Floridian, Old Key West Resort, Polynesian Resort, Port Orleans Resort, Port Orleans–Riverside Resort, and the Wilderness Lodge. The Yacht and Beach Club Resorts rent Sunfish sailboats, catamarans, motor-powered pontoon boats, pedal boats, and tiny two-passenger Water Sprites—a hit with children—for use on Bay Lake and the adjoining Seven Seas Lagoon, Club Lake, Lake Buena Vista, or Buena Vista Lagoon. Most hotels rent Water Sprites, but you should check each hotel's rental roster. The Polynesian Resort marina rents outrigger canoes. Fort Wilderness rents canoes for paddling along the placid canals in the area. And you can sail and waterski on Bay Lake and the Seven Seas Lagoon; stop at the Fort Wilderness, Contemporary, Polynesian, or Grand Floridian marina to rent sailboats or sign up for waterskiing.

Sammy Duvall's Water Sports Centre (⊠ Disney's Contemporary Resort ☎ 407/939–7529) offers waterskiing, wakeboarding (like waterskiing on a small surf board; usually done on your knees), and parasailing on Bay Lake. Boat and equipment rental is included with waterskiing (maximum of five people) and wakeboarding (maximum of four people) as are the services of an expert instructor. Each is $125 per hour, plus tax.

Orlando Area

Alexander Creek and Juniper Creek offer wonderful wilderness canoeing, with abundant wildlife and moss-draped oaks and bald cypresses canopying the clean, clear waters. Some of these runs are quite rough—lots of ducking under brush and maneuvering around trees. You must pack out what you pack in. On Alexander Creek, **Alexander Springs Canoe Rental** (⊠ 49525 Rte. 445, Altoona ☎ 352/669–3522) rents canoes for $10 for two hours, $12 for 4 hours, or $26 per day—with $20 cash deposit and I.D.—plus a $3 per person park entrance fee. All canoes must be returned to the beach by 3:45. **Juniper Springs Canoe Rental** (⊠ 2670 E. Hwy. 40 Silver Springs ☎ 352/625–2808) has canoes on Juniper Creek. The cost is $26 for a 7-mi trip of approximately four hours—with $20 cash deposit and I.D. Rentals are available daily 8–noon. ⊠ *Ocala National Forest, just north of the greater Orlando area.*

The St. Johns River winds through pine and cypress woods and past pastures where cows graze placidly, skirting the occasional housing development. There's good bird- and wildlife-watching around the river; herons, ibis, storks, and sometimes bald eagles can be spotted, along with alligators and manatees. It's a favored local boating spot, for everything from a day of waterskiing to a weeklong trip in a houseboat. Rentals are available in Deland (west of I–4 via U.S. 44). For St. Johns River excursions, **Holly Bluff** (⊠ 2280 Hontoon Rd., Deland ☎ 386/822–9992 or 800/237–5105) rents pontoon boats for $750–$1,550 per weekend and full-week boats, ranging in capacity from 4 to 12 people, for $1,000–$2,400. Rates are lower December through February. Luxury houseboats on St. Johns River are available at **Hontoon Landing Resort and Marina** (⊠ 2317 River Ridge Rd., Deland ☎ 904/734–2474; 800/248–2474 in Florida ⊕ www.hontoon.com) for $425–$795 per day and $1,195–$2,395 per week October through January 31, or $1,595–$2,795 per week February 1 through September 31. Pontoons are $100 per day weekdays and $135 weekends, and 16-ft fishing boats are $75 per day. Bargain month is January—when it's cold by Florida standards but simply pleasant if you're from up north—with houseboat rentals dropping as low as $925 for a four-day, midweek rental.

Wekiva River, a great waterway for nature lovers, runs through 6,397-acre **Wekiva Springs State Park** (✉ 1800 Wekiva Circle, Apopka, I–4 Exit 94 ☎ 407/884–2005) into the St. Johns River. Bordered by cypress marshlands, its clear, spring-fed waters showcase Florida wildlife, including otters, raccoons, alligators, bobcats, deer, turtles, and numerous birds. Canoes and camp sites can be rented near the southern entrance of the park in Apopka. Canoes are available for $17 for a half-day and $26 for a full day. The park has 60 camp sites, some of which are "canoe sites," in that they can only be reached via the river itself, while others are "trail sites," meaning you must hike a good bit of the park's 13-mi hiking trail to reach them. Most sites, however, are for the less hardy among us—you can drive right up to them. Sites go for $18.77 a night with electric hook-ups or $16.65 with no electricity.

Orange Lake, a private lake at the Orange Lake Country Club, next to Walt Disney World, has all types of boating—in rowboats, paddleboats, canoes, and jet boats—plus waterskiing and Jet Skis. At **Orange Lake Water Sports** (✉ 8505 W. Irlo Bronson Memorial Hwy., Kissimmee ☎ 407/239–0000), open daily 10–5, pedal boat rentals are $6–$26 per hour, depending on the boat size. Jet Skis are $50 per half hour or $88 per hour, jet boats are $53 per half hour or $90 per hour.

Shingle Creek is shrouded by giant cypress trees dripping with Spanish moss. You can get around on Shingle Creek by airboat or rent a quiet electric swamp boat or a canoe from **Airboat Rentals** (✉ 4266 Irlo Bronson Memorial Hwy., Kissimmee ☎ 407/847–3672), open daily 9–5. Airboats are $27 per hour, swamp boats and electric boats run $27 per hour or $50 per day, and canoes are $5 per hour or $20 per day, with a $20 deposit and a photo I.D.

AFTER DARK

9

FODOR'S CHOICE

Cirque du Soleil, in Walt Disney World

Comedy Warehouse, in Walt Disney World

Fantasmic!, in Walt Disney World

House of Blues, in Walt Disney World

IllumiNations, in Walt Disney World

SpectroMagic, in Walt Disney World

HIGHLY RECOMMENDED

Bob Marley–A Tribute to Freedom, in Universal

Hard Rock Live, in Universal

Hoop-Dee-Doo Revue, in Walt Disney World

Jimmy Buffett's Margaritaville, in Universal

Mulvaney's, in downtown Orlando

Sak Comedy Lab, in downtown Orlando

Thornton Park, in Central Orlando

Updated by
Gary
McKechnie

FOR SOME, ORLANDO IS simply a factory town, and the factories just happen to be theme parks. To others, it's a backwater burg that lacks sophistication and culture. Then there are the preteen girls who see it as the breeding ground for synthetic bubblegum boy groups like *NSync, the Backstreet Boys, and O-Town. Orlando might be all of this, but it is an entertainment capital and as such is obligated to provide evening diversions to everyone who visits.

There are about 13 million travelers who come to Orlando each year, and many are adults traveling without children. After years of denial, Disney heeded the command of the profits and built Pleasure Island and later West Side to create the Downtown Disney entertainment complex. In response, Universal Orlando opened CityWalk to siphon off from Disney what Disney had siphoned off from downtown Orlando, which is now struggling to find its footing amid the increased competition.

If you're here for at least two nights and don't mind losing some sleep, reserve one evening for Downtown Disney and the next for CityWalk. They are both well worth seeing. If you want a one-night blowout, however, head to Disney—believe it or not! By virtue of Disney's status as essentially a separate governmental entity, clubs on Disney property are allowed to stay open later than bars elsewhere; you can get served here until 2 AM if you have the energy for it.

WALT DISNEY WORLD RESORT

When you enter the fiefdom known as Walt Disney World, you're likely to see as many watering holes as cartoon characters. After beating your feet around a theme park all day, there are lounges, bars, speakeasies, pubs, sports bars, and microbreweries where you can settle down with a soothing libation. Your choice of nightlife can be found at various Disney shopping and entertainment complexes—from the casual down-by-the-shore BoardWalk to the much larger multi-area Downtown Disney, which comprises the Marketplace, Pleasure Island, and West Side. Everywhere you look, jazz trios and bluesmen, DJs, and rockers are tuning up and turning on their amps after dinner's done. Plus, two long-running dinner shows provide an evening of song, dance, and dining, all for a single price.

Don't assume that all after dark activities only center around adult bars and expensive shows. After a hot day of walking, thousands of vacationing families find it preferable to take it easy with a refreshing splash in the hotel's themed pool or duck into an old-fashioned ice cream parlor (or poolside bar) for an inexpensive evening together. Even if you head back to your hotel for an afternoon nap or swim, remember that later you can always return to a theme park to catch a wealth of free shows performed at Epcot's pavilions and stages at the Magic Kingdom and Disney–MGM Studios. These shows are often as entertaining as any cover-charging club. Get information on WDW nightlife from the Walt Disney World information hot line (☎ 407/824–2222 or 407/824–4500) or check on-line at www.disney.com. Disney nightspots accept American Express, MasterCard, and Visa. And cash. Lots of it.

Disney's BoardWalk

At the turn of the 20th century, Americans escaping the cities for the Atlantic seaside spent their days on breeze-swept boardwalks above the strand, where early thrill rides kept company with band concerts and other activities. Here, across Crescent Lake from Disney's Yacht and Beach Club Resorts, WDW has created its own version of these amusement areas, a shoreside complex that's complete with restaurants, bars and clubs, souvenir sellers, surreys, saltwater taffy vendors, and shops. When the lights go on after sunset, the mood is festive—the stage is set for plentiful diversions and a romantic stroll. For information on events call the **Board-Walk entertainment hot line** (☎ 407/939–3492 or 407/939–2444).

The **Atlantic Dance Hall** started out as a hypercool room recalling the Swing Era, with martinis, cigars, and Sinatra sound-alikes. That didn't last, so it reopened as a Latin club. That didn't last either, so now it is a typical Top 40 dance club with a DJ Wednesday and Thursday, and a live band on Fridays and Saturdays. How long will this last? Who knows? Next it may become an American Legion hall. You must be 21 to enter. ☎ 407/ 939–2444 or 407/939–2430 ▧ *No cover* ☉ *Wed.–Sat. 9 PM–2 AM.*

Big River Grille & Brewing Works, Walt Disney World's first brew pub, is warm and comfortable, with polished woods and small intimate tables. Brewmasters tending to their potions add to the charm of this retreat. Inside stainless steel vats brew a variety of beers, the most popular being Rocket Red Ale. But if you're not sure what you'd like best, order a $5 sampler that includes from five to eight 4-ounce shots of whatever they have on tap that day, from the Red Rocket, Southern Flyer Light Lager, Gadzooks Pilsener, and Tilt Pale Ale to Sweet Magnolia Brown and Irish Red Lager. Pub grub, sandwiches, and cigars round out the offerings, and a sidewalk café is a great place for people-watching and good conversation. ☎ 407/560–0253 ▧ *No cover* ☉ *Mon.–Thurs. 11:30 AM–1 AM, Fri.–Sun. 11:30 AM–2 AM.*

As with all things Disney, the sports motif at **ESPN Club** is carried into every nook and cranny. The main dining area looks like a sports arena, with a basketball-court hardwood floor and a giant scoreboard that projects the big game of the day. Sportscasters originate programs from a TV and radio broadcast booth, and there are more than 70 TV monitors throughout the facility, even in the rest rooms. If you want to watch NFL on Sunday, get here about two hours before kickoff, because the place is packed for back-to-back games. On special game days, like those of the World Series or Super Bowl, count on huge crowds and call in advance to see if special seating rules are in effect. ☎ 407/939–1177 ▧ *No cover* ☉ *Sun.–Thurs. 11:30 AM–1 AM, Fri.–Sat. 11:30 AM–2 AM.*

At rugged, rockin', and boisterous **Jellyrolls,** comedians act as emcees and play dueling grand pianos nonstop. In a Disney version of "Stump the Band," they promise "You Name It. We Play It." You may have gone to piano bars before, but with the wealth of conventioneers at Disney, this is where you can catch CEOs doing the conga to Barry Manilow's "Copacabana"—if that's your idea of a good time. You must be 21 to enter. ☎ 407/560–8770 ▧ *Sun.–Thurs. $5 after 8 PM, Fri.–Sat. $5 after 7 PM* ☉ *Daily 7 PM–2 AM.*

Downtown Disney

West Side

Disney's West Side is a pleasantly hip outdoor complex of shopping, dining, and entertainment with the main venues being the House of Blues, DisneyQuest, and Cirque du Soleil. Aside from this trio, there are no cover charges. Whether you're club hopping or not, the West Side is worth a visit for its laid-back attitude, waterside location, wide promenade, and diverse shopping and dining. Opening time is 11 AM, closing time around 2 AM; crowds vary with the season, but weeknights tend to be less busy. For entertainment times and more information, call 407/824–4500 or 407/824–2222.

Latin rhythms provide the beat at **Bongos Cuban Café,** an enterprise of pop singer Gloria Estefan. Although this is primarily a restaurant, you may get a kick out of the pre-Castro Havana interior, and the Latin band that plays *muy caliente* music each Friday and Saturday evening. Samba, tango, salsa, and merengue rhythms are rolling throughout the week. Drop by for a beer and a "babalu." ☎ *407/828–0999* ⊘ *Daily 11 AM–2 AM.*

Fodor'sChoice Don't think you've seen the best Walt Disney World has to offer until you've seen *La Nouba*. The surreal show at **Cirque du Soleil** starts at 100 mph and accelerates from there. Although the ticket price is high compared with those for other local shows, you'd be hard-pressed to hear anyone complain. The performance is 90 minutes of extraordinary acrobatics, avant-garde stagings, costumes, choreography, and a thrilling grand finale that makes you doubt Newton's law of gravity. The story of *La Nouba*—derived from the French phrase *faire la nouba* (which translates to "live it up")—is alternately mysterious, dreamlike, comical, and sensual. A cast of 72 international performers takes the stage in this specially constructed, 70,000-square-ft venue. The original music is performed by a live orchestra that you might miss if you don't scrutinize the towers on either side of the stage, which is a technical marvel in itself, with constantly moving platforms and lifts. A couple of hints: call well in advance for tickets to improve your chances of getting front row seats and hire a baby-sitter if necessary—admission is charged for infants. ☎ *407/939–7600 reservations* ✉ *Premium seats (center section) $82 adults, $49 children under 10, general seats, $72 adults, $44 children under 10* ⊘ *Performances Thurs.–Mon. 6 and 9 PM.*

At **DisneyQuest,** an enclosed five-floor video–virtual reality mini-theme park near the entrance to Pleasure Island, they've figured out that some suckers—er, guests—will pay big bucks to play video games. To be fair, once you've shelled out the considerable cover, you can play all day. There are some cutting-edge games here, but save your money if you think you'll quickly tire of electronic arcade noises. ☎ *407/828–4600* ✉ *$33 adults, $26 children 3–9* ⊘ *Daily 10:30 AM–midnight.*

Fodor'sChoice Adjacent to the **House of Blues** restaurant, which itself showcases cool blues alongside its Mississippi Delta cooking, HOB's concert venue has showcased local and nationally known artists including Aretha Franklin, David Byrne, Steve Miller, Los Lobos, the Backstreet Boys, and *NSync. From rock to reggae to R&B, this is arguably the best live-music venue in Orlando, and standing a few feet from your guitar heroes is the way music should be seen and heard. ☎ *407/934–2583* ✉ *Covers vary* ⊘ *Call for show times.*

Downtown Disney Marketplace

Although the Marketplace offers little in the line of typical nightlife, there is hardly a more enjoyable place where the family can spend a quiet evening window shopping, enjoying ice cream at a courtyard café, or strolling among eclectic Disney stores.

Swing by **Cap'n Jack's Restaurant** to gulp down some oysters or sip on a huge strawberry margarita made with strawberry tequila. It's not a lively joint; instead, it's a smart spot for a quiet evening beside the waterfront. ☎ *407/828–3870* ⊘ *Daily 11:30–10:30.*

Pleasure Island

Pleasure Island was Disney's first foray into a nighttime complex, and judging by the crowds, the combination of clubs and stores and entertainment remains an attractive mix. The six-acre park has eight jam-packed clubs—all of which can be accessed with a single admission. Pleasure Island is packed with an across-the-board mix of college kids, young married couples, middle-age business folk, world travelers, and Mom and Pop sneaking out for an evening. Even kids (with an accompanying adult) are allowed in each club, except Mannequins and BET SoundStage Club. Weekends are the busiest, although Thursdays are hopping with Disney World cast members itching to blow their just-issued paychecks.

At the West End Stage, the mistress of ceremonies lets you know that the Island's theme is a nightly New Year's Eve party and leads you through the storyline: to avoid a midnight curfew, dancers—and this is no joke—need to shimmy like maniacs in an energetic effort to disable the evil computer that enforces the deadline. Surprisingly, the audience believes this. When asked to help the cause by shouting "Par-tay!" guests do so with passion and fervor. Don't worry, the dancers never fail to add two extra hours of "partay"-ing by simply boogie-ing that rotten old computer into submission. ⊠ *Off Buena Vista Dr.* ☎ *407/934–7781 or 407/824–2222* ✉ *$21 for entire park; access to shops, clubs, and restaurants free* ◷ *Clubs daily 7 PM–2 AM; shops and restaurants daily 10:30 AM–2 AM.*

The **Adventurers' Club** re-creates a private club of the cabaret-happy 1930s. The walls are practically paved with memorabilia from exotic places; servers entertain you with their patter; and, several times a night, character explorer/actors share tall tales of the adventures they encountered on imaginary expeditions. Stop for a drink and enjoy the scenery or visit the Library for a slapstick show. With all its props and comedy, this is a good option if you're here with kids. ☎ *407/824–2222 or 407/824–4500.*

BET SoundStage Club, backed by Black Entertainment Television, pays tribute to all genres of black music through videos, live performances, and shows by BET's own dance troupe. As the evening progresses, sounds shift from BET's top 10 to old R&B to hip-hop—a blend that's attracted legions of locals who proclaim this the funkiest nightspot in Central Florida (perhaps also the loudest). Even if you're dance-challenged, you might find it hard to resist shakin' your groove thang to the beat-rich music. You must be at least 21 to enter. ☎ *407/934–7666.*

*Fodor's*Choice Gifted comedians at the **Comedy Warehouse** perform various improv games, sing improvised songs, and create off-the-cuff sketches based largely on suggestions from the audience. Each of the evening's five performances is different, but the cast is usually on target. Lines for the free shows start forming roughly 45 minutes before curtain, so get there early for a good seat. It's well worth the wait to watch a gifted comedy troupe work without profanity. ☎ *407/828–2939.*

In case the lava lamps and disco balls don't tip you off, the '70s are back at **8TRAX.** Slip on your bell-bottoms, strap on your platform shoes, and groove to Chic, the Village People, or Donna Summer on disk. After a while, it might seem like you're in your own Quentin Tarantino film. Swing by on Thursdays when the calendar fast-forwards to the 1980s to celebrate the music of that not-so-long-gone era. ☎ *407/934–7160.*

The highest tech club here is **Mannequins,** where an occasional floorshow by Disney dancers goes over the top with suggestive bump-and-grind moves. While the 30-plus crowd may not get much out of it, younger clubhoppers love the New York–style dance palace interior, the Top 40 hits, the revolving dance floor, the elaborate lighting, and special effects like bubbles and snow. You must be at least 21 to be admitted. ☎ *407/934–6375.*

Motion is the latest arrival to the Pleasure Island mix, and it offers a play list of dance music from Zoot Suit Riot to the latest techno junk. This mix of music means that it attracts a cross-section of people who (eventually) hear at least one song they like. The two-story warehouselike club is stark, emphasizing the dance floor and the club's twirling lights and thumping sound system. Motion hits the right tone to attract a young and hip clientele. Doors open nightly at 9 PM (and stay open until 2 AM). ☎ *407/827–9453.*

One of Central Florida's best jazz venues is the **Pleasure Island Jazz Company.** Accomplished soloists or small bands perform nightly. The audience sits at cozy two-top tables in a space reminiscent of a 1930s speakeasy. Between sets, the songs of Dinah Washington, Billie Holiday, and friends are played to keep the mood mellow. The well-stocked tapas bar and assorted wines by the glass add a smooth contemporary touch. ☎ *407/828–5665.*

The three-tier **Rock & Roll Beach Club** is always crowded and throbbing with rock music from the '50s to the '80s. With most clubs playing machine-produced music, it's a treat to hang out where the tunes were created by humans. The live band and disc jockeys never let the action die down, and the sounds attract a moderately older (thirties) crowd. The friendly and fun feel of a neighborhood bar is sustained by the pool tables, pinball machines, Foosball, darts, and video games. ☎*407/934–7654.*

Hotel Bars

Disney-Owned Hotels in Walt Disney World
Now that Walt Disney World has about a dozen resort hotels to accommodate visitors who once spent their nights off-property, hotel lounges have become surprisingly active. Depending on whether the resort is geared toward business or romance, the lounges can be soothing or boisterous—or both. To reach any of these hotel bars directly, you can call the Disney operator at 407/824–4500 or 407/824–2222.

The nautical-theme **Ale and Compass Lounge** is a very small, serene cappuccino-coffee bar that also serves ales and spirits. ⊠ *Yacht Club Resort* ⊘ *Daily 4 PM–midnight.*

At the lovely **Belle Vue Room,** a comfortable 1930s-style sitting room, you can escape the crowds, play board games, savor a quiet drink, and listen to long-ago shows played through old radios. Step out onto the balcony for a soothing view of the village green and lake. ⊠ *Boardwalk Inn* ⊘ *Daily 5 PM–midnight.*

High atop the Contemporary Resort, the lounge adjoining the **California Grill** restaurant offers a great view of the Magic Kingdom, especially when the sun goes down and the tiny white lights on Main Street start to twinkle. Add nightly fireworks (usually at 10 PM), and there's no better place to order a glass of wine and enjoy the show. An observation deck, which extends to the end of the hotel, adds a breezy vantage point from which to see all this, plus surrounding Bay Lake. Hot tip: You'll need a reservation for the Grill in order to gain access to the observation deck. ⊠ *Contemporary Resort* ⊘ *Daily 5:30 PM–midnight; dinner 6–10 PM.*

Befitting its location in Old Port Royale (which has an island market–style setting), **Captain's Tavern** serves tropical drinks, beer, wine, and cocktails. It may not be Margaritaville, but it's close enough. ⊠ *Caribbean Beach Resort* ⊘ *Daily 5 PM–10 PM.*

At **Copa Banana,** in the Dolphin Hotel, a DJ, karaoke, and specialty drinks keep the clientele entertained and tipsy. Because the Dolphin is a business hotel, count on sharing a fruit slice–shape table with after-hours suits. If you're annoyed by Peterson from accounting, the large-screen

TV may provide a diversion. Although it's on-property, the Dolphin is not a Disney hotel. ☒ *Dolphin Hotel* ☉ *Daily 8 PM–2 AM.*

At the sprawling southwestern-Mexican–theme Coronado Springs Resort, Disney added **Francisco's Lounge** to slake the thirst of conventioneers. At the open-air cantina near the convention hall entrance, cool tile floors and umbrellas are a backdrop for house-specialty margaritas. Bottoms up. ☒ *Coronado Springs Resort* ☉ *Weekdays 1 PM–midnight, weekends noon–1 AM.*

Martha's Vineyard Lounge is a cozy, refined hideaway where you can settle back and sip domestic and European wines. Each evening 18 wines are poured for tasting. After facing the madding crowd, it's worth a detour if you're looking for a quiet retreat and a soothing glass of zinfandel. ☒ *Beach Club Resort* ☉ *Daily 5:30 PM–10 PM.*

At the stylish Grand Floridian, **Mizner's** is tucked away at the far end of the second floor of the main lobby. Even on steroids, this place wouldn't approach rowdy—it's a tasteful getaway where you can unwind with ports, brandies, and mixed drinks while overlooking the beach and the elegance that surrounds you. ☒ *Grand Floridian* ☉ *Daily 5 PM–1 AM.*

Narcoossee's is a restaurant with a bar inside that serves ordinary beer in expensive yard glasses, but the porch-side views of the Seven Seas Lagoon (and the nightly Electrical Water Pageant) are worth the premium you pay. Find a nice spot and you can also watch the Magic Kingdom fireworks. ☒ *Grand Floridian* ☉ *Daily 5 PM–10 PM.*

At the **Tambu Lounge** (beside 'Ohana's restaurant), Disney bartenders ring up all the variations on rum punch and piña coladas. Festooned with South Seas–style masks, totems, and Easter Island head replicas, this place is exotic—with the exception of the large screen TV. ☒ *Polynesian Resort* ☉ *Daily 1 PM–midnight.*

Nestled within a carbon copy of the magnificent Yellowstone Lodge, the **Territory Lounge** at the Wilderness Lodge is a frontier-theme sanctuary that pays tribute to the Corps of Discovery (look overhead for the trail map of Lewis and Clark). A full liquor bar (plus beers, of course) is offered—but you may get just as big a kick looking at the props on display: surveying equipment, daguerreotypes, large log beams, parka mittens, maps, and what the lounge claims is a pair of Teddy Roosevelt's boots. ☒ *Wilderness Lodge* ☉ *Daily 4 PM–midnight.*

Victoria Falls is the central lounge at the extraordinary Animal Kingdom Lodge. The second-floor retreat overlooks the Boma restaurant, and the exotic feel of an obligatory safari theme extends to leather directors' chairs, native masks, and the sounds of a stream flowing past. Across the hall near the front desk, a small alcove beckons. Although no drinks are served in the sunken den called the Sunset Overlook—with artifacts and photos from 1920s safaris of Martin and Osa Johnson—it is a popular spot for late-night conversation. ☒ *Animal Kingdom Lodge* ☉ *Daily 5:30 PM–midnight, dinner 6–10 PM.*

Other Hotels in Walt Disney World

There are a number of nightspots a short drive away at the non-Disney hotels of Walt Disney World. Two of the best of these clubs are at the Wyndham Palace Resort & Spa in Lake Buena Vista.

Lively entertainment and good drink specials draw an energetic young crowd of Disney cast members to the **Laughing Kookaburra**, the Palace's unrefined nightspot. Tuesday is Ladies Night, Wednesday is Hump Night with an all-night happy hour, and Thursday is Ladies Night again. Friday brings the Birthday Bash (if your birthday falls today or in the previous six days, you drink free), and then it's a '70s Saturday night. Oh, what a week it is. All ages are allowed in until 9 PM when you'll need to be 21 to stay. ⊠ *Wyndham Palace Resort & Spa, Lake Buena Vista* ☎ *407/827–3722* ☉ *Weekdays 5 PM–2 AM, weekends 7 PM–2 AM.*

The 27th-floor **Top of the Palace Lounge** offers not only a dazzling view of the Disney empire but also a complimentary champagne toast at sunset each evening—a clock in the lobby lets you know when that is. Considering that this is the highest vista at WDW, file this one away under "worth a detour"—it's a pleasant precursor to dinner at the stylish Arthur's 27 next door. ⊠ *Wyndham Palace Resort & Spa, Lake Buena Vista* ☎ *407/827–3591* ☉ *Daily 5 PM–1 AM.*

Disney's Wide World of Sports

Disney's Wide World of Sports Complex is suspiciously empty when no games are being played, but when the games begin there's plenty of action over at the **Official All-Star Cafe.** Within this stadium-size space is a restaurant and souvenir equipment donated by Andre Agassi, Monica Seles, Tiger Woods, Lou Holtz, and company. For a drink, skip the restaurant and head to the bar in front, and afterward check out the huge billiard room in back. If you subscribe to 48 premium sports channels, then this place is a must-see. Otherwise, just take a look if you're here on game day. ⊠ *690 S. Victory Way* ☎ *407/824–8326* ☉ *Daily 11–11, bar until midnight.*

Celebration

It may not be "nightlife" per se, but a few minutes down the road from the rest of Disney is the Utopian community of **Celebration.** In addition to its homes and school and offices, there's a downtown cluster of shops, restaurants, and a movie theater. Although Celebration's artificial perfection recalls an episode of the *Twilight Zone*, at night everything seems almost real and you can walk around and check out the Celebration Town Tavern, Columbia Restaurant, Barnie's Coffee & Tea Co., bookstores, boutiques, toy shops, and the two-screen AMC Theatre, (☎ *407/566–1403*). ☎ *407/824–4321.*

Dinner Shows

★ The **Hoop-Dee-Doo Revue**, staged at Fort Wilderness's rustic Pioneer Hall, may be corny, but it's also the liveliest dinner show in Walt Disney World. A troupe of jokers called the Pioneer Hall Players stomp their feet, wisecrack, and sing and dance, while the audience chows down on barbecued ribs, fried chicken, corn on the cob, strawberry shortcake, and all the fixin's. There are three shows nightly, and the prime times sell out months in advance in busy seasons. But you're better off eating dinner too early or too late rather than missing the fun altogether—so take what you can get. And if you arrive in Orlando with no reservations, try for a cancellation. ⊠ *Fort Wilderness Resort* ☎ *407/939–3463 advance tickets; 407/824–2803 day of show* 🍽 *$40.50 adults, $20.50 children 3–11* ☉ *Daily 5, 7:15, and 9:30.*

The **Polynesian Luau** is an outdoor barbecue with entertainment in line with its colorful South Pacific style. Its fire jugglers and hula-drum dancers are entertaining for the whole family, if never quite as endearing as the napkin twirlers at the Hoop-Dee-Doo Revue. The hula dancers' navel maneuvers, however, are something to see. You should try to make reservations at least a month in advance. This is a smoke-free establishment. ⊠ *Polynesian Resort* ☎ *407/939–3463 advance tickets; 407/824–1593 day of show* ▤ *$40.50 adults, $20.50 children 3–11* ⊙ *Tues.–Sat. 5:15 and 8.*

Fireworks, Light Shows & Parades

Both in the theme parks and around the hotel-side waterways, Walt Disney World offers up a wealth of fabulous sound-and-light shows after the sun goes down. In fact, WDW is one of the earth's largest single consumers of fireworks—perhaps even rivaling mainland China. Traditionally, sensational short shows have been held at the Magic Kingdom at 10. Times vary during the year, so check with Guest Services just to be certain. For a great, unobstructed view of the Fantasy in the Sky fireworks above Cinderella Castle at the Magic Kingdom, head to the second floor of the Main Street Train Station—but get there early. You can also find fireworks at Pleasure Island as part of the every-night-is-New Year's Eve celebrations—an event that's worth the wait into the wee hours.

Fireworks are only part of the evening entertainment. Each park hosts shows staged with varying degrees of spectacle and style. For the best of the best, head to Epcot which hosts visiting shows that are free with admission. Recently, Epcot has welcomed Lords of the Dance as well as Broadway's *Blast!* to perform abbreviated, albeit highly energetic, samples of their shows. Regular performers include a Beatles sound-alike group in the United Kingdom, acrobats in China, mimes in France, musicians in a smaller African kiosk, and rock and roll bagpipers in Canada. Catching any of these parades and/or performances easily soothes the sting of what you may feel is an overpriced admission.

Electrical Water Pageant

One of Disney's few remaining small wonders is this 10-minute floating parade of sea creatures outlined in tiny lights, with an electronic score highlighted by Handel's *Water Music*. Don't go out of your way, but if you're by Bay Lake and the Seven Seas Lagoon, look for it from the beaches at the Polynesian (at 9), the Grand Floridian (9:15), Wilderness Lodge (9:35), Fort Wilderness (9:45), the Contemporary (10:05), and, in busy seasons, the Magic Kingdom (10:20). Times occasionally vary, so check with Guest Services.

Fantasmic!

Fodor'sChoice Fantasmic!, the Disney–MGM big after-dark show, is held once nightly (twice on weekends and in peak seasons) in a 6,500-seat amphitheater. The special effects are superlative indeed, as Mickey Mouse in the guise of the Sorcerer's Apprentice emcees a revue full of song and dance, pyrotechnics, and special effects. This is an extremely popular show (and, strangely, often a tearjerker) so the crowds are usually heavy. For the best seats, arrive very early or dine at the Studio's Brown Derby, Hollywood & Vine, or Mama Melrose and you'll receive a voucher for special seats.

IllumiNations: Reflections of the Earth

Fodor'sChoice It's worth sticking around for the grand finale of a day in Epcot. The laser and fireworks show on the World Showcase lagoon takes place around 9 PM as orchestral music fills the air accompanied by the stirring whoosh and boom of fireworks, lasers, and neon images exploding and flashing in time with the music. Check the wind direction before staking a claim, since smoke can cloak some views. Some of the better vantage points are the Matsu No Ma Lounge in the Japan pavilion, the patios of the Rose and Crown in the United Kingdom pavilion, and

Cantina de San Angel in Mexico. Another good spot is the World Show-case Plaza between the boat docks at the Showcase entrance, but this is often crowded with those who want to make a quick exit after the show. If you decide to join them here, claim your seat at least 45 minutes in advance. It's worth waiting to see this spectacle.

SpectroMagic

Fodor'sChoice This splendidly choreographed parade of lights is one of the Magic King-dom's don't-miss attractions. It's a colorful, flickering, luminescent pa-rade with cartoonish floats and a complete lineup of favorite Disney characters. Times vary, so check the schedule before you set out, or ask any Disney staffer while you're in the park. The early showing is for parents with children, and the later ones attract night owls and others with the stamina and the know-how to enjoy the Magic Kingdom's most pleasant, least-crowded time of day.

Tapestry of Dreams

A popular holdover from Epcot's Millennium Celebration, this is one of the most spectacular parades in the country. Backed by the talent of *The Lion King*'s Michael Curry, 120 towering puppets (attached to parad-ing performers) march around the World Showcase accompanied by 720 drums and 30 drummers. Giant torch towers set the stage for this event, which, although filled with some hard-to-understand symbolism, is a mighty impressive, eclectic collection of costumes, colors, motion, and music. Don't panic if you miss the first one—it steps off twice each evening, usually around 6 and 8 (but call or ask a cast member for exact times). Instead of running one extremely long parade, they've created several shorter, identical ones that appear from different points and pass in re-view by each pavilion. Wherever you stand, you won't miss it.

Movies

Some nights, your feet won't walk even one more step. Try the **AMC 24 Theatres** (⊠ Downtown Disney West Side ☎ 407/827–1309 ticket of-fice; 407/298–4488 show times). The cinema is state-of-the-art and plays the latest films.

UNIVERSAL ORLANDO RESORT

At Universal, the after-hours action has seeped out of the parks and into CityWalk, an eclectic and eccentric 30-acre pastiche of shops, restau-rants, clubs, and concert venues. CityWalk's attitude is as hip and sassy as anywhere in the Universal domain.

Universal Orlando's CityWalk

Armed with a catchy headline ("Get a Nightlife"), **CityWalk** met the chal-lenge of diverting the lucrative youth market from Disney and down-town Orlando. It did so by creating an open and airy gathering place that includes clubs ranging from quiet jazz retreats to over-the-top dis-cotheques. On weeknights the crowd is a mix of families and conven-tioneers; weekends draw a decidedly younger demographic who are still arriving into the wee hours.

Although clubs have individual cover charges, it's far more economical to pay for the whole kit and much of the caboodle. You can buy a Party Pass (a one price–all clubs admission) for $9.49; a Party-Pass-and-a-Movie for $12.72; a Party-Pass-and-a-Meal combination for $18, which includes a meal from a preset menu, drinks, gratuity, and tax; or a Movie-and-a-Meal, which is also $18 but does not include admission to CityWalk.

Making these deals even better is the fact that, after 6 PM, the $7 parking fee drops to free. It is, however, a long walk from the parking garage to CityWalk (even longer when you stumble out at 2 AM and realize it's a ¼-mi walk to your car). Then again, you shouldn't be driving in this condition, so have a good time and call a cab. Taxis run at all hours (⇨ Taxis *in* Smart Travel Tips A to Z). ☎ 407/224–2692; 407/363–8000 *Universal main line* ⊕ *www.citywalkorlando.com.*

Why spend your time watching a movie when you're on vacation? Who cares? It's your vacation. The 20-screen, 5,000-seat, bilevel **Loew's Universal Cineplex** (☎ 407/354–5998 recorded information and tickets; 407/354–3374 box office) offers an escape from the crowds. You can purchase tickets in advance by telephone.

★ The beauty of **Bob Marley–A Tribute to Freedom** is that even if you can't dance, you can pretend you can by simply swaying to syncopated reggae rhythms. The museum-club is modeled after the "King of Reggae's" home in Kingston, Jamaica, complete with intimate low ceilings and more than 100 photographs and paintings reflecting pivotal moments in Marley's life. Off the cozy bar is a patio area where you can be jammin' to a (loud) live band that plays from 8 PM to 1:30 AM nightly. You must be 21 or over to be admitted on Friday and Saturday after 10 PM. ☎ 407/224–2692 ✉ $5 *after 8 PM* ☉ *Weekdays 4 PM–2 AM, weekends 2 PM–2 AM.*

CityWalk meets the needs of older folks who prefer a quiet, cool, sophisticated place to chill out with **CityJazz.** In the beautiful, tiered room, soft lighting, rich woods, and candlelight create a perfect backdrop for all types of jazz, yet they also manage to also feature live high-energy funk, soul, and rock. To pay tribute to members of the Down Beat Hall of Fame, there's memorabilia from Ella Fitzgerald, Duke Ellington, Lionel Hampton, Count Basie, and other legends. Performers such as Merl Saunders, Paul Howards, and Steve Reid have played here. With a hot act and a cool martini, you can't do much better than this. ☎ 407/224–2692 *or* 407/224–2189 ✉ $5, *special performance ticket prices* $6–$35 ☉ *Sun.–Thurs. 8:30 PM–1 AM, Fri.–Sat. 8:30 PM–2 AM.*

You must be at least 21 to enter **the groove** (note the hip lowercase lettering), a cavernous hall where every nook and cranny is filled with techno pop. The very sound of the place can be terrifying to the uninitiated: images flicker rapidly on several screens and the combination of music, light, and mayhem appeals to an under-30 crowd. They know enough to escape the dance floor into three rooms: the '70s-style Green Room, filled with beanbag chairs and everything you threw out when Duran Duran hit; the sci-fi Blue Room; and the Red Room, which is hot and romantic in a bordello sort of way. Prepare yourself for lots of fog, lots of swirling lights, lots of motion. ☎ 407/224–2692 ✉ $5 ☉ *Daily 9 PM–2 AM, Thurs.–Sat. 9 PM–3 AM.*

You could travel all over the world and never find a larger **Hard Rock Cafe,** where there's great food, loud music, and lots of eye candy. The best items adorn a room on the second floor: Beatles rarities such as cutouts from the *Sgt. Pepper* cover, John Lennon's famous "New York City" T-shirt, Paul's original lyrics for "Let It Be," and the doors from London's Abbey Road studios. Wow. Start with dinner and stay for the show,
★ since much of the attraction here is at the adjoining **Hard Rock Live.** The concert hall's exterior resembles Rome's Colosseum, and almost every evening an entertainer performs here; occasionally it's one you recognize (Ringo, Elvis Costello, Jerry Lee Lewis, etc.). Although the seats are hard and two-thirds don't face the stage, it's one of Orlando's top venues. Cover prices vary. Warning: you can't bring large purses or bags

inside and there are no lockers at CityWalk, so leave big baggage in your car. ☎ 407/224–2692 ⊕ *www.hardrocklive.com* ☉ *Daily from 11 AM, with a varying closing time, generally around midnight.*

Jimmy Buffett may be the most savvy businessman in America. He took a concept, wrapped it up in a catchy tune, and parlayed it into books, ★ clothing, musicals, and **Jimmy Buffett's Margaritaville.** It seems that Florida law requires residents to play Buffett music 24 hours a day, but if you're from out of state you might still not be over "Cheeseburger in Paradise." Attached to the restaurant are three bars (Volcano, Land Shark, and 12 Volt). There's a Pan Am Clipper suspended from the ceiling, music videos projected onto sails, limbo and Hula-Hoop contests, a huge margarita blender that erupts "when the volcano blows," live music nightly, and all the other subtleties that give Parrotheads a place to roost. ☎ 407/224–2692 ⊕ *www.margaritaville.com* ✉ *$5 after 8 PM* ☉ *Daily 11:30 AM–2 AM.*

Florida's Hispanic population is the fastest-growing ethnic group in the state, and the **Latin Quarter** seems to have attracted all who live in Orlando. It's easy to overlook the restaurant here, as most attention is paid to the nightclub, which is crowded with party-goers in eye-catching clothing. The club feels like a 21st-century version of Ricky Ricardo's Tropicana, although the design is based on a mix of Aztec, Incan, and Maya architecture. There's even an Andes mountain range, complete with waterfalls, around the dance floor. If you can get your hips working overtime, pick a rhumba from 1 to 10 and swivel . . . and tango and merengue and salsa . . . ☎ 407/224–2692 ⊕ *www.thelatinquarter.com* ✉ *$5; price may vary for certain performances* ☉ *Mon.–Thurs. 5 PM–2 AM, Fri.–Sat. noon–2 AM.*

The **Motown Cafe**, the club closest to the CityWalk parking lot, is more restaurant than bar but still worth seeing. The usual retinue of rock-star stuff (such as the Jackson 5's basketball uniforms) is here, along with great statues of Little Stevie Wonder and the Supremes. Each evening the house band (alternating between Supremes or Temptations look-alikes) rekindles Motown hits, with virtually everyone finding it hard to stay seated through a good Smokey Robinson song. ☎ 407/224–2692 ✉ *$5 after 9 PM* ☉ *Sun.–Thurs. 11:30 AM–11 PM, Fri.–Sat. 11:30 AM–2 AM.*

Pat O'Brien's is a legend in New Orleans, and this exact reproduction of the original is doing all right in Orlando, with its flaming fountain, dueling pianists, and balcony that re-creates the Crescent City. The draw here is the Patio Bar, where abundant tables and chairs allow you to do nothing but enjoy a respite from the madding crowd—and drink a potent, rum-based hurricane. ☎ 407/224–2692 ⊕ *www.patobriens. com* ✉ *$5 after 8 PM* ☉ *Patio Bar daily 4 PM–2 AM; Piano Bar Sun.–Thurs. 8 PM–2 AM, Fri.–Sat. 6 PM–2 AM.*

ORLANDO & KISSIMMEE

For several years, downtown Orlando clubs had a monopoly on nighttime entertainment—which came to a close when Disney and Universal muscled their way in. Nightspots still attract office workers after hours, but the once-popular Church Street Station entertainment complex has closed. Down Orange Avenue, cool clubs are now sitting beside grungy tattoo and piercing parlors that are making the downtown area look tired and seedy. Despite this, there are some gems in the surrounding neighborhoods and clubs that are worth a visit—if you're willing to seek them out.

The Arts

When the fantasy starts wearing thin, check out the Orlando arts scene in the *Orlando Weekly* (⊕ www.orlandoweekly.com) a local entertainment and opinion newspaper that accurately tracks Orlando culture, lifestyles, and nightlife. Perhaps your best source of up-to-the-week information is in Friday's *Orlando Sentinel* (⊕ www.orlandosentinel.com). The handy "Calendar" section carries reviews of plays, nightclubs, live music venues, restaurants, and attractions, and also contains a few tourist-oriented coupons.

The area has a fairly active agenda of dance, classical music, opera, and theater, much of which takes place at the **Carr Performing Arts Centre** (⊠ 401 W. Livingston St., Orlando ☎ 407/849–2577 ⊕ www.orlandocentroplex. com). The **Broadway Series** (☎ 407/839–3900 Ticketmaster) has top-notch touring shows such as *Beauty and the Beast, Fame,* and *Fosse.*

The downtown Orlando Arena was given a name change thanks to a large check from a major corporation; the clunkily named **TD Waterhouse Centre** (⊠ 600 W. Amelia St., Orlando ☎ 407/849–2020 ⊕ www. orlandocentroplex.com) plays host to many big-name performers and sports events.

During the school year, the Bach Festival organization at **Rollins College** (⊠ Winter Park ☎ 407/646–2233) has a three-part concert series that is open to the public and is usually free. The choral series is held at Rollins's Knowles Memorial Chapel. The second part, the visiting-artists series at the Annie Russell Theater, showcases internationally celebrated artists who have performed at venues such as Carnegie Hall. The last week in February, internationally recognized artists appear at the **Bach Music Festival** (☎ 407/646–2182 ⊕ www.bachfestivalflorida.org), a Winter Park tradition since 1936 and the last in the trilogy. The festival is held at the Annie Russell Theater and the Knowles Memorial Chapel and culminates on Sunday afternoon with "Highlights," which includes short performances by several of the artists who appeared during the week. While at Rollins, contact the **Annie Russell Theater** (☎ 407/646–2501) for information about its regular series of student productions.

Downtown Orlando Clubs & Bars

:08 is a country-theme nightclub with rather unusual attractions in the heart of downtown. In addition to presenting country artists like Trisha Yearwood and Marty Stuart, the club sponsors Buck and Bull Night on Saturday, when professional cowboys entertain the crowd by ridin' real live snortin' bulls. Frontier Fridays are highlighted by dance lessons, ladies' drink specials, country karaoke, and music by live country bands. The club's name reflects the length of time a cowboy has to stay on a rodeo's buckin' bull or bronco to make it to the next round (or seek psychological counseling). If you're interested in a discount, bull riders receive free parking, free admission, and a sandwich. ⊠ 100 W. Livingston St. ☎ 407/839–4800 ⊠ $5 ages 21 and older, $7 ages 18–20 ☉ Fri.–Sat. 8 PM–3 AM.

At **Howl at the Moon,** patrons shout or sing the pop classics of yesteryear and favorites such as "Time Warp" and "Hokey Pokey." This isn't karaoke: at this dueling piano bar everybody sings at once, so the noise level is just below a sonic boom. Toss back a couple of long-neck beers or a house-specialty drink served in a souvenir glass. Piano players keep the music rolling all evening, and the wait staff adds to the entertainment by singing and dancing. No food is served, but the management encourages you to bring your own or order out; several nearby restaurants deliver. You must be 21 or older. ✉ *Church Street Marketplace, 55 W. Church St., 2nd floor* ☎ *407/841–4695 or 407/841–9118* ✉ *$3 Wed., $2 Thurs., $4 Fri., $5 Sat., free Sun.* ☉ *Daily 6 PM–2 AM.*

★ As popular as any other place in the area, **Mulvaney's** is clearly downtown's most frequented Irish pub. Seven nights a week the wood-panel bar is packed with pub crawlers fond of simple fare, imported ales, and live entertainment, especially authentic Irish folk music. ✉ *27 W. Church St.* ☎ *407/872–3296* ✉ *No cover* ☉ *Weekdays 11 AM–2 AM, Sat. noon–2 AM, Sun. 1 PM–2 AM.*

★ Refreshingly free of stand-up comedians, lively **Sak Comedy Lab** is the arena for Orlando's most popular comedy troupe. The regular cast performs the Duel of Fools show and the late-night Fool Jam; the Sak Comedy Lab Rats are apprentices with potential. Each show, consisting of experimental comedy, improv challenges, and audience participation, lasts approximately 90 minutes. To make someone in your group the star of the show, for $100 you can surprise them with a "Slice of Life" scene based on their work, hobbies, and personality. Call in advance for the questionnaire. Wayne Brady, star of *Whose Line Is It Anyway?*, got his start here. ✉ *380 W. Amelia Ave.* ☎ *407/648–0001* ⊕ *www.sak.com* ✉ *Duel of Fools and Fool Jam $10–$13; Lab Rats $5* ☉ *Duel of Fools Thurs.–Sat. 8 PM; Fool Jam Fri.–Sat. 10 PM; Lab Rats Tues. and Wed. 9 PM.*

The **Social** is perhaps the favorite live-music venue of locals and a good place to see touring and local musicians. It serves full dinners Wednesday through Saturday and offers up live music seven nights a week. You can sip trademark martinis while listening to anything from alternative rock to rockabilly to undiluted jazz. Several now-national acts got their start here, including Matchbox Twenty and Seven Mary Three. ✉ *54 N. Orange Ave.* ☎ *407/246–1599* ⊕ *sapphiresupperclub.com* ✉ *$5–$18, depending on entertainment* ☉ *Sat.–Thurs. 8 PM–2 AM, Fri. 5 PM–2 AM.*

★ A short walk east from the main streets of downtown is hip **Thornton Park**. Adjacent to Lake Eola, the 1920s residential neighborhood is dotted with sidewalk cafés, smoothie stands, and casual restaurants. Part of the fun is finding the newly trendy nightspots that have set up shop cheek-by-jowl with the neighborhood's old-timers like Burton's Frosted Mug, a classic watering hole. For a smooth and easy libation, evening walk, or pleasing meal, you may want to make tracks for this Coconut Grove–style neighborhood. ✉ *Washington and Summerlin Aves.*

Wally's is one of Orlando's last traditions, a longtime favorite hangout for a cross-section of cultures and ages. Some would say it's a dive, but that doesn't matter to the lawyers, students, bikers, and barflies who land here to drink amidst the go-go dancer wallpaper and '60s-era interior. Just grab a stool at the bar to take in the scene and down a cold one. ✉ *1001 N. Mills Ave.* ☎ *407/896–6975* ☉ *Daily 7:30 PM–1 AM.*

Clubs & Bars Around I-Drive

International Drive embodies all the stereotypes of mass-market tourism: T-shirt shops, discount ticket kiosks, and a clutter of chain restaurants and strip malls. Of course, these businesses are supported by a host of hotels and the thousands of travelers who bunk down here each night. It's certainly not the most picturesque spot in town, but if you're in the neighborhood, there are countless retreats where you can watch a game and drink a brew.

If pubs could be reinvented in America instead of England, then the perfect prototype would be the **Cricketers Arms,** which is tucked in a back alley of the Mercado shopping complex. Locals crowd this English-style, American-looking pub to hear good Florida bands. Tables are small and closely packed inside, but you can always grab one outside on the sidewalk (nice at night) or go to the back patio. ⊠ *In the Mercado, 8445 International Dr.* ☎ *407/354–0686* ⊕ *www.cricketersarmspub.com* ✉ *No cover except for televised soccer matches ($10)* ⊙ *Daily 11* AM–*2* AM ⊟ *AE, MC, V.*

He never won a Super Bowl (perhaps because he wore unlucky number 13), but Miami Dolphin quarterback Dan Marino has had better luck with **Dan Marino's Town Tavern.** More sophisticated than a locker room, it has secluded booths and an oblong, football-shape bar that seems to have struck a chord with locals who linger over the Marino Margaritas (no, they don't contain Gatorade). This is more restaurant than bar—until around 9 PM, when the bar comes to life. It's not wild, just a calming place for a quiet drink. Be sure to have your server validate your parking ticket. ⊠ *Pointe*Orlando, 9101 International Dr.* ☎ *407/363–1013* ✉ *No cover; parking $2, free with validation* ⊙ *Sun.–Thurs. 11* AM–*midnight, Fri.–Sat. 11* AM–*1* AM ⊟ *AE, MC, V.*

Friday's national empire explains how it could afford to build a sports bar the size of Delaware. You enter **Friday's Front Row Sports Grille & Restaurant** on an incline, giving you the sense that you're walking into a sports stadium. To the right is the dining area; if you're here for drinks, walk past the bleachers toward the back and join the locals, who come here to play trivia games, eat the bar food, talk stats, and ogle autographed pictures. The fun continues upstairs, and upstairs beyond that. This is a sports bar that's been super-sized. ⊠ *8126 International Dr.* ☎ *407/363–1414* ✉ *No cover* ⊙ *Daily 11* AM–*2* AM ⊟ *AE, D, DC, MC, V.*

JB's Sports Bar & Restaurant has been around since 1987, surviving on the sports-mindedness of Universal employees, Disney cast members, and locals. Weeknights are fine, but on weekends and during big games, the place is like a frat-house party, with 28 TVs broadcasting the action and beer flowing nonstop. You can shoot some darts during commercials. JB's is in a shopping plaza, and its appearance is as basic as its bar food: hot dogs, wings, and sandwiches. Head for the enclosed patio if you need a break from the noise. ⊠ *4880 S. Kirkman Rd.* ☎ *407/293–8881* ✉ *No cover except for special pay-per-view events* ⊙ *Daily 11* AM–*2* AM ⊟ *AE, D, DC, MC, V.*

The **Orlando Ale House,** a nice retreat for a beer, would look so much better if it weren't in a strip mall. The large interior has booths and brass rails and standard-issue pool tables, dart boards, and TV screens. There's a raw bar, and you can order sandwiches, burgers, pastas, and fried foods. Beer is the big seller here, especially on Monday and Thursday, when you can buy a pitcher for $5. During the Monday through Friday 11 AM to 7 PM happy hour, draft beers and margaritas are $1. ⊠ *5573 S. Kirkman Rd.* ☎ *407/248–0000* ✉ *No cover* ⊙ *Daily 11* AM–*2* AM ⊟ *AE, D, MC, V.*

The **Players Grill,** one of several drinkeries at Pointe*Orlando, is ostensibly the "Home of the NFL Players." At least you can see their artifacts on display en route to the upscale restaurant upstairs or the sports bar on the ground level. Drink specials change with the sporting event. The pool tables, pinball machines, and darts are staples. ⊠ *Pointe*Orlando, 9101 International Dr.* ☎ *407/903–1974* ✉ *No cover* ⊙ *Weekdays 4–10:30, weekends 11* AM–*midnight* ⊟ *AE, D, DC, MC, V.*

Dinner Shows

Dinner shows are an immensely popular form of nighttime entertainment around Orlando. For a single price, you get a theatrical production and a multicourse dinner. Performances run the gamut from jousting to jamboree tunes and meals tend to be better than average; unlimited beer, wine, and soda are usually included, but mixed drinks (and often *any* drinks before dinner) cost extra. What the shows lack in substance and depth they make up for in grandeur and enthusiasm. The result is an evening of light entertainment, which youngsters in particular enjoy. Seatings are usually between 7 and 9:30, and there are usually one or two performances a night, with an extra show during peak periods. You might sit with strangers at tables for 10 or more, but that's part of the fun. Always reserve in advance, especially for weekend shows.

If you're in Orlando off-season, try to take in these dinner shows on a busy night—a show playing to a small audience can be uncomfortable. Be on the lookout for discount coupons: you can find them in brochure racks in malls, in hotels, and at the Orlando/Orange County Convention & Visitors Bureau. Since performance schedules can vary depending on the tourist season, it's always smart to call in advance to verify show times. When buying tickets, ask if the cost includes a gratuity—servers anxious to pocket more cash may hit you up for an extra handout.

Orlando

If Sherlock Holmes has always intrigued you, head for **Sleuths Mystery Dinner Show,** where your four-course meal is served up with a healthy dose of conspiracy. There are nine rotating whodunnit performances staged throughout the year, and each stops short of revealing the perpetrator. The show begins at a wedding, class reunion, anniversary party, etc., and over appetizers the short play you're watching ends in murder. Discuss the clues over dinner, question the still-living characters, and solve the crime during dessert. Did the butler do it? There are three theaters, which accounts for the frequent performances. ⊠ *7508 Universal Blvd.* ☎ *407/363–1985 or 800/393–1985* ⊕ *www.sleuths.com* ⊠ *$41.95 adults, $23.95 children 3–11* ⊙ *Weekdays 7:30, sometimes 8:30; Sat. 6, 7:30, and 9; Sun. 7:30* ⊟ *AE, D, MC, V.*

Kissimmee

On the outside, **Arabian Nights** is an elaborate palace. It's more like an arena within, with seating for more than 1,200. Its dinner show includes eerie fog, an Arabian princess, a buffoonish genie, a chariot race, an intricate western square dance on horseback, and 60 fabulous horses that perform in such acts as bareback acrobatics by gypsies. You'll be served during the show, so you might not end up paying much attention to the food—which is not a bad idea since the meal of prime rib or vegetable lasagna is functional, not flavorful. Extra shows are added in summer. Make reservations in advance. ⊠ *6225 W. Irlo Bronson Memorial Hwy., Kissimmee* ☎ *407/239–9223; 800/553–6116; 800/533–3615 in Canada* ⊕ *www.arabian-nights.com* ⊠ *$44 adults, $27 children 3–11* ⊙ *Shows nightly, times vary* ⊟ *AE, D, MC, V.*

Capone's Dinner and Show returns to the gangland Chicago of 1931, when mobsters and their dames represented the height of underworld society. The evening begins in an old-fashioned ice cream parlor, but say the secret password and you are ushered inside Al Capone's private Underworld Cabaret and Speakeasy. Dinner is an unlimited Italian buffet that's heavy on pasta. ⊠ *4740 W. Irlo Bronson Memorial Hwy.* ☎ *407/ 397–2378* ⊕ *www.alcapones.com* ⊠ *$39.95 adults, $23.95 children 4–12* ⊙ *Daily 7:30* ⊟ *AE, D, MC, V.*

In a huge, ersatz-medieval manor house, **Medieval Times** portrays a tournament of sword fights, jousting matches, and other games on a good-versus-evil theme. No fewer than 30 charging horses and a cast of 75 knights, nobles, and maidens participate. Sound silly? It is. But it is also a true extravaganza. That the show takes precedence over the meat-and-potatoes fare is obvious: everyone sits facing forward at long, narrow banquet tables stepped auditorium-style above the tournament area. Additional diversions include tours through a dungeon and torture chamber and demonstrations of antique blacksmithing, woodworking, and pottery making. ⊠ *4510 W. Irlo Bronson Memorial Hwy.* ☎ *407/239–0214 or 800/229–8300* ⊕ *www.medievaltimes.com* ✉ *$45.95 adults, $29.95 children 3–11* ☉ *Castle daily 9–4, village daily 4:30–8, performances usually daily at 8 but call ahead* ⊟ *AE, D, MC, V.*

Movies

Check out the impressive **Muvico Pointe 21** (⊠ Pointe＊Orlando, 9101 International Dr., Orlando ☎ 407/903–0555). It has 21 screens and stadium seating. Admission is $7.75 after 6 PM and $5.75 for matinees.

THE SPACE COAST

FODOR'S CHOICE

Kennedy Space Center Visitor Complex, in Titusville

Merritt Island National Wildlife Refuge, in Titusville

Ron Jon Surf Shop, in Cocoa Beach

Surfing off Cocoa Beach

HIGHLY RECOMMENDED

RESTAURANTS   Bernard's Surf, in Cocoa Beach

Dixie Crossroads, in Titusville

Mango Tree Restaurant, in Cocoa Beach

Spanish River Grill, in New Smyrna Beach

Toni and Joe's, in New Smyrna Beach

HOTELS   Cocoa Beach Hilton Oceanfront, in Cocoa Beach

Inn at Cocoa Beach, in Cocoa Beach

Riverview Hotel, in New Smyrna Beach

Wakulla Suites Resort, in Cocoa Beach

SIGHTS   Atlantic Center for the Arts, in New Smyrna Beach

Brevard Zoo, in Melbourne

Canaveral National Seashore, in Titusville

Updated by
Gary
McKechnie

ONE SMALL STEP FROM ORLANDO; one giant leap from Toledo. The most direct route from Greater Orlando to the coast, the Beeline Expressway (Route 528), is arrow-straight, cut through forests of long-needle pine, and laid across the yawning savannas at the very southern tip of the south-to-north St. Johns River, which begins life as a tiny stream in a place called Hell and Blazes, Florida. In this extremely flat countryside of cedars, red maples, and palmettos, American egrets, blue herons, and shy limpkins wade and fish for dinner; ibises tend their chicks; and graceful anhingas perch where they can, spreading their wings to dry. High above watery prairies, hawks hunt and ospreys soar over their nests that crown stately sabal palms, Florida's official tree. It feels a million miles from the artificial worlds of the theme parks, and it's one good reason to make the one-hour trip from Orlando directly east to the coast.

The laid-back little towns and beach communities from Cocoa Beach north to New Smyrna Beach are another reason to venture out of Orlando in this direction. Moreover, the area is home to the Kennedy Space Center and also offers water sports, fishing, golf, nature, nightlife, a great zoo, and some distinctive shopping.

As this book went to press, the space shuttle launch schedule was under review. Call ☎ 800/KSC–INFO (572–4636) for the most recent information. If you're lucky enough to be in this area during a space shot, you'll be treated to a spectacular sight. For the closest access possible, you can purchase tickets in advance for the space shuttle launches by calling ☎ 321/449–4444 or visiting ⊕ www.kennedyspacecenter.com.

Exploring the Space Coast

Although just 50 mi separate the Space Coast and Orlando, they're a world apart. In the small oceanfront towns of Cocoa Beach, Titusville, New Smyrna Beach, and Cape Canaveral, you won't find a lot of glitz, glamour, or giddy attractions. Mainly, it's sun, sand, and surf.

Besides the beach, there's one major attraction in the area: Kennedy Space Center Visitor Complex. The other sights tend to be rather low-key, funky, and offbeat. Still, there's plenty to see and do—or not do. Probably the nicest thing about Cocoa Beach and its neighbors is their laid-back style, which is very easy to get used to.

If you have the time, the best plan is to set aside two or three days to enjoy the area. But the Space Coast can also be enjoyed as a one- or two-day trip from Orlando.

About the Restaurants & Hotels

WHAT IT COSTS				
$$$$	**$$$**	**$$**	**$**	**¢**
RESTAURANTS over $30	$22–$30	$15–$22	$8–$15	under $8
HOTELS over $220	$160–$220	$110–$160	$70–$110	under $70

Restaurant prices are per person for a main course at dinner. Hotel prices are for two people in a standard double room in high season, plus 10%–12% tax.

Cocoa

50 mi east of downtown Orlando, 60 mi east of WDW.

Not to be confused with the seaside community of Cocoa Beach, the small town of Cocoa sits smack dab on mainland Florida and faces the Intracoastal Waterway, known locally as the Indian River. There's a plan-

10

If you have
- **2 days**

For a reprieve from Disney take this surf-and-turf tour of the Space Coast. From Orlando, drive the Beeline Expressway (Route 528) east. Just past mile marker 30, take the exit for Route 520 and head east. Be advised that this is a very narrow two-lane road that attracts anxious motorists, and the danger increases after dark. From the exit off the Beeline, it's about 9½ mi to the **Lone Cabbage Fish Camp.** Stop in for a touch of real down-home Florida. Here you can fish from the dock, get some gator tail for lunch, and take an airboat ride—a genuine Florida experience. Continue east on 520 and you'll have to drive past a mess of city traffic to reach **Cocoa Village,** a restored neighborhood of more than 50 shops and restaurants nestled on the west side of the Intracoastal Waterway. If you want to shop, it's best to come here sometime between midmorning and midafternoon. Saturday tends to be more crowded than weekdays, and on Sunday many of the shops are closed. To explore the entire Cocoa Village area, allow at least an hour; triple that if you plan to do some serious browsing in the shops.

Proceed farther east on 520 to **Cocoa Beach.** 520 deadends in A1A, the coastal highway know as Atlantic Avenue in Cocoa Beach. When you take a right (south) here, almost immediately on your left is the **Ron Jon Surf Shop.** It's a two-story display of all the surfing and beach gear you could ever use, and it's open 24 hours a day. Check into your hotel and spend the rest of the day soaking up the sun.

On Day 2, head north on A1A to the **Kennedy Space Center Visitor Complex.** Follow the signs to 528 (Orlando) and take the exit for Route 3 (heading north). From here, it's about a 20-minute drive. Spend the day learning the story of America's exploration of space. Be sure to include a stop at the **United States Astronaut Hall of Fame,** which, in 2002, became part of the KSC Visitor Complex. It's a fun attraction, and one of the few places where you can test your skills landing the shuttle on a simulator. On your way back, retrace your route; at the end of Route 528, follow the signs for **Port Canaveral.** You're likely to see several giant cruise ships at dock, and you get another good view of Kennedy Space Center's launchpads.

If you have
4 days

Allowing yourself that extra day or two will give you an opportunity to explore at a more leisurely pace. This itinerary picks up on Day 3—your day to get back to nature. From the beach head north on A1A to U.S. 1 on the mainland and go north to Route 406. Turn east on Route 406 and then right on Route 402 and look for signs to the **Merritt Island Wildlife Refuge.** Take a drive through the refuge (just continue on Route 402) and then either head to Playalinda Beach, the southernmost beach of the **Canaveral National Seashore,** where you can get great views of the launchpads, or retrace your drive back to U.S. 1 and head north to New Smyrna Beach. Follow the signs to A1A and stop at the public beach or drive on down to one of the northern beaches at the **Canaveral National Seashore.** There's a northern and southern entrance to the national seashore but these two roads don't connect, so you'll need to head back to U.S. 1 to return to Cocoa Beach for Day 4. Jump-start the day with a brisk walk or jog along the beach to witness a spectacular sunrise. When you've had enough sun and sand, head for the low-key shops and restaurants of **Cocoa Beach Pier.**

etarium and a museum, as well as a rustic fish camp along the St. Johns River, a few miles inland. Perhaps Cocoa's most interesting feature is restored **Cocoa Village.** Folks in a rush to get to the beach tend to overlook this Victorian-style village, but it's worth a stop. Within the cluster of restored turn-of-the-20th-century buildings and cobblestone walkways, visitors can enjoy several restaurants, indoor and outdoor cafés, snack and ice cream shops, and almost 50 specialty shops and art galleries. To get to Cocoa Village, head east on Route 520—named King Street in Cocoa—and when the streets get narrow and the road curves, make a right onto Brevard Avenue; follow the signs for the free municipal parking lot.

As its name suggests, **Porcher House** was the home of E. P. Porcher, one of Cocoa's original pioneers and the founder of the Deerfield Citrus groves. The Porcher Home, built in 1916 and now a national historic landmark, is an example of 20th-century classical revival–style architecture incorporating local coquina rock. The house is open to the public for unguided tours. ✉ *434 Delannoy Ave., Cocoa Village* ☎ *321/639–3500* ✉ *Donation welcome* ☉ *Weekdays 9–5.*

The **Astronaut Memorial Planetarium and Observatory,** one of the largest public-access observatories in Florida, has a 24-inch telescope through which visitors can view objects in the solar system and deep space. On the campus of Brevard Community College, the planetarium has two theaters, one showing a changing roster of nature documentaries; the other hosting laser light as well as changing planetarium shows. **Science Quest Demonstration Hall** features hands-on exhibits, including scales calibrated to other planets. On the moon, big Vegas Elvis would have weighed just 62 pounds. The **Astronauts Hall of Fame** (not to be confused with the one near the Kennedy Space Center) displays exhibits on space travel. Show schedules and opening hours may vary, so it's best to call ahead. Travel 2½ mi east of I–95 Exit 75 on Route 520, and take Route 501 north for 1¾ mi. ✉ *1519 Clearlake Rd.* ☎ *321/634–3732* ⊕ *www.brevard.cc.fl.us/planet* ✉ *Observatory and exhibit hall free; film or planetarium show $6 adults, $4 children 12 and under; both shows $10 adults, $6 children; laser show $6; Triple Combination: planetarium, movie, laser show $14 adults and children* ☉ *Call for current schedule.*

To see what the local lay of land looked like in other eras, check out the **Brevard Museum of History and Natural Science.** Hands-on activities for children are the draw here. Not to be missed is the **Windover Archaeological Exhibit** of 7,000-year-old artifacts indigenous to the region. In 1984, a shallow pond revealed the burial ground for more than 200 Native Americans who lived in the area about 7,000 years ago. Preserved in the muck were bones and, to the archaeologists' surprise, the brains of these ancient people. Don't overlook the hands-on discovery rooms and the **Collection of Victoriana.** The museum's **nature center** has 22 acres of trails encompassing three distinct ecosystems—sand pine hills, lake lands, and marshlands. ✉ *2201 Michigan Ave.* ☎ *321/632–1830* ⊕ *www.brevardmuseum.com* ✉ *$5 adults, $2.50 children under 17; trails free* ☉ *Tues.–Sat. 10–4; Nov.–Apr., also some Sun. 1–4.*

The **Lone Cabbage Fish Camp** is a strange old Florida riverfront restaurant and attraction. In reality just a clapboard shack, it's offbeat and extremely casual. There's a dock where you can buy bait and fish, a Florida Cracker restaurant inside, and if you want to see the river's wildlife up close, there are airboat rides—including specially arranged nighttime tours as well as longer and more thrilling rides aboard shorter and more nimble watercraft. Naturally, there are souvenir T-shirts to memorialize your

10

Beaches

On Florida's mid-Atlantic coast from New Smyrna Beach and Canaveral National Seashore south to Sebastian Inlet, there are about 120 mi of wide, sandy beaches. Although the winter season alone counts about 650,000 vacationers, the area's beaches are much less densely developed than Daytona's. From New Smyrna Beach south to Satellite, the offshore incline is gentle and waters are shallow for some distance out, and bottoms are smooth. Below Satellite Beach, which is south of Cocoa Beach, beaches tend to be rocky, with an uneven bottom. Remember: there are sharks off Florida's coast. Lifeguards and locals know when there's been a lot of shark activity and with their advice, you can decide if you want to swim or not. Chances are the waters will be safe. More of a danger than sharks, however, are rip currents. When the receding waves break through a sandbar, the current can pull you out to sea. If you're caught in a riptide, stay calm and swim parallel to the shore until you're out of the force of the flow before trying to swim to shore. Again, ask locals and lifeguards about the water conditions before going in.

Casting Your Line

There are many hot spots for local fishing. Check Florida Today, the local newspaper, or bait-and-tackle shops to find out what's biting where. You can surf cast for bluefish, pompano, sea bass, and flounder; success is mixed and depends on the season. Or try your hand at pier fishing. (Most major beach towns have lighted piers, and admission is usually $1–$4.) Here anglers sometimes pull in mackerel, trout, sheepshead, and tarpon. Because it's on the Intracoastal Waterway rather than the Atlantic, the Titusville pier has good shrimping, too. You can also fish from some of the bridges that cross the inland waterway, also known here as the Indian River.

Catch of the Day

The Space Coast area is dotted with casual eateries with a heavy emphasis on the fruits of the sea. There are a few upscale dining establishments in Cocoa, Cocoa Beach, and New Smyrna Beach, but for the most part the eatin' is easy.

Lodging

Most lodging in Cocoa Beach is on Route A1A around its intersection with Route 520. Small motels abound; the few larger hotels are part of popular chains. In New Smyrna Beach, motels dot A1A. Such factors as season, upcoming NASA space shuttle launches, and especially spring break all affect room rates. The high season usually runs between February 1 and April 30, and rates drop considerably after.

Surfing

Cocoa Beach is the self-proclaimed Small Wave Capital of the World—an unusual title, yet one the locals hold in high regard. Those who like to hang 10 in the Pacific, however, will find the waves here quite tame. Of course, when there's a major storm or good hurricane a-brewing, then surf's up and you can catch quite a wave. Cocoa Beach's main tourist attraction, the collection of Ron Jon Surf Shops, is a tribute to the town's principal claim to fame. New Smyrna Beach also is popular with surfers, and there's a cluster of surf shops at the main entrance to the beach.

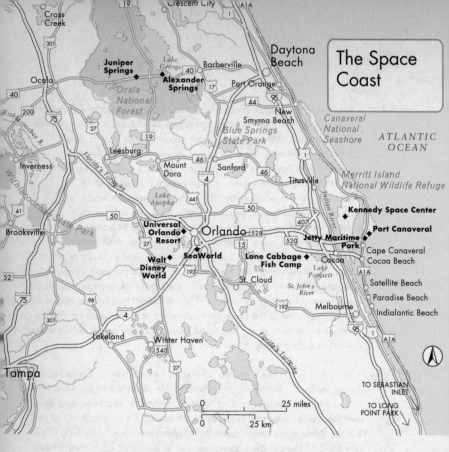

visit. The camp is about 9 mi west of Cocoa's city limits, 4 mi west of I–95. ✉ *8199 Rte. 520* ☎ *321/632–4199* ⊕ *www.twisterairboatrides. com* ✉ *Airboat ride $17 adults, $8.50 children under 12* ☉ *Airboat rides daily 10–6.*

Where to Stay & Eat

$$–$$$ ✕ **Café Margaux.** Dine inside or out at this charming, cozy Cocoa Village spot with its eclectic, creative mix of French and Italian cuisine. The lunch menu features black sesame–coated chicken over mesclun greens, as well as lump crab cakes over pancetta and roasted corn relish. Dinners are equally exotic, with oak-smoked Norwegian salmon rosettes, and samplers like a baked Brie coated in pecans. ✉ *220 Brevard Ave.* ☎ *321/639–8343* ⊕ *www.margaux.com* ▭ *AE, DC, MC, V* ☉ *Closed Sun. and Tues.*

$$ ✕ **Black Tulip Restaurant.** Two intimate dining rooms invite romance at this Cocoa Village bistro, which takes pride in its 50-plus label wine menu. Appetizers include tortellini with meat sauce and crab-stuffed mushrooms. Select such entrées as fettuccine primavera Alfredo; sautéed pork loin simmered with apples, brandy, and cream; roast duckling with peaches and cashews; or fillet medallions with artichoke sauce. Lighter lunch selections include sandwiches, salads, and quiches. Don't miss the chocolate mousse pie and warm apple strudel. ✉ *207 Brevard Ave.* ☎ *321/ 631–1133* ⊕ *www.blacktulip.com* ▭ *AE, DC, MC, V.*

$ ✕ **Paradise Alley Cafe.** The small and active eatery in the heart of Cocoa Village looks a little like Margaritaville, and the menu follows suit. There are tropical kebabs, blackened seafood, gumbo, and dishes taken from the Deep South, Native America, Caribbean, South and Central America. ⊠ *234 Brevard Ave.* ☎ *321/635–9032* ☐ *AE, MC, V.*

¢–$ ✕ **Lone Cabbage Fish Camp.** This is down-home, no-nonsense dining in a rustic setting. Set your calorie counter for plates of catfish, frogs' legs, turtle, and alligator (as well as burgers and hot dogs). There's a fish fry and country-and-western hoedown every Sunday. ⊠ *8199 Rte. 520* ☎ *321/632–4199* ☐ *AE, MC, V.*

$ ⊡ **Indian River House Bed & Breakfast.** Three miles north of the Cocoa Village, this charming 1903 home overlooks the Intracoastal Waterway. Three rooms have water views and all are individually and comfortably decorated. You can spot the space shuttle as well as dolphins and egrets from the dock, where canoes and kayaks await guests. A full breakfast is included. ⊠ *3113 Indian River Dr., 32922* ☎ *321/631–5660* ⊕ *www.indianriverhouse.com* ⇆ *4 rooms* ⌂ *Dock, boating, bicycles* ☐ *MC, V.*

Nightlife & the Arts

In 1918, this building was a Ford dealership that sold Model T's. After that, it evolved into the Aladdin Theater, a vaudeville house, and then did a turn as a movie theater before being purchased by Brevard Community College. Today, the **Cocoa Village Playhouse** (⊠ 300 Brevard Ave. ☎ 321/636–5050) is the area's community theater. The September through June performance schedule has musicals featuring local talent. The rest of the year the stage hosts touring professional productions, concerts, and, in summer, shows geared to children on vacation.

Shopping

You could spend hours browsing in the many boutiques and shops of **Cocoa Village,** along Brevard Avenue and Harrison Street, which has the densest concentration of shops. Kids come to a screeching halt when they catch sight of the dizzying array of toys displayed in the storefront windows of **Annie's Toy Chest** (⊠ 403 Brevard Ave. ☎ 321/632–5890 ⊕ www.anniestoychest.com). The **Bath Cottage** (⊠ 425 Brevard Ave. ☎ 321/690–2284 ⊕ www.bathcottage.com) carries just about everything for the bathroom, from fine soaps to aromatherapy candles, plush towels, and elegant shower curtains. It also has one-of-a-kind accessories for the home including colorful blown-glass balls, drawer pulls, and table lamps.

For some terrific sculptures of fish, follow the brick path back to the **Harry Phillips Gallery** (⊠ 116-B Harrison St. ☎ 321/636–4160). If you like to cook, or even just like to eat, spend some time wandering through the huge array of kitchen and cooking items—handsome ceramic bowls, colorful glassware, regional cookbooks, exotic soup mixes—and gourmet ingredients at **The Village Gourmet** (⊠ 19 Stone St. ☎ 321/636–5480). Take a break from the heat with a hand-packed ice cream cone from the **Village Ice Cream & Sandwich Shop** (⊠ 120 Harrison St. ☎ 321/632–2311).

Cocoa Beach

65 mi east of Orlando, 70 mi east of WDW.

After crossing a long and high bridge just east of Cocoa Village, you'll be dropped down upon a barrier island. A few miles further and you'll

Fodor'sChoice reach the Atlantic Ocean and picture-perfect **Cocoa Beach** at Route A1A. This is one of the Space Coast's nicest beaches, with many wide stretches that are excellent for biking, jogging, power walking, or strolling leisurely. In some places there are dressing rooms, showers, playgrounds, picnic areas with grills, snack shops, and surf-side parking lots. Beach vendors offer necessities, and guards are on duty in summer. Cocoa Beach is considered the capital of Florida's surfing community.

Stretching far over the Atlantic, the **Cocoa Beach Pier** (⊠ 401 Meade Ave. ☎ 321/783–7549 ⊕ www.cocoabeachpier.com) is a local gathering spot as well as a beachside grandstand for space shuttle launches. There are several souvenir shops, bars, and restaurants, as well as a bait-and-tackle shop. It costs $3 to park here, and another $1 for access to the fishing part of the pier that dangles 800 ft out into the Atlantic. Don't expect pristine Disney cleanliness here; this is a weather-beaten, sandy hangout for people who love the beach.

When the children have had enough of the beach, take them to **Jungle Village Family Fun Center** to tire them out. There are mazes to climb around and get lost in, three tracks of go-carts for children and adults, 70 video games, a "soft play" playground, batting cages for both softball and hard ball, laser tag, and 36 holes of miniature golf with a jungle theme featuring Pinky, a life-size elephant who sports pachyderm-size sunglasses. Hey, it's Florida. Don't go in the middle of the day in summer; you could wilt from the drop-dead heat. ⊠ *Rte. A1A, 2½ mi north of Rte. 520* ☎ *321/783–0398 or 321/783–0595* ✉ *Park free; go-carts $5.50 for people over 60″, $4.50 50″–60″, $3.50 40″–49″; miniature golf and laser tag $5 for adults and children; call for off-season price specials* ☉ *Daily 10 AM–midnight.*

Where to Stay & Eat

★ $$–$$$$ ✕ **Mango Tree Restaurant.** Candles, fresh flowers, and rattan basket chairs set a romantic mood in the intimate dining room, designed to evoke the feel of a South Pacific plantation. *Lobsterocki* (Maine lobster wrapped in bacon with teriyaki cream sauce), baked Brie, or rare seared tuna are good appetizer choices. For a main course, try the Indian River crab cakes, coq au vin, or veal Française (scallopini with mushroom sauce). ⊠ *118 N. Atlantic Ave.* ☎ *321/799–0513* ⊕ *www.themangotreerestaurant. com* ⊟ *AE, MC, V* ☉ *Closed Mon. No lunch.*

★ $$–$$$ ✕ **Bernard's Surf.** Since 1948, this popular family operation has featured numerous fresh seafood entrées, from swordfish, cobia, and pompano to lobster and shrimp. The house specialty is snapper under a creamy seafood sauce. Landlubbers can choose pork chops or steak. Be sure to try the tableside Caesar salad, and save room for the unbeatable cheesecake, topped with raspberries and chocolate. ⊠ *2 S. Atlantic Ave.* ☎ *321/783–2401* ⊕ *www.bernardssurf.com* ⊟ *AE, D, DC, MC, V* ☉ *No lunch.*

$$ ✕ **Heidelberg.** As the name suggests, the cuisine here is definitely German, from the sauerbraten served with potato dumplings and red cabbage to the beef Stroganoff and spaetzle to the classically prepared Wiener schnitzel. All the soups and desserts are homemade; try the apple strudel and the rum-zapped almond-cream tortes. The atmosphere is elegant, with crisp linens and fresh flowers. You can also dine inside the jazz club where there's live music every day but Monday. It's not just local talent, either; jazz greats like Boots Randolph and Mose Allison have played here. ⊠ *7 N. Orlando Ave., opposite City Hall* ☎ *321/ 783–6806* ⊕ *www.heidisjazzclub.com* ⊟ *AE, MC, V* ☉ *Closed Mon. No lunch Sun.*

$–$$ ✕ **Alma's Italian Restaurant.** A local favorite for more than 30 years, Alma's is crowded on weekends, but five separate dining rooms keep the place from feeling jammed. The specialties of the house are fresh-caught grouper Italian style and veal Parmesan. The cellar stocks more than 200 imported and domestic wines, and the atmosphere is warm and casual, courtesy of red-checked tablecloths, stone floors, dim lighting, and a large stained-glass window. ⊠ *306 N. Orlando Ave.* ☎ *321/783–1981* ⊟ *AE, DC, MC, V* ☉ *No lunch.*

$–$$ ✕ **Atlantic Ocean Grille.** Five hundred feet over the water in the shopping, dining, and entertainment complex on Cocoa Beach Pier, this restaurant has floor-to-ceiling windows that overlook the ocean. Among the excellent fresh-fish options are mahimahi and grouper, which you can order broiled, blackened, grilled, or fried. ✉ *401 Meade Ave.* ☎ *321/783–7549* ➛ *AE, D, DC, MC, V.*

$–$$ ✕ **Fischer's Bar and Grill.** This casual eatery, owned by the same family that runs the more upscale Bernard's Surf, is a perfect spot for winding down after a tough day at the beach. Although complete dinners are available, people tend to come for the salads, pasta, burgers, and platters of tasty fried shrimp. The family's fleet of fishing boats brings in fresh seafood daily. Happy hour is from 4 to 7. ✉ *2 S. Atlantic Ave.* ☎ *321/783–2401* ⊕ *www.bernardssurf.com* ➛ *AE, DC, MC, V.*

$–$$ ✕ **Rusty's Seafood & Oyster Bar.** Oysters, prepared raw, steamed, or casino style, are just one of the draws at this casual eatery with a Hooters motif—waitresses are dressed in very short shorts. Other popular menu items include seafood gumbo, spicy wings, steamed crab legs, burgers, and baskets of fish-and-chips, clam strips, or fried calamari. It's a popular spot with the locals. There are two locations: the first is in the same building as Bernard's Surf; the other is at Port Canaveral. ✉ *2 S. Atlantic Ave.* ☎ *321/783–2401* ✉ *628 Glen Cheek Dr., Port Canaveral* ☎ *321/783–2033* ⊕ *www.bernardssurf.com* ➛ *AE, D, DC, MC, V.*

¢–$ ✕ **The Boardwalk.** At this popular open-air bar on Cocoa Beach Pier, finger food reigns, and you can count on live entertainment Monday, Wednesday, and Friday through Sunday evenings. At the very popular Friday-night Boardwalk Bash there are $7 lobsters and $2 ribs. ✉ *401 Meade Ave.* ☎ *321/783–7549* ⊕ *www.cocoabeachpier.com* ➛ *AE, D, DC, MC, V.*

¢–$ ✕ **Oh, Shucks!** In the only open-air seafood bar on the beach, the main item is oysters, served on the half shell. It also serves burgers plus live entertainment on Friday and Saturday. ✉ *401 Meade Ave.* ☎ *321/ 783–7549* ➛ *AE, D, DC, MC, V.*

★ **$$–$$$$** 🏨 **Inn at Cocoa Beach.** One of the area's best, this charming oceanfront inn has spacious, individually decorated rooms with four-poster beds, upholstered chairs, balconies or patios, and ocean views. Deluxe rooms are much larger, with a king-size bed, sofa sitting area and most with dining table. Jacuzzi rooms are different sizes; several with fireplaces, all with beautiful ocean views. Included in the rate are evening wine and cheese and a sumptuous Continental breakfast. ✉ *4300 Ocean Beach Blvd., 32931* ☎ *321/799–3460; 800/343–5307 outside Florida* 🖷 *321/ 784–8632* ⊕ *www.theinnatcocoabeach.com* ➛ *50 rooms* ♨ *Dining room, pool, gym, beach* ➛ *AE, D, MC, V.*

$$$ 🏨 **Doubletree Oceanfront Hotel.** Light and airy rooms are comfortably furnished with blond rattan and colorful pastel prints; many are oceanfront with superb water views and private balconies. This well-maintained five-story hotel is popular with families and is also a favorite of Orlandoans as a weekend getaway. ✉ *2080 N. Atlantic Ave., 32931* ☎ *321/783–9222 or 800/552–3224* 🖷 *321/783–6514* ⊕ *www. cocoabeachdoubletree.com* ➛ *138 rooms, 10 suites* ♨ *Restaurant, 2 pools, wading pool, gym, bar* ➛ *AE, DC, MC, V.*

$$–$$$ 🏨 **Holiday Inn Cocoa Beach Resort.** When two adjacent beach hotels were redesigned and a promenade park landscaped between them, the Holiday Inn Cocoa Beach Resort was born. Public rooms are plush, modern, and designed in bright tropical colors. Lodging options include standard and king rooms; oceanfront suites, which have a living room with sleeper sofa; villas; or bilevel lofts. KidsSuites are rooms with an adult area as well as a kids' playroom. ✉ *1300 N. Atlantic Ave., 32931* ☎ *321/783–2271 or 800/206–2747* 🖷 *321/784–8878* ⊕ *www. holidayinnsofcentralflorida.com* ➛ *500 rooms, 119 suites* ♨ *Restau-*

rant, snack bar, 2 tennis courts, pool, hair salon, shuffleboard, volleyball, 2 bars, baby-sitting, children's programs (ages 3–12), laundry facilities ⊟ *AE, DC, MC, V.*

★ **$–$$$** ⊞ **Cocoa Beach Hilton Oceanfront.** At seven stories, this hotel is one of the tallest buildings in Cocoa Beach and also one of the best. Dense natural foliage separates the property from the roadway. Rooms are comfortably but not lavishly furnished. Most have ocean views, but for true drama get a room on the east end, facing the water. The hotel's best feature is its location, right on the beach. In season, a band plays reggae music poolside on weekends. ⊠ *1550 N. Atlantic Ave., 32931* ☎ *321/799–0003 or 800/526–2609* ⊟ *321/799–0344* ⊕ *www.cocoabeachhilton.com* ⇌ *296 rooms* ⌂ *Restaurant, pool, beach, bar, video game room, baby-sitting* ⊟ *AE, D, DC, MC, V.*

★ **$–$$$** ⊞ **Wakulla Suites Resort.** This popular, two-story motel is clean and comfortable and just off the beach. Some rooms are a block away from the water, and a few are just a walk down the boardwalk. The bright rooms are fairly ordinary, decorated in tropical prints. Completely furnished five-room suites, designed to sleep six, are great for families; each comprises two bedrooms and a living room, dining room, and fully equipped kitchen. ⊠ *3550 N. Atlantic Ave., 32931* ☎ *321/783–2230 or 800/992–5852* ⊟ *321/783–0980* ⊕ *www.wakulla-suites.com* ⇌ *116 suites* ⌂ *2 pools, shuffleboard* ⊟ *AE, D, DC, MC, V.*

$$ ⊞ **Cocoa Beach Oceanside Inn.** This five-story property is right on the beach, adjacent to the Cocoa Beach Pier. All rooms are done in the typical tropical Florida pastel style that seems to cool you off after a day in the sun, and each has an oceanfront balcony. After the salty sea, the freshwater pool is nice. A Continental breakfast is included in the room rate; the on-site restaurant serves breakfast only. ⊠ *1 Hendry Ave., 32931* ☎ *321/784–3126 or 800/874–7958* ⊟ *321/799–0883* ⊕ *www.cocoabeachoceansideinn.com* ⇌ *76 rooms* ⌂ *Restaurant, pool, beach, bar* ⊟ *AE, D, MC, V* �⍟ *CP.*

$–$$ ⊞ **Ocean Suite Hotel.** A boxy five-story building with a great location, this property is just a half block south of Cocoa Beach Pier. Ideal for families or business travelers, each suite has two TVs, a separate living room, wet bar area with sink, refrigerator, microwave, dinette set, hideaway sofa bed, two telephone lines with data ports, and desks. All suites have a private balcony. Breakfast is the only meal served at the on-site restaurant. ⊠ *5500 Ocean Beach Blvd., 32931* ☎ *321/784–4343 or 800/367–1223* ⊟ *321/783–6514* ⊕ *www.oceansuiteshotel.com* ⇌ *50 suites* ⌂ *Restaurant, pool, bar* ⊟ *AE, D, DC, MC, V.*

Nightlife

The **Cocoa Beach Pier** (⊠ 401 Meade Ave. ☎ 321/783–7549) is for locals, beach bums, surfers, and people who don't mind the weatherworn wood and sandy, watery paths. At the Mai Tiki they claim that "No Bar Goes This Far," which is true, considering it's at the end of the 800-ft pier. Come to the Boardwalk Friday night for the Boardwalk Bash, with live acoustic and rock-and-roll music; drop in Saturday for more live music; and come back Wednesday evening to catch the reggae band. Oh, Shucks! has live bands Friday and Saturday nights.

Coconuts on the Beach (⊠ 2 Minuteman Causeway ☎ 321/784–1422), a beachfront hangout that's long been the local party place, is popular with the younger crowd. There are karaoke nights, ladies' nights, 25¢-beer nights, and volleyball tournaments, plus live music on Thursday, Friday, and Saturday. Burgers, salads, and sandwiches are on the menu. For some great live jazz, head to **Heidi's Jazz Club** (⊠ 7 Orlando Ave. ☎ 321/783–4559 ⊕ www.heidisjazzclub.com). Local and nationally known musicians play Tuesday through Sunday, with showcase acts usually appearing on weekends.

Outdoor Activities & Sports

The **Space Coast Office of Tourism** (☎ 321/868–1126 or 800/936–2326 ⊕ www.space-coast.com) publishes a lengthy, detailed, and extensive listing of outdoor adventures, from horseback rides to airboat rides to sea turtle walks. It also lists surfing and sailing schools and fishing charters.

The **Cocoa Beach Country Club** (✉ 5000 Tom Warriner Blvd. ☎ 321/868–3351) is actually an extensive public sports complex that's owned by the city and open to anyone. Its facilities include a 27-hole championship golf course; an Olympic-size swimming pool; 10 lighted tennis courts; a restaurant and snack bar; and a riverside pavilion with picnic tables. Seventeen lakes on the golf course provide a habitat which attracts an abundance of waterfowl and other birds, with species listed and information offered at each hole.

BIKING   Although there are no bike trails as such in the area, cycling is allowed on the beaches and the Cocoa Beach Causeway. Bikes can be rented hourly, daily, or weekly at **Ron Jon Surf Shop** (✉ 4151 N. Atlantic Ave., Rte. A1A ☎ 321/799–8888). The rates range from $5 for two hours to $50 for the week. Locks are available.

FISHING   The **Cocoa Beach Pier** (✉ 401 Meade Ave. ☎ 321/783–7549) has a bait-and-tackle shop and a fishing area. Although most of the pier is free to walk on, there's a $1 charge to enter the fishing area at the end of the 800-ft-long boardwalk, and $3.50 to fish. If you didn't bring your own fishing gear, they rent rods and reels here.

SURFING   If you can't tell a tri-skeg stick from a hodaddy shredding the lip on a gnarly tube, then you may want to avail yourself of the **Cocoa Beach Surfing School** (✉ 150 E. Columbia Lane ☎ 321/868–1980 ⊕ www.cocoabeachsurfingschool.com). They teach grommets (dudes) and gidgets (chicks) from kids to seniors. Rates are $45 for a one-hour private lesson and $40 for a one-hour semi-private (two people). For a three-hour lesson rates are $75 for a semi-private and $50 for a group of three or more. No credit cards; cash and traveler's checks only.

Shopping

Merritt Square Mall (✉ 777 E. Merritt Island Causeway, Rte. 520, Merritt Island ☎ 321/452–3272 ⊕ www.merrittsquare.com), the area's only major shopping mall, is about a 20-minute ride from the beach. Stores include Burdines, Dillard's, JCPenney, Sears Roebuck, Bath & Body Works, Foot Locker, Waldenbooks, and roughly 100 others. There's a six-screen multiplex, along with a food court and several popular restaurant chains.

Fodor'sChoice   It's impossible to miss the **Ron Jon Surf Shop** (✉ 4151 N. Atlantic Ave., Rte. A1A ☎ 321/799–8888 ⊕ www.ronjons.com). With a giant surfboard and an aqua, teal, and pink art-deco facade, Ron Jon takes up nearly two blocks along A1A. What started in 1963 as a small T-shirt and bathing suit shop has evolved into a 52,000-square-ft superstore that's open every day 'round the clock. The shop has water-sports gear as well as chairs and umbrellas for rent, and sells every kind of beachwear, surf wax, plus the requisite T-shirts and flip-flops. For up-to-the-minute surfing conditions, call the store and press 3 and then 7 for the **Ron Jon Surf and Weather Report. Ron Jon Watersports** (✉ 4151 N. Atlantic Ave. ☎ 321/799–8888) features the latest in surfing rentals, including glass and foam surfboards, body boards, scuba equipment, and kayaks.

Melbourne

20 mi south of Cocoa.

Despite its dependence on the high-tech space industry, this town has a decidedly laid-back atmosphere.

★ It took 20,000 volunteers two weeks to turn 56 acres of forest and wet-lands into the **Brevard Zoo,** the only AZA-accredited zoo built by a community. Stroll along the shaded boardwalks and get a close-up look at alligators, crocodiles, giant anteaters, marmosets, jaguars, eagles, river otters, kangaroos, exotic birds, and kookaburras. Alligator, crocodile, and river otter feedings are held on alternate afternoons—al-though the alligators do not dine on the otters. Stop by **Paws-On,** an interactive learning playground where kids and adults can crawl into human-sized gopher burrows, beehives, and spider webs; get cozy with a wide range of domestic animals in **Animal Encounters;** have a bird hop on your shoulder in the **Australian Free Flight Aviary;** and step up to the **Wetlands Outpost,** an elevated pavilion that's a gateway to 22 acres of wetlands through which you can paddle kayaks and keep an eye open for the 4,000 species of wildlife that live in these waters and woods. **Overnight Zoo Safaris** for kids ages 7–14 include a nighttime zoo safari by flashlight and marshmallows cooked over a campfire. Pic-nic tables, a snack bar, and a gift shop complete the daytime picture. ✉ *8225 N. Wickham Rd.* ☎ *321/254–9453* ⊕ *www.brevardzoo.org* 🖭 *$7 adults, $5 children 2–12; kayaks $3 per person; train ride $2* ☉ *Daily 10–5.*

The **King Center** is one of the premier performance centers in Central Florida. Oddly enough, top-name performers often bypass Orlando to appear in this comfortable 2,000-seat hall. Call ahead for a performance schedule. ✉ *3865 N. Wickham Rd.* ☎ *321/242–2219 box office* ⊕ *www. kingcenter.com.*

> **off the beaten path**

Satellite Beach. The beaches of this sleepy little community just south of Patrick Air Force Base, about 15 mi south of Cocoa Beach on A1A, are almost always free of crowds.

Paradise Beach. Small and scenic, this 1,600-ft stretch of sand is part of a 10-acre park north of Indialantic, about 20 mi south of Cocoa Beach on A1A. It has showers, rest rooms, picnic tables, a refreshment stand, and lifeguards in summer.

Outdoor Activities & Sports

Even though they play at South Florida's Pro Player Stadium during the season, baseball's **Florida Marlins** (✉ 5800 Stadium Pkwy. ☎ 321/633–9200 ⊕ www.flamarlins.com) use Melbourne's Space Coast Stadium for their spring-training site. Seats are still pretty cheap: $6–$15. For the rest of the season, the facility is home to the Brevard County Manatees, one of the Marlins' minor-league teams.

Sebastian

22 mi south of Melbourne.

One of only a few sparsely populated areas on Florida's east coast, this little fishing village has as remote a feeling as you're likely to find any-where between Jacksonville and Miami Beach.

The 578-acre **Sebastian Inlet State Recreation Area** is so popular that it's the only Florida state park open 24 hours a day, 365 days a year. Popular doesn't mean crowded, thankfully, just blessed with a wide range of activities. It offers 3 mi of interesting beach that's good for swimming, surfing, and snorkeling. The beach is rocky and the sand coarser than elsewhere along the coast, and the underwater drop-off is often sharp. It's fun for treasure hunters, because storms occasionally wash up coins from the area's ancient Spanish shipwrecks. Sebastian is also a favorite destination for Florida anglers. Warning: bring mosquito repellent. The park has a bathhouse, a concession, a fishing jetty, a boat ramp, and campsites. ⊠ *9700 S. Rte. A1A, Melbourne Beach* ☎ *321/984–4852* ⊕ *www.dep.state.fl.us/parks* ☎ *$3.25* ☉ *Daily 24 hrs, bait and tackle shop daily 8–6, concession stand daily 9–5.*

At the southern tip of Sebastian Park across the border in Indian River County is the **McLarty Treasure Museum,** built to commemorate the loss of a fleet of Spanish treasure ships in a hurricane. Don't miss the dramatic movie *The Queen's Jewels and the 1715 Fleet.* Filmed by the Arts & Entertainment television network, it's a riveting tale of the 11 ships that sank in one devastating hurricane in 1715. These ships are the source of most of the treasure that still washes ashore along this part of the Florida coastline. You'll have to pay the park admission before you can reach the museum. ⊠ *13180 N. Rte. A1A* ☎ *561/589–2147* ☎ *$1 ages 6 and older* ☉ *Daily 10–4:30.*

Port Canaveral

5 mi north of Cocoa.

This once-bustling commercial fishing area is still home to a small shrimping fleet, charter boats, and party fishing boats, but its main business these days is as a cruise-ship port. Cocoa Beach itself isn't the spiffiest place around, but what *is* becoming quite clean and neat is the north end of the port where the Carnival, Disney, and Royal Caribbean cruise lines set sail. Port Canaveral is now Florida's second-busiest cruise port, which makes this a great place to catch a glimpse of these giant ships even if you're not headed out to sea.

Jetty Maritime Park serves a wonderful taste of the real Florida. At Port Canaveral's south side, there are assorted restaurants and marine shops, a 4½-acre beach, more than 150 campsites for tents and RVs, picnic pavilions, and a 1,200-ft-long fishing pier that doubles as a perfect vantage point from which to watch a lift-off of the space shuttle. A jetty constructed of giant boulders adds to the landscape, and a walkway that crosses it provides access to a less-populated stretch of beach. Real and rustic, this is Florida without the theme park varnish. ⊠ *400 E. Jetty Rd., Cape Canaveral* ☎ *321/783–7111* ☎ *$3 per car, $7 for RVs, for either fishing or beach: Camping $24 for basic, $28 with water/electric, $31 full hook-up* ☉ *Daily 7 AM–9 PM.*

Where to Stay & Eat

$–$$$ 🏨 **Radisson Resort at the Port.** This resort directly across the bay from Port Canaveral is not on the ocean, but it does provide complimentary transportation to the beach, Ron Jon Surf Shop, and the cruise ship terminals at Port Canaveral. Rooms have wicker furniture, hand-painted wallpaper, coffeemakers, and ceiling fans. The pool is tropically landscaped and replete with a cascading 95-ft mountain waterfall. ⊠ *8701 Astronaut Blvd., 32920* ☎ *321/784–0000 or 800/333–3333* ☎ *321/784–3737* ⊕ *www.radisson.com* ⇄ *284 rooms* ♿ *Restaurant, 2 tennis* courts, 2 pools, health club, hot tub, playground, laundry service, business services, convention center, airport shuttle ☰ AE, DC, MC, V.

Outdoor Activities & Sports

Cape Marina (✉ 800 Scallop Dr. ☎ 321/783–8410 ⊕ www.capemarina. com) books 8-, 10-, and 16-hour fishing charters in search of the elusive wahoo, tuna, dolphin, mackerel, snapper, grouper, amberjack, marlin, and sailfish.

Titusville

17 mi north of Cocoa.

This small community is home to the Kennedy Space Center, the nerve center of the U.S. space program. Several attractions here are devoted to the history of space exploration.

Fodor'sChoice The must-see **Kennedy Space Center Visitor Complex,** just southeast of Titusville, is one of Central Florida's most popular sights. Following the lead of the theme parks, they've switched to a one-price-covers-all admission. At the **Astronaut Encounter,** an astronaut hosts a daily Q&A session to tell visitors about life in zero gravity, providing insights to an experience only a few hundred people have ever shared. If you'd like to have a closer encounter with an astronaut, you can purchase a special ticket option to **Dine with an Astronaut** for $55.95 for adults and $35.95 for kids—which includes your regular KSC admission. No, it's not freeze-dried food and Tang. Other exhibits include the fascinating **Early Space Exploration,** which highlights the rudimentary yet influential Mercury and Gemini space programs; **Robot Scouts,** a walk-through exhibit of unmanned planetary probes; and the **Exploration in the New Millennium** display, which offers you the opportunity to touch a piece of Mars. Don't miss the outdoor **Rocket Garden,** with walkways winding beside spare rockets from early Atlas spacecraft to a Saturn 1. There's also a museum filled with exhibits on spacecraft that have explored the last frontier, and a theater showing several short films. A full-scale reproduction of a space shuttle, *Explorer,* is displayed and you can walk through the payload bay, cockpit, and crew quarters. Children love the space playground, with a one-fifth-scale space shuttle–space station gym.

The most moving exhibit is the **Astronauts Memorial,** a tribute to those who have died while in pursuit of space exploration. The memorial was financed mostly by Floridians who purchased *Challenger* license plates, and will continue to receive funding from Floridians who now are dealing with the *Columbia* tragedy. The 42½-ft-high by 50-ft-wide "Space Mirror" tracks the movement of the sun throughout the day, using reflected sunlight to illuminate brilliantly the names of the 23 fallen astronauts that are carved into the monument's 70,400-pound polished granite surface.

To get the most out of a visit to the space center, take the **KSC Visitor Complex** bus tour (included with admission), which is the only way to see much of the working part of the facility up close. Buses depart every 15 minutes and head to the Launch Complex 39 Observation Gantry, which has an unparalleled view of the twin space-shuttle launchpads. At the Apollo Saturn V Center, don't miss the presentation at the Firing Room Theatre, where the launch of the Apollo VIII is re-created with a ground-shaking, window-rattling lift-off. At the Lunar Surface Theatre, recordings from Apollo XI offer an eerie and awe-inspiring reminder that when Armstrong and Aldrin landed, they had less than 30 seconds of fuel to spare. In the hall it's impossible to miss the 363-ft-long (or tall?) Saturn V rocket. A spare built for a moon mission that never took place, this 6.2-million-pound spacecraft was launched with enough thrust to throw a fully loaded DC-3 all the way to the sun and back!

For an added fee and a more in-depth experience, take the **NASA Up Close** tour, which brings visitors to sights seldom accessible to the public, such as the NASA Press Site Launch Countdown Clock, the Vehicle Assembly Building, the shuttle landing strip, and the 6-million-pound crawler that transports the shuttle to its launchpad.

IMAX films are projected onto 5½-story screens in the only back-to-back twin **IMAX theater complex** in the world. The thunderous sound systems might make you think you're at an actual launch. In the IMAX I Theater, *The Dream Is Alive,* an awesome 40-minute film narrated by Walter Cronkite and shot mostly by the astronauts, takes you from astronaut training and a thundering shuttle launch to an astronaut's-eye view of life aboard the shuttle while in space. The latest film, **Apollo 13: The IMAX Experience** can eat up a lot of time (it's nearly two hours), but if you haven't seen the movie or if you don't know how the mission played out, you can see it here on the very large silver screen. **Space Station IMAX 3-D** follows astronauts and cosmonauts on their missions, with the 3-D effects putting you in space with them. Whatever you choose, while you're waiting for a movie to start, step around the corner for a look at the intriguing recap of the Hubble telescope and get an instant education on how you can measure distances and years between us and the farthest galaxies. When you reach Kennedy Space Center grounds, tune your car radio to AM 1320 for attraction information. ⊠ *Rte. 405, Kennedy Space Center* ☎ *321/452–2121 or 800/572–4636* ⊕ *www.kennedyspacecenter.com* ⊠ *Maximum Access Badge, includes bus tour and all IMAX movies: $26 adults, $16 children 3–11; NASA Up Close Tour: $20 adults and children, Two-day Maximum Access Admission combining the Visitor Complex and the Astronaut Hall of Fame, $31 adults, $21 children 3–11* ☉ *Space Center daily 9 AM–5:30, last regular tour 3 hrs before closing; closed certain launch dates, so call ahead; IMAX I and II Theaters daily 10–5:40.*

Once an independent attraction, the **United States Astronaut Hall of Fame** received $700,000 in improvements and computer upgrades when it became part of the Kennedy Space Center Visitor Complex in December 2002. The original Mercury 7 team and the later Gemini, Apollo, Skylab, and shuttle astronauts have donated their time and energy to make this the world's premium archive of personal stories, authentic memorabilia, and equipment, which tells the story of human space exploration. Complementing the memorabilia are extremely fun and popular interactive displays inside the **Astronaut Adventure.** You can pull 3-Gs in a mock G-force trainer, and go through a hair-raising simulated jet-aircraft dogfight complete with 360° barrel rolls. One of the more challenging activities is a mighty tricky space shuttle simulator that lets you try your hand at landing the craft—and afterward replays a side view of your rolling and pitching descent. For a quiet interlude, view videotapes of historic moments in the space program and marvel at the relatively archaic Sigma 7 Mercury space capsule used by Wally Schirra. Gus Grissom's spacesuit, colored silver only because NASA thought silver looked more "spacey," and a flag that made it to the moon, are also displayed. The exhibit, **First on the Moon,** focuses on crew selection for *Apollo 11* and the Soviet Union's role in the space race. This is also home to **U.S. Space Camp,** which offers young people a hands-on learning environment that budding astronauts will love; five-day programs are available for ages nine and up, and parent-child weekend programs are also offered. ⊠ *6225 Vectorspace Blvd., off Rte. 405, Kennedy Space*

Center ☎ *321/269–6100* ⊕ *www.kennedyspacecenter.com* ✉ *$13.95 adults, $9.95 children 6–12; Two-day Maximum Access Admission combining the Kennedy Space Center Visitor Complex and the Astronaut Hall of Fame, $31 adults, $21 children 3–11* ⊙ *Daily 9–5.*

Although its exterior looks sort of squirrelly, what's inside the **Valiant Air Command Warbird Air Museum** is certainly impressive. Aviation buffs won't want to miss memorabilia from both world wars, Korea, and Vietnam, as well as extensive displays of vintage military flying gear and uniforms. There are posters used to identify Japanese planes, plus there's a Huey helicopter and the cockpit of an F-106 that you can sit in (but can't start). In the north hangar, it looks like activity day at the senior center as a team of retirees are busy volunteering their time to restore old planes. It's an inspiring sight, and a good place to hear some war stories. In the lobby gift shop they sell real flight suits ($40), old flight magazines, bomber jackets, books, and T-shirts. ✉ *6600 Tico Rd.* ☎ *321/268–1941* ⊕ *www.vacwarbirds.org* ✉ *$9 adults, $5 children 4–12* ⊙ *Daily 10–6.*

If you're interested in getting closer to the wildlife of the Merritt Island National Wildlife Refuge or other local scenic waterways, check out **A Day Away Kayaking Tours** with Rick Shafer. He leads guided ecotours for all levels of experience in which you might paddle alongside dolphins, manatees, herons, bald eagles, and submarines. History lessons complement the nature tour, as you learn that in the Indian River and Mosquito Lagoons, an estuary island was home to Native Americans as early as 7000 BC. Tours, which may also include some light fishing, last one to five hours and start at $25 per person, cash only, refreshments included. ☎ *321/268–2655* ⊕ *www.kayaknaturetours.com.*

★ The 57,000-acre **Canaveral National Seashore,** home to more than 250 species of birds and other animals, is an unspoiled area of hilly sand dunes, grassy marshes, and seashell-sprinkled beaches. Surf and lagoon fishing are available, and a hiking trail leads to the top of a Native American shell midden at Turtle Mound. A visitor center is on Route A1A. Weekends are busy, and parts of the park are closed before launches, sometimes as much as two weeks in advance, so call ahead.

Part of the national seashore, remote **Playalinda Beach** has pristine sands and is the longest stretch of undeveloped coast on Florida's Atlantic seaboard. Its isolation explains why a remote strand of the beach is popular with nude sunbathers. Aside from them, hundreds of giant sea turtles come ashore here May through August to lay their eggs. There are no lifeguards, but park rangers patrol. Eight parking lots anchor the beach at 1-mi intervals. Take bug repellent in case of horseflies. To get here, follow U.S. 1 north into Titusville to Route 406 (I–95 Exit 80), follow Route 406 east across the Indian River, and then take Route 402 east for 12 mi. ✉ *Southern end: Rte. 402* ☎ *321/267–1110* ✉ *Northern end: 7611 S. Atlantic Ave., New Smyrna Beach* ☎ *386/428–3384* ⊕ *www. nps.gov/cana* ✉ *$5 per car* ⊙ *Apr.–Oct., daily 6 AM–8 PM; Nov.–Mar., daily 8 AM–6 PM.*

If you prefer wading birds over waiting in line, don't miss the 140,000-acre **Merritt Island National Wildlife Refuge,** which adjoins the Canaveral National Seashore. You can borrow field guides and binoculars at the visitor center to track down various types of falcons, osprey, eagles, turkeys, doves, cuckoos, loons, geese, skimmers, terns, warblers, wrens, thrushes, sparrows, owls, and woodpeckers. One of the most enjoyable pleasures is found in the sublime beauty of nature on the self-guided, 7-mi driving tour along **Black Point Wildlife Drive.** The dirt road takes

FodorśChoice

you back in time, where there are no traces of encroaching malls or mankind and it's easy to visualize the Indian tribes who made this their home 7,000 years ago. On the **Oak Hammock Foot Trail,** you can see wintering migratory waterfowl and learn about the plants of a hammock community. If you exit the north end of the refuge, look for the **Manatee Observation Area** just north of the Haulover Canal (maps are at the visitor center). They usually show up in spring and fall. There are also fishing camps scattered throughout the area. The refuge is closed four days prior to a shuttle launch. ✉ *Rte. 402, across Titusville causeway* ☎ *321/861–0667* ⊕ *merrittisland.fws.gov* ✑ *Free* ☉ *Daily sunrise–sunset, Visitor Center open Mon.–Fri. 8–4:30, Sat. 9–5.*

Where to Stay & Eat

★ **$–$$$** ✕**Dixie Crossroads.** This sprawling restaurant is always crowded and festive, but it's not just the atmosphere that draws the throngs; it's the seafood. The specialty is the difficult-to-cook rock shrimp, which is served fried or broiled. Other standouts include the clam strips and the all-you-can-eat catfish. Often, the wait for a table can last 90 minutes, but if you don't have time to wait, you can order takeout or eat in the bar area. ✉ *1475 Garden St., 2 mi east of I–95 Exit 80* ☎ *321/268–5000* ⌕ *Reservations not accepted* ▤ *AE, D, DC, MC, V.*

$$ ⊡**Holiday Inn Riverside–Kennedy Space Center.** Because it offers great views of lift-offs, this hotel books up fast when a launch at the Kennedy Space Center is scheduled. Rooms are comfortable but modestly furnished. The beach is a car ride away, but there's a big pool. ✉ *4951 S. Washington Ave., 32780* ☎ *321/269–2121 or 800/465–4329* ⎙ *321/267–4739* ⊕ *www.holidayinnksc.com* ☞ *117 rooms* ⌕ *Restaurant, pool, wading pool, lounge, playground* ▤ *AE, D, DC, MC, V.*

New Smyrna Beach

35 mi north of Titusville.

This small town has a long dune-lined beach that abuts the north end of the Canaveral National Seashore. Behind the dunes sit beach houses, small motels, and an occasional high-rise. Canal Street, on the mainland, and Flagler Avenue, home to many beachside shops and restaurants, have both been "street-scaped" and are now lined with wide, brick sidewalks and stately palm trees. The town is also known for its internationally recognized artists' workshop.

★ Changing every two months, the gallery exhibits at the **Atlantic Center for the Arts** feature the works of internationally known artists—sculpture, mixed media, video, drawings, prints, and paintings. Intensive three-week workshops are periodically run by visual, literary, and performing master artists; faculty have included playwright Edward Albee, the late poet and author James Dickey, and sculptor Beverly Pepper. ✉ *1414 Art Center Ave.* ☎ *386/427–6975* ⊕ *www.atlanticcenterforthearts.org* ✑ *Free* ☉ *Weekdays 9–5, Sat. 10–2.*

Smyrna Dunes Park is on the northern tip of its barrier island. Here 1½ mi of boardwalks crisscross sand dunes and delicate dune vegetation as they lead to beaches and a fishing jetty. Botanical signs identify the flora, and there are picnic tables and an information center. ✉ *N. Peninsula Ave.* ✑ *$3* ☉ *Daily 7–sunset.*

The town's **public beach** extends 7 mi from the northernmost part of the barrier island south to the Canaveral National Seashore. It's mostly hard-packed white sand and, at low tide, can be stunningly wide. The beach is lined with heaps of sandy dunes, but please don't disturb them. The dunes are endangered, and it's against the law to walk or play on them or to pick the sea grass that helps to stabilize the dunes. Be aware that from sunrise to sunset cars are allowed on certain sections of the beach (speed limit: 10 mph).

★ The entrance to the north end of the **Canaveral National Seashore** begins at the south end of the public beach. ✉ *7611 S. Atlantic Ave.* ☎ *386/428–3384* ✑ *$5 per car* ☉ *Apr.–Oct., daily 6 AM–8 PM; Nov.–Mar., daily 8 AM–6 PM.*

Where to Stay & Eat

$–$$$$ ✕ **Norwood's** Since 1946, this seafood restaurant has been one of the area's most popular places, thanks to its fresh fish (prepared any style), Angus beef, fresh oysters and scallops, and decadent desserts. Another attraction is its impressive selection of wines, with more than 30,000 bottles of 1,400 different wines in stock. Credit Southern hospitality honed over a half-century for the exemplary service. ✉ *400 E. 2nd Ave.* ☎ *386/428–4621* ☰ *AE, MC, V.*

$–$$ ✕ **New Smyrna Steakhouse.** Locals and visitors flock to this dark and busy spot to dine on giant steaks, spicy ribs, and juicy cheeseburgers. Try the 12-ounce New York strip or sirloin, the 20-ounce porterhouse, the 8-ounce filet mignon, or a rack of tender ribs. Other good choices are the Cajun pizza, shrimp Caesar salad, and mesquite chicken. Booths are lit by individual, low-hanging lamps that provide intimacy but still enough light to read the menu. ✉ *723 3rd Ave.* ☎ *386/424–9696* ☰ *AE, MC, V.*

★ **$–$$** ✕ **Spanish River Grill.** Chef-owners Michelle and Henry Salgado preside over this first-rate Cuban spot, where everything is made from scratch. Start with fried green plantains or black-bean soup, then move on to a tender rib-eye steak stuffed with chorizo, incredibly fresh grilled fish, or the roasted sour-orange chicken. The wine list includes many reasonably priced selections. Ocher walls, crisp table linens, and romantic lighting provide an intimate setting. ✉ *737 E. 3rd Ave.* ☎ *386/424–6991* ☰ *AE, MC, V* ☉ *Closed Mon.*

★ **¢** ✕ **Toni and Joe's.** This longtime, ultracasual favorite (no shoes required) opens right onto the beach and has a large terrace perfect for people-watching. Head here for the famous hoagies: long rolls of fresh bread stuffed with steak slices, cheese, sweet peppers, and onions and heated until the cheese is perfectly melted. ✉ *309 Buenos Aires* ☎ *386/427–6850* ☰ *No credit cards* ☉ *Closed Mon. No dinner.*

$$–$$$ ▦ **Holiday Inn Hotel Suites.** Families like these comfortable suites, which sleep up to eight people. Bedrooms are raised and set behind the living room, which opens out to a balcony and a spectacular view of the ocean. The furnishings are contemporary, and each unit has a full kitchen. ✉ *1401 S. Atlantic Ave., 32169* ☎ *386/426–0020* 🖷 *386/423–3977* ⊕ *www.basshotel.com* ⇌ *101 suites* ⌂ *Restaurant, pool, beach, bar* ☰ *AE, MC, V.*

$–$$ ▦ **Little River Inn Bed & Breakfast.** A formal driveway leads to this charming bed-and-breakfast in an Old Florida home built in 1883. The house, set on a slight rise across the road from the peaceful marshes of the Indian River, is surrounded by nearly 2 acres of oak trees and manicured green lawns. All guest rooms have views of the river. You can breakfast in the sunny dining room, relax in a rocker on the wide terrace, or settle in a corner of the living room with a good book. A full breakfast is included in the rate. ✉ *532 N. Riverside Dr., 32168* ☎ *386/424–0100* 🖷 *386/424–9350* ⊕ *www.little-river-inn.com* ⇌ *6 rooms* ⌂ *Bicycles* ☰ *AE, MC, V.*

★ **$–$$** ▦ **Riverview Hotel.** Built in 1886, this pink B&B is set back from the Intracoastal Waterway. Individually furnished rooms open out to plant-filled verandas and balconies with views of water or a private courtyard and pool. Most rooms are around $100, but champagne in the Executive Suites bump the prices. A complimentary Continental breakfast is served in your room. ⊠ *103 Flagler Ave., 32169* ☎ *386/428–5858 or 800/945–7416* 🖷 *386/423–8927* ⊕ *www.volusia.com/riverview* 🛏 *18 rooms* ⚷ *Restaurant, pool, bicycles* ▤ *AE, D, DC, MC, V.*

Outdoor Activities & Sports

FISHING From trolling on the marsh flats to hitting the open water, the Space Coast is a great place to get hooked. There's big bass on the St. Johns River, giant redfish, trout, and snook on the Indian River Lagoon, and excellent deep sea sites for dolphin, grouper, king mackerel, wahoo, blue and white marlin, sailfish, tuna, and snapper offshore in the Atlantic. There are approximately 40 charter captains setting sail from Cape Canaveral, and they are all licensed, insured, and experienced. You can find a complete listing of the hale and hearty skippers of the **Canaveral Charter Captains** organization at www.fishingspacecoast.org as well as their peers at the **Indian River Guides Association** at www.irga.org. Check individual charter listings for prices and hours.

THE SPACE COAST A TO Z

To research prices, get advice from other travelers, and book travel arrangements, visit www.fodors.com.

Arriving & Departing

AIR TRAVEL

The nearest major airport is Orlando International Airport, a one-hour ride from the Space Coast. The Cocoa Beach Shuttle provides transportation to and from the airport; reservations are required. American Eagle, Continental, Delta, Spirit, and US Airways provide some service to Melbourne International Airport, approximately a half-hour drive from Cocoa. The Melbourne Airport Shuttle and Taxi ferries arriving and departing passengers.

🛪 Airport Information **Cocoa Beach Shuttle** ☎ 321/784–3831. **Melbourne Airport Shuttle and Taxi** ☎ 321/724–1600. **Melbourne International Airport** ☎ 321/723–6227. **Orlando International Airport** ☎ 321/825–2001.

CAR TRAVEL

The Beeline Expressway (Route 528) is accessible from either I–4 or Florida's Turnpike. Tolls for the trip from Orlando add up to $3 for a car. If you take the Beeline directly to the coast, you'll end up in Port Canaveral, about 6 mi north of Cocoa Beach. The coast is about 90 minutes from WDW and 60 minutes from Orlando.

Route 520, which is reached from the Beeline—take Exit 31 just past mile marker 30—is a slightly less direct but more scenic route, at least until you hit the pit of Cocoa and its strip malls and unchecked growth. Continuing east on Route 520 past Cocoa, you'll reach the beach and Route A1A, the beach's main artery.

Route 50, known in Orlando as Colonial Drive, is also a straight shot to the coast. You have to get through some traffic, but once you're on the outskirts of Orlando, it's smooth sailing as long as it's not during the morning or evening rush hour. Route 50 dead-ends at A1A in Titusville, north of the access road to the Kennedy Space Center Visitor Complex. If you're going to the center for the day, Route 50 is actually a more direct route than the Beeline.

If your destination is New Smyrna Beach, follow the Beeline Expressway to Route 407. Take Route 407 to I–95 north to Exit 249 (State Rd.

44) and go east 5 mi. The trip takes about 75 minutes from Orlando and about 95 minutes from WDW.

Getting Around

BY BUS

Chances are that you'll never ride a bus when you're here, but if you do the Space Coast Area Transit is the provider of local bus service. The fare is $1 for adults, 50¢ for senior citizens, people with disabilities, or students with valid ID cards. Route 9 runs between Merritt Square Mall and all major points between Port Canaveral and Cocoa Beach.

🚌 Bus Information **Space Coast Area Transit** ☎ 321/633-1878 ⊕ www.ridescat.com.

BY CAR

The Space Coast is easy to navigate. On the beach, the main thoroughfare is A1A, known as Atlantic Avenue in Cocoa Beach and in New Smyrna Beach and by other names in some beach towns. The area around the intersection of A1A and Route 520 in Cocoa Beach tends to be congested at almost all hours. In general, however, traffic here can be somewhat lighter than in other towns along the coast. The principal route on the "mainland" is U.S. 1, which goes by various local names such as Dixie Highway and is generally not traffic-logged except in the middle of towns.

Contacts & Resources

CAR RENTALS

If you're driving from Orlando International Airport, you may find that although a few major car-rental companies are in the main terminal on Level 1, many are a bus ride away (buses run quite frequently). Several car-rental companies have offices on the Space Coast.

🚗 Major Agencies **Avis** ☎ 800/331-2112. **Budget** ☎ 800/527-0700. **Hertz** ☎ 800/654-3131.

EMERGENCIES

Dial **911** for police, fire, or ambulance.

🏥 Hospitals **Bert Fish Medical Center** ⊠ 401 Palmetto St., New Smyrna Beach ☎ 386/424-5000. **Cape Canaveral Hospital** ⊠ 701 W. Cocoa Beach Causeway, Rte. 520, Cocoa Beach ☎ 321/799-7111.

GUIDED TOURS

AIRBOAT TOURS   Daily from 10 to 6, 30-minute airboat rides on the St. Johns River are available at Lone Cabbage Fish Camp. Prices are $17 for adults, $8.50 children under 12; reservations are essential.

🚤 **Lone Cabbage Fish Camp** ⊠ 8199 Rte. 520, Cocoa ☎ 321/632-4199 ⊕ www.twisterairboatrides.com.

VISITOR INFORMATION

A good source for launch as well as area information is the Space Coast Office of Tourism. The Cocoa Beach Area Chamber of Commerce also offers information about dates for rocket launches.

🏢 **Cocoa Beach Area Chamber of Commerce** ⊠ 400 Fortenberry Rd., Merritt Island 32952 ☎ 321/459-2200 ⊕ www.cocoabeachchamber.com. **Cocoa Village Association** ⊠ Brevard Ave., south of Rte. 520, Box 1, Cocoa Village 32923 ☎ 321/631-9075 ⊕ www.cocoavillage.com. **New Smyrna Beach Chamber of Commerce** ⊠ 115 Canal St., New Smyrna Beach 32168 ☎ 386/428-2449. **Space Coast Office of Tourism** ⊠ 2725 St. Johns St., Melbourne 32940 ☎ 321/868-1126 or 800/936-2326 ⊕ www.space-coast.com. **Titusville Area Chamber of Commerce** ⊠ 2000 S. Washington Ave., Titusville 32780 ☎ 321/267-3036 ⊕ www.titusville.org.

INDEX

NOTES

NOTES